AF513078

About Pearson

Pearson is the world's learning company, with presence across 70 countries worldwide. Our unique insights and world-class expertise comes from a long history of working closely with renowned teachers, authors and thought leaders, as a result of which, we have emerged as the preferred choice for millions of teachers and learners across the world.

We believe learning opens up opportunities, creates fulfilling careers and hence better lives. We hence collaborate with the best of minds to deliver you class-leading products, spread across the Higher Education and Test Preparation spectrum.

Superior learning experience and improved outcomes are at the heart of everything we do. This product is the result of one such effort.

Your feedback plays a critical role in the evolution of our products and you can contact us - reachus@pearson.com. *We look forward to it.*

NVision

FOUNDATION SCIENCE

CLASS 6

Third Edition

Pearson

The aim of this publication is to supply information taken from sources believed to be valid and reliable. This is not an attempt to render any type of professional advice or analysis, nor is it to be treated as such. While much care has been taken to ensure the veracity and currency of the information presented within, neither the publisher nor its authors bear any responsibility for any damage arising from inadvertent omissions, negligence or inaccuracies (typographical or factual) that may have found their way into this book.

Copyright © 2026 Pearson India Education Services Pvt. Ltd

This book is sold subject to the condition that it shall not, by way of trade or otherwise, be lent, resold, hired out, or otherwise circulated without the publisher's prior written consent in any form of binding or cover other than that in which it is published and without a similar condition including this condition being imposed on the subsequent purchaser and without limiting the rights under copyright reserved above, no part of this publication may be reproduced, stored in or introduced into a retrieval system, or transmitted in any form or by any means (electronic, mechanical, photocopying, recording or otherwise), without the prior written permission of both the copyright owner and the publisher of this book.

ISBN 978-93-713-6649-6

First Impression

Published by Pearson India Education Services Pvt. Ltd, CIN: U72200TN2005PTC057128.

Head Office: 1st Floor, Berger Tower, Plot No. C-001A/2, Sector 16B, Noida - 201 301, Uttar Pradesh, India.
Registered Office: 6th Floor, Tower A, Unit A and B , International Tech Park, CapitaLand,
200 Feet Radial Road, Zamin Pallavaram, Old Pallavaram, Chennai – 600117, Tamil Nadu, India.

Website: in.pearson.com, Email: companysecretary.india@pearson.com

Compositor: SRS Global, Puducherry

Printed in India by Saurabh Printers Pvt. Ltd.

Contents

Preface

The *NVision* series has been meticulously designed to help students excel not only in their school curriculum but also in national and international Olympiads such as **NSO, IOM, IMO, NSTSE, IOS** and others. The primary aim of this series is to **support students in realising their full academic potential** through a well-structured, concept-driven approach.

In this latest edition, **all volumes have been comprehensively updated in line with the newly released NCERT textbooks for Grades 6 to 8** and the **revised curriculum framework for Grades 9 and 10 (2024–25 onwards)**. These updates ensure complete alignment with the latest CBSE guidelines, competency-based learning objectives and the current patterns of school and competitive examinations.

Book Components

- **Theory:** The theoretical portion of each chapter seamlessly integrates **concise explanations, conceptual notes, and solved examples** to make learning intuitive and effective. *Theory-based exercises* have been placed strategically at key checkpoints to reinforce understanding. The use of diagrams, tables, and illustrative figures enhances conceptual clarity and engagement.
- **Assessment Level 1 — Concept Building Exercise (CBE):** These exercises focus on **concept assimilation and mastery at the school level**. They include *fill-in-the-blanks, true/false, match the following, assertion-reason, case-based, comprehension-type, and descriptive questions*. The pattern mirrors the latest **CBSE question formats**, including **competency-based and case-integrated questions**. Students are advised to maintain a separate notebook for solving these exercises neatly and systematically.
- **Assessment Level 2 — Competitive Level Exercise (CLE):** Once students are confident with basic concepts, this section elevates their preparation to **competitive standards**. It features multiple-choice questions *(MCQs), Higher-Order Thinking Skill (HOTS) questions, and Olympiad-style problems* that enhance analytical reasoning and exam temperament.
- **Archive Corner:** This section contains **selected questions from previous years' Olympiads and national competitive examinations** like NSO, IOM, IOS, NTSE, and IMO. Solving these helps students assess their preparedness and compare their understanding with real examination standards.

After completing the theory and exercises, students will develop both a **strong conceptual foundation** and **sharp problem-solving skills**. To maximise results, students should solve all exercises in a fair notebook and preserve it carefully for future revision.

Parents are encouraged to **monitor their child's progress** regularly—not necessarily by checking every answer, but by ensuring that work is done consistently and neatly. This involvement reinforces the value of learning and motivates students to stay disciplined and sincere in their academic journey.

With the combined efforts of **students, parents, and teachers**, this book aims to nurture clarity of thought, curiosity and confidence—empowering learners to envision success truly.

Prashant Jain
B. Tech (CSE), IIT Bombay
Lead Author, NVision Series

About the Authors

Prashant Jain (*Series Lead Author)*
Prashant Jain is one of India's most admired Mathematics educators, celebrated for his clarity of thought, innovative teaching methods, and exceptional track record of producing top JEE and Olympiad results. An alumnus of IIT Bombay with a B.Tech. in Computer Science and Engineering (AIR 42, IIT JEE 2008), Prashant brings analytical precision and creative pedagogy together to make complex mathematical ideas beautifully simple.

A Gold Medalist in the Indian National Chemistry Olympiad (INChO) and a qualifier of INPhO, he combines Olympiad-level depth with IIT-JEE practicality. Currently serving as the National Outcomes Head at Unacademy, he has previously been a senior faculty member at Resonance Kota and Nucleus Education, guiding thousands of students to success in the IIT-JEE, IOQM, ISI, and CMI exams.

Over the past decade, Prashant has authored more than 20 bestselling books with Pearson, including the highly acclaimed Nvision series, IOQM Mathematics, and multiple foundational and advanced titles that have become trusted companions for aspirants across India. His books are known for their conceptual depth, structured progression, and problem-solving elegance—embodying his signature philosophy, 'Simple Formulation, Amazing Manipulation'.

Beyond the classroom, Prashant is deeply involved in designing national-level academic strategies and excellence frameworks across more than 65 Unacademy centres. A passionate mentor and innovator, he continues to inspire students through his digital platforms—YouTube (Prashant Jain [IIT B, AIR 42]) and Instagram (@prashantjain0042)—where he simplifies mathematics for learners across the nation.

Harshit Goyal (*Lead Author – Physics*)
Mr. Goyal completed his B.Tech and M.Tech from IIT (BHU) 2014. He opted teaching as a career out of passion and has been associated with Resonance, Kota, as Head of Faculty Training and Teaching - Physics. He has an experience of teaching more than 7000 students, and also lead the annual course designing and planning for foundation and senior classes.

He was also the Co-founder and Chief Product Officer at Eduncle India Pvt. Ltd. and currently working with one of the EdTech unicorns in India.

Ashutosh Gautam (*Lead Author – Chemistry*)
Popularly known as AG Sir, Mr. Gautam is the Founder-Director at Talking Textbook Institute, Kota. He is also the Head of Department, Organic Chemistry, at ISAC Learning, Kota and a Chemistry tutor at PhysicsWallah. He has previously been associated with institutes like Unacademy, Bansal Classes, Nucleus Education, Amazon Academy, etc. Having taught and mentored 10000+ students, Mr. Gautam has a strong social media presence and followers for online classes and YouTube videos.

Nisha Gautam (*Lead Author – Biology*)
Director and Head of Department, Biology, at Proton Tutorials since 2012, Mrs. Gautam has been previously associated with institutes like Allen Career Institute and Unacademy. She has published research paper in Indian Journal of Food Science and Technology and have taught and mentored 10000+ students till date.

Harshita Sharma (*Co-Author – Biology*)
Mrs. Sharma has a rich teaching experience in the Test Preparation section at Resonance, Kota and Surat and has also been associated with Resonance as Head of Department, Biology.

Dr. Bela Kalwadia (*Co-Author – Chemistry*)
Dr. Kalwadia has an extensive teaching experience in Kota and has previously been associated with institutes like Resonance, Nucleus, and Motion Education. Besides working as a Research Scientist at Insecticides (India) Ltd. for 5 years, Dr. Kalwadia has published several research papers and owns patents as well.

Charry Yadav (*Co-Author – Physics*)
Ms. Charry Yadav, M.Sc. (Physics), B.Ed., is an accomplished educator with an impressive teaching career since 2015. Her expertise in Physics is enhanced by her dedication to innovative and effective teaching methodologies. She has made significant contributions to reputed institutes, including Unacademy, Vyas Education, Nucleus Education, and Paravyom Education, where she has guided students in shaping their academic journeys.

Chapter Insights

Learning Outcomes

These outline the targets the chapter aims to achieve. It gives the learner a to-do list to adhere to while going through the chapter.

Learning Outcomes

After reading this chapter, you would be able to:

- explain measuring units and systems of units.
- understand area and volume of different objects and their calculation.
- explain rest and motion and why they are relative terms.
- understand different types of motion along with examples.
- explain relation between distance, time, and speed.

Geekspeak

- Transportation
- Physical quantity
- System of measurement
- Measurement of length
- Area and Volume
- Rest and motion
- Linear motion
- Random motion
- Periodic motion
- Distance
- Speed

Geekspeak

This introduces the learner to the keywords they shall learn from the chapter.

Introduction

This provides the learner with a basic summary of what to expect from the chapter.

Introduction

A mineral was discovered by a shepherd in the town of magnesia which was found to have a wondrous property—It could attract pieces of iron towards it. This mineral is called magnetite or lodestone.

Magnetite

H1
This outlines the first concept to be taught in the chapter.

Types of Substances and Magnet

The types of magnetic substances are discussed as follows:

- **Magnetic Substances:** Those substances which are attracted by magnets are called magn
  Example: Iron, Cobalt, Nickel, Steel, etc.
- **Non-Magnetic Substances:** Those substances which are not attracted by magnets are called
  Example: Plastic, Rubber, Glass, etc.

Properties of Bar Magnet

The properties of a bar magnet are discussed as follows:

- It attracts small pieces of iron towards itself.
- Each magnet has two poles. The magnetic pull seems to come from two points r regions of attraction are called the magnetic poles. All magnets have maximum attı magnet remain slightly inside from the end points.

H2
This builds on the first concept and outlines the second concept to be taught in the chapter.

H3
This builds on the first and second topics and outlines the third concept to be taught in the chapter.

For Time

The units used for the measurement of time are as follows:

- **Year:** The time taken by the earth to complete one revolution around the sun.
  1 year = $365\frac{1}{4}$ days
- **Lunar Month:** One lunar month is the time in which the moon completes one revolution around the earth.
  1 Lunar month = 27.3 days
- **Millennium:** A millennium is of 1000 years.
- **Solar Day:** The time taken by the earth to complete one rotation on its own is called solar day.

Competition Corner

Uniform Motion
A body has a uniform motion if it covers equal distances in equal intervals of time, no matter how small these time intervals may be.
For example, a car running at a constant speed of 10 m/s, will cover equal distances of 10 metre, in every second. Hence, its motion will be uniform.

Non-Uniform Motion
A body has a non-uniform motion if it cover unequal distances in equal intervals of time. For example, if we drop a ball from the roof of a building, we will find that it covers unequal distances in equal intervals of time. It covers
4.9 metre in the 1st second,
14.7 metre in the 2nd second,
24.5 metre in the 3rd second, and so on.

Competition Corner
Attain competitive edge by learning some additional definitions to help with basic concept-learning.

Intext Questions
Learn while applying your concepts with these questions provided alongside concepts to enhance assimilation.

❖ INTEXT QUESTIONS

1. **A football field is 0.5 km long. How many meters long is the football field?**
   Solution: 1000 m = 1 km
   $\therefore$ 0.5 km = 0.5 × 10^3 m = 500 m
2. **Sunita bought 700 grams of sugar to make a cake. How many kg of sugar did she buy?**
   Solution: 1000 grams = 1 kg

Check Point 1

1. The temperature of two bodies differs by 1°C. How much will they differ on the Fahrenheit scale?
2. Express 45°C in Kelvin.
3. A copper rod at 50°C is dropped into a bucket containing water at 50°C. Will the heat flow or not in this case?
4. What are the various means used by a pizza delivery man to keep the pizza hot?
5. Why do we have to shake the thermometer before taking temperature in a clinical thermometer?

Check Points
Self-analyse your learning by answering some questions based on recently learnt concepts.

Testing Room
Satisfy your scientific curiosity by performing fun little experiments and observing the results.

Testing Room 1

To measure the height of a person.
Materials required: Measuring tape, a thick book, and a pencil.
Procedure: To measure the height of your friend, make him / her stand absolutely straight with his/her back against a wall. Place a thick rigid book on his/her head and make a mark on the wall where the underside of the book touches the wall. Measure the length from this mark to the floor with the help of the measuring tape. This gives the height of your friend make sure he/she is not wearing shoes to gain some extra inches.

Keystone

Everything we see can be classified into living and non-living categories.

Keystone
Enhance the knowledge of trivia with fun little tidbits about surrounding things.

Structural Outline
Quickly revise the concepts learnt by going through this simple flowchart that summarises the key ideas.

STRUCTURAL OUTLINE

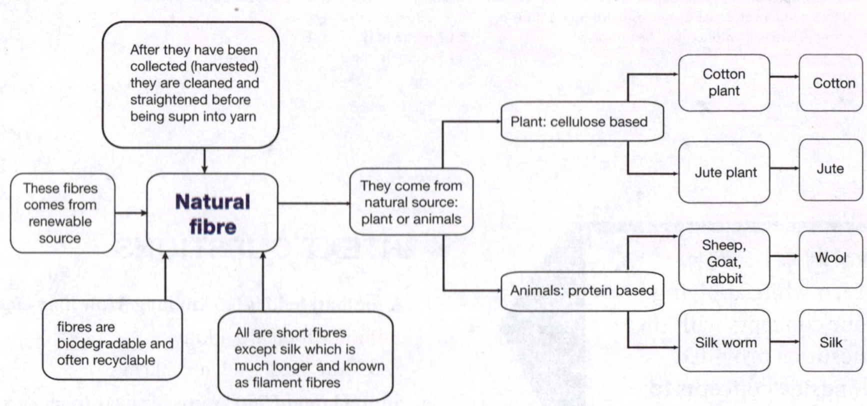

Abridgement
Make learning a smooth journey by availing these bridges that connect the learning between classes.

ABRIDGEMENT

Types of fibres:

- Fibres may be of three types -

  (i) Natural fibres

  Natural fibres: Fibres obtained from plants and animals are known as natural fibres. Natu short fibres.

  Examples: Wool, cotton, silk (it can be obtained up to 1 km length)

  (ii) Synthetic fibres

  Synthetic fibres: Fibres synthesized by human beings are known as synthetic fibres. continuous filament fibres.

EXEMPLIFICATION

1. **Explain how jute is obtained from jute plants.**

   Solution: The jute plant is normally harvested at flowering stage. The stems of harve immersed in water for 10 to 15 days. The stems rot (the process is called retting) and These fibres are converted into yarns to make fabrics.

2. **What are looms?**

   Solution: The devices on which fabrics are woven are called looms. Looms are eitl operated.

3. **What happens when a yarn from a torn sock is pulled?**

   Solution: When we pull a yarn from a torn sock then a single yarn gets pulled ou unravels. Socks are made up of knitted fabrics from a single yarn.

4. **What were the materials used by people in ancient times in place of clothes?**

   Solution: It appears that in those days people used the bark and big leaves of trees or a of clothes.

5. **What happened when people began to settle in agricultural communities?**

   Solution: When people began to settle in agricultural communities, they learnt to wea and baskets. Vines, animal fleece or hair were twisted together into long strands. Th

Exemplification
Enhance concept learning with examples that have been solved for your benefit.

NCERT Compendium
Solutions of all intext NCERT exercises have also been provided in NCERT Compendium.

NCERT COMPENDIUM

1. Some lengths are given in Column I of Table below. Some units are given in Column II. Match the lengths with the units suitable for measuring those lengths.

Column I	Column II
Distance between Delhi and Lucknow	Centimetre
Thickness of a coin	Kilometre
Length of an eraser	Metre
Lenth of school ground	Millimetre

Solution: Distance between Delhi and Lucknow – kilometre
Thickness of a coin – millimetre
Length of an eraser – centimetre
Length of school ground – metre

2. Read the following statements and mark True (T)

6. Take a tumbler or a bottle. Measure the length of the curved part of the base of glass or bottle and record it.

   Solution: The length of curved part is 8 cm.

7. Measure the height of your friend and express it in (i) metres (ii) centimetres and (iii) millimetres.

   Solution: (i) 2.25 foot = 0.68 m (ii) 68 cm (iii) 680 mm

8. You are given a coin. Estimate how many coins are required to be placed one after the other lengthwise, without leaving any gap between them, to cover the whole length of the chosen side of a notebook. Verify your estimate by measuring the same side of the notebook and the size of the coin using a 15-cm scale.

   Solution: 7 coins are required. Estimated length

Level 1

Fixed Response Type

Multiple Choice Questions

1. Why do different students get different measurements when they use their hand spans to measure the same desk?
   (A) They are not measuring carefully.
   (B) The desk changes its length.
   (C) Handspans vary from person to person.

Level 1 MCQ
Learn to avoid confusions by confidently answering the questions asked in this exercise.

Fill in the Blanks
Fill in the gaps in your learning by finding answers to the blanks in the sentences.

Fill in the Blanks

1. No trade is possible without____________ (transportation/Sun)
2. The determination of the size or magnitude of something is called________(motion/ measurement).
3. There are _______ millimeters in one centimeter. (1 / 10)
4. SI unit of length is__________. (m^2/m)

True/False

1. Prehistoric people used animals to carry their loads.
2. Millimeter is the most appropriate unit to measure the length of a pencil.
3. S.I system was introduced in year 1990.
4. S.I unit of length is centimeter.
5. When a body moves around a fixed point, it is

True/False
Double-check your concepts by fact-checking your answers.

Match Type Questions
This exercise is like solving a puzzle. Find the best match so two halves of a sentence can fit together.

Match Type Questions

1. Match the Column A with Column B

Column A	Column B
(i) Unit of length	(a) Motion along straight line
(ii) Linear motion	(b) Oscillatory Motion
(iii) Unit of mass	(c) Metre
(iv) To and fro periodic motion	(d) Pound

Assertion and Reason Type Questions
This exercise enhances learners' analytical skills by providing them with assertions that may or may not be justified by a list of accompanying reasons.

Assertion and Reason Type Questions

Read the given statements and select the correct option.

(A) Both A and R are true and R is the correct explanation of A.
(B) Both A and R are true but R is not the correct explanation of A.
(C) A is true but R is false.
(D) A is false but R is true.

1. **Assertion:** The displacement of a body may be zero, though distance can be finite.
   Reason: If a body moves such that finally it arrives at initial point, then displacement is zero while distance is finite.
2. **Assertion:** In International system of units the unit of length is centimetre.
   Reason: If a centimetre is divided into ten equal parts then each part is equal to a millimetre.
3. **Assertion:** In ancient times bullock cart was

Comprehension Type Questions

Directions: Read the passage (s) given below and answer the questions that follow.

Passage-I: A system having a set of standard units of measurement which was accepted all over the world is called International system of units (S.I. system).

1. The S.I. system of units is based on
   (A) F.P.S. system (B) Metric system
   (C) both of these (D) None of these
2. The metric system of units was created by
   (A) Germans (B) Indians
   (C) Chinese (D) French
3. In S.I. system of units, the standard unit of distance is

Comprehension Type Questions
This exercise tests concept learning by checking for a learner's level of understanding.

Very Short Answer Type Questions
Summarise your learning in a few words by answering these questions.

Free Response Type

Very Short Answer Type Questions

1. Define transportation.
2. Give an example of circular motion.
3. How will you measure the length of curved line?
4. Distinguish between the state of rest and motion.
5. Name the SI unit of measurement for temperature.
6. Define distance along with its SI unit.
7. Name the device used to measure the distance traveled by a vehicle.

Short Answer Type Questions

1. What are the advantages of Modern means of transport?
2. What are the disadvantages of modern means of transport?
3. Explain the type of motion exhibited by the hands of a clock.
4. State the importance of measurements.
5. Discuss the use of divider.
6. Why could you not use an elastic measuring tape to measure distance?
7. If a train travels 120 kilometers in 2 hours, calculate its speed.

Short Answer Type Questions
Summarise your learning in a short sentence by answering these questions.

Long Answer Type Questions
Elaborate on concepts learnt by knowing exactly what to include in these long-answer type questions.

Long Answer Type Questions

1. What are the advantages of wheel?
2. Explain how you will measure the average speed of the journey between your home and school.
3. While measuring the length of a knitting needle the reading of the scale at one end is 5 cm & at the other end is 23.2 cm. What is the length of the needle?

Numerical Based Questions

1. A boy was riding his bicycle at a speed of 10 m/s. He covered 1 km. Calculate the time taken by him.
2. A boy is cycling and follows the path as shown in the figure. The total trip consists of four straight line path AB, BC, CD and DE. At the end of the journey, what is the boy's displacement from the starting point?

A E

Numerical Based Question
Play with numbers in this fun activity that checks for your understanding of mathematical concepts.

Case Based Questions
This exercise enhances learners' analytical skills by providing them with practical situations where they can apply the theories learnt.

Case Based Questions

Passage: Read the following table and answer the question from 1–3.

P	Q	R
Magnets	Magnetic substances	Non-magnetic substances

1. Articles from which of these groups can be attracted by magnets but cannot attract other objects?
(A) P (B) Q
(C) R (D) P and Q

LEVEL 2

Multiple Choice Questions

1. Standard units of measurement were introduced primarily to:
   (A) Make mathematics easier.
   (B) Ensure consistency in global trade and science.
   (C) Reduce the number of measuring tools needed.
   (D) Make measurements faster.

Level 2 MCQ
Learn to avoid confusions by confidently answering the questions asked in this exercise.

Higher Order Thinking Skills (HOTS)
Apply theories at a higher level by applying your learning and analysing these higher order thinking questions.

Higher Order Thinking Skills (HOTS)

1. Two identical metal balls A and B moving in opposite directions hit each other at point X as shown in the figure. Changes are most likely to be appear in their

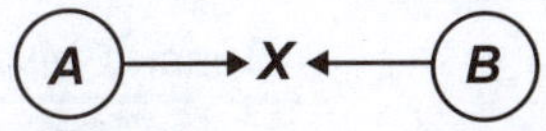

1. Shapes 2. Speeds
3. Directions 4. Volumes
(A) 1 and 3 only (B) 2 and 3 only

ARCHIVE CORNER

1. A cyclist moves from a certain point P and goes round a circle of radius a and reaches Q, exactly at the other side of the point P as shown in figure. The displacement of the cyclist would be

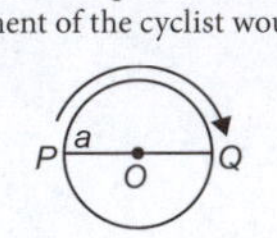

(A) πa (B) $2\pi a$
(C) 2a (D) $2\pi/a$

2. A scientist needs to measure distances ranging from atomic dimensions to astronomical distances. The choice of measurement technique depends primarily on:
   (A) Cost of equipment
   (B) Unit of measurement and required precision
   (C) Personal preference
   (D) Speed of measurement

7. Match the following and select the correct option from the codes given below.

Column A	Column B
(i) Railway engine	(a) Quintal
(ii) Packet of chilli powder	(b) kg
(iii) Sack of wheat	(c) mg
(iv) Huge bag of sand	(d) g
(v) Aspirin tablet	(e) Metric ton

(A) (i)–(e), (ii)–(d), (iii)–(a), (iv)–(b), (v)–(c)
(B) (i)–(a), (ii)–(b), (iii)–(c), (iv)–(d), (v)–(e)
(C) (i)–(b), (ii)–(d), (iii)–(e), (iv)–(c), (v)–(a)
(D) (i)–(c), (ii)–(b), (iii)–(d), (iv)–(e), (v)–(a)

8. Which of the following motions is/are periodic as well as oscillatory motion?

Archive Corner
Reassess your learning by understanding and remembering questions you have already answered and concepts you have already learnt.

Answer Key
Cross-check your answers by referring to this comprehensive list provided.

ANSWER KEY

Level 1

Fixed Response Type

Multiple Choice Questions

1. C	2. B	3. B	4. A	5. B	6. C	7. A	8. D	9. B	10. C
11. D	12. A	13. A	14. A	15. B	16. C	17. A	18. C	19. B	20. B
21. C	22. B	23. C	24. B	25. A					

Fill in the Blanks

1. Transportation 2. Measurement 3. 10 4. m
5. Periodic 6. Car moving on a straight road 7. Linear

CHAPTER 1: MEASUREMENT OF LENGTH AND MOTION

Check Point 1

1. Bus, train
2. Helicopter, aeroplane
3. Boat, ship
4. Primitive mode of transportation was mostly based on simple machines, like wooden cart, wooden rafts made of woods, etc. Also, they use animals to some extent. While modern mode of transportation is mostly using fuels and engines to increase their speed. They are made up of metals.
5. Primitive mode of transportation was made up of wood because at that time, the most easily accessible and available thing was wood which is obtained from trees.
6. (a) $5\ \mu m = 5 \times 10^{-6}$ m

12. $18\ km\ h^{-1} = 18 \times 10^3 / (60 \times 60) = 5$ m in 1 second

Check Point 2

13. Scale C is suitable for measuring up to 10 cm length.
14. $500\ m = 500 \times 10^{-3}\ km = 0.5\ km$
15. 1 millimeter < 1 centimeter < 1 meter < 1 kilometer
16. $1.65\ m = 1.65 \times 10^2\ cm = 165\ cm$

    $1.65\ m = 1.65 \times 10^3\ mm = 1650\ mm$
17. Perimeter of square park = 4 × side = 4 × 300 m = 1200 m

    Cost of fencing = Cost of 1 meter × Perimeter = Rs. 25 × 1200 = Rs. 30,000

Hints and Explanations
Address any and all gaps in learning by referring to hints and explanations provided for better understanding of concepts and questions.

CHAPTER 1

Measurement of Length and Motion

Learning Outcomes

After reading this chapter, you would be able to:

- explain measuring units and systems of units.
- understand area and volume of different objects and their calculation.
- explain rest and motion and why they are relative terms.
- understand different types of motion along with examples.
- explain relation between distance, time, and speed.

Geekspeak

- Transportation
- Physical quantity
- System of measurement
- Measurement of length
- Area and Volume
- Rest and motion
- Linear motion
- Random motion
- Periodic motion
- Distance
- Speed

Introduction

In daily life, the importance of measurement is well known. When we become ill we always drink medicine by measuring it using measuring cup. When we buy fruits and vegetables, the shopkeeper measures it using beam balance. We buy dresses according to our body measurements. In addition, when go on a picnic we always have an approximation that how much time will be spent on a journey for our convenience. Thus, we can observe that the measurement is an integral part of everyday life.

Transportation and Physical Quantities

The process of transportation and physical quantities used for the measurement are discussed as follows:

Transportation

The process of travelling or moving people or goods from one place to another is called transportation. Transportation takes people to where they want to go and brings to them what they need. Trade is possible because of transportation only. Transportation is an integral part of our lives from ancient times. Prehistoric people used to mainly travel and even carry goods on foot as there were no other means available to them. It was noted that from around 5000 B.C. itself, people began to use animals to haul their loads. Later on, after the invention of wheel, wagons and sailing vessels (as shown in the Fig. 1.1) were invented to ease.

Figure 1.1 **Transportation: Past, Present and Future**

People used to drag their loads along the ground. With time, they learnt to make sledges from logs, poles, rawhide, etc., which enable them to transport their load. In addition, they also started to build wooden rafts from logs or reeds to transport goods across water. As time passed by, they learnt to build canoes that could be paddled by hand or with poles, which ultimately led to the making of boats (as shown in the Fig. 1.2). These boats were of very fragile nature and were mainly used across rivers and lakes.

Figure 1.2 **Water Transportation**

Physical Quantities

The quantities that can be measured by an instrument and follow laws of physics are called physical quantities.
For example: mass, length, time, speed, velocity, acceleration, force, temperature, pressure, density, etc.

Competition Corner

Classification of Physical Quantities

Physical quantities classified on the basis of their dependency are discussed as follows:

- **Fundamental quantities:** The physical quantities that are independent of one another are called fundamental quantities. The units in which these quantities are measured are called fundamental units.
  For example: mass, length, time, temperature.
- **Derived quantities:** The physical quantities, which can be expressed in terms of fundamental quantities, are called derived quantities. The units in which these quantities are measured are called derived units.
  For example: speed of a particle can be written as distance travelled by it in unit time.

$$\textbf{Speed} = \frac{\text{Distance}}{\text{Time}} \text{ or } \frac{\text{Length}}{\text{Time}}$$

Measurement

Measurement is an integral part of our day to day life. Measurement is the comparison of an unknown quantity with a known standard quantity of the same type. The standard quantity used for comparison is called the unit. To represent the measurement, the following things are needed.

- **Unit:** A unit of measurement is a definite magnitude of quantity, defined and adopted by convention or by law and used as standard for measurement of the same quantity.
- **Numerical Value:** It expresses the magnitude of quantity, that is, how many times the amount is in the quantity.

  Therefore, we can represent the measurement using following formula

Measure of a physical quantity (M) = Numerical value (N) × Unit (U)

For example: If the mass of certain quantity of rice is 8 kg, it means the unit of mass is kilogram (kg) and the magnitude of the given quantity of rice is eight times this unit.

Some Special Units

Some special units of measurement are discussed below:

For Length

The units used for the measurement of length are as follows:

- **Micron (μ):** A micron is one millionth part (10^{-6}) of a metre and is denoted by the symbol μ. It is also called micrometre.

  1 micron = 10^{-6} metre = 10^{-4} cm = 10^{-3} mm
- **Angstrom (Å):** An angstrom is (10^{-10}) times of a metre. It is denoted by the symbol Å.

  1 Å = 10^{-10} m = 10^{-8} cm
- **Light Year:** A light year can be defined as the distance travelled by light in vacuum in one year.

  1 light year = 9.46×10^{15} m
- **Parsec:** A parsec is the quantity used to measure distances in space.

  1 Parsec = 3.26 light year

For Mass

The units used for the measurement of mass are as follows:

- **Quintal:** One quintal is equal to hundred kg.

  1 quintal = 100 kg = 10^2 kg
- **Metric Tonne:** One metric tonne is equal to thousand kg.

  1 metric tonne = 1000 kg = 10^3 kg

For Time

The units used for the measurement of time are as follows:

- **Year:** The time taken by the earth to complete one revolution around the sun.

  1 year = $365\frac{1}{4}$ days
- **Lunar Month:** One lunar month is the time in which the moon completes one revolution around the earth.

  1 Lunar month = 27.3 days
- **Millennium:** A millennium is of 1000 years.
- **Solar Day:** The time taken by the earth to complete one rotation on its own is called solar day.

  1 solar day = 86400 sec
- **Shake:** 1 shake = 10^{-8} second

The Smallest and the Biggest Units

The smallest and the biggest units of distance and time are as follows:

The smallest practical unit of distance is Fermi. 1 fermi = 10^{-15} m

The biggest unit of distance is parsec. 1 parsec = 3.26 light year

The smallest unit of time is shake. 1 shake = 10^{-8} second

The largest unit of time is Millennium. 1 millennium = 1000 year

Example:

- 1 μm = 1 micrometre = 10^{-6} m
- 1 nm = 1 nanometre = 10^{-9} m
- 1 km = 1 kilometre = 10^{3} m
- 1 mm = 1 millimetre = 10^{-3} m
- 1 MHz = 1 megahertz = 10^{6} Hz
- 1 GHz = 1 gigahertz = 10^{9} Hz

❖ INTEXT QUESTIONS

1. A football field is 0.5 km long. How many meters long is the football field?

Solution: 1000 m = 1 km

∴ 0.5 km = 0.5 × 10^3 m = 500 m

2. Sunita bought 700 grams of sugar to make a cake. How many kg of sugar did she buy?

Solution: 1000 grams = 1 kg

$$700\text{ g} = \frac{700}{1000}\text{ kg} = 0.7\text{ kg}$$

3. Convert 64 km/h into m/s.

Solution: $64\frac{\text{km}}{\text{h}} = \frac{64\times 1000\text{m}}{60\times 60\text{s}} = \frac{160}{9}\frac{\text{m}}{\text{s}}$

4. Convert 36 g/cm³ into kg/m³.

Solution: 36 g/cm³

$$36\times\frac{1}{1000}\text{kg}\times\frac{1}{(100)^{-3}\text{ m}^3} = 36\times 10^3\text{ kg/m}^3$$

Note: To convert $\frac{\text{km}}{\text{hour}}$ into $\frac{\text{m}}{\text{sec}}$, multiply it by $\frac{5}{18}$.

Check Point 1

1. Give two examples of modes of transport on land.
2. Give two examples of modes of transport in air.
3. Give two examples of modes of transport on water.
4. Compare the primitive mode of transportation to that of modern mode of transportation.
5. Why where the primitive mode of transportation made up of wood?
6. Convert the following in metre:
   (i) 5 μm (ii) 3 km (iii) 20 mm (iv) 73 picometer (v) 7.5 nm
7. Convert 5 metric tonne into gram.
8. Convert 1560 gram in kilogram.
9. Density of mercury is 13.6 gcm^{-3}, then its value in MKS system will be ________.
10. How many metres are there in 1 light year?
11. The volume of a cube of side 1 cm is equal to ________ m³.
12. A vehicle moving with a speed of 18 km h^{-1} covers ________ m in 1 s.

Measuring Physical Quantities

Nowadays, the measurement of physical quantities can be done by using appropriate instruments. Let's discuss the history of measurement and instruments we use.

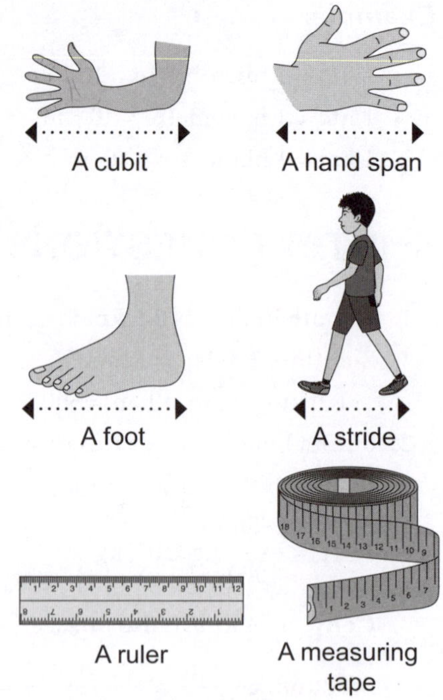

Figure 1.3 **Units for Length Measurement**

History of Length Measurement

In ancient times, different body parts were used to measure length as no other means were available to them. The distance between the tip of the thumb and the tip of the little finger of a fully stretched hand was termed a hand span. The distance between the tip of the middle finger and the elbow was termed as Cubit. Foot, stride, fathom, and yard are some more units based on the length of body parts (as shown in the Fig. 1.3). However, it was soon realised that these units were not very reliable, as the length of body parts can vary from person to person. We need standard units of length and other physical quantities to obtain the same value for a measurement. However, people across the world might adopt different standard units. For example, gram and pound are units of mass used by people of different countries. To solve this problem, we need a set of standard units that is acceptable throughout the world.

Drawbacks

Measuring units as above, which were based on men's body measurements were not accurate and failed because not all men were of the same size. That varies from person to person (as shown in the Fig. 1.4). In modern measuring systems, the measuring tools consist of units based on measurement standards agreed upon by users of the system.

Standard Measurement System

The standard measuring system is designed to provide common measuring unit for everyone.

Figure 1.4 **Drawbacks of Measuring Units**

- **F.P.S. System:** In this system, the unit of length, mass, and time are foot, pound, and second, respectively.
- **C.G.S. System:** In this system, the unit of length, mass, and time are centimetre, gram, and second, respectively.
- **M.K.S. System:** In this system, the unit of length, mass, and time are metre, kilogram, and second, respectively.
- **S.I. System:** In 1960, International Bureau of weights and measurements set up a new system that is the extension of M. K. S. system and units of all physical quantities can be expressed in these terms. The new system is called 'International system of units or S.I. units'.

The SI system of units was adopted in 1960 by the General Conference of Weights and Measures. SI is the short form of system of International Units (in French). The SI unit of length is the metre. Other common standard units of length are inch, millimetre, centimetre, kilometre, and so on.

Standard units are those that have a fixed quantity, and therefore, do not vary from person to person and place to place. For example, the metric system, created by the French in 1790, is a standard set of units.

Adopting standard units of measurement solves only half the problem. People in different countries may be using different sets of standard units for measurement. For example, gram and pound are set of units of mass. The adoption of SI units has made it easier for scientists of different countries to communicate their results to one another.

Competition Corner

Seven fundamental units and derived units are shown in the following tables.

Table Units of Seven Fundamental Physical Quantities

Basic Quantity	S.I Unit	
	Name	**Symbol**
Length	metre	m
Mass	kilogram	kg
Time	second	s
Electric Current	ampere	A
Temperature	kelvin	K
Amount of Substance	mole	mol
Luminous intensity	candela	Cd

Table Derived Units of Some Physical Quantities

Derived Physical Quantity	Formula or Relation with other Physical Quantities	Derived Unit	Symbol
Area	Length × Breath	m × m	m^2
Volume	Length × Breath × Height	m × m × m	m^3
Frequency	1/Time period	1/second	Hz
Density	Mass/Volume	kg/m^3	$kg\ m^{-3}$
Speed	Distance/Time	m/s	ms^{-1}
Velocity	Displacement/Time	m/s	ms^{-1}
Acceleration	Change in velocity/Time	m/s/s	ms^{-2}
Force	Mass × Acceleration	$kg \times m/s^2 = kg.m.s^{-2}$	Newton = N
Pressure	Force/Area	$Newton/m^2$	Pascal = Pa

S.I. Prefixes

The magnitude of physical quantities varies over a wide range. Therefore, to express the very large magnitude as well as very small magnitude more compactly, "CGPM" (General conference on weight and measures) recommended some standard prefixes for certain power of 10.

Table Some Standard Prefixes for Certain Power of 10

Power of 10	Prefix	Symbol
10^{18}	exa	E
10^{15}	peta	P
10^{12}	tera	T
10^{9}	giga	G
10^{6}	mega	M
10^{3}	kilo	k
10^{2}	hecto	h
10^{1}	deca	da
10^{-1}	deci	d
10^{-2}	centi	c
10^{-3}	milli	m
10^{-6}	micro	μ
10^{-9}	nano	n
10^{-12}	pico	p
10^{-15}	femto	f
10^{-18}	atto	a

We need to choose appropriate unit for the length of specific object to be measured. For example, we use metre to measure the length of a piece of cloth, kilometre to measure the distance from one place to another, millimetre to measure the thickness of the hair, and so on. Units of length can be interconverted by multiplying or dividing their values by 10, 100, 1000, and so on.

A commonly used unit for measuring large distances is 'kilometre' (represented as km). Commonly used units for measuring small distances are the centimetre (cm) and millimetre (mm).

1000 m = 1 km 100 cm = 1 m 1000 mm = 1 m

For measuring lengths smaller than the metre, its sub-multiples are used. For lengths greater than the metre, its multiples are used. Those are given in Table 1.1:

Table 1.1 Some Units for Length Measurements

Name of the Unit	Symbol	Relation in terms of metre
millimetre	mm	1/1000
centimetre	cm	1/100
decimetre	dm	1/10
metre	m	1
decametre	dam	10
hectometre	hm	100
kilometre	km	1000

Relation between some units

10 mm =1 cm, 10 cm = 1 dm, 10 dm = 1 m; 10 m = 1 dam, 10 dam = 1 hm, 10 hm = 1 km

Measurement of Length

The measurement of length can be done by following ways:

Using Ruler

Figure 1.5 A Ruler

The length of an object can be calculated by knowing the distance between its ends. It can be measured using a ruler (as shown in the Fig. 1.5), a measuring tape, a metre rod, and so on, whichever is convenient for the required purpose.

While measuring length using a ruler, we have to take the following precautions (as shown in the Fig. 1.6 and 1.7):

- Care should be taken to keep the ruler along the length of the object.

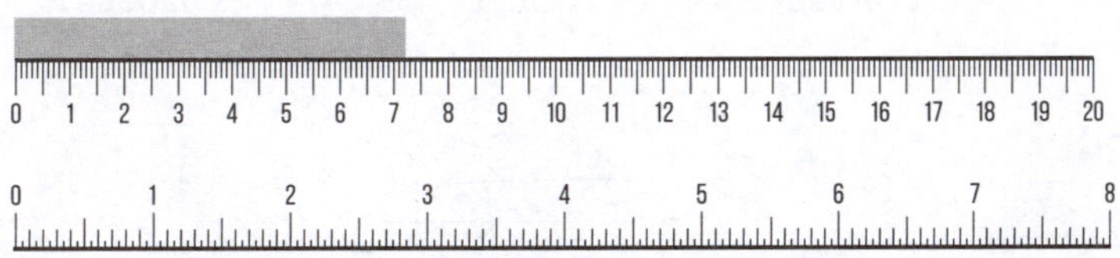

Figure 1.6 The Ruler Should be Kept Along the Length of the Object

- If the edge of the ruler is worn out or broken, the measurement should be started from any other mark that is fully clear.

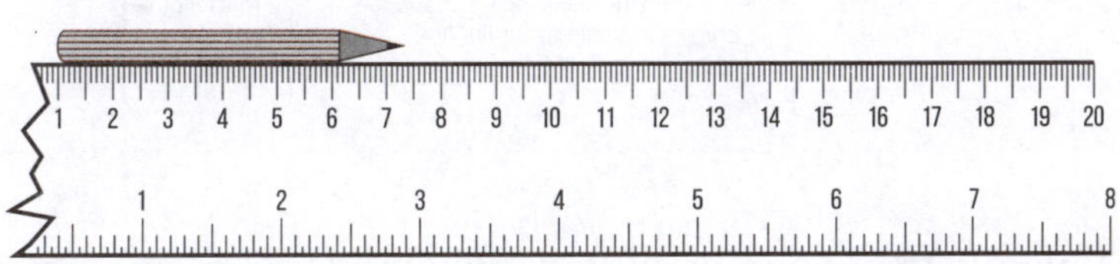

Figure 1.7 Measurement Should only be Started from a Mark that is Fully Clear

Therefore, the length of the object will be " final point – initial point".

- Eyes should be exactly above the point where the measurement is to be taken.

Testing Room 1

To measure the height of a person.
Materials required: Measuring tape, a thick book, and a pencil.
Procedure: To measure the height of your friend, make him / her stand absolutely straight with his/her back against a wall. Place a thick rigid book on his/her head and make a mark on the wall where the underside of the book touches the wall. Measure the length from this mark to the floor with the help of the measuring tape. This gives the height of your friend make sure he/she is not wearing shoes to gain some extra inches.

Using Divider to Measure Length

A divider is used to measure the distance between two points (as shown in the Fig. 1.8). The divider should be correctly used to get a fairly accurate measurement. The divider is placed such that its two pointed ends are at the two ends of the length to be measured. Then, without disturbing the divider, the distance between the two marked points is measured with a ruler.

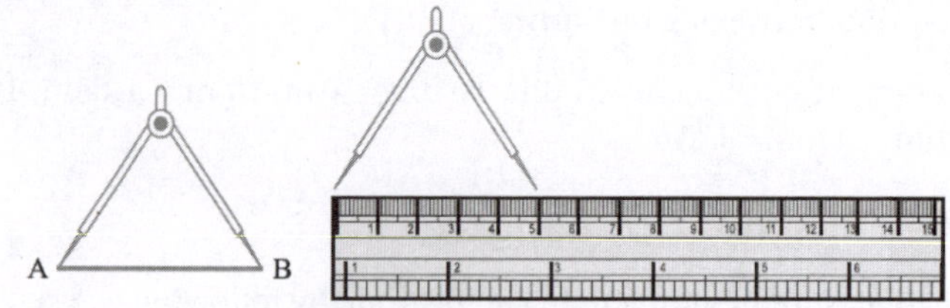

Figure 1.8 **Measurement of a Length Using Divider**

Measuring the Length of a Curved Line

We can measure the length of a curved line using a string. The string is placed along the curved line and its ends are marked on the string. The length of the string between the marked points is measured with a ruler.

Testing Room 2

To measure the length of a curved line using a metre scale.

What you need:

- **A thread**
- **A ruler**
- **A paper**

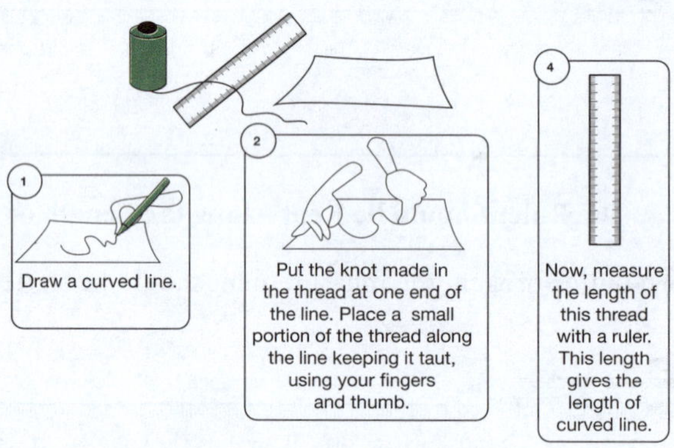

Testing Room 3

Can you measure the thickness of a thin wire?

What you need

1. A pencil
2. A ruler
3. A thin wire

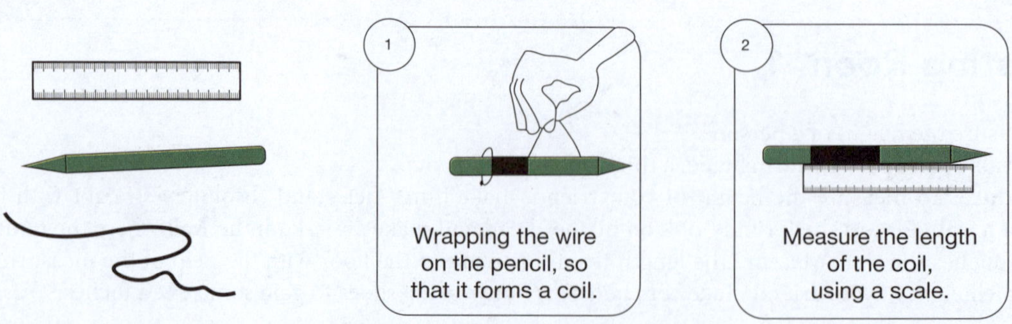

Now, divide the length with the number of turns. You will get the thickness of the wire.

We have seen how we can measure very small lengths or thickness using indirect methods. However, the same lengths can also be measured using special instruments such as the Vernier Calliper and the Screw Gauge in the laboratory (as shown in the Fig. 1.9).

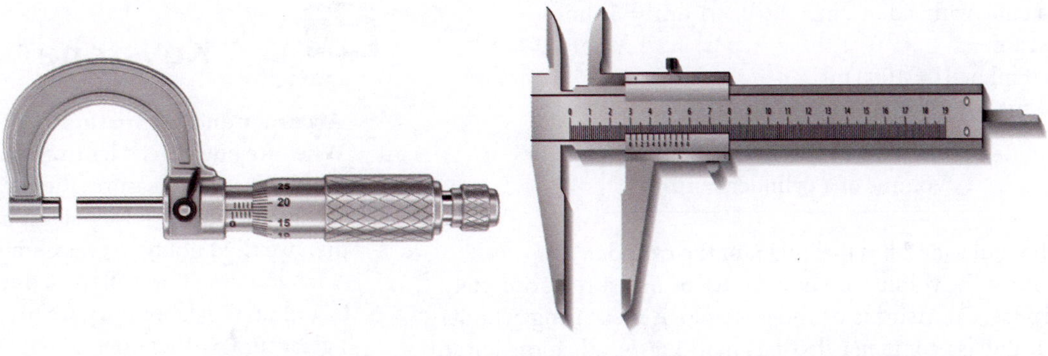

Figure 1.9 **Special Measuring Instruments (a) Screw Gauge (b) Vernier Calliper**

Measurement of Area

The amount of surface covered by the object is called its area. The measurement of area counts two dimensions.
The SI unit of area is square metre, represented as m^2. This is the area covered by a square whose length and breadth are 1 m each.
The area of regular surfaces (squares, rectangles, etc.) can be measured by using the following formula:

Area of a square = Length × Length
Area of a rectangle = Length × Breadth

Let us convert the units of area.

Example: How many m^2 are equal to 1 cm^2 area?

Solution: $1\ cm^2 = 1\ cm \times 1\ cm = (1/100)\ m \times (1/100)\ m = (1/10000)\ m^2 = 10^{-4}\ m^2$

Measurement of Volume

The amount of space occupied by an object is its volume. The SI unit of volume is the cubic metre, represented as m^3.
The litre (represented as l) is an important unit of volume used in the everyday life.
1 litre = 1000 ml
1 m^3 = 1000 litres
The litre is also known as 1000 cm^3.
Since 1 litre = $(1/1000)\ m^3$.

$$1 \text{ litre} = \frac{(100\text{cm})^3}{1000} = 1000\ \text{cm}^3$$

The volume of a liquid is more often expressed in millilitres.
The volume of a solid that has a regular shape can be calculated using a mathematical formula. The formula for determining the volumes of some regular solids are:

Volume of a cube = l^3

where l is the length of the side of the cube.

Volume of a cuboid = l × b × h

where l is the length, b is the breadth, and h is the height of the cuboid.

For example: Volume of a cube of side 1 m = 1 m × 1 m × 1 m = 1 × 1 × 1 m^3 = 1 m^3
Volume of a cube of side 1 cm = 1 cm × 1 cm × 1 cm = 1 × 1 × 1 cm^3 = 1 cm^3
Volume of a cube with side 10 cm = 10 × 10 × 10 cm^3 = 1000 cm^3

Volume of a cube with side 1 dm = $1 \times 1 \times 1$ dm^3 = 1 dm^3
1000 cm^3 = 1 dm^3
1 litre = 1000 ml or 1l = 1000 ml
or 1 cm^3 = 1 ml

$$\text{Volume of a cylinder} = \pi r^2 h$$

where r is the radius and h is the height of the cylinder.
In the laboratory, the volume of a liquid must be measured accurately. For this purpose, a measuring cylinder is used. A measuring cylinder is a cylindrical glass container that has markings/graduations on it. Measuring cylinders are available in different sizes, ranging from 10 ml to 1000 ml (i.e., 10 cm^3 to 1000 cm^3).

Keystone

Accuracy and Estimation
When we buy vegetables from market, the shopkeeper measures them very accurately but when we put salt in curry, then we need not be very accurate. A rough estimation will work fine. In addition, in laboratory, we need a high accuracy. Therefore, sometimes measurements have to be accurate, while other times a rough estimation is good.

Check Point 2

13. You are provided with three scales: A, B, and C as shown in figure to measure a length of 10 cm. For the correct measurement of the length, which scale can be used?

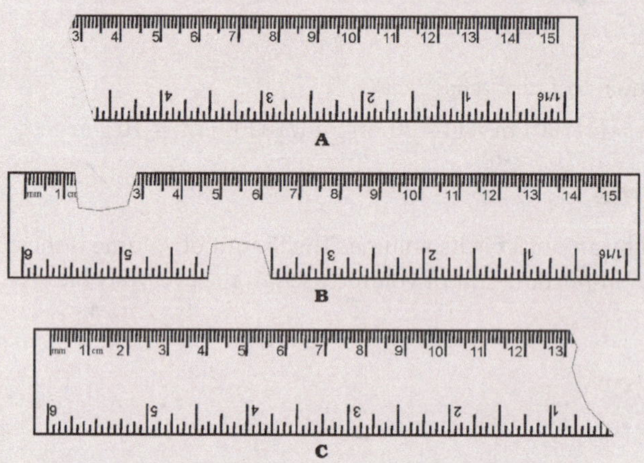

14. 500 m = ________ km.

15. Arrange the following lengths in increasing magnitude.
1 meter, 1 centimetre, 1 kilometre, 1 millimetre.

16. Height of a person is 1.65 m. Express it in cm and mm.

17. Find the cost of fencing a square park of side 300 m at the rate Rs. 25 per metre.

Concept of Rest and Motion

The concept of rest and motion is discussed as follows:

Rest

An object is said to be at rest if it does not change its position with respect to its surroundings with the passage of time.

Motion

A body is said to be in motion if its position changes continuously with respect to the surroundings (or with respect to an observer) with the passage of time.

Rest and Motion are Relative Terms

Motion is relative rather than an absolute term.

An object may be in motion with regard to another object but it may be stationary with respect to a third object. For example, suppose you are sitting in a train (as shown in the Fig. 1.10) and a person is standing alongside the tracks. The person standing along the tracks will see you and everyone else on the train as being in motion. But the person sitting next to you on a train will be stationary with respect to you.

Even as you sit reading this page, it means that when you are at rest, you are moving rapidly around sun because the earth is rotating on its axis. You are also moving along with the earth as the earth revolves around the sun (as shown in the Fig. 1.11). In addition, the sun, the earth and rest of the planets in our solar system are involved in the general rotation of our galaxy within the universe.

Figure 1.10 **Boy is Sitting Inside the Train**

Figure 1.11 **Earth is Revolving Around the Sun**

Types of Motion

The motion can be classified into various types depending on the path or trajectory they followed during the movement.

Linear Motion (or Translatory Motion)

Linear motion is divided into two categories: Rectilinear motion and Curvilinear motion.

The motion along a straight line is known as rectilinear motion.

For example: the motion of a moving car (as shown in the Fig. 1.12), a person running, a stone being dropped, motion of a train on a straight track

Figure 1.12 **Car in Linear Motion**

The motion along a curve is known as curvilinear motion.

Example: Motion of an ant along a thread

Random Motion

The motion that does not follow a fixed direction or pattern is called random motion. Consider the movement of a bird in flight, flying of butterflies in free sky, a hockey player running after the ball (as shown in the Fig. 1.13), an ant crawling on a sheet of paper, children running in a playground. All the above do not follow a set pattern and hence are examples of random motion.

Figure 1.13 **Butterflies and Ball are in Random Motion**

Periodic Motion

A motion in which a body repeats its path in the fix interval of time is called periodic motion.

Types of Periodic Motion

There are two types of periodic motion discussed as follows:

- **Circular Motion**

  A periodic motion in which a body revolves around a fixed point on the circular path is called circular motion.

  For example: Motion of the tip of the clock's arm, motion of the moon around the earth, motion of giant wheel and motion of a point on circular disk in a thread (as shown in the Fig. 1.14)

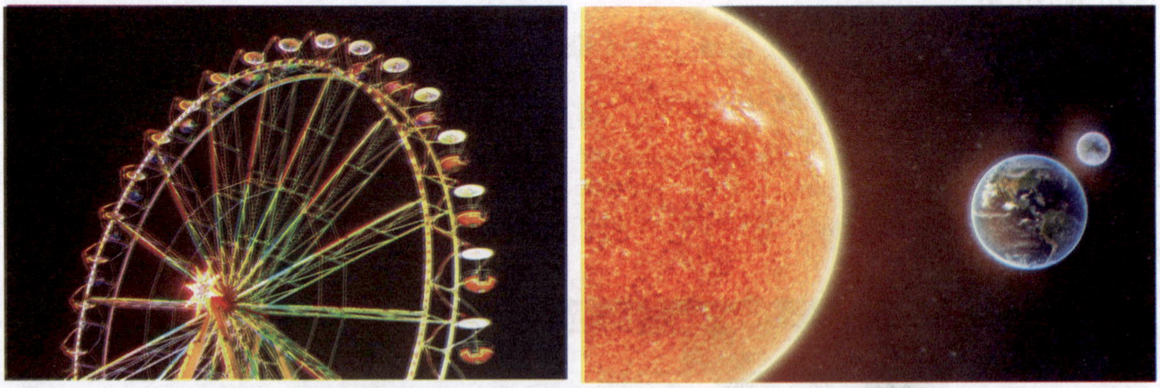

Figure 1.14 **Examples of Circular Motion**

- **Oscillatory Motion**

  The to and fro periodic motion of a body about a fix point is called oscillatory motion.

  For example: the motion of a simple pendulum, a body suspended from a spring, motion of a swing (also called to and fro motion)(as shown in the Fig. 1.15).

Figure 1.15 Examples of Oscillatory Motion

Combined Motion

Sometimes body possesses two types of motion at the same time. For example, the wheel of a moving car rotates as well as moves forward, when you roll a coin on the table it moves in circular path as well as moves forward (as shown in the Fig. 1.16).

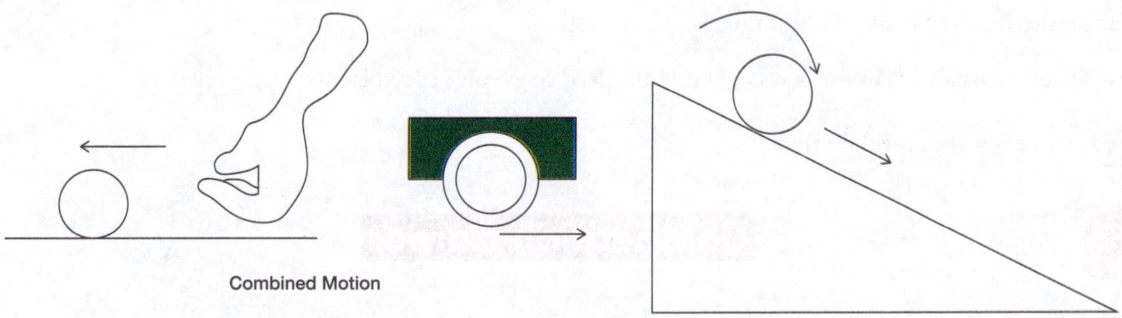

Figure 1.16 Examples of Combined Motion

Competition Corner

Reference Point

Reference point is the point from where we start observing the motion of bodies or we start measurement of length or distance. This measurement of distance from reference point will be the position of a body.

Distance

Distance is the actual path travelled by a body in a given time. Consider a body travelling from A to B along any path between A and B. The actual length of the path that a body travels between A and B is known as the distance.

Here, if the body goes from A to B via C, the distance travel will be ACB.

The distance travelled will be different for different paths between A and B.

Displacement

The distance travelled in a given direction is the displacement. Thus, displacement is the shortest distance between the given points. It is a vector quantity. S.I. unit of distance and displacement is metre.

According to diagram, Path (1) will represent displacement.

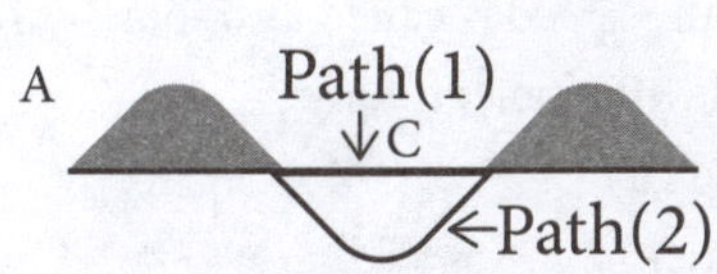

Body Travelling from A to B using different paths

❖ INTEXT QUESTION

5. A body starts from A and moves according to given figure. The body retraces the path after C then reaches to D. Find distance and displacement for each path.

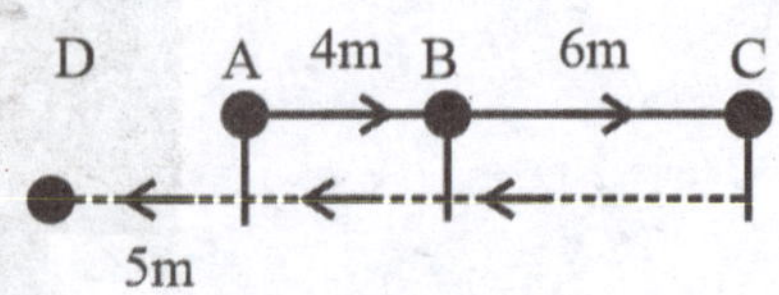

Solution: The distance and displacement for each path is discussed as follows:

Path	Distance	Displacement
AB	4 m	4 m
ABC	10 m	10 m
ABCB	16 m	4 m
ABCA	20 m	0 m
ABCAD	25 m	–5 m

Speed

The distance travelled by a body in a unit time is called its speed.

Therefore, Speed = Distance/Time or $s = \frac{d}{t}$. SI unit of speed or average speed is m/s.

Here d = distance, s = speed and t = time

Competition Corner

Uniform Motion
A body has a uniform motion if it covers equal distances in equal intervals of time, no matter how small these time intervals may be.
For example, a car running at a constant speed of 10 m/s, will cover equal distances of 10 metre, in every second. Hence, its motion will be uniform.

Non-Uniform Motion
A body has a non-uniform motion if it cover unequal distances in equal intervals of time. For example, if we drop a ball from the roof of a building, we will find that it covers unequal distances in equal intervals of time. It covers
4.9 metre in the 1st second,
14.7 metre in the 2nd second,
24.5 metre in the 3rd second, and so on.

Check Point 3

18. Give two examples of periodic motion.
19. Correct the following
    (i) The motion of a swing is an example of rectilinear motion.
    (ii) The instrument used to measure speed is called as odometer.
20. What types of motion do the following objects have?
    (a) The needle of sewing machine
    (b) The smoke from an incense stick
    (c) Wheels of a moving car
21. A motorcycle travels a distance of 248 km in 4 hours. What would be the speed of motorcycle?
22. A body travels along the path of PQR. What is the distance travelled by the body?

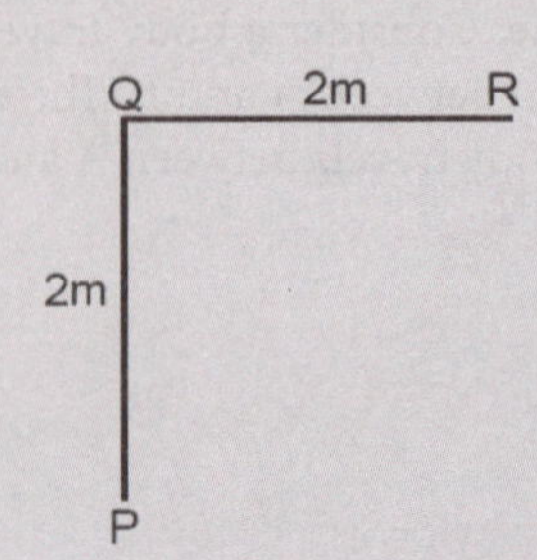

Competition Corner

- Other units of time are
  1 Decade = 10 years; 1 Century = 100 years
  1 Millennium = 10 centuries
- Other unit of length: 1 m = 39.37 inches
- Motion of a body occurs only when a force acts on it. No motion can occurs itself without force.
- **Major Inventions**
  - Aeroplane was invented by Orville and Wilbur Wright.
  - The steam engine was invented by Thomas Newcomen.
  - The light bulb was invented by Thomas Edison.
  - The telephone was invented by Alexander Graham Bell.
- **Time Period of a Simple Pendulum:** Simple pendulum is a small sphere hang through the wire from a fixed point. It does a to and fro motion/ oscillatory motion.

  Let, it starts from A. It will reach at the point at same height as A on opposite side, that is, C.

  The time period of the pendulum will be the time when it again reaches at A. The larger the length of the string, the larger the time period. The time taken by bob from A to B is equal to the time taken by it to B to C and vice-versa in return journey.

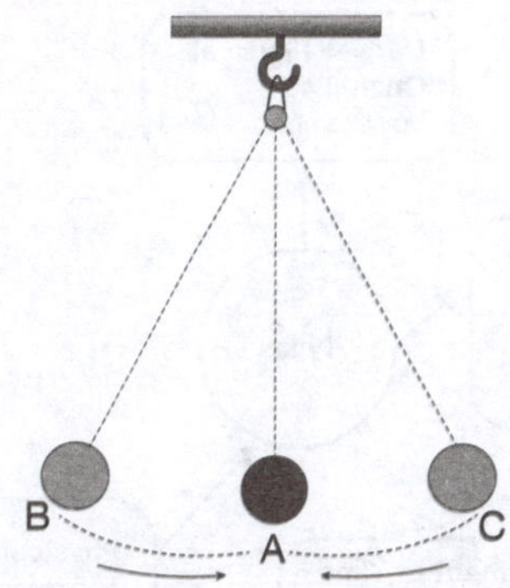

Different Positions of Simple Pendulum

- **Rules for writing SI Units**
  - All the symbols of units should be written is small letters, when they are not the name of scientist.

    Example: kg, m, s.

    If they are name of scientist, then they are written in capital letters.

    Example: N for newton, A for Ampere.
  - Full Stop should not be used after the unit symbol.

    Example: kg not kg.
  - Unit symbol should be written in singular form.

    Example: kg not kgs

STRUCTURAL OUTLINE

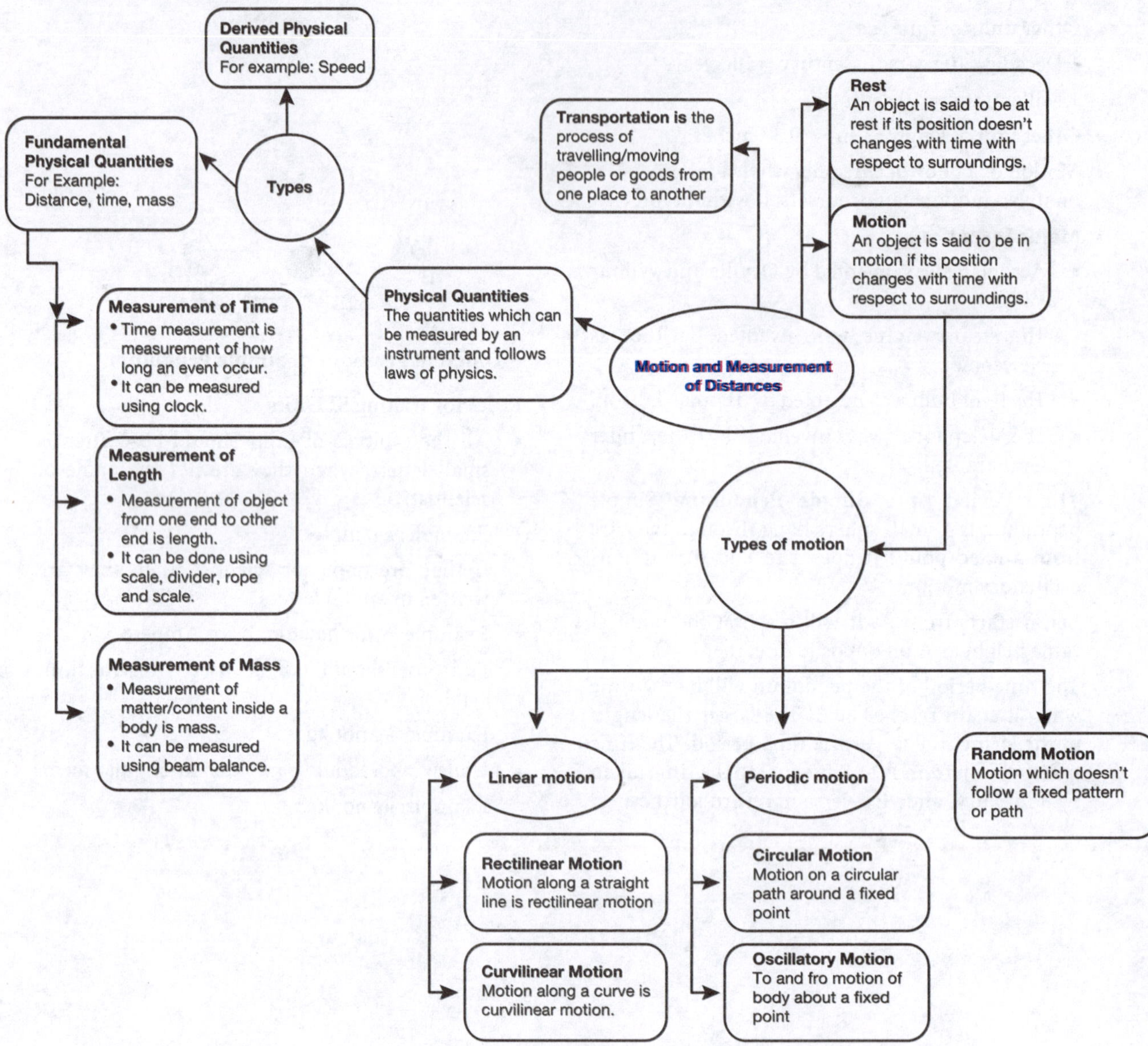

ABRIDGEMENT

- **Speed:** The distance travelled by a body in unit time is called its speed.

  Therefore, speed $= \frac{\text{Distance}}{\text{Time}}$ or $s = \frac{d}{t}$.

  S.I unit of speed or average speed is m/s. It is a scalar quantity.

  - **Average Speed:** For an object moving with variable speed, it is the total distance travelled by an object divided by the total time taken to cover that distance.

    $$\text{Average speed} = \frac{\text{Total Distance Travelled}}{\text{Total Time Taken}}$$

  - **Uniform Speed (or Constant Speed):** When an object covers equal distances in equal intervals of time, it is said to be moving with uniform speed. **Example:** A car moves 10 m in every second so its motion is uniform.
  - **Non-Uniform Motion (or Variable Speed):** If a body covers unequal distances in equal intervals of time or equal distances in unequal intervals of time, then it is said to be moving with non-uniform speed.

    Example: Falling of an apple from a tree, a cyclist moving on a rough road, an athlete running a race, vehicle starting from rest, the motion of a freely falling body etc.

- **Velocity:** It is the rate of change of displacement.

  Therefore, velocity $= \frac{\text{Displacement}}{\text{Time}}$ or it is the distance travelled in unit time in a given direction.

  $$\text{Velocity} = \frac{\text{Distance Travelled in a Given Direction}}{\text{Time Taken}}$$

  S.I. unit of velocity is m/s. It is a vector quantity. (Magnitude of the velocity is known as speed.)

  $1 \text{ km/h} = \frac{5}{18} \text{ m/s}$

  - **Uniform Velocity (or Constant Velocity):** If a body covers equal distances in equal intervals of time in a given direction, then it is said to be moving with constant velocity.
  - **Non-Uniform Velocity (or Variable Velocity):** When a body does not cover equal distances in equal intervals of time, in a given direction (in this case speed is not constant), then it is said to be moving with non-uniform velocity. If speed is constant then also body can have a non-uniform velocity (in this case the direction of motion changes). **Example:** A car moving on a circular road with constant speed.

- **Acceleration:** Mostly the velocity of a moving object changes either in magnitude or in direction or in both when the object moves. Then the body is said to have acceleration. So, it is the rate of change of velocity, i.e., change in velocity in unit time is said to be acceleration. It is a vector quantity. Its S.I. unit is m/s^2 and C.G.S unit is cm/s^2.

  $$\text{Acceleration, } a = \frac{\text{Change in Velocity}}{\text{Time}} = \frac{\text{Final Velocity} - \text{Initial Velocity}}{\text{Time}}$$

  $$\Rightarrow a = \frac{v - u}{t} \Rightarrow v = u + at$$

- **Types of Acceleration**
  - **Positive Acceleration:** If the velocity of an object increases in the same direction, then the object has a positive acceleration. **For example:** A freely falling body.
  - **Negative Acceleration (Retardation):** If the velocity of a body decreases in the same direction, the body has a negative acceleration or it is said to be retardation. **For example:** A train slows down.

EXEMPLIFICATION

Q1. You are sitting in a moving car. Are you at rest or in motion according to the car? Explain.

Solution: You are at rest according to the car because you are not moving with respect to the car.

Q2. Why we shouldn't use our hand for measurement?

Solution: Every person has hands of different length. So, it is not reliable to use hand for measurement.

Q3. Which measuring device can be used for measuring the girth of a thick pole?

Solution: Measuring tape.

Q4. The height of a boy is 2.00 m. Express it into cm and mm.

Solution: The height of a boy in cm is 200 cm and in mm is 2000 mm.

Q5. How motion of ceiling fan and motion of a pendulum are different?

Solution: Motion of ceiling fan is circular motion and motion of a pendulum is periodic motion/oscillatory motion.

Q6. Why can't be elastic tape used to measure distances?

Solution: We can't use elastic tape to measure distances because we will not know how much we stretched the tape during measurement. It will cause error.

Q7. The distance between Rahul's house and Rohit's house is 2500 m. Express it in km.

Solution: 1000 m =1 km. So, 2500 m = 2.5 km.

NCERT COMPENDIUM

1. Some lengths are given in Column I of Table below. Some units are given in Column II. Match the lengths with the units suitable for measuring those lengths.

Column I	Column II
Distance between Delhi and Lucknow	Centimetre
Thickness of a coin	Kilometre
Length of an eraser	Metre
Lenth of school ground	Millimetre

Solution: Distance between Delhi and Lucknow – kilometre
Thickness of a coin – millimetre
Length of an eraser – centimetre
Length of school ground – metre

2. Read the following statements and mark True (T) or False (F) against each.
   (i) The motion of a car moving on a straight road is an example of linear motion.
   (ii) Any object which is changing its position with respect to a reference point with time is said to be in motion.
   (iii) 1 km = 100 cm

Solution: (i) true (ii) true (iii) false

3. Which of the following is not a standard unit of measuring length?
(i) millimetre (ii) centimetre (iii) kilometre (iv) handspan

Solution: (iv) handspan

4. Search for the different scales or measuring tapes at your home and school. Find out the smallest value that can be measured using each of these scales. Record your observations in a tabular form.

Solution:

Different Scales	Smallest value that can be measured
Centimetre scale	1mm
Metre scale	1 cm
Measuring Tape	1 cm

5. Suppose the distance between your school and home is 1.5 km. Express it in metres.
Answer: 1.5 km = 1.5 × 1000 m = 1500 m

6. Take a tumbler or a bottle. Measure the length of the curved part of the base of glass or bottle and record it.

Solution: The length of curved part is 8 cm.

7. Measure the height of your friend and express it in (i) metres (ii) centimetres and (iii) millimetres.

Solution: (i) 2.25 foot = 0.68 m (ii) 68 cm (iii) 680 mm

8. You are given a coin. Estimate how many coins are required to be placed one after the other lengthwise, without leaving any gap between them, to cover the whole length of the chosen side of a notebook. Verify your estimate by measuring the same side of the notebook and the size of the coin using a 15-cm scale.

Solution: 7 coins are required. Estimated length = 7 × 1.5 cm = 10.5 cm

9. Give two examples each for linear, circular and oscillatory motion.

Solution: Linear: The motion of a car on straight road, the motion of a ball rolling down in a straight line
Circular: Motion of Earth around Sun, Motion of stone tied to string
Oscillatory: Motion of bob of pendulum, Motion of a child on swing

10. Observe different objects around you. It is easier to express the lengths of some objects in mm, some in cm and some in m. Make a list of three objects in each category and enter them in the Table below.

Size	Objects
mm	
cm	
m	

Solution: mm: Thickness of wire, Size of ant, Thickness of coin
cm: Size of eraser, Size of notebook, Diameter of coin
m: Length of the room, Length of a cloth, Length of playground

11. A rollercoaster track is made in the shape shown in Figure. A ball starts from point A and escapes through point F.

Identify the types of motion of the ball on the rollercoaster and corresponding portions of the track.

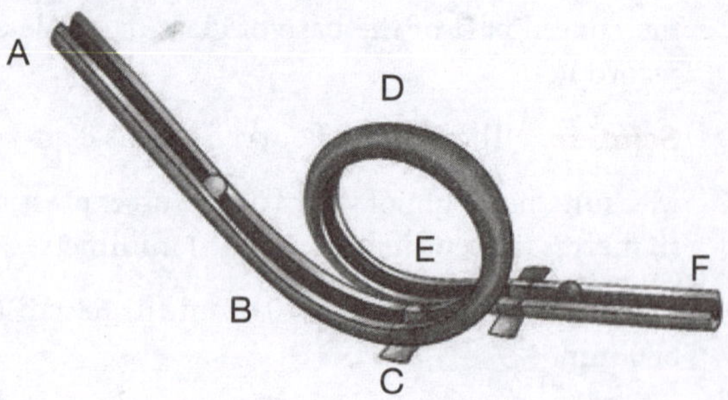

Solution: A to B: Linear motion
C to E: Circular motion
E to F: Linear motion

12. Tasneem wants to make a metre scale by herself. She considers the following materials for it—plywood, paper, cloth, stretchable rubber and steel. Which of these should she not use and why?

Solution: She should not use paper because it may tear down easily.
She should not use cloth because it is very flexible.
She should not use Stretchable rubber because while measuring, it may stretch causing incorrect measurement.

13. Think, design and develop a card game on conversion of units of length to play with your friends.

Solution: Let your creative juices flow. Do it on your own.

ASSESSMENT CORNER

Level 1

Fixed Response Type

Multiple Choice Questions

1. Why do different students get different measurements when they use their hand spans to measure the same desk?
(A) They are not measuring carefully.
(B) The desk changes its length.
(C) Handspans vary from person to person.
(D) The measurement technique is wrong.

2. In which year people began the use of animals to haul their loads?
(A) 6000 BC (B) 5000 BC
(C) 4000 BC (D) 3000 BC

3. Long ago, people developed boats on the pattern of
(A) Streamlined shape of birds
(B) Streamlined shape of fish
(C) Streamlined shape of submarine
(D) Elongated shape of python

4. Which of the following is the slowest mode of transportation?
(A) Bullock cart (B) Aeroplane
(C) Train (D) Car

5. The movement of things and people from one place to another is known as
(A) Measurement (B) Transportation
(C) Unit (D) Cubit

6. The S.I. system of measurement is the abbreviation of
(A) International Measurement System
(B) Standard of India
(C) International System of Units
(D) International Standard of Units

7. The S.I. unit of mass is
(A) kilogram (B) centigram
(C) milligram (D) tonne

8. If the mass of the bag carried by Neha is 1.5 kg, then what will be the mass in grams?
(A) 1.5 g (B) 15 g
(C) 150 g (D) 1500 g

9. One metre square is equal to
(A) 100,000 centimetre square
(B) 10,000 centimetre square
(C) 1000 centimetre square
(D) 100 centimetre square

10. 1 cm^2 is equal to
(A) 1/100 m^2 (B) 1/1000 m^2
(C) 1/10000 m^2 (D) 1/10 m^2

11. Second is the SI unit of
(A) Length (B) Mass
(C) Temperature (D) Time

12. The area of rectangle is given as the product of length and
(A) Breadth (B) Side
(C) Volume (D) None of these

13. 1 mm is equal to
(A) 1/10 cm (B) 1/100 cm
(C) 1/1000 cm (D) 1 cm

14. 1 cm^3 = _____ m^3
(A) 10^{-6} (B) 10^{-3}
(C) 10^9 (D) 10^6

15. Which of the following is a standard unit of length?
(A) Foot (B) Meter
(C) Inch (D) Yard

16. A student wants to measure the thickness of a single coin. Which measuring tool would be most appropriate?
(A) Measuring tape (B) 30 cm ruler
(C) Vernier callipers (D) Meter stick

17. When a bus is passing by a standing man, then we can say that
(A) the bus is in motion
(B) the man is in motion
(C) both are in motion
(D) both are at rest

18. Which unit is larger?
(A) Centimeter (B) Millimeter
(C) Kilometer (D) Meter

19. The reference point in motion is important because:
(A) It makes objects move faster.
(B) It determines whether an object appears to be in motion or at rest.
(C) It changes the speed of objects.
(D) It affects the size of objects.

20. S.I unit of speed is
(A) ms (B) $\frac{m}{s}$
(C) $\frac{m}{s^2}$ (D) none of these

21. A child on a swing exhibits which combination of motions?
(A) Only linear motion
(B) Only circular motion
(C) Oscillatory and curved motion
(D) Random and circular motion

22. The concept of rest and motion tells us how:
(A) All objects move at the same speed.
(B) The state of rest or motion depends on the reference point.
(C) Only fast objects appear to move.
(D) Motion is always in a straight line.

23. Which of the following tools is best suited to measure the diameter of a small ball?
(A) Measuring tape (B) Ruler
(C) Vernier caliper (D) Protractor

24. Motion of the point on blade of a moving fan
(A) Linear (B) Circular
(C) Oscillatory (D) Vibrational

25. The motion which repeats itself after a regular interval of time
(A) Periodic (B) Non Periodic
(C) Rotational (D) Vibrational

Fill in the Blanks

1. No trade is possible without____________ (transportation/Sun)

2. The determination of the size or magnitude of something is called_______(motion/ measurement).

3. There are_______millimeters in one centimeter. (1 / 10)

4. SI unit of length is_________. (m^2/m)

5. A body repeating its motion after certain interval of time is in_________ motion. (Periodic/Non Periodic)

6. ________ represents motion in a straight line. (Spinning top/ Car moving on a straight road)

7. A stone thrown up in the air is an example of __________ motion. (linear/rotational)

8. _______ is not a non-standard unit of measurement. (Footstep / Meter)

9. In rectilinear motion, object moves in a _________ line. (straight/zig-zag)

10. Motion of a child on a swing is called as _____. (Periodic/Non Periodic)

11. Motion of the needle of a sewing machine is called as __________. (Oscillatory/linear)

12. Motion of the wheel of a bicycle is_________. (linear/Circular)

True/False

1. Prehistoric people used animals to carry their loads.

2. Millimeter is the most appropriate unit to measure the length of a pencil.

3. S.I system was introduced in year 1990.

4. S.I unit of length is centimeter.

5. When a body moves around a fixed point, it is said to have linear motion.

6. km/h, m/s, km/min, m/min, m/h are the units of speed.

7. Motion of earth around sun is random motion.

Match Type Questions

1. Match the Column A with Column B

Column A	Column B
(i) Unit of length	(a) Motion along straight line
(ii) Linear motion	(b) Oscillatory Motion
(iii) Unit of mass	(c) Metre
(iv) To and fro periodic motion	(d) Pound

(A) (i)–(a), (ii)–(c), (iii)–(b), (iv)–(d)
(B) (i)–(c), (ii)–(a), (iii)–(d), (iv)–(b)
(C) (i)–(d), (ii)–(a), (iii)–(c), (iv)–(b)
(D) (i)–(c), (ii)–(b), (iii)–(a), (iv)–(d)

2. Match the following using the most convenient unit.

Column A	Column B
(i) One rupee coin	(a) m^2
(ii) Cricket field	(b) Hectare
(iii) Paddy field	(c) km^2
(iv) Country	(d) cm^2

(A) (i)–(b), (ii)–(d), (iii)–(a), (iv)–(c)
(B) (i)–(d), (ii)–(a), (iii)–(b), (iv)–(c)
(C) (i)–(c), (ii)–(d), (iii)–(a), (iv)–(b)
(D) (i)–(a), (ii)–(b), (iii)–(d), (iv)–(c)

3. Match the Column A with Column B

Column A	Column B
(i) A wheel rolling on the surface	(a) Non-uniform motion
(ii) A ball falling vertically downwards	(b) Rectilinear motion
(iii) The motion of watch hands	(c) Translatory as well as rotatory motion
(iv) The motion of a train when approaches towards a station	(d) Uniform motion

(A) (i) → (b); (ii) → (a); (iii) → (c); (iv) → (d)
(B) (i) → (c); (ii) → (b); (iii) → (d); (iv) → (a)
(C) (i) → (a); (ii) → (c); (iii) → (d); (iv) → (b)
(D) (i) → (d); (ii) → (b); (iii) → (a); (iv) → (c)

Assertion and Reason Type Questions

Read the given statements and select the correct option.

(A) Both A and R are true and R is the correct explanation of A.
(B) Both A and R are true but R is not the correct explanation of A.
(C) A is true but R is false.
(D) A is false but R is true.

1. **Assertion:** The displacement of a body may be zero, though distance can be finite.
Reason: If a body moves such that finally it arrives at initial point, then displacement is zero while distance is finite.

2. **Assertion:** In International system of units the unit of length is centimetre.
Reason: If a centimetre is divided into ten equal parts then each part is equal to a millimetre.

3. **Assertion:** In ancient times bullock cart was used as a means of transport.
Reason: Aeroplanes were developed only in 1800 AD.

4. **Assertion:** Speed can be negative
Reason: Speed can be positive or zero only.

Comprehension Type Questions

Directions: Read the passage (s) given below and answer the questions that follow.

Passage-I: A system having a set of standard units of measurement which was accepted all over the world is called International system of units (S.I. system).

1. The S.I. system of units is based on
(A) F.P.S. system (B) Metric system
(C) both of these (D) None of these

2. The metric system of units was created by
(A) Germans (B) Indians
(C) Chinese (D) French

3. In S.I. system of units, the standard unit of distance is
(A) kilometre (B) metre
(C) centimetre (D) All of these

Passage II: Consider the below figures to solve question 4-6.

(i)

(ii)

(iii)

(iv)

4. Look at the pictures above and arrange them in correct chronological order starting from ancient times.
(A) (i), (iii), (ii), (iv)
(B) (iii), (i), (ii), (iv)
(C) (ii), (iii), (i), (iv)
(D) (iv), (iii), (ii), (i)

5. Which means of transport makes use of steam engine?
(A) (i) (B) (ii)
(C) (iii) (D) (iv)

6. Which means of transport used the invention of wheel?
(A) (i) (B) (i) and (ii)
(C) (i), (ii) and (iii) (D) All of these

Free Response Type

Very Short Answer Type Questions

1. Define transportation.
2. Give an example of circular motion.
3. How will you measure the length of curved line?
4. Distinguish between the state of rest and motion.
5. Name the SI unit of measurement for temperature.
6. Define distance along with its SI unit.
7. Name the device used to measure the distance traveled by a vehicle.

Short Answer Type Questions

1. What are the advantages of Modern means of transport?
2. What are the disadvantages of modern means of transport?
3. Explain the type of motion exhibited by the hands of a clock.
4. State the importance of measurements.
5. Discuss the use of divider.
6. Why could you not use an elastic measuring tape to measure distance?
7. If a train travels 120 kilometers in 2 hours, calculate its speed.
8. State the difference between circular motion & oscillatory motion with example.

Long Answer Type Questions

1. What are the advantages of wheel?
2. Explain how you will measure the average speed of the journey between your home and school.
3. While measuring the length of a knitting needle the reading of the scale at one end is 5 cm & at the other end is 23.2 cm. What is the length of the needle?
4. Explain the motion that repeats itself after a fixed interval of time with examples.
5. Rohan is trying to find out the length of his room. Help him by explaining the method.
6. Write down the similarities (in motion) between:
(i) Movement of the earth about its axis and the movement of the rotating top.
(ii) The birds in the sky and fish in a pond.
7. How can you measure the time period of one year?
8. Find the speed of Vijay if he covers a distance of 20 km in 0.5 hour.
9. Convert the followings
(i) 54 km/h = ? m/s (ii) 30 m/s = ? km/h

Numerical Based Questions

1. A boy was riding his bicycle at a speed of 10 m/s. He covered 1 km. Calculate the time taken by him.
2. A boy is cycling and follows the path as shown in the figure. The total trip consists of four straight line path AB, BC, CD and DE. At the end of the journey, what is the boy's displacement from the starting point?

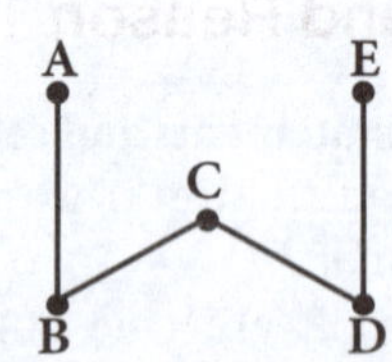

3. A body travels from A to B to C to D to E as shown in figure. The distance between A and E is 2 cm. What is the distance moved by the moving body?

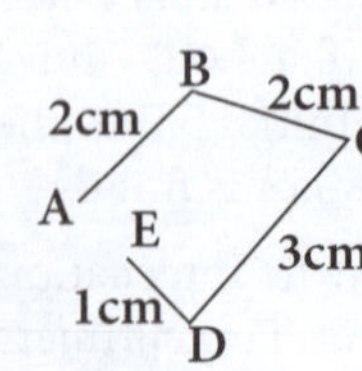

Case Based Questions

Directions: Read the passage given below and answer the questions that follow.

Passage: Observe a tailor working on a sewing machine. The sewing machine remains at the same location while its wheel moves with a circular motion. It also has a needle that moves up and down continuously, as long as wheel rotates.

1. Select the one that remains at rest when you were making the above observation.
(A) Tailor
(B) Sewing machine
(C) Both tailor and sewing machine
(D) None of the above is correct

2. In this observation the circular motion was observed in
(A) Wheel of machine
(B) Needle of machine
(C) Both (A) and (B)
(D) None of the above is correct

3. The up and down motion of the needle of sewing machine can be classified as
(A) rotatory motion (B) circular motion
(C) periodic motion (D) None of these

Level 2

Multiple Choice Questions

1. Standard units of measurement were introduced primarily to:
(A) Make mathematics easier.
(B) Ensure consistency in global trade and science.
(C) Reduce the number of measuring tools needed.
(D) Make measurements faster.

2. Measurement means the comparison of
(A) two known quantities
(B) two unknown quantities
(C) an unknown quantity with all known quantities of different kind
(D) an unknown quantity with some known quantity of same kind

3. The smallest time measured by a wrist watch accurately is
(A) 1 milli second (B) 60 second
(C) 1 second (D) 1 hour

4. Error occurs when:
(A) The measuring tool is broken.
(B) The object being measured is too small.
(C) The observer's eye is not positioned correctly.
(D) The measurement is taken too quickly.

5. The standard unit of measuring large distances, such as the distance between cities, is:
(A) Centimeter (B) Kilometer
(C) Meter (D) Millimeter

6. An example of translatory motion is
(A) a car moving on a curved path
(B) a ball tied to a string and whirled around
(C) a striker moving across a carrom board
(D) the child moving on a swing

7. A marble rolling down a ramp demonstrates:
(A) Only rotational motion.
(B) Only translational motion.
(C) Both rotational and translational motion.
(D) Only oscillatory motion.

8. The distance covered by a moving object in unit time is called:
(A) Distance (B) Displacement
(C) Speed (D) Velocity

9. Which of the following units is used to measure the length of very small objects like bacteria?
(A) Meter (B) Centimeter
(C) Millimeter (D) Micrometer

10. The motion of planets around the Sun is best described as:
(A) Linear motion
(B) Oscillatory motion
(C) Circular/elliptical motion
(D) Random motion

11. When measuring the circumference of a cylindrical pipe, a flexible measuring tape is preferred over a rigid ruler because:
(A) It is cheaper
(B) It can follow the curved surface accurately
(C) It is easier to read
(D) It is more durable

Direction: Refer to the given figure and answer questions:

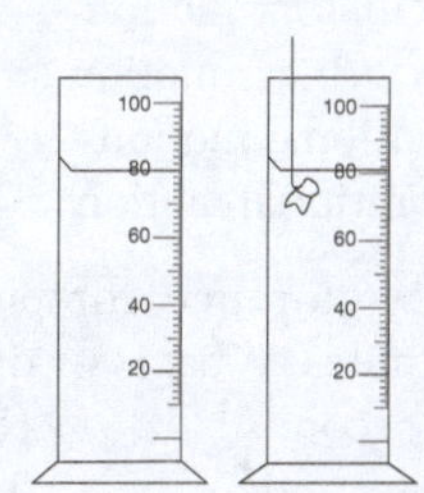

12. Given figure shows a measuring cylinder before and after the immersion of an irregular solid object. The volume of the object is
(A) 82 cm^3 (B) 12 cm^3
(C) 30 cm^3 (D) 18 cm^3

13. To measure the thickness of a thin sheet of paper, the most suitable unit would be:
(A) Meter (B) Millimeter
(C) Centimeter (D) Kilometer

ASSESSMENT CORNER

14. The period of a pendulum refers to:
(A) The maximum distance it travels.
(B) The time taken for one complete oscillation.
(C) The number of oscillations per minute.
(D) The height from which it is released.

15. Which of the following statements is incorrect regarding the symbol used for a unit of a physical quantity?
(A) The symbol named after scientist should have capital letter.
(B) They take plural forms.
(C) They can be written in full.
(D) They should be written only in the agreed symbols.

16. Two friends measure the length of the same table using different units. One uses meters and the other uses feet. Why might their measurements differ, and how can they standardize their results?
(A) Different measurement tools; use a ruler
(B) Different unit systems; convert all measurements to a common unit
(C) Different measurement techniques; use the same technique
(D) Different perspectives; measure from the same point

17. In which scenario would you use millimetres as the preferred unit?
(A) Measuring the distance between two cities.
(B) Measuring the length of a football field.
(C) Measuring the thickness of a book.
(D) Measuring the height of a building.

18. The motion of the blades of a food processor is an example of
(A) oscillatory motion
(B) curvilinear motion
(C) rotational motion
(D) vibrational motion

19. A merry-go-round completes four rotations in two minutes. What is its time period of rotation?
(A) 15 seconds (B) 30 seconds
(C) 45 seconds (D) 60 seconds

20. Which of the following statements is false?
(A) The motion of a swing is rectilinear as well as circular.
(B) A guitar shows vibratory motion.
(C) Pendulum of a clock shows oscillatory motion.
(D) A ceiling fan shows rotatory motion

21. A pendulum completes 20 oscillations in 10 seconds. What is the time period of the pendulum?
(A) 0.5 seconds (B) 1 second
(C) 2 seconds (D) 0.1 seconds

22. A measurement consists of
(A) number only (B) unit only
(C) both (A) and (B) (D) None of these

23. A rectangular garden measures 25.5 meters in length and 18.75 meters in width. What is the perimeter in centimetres?
(A) 8850 cm (B) 8825 cm
(C) 8875 cm (D) 8800 cm

24. If a body is moving on a straight path, covering equal distances in equal interval of time. What does it signify about the motion?
(A) The object is stationary
(B) The object is moving with uniform speed
(C) The object is accelerating
(D) The object is decelerating

25. If a measuring tape shows readings from 5.2 cm to 23.7 cm when measuring a pencil, what is the actual length of the pencil?
(A) 28.9 cm (B) 18.5 cm
(C) 23.7 cm (D) 18.9 cm

26. A student needs to convert 3.75 kilometres to millimetres. The correct answer is:
(A) 3,750 mm (B) 37,500 mm
(C) 375,000 mm (D) 3,750,000 mm

27. Which of the following scenarios represents periodic motion, and why is it categorized as such?
(A) A car moving on a highway; because it moves in a straight line
(B) A child on a swing; because it repeats its motion at regular intervals
(C) A stone falling from a height; because it accelerates due to gravity
(D) A ball rolling on the ground; because it eventually stops

28. A pendulum completes 15 oscillations in 30 seconds. What is its time period?
(A) 0.5 seconds (B) 2 seconds
(C) 15 seconds (D) 45 seconds

29. You have a metal rod and need to measure its length. What tool and method would you choose?
(A) Ruler; measure once
(B) Measuring tape; measure once
(C) Vernier caliper; take multiple measurements and average them
(D) Thread; wrap around and measure the thread

30. To measure the internal diameter of a test tube accurately, you should:
(A) Place the ruler inside the tube.
(B) Measure from the outside and guess.
(C) Use vernier callipers and position your eye at the level of measurement.
(D) Estimate the measurement.

31. How does using different units of measurement affect the outcome when comparing the lengths of two objects?
(A) It creates inaccuracies; use any unit
(B) It requires conversion to a common unit to accurately compare
(C) It makes no difference; results are the same
(D) It makes measurements easier; choose any unit

32. A racing track is circular with a radius of 70 meters. The distance covered in one complete round is:
(A) 140 meters (B) 220 meters
(C) 440 meters (D) 490 meters

33. A car is moving with a uniform speed of 60 km/h. How far will it travel in 2.5 hours?
(A) 120 km (B) 150 km
(C) 180 km (D) 240 km

34. When a bus travelling at constant speed overtakes a stationary car, a passenger in the bus observes that the car:
(A) Moves forward relative to the bus
(B) Moves backward relative to the bus
(C) Remains stationary
(D) Moves upward

35. If you have only a 15 cm ruler to measure a 2-meter rope, how many ruler lengths would you need to measure?
(A) About 13 ruler lengths
(B) About 15 ruler lengths
(C) About 17 ruler lengths
(D) About 10 ruler lengths

36. Which of the following illustrates rectilinear motion?
(A) Falling of a stone freely from some height
(B) A moving bus on a straight road
(C) Both the above
(D) None of the above

37. An object moves in a circular path with a constant speed. Which statement is true about its motion?
(A) The object is in rectilinear motion
(B) The object is changing direction
(C) The object is not changing directions
(D) The object's speed is variable

38. A bicycle wheel has a diameter of 60 cm. How many complete rotations will it make to travel 50 meters?
(A) 25 rotations (B) 26 rotations
(C) 27 rotations (D) 28 rotations

39. To avoid error while reading a measurement, your eye should be:
(A) Above the scale
(B) Below the scale
(C) At the same level as the measurement mark
(D) At any convenient position

40. A student measures a textbook's thickness as 2.5 cm using 200 pages. The thickness of one page is approximately:
(A) 0.0125 mm (B) 0.125 mm
(C) 1.25 mm (D) 12.5 mm

41. How can you measure the boundary of the stem of a tree?
(A) Using a measuring tape
(B) Using a long ruler
(C) Using Divider
(D) Using a thread and ruler

42. The motion of a coin moving over a carromboard can be classified as
(A) rectilinear motion (B) circular motion
(C) periodic motion (D) rotatory motion

43. A ball is rolling with a uniform speed of 20 m/s. What will be the speed of the ball after 5 mins?
(A) 0 m/s (B) 10 m/s
(C) 20 m/s (D) 40 m/s

44. When converting a measurement from meters to kilometers, what should be done?
(A) Multiplication by 1000
(B) Division by 1000
(C) Addition of 1000
(D) Subtraction of 1000

45. Two objects, A and B, move in opposite directions along a straight path. If A travels 60 km/h and B travels 40 km/h, how far apart will they be after 1 hour?
(A) 20 km (B) 60 km
(C) 100 km (D) 40 km

46. Select the precaution that has to be taken while taking a measurement of length
(A) the scale be placed in contact with the object
(B) the eye should be placed exactly in front or on top of the point where the measurement is to be Taken
(C) Both the above
(D) None of the above

47. Select the one that is an example of periodic motion
(A) A car taking a turn on a curved road
(B) March past of soldiers
(C) A bird flying in air
(D) A lift moving down

48. If a snail moves 12 millimetres per minute, how far will it travel in 2.5 hours?
(A) 30 mm (B) 300 mm
(C) 1800 mm (D) 3000 mm

49. When measuring a curved path using a measuring tape, you should:
(A) Stretch the tape straight across
(B) Let the tape follow the curved path
(C) Estimate the length
(D) Use a ruler instead

Higher Order Thinking Skills (HOTS)

1. Two identical metal balls A and B moving in opposite directions hit each other at point X as shown in the figure. Changes are most likely to be appear in their

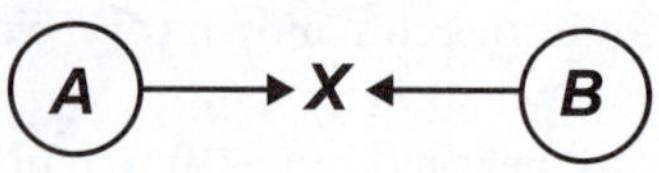

1. Shapes 2. Speeds
3. Directions 4. Volumes
(A) 1 and 3 only (B) 2 and 3 only
(C) 2 and 4 only (D) 1, 2 and 3 only

2. A simple pendulum oscillates between point P and Q shown in figure and its time period is T. If time taken to go from R to Q is t, which of the following relation is correct?

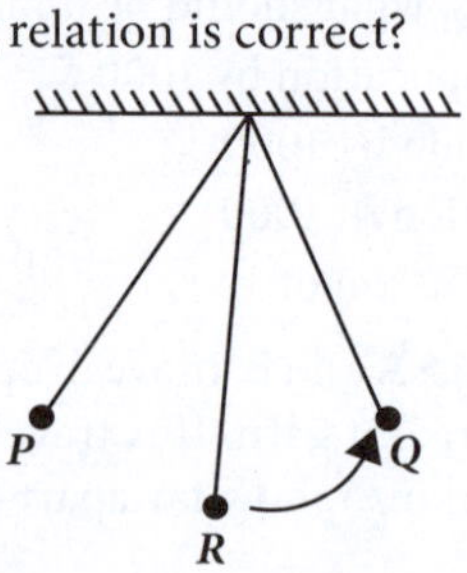

(A) $t = T$ (B) $t = \frac{T}{2}$
(C) $t = \frac{T}{4}$ (D) $t = \frac{T}{8}$

3. A circular disk with a stick moving about its axis through the centre is shown in the figure. Which of the following type of motion is described by the stick?

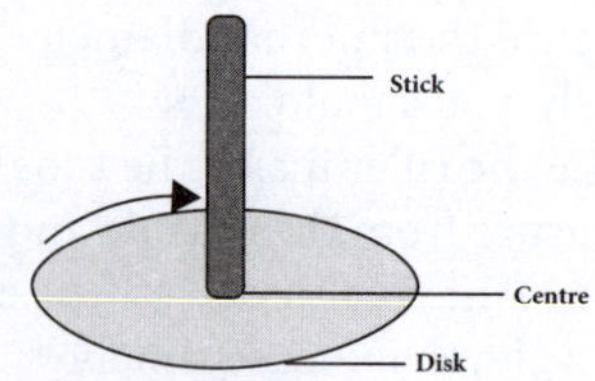

(A) Rotatory motion
(B) Periodic motion
(C) Rectilinear motion
(D) Circular motion

4. A ball is rolling down on an inclined plane as shown in the figure. Which type of motion, the ball is undergoing?

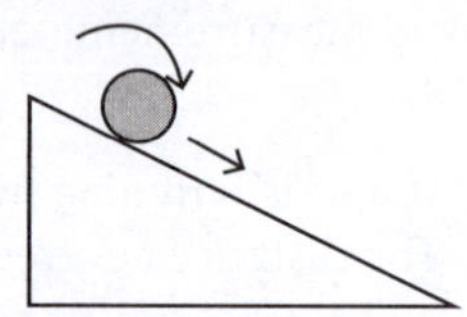

(A) Circular and linear
(B) Periodic and rotational
(C) Rotational and linear
(D) Translatory only

5. Read the given statements and select the correct option.
Statement 1: When we see the trees near the track from a moving train, they appear to be moving.
Statement 2: The position of a tree near the track with respect to a moving train changes.
(A) Both statements 1 and 2 are true and statement 2 is the correct explanation of statement 1.
(B) Both statements 1 and 2 are true but statement 2 is not the correct explanation of statement 1.
(C) Statement 1 is true and statement 2 is false.
(D) Statement 1 is false and statement 2 is true.

6. A passenger in a rotating Ferris wheel experiences different motion classifications depending on the reference frame. From the ground, the passenger exhibits:
(A) Only linear motion
(B) Only rotational motion
(C) Circular motion
(D) No motion

7. There are four pendulums as shown in the given figure. Which of the following pendulums has the longest time period?

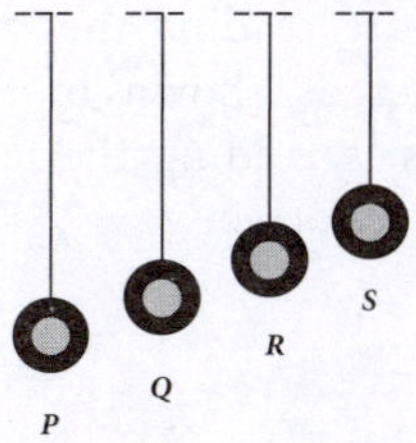

(A) P (B) Q
(C) R (D) S

8. When observing a spinning wheel, different points on the wheel exhibit different types of motion. The centre of the wheel shows:
(A) Circular motion only
(B) Linear motion only
(C) No motion relative to the wheel
(D) Oscillatory motion

9. Which of the following pairs relating different units are incorrect?
(i) 10 cm = 1 dm
(ii) 20 m = 2000 km
(iii) 30 mm = 30000 cm
(iv) 40 m = 400 dm
(A) (i) and (ii) (B) (ii) and (iii)
(C) (iii) and (iv) (D) (i) and (iv)

10. Match the column I with column II and select the correct option from the given codes.

Column - I		Column - II
(i)	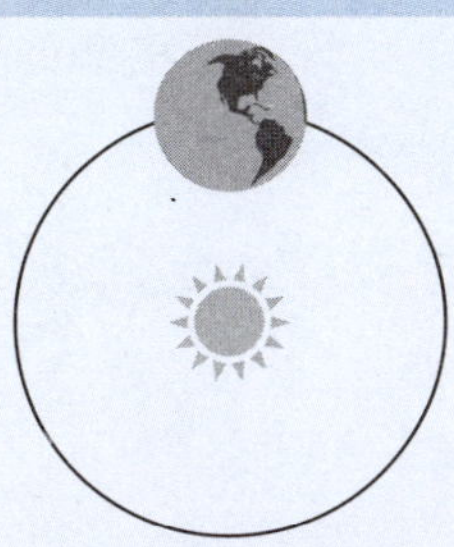	(a) Circular motion
(ii)		(b) Periodic motion
(iii)	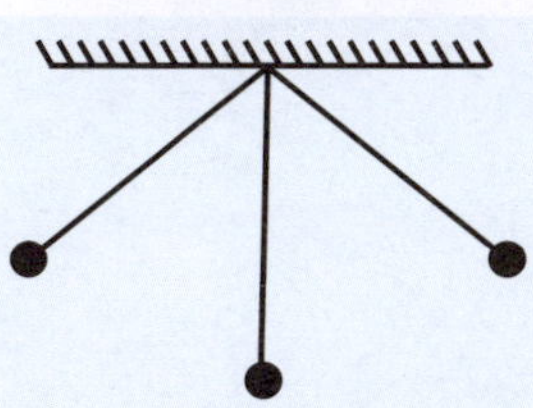	(c) Oscillatory

	(i)	(ii)	(iii)
(A)	(a), (c)	(b), (c)	(a), (b)
(B)	(a), (b)	(a), (c)	(b), (c)
(C)	(a), (b)	(a), (b)	(b), (c)
(D)	(b), (c)	(a), (b)	(a), (c)

11. A pendulum bob pivoted at point A, starts swinging from point B. Assuming that there is no loss of energy to the surroundings, at which position will the bob next come to a momentary rest?

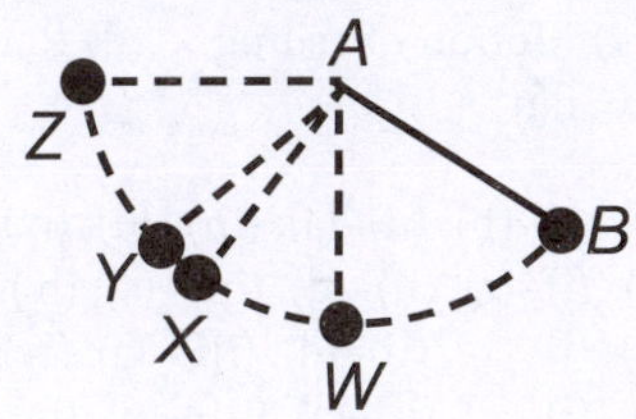

(A) W
(B) X
(C) Y
(D) Z

12. Two trains travelling in the same direction, parallel to each other at 60 km/h each, will appear to a passenger in one train that the other train is moving at:
(A) 60 km/h
(B) 0 km/h
(C) 30 km/h
(D) 120 km/h

13. Match column-A with column-B and select the correct option.

Column A	Column B
(i) Car on a bank road	(a) Rectilinear motion
(ii) Apple falling from a tree	(b) Oscillatory motion
(iii) Moving top	(c) Curvilinear motion
(iv) Kid on a swing	(d) Rotatory motion

(A) (i)–(c), (ii)–(b), (iii)–(d), (iv)–(a)
(B) (i)–(c), (ii)–(a), (iii)–(d), (iv)–(b)
(C) (i)–(d), (ii)–(a), (iii)–(b), (iv)–(c)
(D) (i)–(d), (ii)–(b), (iii)–(a), (iv)–(c)

14. Match column-A with column-B and select the correct option from the given codes.

Column A	Column B
(i) Movement of Snake	(a) Oscillatory motion
(ii) Kids on see-saw	(b) Rotatory motion
(iii) Players playing football	(c) Curvilinear motion
(iv) Motion of ceiling fan	(d) Random motion

(A) (i)–(b), (ii)–(a), (iii)–(d), (iv)–(c)
(B) (i)–(c), (ii)–(d), (iii)–(a), (iv)–(b)
(C) (i)–(b), (ii)–(d), (iii)–(a), (iv)–(c)
(D) (i)–(c), (ii)–(a), (iii)–(d), (iv)–(b)

15. Which of the following conversions is/are incorrect?
(i) 10 decades = 1 century
(ii) 100 centuries = 1 millennium
(iii) 100 inches = 2.54 metres
(iv) 100 millimetres = 10 centimetres
(A) (ii) only (B) (iv) only
(C) (i) and (ii) only (D) (iii) and (iv) only

16. When analysing the motion of a rolling coin, which statement is most accurate?
(A) It exhibits only rotational motion.
(B) It exhibits only translational motion.
(C) Different parts of the coin exhibit different combinations of motion.
(D) All parts move identically.

17. Four boys are reading the temperature on the thermometer as shown in the figure. Which of the boys is reading the temperature on the thermometer correctly?

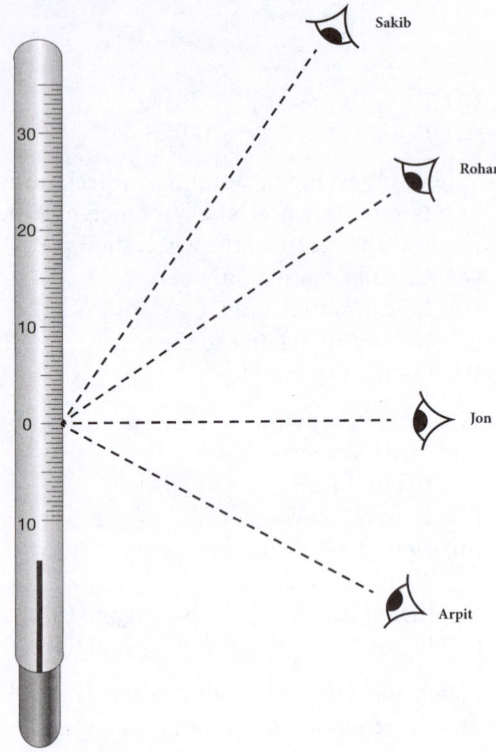

(A) Sakib (B) Jon
(C) Arpit (D) Rohan

ARCHIVE CORNER

1. A cyclist moves from a certain point P and goes round a circle of radius a and reaches Q, exactly at the other side of the point P as shown in figure. The displacement of the cyclist would be

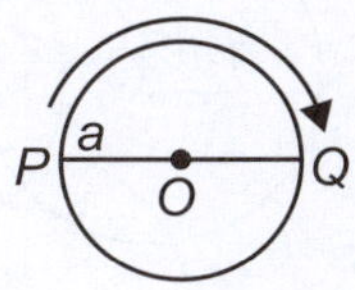

(A) πa (B) 2πa
(C) 2a (D) 2π/a

2. A scientist needs to measure distances ranging from atomic dimensions to astronomical distances. The choice of measurement technique depends primarily on:
(A) Cost of equipment
(B) Unit of measurement and required precision
(C) Personal preference
(D) Speed of measurement

3. In circular motion, the
(A) Direction of motion is fixed
(B) Direction of motion changes continuously
(C) Acceleration is zero
(D) Velocity is constant.

4. A piece of thread folded 6 times is placed along a 15 cm long measuring scale as shown in the figure. The length of the thread is between

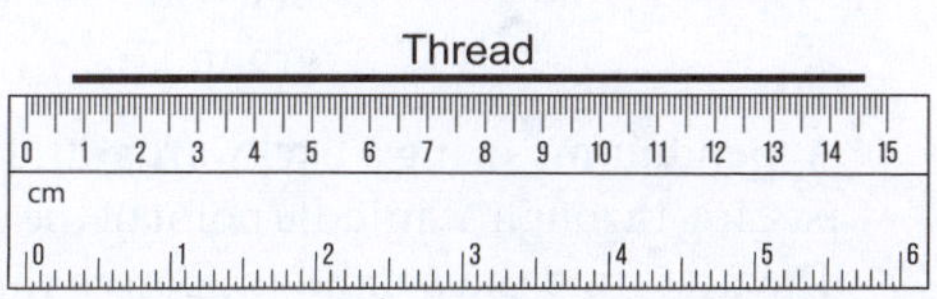

(A) 0.15–0.50 m (B) 0.50 m–1.0 m
(C) 1.0 m–1.5 m (D) 1.5 m–2.0 m

5. In comparing the motion of a child on a swing with a pendulum in a clock, both exhibit periodic motion, but they differ in:
(A) Both have identical time periods.
(B) The swing has a constant time period, while the pendulum's time period changes.
(C) Their time periods depend on different factors, like length and amplitude.
(D) Neither actually exhibits periodic motion.

6. One centimeter on a scale is divided into 20 equal divisions. The least count (minimum value) of this scale is
(A) 20 cm (B) 1 mm
(C) 0.1 mm (D) 0.5 mm

7. Match the following and select the correct option from the codes given below.

Column A	Column B
(i) Railway engine	(a) Quintal
(ii) Packet of chilli powder	(b) kg
(iii) Sack of wheat	(c) mg
(iv) Huge bag of sand	(d) g
(v) Aspirin tablet	(e) Metric ton

(A) (i)–(e), (ii)–(d), (iii)–(a), (iv)–(b), (v)–(c)
(B) (i)–(a), (ii)–(b), (iii)–(c), (iv)–(d), (v)–(e)
(C) (i)–(b), (ii)–(d), (iii)–(e), (iv)–(c), (v)–(a)
(D) (i)–(c), (ii)–(b), (iii)–(d), (iv)–(e), (v)–(a)

8. Which of the following motions is/are periodic as well as oscillatory motion?

(i)  (ii) 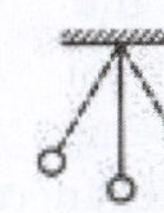

(iii) 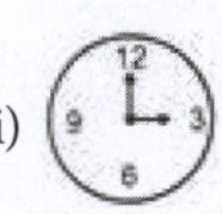

(iv) 

(A) (i), (ii) and (iii) (B) (ii) only
(C) (i), (iii) and (iv) (D) (iii) only

9. Which of the following statements is correct?
(A) Motion of soldiers on march past is a circular motion.
(B) Motion of a train along a curved track on hills is the example of curvilinear motion.
(C) Every circular motion is also a oscillatory motion.
(D) Hockey player running after a ball is a combined motion.

10. Four pieces of wooden sticks P, Q, R and S are placed along the length of 15 cm long scale as shown in figure. What is the average length of these sticks?

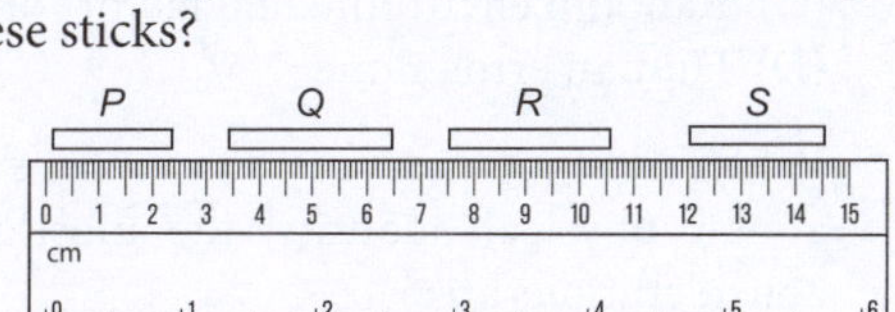

(A) 2.0 cm (B) 2.5 cm
(C) 2.6 cm (D) 2.9 cm

Direction for 11 and 12: Observe the given situation and answer the following question. Rahul and Ravi are playing in a ground. They start running from the same point X simultaneously in the ground and reach point Y at the same time by following paths marked 1 and 2 respectively, as shown in the figure.

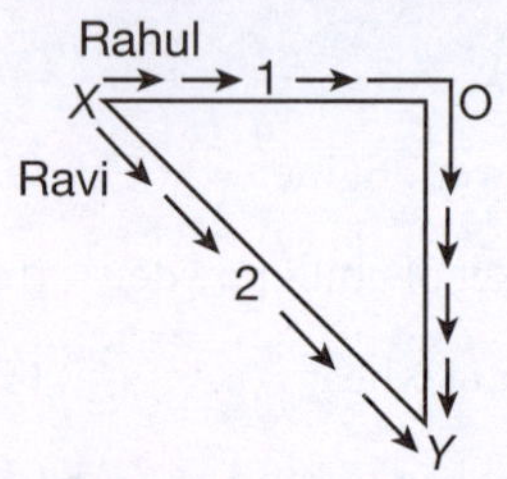

11. Which one of the following paths does show the displacement?
(A) XY (B) XOY
(C) XOYX (D) XYO

12. Which of the following is correct statement for the given situation?
(A) Rahul covers a longer distance with a lower speed.
(B) Rahul covers a longer distance with a higher speed.
(C) Rahul and Ravi both cover different distances with same speed.
(D) Ravi covers a shorter distance with higher speed.

13. When measuring very small distances like the width of a hair, conventional rulers become inadequate because:
(A) They are too expensive
(B) The measurement scale is too large compared to the object being measured.
(C) They are not available in small sizes.
(D) They break easily

14. When comparing the accuracy of measuring the same distance using different methods (pacing, ruler, measuring tape), the variation in results is primarily due to:
(A) The distance is actually changing
(B) Different levels of precision and errors in each method
(C) Random environmental factors only
(D) Human error alone

15. When designing a measurement system for a new physical quantity, the most important considerations are:
(A) Making it different from existing systems
(B) Reproducibility, universality, and appropriate scale
(C) Using familiar body parts as references
(D) Making calculations simple

16. Study the given Venn diagram. Which of the motions described by different bodies are most likely to be I, II and III?

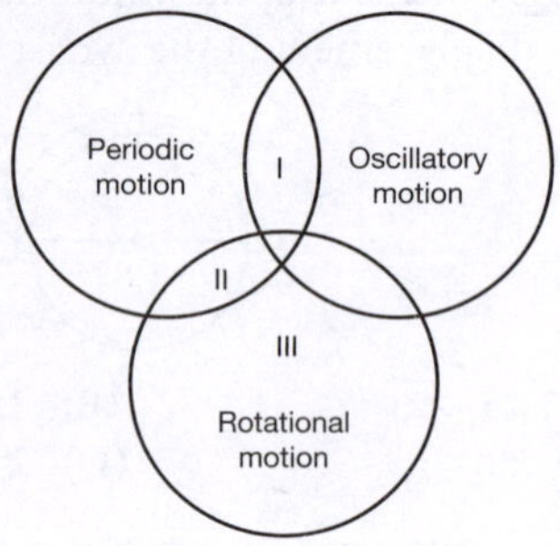

	I	II	III
(A)	Hands of clock	Motion of moon around the earth	The blades of a fan
(B)	Motion of a top	The wheels of a bullock cart	Ball moves around its centre
(C)	To and fro motion of a swing	Hands of a clock	Motion of a top
(D)	Motion of skin of table	Child playing in a play ground	A flying bird

17. A pendulum swings backwards and forwards passing through Y, middle point of the oscillation The first time the pendulum passes through Y, a stopwatch is started.

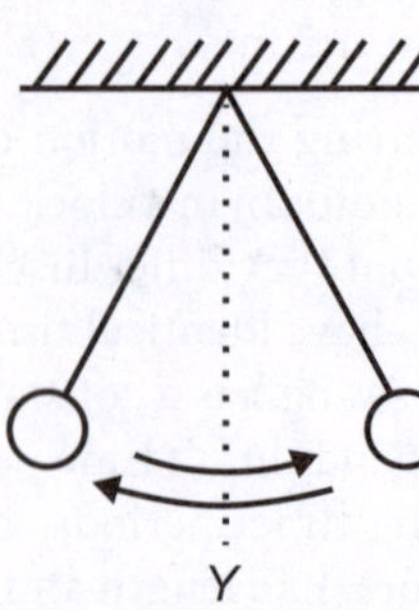

The twenty-first time the pendulum pass through Y, the stopwatch is stopped. The reading is T. What is the time period of the pendulum?
(A) T/40 (B) T/21
(C) T/20 (D) T/10

ANSWER KEY

LEVEL 1

Fixed Response Type

Multiple Choice Questions

1. C	2. B	3. B	4. A	5. B	6. C	7. A	8. D	9. B	10. C
11. D	12. A	13. A	14. A	15. B	16. C	17. A	18. C	19. B	20. B
21. C	22. B	23. C	24. B	25. A					

Fill in the Blanks

1. Transportation	2. Measurement	3. 10	4. m
5. Periodic	6. Car moving on a straight road		7. Linear
8. Meter	9. Straight	10. periodic	11. Oscillatory
12. circular			

True/False

1. True	2. False	3. False	4. False
5. False	6. True	7. False	

Match Type Questions

1. B 2. B 3. B

Assertion Reason Type Questions

1. A 2. D 3. C 4. D

Comprehension Type Questions

1. B 2. D 3. B 4. A 5. C 6. D

Free Response Type

Short Answer Type Questions

7. 60 km/hr

Long Answer Type Questions

3. 18.2 cm	7. 6000 m	8. 40 km/hr	9. (i) 15 m/s, (ii) 108 km/hr

Numerical Based Questions

1. 100 s	2. AE	3. 8 cm

Case Based Questions

1. C 2. A 3. C

Level 2

Multiple Choice Questions

1. B	2. D	3. C	4. C	5. B	6. A	7. C	8. C	9. D	10. C
11. B	12. B	13. B	14. B	15. B	16. B	17. C	18. C	19. B	20. A
21. A	22. C	23. A	24. B	25. B	26. D	27. B	28. B	29. A	30. C
31. B	32. C	33. B	34. B	35. A	36. C	37. B	38. C	39. C	40. B
41. A	42. A	43. C	44. B	45. C	46. C	47. B	48. C	49. B	

Higher Order Thinking Skills (HOTS)

1. B	2. C	3. A	4. C	5. A	6. C	7. A	8. C	9. B	10. C
11. C	12. B	13. B	14. D	15. A	16. C	17. B			

Archive Corner

1. C	2. B	3. B	4. B	5. C	6. D	7. A	8. B	9. B	10. C
11. A	12. B	13. B	14. B	15. B	16. C	17. D			

CHAPTER 2

Exploring Magnets

Learning Outcomes

After reading this chapter, you would be able to:

- explain what a magnet and a magnetic substance is.
- understand the types of magnets and the classification of magnets.
- explain what electromagnet is.
- understand different methods of demagnetization.
- explain what magnetic compass is.

Geekspeak

- Magnetic substance
- Magnet
- Natural magnet
- Artificial magnet
- Temporary magnet
- Permanent magnet
- Electromagnet
- Method of demagnetization
- Magnetic compass

Introduction

A mineral was discovered by a shepherd in the town of magnesia which was found to have a wondrous property—It could attract pieces of iron towards it. This mineral is called magnetite or lodestone.

Magnetite

Types of Substances and Magnet

The types of magnetic substances are discussed as follows:

- **Magnetic Substances:** Those substances which are attracted by magnets are called magnetic substances.
  Example: Iron, Cobalt, Nickel, Steel, etc.
- **Non-Magnetic Substances:** Those substances which are not attracted by magnets are called non-magnetic substances.
  Example: Plastic, Rubber, Glass, etc.

Definition of Magnet

A magnet is a material or object capable of attracting iron and aligns itself in the north-south direction. Magnetic effect can act through non-magnetic materials.

Types of Magnets

There are two types of magnets discussed as follows:

i. **Natural magnet:** A magnet which occurs naturally and is not made by any artificial means is called a natural magnet.
   Example: Magnetite is an ore of iron [Fe_3O_4].

ii. **Artificial magnet:** A substance to which properties of the natural magnet are imparted by artificial means is called artificial magnet.
   Example: Bar magnet, Horseshoe magnet.

Temporary and Permanent Magnets

The temporary and permanent magnets are distinguished on the magnetizing property of the substance.

- **Temporary Magnets:** The magnets which cannot retain their magnetism for a long time are called temporary magnets. Temporary magnets are made of soft iron.
  Example: Electromagnet
- **Permanent Magnets:** The magnets which retain their magnetism for a very long time are called permanent magnets. Permanent magnets are generally made of steel.
  More powerful permanent magnets are made from AlNiCo (an alloy of Aluminium, Nickel, and Cobalt) or from Ferrite. Ferrite made permanent magnets are quite strong.

Keystone

All magnets produce a magnetic force, called a magnetic field. This field travels from a magnet's north pole to south and is completely invisible to the human eye, however, iron filings can be used to show these fields.

Shapes of Magnet

The different shapes of artificial magnets are shown in the Fig. 2.1. The bar magnet and magnetic needle can also be used as a magnetic compass to know the north and south directions. Each magnet has two poles North and South, no matter what their shape is.

Figure 2.1 **Magnets of Different Shapes**

Electromagnet

When an electric current flows through a coil of wire the coil behaves like a magnet (as shown in Fig. 2.2).

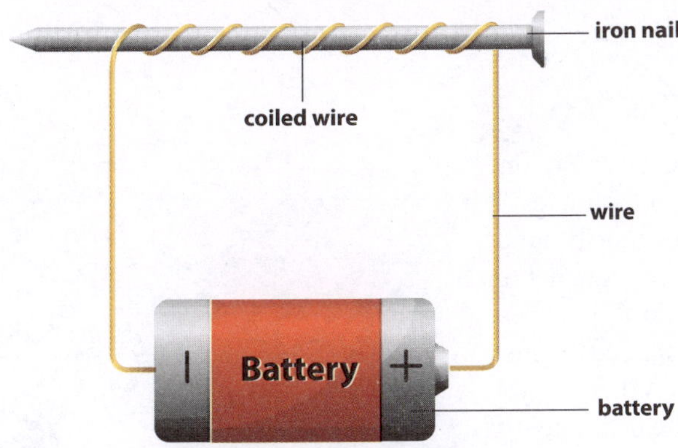

Figure 2.2 **Electromagnet**

When electric current is passed through a copper wire wound over an iron nail, it starts behaving as a magnet and attracts steel paper clips. This makes it an electromagnet.

Properties of Bar Magnet

The properties of a bar magnet are discussed as follows:

- It attracts small pieces of iron towards itself.
- Each magnet has two poles. The magnetic pull seems to come from two points near the ends. These preferred regions of attraction are called the magnetic poles. All magnets have maximum attraction at their poles. Poles of a magnet remain slightly inside from the end points.

Testing Room 1

Spread out some iron fillings over a sheet of paper. Now, move a bar magnet in the fillings taking care that all parts of the magnet move through iron fillings and observe how the iron fillings are distributed all over the magnet.

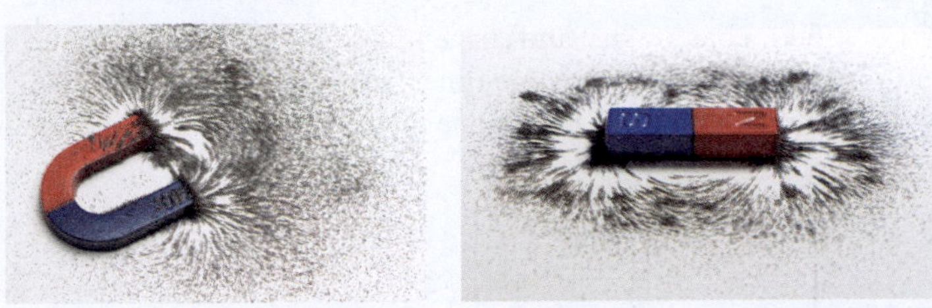

Properties of Magnet

We will notice that most of the iron fillings cling near the ends of the magnet while there are a few iron fillings near the middle.

Repeat the experiment with a horseshoe magnet. This experiment explains the attractive property of magnets.

- **Poles of Magnet:** The points on the magnet which have maximum attraction property are called poles of the magnet. The pole of the magnet lies slightly inside from the end. If 'l' is length of magnet, then the distance between 2 poles is around 0.84 l.

- A freely suspended magnet always aligns itself along the north-south direction. The end of the magnet that points towards the north is called the North pole (N-pole) or north seeking pole and the other end of the magnet pointing towards the South is called the South-pole (S-pole) or south seeking pole because our Earth behaves like a magnet.
- Like poles of the magnets repel each other, while unlike poles attract each other (as shown in Fig. 2.3).

Figure 2.3 **Force of Attraction and Repulsion Between the Poles of Magnet**

Testing Room 2

Take two bar magnets. Suspend one magnet with a piece of thread. It will come to rest in the north south direction. Hold the other magnet in your hand and bring its north pole near the north pole of the suspended magnet, as shown in figure (a). What do you see? You will find that the north pole of the suspended magnet is repelled, i.e., the north pole moves away.

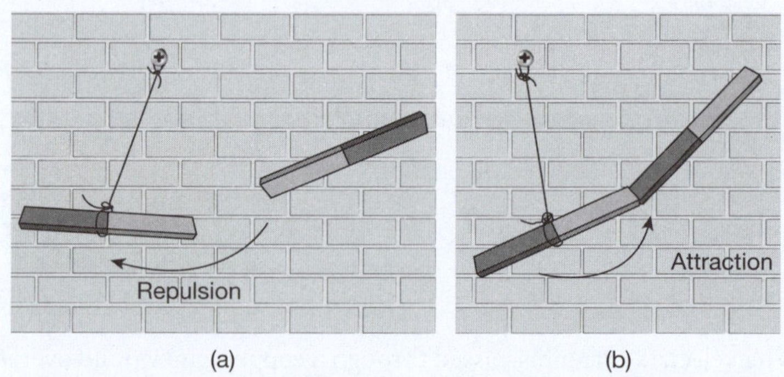

Now bring the south pole of the magnet in the hand near the north pole of the suspended magnet (figure-b). You will find that the north pole of the suspended magnet will be attracted towards the south pole of the other magnet, i.e., north pole of the suspended magnet will come close to the south pole of the magnet in hand.

- Magnetic poles always exist in pair. A single north or south pole cannot exist.
- Repulsion is the surest test of magnetism. A magnet can attract magnet and magnetic substances but it will always repel a magnet only.

Testing Room 3

Take a bar magnet and suspend it freely as shown in figure, or float it on a block of wood in water. The magnet comes to rest after some time. Disturb it a little from its position of rest and see what happens.
You will find that the magnet always comes to rest in the north-south direction.

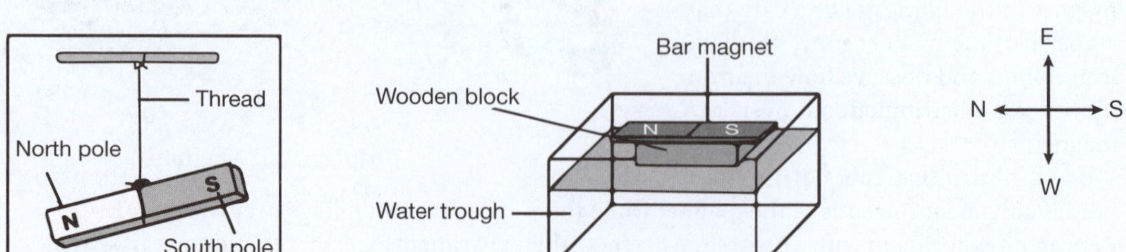

Competition Corner

Magnetic Field Lines: Magnetic field lines are imaginary lines where a tangent to it at any point gives the direction of magnetic field at that point in space.

Magnetic field lines are drawn to represent a magnetic field. Magnetic field lines can be drawn with the help of magnetic compass. Magnetic field lines are also called as magnetic lines of force.

Magnetic Field Lines

❖ INTEXT QUESTIONS

1. What are the different type of magnets and where are the poles located?

   Solution: In a bar magnet the poles are located at the ends of the bar. In a horseshoe magnet the poles are located at the two free ends of the 'U' shape. In a cylindrical magnet the poles are located at the two circular ends of the cylinder

2. It is advised to keep the magnets away from television, mobiles, CDs, and computers. Explain why?

   Solution: Television, mobiles, CDs, computers and many more devices are made up of magnetic materials and have magnets in it. If you bring a magnet closer to it, it will spoil these devices.

3. Name the country in which magnetism was discovered?

   Solution: Magnetism was discovered in Greece.

4. List some non-magnetic substances.

   Solution: Plastic, wood, rubber, glass, etc.

5. What is lodestone?

   Solution: Lodestone is a compound of iron that has the properties of a magnet.

Check Point 1

1. It was observed that a pencil sharpener gets attracted by both the poles of a magnet though its body is made of plastic. Why is it so?
2. A bar magnet has no marking to indicate its poles. How would you find out near which end is the north pole?

Methods of Magnetizing and Demagnetizing

By magnetizing method, a substance is converted into a magnet. By demagnetizing method, a magnet loses its magnetic properties.

Magnetization

The process of making a substance a magnet is known as magnetization. The methods by which an ordinary piece of magnetic material, like iron or steel, can be made into a magnet are single touch method, double touch method, and electrical method. Let us study each method separately.

Single Touch Method

A piece of magnetic material, like iron or steel (a nail, knitting needle, bolt, etc.) is taken and placed on a bench or a table. A bar magnet is brought close to the magnetic material (say an iron piece AB). One end of the bar magnet is stroked against it, moving from end A to end B of the iron piece (as shown in Fig. 2.4).
When the bar magnet reaches end B, it is lifted, and the stroke is repeated from end A to end B. This procedure is repeated several times, keeping two things in mind.

- The same pole of the bar magnet should be used every time.
- Strokes should be in the same direction.

By stroking the iron piece with the north pole of the bar magnet, end A becomes the north pole and end B the south pole.

Double Touch Method

The iron piece to be magnetized, say AB, is placed on a bench and two bar magnets of equal strengths are taken (as shown in Fig. 2.5). Here, the opposite poles of both the magnets are stroked, at the same time, from the centre to the opposite ends of the iron piece being magnetized. This step is repeated many times.
Then, the end A of the iron piece becomes the North pole and end B becomes the South pole.

Keystone

Earth's core is made up of mostly iron, which has given the Earth its own magnetic field, with both a north and south facing pole. The Earth's magnetic field protects the planet by deflecting solar winds and charged particles from the sun.

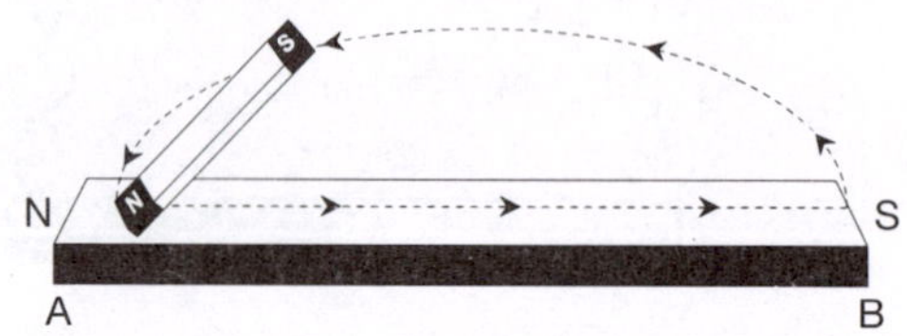

Figure 2.4 **Single Touch Method**

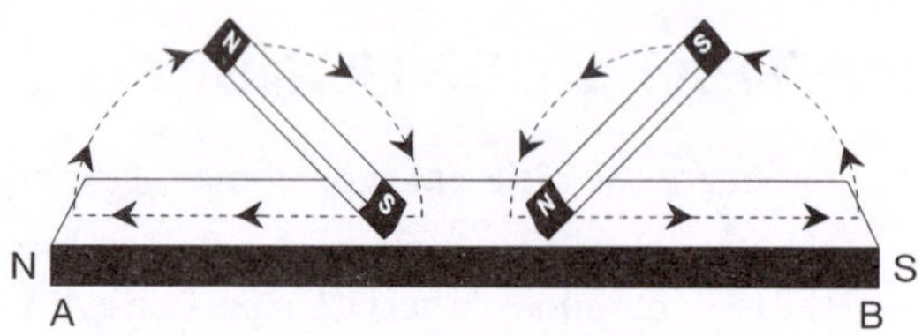

Figure 2.5 **Double Touch Method**

Competition Corner

Electrical Method

Hans Christian Oersted, a Danish scientist, discovered in 1819 that a wire carrying electric current behaves like a magnet. This discovery provided the best method to make magnets, by using an electric current.

A long, insulated copper wire is taken. About 300 or more turns of the wire are wound around a glass or cardboard tube. The turns of the wire are kept as close together as possible. The ends of the wire are connected to a source of electric current and a switch. A knitting needle is put inside the tube and the current switched on for a short period of time.

When the needle is removed from the tube, it behaves like a magnet.

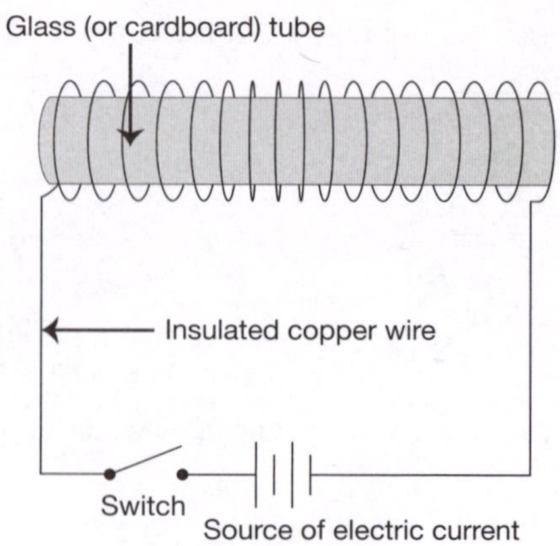

Electrical Method

Demagnetization

The process of losing magnetic properties by a magnet is known as demagnetization.

A magnet can be demagnetized by:

- If the magnet is stored without using magnetic keepers.

  Self-demagnetization: Magnets tend to become weak after some time. This weakening is called self-demagnetization. Small pieces of soft iron are placed in contact with their opposite poles. These pieces of soft iron are called magnetic keepers (as shown in Fig. Fig. 2.6).
- Dropping it from a height or by rough handling.
- Heating or hammering the magnet (as shown in Fig. 2.7).

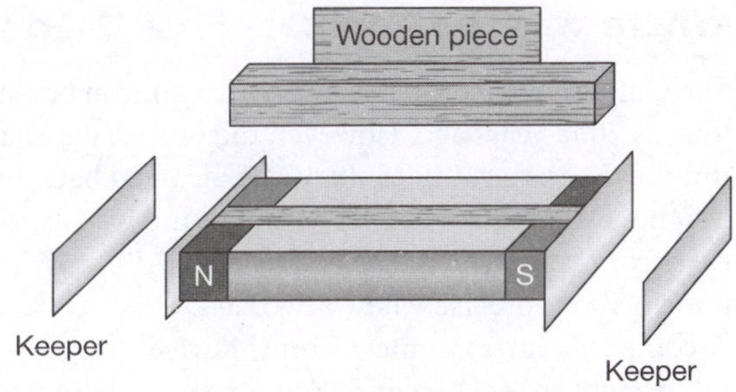

Figure 2.6 Storing Magnets by Using Magnetic Keepers

Precautions while Using Magnet

The precautions that must be taken care while using a magnet are discussed as follows:

- Magnets lose their properties if they are heated, hammered, or dropped from a height.
- Magnets become weak if they are not stored properly. Magnets should be kept in magnetic keepers. A magnetic keeper consists of a wooden piece with two magnets on its two sides with their unlike poles on one side. Two pieces of soft iron are to be placed across their ends.

  However, for a horseshoe magnet, one piece of soft iron is sufficient.
- Keep magnets away from cassettes, mobiles, T.V., CDs, and computers as they are weakened by these devices.

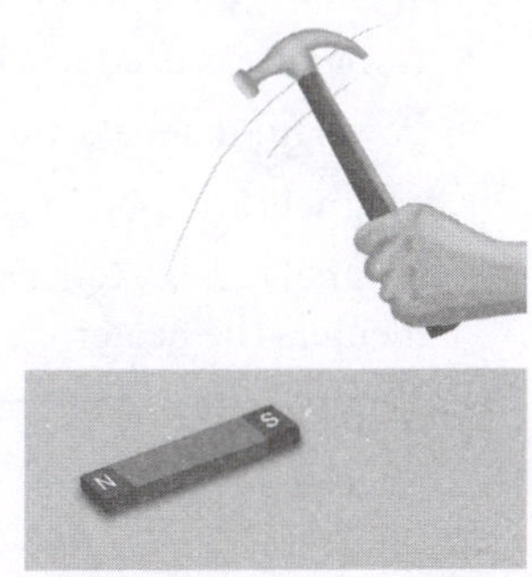

Figure 2.7 Hammering the Magnet

Check Point 2

3. How can you safely store a bar magnet so that they do not lose their magnetic property?
4. If you put a bar magnet near a television for a long period of time, what will happen?
5. You and your friends were decorating the class bulletin board. You dropped the box of stainless-steel pins by mistake. You tried to collect the pins using a bar magnet. You did not succeed. What could be the reason for this?

Magnetic Compass

When people think of instruments that help with direction finding, the first one that comes in mind is the magnetic compass (as shown in Fig. 2.8). It is the oldest instrument for navigation and has been a vital tool for navigators at sea for centuries. The compass allows ships to steer a selected course. By taking bearings of visible objects with a compass, the navigator is also able to fix a ship's position on a chart. It works on the fact that a freely suspended magnet always align itself in north-south direction. There are four cardinal directions or cardinal points marked on the compass as four main directions: north (N), east (E), south (S), and west (W). And there are four ordinal directions or intercardinal directions marked as northeast (NE), southeast (SE), southwest (SW), and northwest (NW).

Figure 2.8 Magnetic Compass

Where was the Compass First Used?

The Chinese were probably aware that an iron bar stroked with a lodestone acquired a directional north-south property as long as 2000 years ago. However, the precise date at which this knowledge was used to create the first magnetic compass is unknown. By the 10th century, the idea had been brought to Europe, probably from China, by Arab traders.

Magnetic compasses of a very simple kind were certainly in use in the Mediterranean as early as the 12th century. However, early compasses were not very reliable. Although the magnetic compass was in general use in the Middle Ages, little was known about precisely how it worked.

A compass is an extremely simple device. A magnetic compass (as opposed to a gyroscopic compass) consists of a small, lightweight magnet balanced on a nearly frictionless pivot point. The magnet is generally called a needle. One end of the needle is often marked "N" for North or coloured in some way to indicate that it points toward North. On the surface, that's all there is to a compass.

Uses of Magnets

The uses of magnets are discussed as follows:

- A magnet is used in a compass to show the direction.
- Powerful magnets are used to lift objects.
- Magnets are used in generators and motors.
- Magnet can prevent corrosion in a water heater. The magnetic calcium particles are attracted by the magnets before it enters the heater.
- Magnets are used in medical equipment.

Check Point 3

6. How does magnetic compass help in navigation?
7. What type of stone was used for navigation before the invention of magnetic compass?
8. What are the letters and numbers marked on the magnetic compass and how many degrees apart are they?
9. Can a compass be used to find east-west direction at any place?
10. How will you identify the north pole of the magnetic compass by simply looking at it?

Competition Corner

Evidence of the Existence of Earth's Magnetic Field

Our earth itself has a magnetic field and it behaves like a magnet. The existence of earth's magnetic field is based on the following fact:

- **A freely suspended magnetic needle always rests in the geographic north-south direction:** When a magnetic needle is suspended such that it is free to rotate in horizontal plane, it always rests indicating the geographic north-south direction. It is clear that the north pole of a magnet will point towards the geographic north only

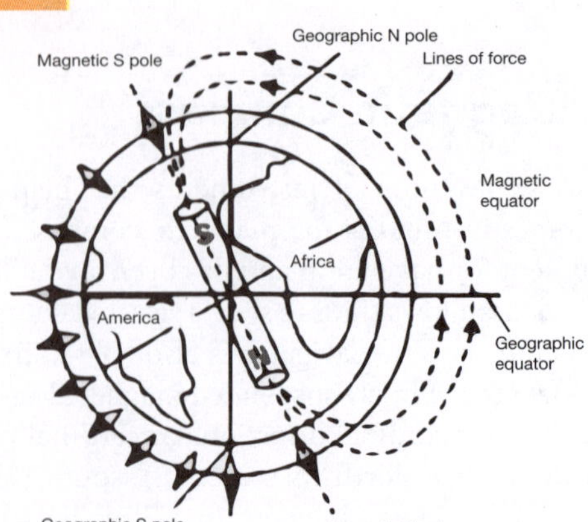

when there is a magnetic south pole attracting it. Thus, there must be the south pole of the earth's magnet in the geographic north and the pole of the earth's magnet in the geographic south.

A Current Carrying Wire is a Magnet

In 1820, a Danish physicist, Hans Christian Oersted, discovered that there was a relationship between electricity and magnetism. By setting up a compass near a wire carrying an electric current, Oersted showed that moving electrons can create a magnetic field.

The magnetic field created by electric current goes in circles around the wire.

STRUCTURAL OUTLINE

Fun with Magnets

A magnet is a material that produces a magnetic field which attracts magnetic materials like iron, cobalt, nickel, steel, etc. and their alloys

Non-magnetic Materials

- The materials which don't gets attracted by a magnet are known as non-magnetic materials.
  Example – wood, glass, etc.

Magnetic Materials

- The materials which are attracted by a magnet are known as magnetic materials.
  Example – Iron, cobalt, nickel, and steel.

Types of Magnets

Natural Magnet

A lodestone or magnet is a piece of magnetic material that are naturally found in the Earth

Artificial Magnet

- Substances on which magnetic properties are imparted by artificial means are known as artificial magnets.
- Example: Horseshoe magnet, bar magnet, ring magnet, button magnet.

Methods of Making Artificial Magnets

- Single touch method: An iron nail can be made into a magnet by stroking it several time with a strong magnet
- Double touch method: An iron strip can be made into a magnet by stroking with two bar magnets.
- By using electricity: When electric current is passed through a coil wound around a steel rod, it behaves like a magnet.

Properties of Magnet

- A magnet always has two poles, north pole, and south pole.
- Magnetic strength is maximum at poles.
- The freely suspended magnet always comes to rest in the north-south direction.
- Magnetic poles cannot be isolated.
- Like poles repel and unlike poles attract each other.

Cautions while Handling Magnets

- Magnets must not be hammered or dropped from a height.
- A magnet can be demagnetized by heating it for a long time.
- Keep the magnet always away from electronic devices.

Storage of Magnet

- Bar magnet should always be stored in pairs between soft iron pieces called keepers.
- Horseshoe magnet needs only one keeper.

EXEMPLIFICATION

1. **Name the poles of a magnet. Where do we find them on a bar magnet?**

   Solution: There are two poles of the magnet, north and south pole. We can find them at the ends of a bar magnet.

2. **What are magnetic substances? Give some examples.**

   Solution: The substances which are attracted towards a magnet/ magnetic field are known as magnetic substances.

   For example: iron, nickel, cobalt, etc.

3. **Explain any one way by which a magnetic substance can be magnetized?**

   Solution: Single Touch Method: A piece of any magnetic material, like iron or steel (a nail, knitting needle, bolt etc) is taken and placed on a bench or a table. A bar magnet is brought close to the magnetic material (say an iron piece AB). One end of the bar magnet is stroked against it, moving from end A to end B of the iron piece.

   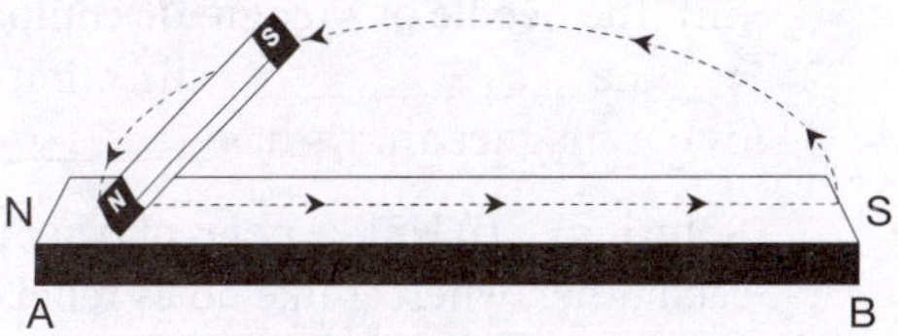

   Single Touch Method

   When the bar magnet reaches end B, it is lifted, and the stroke repeated from end A to end B. This procedure is repeated several times, keeping two things in mind:

   1. The same pole of the bar magnet should be used every time.
   2. Strokes should be in the same direction.

   By stroking the iron piece with the north pole of the bar magnet, end A becomes the north pole and end B the south pole.

4. **What are the ways by which a magnet can be demagnetized?**

   Solution: Magnet can be demagnetized by:

   1. If the magnet is stored without using magnetic keepers.
   2. Dropping it from a height or by rough handling.
   3. Heating or hammering the magnet.

5. **How can we care for our magnets?**

   Solution: We can care for our magnets as follows:

   1. Magnets lose their properties if they are heated, hammered, or dropped from a height. So, we must avoid these.
   2. Magnets become weak if not stored properly. Magnets should be kept in magnetic keepers. A magnetic keeper consists of a wooden piece with two magnets on its two sides with their unlike poles on one side. Two pieces of soft iron called keepers are to be placed across their ends.

      However, for a horseshoe magnet one piece of soft iron/ keeper is sufficient.
   3. We must Keep magnets away from cassettes, mobiles, T.V., CD's, computers as they are weakened by these devices.

6. **Write some uses of magnets.**

   Solution: Some uses of magnets are as follows:

   - A magnet is used in a compass to show the direction.
   - Powerful magnets are used to lift objects.
   - Magnets are used in generators and motors.
   - Prevents corrosion in a water heater. The magnetic calcium particles are attracted by the magnets before it enters the heater.
   - Magnets are used in medical equipment.

7. **What is self-demagnetization? How this can be prevented?**

   Solution: Magnets tend to become weak after some time. This weakening is called self-demagnetization.

   Self-demagnetization can be prevented by using small pieces of soft iron which are placed in contact with their opposite poles. These pieces of soft iron are called magnetic keepers.

NCERT COMPENDIUM

1. Fill in the blanks

(i) Unlike poles of two magnets __________ each other, whereas like poles __________ each other.

(ii) The materials that are attracted towards a magnet are called ______________.

(iii) The needle of a magnetic compass rests along the ______________ direction.

(iv) A magnet always has ______________ poles.

Solution: (i) Unlike poles of two magnets **attract** each other, whereas like poles **repel** each other.

(ii) The materials that are attracted towards a magnet are called **magnetic material**.

(iii) The needle of a magnetic compass rests along the **North-South** direction.

(iv) A magnet always has **two** poles.

2. State whether the following statements are True (T) or False (F).

(i) A magnet can be broken into pieces to obtain a single pole.

(ii) Similar poles of a magnet repel each other.

(iii) Iron filings mostly stick in the middle of a bar magnet when it is brought near them.

(iv) A freely suspended bar magnet always aligns with the north-south direction.

Solution: (i) False (ii) True (iii) False (iv) True

3. Column I shows different positions in which one pole of a magnet is placed near that of the other. Column II indicates the resulting interaction between them for different situations. Fill in the blanks.

Column I	Column II
N – N	_______
N – ________	Attraction
S – N	_______
_________-S	Repulsion

Solution: Repulsion, South, Attraction, South

4. Atharv performed an experiment in which he took a bar magnet and rolled it over a heap of steel U-clips (Figure).

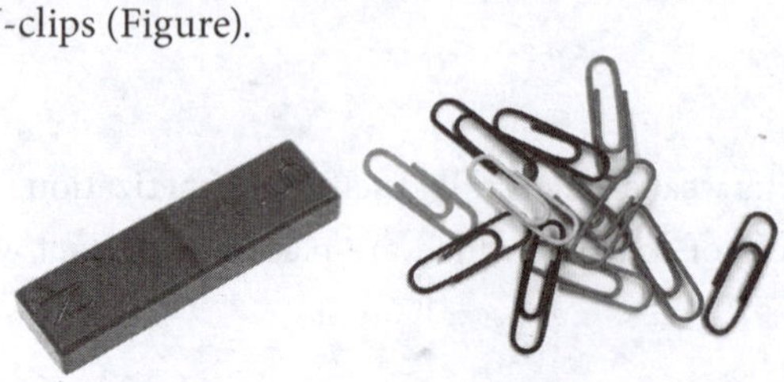

According to you, which of the options given in Table below is likely to be his observation?

	Position A	Position B	Position C
(i)	10	2	10
(ii)	10	10	2
(iii)	2	10	10
(iv)	10	10	10

Solution: (i)

5. Reshma bought three identical metal bars from the market. Out of these bars, two were magnets and one was just a piece of iron. How will she identify which two amongst the three could be magnets (without using any other material)?

Solution: Reshma should try to bring two metal bars towards each other. The one attracting the other is the magnet.

6. You are given a magnet which does not have the poles marked. How can you find its poles with the help of another magnet which has its poles marked?

Solution: Bring the north pole of known magnet closer to the unknown magnet. If they repel then mark the north pole. If they attract, then mark it south.

7. A bar magnet has no markings to indicate its poles. How would you find out near which end its North pole is located without using another magnet?

Solution: Hang the magnet and let it settle. It will align itself with north south direction.

8. If the earth is itself a magnet, can you guess the poles of earth's magnet by looking at the direction of the magnetic compass?

Solution: Since unlike poles attract each other. Thus, magnetic compass north will point towards earth's magnet south pole.

9. While a mechanic was repairing a gadget using a screw driver, the steel screws kept falling down. Suggest a way to solve the problem of the mechanic on the basis of what you have learnt in this chapter.

Solution: Mechanic can use a magnet to stop the steel screw from falling.

10. Two ring magnets X and Y are arranged as shown in Figure. It is observed that the magnet X does not move down further.

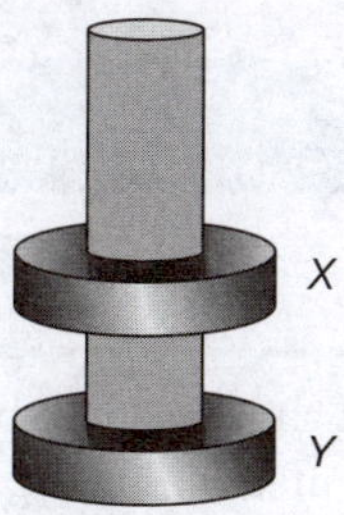

What could be the possible reason? Suggest a way to bring the magnet X in contact with magnet Y, without pushing either of the magnets.

Solution: Like poles must be facing towards each other. Turn the magnet X.

11. Three magnets are arranged on a table in the form of the shape shown in Figure. What is the polarity, N or S, at the ends 1, 2, 3, 4 and 6 of the magnets? Polarity of one end (5) is given for you.

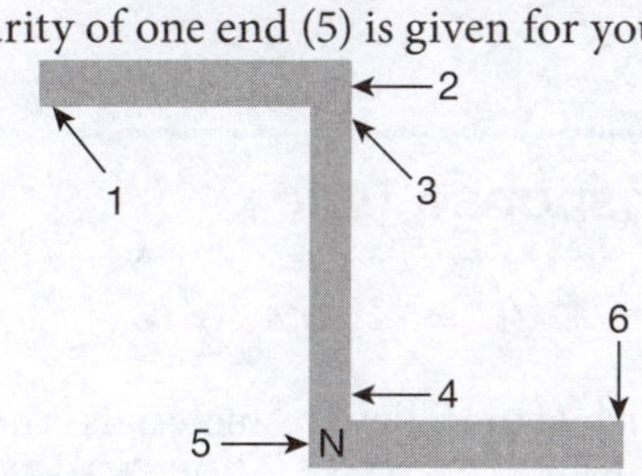

Solution: 1-North, 2-South, 3-North, 4-South, 6-South

ASSESSMENT CORNER

Level 1

Fixed Response Type

Multiple Choice Questions

1. Which of the following materials is not magnetic?
   (A) Iron (B) Nickel
   (C) Copper (D) Cobalt
2. Which material will not get attracted to a magnet?
   (A) Iron (B) Cobalt
   (C) Wood (D) Nickel
3. The chemical formula of magnetite (natural magnet) is:
   (A) Fe_2O_3 (B) Fe_3O_4
   (C) FeO (D) FeO_2
4. When a bar magnet is suspended freely, it always comes to rest in which direction?
   (A) East-West (B) North-South
   (C) Any Direction (D) South-East
5. What happens when you bring two like poles of two magnets together?
   (A) They attract each other
   (B) They repel each other
   (C) They neutralize each other
   (D) Nothing happens
6. Which of the following objects can be used to detect a magnet?
   (A) Wooden block (B) Compass
   (C) Rubber band (D) Plastic bottle
7. A bar magnet is immersed in a heap of iron fillings and pulled out. The amount of iron filling clinging to the:
   (A) North pole is almost equal to the south pole.
   (B) North pole is much more than the south pole.
   (C) North pole is much less than the south pole
   (D) It will be the same all along its length.
8. Natural magnets are _____ the artificial magnets.
   (A) stronger than (B) of equal strength as
   (C) weaker than (D) None of the above
9. The ends of a bar magnet where the magnetic force is maximum are called
   (A) Equators (B) Centres
   (C) Poles (D) Nodes
10. North pole of a magnet can be identified by:
    (A) Another magnet having its poles marked as north pole and south pole.
    (B) Using an iron bar.
    (C) Using iron filings.
    (D) None of these
11. Which of the following is a natural magnet?
    (A) Iron (B) Copper
    (C) Lodestone (D) Aluminium
12. What happens if you break a bar magnet into two pieces?
    (A) Each piece becomes a new magnet.
    (B) Only one piece acts as a magnet.
    (C) Neither piece is magnetic.
    (D) The south pole disappears.
13. Which of the following cannot be turned into a magnet?
    (A) Steel (B) Plastic
    (C) Iron (D) Cobalt
14. Which property of magnets is used in a compass?
    (A) Attractive (B) Repulsive
    (C) Directive (D) Magnetising
15. Maximum iron filings cling to which part of a bar magnet?
    (A) Middle (B) At the ends
    (C) Equator (D) Side
16. What is the space around a magnet where its force is effective called?
    (A) Magnetic field (B) Magnetic domain
    (C) Magnetic pole (D) Magnetic force
17. Which shape is not commonly used to make artificial magnets?
    (A) Bar (B) Horse-shoe
    (C) Disc (D) Triangle
18. A bar magnet is divided in two pieces. Which of the following statement is true?
    (A) The bar magnet is demagnetized.
    (B) The magnetic field of each separated piece become stronger.
    (C) The magnetic poles are separated.
    (D) Two new bar magnets are created.
19. ALNICO is an example of _________ magnet:
    (A) Permanent (B) Temporary
    (C) Both (A) and (B) (D) None of these

20. Which of the following actions may destroy the magnetism of a magnet?
(A) Keeping in a keeper
(B) Heating
(C) Storing with unlike poles together
(D) Suspending it

21. What is the best test to check if a material is a magnet?
(A) Attraction (B) Repulsion
(C) Induction (D) Deflection

22. _________is a device used by pilots and navigators used to find the direction.
(A) Barometer
(B) Thermometer
(C) Magnetic compass
(D) None

23. What would happen if a magnet is cut into three pieces?
(A) Only one piece will be magnetic
(B) Only two pieces will be magnetic
(C) All three pieces will be magnetic
(D) None of the pieces will be magnetic

24. Which pole of a magnet points towards geographic North?
(A) South (B) East
(C) North (D) West

25. How many degrees apart is the EAST direction from the SOUTH-EAST direction in a magnetic compass?
(A) 90 Degree (B) 45 Degree
(C) 180 Degree (D) 60 Degree

26. Which material would be best for making a temporary magnet?
(A) Copper (B) Aluminium
(C) Steel (D) Soft iron

27. Why do magnets lose their magnetism when heated?
(A) The magnetic domains align
(B) The magnetic domains scatter
(C) The magnet becomes softer
(D) The magnet becomes harder

28. Why are keepers used to store magnets?
(A) To beautify
(B) To increase weight
(C) To prevent loss of magnetism
(D) To break them easily

29. Which of these is not attracted by a magnet?
(A) Steel (B) Copper
(C) Nickel (D) Iron

30. The region around a magnet where its influence can be detected is known as?
(A) Magnetic field (B) Electric field
(C) Gravitational field (D) Neutral zone

31. Fill in the blanks with a correct combination of words.
(i) were discovered by an old (ii) named (iii) he had a (iv) stick. The stick had an iron casing at its lower end which was attracted by a rock. This rock which behaved like a magnet was given the name (v).
(A) (i) – Magnetite, (ii) – Cobalt, (iii) Magnet, (iv) – Plastic, (v) – Magnes
(B) (i) – Magnes, (ii) – Painter, (iii) Magnet, (iv) – Rubber, (v) – Magnetite
(C) (i) – Magnets, (ii) – Shepherd, (iii) Magnes, (iv) – Wooden, (v) – Magnetite
(D) (i) – Magnets, (ii) – Cobbler, (iii) Magnes, (iv) – Wooden, (v) – Magnetite

32. How would you identify the poles of an unmarked bar magnet using a second magnet?
(A) By heating the magnet
(B) By checking for induced magnetism
(C) By testing for repulsion with the marked poles
(D) By rubbing both magnets together

33. What is the primary reason magnets are used in speakers?
(A) To produce sound
(B) To amplify sound
(C) To convert electrical energy to mechanical energy
(D) To convert sound energy to electrical energy

34. Choose the correct option for the given figure.

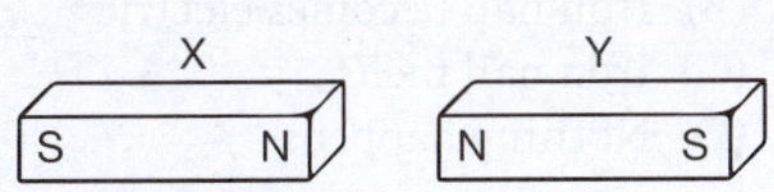

(A) Magnet X and Y will attract each other.
(B) Magnet X and Y will repel each other.
(C) No force will be experienced by them.
(D) All the above.

35. What is a magnetic keeper?
(A) A device to make magnets stronger
(B) A device to demagnetize a magnet
(C) A piece of soft iron placed across the poles of a magnet
(D) A magnet used for attracting iron objects

36. Which of the following factors does not affect the magnetic strength of a magnet?
(A) Material (B) Shape
(C) Color (D) Size

37. You are given a mixture of sand, iron filings, and wood shavings. How will you separate iron filings?
(A) Use a magnet (B) Add water
(C) Dry in sunlight (D) Blow air

38. Why do like poles of two magnets repel each other?
(A) Because of gravitational force
(B) Because of magnetic force
(C) Because of electrostatic force
(D) Because of nuclear force

39. How does Earth's magnetic field affect a compass?
(A) It repels the compass needle
(B) It attracts the compass needle
(C) It aligns the compass needle north-south
(D) It has no effect on the compass needle

40. You need to retrieve a key that has fallen into a narrow metal pipe. Which tool will you use?
(A) Plastic rod (B) Iron rod
(C) Magnet (D) Wooden stick

41. North Pole of a magnetic needle is usually painted ________.
(A) Black (B) Blue
(C) Red (D) Orange

42. North pole of a magnet can be identified by:
(A) Using iron nails.
(B) Another magnet without marked poles.
(C) Using a steel bar.
(D) Another magnet having marked north and south pole.

43. If you rub an iron nail with a bar magnet in one direction several times, what would you observe?
(A) Iron nail becomes a temporary magnet
(B) Iron nail becomes electric
(C) Iron nail melts
(D) Nothing happens

44. South pole of a freely suspended magnet is attracted towards the __________ direction of Earth.
(A) East (B) West
(C) North (D) South

45. Which experiment would best show that like poles repel and unlike poles attract?
(A) Bringing two N poles together
(B) Bringing N and S poles together
(C) Bringing two S poles together
(D) All of these

46. Observe the pictures A and B given in figure carefully.

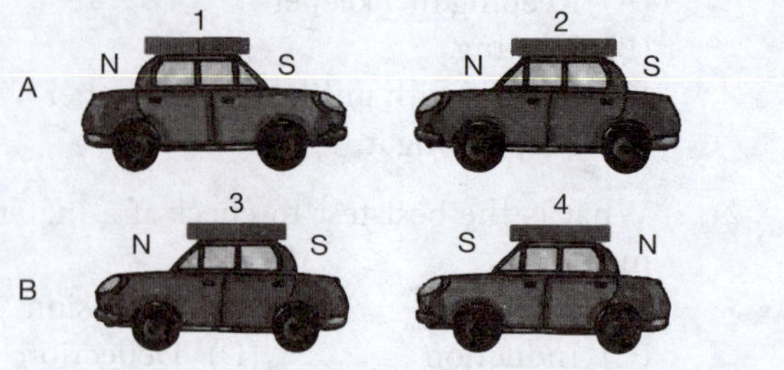

Which of the following statement is correct for the above given pictures?
(A) In A, cars 1 and 2 will come closer and in B, cars 3 and 4 will come closer.
(B) In A, cars 1 and 2 will move away from each other, and in B, cars 3 and 4 will move away.
(C) In A, cars 1 and 2 will move away from each other, and in B, 3 and 4 will come closer to each other.
(D) In A, cars 1 and 2 will come closer to each other, and in B, 3 and 4 will move away from each other.

47. The arrangement to store two magnets is shown by figures (a), (b), (c) and (d) in figure. Which one of them is the correct arrangement?

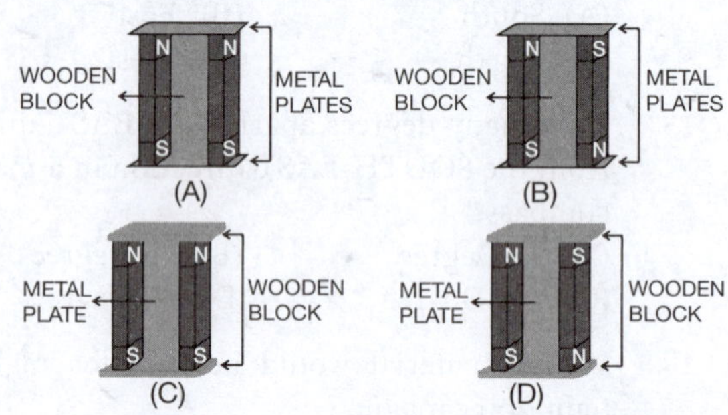

48. Three magnets A, B and C were dipped one by one in a heap of iron filings. Figure shows the amount of the iron filing sticking to them.

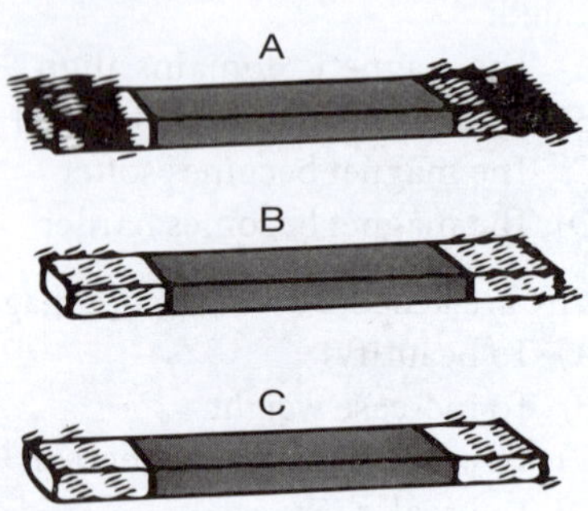

The strength of these magnets will be
(A) A > B > C (B) A < B < C
(C) A = B = C (D) A < B > C

49. If you want to keep magnets for a long time, what should you avoid?
(A) Use magnetic keepers
(B) Heat or hammer
(C) Store unlike poles together
(D) Store in pairs

50. To make a simple electromagnet, which two components are essential?
(A) Copper wire and iron rod
(B) Copper wire and aluminium rod
(C) Plastic wire and iron rod
(D) Gold wire and iron rod

Fill in the Blanks

1. When a bar magnet is broken, each of the broken parts will have ________________ pole/poles.

2. In a bar magnet, magnetic attraction is ________________ near its ends.

3. When a suspended magnet comes to rest, one pole always points towards the ________________ and the other pole always points towards the ________________.

4. Cobalt is a __________ material.

5. In the olden days, sailors used to find direction by suspending a piece of ________________.

6. A magnet always has ________________ poles.

True/False

1. There are 5 poles for each magnet.

2. Natural magnets were discovered in Greece.

3. Like poles repel each other.

4. Minimum iron filings stick in the middle of a bar magnet when it is brought near them.

5. Bar magnets never point towards the north-south direction.

6. A compass can't be used to find East-West direction at any place.

7. Plastic is a magnetic material.

Match Type Questions

1. Match the following:

Column-A	Column-II
(i) N-N	(a) Ebonite
(ii) Nonmagnetic substance	(b) Attraction
(iii) S-N	(c) Cobalt
(iv) Electromagnet	(d) Repulsion
(v) Magnetic Substance	(c) Soft iron

(A) (i)–d, (ii)–a, (iii)–b, (iv)–e, (v)–c
(B) (i)–a, (ii)–b, (iii)–c, (iv)–d, (v)–e
(C) (i)–a, (ii)–c, (iii)–e, (iv)–b, (v)–d
(D) (i)–a, (ii)–d, (iii)–b, (iv)–e, (v)–c

2. Match the following:

Column-A	Column-II
(i) Magnet attracts	(a) rests along a particular direction.
(ii) Electromagnet	(b) soft iron.
(iii) Magnet if suspended freely	(c) another magnet.
(iv) Poles of a magnet can be identified by	(d) iron filings.

(A) a-iii, b-ii, c-iv, d-i (B) a-i, b-iii, c-ii, d-iv
(C) a-iv, b-iii, c-ii, d-i (D) a-iii, b-iv, c-i, d-ii

Assertion and Reasons Type Questions

Directions: Study both statements and mark your answer using the codes given blow.
(A) Both A and R are true, and R is the correct explanation of A.
(B) Both A and R are true, but R is not the correct explanation of A.
(C) A is true but R is false.
(D) A is false but R is true.

1. **Assertion:** Rubber is not attracted by a magnet.
Reason: Rubber is a non-magnetic material.

2. **Assertion:** A compass can be used to find the north-south direction.
Reason: A compass has a small magnet inside it.

3. **Assertion:** A bar magnet is an artificial magnet.
Reason: Natural magnet is magnetite.

Comprehension Type Questions

Directions: Read the passage (s) given below and answer the questions that follow.

Passage: A compass is an extremely simple device. A magnetic compass (as opposed to a gyroscopic compass) consists of a small, lightweight magnet balanced on a nearly frictionless pivot point. The magnet is generally called a needle. One end of the needle is often marked "N" for North or coloured in some way to indicate that it points toward North. On the surface, that's all there is to a compass.

1. What does a compass consist of?
   (A) Magnet (B) Stone
   (C) Pipe (D) Crystal
2. Which direction is shown by the coloured end of a magnetic needle?
   (A) East (B) West
   (C) North (D) South
3. What do we call the magnet inside magnetic compass?
   (A) Magnetic Compass
   (B) Magnetic needle
   (C) Magnetic stone
   (D) None of these

Free Response Type

Very Short Answer Type Questions

1. Magnetic keeper is made up of which metal?
2. What is the strength of a bar magnet at the centre of the magnet?
3. If a bar magnet is cut in 5 equal parts, how many north & south poles come from it?
4. Name three magnetic materials.
5. What are the methods of demagnetizing a permanent magnet?
6. What are the different types of magnets?
7. How will you test that 'tea dust' is not adulterated with iron powder?
8. Does Earth have a magnetic field?

Short Answer Type Questions

1. What is an electromagnet?
2. What is a magnet?
3. Distinguish between temporary and permanent magnets.
4. What is magnetic and non-magnetic material? Explain with example.
5. What factors does electromagnetism depend on?
6. Explain directive property of a magnet.
7. Four identical iron bars were dipped in a heap of iron filings one by one. The figure below shows the amount of iron filings sticking to each of them.

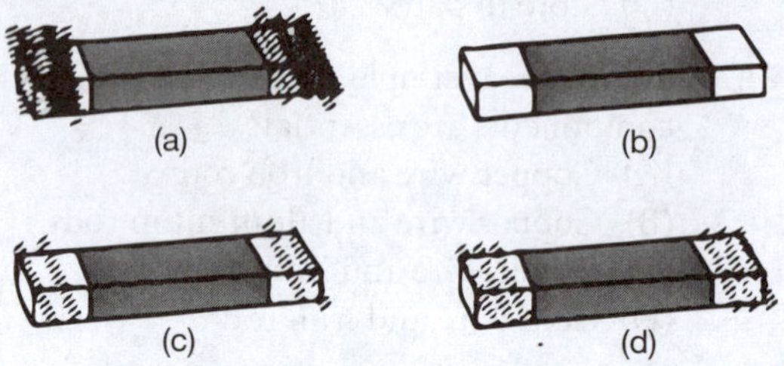

   (a) Which of the iron bar is likely to be the strongest magnet?
   (b) Which of the iron bars is not a magnet? Justify your answer.
8. A toy car has a bar magnet laid hidden inside its body along its length. Using another magnet how will you find out which pole of the magnet is facing the front of the car?
9. You are provided with two identical metal bars. One out of the two is a magnet. Suggest two ways to identify the magnet.

Long Answer Type Questions

1. Draw the diagram of a magnetic compass and explain its uses.
2. "Repulsion is the surest test of a magnet" Explain.
3. How can you say that an artificial electromagnet is much stronger than a natural magnet?
4. Discuss the properties of a bar magnet.
5. How will you make an electromagnet? Explain the process.
6. Three identical iron bars are kept on a table. Two out of three bars are magnets. In one of the magnets, the north-south poles are marked. How will you find out which of the other two bars is a magnet? Identify the poles of this magnet.
7. Describe the steps involved in magnetising an iron strip with the help of a magnet.
8. The figure below shows a magnetic compass. What will happen to the position of its needle if you bring a bar magnet near it? Draw a diagram to show the effect on the needle on bringing the

bar magnet near it. Also draw the diagram to show the effect when the other end of the bar magnet is brought near it.

9. Suggest an activity to prepare a magnetic compass by using an iron needle and a bar magnet.

10. Boojho kept a magnet close to an ordinary iron bar. He observed that the iron bar attracts a pin as shown in the figure below.

What inference could he draw from this observation? Explain.

11. A bar magnet is cut into two pieces A and B, from the middle, as shown in figure.

Will the two pieces act as individual magnets? Mark the poles of these two pieces. Suggest an activity to verify your answer.

12. Suggest an arrangement to store a U shaped magnet. How is this different from storing a pair of bar magnets?

Numerical Based Questions

1. If a bar magnet is cut in 2 equal parts, how many north & south poles come from it?
2. If a bar magnet is cut in 7 unequal parts, how many north & south poles come from it?

Case Based Questions

Passage: Read the following table and answer the question from 1–3.

P	Q	R
Magnets	**Magnetic substances**	**Non-magnetic substances**

1. Articles from which of these groups can be attracted by magnets but cannot attract other objects?
   (A) P (B) Q
   (C) R (D) P and Q
2. A few examples of substances are given below.
   Iron, Cobalt, Nickel
   To which group do they belong?
   (A) P (B) Q
   (C) R (D) P and R
3. After repeated rubbing with a magnet in the same direction, a piece of substance fails to get magnetized. To which group does it belong?
   (A) P and Q (B) Q and R
   (C) Q (D) R

Level 2

Multiple Choice Questions

1. A student designs a magnetic game where a metal ball is moved on a board without touching it directly. Which principle is being applied?
   (A) Friction (B) Gravity
   (C) Magnetism (D) Electricity
2. Which of the following best describes the alignment of magnetic domains in a magnet?
   (A) Randomly aligned
   (B) Partially aligned
   (C) Fully aligned in one direction
   (D) Aligned at right angles to each other
3. What is the most likely cause if a previously strong magnet has become weak?
   (A) Stored with keepers
   (B) Stroked with another magnet
   (C) Heated or dropped
   (D) Covered in paper
4. A bar magnet is suspended with a piece of string, and another rod brought close to it as shown. The rod repels the magnet.

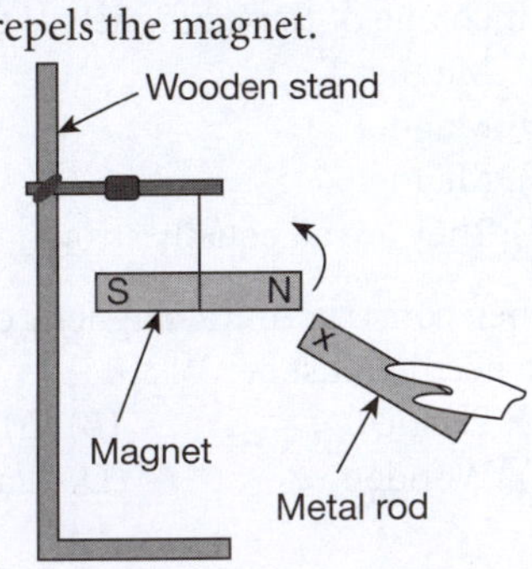

Which one of the following statements is correct?
(A) The rod is non-magnetic.
(B) The rod has a south pole at X.
(C) The rod has a north pole at X.
(D) The rod is made of wood.

5. Mary wanted to find out if a nail was magnetized. She put the nail near a magnet, a compass, and a paper clip. She recorded her observations below:
1. It repelled one end of the magnet.
2. It was attracted by the other end of the magnet.
3. It attracted the paper clip.
4. It caused the compass needle to move.

From which of the above observations can she be certain that the nail was magnetized?
(A) 1, 2, 3 and 4 (B) 1 only
(C) 2 and 3 only (D) 1 and 4 only

6. What would you observe if a dry leaf is placed between a magnet and some iron filings?
(A) No attraction
(B) Iron filings still get attracted
(C) Attraction decreases
(D) Magnet is demagnetised

7. Four thumbtacks were attracted to a magnetized steel bar. Eamonn brought one end of a strong bar magnet close to the tip of the fourth thumbtack as shown in the diagram.

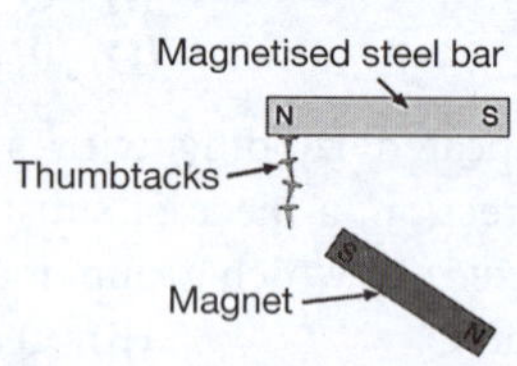

Which one of the following did Eamonn observe?
(A) The fourth thumbtack moved towards the magnet.
(B) The fourth thumbtack fell to the ground.
(C) The fourth thumbtack did not move.
(D) The fourth thumbtack moved away from the magnet.

8. Magnet X can hold a maximum of 5 paper clips, magnet Y can hold a maximum of 3 paper clips, magnet Z can hold a maximum of 7 paper clips. Which one of these magnets is the weakest?
(A) Magnet X
(B) Magnet Y
(C) Magnet Z
(D) They are all equally strong.

9. When constructing a magnetic compass at home, the needle must be:
(A) Plastic (B) Magnetised metal
(C) Wooden (D) Paper

10. What would happen when the magnet is held near the cork as shown in the diagram?

(A) The cork would move towards the magnet because of the magnetic force of repulsion.
(B) The cork would move towards the magnet because of the magnetic force of attraction.
(C) The cork would move away from the magnet because of the magnetic force of repulsion.
(D) The cork would move away from the magnet because of the magnetic force of attraction.

11. Vishnu brings a magnet near 3 pins made up of different materials. Pins Y and Z get attracted whereas pin X remains in its places as shown below.

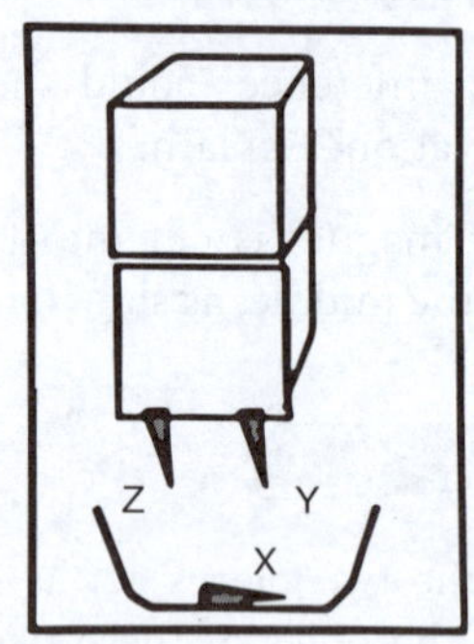

What materials are pins X, Y, and Z made up of?

(A)	Pin X Copper	Pin Y Iron	Pin Z Steel
(B)	Pin X Steel	Pin Y Nickel	Pin Z Aluminium
(C)	Pin X Copper	Pin Y Brass	Pin Z Cobalt
(D)	Pin X Iron	Pin Y Copper	Pin Z Brass

12. Vikram is going to dip a bar magnet into a container of iron filings. Which part of the bar magnet will he observe attract the most amount of the iron filings?

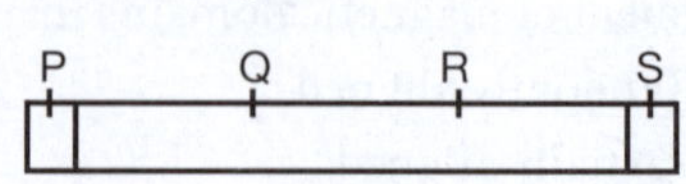

(A) P & Q (B) P & S
(C) R & S (D) P, Q & R

13. Why is steel not used for making temporary magnets?
(A) It is expensive
(B) It is hard to magnetize and demagnetize
(C) It rusts easily
(D) It does not conduct electricity

14. If two magnets are arranged so that both north poles are close, what will happen?
(A) They attract (B) They repel
(C) No effect (D) Stick together

15. To instantly identify the weak pole of a magnet, what would you use?
(A) Copper filings (B) Another strong magnet
(C) Bar of wood (D) Thread

16. Which reasoning best explains why a magnetic compass fails near a large iron structure?
(A) Earth's magnetism is weaker there.
(B) Iron interferes with the compass needle.
(C) Compass magnetises iron.
(D) Compass is wrongly built.

17. Three compasses are placed near a bar magnet as shown. Which of the compasses has/have the needle pointing in the correct direction?

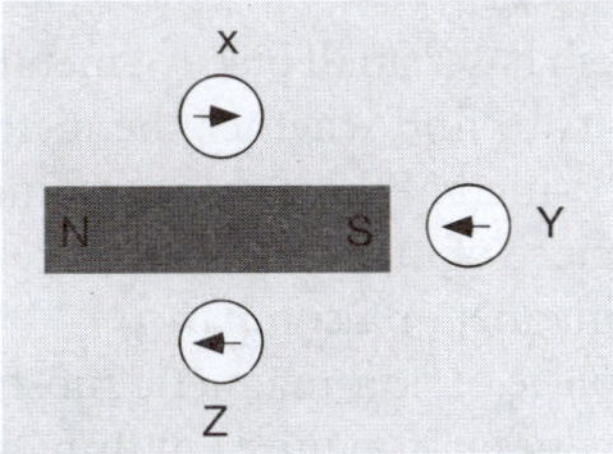

(A) Compass X
(B) Compasses Y and X
(C) Compasses X and Z
(D) Compass Y

18. The needle of the compass is made of a magnet because it
(i) Attracts metal.
(ii) Gets deflected when a magnet is brought near to it.
(iii) Comes to rest in the east-west direction.
(iv) Comes to rest in the north-south direction.
Which of the above statements is/are correct?
(A) (i) & (ii) (B) (i), (ii) & (iii)
(C) (ii) & (iv) (D) (ii) only

19. How can you make a bar magnet from a piece of iron?
(A) By heating the iron
(B) By cooling the iron
(C) By rubbing it with another magnet
(D) By placing it in a magnetic field

20. Alnico is an alloy composed of four different metals. Which one of the following metals is not contained in this magnet?
(A) Calcium (B) Iron
(C) Cobalt (D) Aluminium

21. Why do maximum filings cling to poles and not to the middle of a bar magnet?
(A) Poles have a stronger field.
(B) Middle is magnetic.
(C) Middle is repelled.
(D) Field is the same everywhere.

22. Why can a magnet not be isolated into north-pole only?
(A) Only South is possible.
(B) Poles exist in pairs.
(C) North is heavier.
(D) It is man-made.

23. The four basic points on a compass are classified as:
(A) Northings (B) Cardinal points
(C) Legend points (D) Eastings

24. Read the following table and answer the questions from.

P	Q	R
Magnets	Magnetic substances	Non-magnetic substances

Articles from which of these group(s) can be attracted by a magnet?
(A) Only P and Q (B) Only Q and R
(C) Only Q (D) R

25. Read the following table and answer the questions from.

P	Q	R
Magnets	Magnetic substances	Non-magnetic substances

An object is repelled by a magnet. To which group does it belong?
(A) P (B) Q
(C) R (D) Q and R

26. Read the following table and answer the questions from.

P	Q	R
Magnets	Magnetic substances	Non-magnetic substances

To which group does a ring made up of copper belong?
(A) P (B) Q
(C) R (D) Either Q or P

27. How does the strength of a magnetic field vary with distance from the magnet?
(A) Increases with distance
(B) Decreases with distance
(C) Remains constant
(D) Fluctuates

28. A suspended magnet always settles in North-South direction because:
(A) Earth pulls it
(B) Earth has a magnetic field.
(C) Air pushes it
(D) Thread guides it

29. Which of the following statements is true?
(A) The north pole of a magnet will attract the north pole of another magnet.
(B) Artificial magnets can be made from non-magnetic materials also.
(C) Lodestone is an artificial magnet.
(D) Isolated magnetic poles do not exist.

30. If an iron bar is placed close to a magnet without touching, what happens to the bar?
(A) It is magnetised by induction
(B) It becomes non-magnetic
(C) It heats up
(D) Nothing

31. In which direction does a magnet always point when suspended freely?
(A) South-West (B) North-South
(C) East-West (D) West-South

32. A student finds their compass needle isn't pointing North in class, which is most probable?
(A) Magnet nearby
(B) Rust on the compass
(C) Poor painting
(D) Strong sunlight

33. Why might a magnet stored near an electric motor become weaker?
(A) Motor creates heat/vibrations
(B) Motor attracts the magnet
(C) Magnets demagnetise in cold
(D) Motor blocks Earth's field

34. What would happen if you tried to separate a north pole from a bar magnet?
(A) You get only north
(B) You get two magnets, each with both poles
(C) No magnet
(D) Poles disappear

35. Rakesh has one bar magnet, two iron pieces and all of them are of the same size and shape. Which of the following can be used for identifying them?
(i) Another magnet
(ii) A compass
(iii) A piece of thread
(A) Only (i) and (ii)
(B) Only (ii) and (iii)
(C) Only (i) and (iii)
(D) All the three

36. What will happen if you drop a magnet repeatedly?
(A) It becomes stronger
(B) It becomes weaker
(C) It changes polarity
(D) It remains unchanged

37. How is a compass useful to us?
(A) In finding the altitude of a place.
(B) In finding only the north of a place.
(C) In finding all the directions of a place.
(D) In making artificial magnets.

38. In a game, a ring magnet floats above another ring magnet placed on a pencil. What is happening?
(A) Their like poles repel
(B) Their like poles attract
(C) Gravity only
(D) Rings are magnetised

39. Nikhilesh has a small piece of metal and a thread. He wants to find whether the metal is a magnet or not. Which of these things would he need?
(A) A piece of magnetic substance.
(B) A magnet or a compass.
(C) A piece of non-magnetic substance.
(D) He does not require anything more.

40. A magnet shaped like a disc and another shaped like a bar are of the same material. Which will likely have stronger poles?
(A) Bar magnet (B) Disc
(C) Both are the same (D) Neither

41. If a compass is kept inside a closed iron box, what would happen?
(A) Still points North
(B) Gives the wrong direction
(C) Stops working
(D) Becomes attracted to the box

42. Bhavya placed a magnet near a metal ball and observed that the ball moved away. What does she conclude about the metal ball?
(A) It is a magnet.
(B) It is made up of aluminium.
(C) It is made up copper.
(D) It is not a magnet.

43. Two magnets are placed close to each other as shown below. Which set will attract each other?

(A) 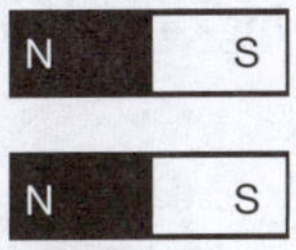

(B) 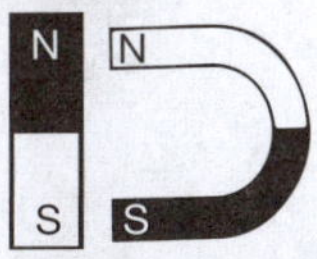

(C) 

(D) 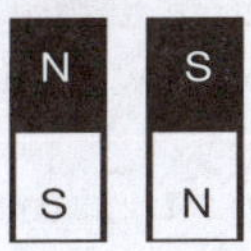

44. Which of these can explain why a magnet lifts more pins when cold than when hot?
(A) Cold increases strength
(B) Heat weakens magnets
(C) Pins are lighter when cold
(D) Air helps at low temperatures

45. Why should we pivot the compass needle on a sharp pin?
(A) To minimize the magnetic effect on the pin.
(B) To maximize the magnetic effect on the pin.
(C) To minimize the friction between the pin and the compass needle.
(D) To ensure that the compass needle will not drop from the pivoted point.

46. Which type of magnet is used in electric motors?
(A) Bar magnet (B) Electromagnet
(C) Horseshoe magnet (D) Natural magnet

47. Which of the following diagrams shows magnetic repulsion?

(A) 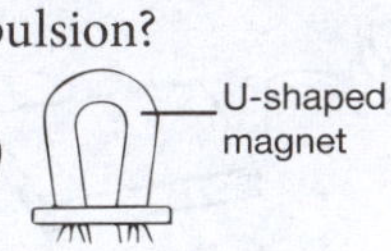

(B) 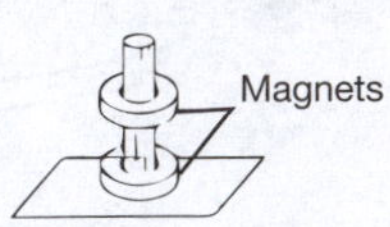

(C) 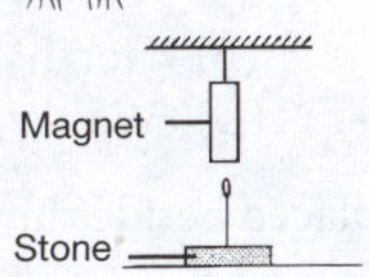

(D) 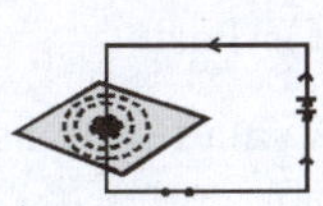

48. How can the strength of a temporary magnet be increased?
(A) By cooling it
(B) By rubbing it with another magnet
(C) By making the turns of coil closer
(D) By exposing it to sunlight

49. Which of the following does NOT contain a magnet in it?
(A) A torch (B) A radio
(C) A fan (D) Both (B) and (C)

50. In many household articles, magnets in the lids/covers are present. Why are magnets used in such instances?
(A) To facilitate their frequent usage.
(B) To ensure safety of the contents.
(C) To make the articles airtight.
(D) To make the articles look beautiful.

51. What property of a magnet is utilized in a magnetic door lock?
(A) Attraction (B) Repulsion
(C) Magnetic field (D) Magnetic domains

52. Which of the following objects does NOT make use of a magnet?

(A) 
Refrigerator

(B) 
Telephone

(C) 
Television

(D) 

Dry cell

53. A magnet in the form of a cube is placed on a piece of cork that floats on water. The cube is marked with four directions. W, X, Y and Z and the compass needle which pionts in the direction as shown in the figure.
Which of the following denotes the N-pole and S-pole of the magnet?

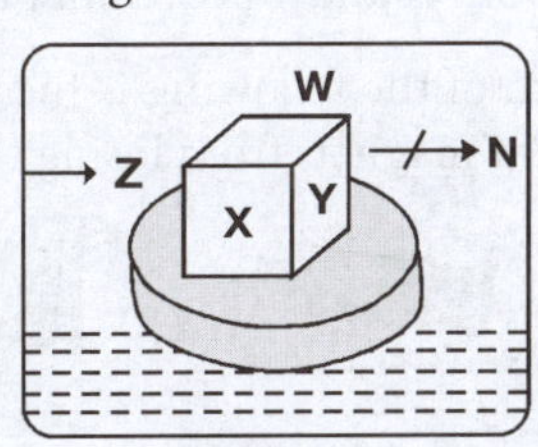

(A) N-pole W S-pole X
(B) N-pole X S-pole Y
(C) N-pole Y S-pole Z
(D) N-pole Z S-pole W

54. A weak magnet Y is placed near a strong magnet X as shown in the figure. How will the magnets move?

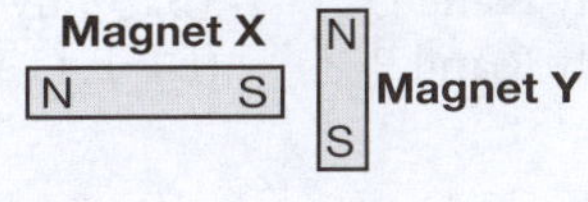

(A) Y will move away.
(B) X will turn in a clockwise direction.
(C) Y will turn in an anti-clockwise direction.
(D) Both X and Y will turn clockwise.

55. Which of the following figures does NOT show the poles correctly?

(A) 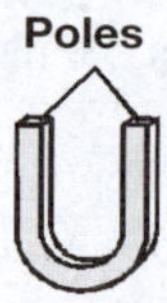

(B) 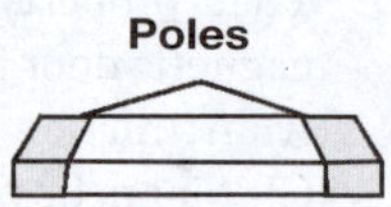

(C) 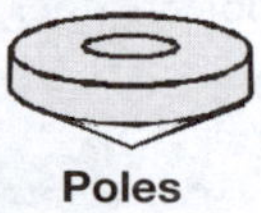

(D) 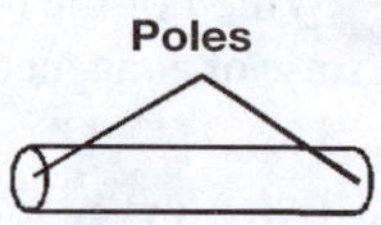

56. Ganeshan set up an experiment using two bar magnets one of which is marked N (North pole) and S (South pole) as shown in the figure. He noticed that the upper magnet is suspended in the air.

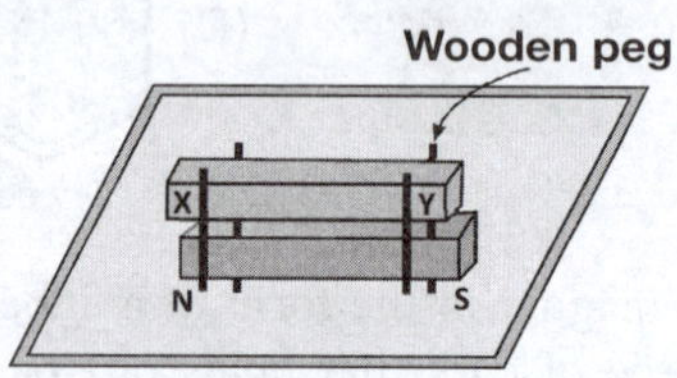

Identify X and Y poles of upper magnet.
(A) X is the north pole, Y is the south pole.
(B) X is the south pole, Y is the north pole.
(C) Both X and Y are north poles.
(D) Both X and Y are south poles.

57. Which of the following is the correct method to prevent magnets from losing their magnetism?

(A) 

(B) 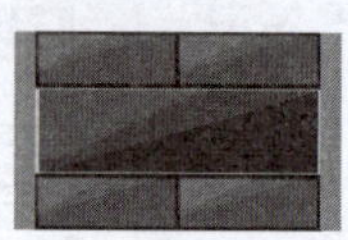

(C) 

(D) 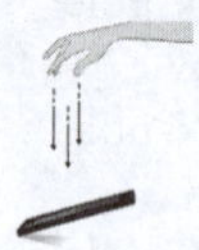

58. Which of the following shapes of a magnet are possible?

P Q R

(A) Only P and Q (B) Only Q and R
(C) Only R and P (D) P, Q and R

Higher Order Thinking Skills (HOTS)

1. Which one of the following can be attracted by a magnet?

(A) 
Nickel rod

(B) 
Copper wire

(C) 
Aluminium can

(D) 
Silver ring

2. A student tries to magnetize a short steel rod. Which of the following tests will show that he has succeeded?
(A) Both ends of a magnet attract the rod.
(B) One end of a magnet repels the rod.
(C) The rod picks up a small piece of paper.
(D) When freely suspended, the rod points in any direction.

3. What is the main reason that magnets lose their magnetism when heated?
(A) The magnetic domains get aligned
(B) The magnetic domains become random
(C) The magnet expands
(D) The magnet contracts

4. Which part of a magnet has the strongest magnetic force?
(A) Center (B) North pole
(C) South pole (D) Both poles

5. A small plotting compass is placed between two strong magnets. The tip of the arrow represents the N-pole of the compass. What is the polarity of the end P of the right hand side magnet?

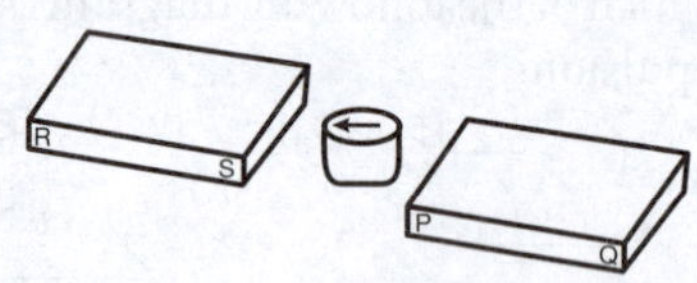

(A) South (B) North
(C) East (D) West

6. A small compass is placed beside the middle of a bar

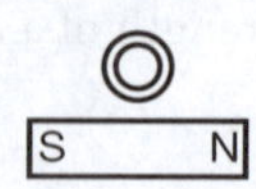

In which direction will the compass needle point?

(A)  (B) 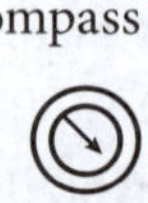

(C)  (D) 

7. If a piece of metal was thought to be a magnet, which one of the following observations would offer conclusive evidence?
   (A) It attracts a known magnet.
   (B) It repels a known magnet.
   (C) It attracts a steel screwdriver.
   (D) None of these

8. Which of the following iron cores has more strength as compared to others?

(A) 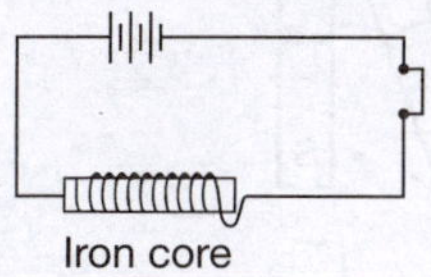

(B) 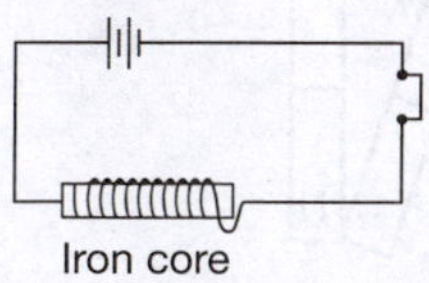

(C) 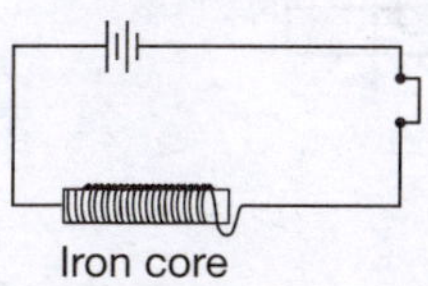

(D) 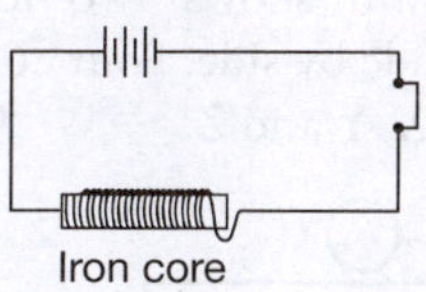

9. Three magnets X, Y, and Z were dipped one by one in a heap of iron filings. The figure below shows the amount of the iron filings attracted by them.

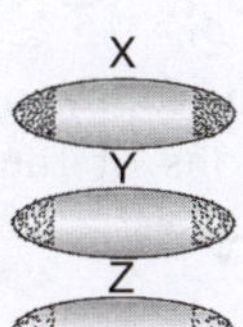

The strength of these magnets will be in the order
   (A) X > Y > Z (B) X < Y < Z
   (C) X = Y = Z (D) X < Y > Z

10. To demagnetize a magnet using the heating method. Which of the following is the correct step?
   (A) Heat the magnet to become red hot and allow it to cool in the east-west direction.
   (B) Heat the magnet to become red hot and allow it to cool in the north-south direction.
   (C) Heat the magnet in boiling water and allow it to cool in the north - south direction.
   (D) Both A and B.

11. The north pole of a bar magnet picks up an iron nail. Which of the following options is correct regarding the pole(s) induced in the nail?
   (A) South pole only
   (B) North pole only
   (C) A north pole and a south pole
   (D) None of these

12. A plotting compass is moved slowly towards the metal bar along the path as shown in figure. The final position of the compass needle is shown in the given figure.

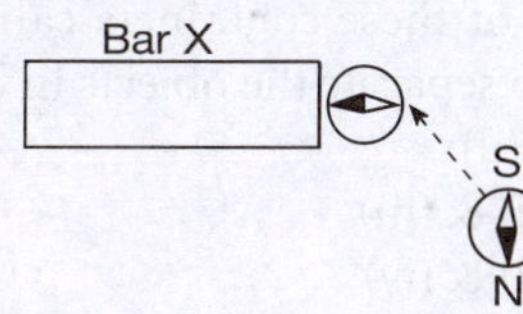

What can you conclude about bar X based on the diagram?
   (A) Bar X is a magnetic material.
   (B) Bar X is a magnet.
   (C) Bar X is a non-magnetic material.
   (D) Bar X is either a magnet or a magnetic material.

13. Four plotting compasses are placed near a bar magnet. One compass appears like this ( ). What is a possible position for the compass? (Ignore any effects of the Earth's magnetic field.)

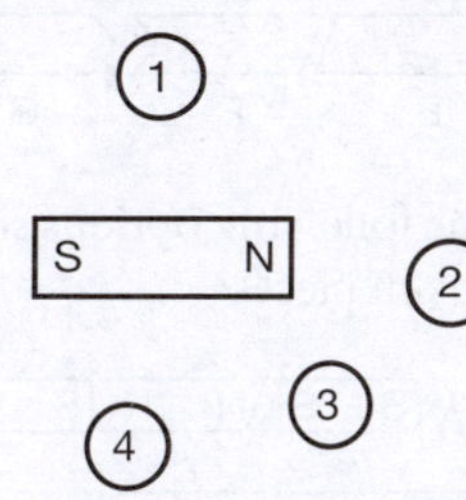

   (A) 1 (B) 2
   (C) 3 (D) 4

14. The figure shows a ring magnet, X, 'floating' above another ring magnet, Y. This is because:

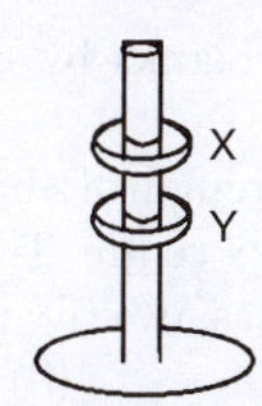

   (A) Magnet X is lighter than magnet Y.
   (B) Magnet Y is more powerful than magnet X.
   (C) The like poles of both magnets are facing each other, and they repel each other
   (D) The unlike poles of both magnets are facing each other, and they attract each other.

ASSESSMENT CORNER

15. Magnet can be made weaker by:
(A) Keeping it wrapped in cotton wool.
(B) Using it as a hammer.
(C) Storing it in a cool room.
(D) Playing with it.

16. Reeta puts two different objects in each of the following containers.
Container (i): Copper coin and iron nail
Container (ii): Steel nail and aluminium earring
Container (iii): Marble and gold coin
Container (iv): Nickel coin and steel nail
In which of these containers can she can use a magnet to separate the objects in containers.
(A) (i) & (ii)
(B) (i), (ii) & (iii)
(C) (i), (ii) & (iv)
(D) (i), (ii), (iii) & (iv)

17. You should not store a floppy disk near a magnet because
(A) The magnet will rust.
(B) The magnet will become weaker.
(C) The information in the disk may be erased.
(D) The magnet will break the disk.

18. A bar magnet gets broken into four pieces E, F, G and H.

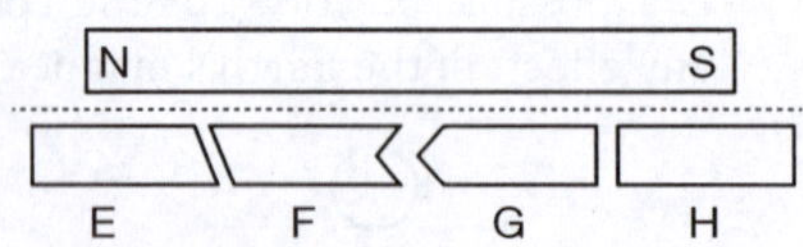

Which of the following options shows the correct poles in broken pieces?

(A) 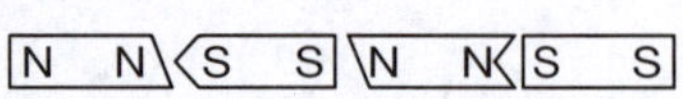

(B) 

(C) 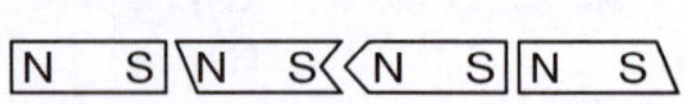

(D) 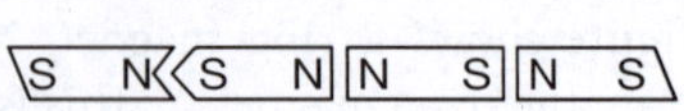

19. Fill in the blanks by choosing an appropriate option.
Magnetic strength of a bar magnet is (i) at its poles and (ii) at its centre. Two (iii) poles attract each other whereas, two (iv) poles repel each other.

	(i)	(ii)	(iii)	(iv)
(A)	Maximum	Minimum	Opposite	Similar
(B)	Maximum	Maximum	Opposite	Similar
(C)	Minimum	Minimum	Similar	Opposite
(D)	Minimum	Maximum	Similar	Opposite

20. Which of the following arrangements of four bar magnets is not possible?

(A) 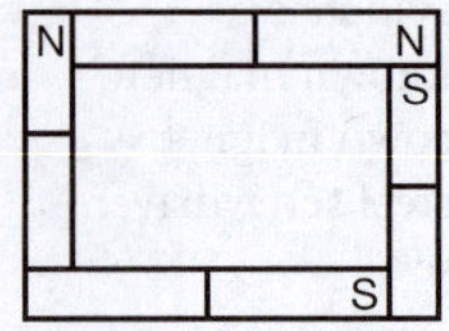

(B) 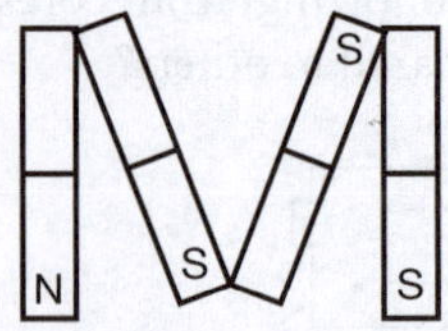

(C) 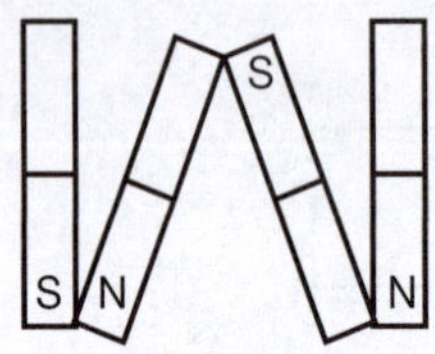

(D) 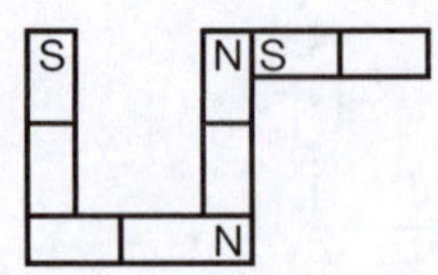

21. The given diagram shows two identical bar magnets placed side by side. Four compasses are positioned at W, X, Y and Z.

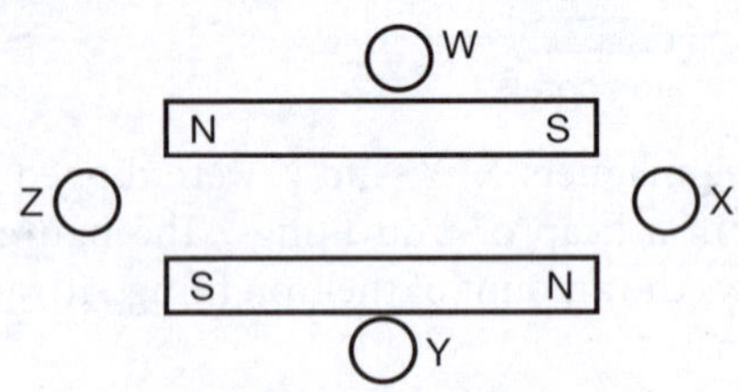

Which of the following options correctly shows the deflections of the compass needles in the given compasses?

	W	X	Y	Z
(A)	↓	←	↑	→
(B)	←	↓	→	↑
(C)	→	↑	←	↓
(D)	↑	→	↓	←

22. A compass is placed between two magnets as shown in the diagram. Magnet X is stronger than magnet Y. In which direction will the compass needle point?

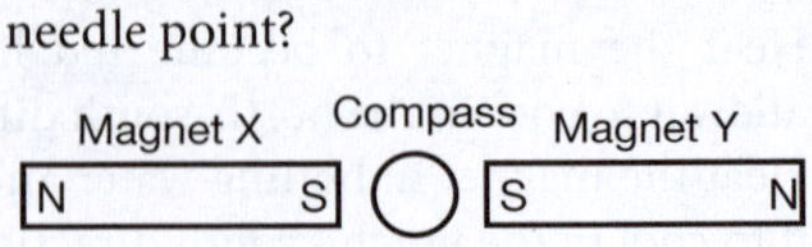

(A)  (B) 

(C)  (D) 

23. The figure shows two pieces of steel P and Q arranged in line with a bar magnet.

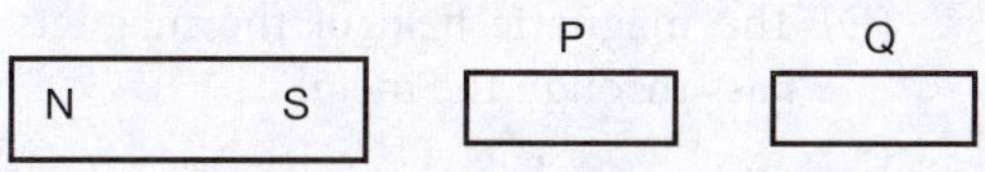

Which of the following are true forces on P and Q?

	Force on P	Force on Q
(A)	Attractive	Repulsive
(B)	Attractive	Attractive
(C)	Repulsive	Repulsive
(D)	Repulsive	Attractive

24. Three magnets P, Q, and R were dipped one by one in a heap of iron filings. Figure shows the amount of the iron filings sticking to them. The strength of these magnets will be

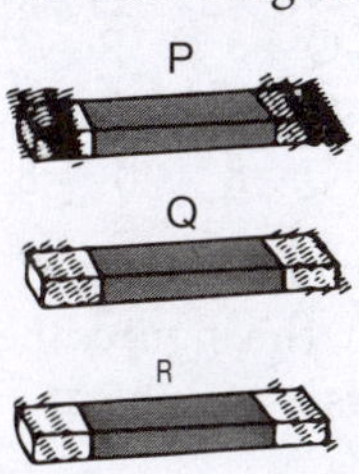

(A) P > Q > R (B) P < Q < R
(C) P = Q = R (D) P < Q > R

25. Aqil used a strong magnet to stroke the iron nail fifty times in the same direction continuously. After stroking, he wanted to test it by bringing a compass near the tip of the nail. Which one of the following diagrams shows the correct observation?

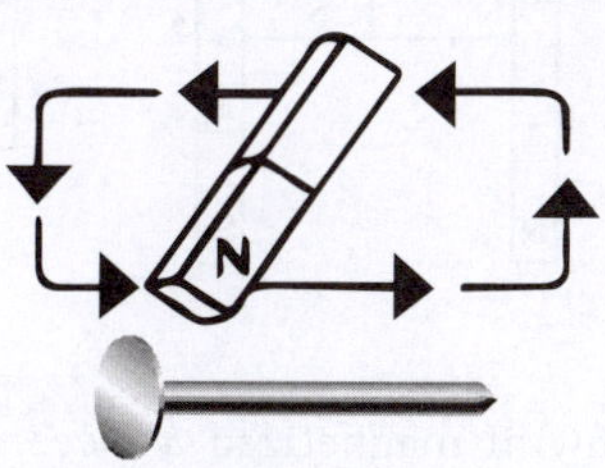

(A) 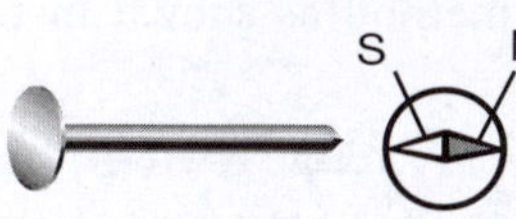

(B) 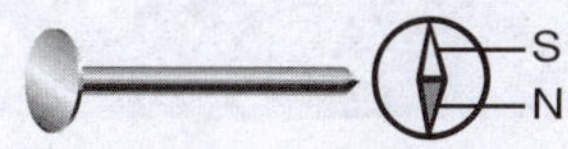

(C) 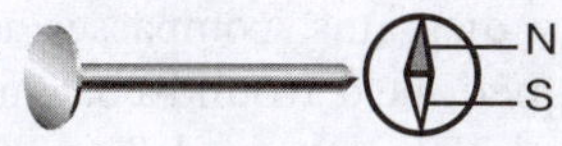

(D) 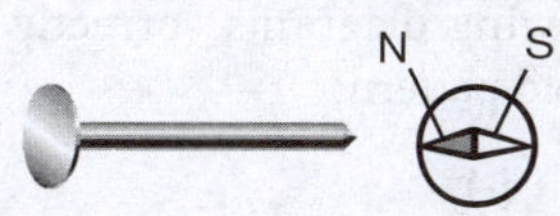

26. Mohit created a temporary magnet using the stroking method. Which of the following options shows the correct poles of his new magnet when it is stroked in the direction indicated?

(A) 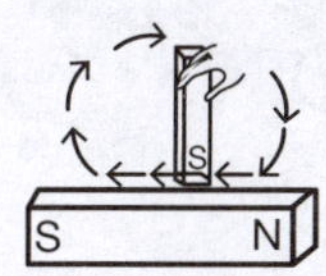

(B) 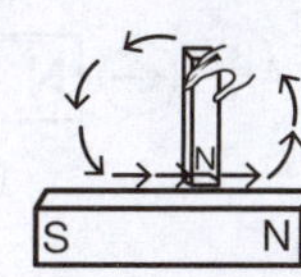

(C) 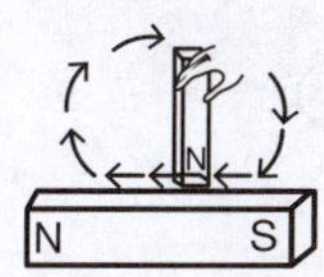

(D) 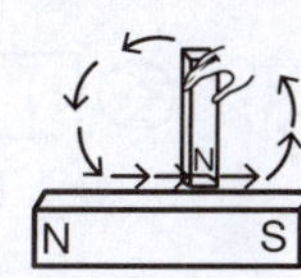

27. The figure shows two iron nails X and Y hanging from a magnet. Which of the following statements is incorrect?

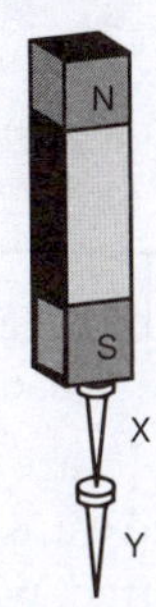

(A) Top of nail Y is north pole, and bottom of nail Y is south pole.
(B) Top of nail X is north pole, and bottom of nail X is south pole.
(C) Magnetic properties are induced into both the nails—X and Y.
(D) Magnetic properties are induced only into the nail X.

ARCHIVE CORNER

1. In the given diagrams, compasses are used to plot the magnetic field around a bar magnet with poles marked N (north) and S (south). Which of the following diagrams correctly shows the expected field pattern?

(A) 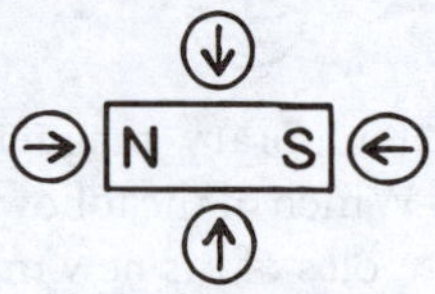

(B) 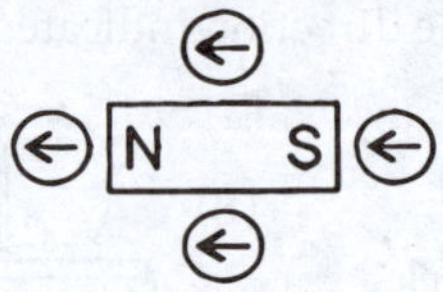

(C) 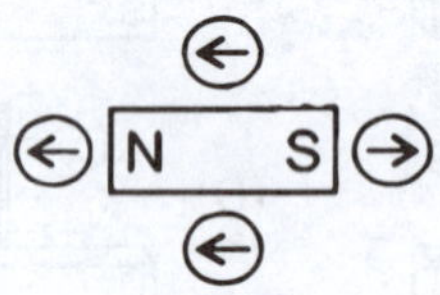

(D) 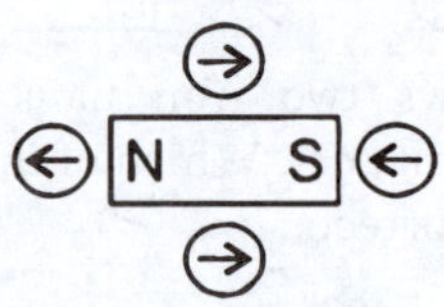

2. Observe the given figure and identify the correct statements

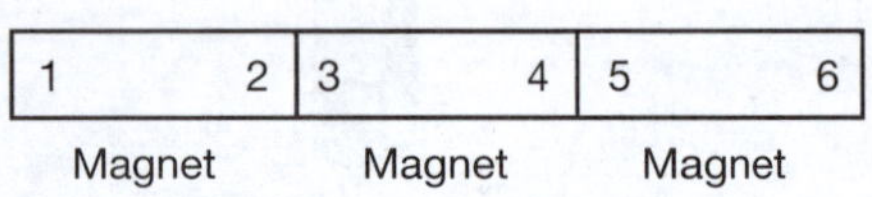

(i) Poles 1, 3, and 5 are unlike poles.
(ii) Poles 2, 4, and 6 are like poles.
(iii) Pole 1 will attract pole 3 and 5.
(iv) Pole 4 will be attracted by pole 1.

(A) Only (i) and (iii)
(B) Only (ii) and (iv)
(C) Only (i) and (ii)
(D) Only (iii) and (iv)

3. Two bar magnets suspended by string, are separated by a piece of metal. Which of the following statements best explain the outcome shown in the diagram?

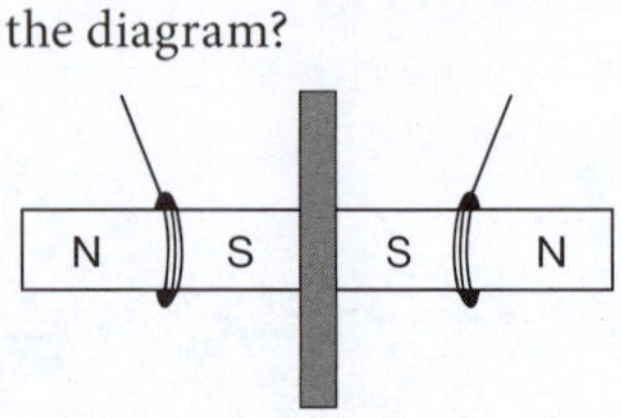

(A) Only like poles attract.
(B) The magnets have lost their magnetic forces.
(C) The metal exerts a magnetic field which attracts the magnets.
(D) The magnetic field of the magnets cannot pass through the metal.

4. Lisa did an experiment to find out which part of the magnet attracts the most pins. Which of the following readings is correct regarding the number of pins attracted by the different parts of the magnet?

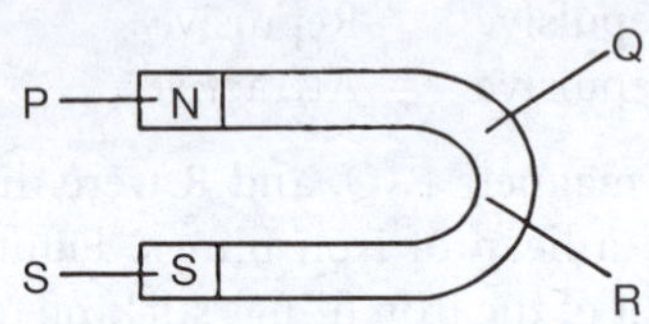

(A) P – 8 Q – 1 R – 2
(B) P – 8 Q – 3 R – 3
(C) P – 3 Q – 2 R – 3
(D) P – 1 Q – 8 R – 8

5. Study the arrangement of three bar magnets as shown in the figures below. Which of the arrangements is possible?

(A) 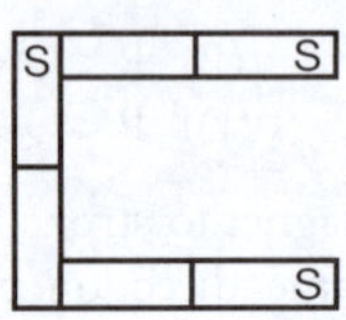

(B) 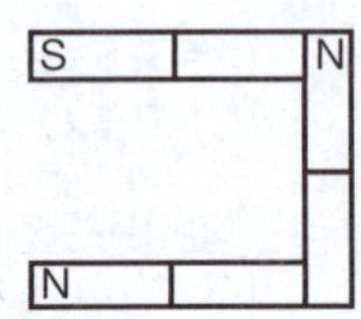

(C) 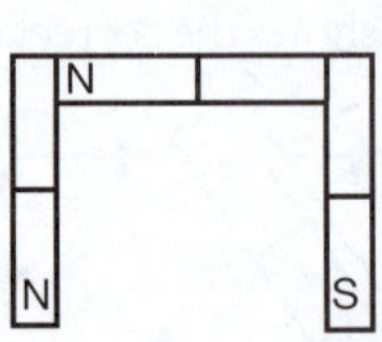

(D) 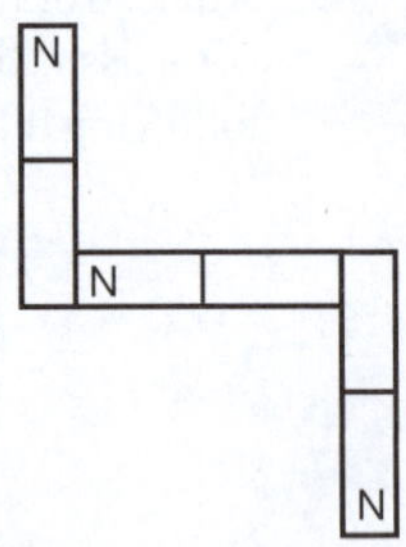

6. Ashwini magnetized a piece of iron rod using the stroking method as shown in the diagram below.

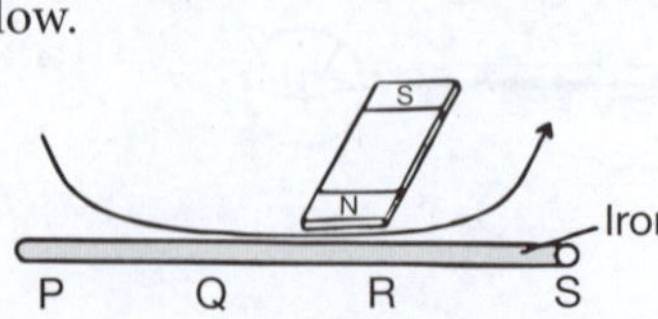

Which part of the iron rod becomes the north-seeking pole?

(A) P
(B) Q
(C) R
(D) S

ARCHIVE CORNER

7. What will happen when three bar magnets are hung in the manner as shown below?

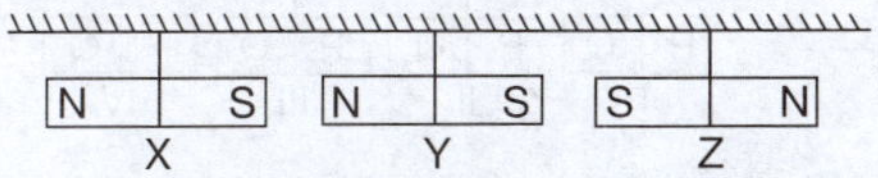

(A) Nothing will happen.
(B) Magnet Y will turn round and round.
(C) Magnet Y will move towards magnet Z.
(D) Magnet Y will move towards magnet X.

8. Magnets lose their properties significantly if they are:
(A) left in the open.
(B) touched with iron.
(C) dropped from a height repeatedly.
(D) None of these.

9. A matchbox containing an unknown object is placed on a thin sheet of glass in the experimental set up shown in the figure

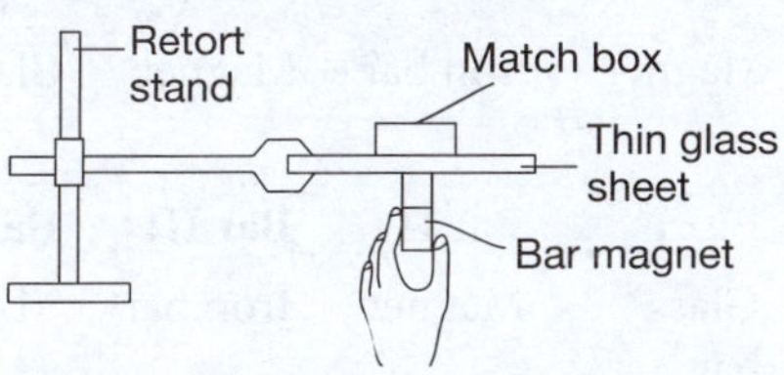

When the bar magnet moves, it is able to drag the match box along. What is most likely to be found in the matchbox?
(A) Marble
(B) Toothpick
(C) Ten-cent coin
(D) Steel ball bearing

10. Arpita is standing in the middle of a crossroad with a compass. The red portion of the compass needle is pointing towards her. If she wants to go east, she should turn
(A) Right and then go straight.
(B) Left and then go straight.
(C) Right and then go left.
(D) Left and then go right.

11. How many north and south poles are present in a magnet if it is broken into 6 pieces without loss of magnetism?
(A) Six (B) Twelve
(C) Two (D) Zero

12. Two magnets are placed in a container as shown in the figure by some external force. What would happen if the force on magnet P is removed?

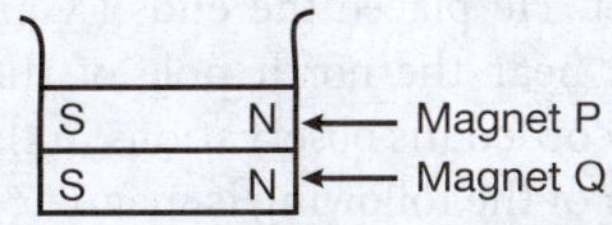

(A) Magnet P will attract magnet Q.
(B) Magnet P will repel magnet Q.
(C) Both magnets will demagnetize each other.
(D) Both magnets will produce electric current.

13. Read the given statements, select the correct option.
Statement 1: When a horseshoe magnet is brought close to pile of iron filings, more filings will be attracted to the U shaped part of the magnet.
Statement 2: Horseshoe magnet has only one pole, the U-shaped part.
(A) Both statement 1 and 2 are true, and statement 2 is the correct explanation of statement 1.
(B) Both statement 1 and 2 are true, but statement 2 is not the correct explanation of statement 1.
(C) Statement 1 is true but statement 2 is false.
(D) Both statement 1 and 2 are false.

14. Which of the following is incorrect?
(A) To increase the magnetic strength, increase the number of strokes while creating magnets.
(B) To increase the magnetic strength, increase the number of coils around the nail.
(C) Magnetic force is pulling force only.
(D) Magnet may lose its magnetic property when heated to a very high temperature.

15. Which of the following is the best way to keep magnets?

(A) 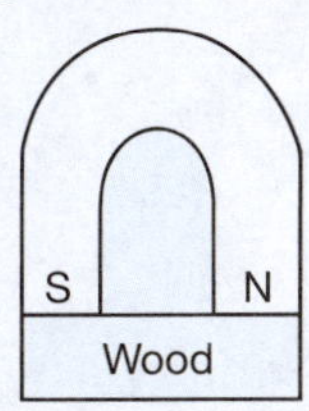

(B) 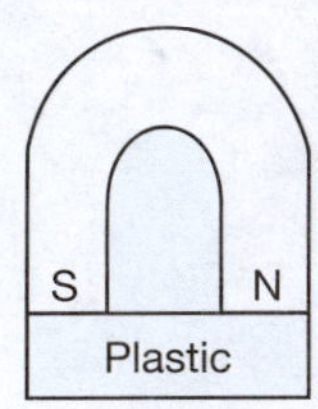

(C) 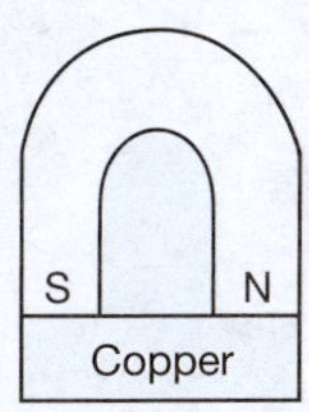

(D) 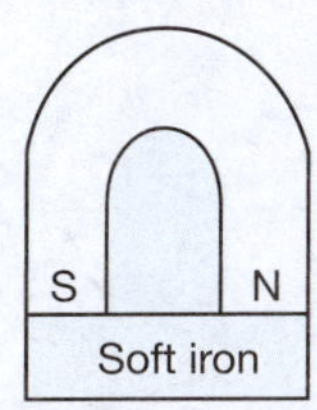

16. Arun suspended a bar magnet on a string as shown in the diagram below. He brought 3 bar-shaped objects P, Q, and R towards the bar magnet. He placed the ends (X and Y) of each object, near the north pole of the bar magnet and recorded his observations in the table below. Which of the following is magnet?

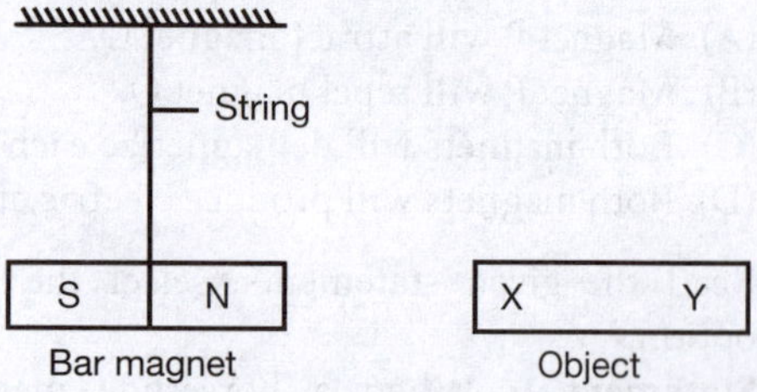

Object	End X brought near to N pol	End Y brought near to N pole
P	N pole repelled	N pole attracted
Q	N pole attracted	N pole repelled
R	N pole remains stationary	N pole remains stationary

(A) P only
(B) Q only
(C) P and Q only
(D) P and R only

17. When Asha suspended four bars of different materials from a pole and brought the north pole of a bar magnet near part P and Q of each bar one by one as shown in the figure below, she recorded her observations as follows:

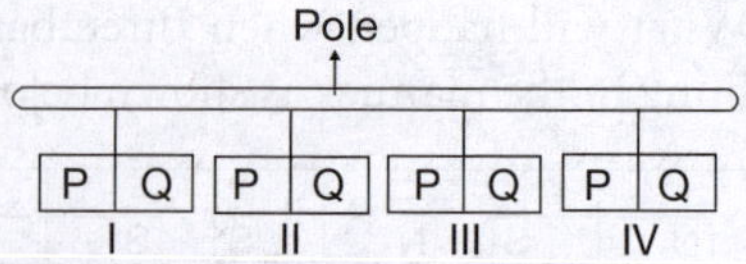

Bar	Part P	Part Q
I	Pushed	Pulled
II	Nothing happened	Nothing happened
III	Pulled	Pushed
IV	Pulled	Pulled

(A)

Bar I	Bar II	Bar III	Bar IV
Magnet	Stainless steel bar	Magnet	Iron bar

(B)

Bar I	Bar II	Bar III	Bar IV
Magnet	Iron bar	Magnet	Glass bar

(C)

Bar I	Bar II	Bar III	Bar IV
Glass bar	Magnet	Iron bar	Magnet

(D)

Bar I	Bar II	Bar III	Bar IV
Magnet	Iron bar	Glass bar	Stainless steel bar

ANSWER KEY

Level 1

Fixed Response Type

Multiple Choice Questions

1. C	2. C	3. B	4. B	5. B	6. B	7. A	8. C	9. C	10. A
11. C	12. A	13. B	14. C	15. B	16. A	17. D	18. D	19. A	20. B
21. B	22. C	23. C	24. C	25. B	26. D	27. B	28. C	29. B	30. A
31. C	32. C	33. B	34. B	35. C	36. C	37. A	38. B	39. C	40. C
41. C	42. D	43. A	44. D	45. D	46. D	47. B	48. A	49. B	50. A

Fill in the Blanks

1. 2
2. More
3. North, South
4. Magnetic
5. lodestone
6. 2

True/False

1. False
2. True
3. True
4. True
5. False
6. False
7. False

Match Type Questions

1. A
2. A

Assertion and Reason Type Questions

1. A
2. A
3. B

Comprehension Type Questions

1. A
2. C
3. B

Free Response Type

Numerical Based Questions

1. 4
2. 14

Case Based Questions

1. B
2. B
3. D

Level 2

Multiple Choice Questions

1. C	2. C	3. C	4. C	5. A	6. B	7. A	8. B	9. B	10. C
11. A	12. B	13. B	14. B	15. B	16. B	17. B	18. C	19. C	20. A
21. A	22. B	23. B	24. A	25. A	26. C	27. B	28. B	29. D	30. A
31. B	32. A	33. A	34. B	35. A	36. B	37. C	38. A	39. B	40. A
41. B	42. A	43. D	44. B	45. C	46. B	47. B	48. C	49. A	50. B
51. A	52. D	53. C	54. C	55. C	56. A	57. B	58. D		

Higher Order Thinking Skills (HOTS)

1. A	2. B	3. B	4. D	5. B	6. D	7. B	8. D	9. A	10. A
11. C	12. B	13. C	14. C	15. B	16. A	17. C	18. C	19. A	20. C
21. C	22. C	23. B	24. A	25. D	26. D	27. D			

Archive Corner

1. D	2. D	3. D	4. B	5. C	6. A	7. D	8. C	9. D	10. B
11. B	12. B	13. D	14. C	15. D	16. C	17. A			

ANSWER KEY

CHAPTER 3

Temperature and Its Measurement

Learning Outcomes

After reading this chapter, you would be able to:

- explain temperature.
- discuss the types of thermometer.

Geekspeak

- Temperature
- Clinical and laboratory thermometer

Introduction

- Heat is a form of energy which causes the sensation of hotness or coldness.

  For example, if we dip our finger in hot water, we have a sensation of hotness. Similarly, if we touch a block of ice, the sensation is that of coldness. In the former case, the heat energy moves into the finger, while in the latter, it moves out of the finger. Thus, hotness or coldness basically indicates whether heat energy is flowing into our body or out of it.
- The amount of heat energy present in a body is determined by the total sum of the kinetic energy and potential energy of its molecules.

Temperature

Temperature is the effect of heat energy which determines the thermal state of a given substance. In other words, it determines the degree of hotness or coldness of a substance.
When two bodies at different temperatures are brought in contact with each other, the heat energy always flows from a body at higher temperature to a body at lower temperature, till the temperatures equalize. Thus, it is the temperature of a body which determines the direction of flow of heat energy. If a body is at a higher temperature than its surroundings, it means that heat energy will flow out of the body into the surroundings.
Measurement of Temperature: The instrument used for measuring temperature is called thermometer (as shown in Fig. 3.1).

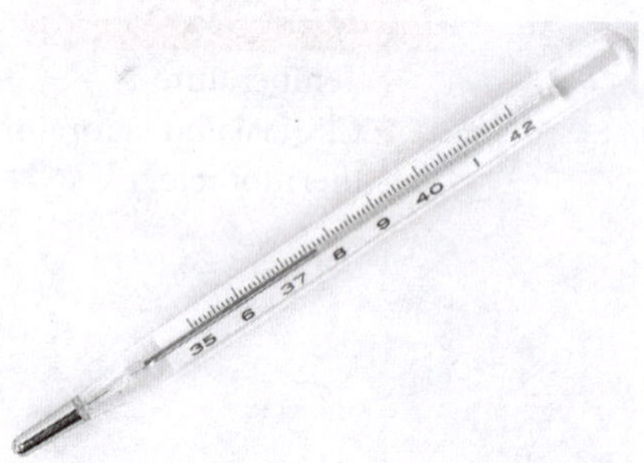

(a) Mercury Thermometer

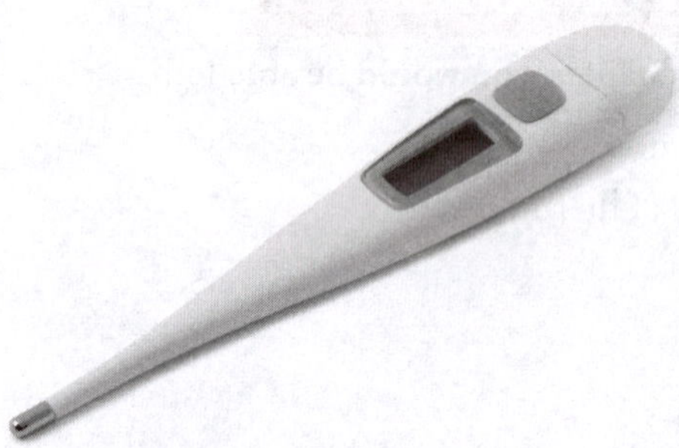

(b) Digital Thermometer

Figure 3.1 Thermometer

Competition Corner

Different Scales of Temperature

- **Celsius or Centigrade Scale:** As the name suggests, this scale has 100 divisions between the upper and lower standard points. This scale was introduced by a Swedish astronomer Celsius, and is known after his name. Each division on this scale is called one degree centigrade or one degree Celsius and is written as °C. More sensitive thermometers have 200 divisions between standard points and each division is equal to ½ °C. Sometimes these thermometers are called half °C thermometers.
- **Fahrenheit Scale:** This scale was introduced by Fahrenheit. On this scale, 32°F represents the melting point of ice and 212°F the steam point. Zero is marked 32°F below the ice point. The length in between the standard points is divided into 180 equal parts. Each division on this scale is called 1°F.

  This scale is widely used for meteorological and clinical purposes.

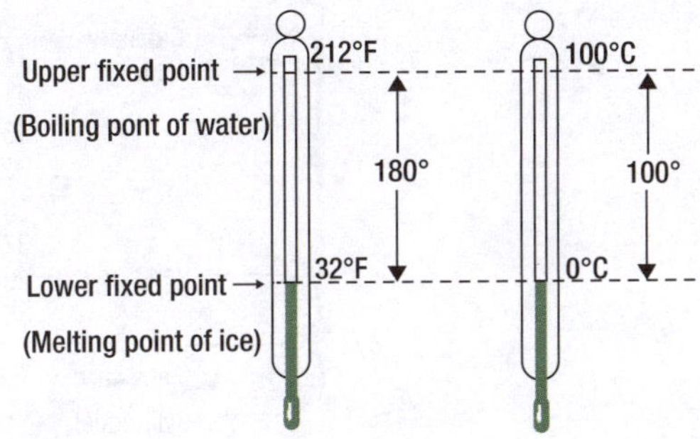

Upper and Lower Fixed Points

  - **Relation between Celsius and Fahrenheit scales:**

    If T_C and T_F are temperature values of a body on Celsius scale and Fahrenheit scale respectively, then

$$\frac{T_C - 0}{100} = \frac{T_F - 32}{180} \Rightarrow \frac{T_C}{5} = \frac{T_F - 32}{9}$$

    The above relation is very useful for converting temperatures from one scale to another.

- **Kelvin Scale:** The scale of measurement of temperature in which the lowest temperature is zero Kelvin (–273°C) is called Kelvin scale. This is also called S.I. scale of temperature.
  - **Characteristics of Kelvin scale:**
    - There cannot be any temperature below zero Kelvin.
    - The temperature is expressed in (K), but no degree symbol is attached to it.
    - Rise in temperature in Kelvin = Rise in temperature in degree Celsius.
  - **Relation between different temperature scales:**

$$\frac{T_C}{5} = \frac{T_F - 32}{9} = \frac{T_K - 273}{5}$$

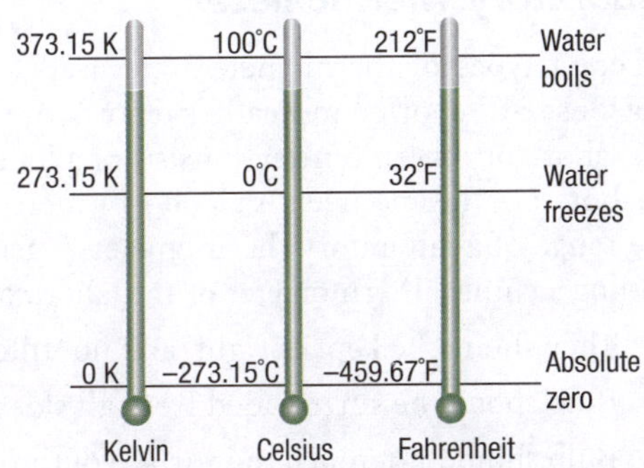

Comparison Between All Three Scales of Temperature

Types of Thermometer

The types of thermometer used for measuring temperature are discussed below:

Clinical Thermometer

Clinical thermometer is a specially adapted Fahrenheit thermometer used by doctors to record the temperature of human body. It consists of a long, narrow, uniform glass tube which has a bulb filled with mercury at one end.

The markings are from 95°F to 110°F, because the temperature of the human body does not fall below 95°F or rise above 110°F, as in either case death occurs. Some clinical thermometers have centigrade scale, marked between 35°C and 43°C, the normal temperature of human body being 37°C. Before using the thermometer, it should be washed with water and then jerked so that the mercury flows back into the bulb (as shown in Fig. 3.2).

There is a kink in mercury thermometer to prevent the mercury to go back in its bulb and gives time to observe the reading after measurement. Now a days digital thermometers are widely used in place of mercury thermometer as mercury is very toxic material and very difficult to dispose. These thermometers work on batteries. These show readings when metallic end comes in contact with the person's body. There are also infrared thermometers which measure temperature without touching the person's body.

We keep thermometer under the tongue or under the armpits. There is a slight difference in the reading for both. The temperature shown by thermometer kept under the armpit is lower than the temperature shown by keeping the thermometer under the tongue.

Now a days, digital thermometers are widely used in place of mercury thermometer.

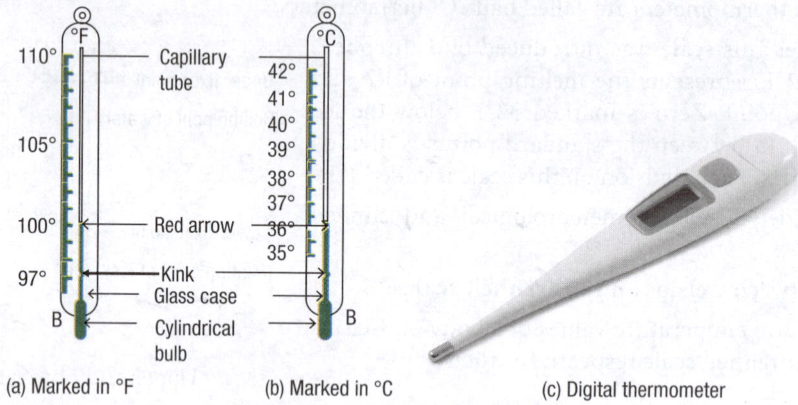

Figure 3.2 Clinical Thermometer

Laboratory Thermometer

Different types of thermometers are used for different purposes. The maximum and minimum temperatures of the previous day, reported in weather reports, are measured by a thermometer called the maximum-minimum thermometer. The laboratory thermometer consists of a long transparent glass tube having a bulb at one end. The liquid generally used in laboratory thermometer is alcohol or mercury.

The range of a laboratory thermometer is generally from –10°C to 110°C. In addition to the precautions needed while reading a clinical thermometer or the laboratory thermometer:

- They should be kept upright, and not tilted.
- Bulb should be surrounded from all sides by the substance of which the temperature is to be measured.
- Bulb should not touch the surface of the container.
- The Reading must be taken keeping the mark in line to the eye level.

Maximum-Minimum Thermometer

A maximum-minimum thermometer, also known as a Six's thermometer, is a type of thermometer that records the highest and lowest temperatures reached over a specific period, typically 24 hours. It's a crucial tool for monitoring temperature fluctuations in various settings, such as weather stations, greenhouses and schools. It usually consists of a U-shaped glass tube containing mercury and two movable steel indices (or markers). When the temperature rises, the alcohol in the bulb expands, pushing the mercury column and moving one index to record the maximum temperature. Conversely, when the temperature drops, the alcohol contracts, and the mercury column moves in the opposite direction, pushing the other index to record the minimum temperature.

The maximum temperature is read at the end of the mercury column, which is pushed up by the expanding alcohol. The minimum temperature is read at the end of the mercury column that was pushed down by the contracting alcohol.

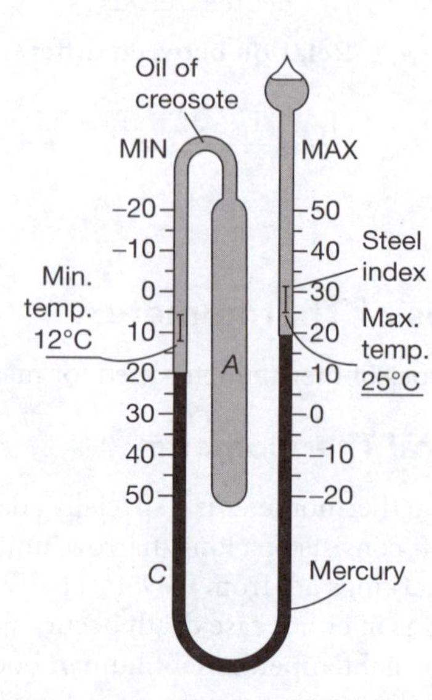

Figure 3.3 Maximum-Minimum Thermometer

Units of Heat Energy

Heat energy is measured in calories. The quantity of heat energy required to raise the temperature of 1 g of pure water through 1°C (14.5°C to 15.5°C) is called one calorie. The calorie is a very small unit of heat energy for practical purposes. Thus, a bigger unit, called kilocalorie, is used.

The quantity of heat energy required to raise the temperature of 1 kg of pure water through 1°C is called one kilocalorie.

> **Keystone**
>
> According to 'Dolbear's Law', you can calculate the temperature in degrees Fahrenheit by counting the number of chirps produced in 14 seconds by the snowy tree cricket and adding 40.

$$1 \text{ kilocalorie} = 1000 \text{ calories}$$

Kilocalorie is sometimes called Big Calorie or Doctor's Calorie or Calorie (with capital C). The energy value of foods and fuel is measured in kilocalories.

We know energy is measured in Joules. As heat is a form of energy, it should also be measured in Joules, rather than calories or kilocalories, for strict scientific purposes. However, doctors still continue with kilocalories.

The following are the equivalent of calorie and kilocalorie in joules:

- 1 calorie = 4.186 J = 4.2 J (approx.)
- 1 kilocalorie = 4186 J = 4200 J (approx.)

❖ INTEXT QUESTIONS

1. **At what temperature, if any, do the following pairs of scales give the same reading?**

   (a) Celsius and Fahrenheit (b) Fahrenheit and Kelvin (c) Kelvin and Celsius

   Solution: If the temperature is θ at which the reading of two scales coincides, then from

   $$\frac{T_C - 0}{100} = \frac{T_F - 32}{180} = \frac{T_K - 273.15}{100}$$

   (a) $\frac{\theta}{100} = \frac{\theta - 32}{180}$, i.e., $\theta = -40°$

   i.e., reading of Celsius and Fahrenheit scale coincides at –40°.

   (b) $\frac{\theta - 32}{180} = \frac{\theta - 273.15}{100} \Rightarrow \theta = 574.6°$

   i.e., reading of Fahrenheit and Kelvin scale coincides at 574.6°.

   (c) $\frac{\theta - 273}{100} = \frac{\theta}{100}$, which is not possible.

   So, reading of Celsius and Kelvin scale can never coincide.

2. Find the value of 5°C in °F and K scales, respectively.

   Solution: Relation between Celsius and Fahrenheit scale:

   $$\frac{C}{5} = \frac{F - 32}{9}$$

   So, the corresponding value of 5°C in Fahrenheit scale is:

   $$\frac{5}{5} = \frac{F - 32}{9} \Rightarrow F = 41°F$$

   Relation between Celsius and Kelvin scale:

   T(K) = T(°C) + 273 = 5 + 273 = 278 K

Check Point 1

1. The temperature of two bodies differs by 1°C. How much will they differ on the Fahrenheit scale?
2. Express 45°C in Kelvin.
3. A copper rod at 50°C is dropped into a bucket containing water at 50°C. Will the heat flow or not in this case?
4. What are the various means used by a pizza delivery man to keep the pizza hot?
5. Why do we have to shake the thermometer before taking temperature in a clinical thermometer?

Competition Corner

Expansion of matter

- Matter, whenever it receives heat, always expands. The types of matter expand differently as gas expands more than solid or liquid. A metal ball when heated gain energy and all the particles starts vibrating and distance between them increased. As a result, it expands.
- Similarly, when matter loses heat (that is cooling), it contracts. All the particles move closer when the heat is taken from them and the object shrinks.
- Warm objects expand or become larger. Cold objects contract or become smaller.
- Water boils at 100°C, but if you keep on giving the heat energy, this will not increase its temperature, instead this energy is used in changing the state of water. And water starts converting into vapours.
- Similarly, ice melts at 0°C, but if you keep on giving the heat energy, this will not increase its temperature, instead this energy is used in changing the state of ice. And ice starts to melts.

STRUCTURAL OUTLINE

Temperature

Temperature is the degree of hotness and coldness of an object.

- Heat is a form of energy that produces a feeling of hotness and coldness of an object. This effect is known as temperature.
- 1 cal = 4.2 J

Scales of Temperature

Thermometer scales are

- Celsius (°C)
- Fahrenheit (°F)
- Kelvin (K)
  - Relation between three scales:

$$\frac{T_c - 0}{100 - 0} = \frac{T_F - 32}{212 - 32} = \frac{T_K - 273}{373 - 273}$$

Thermometer

Thermometer is an instrument used to measure temperature. It works on the principle of expansion of liquid on heating. Temperature is measured in Celsius and Fahrenheit scale for clinical and digital purpose but for scientific work, Kelvin scale is used.

Different types of thermometers:

- Clinical thermometer
- Laboratory thermometer
- Digital thermometer
- Maximum-minimum thermometer

Heat

Effect of Heat on Matter

Matter contracts when cold

Matter contracts on cooling, causing decrease in volume or shape and size of the matter.

Matter expands on heating

Matter (solid, liquid and gas) expands on heating, causing change in shape and size or volume of the matter.

EXEMPLIFICATION

1. **Define the following terms:**

   (a) Temperature **(b) Thermometer**

   (c) Conductor of heat **(d) Insulator of heat**

   Solution:

   (a) Temperature: The degree of hotness or coldness of a substance is known as temperature.

   (b) Thermometer: The device that measures temperature is known as thermometer.

   (c) Conductor of heat: The substances through which heat energy can easily flow by conduction are called conductors of heat.

   (d) Insulator of heat: The substances which do not allow the heat energy to flow through them easily are called insulators of heat.

2. **(i) What is a clinical thermometer?**

   (ii) Name the liquid used in this thermometer.

   (iii) What is the range of this thermometer?

   (iv) Why are digital thermometers used these days?

   Solution:

   (i) Thermometer that measures our body temperature is called a clinical thermometer.

   (ii) Mercury.

   (iii) 35°C to 42°C.

   (iv) Mercury is a poisonous metal. If a thermometer breaks, when in mouth, one is exposed to mercury. To overcome this, digital thermometers are used these days.

3. **What is the normal temperature of a healthy human body?**

   Solution: 37°C.

4. **What is the range of laboratory thermometer?**

   Solution: –10°C to 110°C.

5. **We cannot use laboratory thermometer to measure our body temperature. Why?**

   Solution: There is no 'kink' in laboratory thermometer. Therefore, the temperature will fall as soon as we remove the thermometer from the mouth and we will not be able to measure the correct temperature of the body.

6. **What is the use of "kink" in clinical thermometers?**

   Solution: 'Kink' provided in the clinical thermometer does not allow the mercury to come down on its own and we can note the measured temperature even after some time.

7. **Why is mercury used in thermometers?**

   Solution: Mercury is the only metal in liquid state at room temperature. It is used in thermometers because it has high coefficient of expansion. Hence, any slight change in temperature is visible when it is used in a thermometer. It also has a high boiling point, which makes it highly suitable to measure high temperature.

NCERT COMPENDIUM

1. The normal temperature of a healthy human being is close to ____________.
(i) 98.6 °C (ii) 37.0 °C
(iii) 32.0 °C (iv) 27.0 °C

Solution: (ii) 37.0 °C

2. 37 °C is the same temperature as
(i) 97.4 °F (ii) 97.6 °F
(iii) 98.4 °F (iv) 98.6 °F

Solution: (iv) 98.6 °F

Relation between Celsius and Fahrenheit scale

$$\frac{C}{5} = \frac{F-32}{9}$$

So corresponding value of 37°C in Fahrenheit scale is

$$\frac{37}{5} = \frac{F-32}{9} \quad \Rightarrow F = 98.6°F$$

3. Fill in the blanks:
(i) The hotness or coldness of a system is determined by its ________________
(ii) The temperature of ice-cold water cannot be measured by a ______________ thermometer.
(iii) The unit of temperature is degree ____________

Solution: (i) The hotness or coldness of a system is determined by its temperature.
(ii) The temperature of ice-cold water cannot be measured by a clinical thermometer.
(iii) The unit of temperature is degree Celsius.

4. The range of a laboratory thermometer is usually
(i) 10 °C to 100 °C (ii) –10 °C to 110 °C
(iii) 32 °C to 45 °C (iv) 35 °C to 42 °C

Solution: (ii) –10 °C to 110 °C

5. Four students used a laboratory thermometer to measure the temperature of water as shown in Figure.

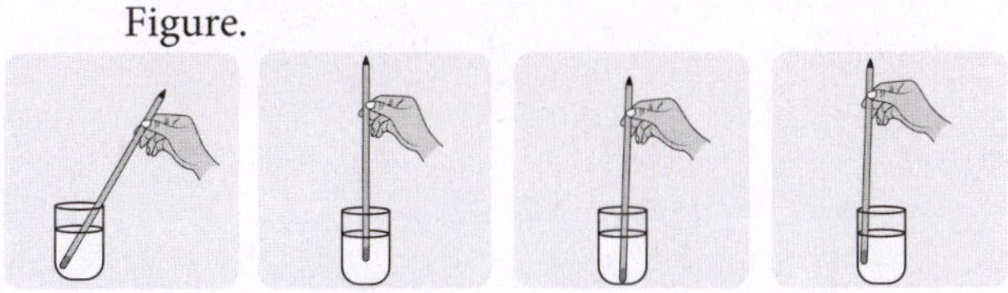

Student 1 Student 2 Student 3 Student 4

Who do you think followed the correct way for measuring temperature?
(i) Student 1 (ii) Student 2
(iii) Student 3 (iv) Student 4

Solution: (ii) Student 2. Thermometer must be upright and should not touch the bottom as well as the boundary of container.

6. Colour to show the red column on the drawings of thermometers (Figure) as per the temperatures written below:

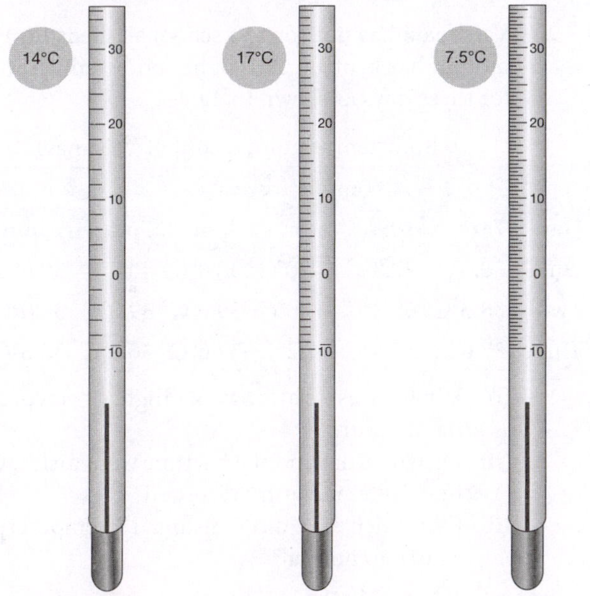

Solution:

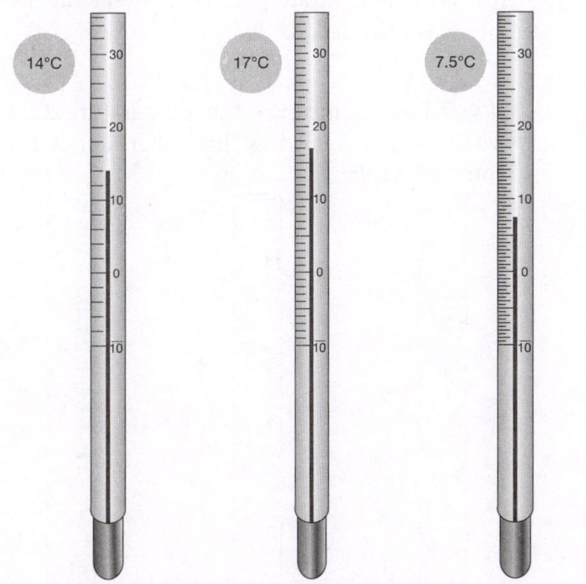

7. Observe the part of thermometer shown in Figure and answer the following questions:

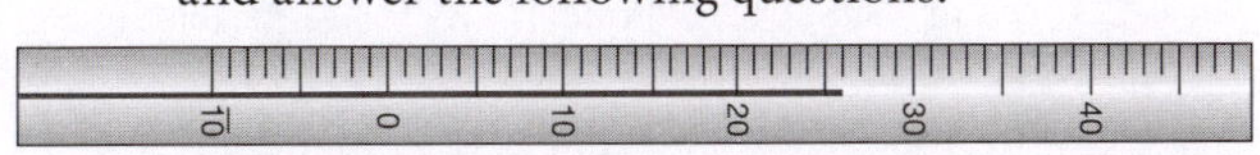

(i) What type of thermometer is it?
(ii) What is the reading of the thermometer?
(iii) What is the smallest value that this thermometer can measure?

Solution: (i) Laboratory Thermometer
(ii) 26 °F
(iii) 1 °F

NCERT COMPENDIUM

8. A laboratory thermometer is not used to measure our body temperature. Give a reason.

Solution: A laboratory thermometer is not used to measure our body temperature because it doesn't have a kink. Thus, we will not be able to measure correct temperature.

9. Vaishnavi has not gone to school as she is ill. Her mother has kept a record of her body temperature for three days as shown in Table .

Table Body temperature record of Vaishnavi

	Temperature at					
Day	**7am**	**10am**	**1pm**	**4pm**	**7pm**	**10pm**
One	38.0°C	37.8°C	38.0°C	38.0°C	40.0°C	39.0°C
Two	38.6°C	38.8°C	39.0°C	39.0°C	39.0°C	38.0°C
Three	37.6°C	37.4°C	37.2°C	37.0°C	36.8°C	36.6°C

(i) What was Vaishnavi's highest recorded temperature?

(ii) On which day and at what time was Vaishnavi's highest temperature recorded?

(iii) On which day did Vaishnavi's temperature return to normal?

Solution: (i)40 °C

(ii) On Day 1 and at 7 pm, the highest temperature was recorded.

(iii) Day three

10. If you have to measure the temperature 22.5 °C, which of the following three thermometers will you use? Explain.

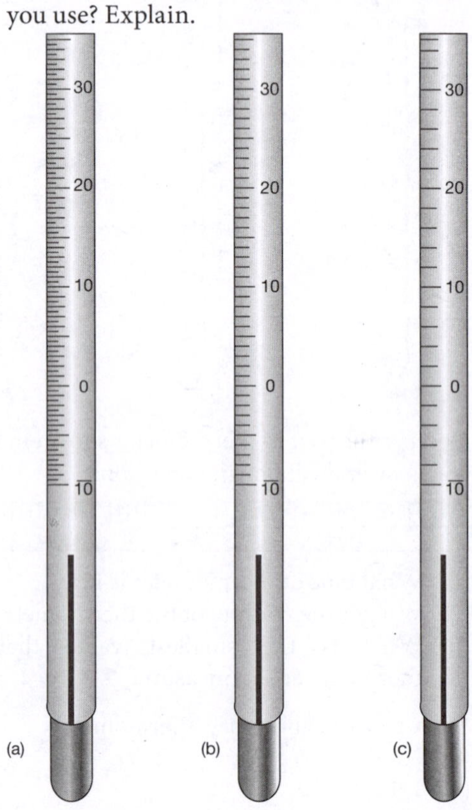

Solution: We will use thermometer b because it can measure upto 0.1 degree correct temperature.

11. The temperature shown by the thermometer in Figure is

(i) 28.0 °C
(ii) 27.5 °C
(iii) 26.5 °C
(iv) 25.3 °C

Solution: (ii) 27.5 °C

12. A laboratory thermometer has 50 divisions between 0 °C and 100 °C. What does each division of this thermometer measure?

Solution: Each division will measure 2 °C.

13. Draw the scale of a thermometer in which the smallest division reads 0.5 °C. You may draw only the portion between 10 °C and 20 °C.

Solution:

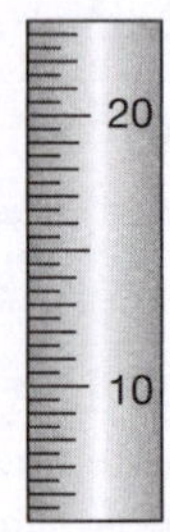

14. Someone tells you that she has a fever of 101 degrees. Does she mean it on the Celsius scale or Fahrenheit scale?

Solution: The temperature is in Fahrenheit scale.

ASSESSMENT CORNER

Level 1

Fixed Response Type

Multiple Choice Questions

1. Convert 293 K into Celsius scale.
(A) 566°C (B) 293°C
(C) 20°C (D) 496°C

2. Which of the following temperature is the highest?
(A) 100 K (B) –20°C
(C) –23°C (D) –13°F

3. The normal temperature of a human body is:
(A) 37°C (B) 38°C
(C) 35°C (D) 98.4°C

4. Fahrenheit scale divides two fixed points into:
(A) 180 parts (B) 212 parts
(C) 100 parts (D) 32 parts

5. Convert 302°F into Celsius scale.
(A) 150° (B) 160°
(C) 140° (D) 170°

6. At what temperature is the reading on Celsius scale half of that on Fahrenheit scale?
(A) 300° (B) 320°
(C) 420° (D) 350°

7. The value of 32°F in centigrade scale is:
(A) 0°C (B) 10°C
(C) 20°C (D) 30°C

8. Heat is closely related with:
(A) Liquid (B) Pressure
(C) Temperature (D) Force

9. Express 55°C in Kelvin.
(A) 328 (B) 132
(C) 133 (D) 134

10. The measure of degree of hotness or coldness of body is called:
(A) Heat energy (B) Celsius
(C) Kelvin (D) Temperature

11. When in thermal contact, the quantity of heat lost by the hotter body is ______________ the amount of heat gained by the colder body.
(A) Equal to (B) Greater than
(C) Less than (D) Cannot say

12. 1 calorie equals to:
(A) 4.2 J (B) 0.42 J
(C) 420 J (D) 4200 J

13. A copper disc with a central hole is heated; the diameter of the hole:
(A) Increases
(B) Decreases
(C) First decreases then increases
(D) First increases then decreases

14. Thermal expansion due to heating at equal temperature will be the least:
(A) In solid (B) In liquid
(C) In gas (D) Equal in all

15. Which of the following conditions enables heat to flow from one body to another identical body?
(A) The difference in the temperatures of the two bodies
(B) The difference in the pressures exerted on the two bodies
(C) The difference in the densities of the two bodies
(D) The difference in the sizes of the two bodies

16. When you heat water in a pot, it boils. What can you infer from the above observation?
(A) Heat is a form of energy
(B) Water can boil by itself
(C) Water develops heat on its own
(D) Water is a universal solvent

17. What must be done to enable mercury in a glass thermometer to respond quickly to changes in temperature?
(A) The bore should be narrow
(B) The wall of stem should be thin
(C) The bulb should contain a lot of mercury
(D) The wall of glass bulb should be thin

18. Which instrument measures the degree of hotness or coldness of a body?
(A) Heat energy (B) Measuring scale
(C) Barometer (D) Thermometer

19. Why is mercury widely used in clinical thermometers?
(i) Mercury is easily available in pure form
(ii) Mercury is opaque
(iii) Mercury has a constant coefficient of expansion

(A) Only (i) and (ii)
(B) Only (ii) and (iii)
(C) Only (i) and (iii)
(D) (i), (ii), and (iii)

20. Which of the following is NOT a scale of temperature?
(A) Kelvin scale (B) Celsius scale
(C) Fahrenheit scale (D) Richter scale

21. How many parts does a Celsius scale have?
(A) 100 (B) 273
(C) 180 (D) 50

22. What is the range of a clinical thermometer?
(A) 0–100°C (B) 32–214°F
(C) 0–273°C (D) 35–42°C

23. Identify the normal human body temperature.
(A) 32°F (B) 212°F
(C) 100.4°F (D) 98.6°F

24. What happens when the temperature of a substance is increased?
(A) Kinetic energy of the molecules of the substance increases
(B) Kinetic energy of the molecules of the substance decreases
(C) The amplitude of vibrations of molecules of the substance about their mean position decreases
(D) It does not cause any change

25. What is temperature?
(A) The rate of expansion of an object
(B) The loss of heat energy
(C) The volume of a gas occupied
(D) The degree of hotness or coldness of a body

26. What does thermometer actually measure?
(A) The total heat energy in a body
(B) The degree of hotness or coldness of a body
(C) The amount of matter in a body
(D) The weight of molecules in a body

27. A student observes that when a laboratory thermometer is taken out of hot water, the mercury level immediately starts falling. This happens because:
(A) Mercury is escaping from the thermometer.
(B) The glass tube is contracting.
(C) Mercury contracts as temperature decreases.
(D) Air pressure is pushing the mercury down.

28. Why is the Kelvin scale considered the most scientific temperature scale?
(A) It uses larger degree intervals.
(B) It starts from absolute zero temperature.
(C) It is easier to use in calculations.
(D) It was invented by scientists.

29. When measuring temperature with a laboratory thermometer, why must the reading be taken while the thermometer is still in the liquid?
(A) The thermometer will break if removed quickly
(B) The liquid level will change immediately upon removal
(C) It prevents contamination of the liquid
(D) The glass becomes too hot to handle

30. A digital thermometer shows 37.2°C while a clinical thermometer shows 37°C for the same person. This difference occurs because:
(A) One of the thermometers is broken.
(B) Digital thermometers are less accurate.
(C) Different thermometers may have slight variations in precision.
(D) Body temperature is constantly changing.

31. Infrared thermometers work by detecting:
(A) The vibration of molecules in the object.
(B) The thermal radiation emitted by the object.
(C) The expansion of materials in the object.
(D) The electrical conductivity of the object.

32. The normal range for a clinical thermometer is 35°C to 42°C. This narrow range exists because:
(A) Human bodies can only survive in this temperature range.
(B) Clinical thermometers are designed specifically for human body measurements.
(C) Mercury cannot expand beyond these temperatures.
(D) Glass thermometers work best in this range.

33. When water boils, its temperature remains constant at 100°C (at sea level) because:
(A) The thermometer stops working at 100°C.
(B) Water cannot get hotter than 100°C.
(C) Energy is being used to convert liquid to vapour rather than to increase the temperature.
(D) The bubbles prevent further heating.

34. Mercury was traditionally used in thermometers because it:
(A) is the cheapest liquid available.
(B) expands uniformly with temperature changes.
(C) is transparent and easy to see.
(D) does not react with glass.

35. The kink in a clinical thermometer serves to:
(A) Make the thermometer easier to hold.
(B) Prevent mercury from flowing back immediately after measurement.
(C) Allow air to enter the thermometer.
(D) Make the scale easier to read.

36. A student needs to measure the temperature of boiling water in a laboratory. Which thermometer should they use and why?
(A) Clinical thermometer, because it's more accurate.
(B) Digital thermometer, because it's safer.
(C) Laboratory thermometer, because it can measure higher temperatures.
(D) Any thermometer will work equally well.

37. If you convert 25°C to Kelvin, the result would be:
(A) 248 K (B) 298 K
(C) 298.15 K (D) 273 K

Fill in the Blanks

1. The coldness of an object is determined by its ________________.

2. Temperature of boiling water can be measured by a ________________ thermometer.

3. Different scales of temperature are ________________.

True/False

1. The S.I. unit of temperature is degree Celsius.

2. The range of a laboratory thermometer is generally from 35°C to 42°C.

Match Type Questions

1. Match Column-I with Column-II and select the correct answer using the code given below the columns.

Column - I	Column - II
(i) Clinical thermometer	(p) Kink
(ii) Laboratory thermometer	(q) Scale marked in °C
(iii) Steel	(r) Good conductor
(iv) Plastic	(s) Bad conductor

(A) (i) → (p), (ii) → (q), (iii) → (r), (iv) → (s)
(B) (i) → (q), (ii) → (p), (iii) → (r), (iv) → (s)
(C) (i) → (q), (ii) → (p), (iii) → (s), (iv) → (r)
(D) (i) → (p), (ii) → (q), (iii) → (s), (iv) → (r)

Assertion and Reason Type Questions

Directions: Study both statements and mark your answer using the codes given blow.
(A) Both A and R are true and R is the correct explanation of A.
(B) Both A and R are true but R is not the correct explanation of A.
(C) A is true but R is false.
(D) A is false but R is true.

1. **Assertion:** When a body A at temperature 50°C is brought in contact with a body B at temperature 30°C, heat flows from the body A to the body B.

Reason: Heat always flows from a body at a low temperature to a body at a high temperature.

2. **Assertion:** Two bodies at the same temperature may contain different amounts of heat.

Reason: Two bodies may require different amounts of heat to maintain or acquire the same temperature.

3. **Assertion:** The flow of heat energy from one body to the other depends upon the amount of heat energy in them.

Reason: Heat flows from lower temperature of the body to higher temperature of the body.

4. **Assertion:** Temperature is a measure of degree of hotness of our body.

Reason: We use a clinical thermometer to measure the degree of hotness of our body.

Comprehension Type Questions

Directions: Read the passage given below and answer the questions that follow.

Passage: A clinical thermometer is used to measure the body temperature of human beings. It consists of a long, narrow, uniform glass tube. It has a bulb at one end. The bulb contains mercury. This thermometer reads temperatures from 35°C to 42°C.

1. A clinical thermometer can be used to measure the body temperature of human beings. A person suffering from fever is likely to show which of the following readings on this thermometer?
(A) 35°C (B) 36°C
(C) 37°C (D) 39°C

2. Why is a clinical thermometer provided with a kink?
(A) To keep the mercury within the range of 35°C to 42°C

ASSESSMENT CORNER

(B) To allow the temperature reading to remain unchanged after taking temperature until a jerk is given
(C) To make the thermometer size smaller
(D) All of the above

3. Which of the following precautions should be taken while using a clinical thermometer?
(A) It should be washed before use
(B) It should be washed after use
(C) It should be washed preferably with some antiseptic
(D) All of the above

Free Response Type

Very Short Answer Type Questions

1. Give some important effects of heat
2. What is temperature?

Short Answer Type Questions

1. Write down the type of thermometer.
2. How will the heat flow, if an iron ball at 40°C is dropped in a mug containing water at 40°C?

Long Answer Type Questions

1. Discuss different temperature scales.

Numerical Based Questions

1. Convert 37°C to °F.
2. Convert 42°C to Kelvin scale.
3. Convert 100°F to °C.
4. Convert 0 K to °C.
5. Convert 76°F to K.

Level 2

Multiple Choice Questions

1. During the day time, the atmospheric temperature rises by 18°F. What is the corresponding rise on Celsius scale?
(A) 10°C (B) 12°C
(C) 14°C (D) 16°C

2. When one litre of water at 30°C is mixed with one litre of water at 50°C, the temperature of the mixture will be:
(A) Between 30°C and 50°C
(B) 80°C
(C) Between 50°C and 80°C
(D) 20°C

3. A pot full of water is put to boil on the stove. Which one of the graphs below shows the correct change in temperature over time?

(A)
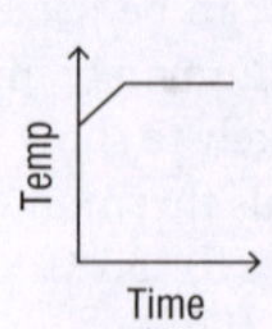

(B)
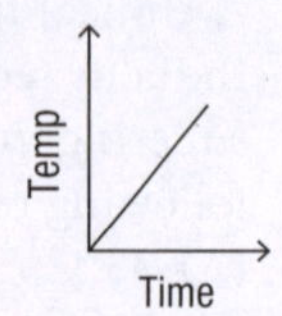

(C)
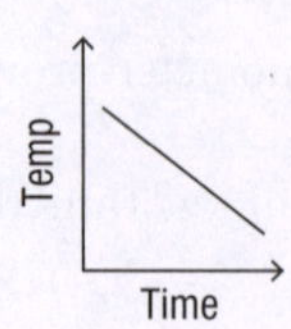

(D)
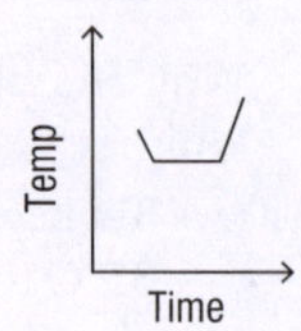

4. Which of the following increases when a liquid becomes a gas at its boiling point?
(A) Average kinetic energy of the molecules
(B) Molecular size
(C) Molecular spacing
(D) Total number of molecules

5. Which statement describes the motion and the arrangement of the molecules in a gas?
(A) Molecules move randomly within an ordered arrangement
(B) Molecules move randomly within a random arrangement
(C) Molecules vibrate about a fixed position within an ordered arrangement
(D) Molecules vibrate about a fixed position within a random arrangement

6.
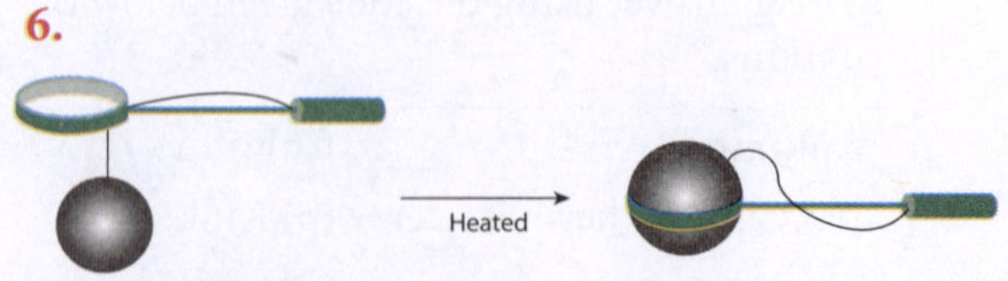

The above experiment shows that heat causes solids to change their:
(A) Size (B) State
(C) Shape (D) Composition

7. When you put a metal key into its metal lock, you find the key is too tight. Which of the following methods will you adopt to make the key fit properly?

(A) Heat the key and lock
(B) Cool the key and heat the lock
(C) Heat the key and cool the lock
(D) Cool the key and lock

8. Which of the paper pins will fall off the metal case first?

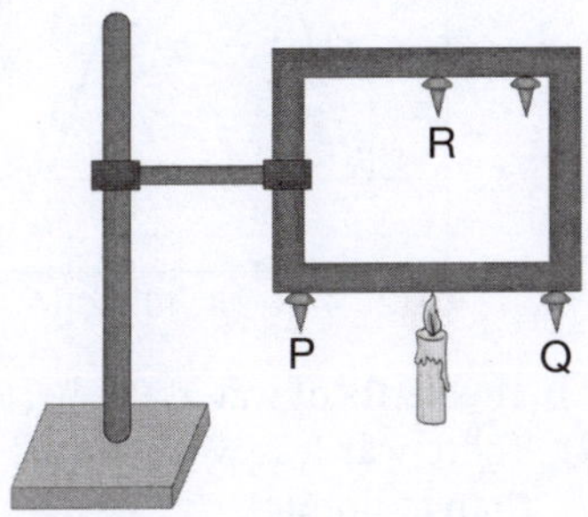

(A) P (B) Q
(C) Both P and Q (D) Both Q and R

9. What does the above specified experiment show?
(A) Wax melts easily
(B) The candle flame conducts heat
(C) The thumbtacks expand when heated
(D) Heat travels from a hot place to a cold place

10. A nurse needs to quickly check the temperature of multiple patients during a pandemic. The most appropriate thermometer to use would be:
(A) Mercury thermometer for accuracy.
(B) Infrared thermometer for safety and speed.
(C) Clinical thermometer for precision.
(D) Laboratory thermometer for reliability.

11. In a science experiment, a student observes ice melting. The temperature reading remains at 0°C throughout the melting process. This demonstrates:
(A) The thermometer is faulty.
(B) Ice cannot change temperature.
(C) Energy is used for changing state, not increasing temperature.
(D) 0°C is the maximum temperature for ice.

12. If a laboratory thermometer reads 80°C when measuring hot oil, and you want to express this in Fahrenheit, the temperature would be:
(A) 144°F (B) 176°F
(C) 212°F (D) 100°F

13. A student accidentally drops a clinical thermometer. Before using it again, they should:
(A) Just check if the glass is cracked.
(B) Shake it vigorously and check the mercury level.
(C) Test it against a laboratory thermometer.
(D) All of the above.

14. During a fever, a child's temperature is measured as 102°F. In Celsius, this would be approximately:
(A) 37°C (B) 39°C
(C) 35°C (D) 41°C

15. A chef wants to check if the oil is hot enough for deep frying (around 180°C). Which thermometer would be most suitable?
(A) Clinical thermometer
(B) Digital cooking thermometer
(C) Infrared thermometer
(D) Room thermometer

16. To convert –10°C to Kelvin, you would:
(A) Add 273.15 to get 263.15 K
(B) Subtract 273.15 to get -283.15 K
(C) Multiply by 273.15
(D) The conversion is impossible for negative temperatures

17. A student measures the room temperature as 22°C. If they wanted to express this in all three temperature scales, the values would be:
(A) 22°C, 72°F, 295 K
(B) 22°C, 73°F, 295.15 K
(C) 22°C, 71.6°F, 295.15 K
(D) 22°C, 68°F, 295 K

18. Compare the advantages and disadvantages: Why are digital thermometers replacing mercury thermometers in most applications?
(A) Digital thermometers are cheaper to manufacture.
(B) Digital thermometers are faster, safer, and more accurate.
(C) Mercury thermometers are becoming obsolete.
(D) Digital thermometers last longer.

19. A student observes three thermometers giving readings of 37.0°C, 37.2°C, and 36.8°C for the same measurement. This variation is most likely due to:
(A) All thermometers are defective.
(B) Temperature fluctuations during measurement.
(C) Different precision levels and calibration of instruments.
(D) Environmental factors affecting the readings.

20. Analyse why the temperature range of a clinical thermometer (35°C–42°C) is much smaller than that of a laboratory thermometer (–10°C to 110°C):
(A) Clinical thermometers use less mercury.
(B) Clinical thermometers are designed specifically for human body temperature measurement.

(C) Laboratory thermometers are made of stronger glass.
(D) Clinical thermometers are more sensitive.

Higher Order Thinking Skills (HOTS)

1. Warm water is poured slowly into a beaker of ice cubes as shown in the figure. Which of the following options is correct when the warm water was poured into the beaker?

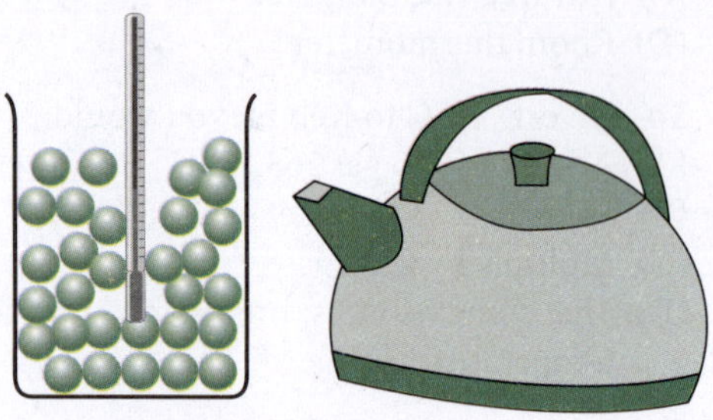

(i) The ice starts to melt
(ii) The glass expands
(iii) The temperature of the ice increases
(iv) The temperature of the warm water decreases
(A) (i) and (iv) only
(B) (ii) and (iv) only
(C) (i), (iii), and (iv) only
(D) All of these

2. The temperature, shown by a mercury-in-glass thermometer, increases. Which of the following is constant?
(A) Density of the mercury
(B) Internal energy of the mercury
(C) Mass of the mercury
(D) Volume of the mercury

3. Hot liquid is poured into a test tube. The figure shows how the temperature of the contents of the test tube changes with time. What is the physical state of the contents of the tube at time 8 minute?

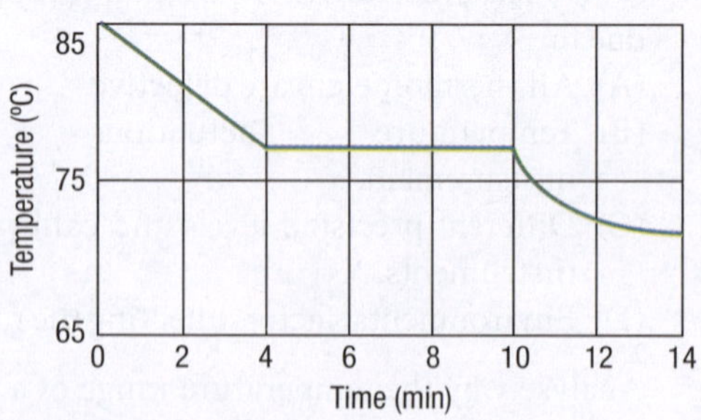

(A) Mixture of liquid and vapour
(B) Mixture of liquid and solid
(C) Liquid
(D) Solid

4. The temperature changes in a closed kettle of water were recorded for 11 minutes and represented in the graph below. Which of the following statement is true?

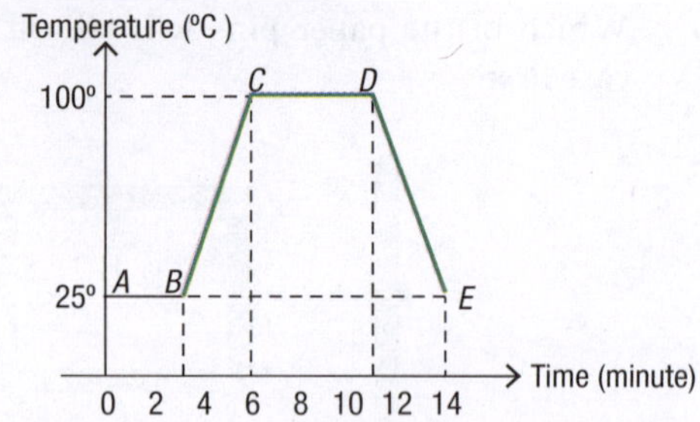

(A) The kettle of water was heated for 6 minutes
(B) There was less water in the kettle at point E than at point A
(C) The water took 6 minutes to reach its boiling point after it was heated
(D) The water in the kettle started boiling at C

5. When you heat a system, its temperature:
(A) Always increases
(B) Sometimes decreases
(C) May stay the same
(D) Always goes up or down, depending on the heat

6. During the formation of rain, when water vapours change back to liquid in the form of rain drops:
(A) Heat is absorbed
(B) Heat is released
(C) Heat is first absorbed and then released
(D) There is no exchange of heat

7. The melting point of a substance is 125°C and its boiling point is 305°C. At 105°C, the substance is in the ___________.
(A) Solid state
(B) Liquid state
(C) Gaseous state
(D) Solid and liquid state

8. A sphere, a cube, and a thin circular plate, all of the same material and same mass, are initially heated to the same high temperature. Then the:
(A) Sphere will cool fastest and cube the slowest
(B) Plate will cool fastest and sphere the slowest
(C) Cube will cool fastest and sphere the slowest
(D) Sphere will cool fastest and plate the slowest

9. A piece of ice is being heated till it turns to water and then to steam. Which of the following statements is true?

(A) The molecules expand as ice changes to steam
(B) The molecules move faster as ice changes to steam
(C) The molecules move closer to each other as ice changes to steam
(D) The intermolecular force of attraction increases as ice changes to steam

10. The length of mercury thread in a mercury thermometer is 2 mm at the ice point and 26 mm at the boiling point of water. What will be the length of mercury thread in this thermometer if it is used to measure a temperature of 75°C?
(A) 18 mm (B) 20 mm
(C) 22 mm (D) 24 mm

11. Aparna heated a bi-metallic strip made of two different types of metals for some time.

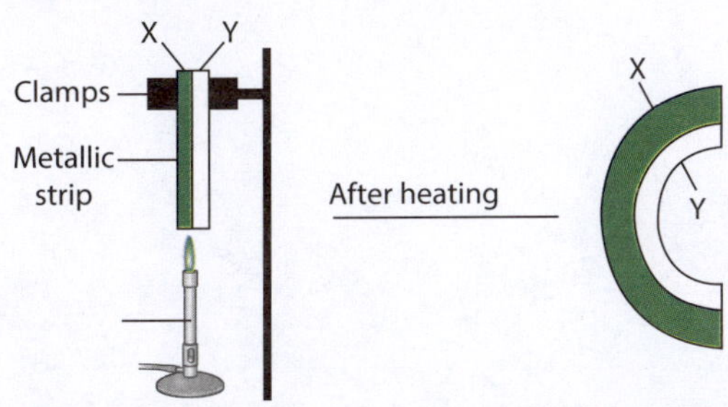

After heating it, she observed that the metallic strip curved as shown in the figure. Which of the following would best explain the conclusion derived by Aparna about the experiment she had done?
(A) Metal X is a better conductor of heat than metal Y
(B) Metal X is a poorer conductor of heat than metal Y
(C) Metal X is of better quality than metal Y
(D) Metal X is more flexible than metal Y

12. Rohan set up an experiment as shown here.

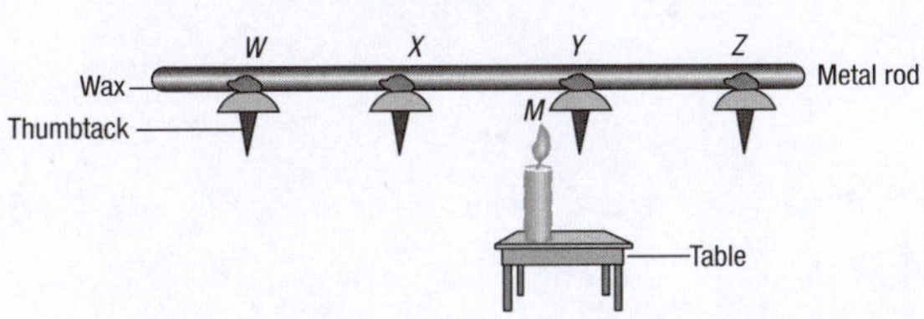

He placed the lighted candle below the metal rod at position M. He used the same amount of wax to hold all the thumbtacks at positions W, X, Y, and Z on the rod. Arrange the thumbtacks according to the time they take to drop from the rod, from the first to the last.
(A) Y, X, W, Z (B) Y, X, Z, W
(C) X, Y, W, Z (D) W, Z, Y, X

13. When comparing the three temperature scales, which statement correctly analyses their relationships?
(A) Celsius and Fahrenheit have the same zero point.
(B) Kelvin and Celsius have the same degree size but different zero points.
(C) All three scales increase at the same rate.
(D) Fahrenheit has the largest degree intervals.

14. A scientist working with liquid nitrogen needs to measure temperatures around –196°C. Analyse which type of thermometer would be most appropriate:
(A) Clinical thermometer cannot measure such low temperatures.
(B) Regular laboratory thermometer would be insufficient.
(C) Specialised cryogenic thermometer would be needed.
(D) Any digital thermometer would work.

15. If you analyse the working principle of different thermometers, what is the fundamental difference between infrared and contact thermometers?
(A) Infrared thermometers are more accurate.
(B) Contact thermometers measure internal temperature, while infrared thermometers measure surface temperature.
(C) Infrared thermometers work faster.
(D) Contact thermometers are safer to use.

16. Analysing the properties of mercury as a thermometric liquid, which factor makes it most suitable for temperature measurement?
(A) It is the only liquid that expands with heat.
(B) It has uniform thermal expansion over a wide temperature range.
(C) It is the most visible liquid.
(D) It conducts electricity well.

17. A student notices that during winter, outdoor temperature drops to –5°C, but water in pipes doesn't freeze immediately. Analysing this situation, the most likely explanation is:
(A) The thermometer reading is wrong.
(B) Water has additives that lower its freezing point.
(C) Underground pipes are insulated by soil temperature.
(D) The measurement location affects the reading.

18. When analysing why mercury thermometers are being phased out despite their accuracy, the primary concern is:

(A) They are too expensive to manufacture.
(B) They break easily and mercury is toxic.
(C) They take too long to give readings.
(D) They are difficult to read accurately.

19. Analyse the temperature conversion: If absolute zero is –273.15°C, why is it exactly 0 K?
(A) It's just a coincidence in the scale design.
(B) The Kelvin scale was specifically designed to start from absolute zero.
(C) Kelvin measurements are more accurate.
(D) The Celsius scale has an error in its zero point.

20. A research team measures the same solution with three different thermometers and gets: 25.0°C, 24.8°C, and 25.3°C. Analysing these results, what can be concluded?
(A) One thermometer is definitely wrong.
(B) The measurements show acceptable precision within instrument error.
(C) The solution temperature is changing rapidly.
(D) All thermometers need recalibration.

ARCHIVE CORNER

1. Direction: Read the given experiment and answer the following questions.
Paper pins are stuck to a metal rod with wax and a lighted candle is kept below the rod as shown in the diagram below.
Which one of the paper pins will fall off the metal rod first?

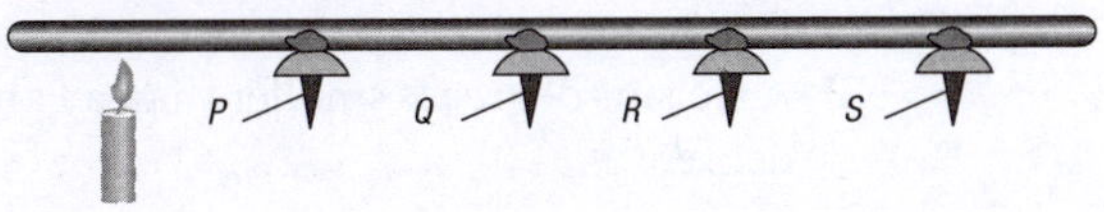

(A) P (B) Q
(C) R (D) S

2. Direction: Read the given experiment and answer the following questions.
Paper pins are stuck to a metal rod with wax and a lighted candle is kept below the rod as shown in the diagram below.
What does this experiment illustrate?

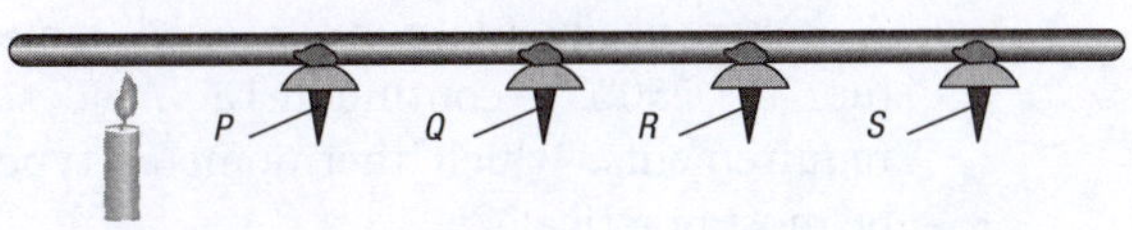

(A) The wax melts easily
(B) The candle flame conducts heat
(C) The thumbtacks expand when heated
(D) Heat gets transferred from the hot part of a body to the cold part

3. Four boxes made of different materials are left in the sun for half an hour. Which one of the boxes will be the hottest after half an hour?

(A) 
Iron

(B) 
Wood

(C) 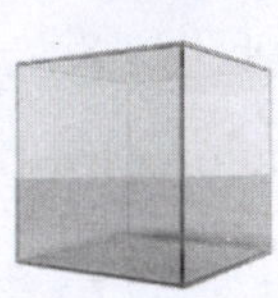
Glass

(D) 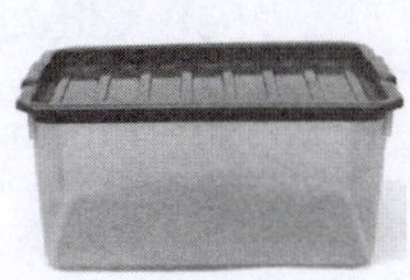
Plastic

4. The bimetallic strip made up of aluminium and copper when heated bends in the direction shown below. Which metal expands more when the two are heated at the same temperature?

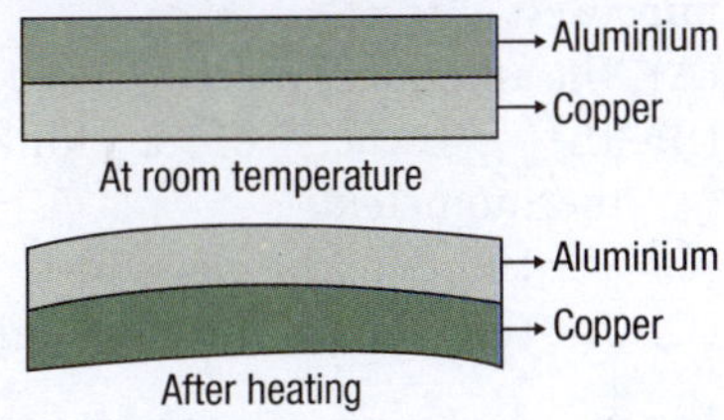

(A) Aluminium expands more than copper
(B) Copper expands more than aluminium
(C) Both aluminium and copper expand by the same amount
(D) Neither aluminium nor copper expands

5. A saucepan is usually made up of two different materials, P and Q. Identify P and Q.

(A) P-Steel, Q-Aluminium
(B) P-Ebonite, Q-Plastic
(C) P-Steel, Q-Ebonite
(D) P-Wood, Q-Ebonite

6. Which of the following statements is incorrect?
(A) A thermometer is read by holding its bulb
(B) A few sharp jerks are given to a clinical thermometer before using it
(C) The black fabric tent is preferred during winter
(D) Shopkeepers selling ice blocks usually cover them with jute sacks

7. Two steel balls P and Q have same readings when measured by thermometers of Celsius readings and Fahrenheit readings, respectively. Then:
(A) Ball P has greater temperature than ball Q
(B) Ball P has lower temperature than ball Q
(C) Both the balls P and Q have same temperature
(D) None of these

8. Which of the following quantities increases when a liquid at room temperature becomes a gas at its boiling point?
(A) The average kinetic energy of the molecules
(B) The molecular size
(C) The total number of molecules
(D) All of these

9. Analysing the design features of clinical vs laboratory thermometers, which structural difference is most significant for their specific purposes?
(A) The amount of mercury used.
(B) The presence of a kink in clinical thermometers.
(C) The length of the glass tube.
(D) The thickness of the glass walls.

10. When analysing temperature measurement accuracy, why might an infrared thermometer give different readings than a contact thermometer on the same object?
(A) Infrared thermometers are always less accurate.
(B) They measure different things—surface vs internal temperature.
(C) Contact thermometers are an outdated technology.
(D) Environmental factors don't affect infrared readings.

11. Analysing the safety concerns: Why are digital thermometers considered safer than mercury thermometers in household use?
(A) Digital thermometers are more accurate.
(B) They eliminate the risk of mercury exposure from broken thermometers.
(C) They are easier to clean.
(D) They work faster.

12. A meteorologist needs to measure air temperature accurately for weather forecasting. Analysing the requirements, which factor would be most important in thermometer selection?
(A) The speed of measurement.
(B) The ability to measure a wide range of temperatures with good accuracy.
(C) The cost of the instrument.
(D) The ease of reading the display.

13. Why does the liquid in a thermometer rise when heated?
(A) Heat makes the liquid lighter.
(B) Molecules move faster and take up more space when heated.
(C) Air pressure pushes the liquid up.
(D) The glass tube contracts, forcing liquid upward.

14. When analysing the relationship between temperature scales, if water freezes at 0°C and 32°F, what can you conclude about the relationship between Celsius and Fahrenheit degree sizes?
(A) They are exactly the same size.
(B) A Fahrenheit degree is smaller than a Celsius degree.
(C) A Celsius degree is smaller than a Fahrenheit degree.
(D) The relationship varies with temperature.

15. A student gets temperature readings of 23.1°C, 23.0°C, and 23.2°C in repeated measurements. This variation indicates:
(A) The thermometer is broken.
(B) Normal measurement uncertainty and instrument precision limits.
(C) The temperature is changing rapidly.
(D) The student is making errors in reading.

16. A baker needs to monitor oven temperature (up to 250°C) continuously. Analysing the requirements, which thermometer type would be most practical?
(A) Clinical thermometer for accuracy
(B) Mercury laboratory thermometer for precision
(C) Digital thermometer designed for high temperatures
(D) Infrared thermometer for safety

17. If you know that 0°C = 32°F and 100°C = 212°F, what can you conclude about converting any Celsius temperature to Fahrenheit?
(A) Multiply by 2 and add 32.
(B) The relationship involves multiplying by $\frac{9}{5}$ and adding 32.
(C) Add 32, then multiply by 1.8.
(D) Subtract 32, then multiply by $\frac{5}{9}$.

ARCHIVE CORNER

ANSWER KEY

Assessment Corner

Level 1

Fixed Response Type

Multiple Choice Questions

1. C	2. B	3. A	4. A	5. A	6. B	7. A	8. C	9. A	10. D
11. A	12. A	13. B	14. A	15. A	16. A	17. D	18. D	19. C	20. D
21. A	22. D	23. D	24. A	25. D	26. B	27. C	28. B	29. B	30. C
31. B	32. B	33. C	34. B	35. B	36. C	37. C			

Fill in the Blanks

1. Temperature 2. Laboratory 3. Celsius, Fahrenheit & Kelvin

True/False

1. False 2. False

Match Type Questions

1. A

Assertion and Reason Type Questions

1. C 2. B 3. C 4. B

Comprehension Type Questions

1. D 2. B 3. D

Numerical Based Questions

1. 98.6°F 2. 315.15K 3. 37.7°C 4. –273.15°C 5. 297.55K

Level 2

Multiple Choice Questions

1. A	2. A	3. A	4. A	5. B	6. A	7. B	8. C	9. D	10. B
11. C	12. B	13. D	14. B	15. B	16. A	17. C	18. B	19. C	20. B

Higher Order Thinking Skills (HOTS)

1. A **2.** D **3.** B **4.** D **5.** C **6.** B **7.** A **8.** B **9.** B **10.** B
11. A **12.** B **13.** B **14.** C **15.** B **16.** B **17.** C **18.** B **19.** B **20.** B

Archive Corner

1. A **2.** D **3.** A **4.** A **5.** C **6.** A **7.** C **8.** A **9.** B **10.** B
11. B **12.** B **13.** B **14.** B **15.** B **16.** C **17.** B

CHAPTER 4

Beyond Earth

Learning Outcomes

After reading this chapter, you would be able to:

- identify different constellations and properties of stars.
- describe all the planets.
- describe the phases of the Moon.

Geekspeak

- The night sky
- Astronomical distances
- Stars
- Galaxies
- Constellation
- The solar system
- Sun
- Planets
- Asteroids
- Comets
- Meteors
- Satellite
- Natural satellite (Moon)

Introduction

The universe is the large spread of space which includes everything—all the stars, planets, satellites and clouds of dust and gases. The branch of science in which we study the universe is called astronomy. In astronomy, various methods and instruments are used for the study of the universe.

The Night Sky

In night, the bright point objects are visible in the sky. These are stars. These stars are visible clearly through a telescope; we can even observe the color of these stars, most stars are yellow in colour and a some are white or red in colour.

The most important characteristic of stars is that they appear to twinkle. Another object visible at night is the Moon, which change its size every night. The Moon does not appear to twinkle.

Astronomical Distances

The billions of stars and other heavenly bodies in the universe are separated by large distances.

To express these extremely large distances, we use two astronomical units—the light year and the parsec.

A light year is defined as the distance travelled by light in one year.

The speed of light is 300,000 km/s and 1 year has 1 × 365 × 24 × 60 × 60 seconds.

$\therefore$ 1 light year = 300000 × 365 × 24 × 60 × 60 km

1 light year = 9.46×10^{12} km

1 parsec is equal to 3.26 light years.

The distance travelled by light at a speed of 300,000 km/s in one minute (60 seconds) is called a **light minute**.

$$1 \text{ light minute} = 3{,}00{,}000 \frac{\text{km}}{\text{s}} \times 1 \text{minute}$$

$$= 3{,}00{,}000 \frac{\text{km}}{\text{s}} \times 60 \text{sec} = 18 \times 10^{6} \text{ km}$$

Keystone

Our universe is expanding: An astronomer observed that these galaxies are not stationary but are moving away from each other. The larger the distance between two galaxies, the faster they move away from each other. This led him to propose and conclude that the universe is expanding.

The Stars

Stars are very heavy bodies that have very high temperature and give out light of their own. Stars are mostly made up of hydrogen. Nuclear fusion reaction is continuously going on inside stars through which the hydrogen is converted into helium. This process generates huge amount of energy which are emitted as light and heat energy. According to their temperature, stars can be of various colors. These colors are similar to the colors shown by a piece of metal when it is heated. The metal in starting glows red hot, then it becomes brighter and yellow to white hot. This is very similar to the color of stars with their temperatures but in reverse order. As the temperature increases it shows color from white to red hot. Our sun is a yellow star and its has surface temperature of about 6000 degree celsius. Since Earth rotates from west to east, thus stars appears to move from east to west in the sky.

Stars appear to twinkle as the light coming from them reaches to us after passing through Earth's atmosphere in which air constantly blows. So, the light observes unsteady which gives the twinkling effect.

INTEXT QUESTIONS

1. **Why do stars appear to us like point objects?**

   Solution: The stars appear to us like point objects, because they are very far away from the Earth. Most of the stars are so much far away, that the light from them takes millions of years to reach the Earth.

2. **Why does the distance between any two stars not change when viewed from the Earth?**

Solution: The distance between any two stars not change when viewed from earth because they are very far away from us, so, the change in distance will not be observed even in few years or few hundreds of years.

3. **Why do stars appear to move from east to west?**

Solution: Stars appear to move from east to west because the Earth rotates about its north-south axis from west to east. This happens due to relative motion.

4. **Why does the pole star (Polaris or Dhruva Tara) not change its position in the sky?**

Solution: The position of pole star relative to the Earth does not change and hence, it appears stationary as it is situated in the direction which is directly above the geographic north-pole of the Earth's axis.

5. **How does the pole star help travellers and sailors at night?**

Solution: Looking at the position of the pole star during the night, one can easily find the geographic directions as the pole star always points in the north direction and hence take the correct route.

6. **Which is the nearest star to the Earth?**

Solution: The star nearest to the Earth is the Sun. The next nearest star is the Alpha Centaury or Proxima Century.

7. **How far is the Sun from the Earth if the light from it reaches us in 8.3 light minutes?**

Solution: 1 light minute = $3{,}00{,}000 \frac{\text{km}}{\text{s}} \times 60\,\text{s}$

$\therefore$ 8.3 light minutes = 300,000 × 60 × 8.3 km = 149,400,000 km = 150,000,000 km (approx).

8. **How far is the nearest star Alpha Centauri from the Earth in kilometres?**

Solution: Alpha Centauri is at a distance of 4.3 light years.

$\therefore$ Distance in kilometres = Distance travelled in one light year × Number of light years

$$= 9.46 \times 10^{12} \frac{\text{km}}{\text{light year}} \times 4.3\,\text{light years} = 40.678 \times 10^{12}\,\text{km}$$

Competition Corner

Big Bang Theory: The whole of the matter of the universe was concentrated in a very dense and hot fire ball about 20 billion years ago, and an explosion occurred. The matter was broken into pieces in the form of stars and galaxies. The faster moving galaxies have gone farther than the slower ones. A galaxy situated at 20 billion light years is the boundary of universe.

- One light year = 30,0000 × 365 × 24 × 60 × 60 km = 9460000000000 kilometres = 9.46×10^{12} kilometres = distance travelled by light in one year
- A galaxy is a cluster of millions of stars along with hydrogen gas and dust. There are millions of galaxies in the universe. In fact, galaxies are the building blocks of the universe.
- The name of our galaxy is the Milky Way. The Milky Way is one of the millions of galaxies which exist in the universe. It contains about a hundred billion stars (or 10^{11} stars). The view of Milky Way galaxy looks like a disc of stars.
- **The** Milky Way is a spiral galaxy. Its mass is 150 solar masses (i.e., 3×10^{41} kg).
- The distance between the Sun and the Earth is about 15 crore kilometres. The light reaches from the Sun to the Earth in about 8.3 minutes. The next nearest star from the Earth is about 4.3 light years away from it known as Proxima Centaury. The brightest star Sirius is about 8.7 light-years away from the Earth.
- A spinning neutron star emits radio waves and is commonly known as a pulsar.

Galaxies

An enormous cluster of billions of stars held together by gravitational forces is called a galaxy. A galaxy is the building block of the universe. There are about 100 billion galaxies (10^{11} galaxies) in the universe and each galaxy has on an average 100 billion stars (10^{11} stars). So, the total number of stars in the universe is about 10^{22}. The two important galaxies in the universe are the Milky Way galaxy and the Andromeda galaxy.

Hubble (American astronomer) made important contribution in the study of galaxies. He divided galaxies into three categories—spiral, elliptical and irregular (Fig. 4.1).

Spiral Galaxies

Spiral galaxies are spiral as shown in Fig.4.1 (a) and range from 20,000 to 100,000 light years in diameter. Our own Milky Way galaxy is an example of spiral galaxy. Approximately 80% of the total galaxies are of this kind. The spiral galaxies have well defined nucleus and a large spheroidal halo composed of stars.

Elliptical Galaxies

Elliptical galaxy is shown in Fig. 4.1 (b). They account for 18% of all the observed galaxies. However, it is estimated that their number is far larger than the observed percentage.

The elliptical galaxies are classified on the basis of their shape into eight categories designated as E_0 to E_7. E_0 galaxies are nearly spherical, whereas a higher number represents an increasing degree of flattening. E_7 is highly flattened. In spite of their oversize, elliptical galaxies are less luminous than spiral galaxies. This is because they are mostly composed of old population stars such as red and yellow stars.

Irregular Galaxies

The small galaxies which lack clear symmetrical form are called irregular galaxies as shown in Fig. 4.1 (c). They comprise 2% of the observed galaxies. In these galaxies, we find lot of dust and large number of blue stars.

(a) (b) (c)

Figure 4.1 Types of Galaxies (a) Spiral Galaxy; (b) Elliptical Galaxy and (c) Irregular Galaxy

The Milky-Way Galaxy

The name Milky Way comes from the Greek word *gala* which means milk. Milky Way is the hazy luminous band of white light seen stretched across the sky at night. Its Indian name is Akash Ganga. Our solar system is a part of the Milky Way. The Milky Way contains more than 100 billion (10^{11}) stars. The Milky Way is called our galaxy and is a spiral galaxy in the form of a disc with a bulge at the centre, tapering off towards the edges. Its diameter is about 10^5 light years and central thickness is about 10^4 light years. The Sun is situated at a distance of 2.7×10^4 light years from the galactic centre. The thickness of disc near the Sun is 1000 light years. The space between the stars in the Milky Way is filled with dust and gases called interstellar matter. About 90% of the interstellar matter is in the form of hydrogen. The mass of the Milky Way is estimated to be nearly 3×10^{41} kg.

As seen from above, the Milky Way galaxy looks like a disc of stars. The stars are not uniformly arranged in the plane of the disc but are arranged in spiral arms.

It is very difficult to find out the shape of our galaxy as the Earth lies within the galaxy. Astronomers have been able to establish the spiral shape of our galaxy by joining together photographs taken from many different directions over many years. Like other galaxies, the Milky Way is rotating about an axis passing through its centre. All the stars in the Milky Way revolve slowly around the galactic centre and complete one revolution in 300×10^6 years.

Constellation

A group of stars which are arranged in a pattern resembling some recognizable figure is called a constellation. There are about 88 constellations that we know. All the stars in a constellation appear to stay together, so its shape remains the same. Four of the well-known constellations are Orion, Ursa Major, Ursa Minor and Cassiopeia.

Orion

Orion is one of the magnificent constellations in the sky. It has seven bright stars. Four of these appear to be arranged in the form of a quadrilateral and the other three form a straight line in the middle (Fig. 4.2). One of the largest stars known as Betelgeuse is situated on one corner of this quadrilateral while another bright star called Rigel, is located on its opposite corner. The arrangement of stars in this constellation resembles a hunter with a belt and a sword. This constellation is visible during the winters in the northern hemisphere.

Some people imagine that the hunter Orion, followed by his dog (the constellation Canis Major), is battling a bull (the constellation Taurus). Canis Major contains a star called Sirius, which is the brightest star in the night sky.

Figure 4.2 Orion

Ursa Major

Ursa major is also known as the Great Bear, the Big Dipper or Saptarishi. Ursa Major contains seven stars, making the pattern of a plough. A line drawn through the pointers of the plough leads us to the Pole star or Polaris (Dhruv Tara) (Fig. 4.3). The Pole star always appears in the same position in the sky as it is directly above the north pole. This constellation is visible during the summers.

Ursa Minor

Ursa minor is also known as the Little Bear or Little Dipper. Ursa Minor also consists of seven stars arranged in a similar manner to those to Ursa Major, but the stars in this constellation are closer together and less bright than in the Ursa Major. The last star in the handle of the Little Dipper is the Pole star itself (Fig. 4.3). Ursa Minor is also known as the Pole star constellation. This also is visible in the summers.

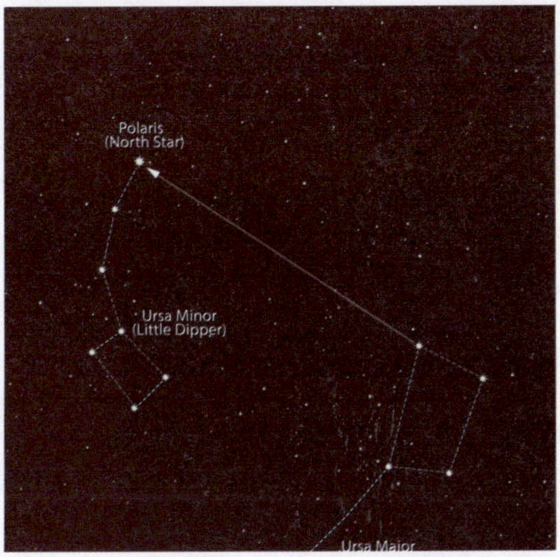

Figure 4.3 Ursa Minor and Major

The pointer of the 'Ursa Major' points out the Pole star. The Pole star is also called Polaris and Dhruv tara.

Cassiopeia

Cassiopeia is another prominent constellation in the northern sky. It is visible during winter in the early part of the night. It looks like a distorted letter W or M (Fig. 4.4).

Figure 4.4 Cassiopeia

Testing Room 1

Observe these given constellations in the sky at night and see if they look exactly the same.

The difference between a galaxy and a constellation is discussed in Table 4.1.

Table 4.1 Differences between a Galaxy and a Constellation

Galaxy	Constellation
It is a group of billions of stars.	It is a group of only a few stars.
It does not form a definite pattern.	The stars are arranged in definite, recognizable patterns.
There are billions centre of galaxies in the universe.	At present, we know of only about 88 constellations.
Very few galaxies are visible to the naked eye.	Many constellations are visible to the naked eye.

Check Point 1

1. The Pole star is a member of the solar system. (True/False)
2. Constellation Orion can be seen only with a telescope. (True/False)
3. A group of stars that appear to form a pattern in the sky is known as a ____________.
4. Shooting stars are actually _________.
5. Milky Way galaxy looks like a _________.

The Solar System

The Sun and all bodies in orbit around it make up the solar system. The centre of the solar system is the Sun. The other members of the solar system include the eight planets, their moons or satellites, a large number of asteroids, thousands of comets and innumerable meteors (Fig. 4.5). These other members of the solar system also revolve around the Sun and are bound to it by strong gravitational forces.

Figure 4.5 Solar System

The Sun

Figure 4.6 The Sun

The Sun is the star closest to the Earth at a distance of 150 million km from the Earth (Fig. 4.6). Light from the Sun takes 8¼ minutes to reach the Earth. The diameter of the Sun is over 109 times the diameter of the Earth and it is 333,000 times as heavy as the Earth. The Sun is made up of hydrogen gas that is continuously being converted into helium at extremely high temperature. The centre of the Sun is thus extremely hot at about 14 million degrees Celsius, while its surface temperature is about 6000 degrees Celsius. Compared to the other stars, the Sun looks enormous to us as it is very close to the Earth. The next nearest star, Alpha Centauri, is several times bigger than the Sun, but it appears tiny as it is much away from us. Sometimes, from some areas on the surface of the Sun, hot gases shoot outward. These are called prominences. There are also some darker, relatively cooler patches (of about 4000°C) on the surface of the Sun. These spots are called sunspots and are of interest to scientists as they are found to interfere with radio and wireless transmission from the Earth. They also produce change in weather on the Earth.

Planets

The word 'planets' is of Greek origin and means 'wanderers'. In Hindi, planets are known as *graha*.

The 'planet' refers to those (bright) heavenly bodies that revolve around the Sun. They look like stars but they do not twinkle. Their observed brightness is only due to the light of the Sun reflected by them. There are eight planets now in our solar system. They move in elliptical shaped paths called orbits around the Sun. The eight planets of our solar system, in increasing order of their distances from the Sun, are Mercury, Venus, Earth, Mars, Jupiter, Saturn, Uranus and Neptune. The planets relatively nearer to the Sun have features that are quite different from those which are 'far off'. We can divide the planets into two categories: Terrestrial planets and Jovian planets.

Mercury, Venus, Earth and Mars are the terrestrial planets. They have solid and rocky surfaces. The Jovian planets are Jupiter, Saturn, Uranus and Neptune. These planets are very large in size and are made up largely of gases.

Mercury (Budh)

Figure 4.7 Mercury (Budh)

Mercury lies closer to the Sun than any other planet. It is a dry, hot and virtually airless planet (Fig. 4.7). It has craters like the Moon, but its interior is similar to that of the Earth. Like the Earth, its interior contains iron and other heavy elements. Mercury is much smaller in size than the Earth. Mercury is a less common planet that appears in the east before sunrise and it is also sometimes called morning star. Being close to the Sun, it takes only 88 Earth days to go once around the Sun. A day on Mercury (the time it takes for Mercury to rotate or spin once with respect to the stars) takes 59 Earth days. One day-night cycle on Mercury takes 175.97 Earth days. Mercury makes a complete orbit around the Sun (a year in Mercury time) in just 88 Earth days.

Venus (Shukra)

Figure 4.8 Venus

Venus is the brightest object in our sky after the Sun and the Moon (Fig. 4.8). Its bright appearance is due to its cloudy atmosphere which reflects almost three-fourth of the Sunlight falling on it.

Venus is almost the same size as the Earth but rotates relatively slowly around its axis. It has no moon or satellite of its own. Venus is even hotter than Mercury although it is relatively farther away from the Sun. This is because of the high percentage of carbon dioxide in its atmosphere. This gas traps most of the Sun's heat falling on it. This is due to an effect called the greenhouse effect. One day on Venus lasts 243 Earth days because Venus spins backwards, with its sun rising in the west and setting in the east. Venus is the most common planet that appears in the east before sunrise and immediately after sunset. So, it is also often called morning and evening star.

Earth (Prithvi)

Figure 4.9 Earth

The Earth is a very unique and special planet of our solar system (Fig. 4.9). Like the other planets, the Earth not only revolves round the Sun but also rotates about an (imaginary) axis of its own. The portion of the Earth facing the Sun at any time has day, the other portion facing away has night.

As the Earth rotates on its axis, 'day and night' follow one another. The axis of rotation of the Earth is known to be tilted with respect to its orbit. It completes one revolution around the Sun in nearly 365¼ days. When the northern hemisphere is tilted towards the Sun, it is summer there. At that time, it is winter in the southern hemisphere. The reverse happens when the northern hemisphere is tilted away from the Sun. Autumn and spring occur when the Earth is in between these two extreme positions in its orbit.

Mars (Mangal)

Figure 4.10 Mars

Mars usually appear reddish in colour (Fig. 4.10), Hence, it is also often known as the red planet. Its surface resembles a cold, high altitude desert. Its atmosphere consists primarily of carbon dioxide, along with small amount of nitrogen, oxygen, water vapour and other gases. Its surface temperature and surface pressure are both very low. These conditions make it unlikely for water to exist in a liquid state on this planet. The diameter of mars is only a little more than half of that of earth. Its mass is, however, only one-tenth of that of the Earth. Therefore, Mars has a low average density as compared to the Earth. Mars has two natural satellites or moons named Phobos and Deimos. One day on Mars takes a little over 24 hours. Mars makes a complete orbit around the Sun (a year in Martian time) in 687 Earth days.

Jupiter (Brihaspati)

Figure 4.11 Jupiter

It is the largest of all planets (Fig. 4.11). According to NASA, Jupiter has 97 confirmed moons and 17 unconfirmed moons as of 30 April, 2025. They are unconfirmed because we are waiting to get more information about them. If the Moons get confirmed, Jupiter will have 114 moons or satellites. This planet has the largest number of moons amongst all the planets. Ganymede is the biggest satellite of Jupiter. Jupiter rotates once about every 10 hours (a Jovian day), but takes about 12 Earth years to complete one orbit of the Sun (a Jovian year).

Saturn (Shani)

Saturn is quite similar to Jupiter in size, mass and composition. It is the second largest planet of the solar family (Fig. 4.12). It is distinguished by its very unique and special system of rings. These rings give it a beautiful appearance. There are three distinct rings surrounding this planet.

These rings can be seen clearly only with the help of a telescope. Galileo was the first to observe these rings with the telescope. According to NASA, Saturn has 274 confirmed moons as of 11 March, 2025. Titan is the biggest satellite of Saturn. Saturn takes about 10.7 hours (no one knows precisely) to rotate on its axis once—a Saturn 'day'—and 29 Earth years to orbit the Sun.

Figure 4.12 Saturn

Uranus (Arun)

It is the third largest planet of the solar system (Fig. 4.13). It, in fact is the third largest planet of the solar system. Its diameter is almost four times than that of the Earth. It can contain as many as (nearly) 64 Earths in it. Hydrogen and methane have been detected in the atmosphere of this planet. This planet is observed to have blue-green colour. This is believed to be because of the presence of methane gas in its cold, clear atmosphere. Its northern hemisphere remains in a four-decade long period of darkness because of the way the planet rotates. So far, 29 satellites or moons of Uranus have been discovered. Titania is the biggest moon of Uranus. Uranus takes about 17 hours to rotate once (a Uranian day), and about 84 Earth years to complete an orbit of the Sun (a Uranian year).

Figure 4.13 Uranus

Neptune (Varun)

It is very far away from the Sun and is visible only through a telescope (Fig. 4.14). It has been named after the Roman sea god Neptune. According to NASA, Neptune has 16 moons or satellites. Triton is the largest satellite of Neptune. Neptune is an ice giant. Most of its mass is a hot, dense fluid of 'icy' materials—water, methane and ammonia—above a small rocky core. Neptune takes about 16 hours to rotate once (a Neptunian day), and about 165 Earth years to orbit the Sun (a Neptunian year).

Figure 4.14 Neptune

Keystone

The number of moons of the Jovian planets keeps changing. With the improvement in observing techniques, many new moons may be discovered.

Asteroids

These are very small planets or planetoids that are found mainly in a belt between the orbit of Mars and Jupiter (Fig. 4.15). Each asteroid has its own orbit and the orbits of all of them are spread over a large distance, forming a band. Astronomers have discovered more than 500 asteroids which are larger than 48 km in diameter. Ceres is the largest of the asteroids discovered till now.

Figure 4.15 Asteroid

Comets

The name comet means a 'hairy star'. Comets are relatively small and icy celestial bodies revolving around the Sun (Fig. 4.16). When a comet comes near the Sun, some of the 'ice' in it turns into gas. The gas and loose dust, free from ice, create a long illuminating tail that streams behind the comet. The tail of the comet could be as long as 800 million kilometres. Comets are visible only when they are near

Figure 4.16 Comet

the Sun. This is because the intense solar heat then vapourizes parts of their icy matter. There are a few 'periodic comets' that appear again and again after a regular (nearly, constant) interval. One of such periodic comets is the Halley's Comet. It appears approximately after every 76 years. It was last seen in the year 1986. It is, therefore, next expected to 'pass by' the Earth in the year 2062.

Meteors

Meteors are pieces of stony or metallic rock widely scattered throughout the solar system (Fig. 4.17). They travel at high speeds around the Sun. When meteors come close enough to the Earth, they are pulled towards the Earth by its gravitational force. As a meteor passes through the Earth's atmosphere, it gets burnt due to the immense heat produced by friction with the atmosphere, leaving a brilliant trail of light behind it. Such a meteor is also called a shooting star. Most of the meteors are so small that they burn up completely in the upper atmosphere, but some of the larger meteors may land on the surface of the Earth producing craters. Such meteors which land on the Earth are called meteorites.

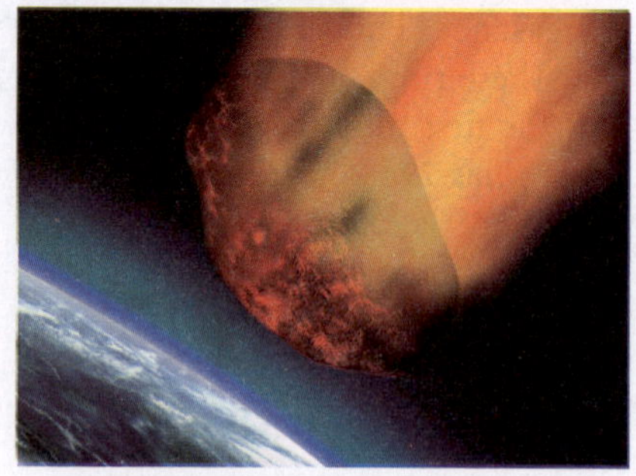

Figure 4.17 Meteors

The difference between stars and planets is discussed in Table 4.2.

Table 4.2 Differences between Stars and Planets

Parameters	Stars	Planets
Light	Stars have their own light.	Planets have no light of their owm. Planets shine because they reflect light receive from the Sun.
Number	Stars are countless in number.	There are only eight planets.
Size	They are very big in size. They appear to be small because they are very far off from the Earth.	They are very small in size.
Motion	They appear to be from east to west.	They actually move round the Sun from west to east (except Uranus).
Matter	Each star is made up of huge mass of extremely hot gases mainly hydrogen and helium.	They are made up of rocks and metals.
Temperature	Extremely high temperature.	Temperature depends on their distance from the Sun.
Twinkling	They twinkle.	They do not twinkle.
Shape	They appear as dot.	They are disc shaped.

Check Point 2

6. Name two objects other than planets which are members of the solar system.
7. Planets move round the Sun from _________.
8. Asteroids are found between the orbits of _____ and________.
9. Neptune has atmosphere similar to that of ________.
10. Name the largest planet of the solar system.

Satellite

A satellite is a small body revolving around a planet. Satellites are of two types:

Natural Satellite (Moon)

The Moon, our nearest neighbour in space, is a natural satellite of the Earth. A satellite is a heavenly body that revolves around a planet. Of the nine planets, **only Mercury and Venus have no satellites or moons** associated with them. **Mars is believed to have 2 moons, Jupiter 63 moons, Saturn 34 moons, Uranus 27 moons, Neptune 13 moons. The Earth, of course, has only one moon** and that, being our nearest neighbour, has been explored and studied the most by the astronomers.

The Moon has no air or water on it. Its diameter is about **(1/4)** of the diameter of the Earth and its mass is about **(1/81)** that of the Earth. It has no light of its own. Its observed silver glow is only due to the light of the Sun reflected by its surface.

The Moon is very much smaller than stars but it appears bigger because of its nearness. This near neighbour is, however, still about **3,84,400 km** away from us. Its surface is covered with hard and loose dirt and it has many uplands (mountains) and valleys that are filled with dry rock materials.

The Moon has a very interesting feature associated with it. It takes the same time **(27 days and 7 hours)** to revolve around the Earth as well as to spin, or rotate, once about its own axis. We, on the Earth, therefore, always see only one side (the '**front**' side) of the Moon. Its other or '**black**' side is not seen from the Earth.

Phases of the Moon

The Moon has no light of its own. The Moon shines and becomes visible to us because it reflects sunlight falling on it towards the Earth. At any point of time, half of the Moon's surface is in direct sunlight and the other half is in shadow. But since the Moon revolves around the Earth and the Earth (along with the Moon) revolves around the Sun, we cannot see the entire sun-lit surface of the Moon from the Earth all the time. We can see only that part of the sun-lit surface of the Moon which is towards us (on the Earth). Thus, we see different amount (or portions) of the sun-lit surface of the Moon from the Earth depending upon the relative positions of the Sun, the Moon and the Earth. Thus, sometimes, we see almost no face of moon (called **new moon**); sometimes, we see less than half the face of the Moon (called **crescent moon**); sometimes, we see half of the Moon; sometimes, we can see more than half of the Moon; and sometimes we see the whole circular face of the Moon (called **full moon**). So, as the Moon revolves around the Earth once every month, the Moon's appearance varies according to how much of its illuminated surface is turned towards the Earth (from where we see it). **The different views of the Moon (as seen from the Earth) are called phases of the Moon**. Some of the phases of the Moon are shown in Fig. 4.18.

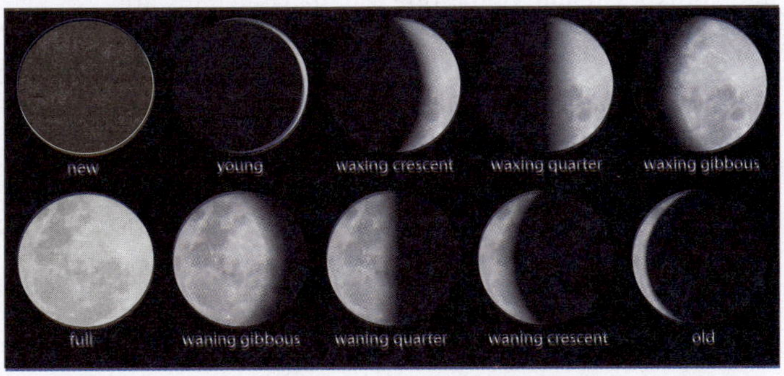

Figure 4.18 Phases of the Moon

On a new moon night, the Moon is a dark ball and hence the new moon is not visible to us in the night sky. On a full moon night, the Moon appears to be a bright ball of light. In between a new moon and full moon, and then between the full moon and the next new moon, we see different shapes of the Moon which are called phases of the Moon.

Testing Room 2

Observe these different phases of the Moon in the sky and name them.

Formation of the Various Phases of the Moon

- When the Moon is on the side of the Earth nearest to the Sun (see position 1 in Fig. 4.18), then the side of the Moon which is lit by the Sun is away from the Earth. And the side of moon which is towards the Earth is in darkness. In this position, the Moon appears to be in darkness from the Earth. This is called new moon. The new moon day is called '**Amavasya**'. In fact, we cannot see the Moon at all on the new moon day (or Amavasya). So, the new moon night (or **Amavasya Night**) is very dark having no moonlight at all.

- As the Moon moves in its orbit around the Earth from position 1 to 2, we can see a small sun-lit portion of its surface. This is called crescent moon. As the Moon moves further from position 2 to position 3 and 4, the sun-lit portion of the Moon facing the Earth becomes bigger and bigger, giving us half moon and more than half moon. This is called the **waxing phase** (increasing phase) of the Moon.
- After two weeks, from new moon day, the Moon reaches in position 5 which is on the side of the Earth farthest from the Sun. In this position, the whole sun-lit side of the Moon is towards the Earth, and we see the Moon as a full round disc of bright light. This is called full moon. The full moon day is called '**Purnima**'. The full moon night (or **Purnima Night**) is very bright because we have the maximum moonlight on that night.
- As the Moon moves around the Earth further from position 5 to positions 6, 7 and 8, the sun-lit portion of the Moon facing the Earth becomes smaller and smaller. This is called the **waning phase** (decreasing phase) of the Moon. And ultimately, the Moon completes the revolution around the Earth and again reaches position 1. So, we have new moon once again. Please note that we can have one new moon and one full moon during a month (which is the time taken by the Moon to complete one revolution around the Earth).

From the above discussion, we conclude that we have '**Amavasya**' on new moon day which changes in two weeks' time into Purnima. And during the next two weeks, Purnima changes into Amavasya again. This process is repeated again and again.

Artificial Satellite

A man-made space-craft placed in orbit around the Earth is called an **artificial satellite** (Fig. 4.19). Artificial satellites are also known as man-made satellites. An artificial satellite is placed in orbit around the Earth with the help of a launch vehicle called rocket.

India has built and launched several artificial satellites. Aryabhatta was the first Indian satellite. Some other Indian satellites are INSAT, IRS, Kalpana-1, EDUSAT, Bhaskara, Rohini, Apple, etc. mentioned in Table 4.3.

Artificial satellites have many practical applications. They are used for forecasting weather, transmitting television and radio signals. They are also used for telecommunication and remote sensing.

Figure 4.19 Artificial Satellites

Keystone

Geosynchronous satellites: Satellites which go round the Earth once in 24 hours are called geo synchronous satellites.

Table 4.3 Artificial Satellites sent by India

Some artificial satellite sent by India are as follows			
Date	**Satellite**	**Date**	**Satellite**
19-Mar-75	Arybhatta	20-Sep-04	EDUSAT
07-Jun-79	Bhaskara-1	22-Dec-05	INSAT 4A
18-Jul-80	Rohini	12-Mar-07	INSAT 4B
19-Jun-81	Apple	02-Sep-07	INSAT 4CR
30-Aug-83	INSET-1B	28-Apr-08	CARTOSA T- 2A
17-Mar-88	IRS-1A	2008	Chandrayaan-1
07-Dec-95	INSET-2C	2010	GSAT-4
26-May-99	OCEANSA T-1 (IRS-P4)	2011	Megha-Tropiques
12-Sep-02	METSAT (Kalpana-1)	2013	Mars Orbiter Mission(MOM)
28-Sep-03	INSET-3E	2019	Chandrayaan-2
17-Oct-03	RESOURCESAT -1 (IRS-P6)		

Table 4.4 Description about the Planets

Planet	Distance from the Sun (Astronomical units miles KM)	Period of revolutions around the Sun (1 planetary year)	Period of rotation (1 planetary year)	Mass (kg)	Diameter (miles/km)	Apparent angular size as seen from the earth	Temperature (Range or Average)	Number of moons
Mercury	0.39 AU 36 million miles 57.9 million km	87.96 Earth days	58.7 Earth days	3.3×10^{23}	3031 miles 4878 km	5–13 arc seconds	100–700 K mean–452 K	0
Venus	0.723AU 67.2 million miles 108.2 million km	224.68 Earth days	243 Earth days	4.87×10^{24}	75821 miles 12,104 km	10–64 arc seconds	726 K	0
Earth	1 AU 93 million miles 149.6 million km	365.26 Days 1 Year	24 Hours	5.98×10^{24}	7926 miles 12,756 km	Not applicable	260–310 K	1
Mars	1.524 AU 141.6 million miles 227.9 million km	686.98 Earth days About 2 Years	24 hrs 37min 1.026 Earth days	6.42×10^{23}	4222 miles 6787 km	4–25 arc seconds	150–310 K	2
Jupiter	5.203 AU 483.6 million miles 778.3 million km	11.862 Earth years 12 Years	9 hrs 54 min 9.84 Earth hours	1.90×10^{27}	88,729 miles 142,796 km	31–48 arc seconds	120 K (Clouds top)	67
Saturn	9839 AU 886.7 million miles 1427 million km	29.456 Earth years 29.5 Years	10 hrs 14 min 10.2 Earth hours	$5.69 \mathrm{x} 10^{26}$	74,600 miles 120,660 km	15–21 arc seconds excluding rings	88 K	62

Planet	Distance from the Sun (Astronomical units miles KM)	Period of revolutions around the Sun (1 planetary year)	Period of rotation (1 planetary year)	Mass (kg)	Diameter (miles/km)	Apparent angular size as seen from the earth	Temperature (Range or Average)	Number of moons
Uranus	19.18 AU 1784 million miles 2871 million km	84.07 Earth years 84 Years	10 hrs 49 min 17.9 Earth hours	8.68×10^{25}	32,600 miles 51,118 km	3–4 arc seconds	59 K	27
Neptune	30.06 AU 2794.4 million miles 4497.1 million km	164.81 Earth years 165 Years	15 hrs 40 min 19.1 Earth hours	1.02×10^{26}	30,200 miles 48,600 km	2.5 arc seconds	48 K	14

Competition Corner

Eclipse: An eclipse happens when one object in space blocks another from view. For example, during a solar eclipse, the **Moon** comes between the **Earth** and the **Sun**. The Moon blocks the Sun for a time so that people on Earth cannot see it.

During a solar eclipse, the Moon passes between the Sun and the Earth. During a lunar eclipse, the Earth passes between the Sun and the Moon.

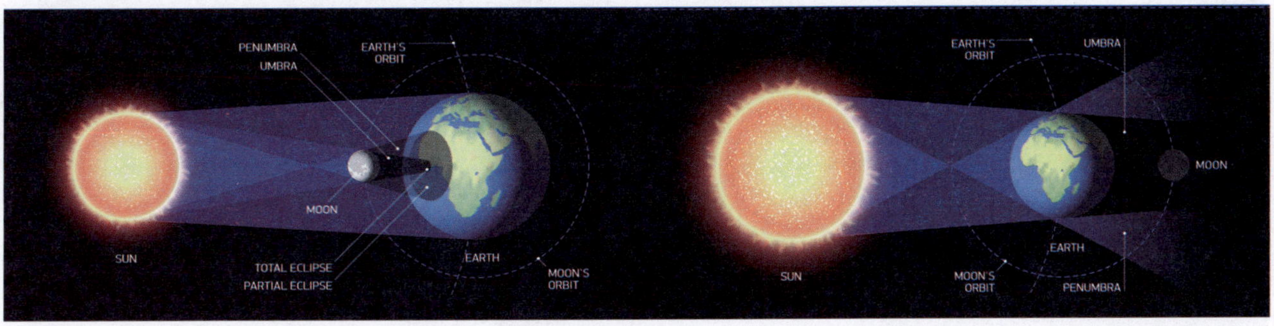

Solar and Lunar eclipse

Check Point 3

11. Instant is an artificial satellite (True/ False).
12. Name any two artificial satellites.
13. ______ was the first Indian satellite.
14. The full moon day is called ______.
15. The new moon day is called ______.

INTEXT QUESTIONS

9. Do stars emit light only during night?

Solution: Stars emit light always, but cannot see them in the day because of the excessive brightness of the Sun.

10. Paheli and Boojho observe a bright object in the night sky which was not twinkling. Paheli says, it is a star and Boojho says it is a planet. Who is correct?

Solution: Boojho is right because only planets cannot twinkle whereas stars emit light from a far distance and they twinkle.

11. State whether the following statements are 'True' or 'False'.

(a) The planet nearest to us is Jupiter.

(b) All the stars are at the same distance from us.

(c) The planets do not emit light of their own.

(d) The planets keep changing their position with respect to stars.

(e) The planet Venus appears in the eastern sky before sunrise.

(f) The plane in which the Earth revolves around the Sun is called the equatorial plane of earth.

Solution: (a) False – Mars and Venus are the nearest planets to earth

(b) False- Different stars are at distance from us

(c) True

(d) True

(e) True

(f) False- Earth revolves around the Sun in the orbital plane

12. John saw the full moon on a particular day. After how many days will he be able to see the full moon again?

Solution: Approximately 29 days

13. In the picture of rotating earth, given in figure, mark the position of the pole star.

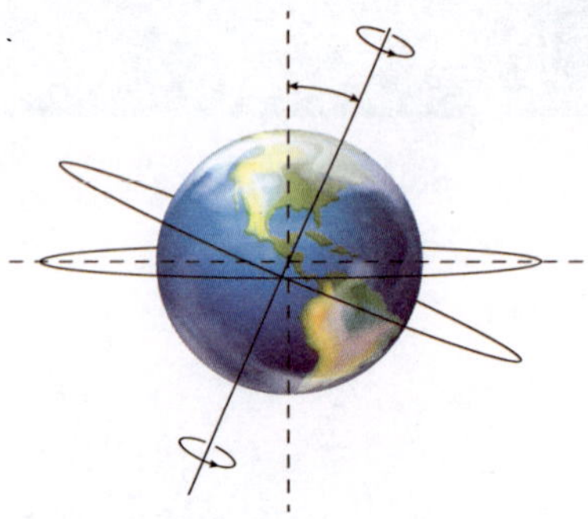

Solution: The position of the polar star is shown in the figure below:

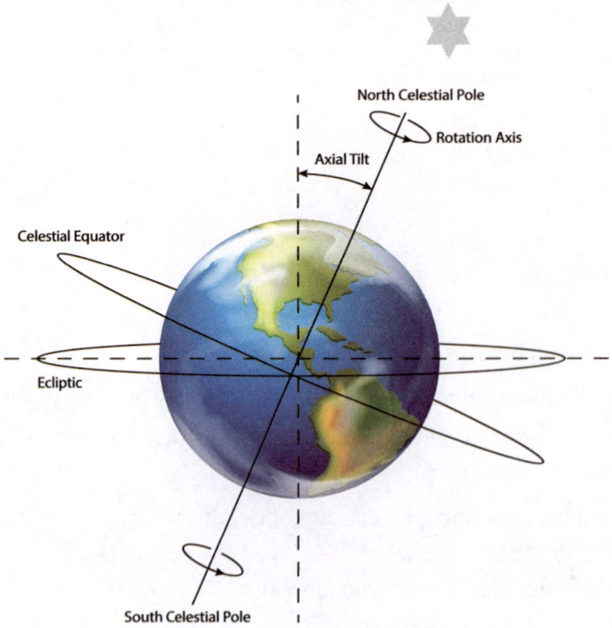

14. In the given figure, out of the positions A, B, C and D which will indicate the position of the Sun? Draw the Sun at the appropriate position.

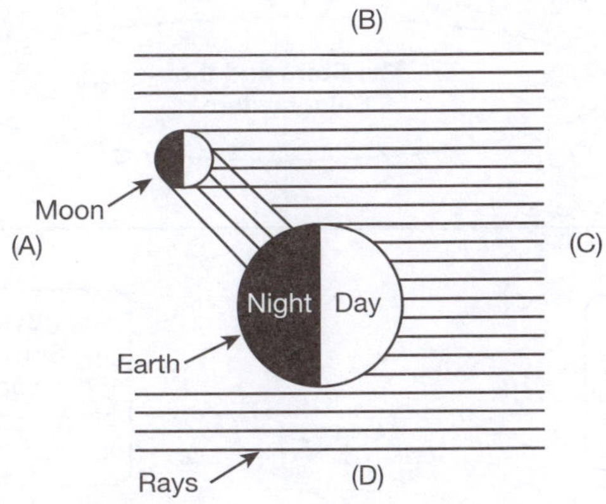

Solution: The sun will be at position (C) as shown the in figure below:

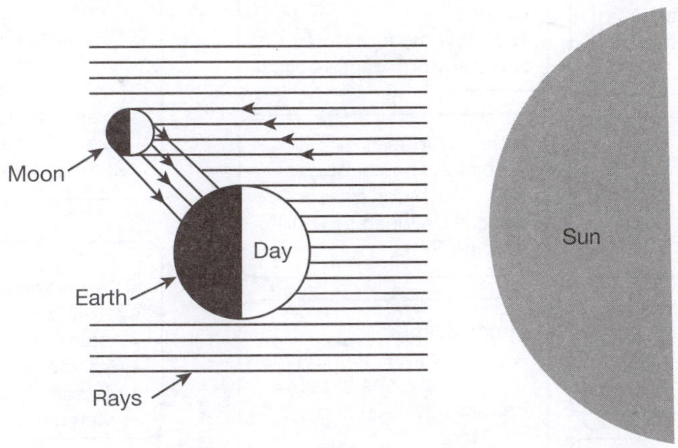

15. In given figure, mark the arrows (←), (→), (↓), or (↑) to show the direction of sunlight.

Solution: The arrows are marked in the figure below:

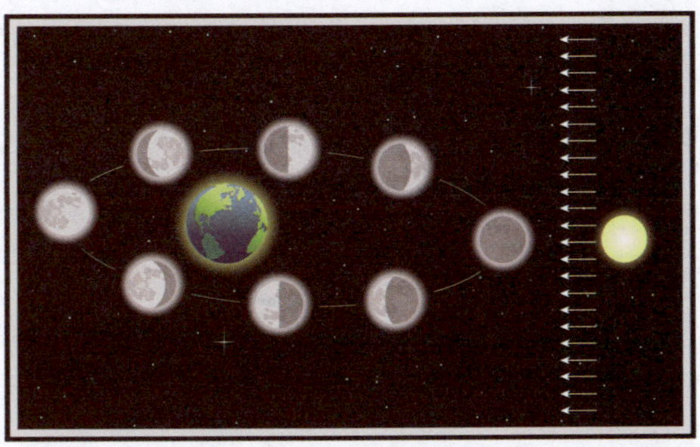

16. A star is ten light-years away from the Earth. Suppose it brightens up suddenly today. After how much time shall we see this change?

Solution: We will see the change after 10 years.

17. Meteors are not visible during the daytime. Explain the reason.

Solution: Meteors are not visible during the daytime because the brightness of a meteor is extremely small compared to that of the Sun.

18. Why does the Moon change its shape daily?

Solution: We see only that part of the Moon from which the light of the Sun is reflected towards us. Hence the Moon changes its shape daily.

STRUCTURAL OUTLINE

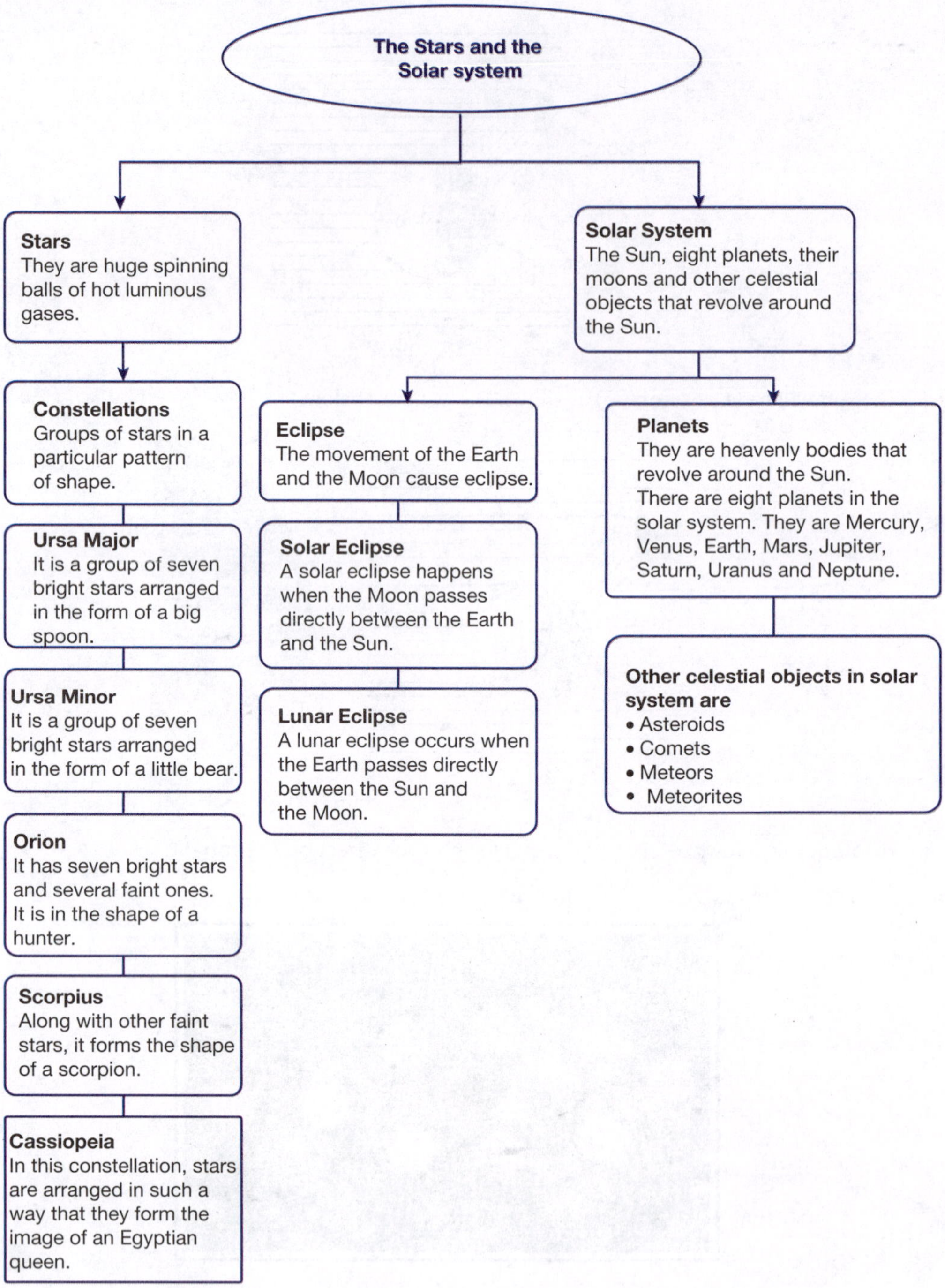

EXEMPLIFICATION

1. Paheli saw the Moon through a glass window at 8:00 p.m. She marked the position of the Moon on the glass pane. She got up at 4 a.m. in the morning. Will the Moon be visible at the same position?

Solution: No, because the position of the Moon keeps changing during the night.

2. Suppose the Moon emits light of its own. Would it still have phases? Justify your answer

Solution: As the Moon does not emit its own light and reflects the light of the Sun, phases are seen. Due to the revolution of the Earth, reflection of different intensities of light fall on the Moon. Hence, the Moon glows continuously, forming phases.

3. The given figure shows comets without their tail. Show the tails of the comets at position A, B and C. In which position will the tail be longest?

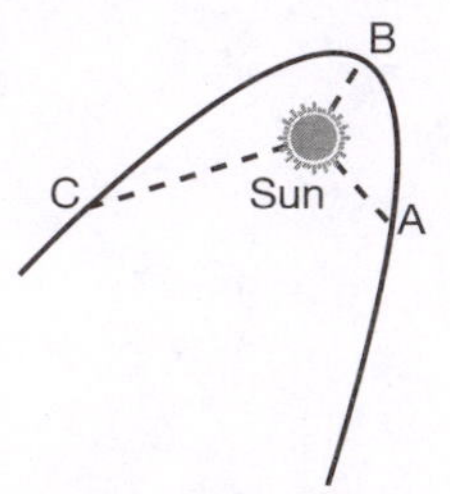

Solution: The tails of the comets at given positions are shown below:

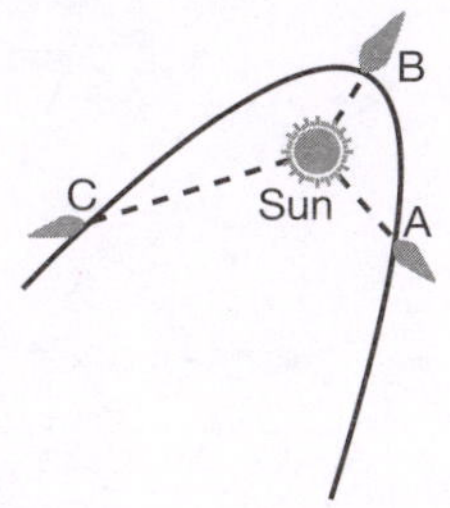

The tail will be longest at position B.

4. Explain why we always see the same side of the Moon.

Solution: We always see the same side of the Moon because the Moon's period of revolution around the Earth is equal to the period of rotation of the Moon on its axis. Hence, we can only the side that faces us.

5. Look at the given figure carefully and answer the following questions:

(a) In which part of the sky would you see the full moon in the evening?

(b) In which part of the sky would you see the crescent moon in the evening?

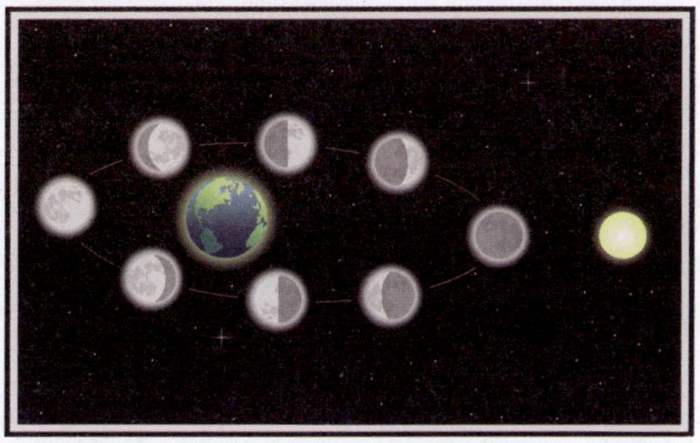

Solution:

(a) We see the full moon in the evening in the eastern part of the sky.

(b) We see the crescent moon in the evening in the western part of the sky.

6. Write the names of all planets in the correct sequence from the Sun.

Solution:

1. Mercury
2. Venus
3. Earth
4. Mars
5. Jupiter
6. Saturn
7. Uranus
8. Neptune

7. Suppose the distance between the Earth and the Sun becomes half of its present distance. What is likely to happen to life?

Solution: Life may no longer exist because some special environmental conditions are needed for the existence and continuation of life on the Earth. The right distance of the Earth from the Sun is necessary so that it has the right temperature range, the presence of water and a suitable atmosphere and a blanket of ozone.

8. Explain how you can locate pole star with the help of the constellation Great Bear (Ursa Major).

Solution: Locate the two end stars of Ursa Major. Imagine a straight line passing through these stars as shown in the Figure 4.3 on page no. 5. Extend this imaginary line towards the north direction. This line will lead to a star which is not too bright. This is a pole star.

NCERT COMPENDIUM

1. Match the column:

Column-I	Column-II
(i) Satellite of Earth	(a) Orion
(ii) Red planet	(b) Venus
(iii) Constellation	(c) Mars
(iv) Planet which is commonly called an evening star	(d) Moon

Solution: I – d, ii – c, iii – a, iv - b

2. (i) Solve the following riddle.
My first alphabet is in MAN but not in CAN
My second alphabet is in ACE and also in FAN
My third alphabet is in RAT and not in CAT
My fourth alphabet is in SUN but not in FUN
I am a planet that moves around the Sun.
(ii) Make two similar riddles by yourself.

Solution: (i) Mars
(ii) My first alphabet is in VAN but not in CAN
My second alphabet is in EAT and also in SEAT
My third alphabet is in NET and not in SET
My last alphabet is in SUN but not in FAN
I am a planet that moves around the Sun.

3. Which of the following is not a member of our Solar System?
(i) Sirius
(iii) Asteroids
(ii) Comets
(iv) Pluto

Solution: Answer: (i) Sirius

4. Which of the following is not a planet of the Sun?
(i) Jupiter
(iii) Neptune
(ii) Pluto
(iv) Saturn

Solution: (ii) Pluto

5. Which is the brighter star, the Pole Star or Sirius?

Solution: Sirius

6. An artist's representation of the Solar System is given in Figure. Is the order of the planets correct? If not, write the correct order in the boxes in the figure.

Solution: Answer: Correct order: Mercury, Venus, Earth, Mars, Jupiter, Saturn, Uranus, Neptune

7. A portion of night sky with stars is shown in Figure. Look carefully and identify the groups of stars that form the patterns—the Big Dipper and the Little Dipper. Draw lines to connect the stars for these patterns and label them. Also, identify and label the Pole Star. You may refer to Fig. from theory part.

Solution:

8. A portion of the night sky is shown in Figure below. Draw lines to connect the stars for Orion and label the star Sirius. You may refer to Fig. from theory part.

Solution:

9. You can see stars fading away at dawn and appearing at dusk. During the day we do not see the stars. Explain why.

Solution: During the day, we do not see the stars because Sun is very bright star during day.

10. During a clear night, try to observe the Big Dipper 3–4 times at an interval of 2 to 3 hours. Also try to locate the Pole Star each time. Does the Big Dipper appear to move? Draw a rough sketch to illustrate this, mentioning the time in each case.
Solution: Yes, the big Dipper appear to move.

11. Think about the night sky and write a poem or a story on it.
Solution: Do it on your own.

ASSESSMENT CORNER

Level 1

Fixed Response Type

Multiple Choice Questions

Directions: Read the following questions carefully and choose the best answers.

1. Stars are mainly made up of
   (A) Oxygen and hydrogen
   (B) Oxygen and nitrogen
   (C) Hydrogen and helium
   (D) Water and helium

2. The Sun is a
   (A) Star (B) Planet
   (C) Galaxy (D) Comet

3. Stars appear motionless because
   (A) They move with the same speed as that of the Earth.
   (B) They do not move at all.
   (C) They are very far away from the Earth.
   (D) Their speed is extremely slow.

4. Galaxies
   (A) Move towards each other
   (B) Move away from each other
   (C) Do not move at all
   (D) None of these

5. Any heavenly body having light of its own is called a
   (A) Planet (B) Star
   (C) Comet (D) Meteorite

6. Galaxies are usually classified on the basis of their
   (A) Mass (B) Size
   (C) Shape (D) None of these

7. The Indian name of Milky way galaxy is
   (A) Akash Ganga (B) Dhruv Tara
   (C) Saptarishi (D) None of these

8. The vast collection of billions of stars is called a
   (A) Universe (B) Galaxy
   (C) Constellation (D) None of these

9. The Milky Way galaxy has a/an
   (A) Elliptical shape (B) Spiral shape
   (C) Irregular shape (D) None of these

10. Orion is the name of a
    (A) Star (B) Planet
    (C) Galaxy (D) Constellation

11. The star that lies close to the axis of rotation of the Earth is
    (A) The pole star (B) Ursa Major
    (C) Minor (D) None of these

12. The star forming a group that has a recognizable shape is called
    (A) Constellation (B) Orion
    (C) Light year (D) Pole star

13. Our Earth as well as the Sun belongs to the galaxy which has a spiral shape called the
    (A) Galaxy (B) Light year
    (C) Milky Way (D) None of these

14. Stars produce heat energy and light due to the fusion of
    (A) Oxygen (B) Hydrogen
    (C) Helium (D) Ozone

15. Distance of stars is expressed in
    (A) km (B) Square meter
    (C) Light year (D) Meter

16. The distance of the star Proxima Centauri from the Earth is
    (A) 4.3 million kilometres
    (B) 8.25 light minute
    (C) 2 million light years
    (D) 4.3 light years

17. The planet which takes the minimum time to revolve around itself is
    (A) Mercury (B) Pluto
    (C) Venus (D) Neptune

18. A star which appears blue will be
    (A) As hot as the Sun
    (B) Cooler than the Sun
    (C) Very cold indeed
    (D) Much hotter than the Sun

19. The average distance of the Earth from the Sun is
    (A) 150 million kilometres
    (B) 100 million kilometres

(C) 120 million kilometres
(D) 110 million kilometres

20. Time taken by Neptune to complete one revolution around the Sun is
(A) 100 years (B) 120 years
(C) 165 years (D) 200 years

21. What is the main difference between a star and a planet?
(A) Stars are smaller than planets.
(B) Stars emit their own light while planets reflect light.
(C) Planets are always closer to Earth than stars.
(D) Stars move around planets.

22. Which of these celestial bodies is not part of our solar system?
(A) Jupiter (B) The Moon
(C) Sirius (D) Mars

23. During which moon phase does a solar eclipse occur?
(A) Full Moon (B) New Moon
(C) First quarter (D) Third quarter

24. Why can't we see stars during the daytime?
(A) Stars only shine at night.
(B) Stars move away during the day.
(C) The Sun's bright light makes stars invisible.
(D) Earth's rotation hides the stars.

25. The Pole Star appears stationary in the sky because:
(A) It doesn't rotate like other stars.
(B) It is located close to Earth's axis of rotation.
(C) It is the brightest star in the sky.
(D) It orbits around Earth.

26. During the day, the surface temperature on the Moon is
(A) –100° C (B) 100° C
(C) –168° C (D) 168° C

27. India first satellite put in the space was
(A) Bhaskara (B) INSAT
(C) Rohini (D) Aryabhatta

28. Phases of the Moon are observed because
(A) The Moon does not reflect sunlight at all.
(B) It is only the sunlight, reflected by some parts of the Moon that reaches the Earth.
(C) The shadow of the Earth falls on the Moon.
(D) Only some parts of the Moon can emit light.

29. GSLV means________.
(A) Geostationary satellite launching vehicle
(B) German satellite launching vehicle
(C) Global satellite locus verification system
(D) None of the above

30. What do you mean by INSAT?
(A) Indian space satellite
(B) Indian national satellite
(C) International space satellite
(D) International satellite

Fill in the Blanks

Directions: Fill in the blanks with the correct answers.

1. A group of billions of stars is called a __________.

2. 1 parsec is equal to __________ light years.

3. Orion constellation is visible during winters in the __________________ hemisphere.

4. The distance between stars is measured in _______________.

5. Saptarishi is also known as__________________.

True/False

Directions: Specify True and False. Write "T" if the statement is correct and "F" if it is incorrect.

1. Constellation Orion can be seen only with a telescope.

2. The Milky Way is a spiral galaxy in the form of disc.

3. Ursa minor is also known as Little bear.

4. The Earth rotates about its axis from east to west.

5. Pole star is a member of the solar system.

Match Type Questions

Directions: Match column A with the corresponding description in column B.

1. Match Column-I with Column-II and mark the correct option.

Column-I	Column-II
(i) Morning star	(a) Meteors
(ii) Saturn's moon	(b) Mars
(iii) Pole star	(c) Titan

ASSESSMENT CORNER

(iv) Phobos	(d) Northern hemisphere
(v) Shooting star	(e) Venus

(A) (i)-(e), (ii)-(c), (iii)-(d), (iv)-(b), (v)-(a)
(B) (i)-(a), (ii)-(c), (iii)-(d), (iv)-(b), (v)-(e)
(C) (i)-(c), (ii)-(e), (iii)-(d), (iv)-(b), (v)-(a)
(D) (i)-(b), (ii)-(c), (iii)-(d), (iv)-(e), (v)-(a)

2. Match Column-I with Column-II and mark the correct option.

Column-I	Column-II
(i) Mars	(a) 67 moons
(ii) Jupiter	(b) 2 moons
(iii) Saturn	(c) 14 moons
(iv) Uranus	(d) 62 moons
(v) Neptune	(e) 27 moons

(A) (i)-(e), (ii)-(c), (iii)-(d), (iv)-(b), (v)-(a)
(B) (i)-(a), (ii)-(c), (iii)-(d), (iv)-(b), (v)-(e)
(C) (i)-(c), (ii)-(e), (iii)-(d), (iv)-(b), (v)-(a)
(D) (i)-(b), (ii)-(d), (iii)-(a), (iv)-(e), (v)-(c)

3. Match the Column I with Column II and select the correct option from the codes given below.

Column-I	Column-II
(i) Made of ice and rocky material	(a) Orion
(ii) Chunks of rocks that have never managed to come together as planet	(b) Meteors
(iii) Shooting stars in the sky	(c) Asteroids
(iv) The hunter	(d) Comets

(A) (i)-(a), (ii)-(b), (iii)-(c), (iv)-(d)
(B) (i)-(d), (ii)-(c), (iii)-(b), (iv)-(a)
(C) (i)-(c), (ii)-(b), (iii)-(a), (iv)-(d)
(D) (i)-(b), (ii)-(a), (iii)-(d), (iv)-(c)

Assertion and Reasons Type Questions

Directions: Study both statements and mark your answer using the codes given blow.

(A) Both A and R are true and R is the correct explanation of A.
(B) Both A and R are true but R is not the correct explanation of A.
(C) A is true but R is false.
(D) A is false but R is true.

1. **Assertion:** Saturn could float if put in water.
Reason: Saturn is less dense than water.

2. **Assertion:** Venus is hotter than Mercury though it is far away from the Sun.
Reason: Cloudy atmosphere of Venus reflects almost 75 percent of the sunlight that falls on it.

3. **Assertion:** Stars twinkle while the planets do not.
Reason: Stars are much bigger in size than the planets.

4. **Assertion:** The Earth has an atmosphere but the Moon does not.
Reason: The Moon is small in comparison to the Earth.

5. **Assertion:** The time period of geostationary satellite is 24 hours.
Reason: Geostationary satellite must have the same time period as the time taken by the Earth to complete one revolution about its axis.

6. **Assertion:** The same face of the Moon is always presented to the Earth.
Reason: The Moon rotates about its own axis in days which is about the same time that it takes to orbit the Earth.

7. **Assertion:** Existence of human life on Venus is highly improbable.
Reason: Venus has extremely high level of carbon dioxide in its atmosphere.

Comprehension Type Questions

Directions: Read the given paragraph and answer the following questions (1–3).

Passage: The Moon has no light of its own. The Moon shines and becomes visible to us because it reflects sunlight falling on it towards the Earth. At any point of time, half of the Moon's surface is in direct sunlight and the other half is in shadow. However, since the Moon revolves around the Earth and the Earth (along with the Moon) revolves around the Sun, we cannot see the entire sun-lit surface of the Moon from the Earth all the time. We can see only that part of the sun-lit surface of the Moon which is towards us (on the Earth). Thus, we see different amount (or portions) of the sun-lit surface of the Moon from the Earth, depending upon the relative positions of the Sun, the Moon and the Earth.

1. Example of natural satellite is
(A) Venus (B) Comet
(C) Moon (D) Sputnik-I

2. Moon is
   (A) Luminous (B) Non-luminous
   (C) Both of them (D) None of them

3. Phases of the Moon are observed because
   (A) The Moon does not reflect sunlight.
   (B) The relative position of the Sun, the Earth and the Moon changes.
   (C) The shadow of the Earth falls on the Moon.
   (D) Only some parts of the Moon can emit light.

FREE RESPONSE TYPE

Very Short Answer Type Questions

Directions: Write one sentence for each of the following questions.

1. Name the star which appears stationary from the Earth.
2. Name the galaxy in which our solar system is situated.
3. Why do stars twinkle?
4. What is a light year?
5. Stars are not visible during the day. Why?
6. Name a star other than the Sun nearest to the Earth.
7. Which two planets have asteroids between them?
8. Name the planet having the largest number of natural satellites.
9. Name the object which appears as a bright ball with a long glowing tail in the sky.
10. Which planet is known as the sister planet of Earth and why?
11. Which comet can be seen every 76 years?
12. What is the Indian name of Ursa Minor?
13. Which planet in the solar system has the longest day?

Short Answer Type Questions

Directions: Write short answer for each of the following questions.

1. Define a satellite.
2. Give the reason the Sun appears to move from east to west.
3. Why is the distance between stars expressed in light years? What do you understand by the statement that a star is eight light years away from the Earth?
4. Name two objects other than planets which are members of the solar system.
5. Why is life on Mercury, Venus and Mars not possible?
6. In which part of the sky can you find Venus if it is visible as an evening star?
7. How many planets are there in our solar system?
8. The Earth is known as the unique planet. Explain.
9. What are the reasons for the occurrence of seasons?
10. Differentiate between meteors and meteorites.

Long Answer Type Questions

Directions: Answer the following questions with the complete explanation.

1. What do you mean by constellation? Explain any three constellations.
2. What do you mean by a galaxy? Explain the different categories of galaxies.
3. What are natural and artificial satellites? Explain the various phases of the Moon.
4. Define an artificial satellite. Write the use of satellites in practical life. Give five examples of satellites which were launched by India.
5. With the help of a diagram, explain the occurrence of (a) solar eclipse (b) lunar eclipse.

Numerical Type Questions

1. How many natural satellites does the Earth have?
2. How many moons does Mars have?
3. The distance of the star Alpha Centauri from the Earth is 4.3 light years. Calculate the distance in kilometres.
4. How many natural satellites does Venus have?
5. How many phases of the Moon are there?

Case Based Questions

Directions: Answer the following questions based on the given case.

Directions: Read the given paragraph and answer the following questions (1–3).

The planets, relatively nearer to the Sun have features that are quite different from those which are 'far off'. We can divide the planets into two categories: The terrestrial planets and the Jovian planets.

Mercury, Venus, Earth and Mars are the terrestrial planets. They have solid and rocky surfaces. The Jovian planets are Jupiter, Saturn, Uranus and Neptune. These planets are very large in size and are made up largely of gases.

1. Which of the following is a Jovian planet?
   (A) Mercury (B) Saturn
   (C) Earth (D) Mars
2. Which of the following is a terrestrial planet?
   (A) Mercury (B) Saturn
   (C) Uranus (D) Neptune
3. A terrestrial planet is largely made up of
   (A) Rocks (B) Gases
   (C) Helium (D) Stars

Level 2

Multiple Choice Questions

1. Consider the following statements. Identify the right ones.
   (i) Stars are celestial bodies that continuously emit light and heat.
   (ii) The Sun is also a star.
   (A) i only (B) ii only
   (C) Both (D) None
2. The following constellation consists of 7 main stars.
   (A) Ursa major (B) Ursa Minor
   (C) Lyra (D) None of these
3. Our Earth as well as the Sun belongs to the galaxy which has a spiral shape called the
   (A) Milky way (B) Galaxy
   (C) Light year (D) Universe
4. Sources of energy in the Sun is
   (A) Excitation of atoms
   (B) Collision of atoms
   (C) Breaking of heavy nuclei
   (D) Combination of light nuclei
5. Ceres is
   (A) Satellite of the mars
   (B) Satellite of the Jupiter
   (C) An asteroid
   (D) A meteorite
6. The tail of a comet usually extends to
   (A) 10 kilometers
   (B) 2 light years
   (C) 800 million kilometers
   (D) 1.5 billion kilometers
7. The number of satellites of Venus is
   (A) One (B) Two
   (C) Three (D) Zero
8. Which planet is also known as 'Red planet'?
   (A) Mars (B) Venus
   (C) Jupiter (D) Mercury
9. A small mass of rock-like material surrounded by vapours of large masses and revolving in highly elliptical orbits are called
   (A) Comets (B) Meteorites
   (C) Asteroids (D) Galaxy
10. The planet which takes the maximum time to rotate on its axis is
    (A) Venus (B) Neptune
    (C) Mercury (D) Saturn
11. The credit for the discovery of rings of the Saturn goes to
    (A) Kepler (B) Galileo
    (C) Newton (D) Copernicus
12. Shukra is Venus, as Shani is to
    (A) Saturn (B) Mars
    (C) Jupiter (D) Mercury
13. Mercury is closer to the Sun than Venus. But Venus is hotter than Mercury because
    (A) Mercury has no atmosphere and Venus has a thick atmosphere which can retain the heat.
    (B) Mercury is mostly made up of sedimentary rocks while Venus contains igneous rocks.
    (C) Both of these
    (D) None of these
14. The biggest satellite of Saturn is
    (A) Eris (B) Ceres
    (C) Xena (D) Titan
15. The biggest star in the sky is
    (A) Sirius (B) Riga
    (C) Betelgeuse (D) Mriga

16. Where do you find the sea of tranquility?
(A) Moon (B) Earth
(C) Mercury (D) Mars

17. The plane formed by the axis of the Earth and orbit is known as the
(A) Symmetric plane (B) Orbital plane
(C) Spherical plane (D) None of these

18. The Earth is slightly bulging in the ______.
(A) South pole (B) North pole
(C) Middle (D) None of these

19. The imaginary line running on the globe that divides it into two equal parts is known as the
(A) Axis (B) Equator
(C) Pole (D) Both A and B

20. ISRO stands for
(A) International society for research on optometry
(B) Indian satellite and radar organization
(C) Indian space research organization
(D) None of these

21. Communication satellites are placed in the
(A) Geostationary orbit
(B) Sun-synchronous orbits
(C) Both A and B
(D) None of these

22. The approximate height of a geostationary satellite is (Given that time period of satellite is 24 hours)
(A) 6400 km (B) 12800 km
(C) 7200 km (D) 36000 km

23. On the day of Amavasya, the phase of the Moon is called
(A) Full moon (B) New moon
(C) Half moon (D) Crescent moon

24. Lunar eclipse occurs when the
(A) Sun comes between the Earth and the Moon.
(B) Moon comes between the Earth and the Sun.
(C) Earth comes between the Sun and the Moon.
(D) Earth and the Moon collide with each other.

25. Which constellation contains the Big Dipper?
(A) Orion (B) Ursa Minor
(C) Ursa Major (D) Canis Major

26. Which planets are called terrestrial planets?
(A) Jupiter, Saturn, Uranus, Neptune
(B) Mercury, Venus, Earth, Mars
(C) All planets in the solar system
(D) Only Earth and Mars

27. What is the correct order of planets from the Sun?
(A) Mercury, Venus, Earth, Mars, Saturn, Jupiter, Uranus, Neptune
(B) Mercury, Venus, Mars, Earth, Jupiter, Saturn, Uranus, Neptune
(C) Mercury, Venus, Earth, Mars, Jupiter, Saturn, Uranus, Neptune
(D) Venus, Mercury, Earth, Mars, Jupiter, Saturn, Neptune, Uranus

28. A lunar eclipse can only occur during which moon phase?
(A) New Moon (B) Full Moon
(C) First quarter (D) Last quarter

29. If you wanted to find the Pole Star at night, which constellation would you use as a guide?
(A) Orion
(B) The Big Dipper (Ursa Major)
(C) Canis Major
(D) Taurus

30. A student observes that the Big Dipper appears to move across the sky during the night. What causes this apparent movement?
(A) The Big Dipper is actually moving through space.
(B) Earth's rotation on its axis.
(C) The Moon's gravitational pull
(D) The Sun's magnetic field

31. If Earth suddenly stopped rotating, what would happen to the day-night cycle?
(A) Days and nights would become six months long each.
(B) There would be no more day-night cycle.
(C) Days would become shorter.
(D) One side of Earth would always face the Sun, creating permanent day and night sides.

32. Why don't we see a solar eclipse every new Moon?
(A) The Moon is too small.
(B) The Moon's orbit is tilted about five degrees relative to Earth's orbit.
(C) Solar eclipses only happen in winter.
(D) The Sun is too far away.

33. Which characteristic would help you distinguish between a terrestrial and Jovian planet?
(A) Colour of the planet
(B) Presence or absence of a solid surface
(C) Distance from other stars
(D) Number of days in a year

34. If light pollution increases in your area, what would happen to your ability to see constellations?
(A) Constellations would appear brighter.
(B) You would see more constellations.
(C) Constellations would become harder to see.
(D) Constellations would change their patterns.

35. A space probe travels beyond Neptune. What type of planets would it have just passed through?
(A) Terrestrial planets (B) Jovian planets
(C) Dwarf planets (D) Asteroid belt

36. If you observe a planet through a telescope and see that it has rings and many moons, it is most likely:
(A) A terrestrial planet
(B) A Jovian planet
(C) An asteroid
(D) A comet

Higher Order Thinking Skills (HOTs)

1. Which of the following planets can be seen with the naked eye?
(A) Mercury, Venus, Mars, Jupiter
(B) Mars, Jupiter, Uranus, Neptune
(C) Mercury, Venus, Uranus, Neptune
(D) Mercury, Mars, Jupiter, Neptune

2. Taking one light year equal to 9.4×10^{15} m and one day equal to 86400 s, what will be the speed of light in light year per day if the speed of light in m s^{-1} is 3×10^8?
(A) 2.75×10^{-3} ly day^{-1} (B) 3.75×10^{-3} ly day^{-1}
(C) 2.75×10^{3} ly day^{-1} (D) 3.79×10^{3} ly day^{-1}

3. Comets spend most of their time __________.
(A) Far away from the Sun
(B) Close to one planet or the other
(C) Very close to Sun
(D) Very close to the Earth

4. Lunar eclipse occurs when the Earth comes in between the Sun and the Moon. Solar eclipse occurs when the Moon comes in between the Sun and the Earth. This suggests that
(A) Both eclipses occur on a new moon day
(B) Solar eclipse occurs on a new moon day
(C) Lunar eclipse occurs on a new moon day
(D) Both eclipses occur on a full moon day

5. Which planet is called the morning star as well as the evening star, depending on its position with respect to the Sun?
(A) Mercury (B) Venus
(C) Mars (D) Saturn

6. Arrange the following planets in increasing order of time required to complete one rotation around the Sun.
(i) Earth (ii) Uranus
(iii) Mars (iv) Jupiter
(A) (i), (ii), (iii), (iv) (B) (i), (iii), (iv), (ii)
(C) (iv), (iii), (ii), (i) (D) (ii), (iii), (i), (iv)

7. Which of the following options is true regarding the number of moons of the given planets?
(A) Mars < Earth < Uranus < Neptune < Jupiter
(B) Earth < Mars < Jupiter < Uranus < Neptune
(C) Earth < Mars < Neptune < Uranus < Jupiter
(D) Jupiter < Earth < Mars < Neptune < Uranus

8. The given diagram shows the night sky in which stars are visible. Identify the star X, and the constellation Y from the figure.

(A) Orion Cassiopeia
(B) Sirius Orion
(C) Pole star Sirius
(D) Pole star Orion

9. Which of the following options correctly represents the relative positions of the Sun (S), Moon (M) and Earth (E) on the day of full moon and new moon?

	Full Moon	New Moon
(A)	MES	MSE
(B)	SME	ESM
(C)	SEM	SME
(D)	ESM	EMS

10. Which of the following statements are correct?
(i) Venus is the hottest planet of the solar system.
(ii) Jupiter is called the red planet as it has a large red spot on its surface.
(iii) Revolving speed of Mercury is fastest of all planets.
(iv) Mars has no natural satellites of its own.
(v) Saturn is the least dense planet among all planets.

ASSESSMENT CORNER

(A) (ii) and (iii) only
(B) (ii), (iv) and (v) only
(C) (i), (iii) and (v) only
(D) (i), (ii), (iv) and (v) only

11. During which season would you expect to see different constellations in the night sky?
(A) The same constellations are visible all year.
(B) Different seasons show different constellations due to Earth's orbit.
(C) Only winter shows constellations.
(D) Seasons don't affect constellation visibility.

12. If you were an astronaut on the International Space Station during a lunar eclipse, what would you observe?
(A) The Moon is disappearing completely.
(B) Earth casting a shadow on the Moon.
(C) The Sun is getting dimmer.
(D) Nothing different from normal.

13. What would happen to Jupiter's classification if scientists discovered it had a solid surface?
(A) It would remain a Jovian planet.
(B) It would be reclassified as a terrestrial planet.
(C) It would become a dwarf planet.
(D) Its classification wouldn't change.

14. If Earth's axis were not tilted, what would happen to the apparent position of constellations throughout the year?
(A) Constellations would appear in the same positions all year.
(B) Constellations would move faster across the sky.
(C) We would see more constellations.
(D) Constellations would disappear.

15. If the Moon's orbit were in the same plane as Earth's orbit around the Sun, what would happen to eclipses?
(A) There would be no eclipses.
(B) We would have both solar and lunar eclipses every month.
(C) Only solar eclipses would occur.
(D) Eclipses would be less frequent.

16. A student wants to observe Saturn's rings. During which time would this be most difficult?
(A) During a new moon in a dark area
(B) During a full moon in the city
(C) During the daytime
(D) Both (B) and (C)

17. Compare the conditions necessary for a solar eclipse versus a lunar eclipse. What is the key difference in the alignment of the Earth, Moon, and Sun?
(A) Solar eclipse: Moon between Earth and Sun; Lunar eclipse: Earth between Moon and Sun
(B) Both require the same alignment
(C) Solar eclipse: Earth between Moon and Sun; Lunar eclipse: Moon between Earth and Sun
(D) The Sun's position doesn't matter for either eclipse.

18. Why do Jovian planets have so many moons compared to terrestrial planets?
(A) They are closer to the asteroid belt.
(B) Their strong gravitational fields can capture more objects.
(C) They are older than terrestrial planets.
(D) They have more solid surfaces for moons to form.

19. If you observe that a celestial object has the following characteristics: it's very large, has no solid surface, has many moons, and is located far from the Sun, what type of object is it?
(A) Terrestrial planet (B) Jovian planet
(C) Asteroid (D) Comet

20. Analyse the relationship between a planet's distance from the Sun and its composition. What pattern exists?
(A) Closer planets are gaseous, farther planets are rocky.
(B) Closer planets are rocky, farther planets are gaseous.
(C) Distance has no effect on composition.
(D) All planets have the same composition.

21. Why do we always see the same side of the Moon from Earth?
(A) The Moon doesn't rotate.
(B) The Moon's rotation period equals its orbital period around Earth.
(C) Earth's gravity stops the Moon's rotation.
(D) The Moon is too small to rotate.

22. Analyse why ancient civilisations used constellations for navigation:
(A) Constellations move in predictable patterns.
(B) Constellations remain in relatively fixed positions and can indicate direction.
(C) Constellations are brighter than individual stars.
(D) Constellations change with the seasons.

ARCHIVE CORNER

Directions: Read the following questions carefully and choose one alternative that best describes the answer.

1. Which of the following statements is incorrect about constellation?
   (A) It is a group of stars that has recognizable shape.
   (B) It appears to move in the sky from east to west.
   (C) It consists of large number of stars but we are able to see only the bright ones.
   (D) All the stars of a constellation are at the same distance from us.

2. Meera's father was born on February 2, 1977. How many complete turns has he gone round the Sun till October 20, 2016?
   (A) 28 (B) 39
   (C) 40 (D) 77

3. Which of the following is an incorrect match?

	Planet	Time to orbit the Sun	Time for one rotation on its axis
(A)	Jupiter	12 years	9 h 55 m
(B)	Mars	687 years	24 h 37 m
(C)	Venus	225 years	243 days
(D)	Neptune	265 years	10 h 7 m

4. The artificial satellites sent into space by India in ascending order of their launching dates are
   (A) APPLE, EDUSAT, ROHINI, INSAT 48
   (B) EDUSAT, ROHINI, APPLE, INSAT 48
   (C) ROHINI, APPLE, EDUSAT, INSAT 48
   (D) INSAT 48, EDUSAT, APPLE, ROHINI

5. Arrange the following planets in decreasing order of time required to complete one revolution around the Sun.
   (i) Earth (ii) Uranus
   (iii) Mars (iv) Jupiter
   (A) (i), (ii), (iii), (iv) (B) (i), (iii), (iv), (ii)
   (C) (iv), (iii), (ii), (i) (D) (ii), (iv), (iii), (i)

6. The force that is responsible for revolution of the Earth around the Sun is
   (A) Electric force
   (B) Magnetic force
   (C) Electromagnetic force
   (D) Gravitational force

7. Compare the density of Jovian planets to terrestrial planets and explain what this tells us about their composition:
   (A) Jovian planets are denser because they contain more rock.
   (B) Terrestrial planets are denser because they're composed mainly of rock and metal.
   (C) Both types have the same density.
   (D) Density has no relationship to composition.

8. Why is Jupiter called a 'failed star'?
   (A) It's made of the same materials as stars but lacks sufficient mass for nuclear fusion.
   (B) It used to be a star but burned out.
   (C) It orbits too close to the Sun.
   (D) It has too many moons.

9. If Earth were located where Mars is now, analyse how this would affect the occurrence of eclipses?
   (A) Eclipses would be more frequent.
   (B) Eclipses on Mars would be less frequent because of its smaller moons.
   (C) There would be no eclipses because Mars' moons are too small.
   (D) Eclipse frequency would remain the same.

10. Evaluate the statement: 'All planets beyond the asteroid belt are gas giants.'—Is this accurate?
    (A) Yes, all outer planets are gas giants.
    (B) No, Uranus and Neptune are ice giants, not gas giants.
    (C) No, some outer planets are terrestrial.
    (D) Yes, but they're called Jovian planets, not gas giants.

11. If you were designing a space mission to study planetary rings, which type of planets would you target and why?
    (A) Terrestrial planets because they're closer.
    (B) Jovian planets because they have prominent ring systems.
    (C) Dwarf planets because they're easier to study.
    (D) Any planet would work equally well.

12. Analyse why the same constellation appears in different positions in the sky at different times of night:
    (A) The constellation is actually moving.
    (B) Earth's rotation causes the apparent movement.
    (C) The atmosphere bends starlight.
    (D) Gravitational forces move the stars.

ANSWER KEY

Assessment Corner

Level 1

Fixed Response Type

Multiple Choice Questions

1. C 2. A 3. C 4. B 5. B 6. C 7. A 8. B 9. B
10. D 11. A 12. A 13. C 14. B 15. C 16. D 17. D 18. D
19. A 20. C 21. B 22. C 23. B 24. C 25. B 26. B 27. D
28. B 29. A 30. B

Fill in the Blanks

1. Galaxy 2. 3.3 3. Northern 4. light year 5. Ursa Major

True/False

1. false 2. true 3. true 4. false 5. false

Match Type Questions

1. A 2. D 3. B

Assertion and Reasons Type Questions

1. A 2. B 3. B 4. B 5. A 6. A 7. A

Comprehension Type Questions

1. C 2. B 3. D

Free Response Type

Short Answer Type Questions

7. 8

Numerical Type Questions

1. 1 2. 2 3. 4.078×10^{13} km 4. 0 5. 8

Case Based Questions

1. B 2. A 3. A

Level 2

Multiple Choice Questions

1. C	2. A	3. A	4. D	5. C	6. C	7. D	8. A	9. A
10. A	11. B	12. A	13. A	14. D	15. A	16. A	17. B	18. C
19. B	20. C	21. A	22. D	23. B	24. C	25. C	26. B	27. C
28. B	29. B	30. B	31. D	32. B	33. B	34. C	35. B	36. B

Higher Order Thinking Skills (HOTS)

1. A	2. A	3. A	4. B	5. B	6. B	7. C	8. B	9. C
10. C	11. B	12. B	13. B	14. A	15. B	16. D	17. A	18. B
19. B	20. B	21. B	22. B					

Archive Corner

1. D	2. B	3. D	4. C	5. D	6. D	7. B	8. A	9. C
10. B	11. B	12. B						

CHAPTER 5

Material Around Us

Learning Outcomes

After reading this chapter, you would be able to:

- define grouping and classification.
- classify different objects based on different properties like appearance, hardness, solubility, transparency, texture, and floatation.
- describe reason why some materials are magnetic, why handles of cooking utensils are made from plastic, and what material are electrical wires made of?

Geekspeak

- Grouping
- Classification
- Appearance
- Hardness
- Solubility
- Texture
- Floatation
- Transparency
- Magnetism
- Conduction

Introduction

We use several objects in our day-to-day lives. Pencils, erasers, books, notebooks, etc., are objects that you might be using a lot. All objects are made of substances called materials. It is very important to use the right materials for making each object. For example, a chalk made of materials like wood or plastic would be useless because it cannot be used to write on a blackboard. Therefore, it is important for us know the properties of different kinds of materials. Let us start by learning more about objects.

Objects

There is a great variety of objects everywhere. We see things around us: chairs, carts, bicycles, utensils, books, clothes, toys, water, stones. All these objects have different shapes, colors and uses. All objects around us are made of one or more materials. These materials include glass, metal, plastic, wood, cotton, paper, mud, and dirt (Fig. 5.1).

Figure 5.1 **Objects Around Us**

Importance of Grouping Things

Virag has a science test tomorrow. He searched his room for hours but cannot find his science textbook! This is because his room is in a mess. Clothes, toys, and other objects are scattered all over the place. This situation could have been avoided if the objects had been grouped properly. Placing similar things together is called grouping.

Grouping makes it easier to find when you need it. If all textbooks had been kept at the same place it would have been very easy to find the Science textbook. Similarly, it would be easy to find a particular shirt if all clothes are kept together. Also, grouping things would make the room look much better.

Have you ever been to a supermarket? Grouping is done in a supermarket by keeping similar items on the same shelf, making it easier for us to find the items we need. If things are not grouped, you might never find your favourite chocolate in a large supermarket.

❖ INTEXT QUESTIONS

1. What is common between salt and sand?

   Solution: Both have mass and are solids.

2. Why do we need to group materials? Give one reason.

   Solution: We often group materials for our convenience. It helps describe their properties.

3. Suggest two bases on which we can group objects.

   Solution:

   (i) Material used in making the object, e.g., wood or metal/plastic.

   (ii) Whether the material of the object is soft or hard, whether the substance dissolves in water or not.

Check Point 1

1. What do you mean by material?
2. Taking an example of three objects, identify the material it is made up of.
3. Name five objects made using paper.
4. Define the term 'Grouping.'
5. 'Grouping of objects helps the shopkeeper.' Justify the statement.

Classification

Grouping is done based on certain similarities between objects.
The process of grouping things on the basis of some similarities and dissimilarities is called classification.
Various objects around us are made up of different kinds of materials. These materials have different properties. The classification or grouping of things can be done on the basis of similarities and dissimilarities in their properties. Let us first study the properties of various materials.

> **Keystone**
>
> Everything we see can be classified into living and non-living categories.

- **Appearance:** Materials usually look different. Wood looks very different than iron. Iron looks different than copper or aluminum. At the same time, there may be some similarities between iron, copper and aluminum that do not exist in wood. These are usually metal. Iron, copper (Fig. 5.2(b)), aluminum and gold (Fig. 5.2(a)) are examples of metals. Some metals often lose their lustre and look dull when exposed to air and moisture (Fig. 5.2(c)).

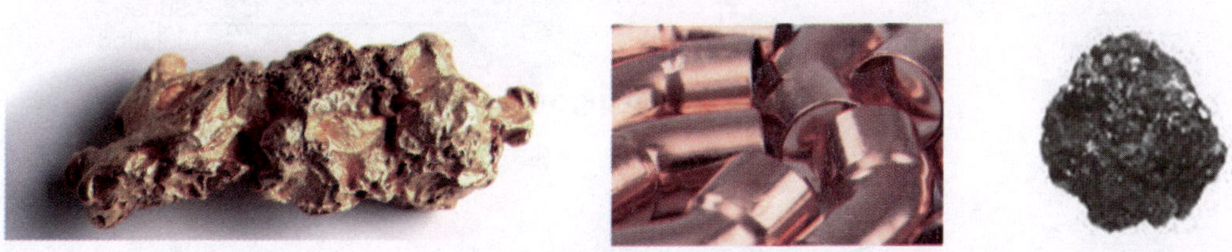

(a) Gold (b) Copper (c) Pyrite

Figure 5.2 **Metals**

Testing Room 1

Aim: To show that certain materials have lustre.

Material required:

- Small pieces of (i) paper (ii) cardboard
- a thin piece of wood
- a small strip of plastic
- thin wires of copper, aluminium, and iron
- heavy scissors or a metal cutter
- sandpaper.

Procedure:

(a) Cut each of the materials with heavy scissors or a metal cutter. Carefully observe the cut surface of each material.
However, in case of thin wires of copper, aluminium and iron, the cut surface is shining.

(b) Rub each of the material with sandpaper. Carefully observe the sand papered surface of the material.
Conclusion (i) We will notice that in case of paper, cardboard, wood, plastic, etc., the cut surface is not shining.
(ii) We will notice that in case of paper, cardboard, plastic and wool, the sand papered surface is not shining. However, in case of thin wires of copper, aluminium and iron, the sand papered surface is shining.

- **Hardness:** When we press different materials with our hands, some of them may be hard to compress while others can be easily compressed.

  There are materials that are easily scratched and materials that are not. Materials that are easily compressed or damaged are called soft materials, and materials that are difficult to compress are called hard materials. For example, cotton and sponge are soft and iron is hard.

- **Solubility:** Some substances, such as sugar and salt, completely dissolve or disappear in water. These substances are water soluble (Fig. 5.3). Other substances, such as sand, chalk powder, do not mix with water and do not disappear after prolonged stirring. These substances are insoluble in water.

  Water plays an important role in the functioning of our bodies because it can dissolve many different substances.

  When two liquids dissolve in one another such as water and milk, they are known as miscible liquids. Liquids such as mustard oil and kerosene do not dissolve in water but form separate layers. Such liquids are known as immiscible liquids.

Figure 5.3 **Dissolving Sugar in Water**

Testing Room 2

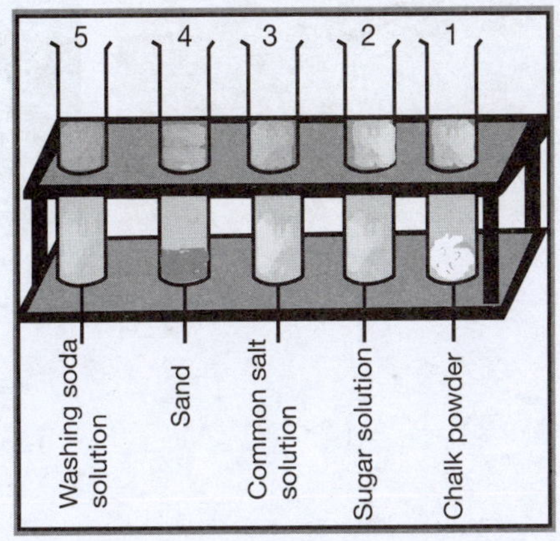

Aim: To prove that some solids are soluble in water.

Material required:

- A rack of test tubes
- water
- common salt
- sugar
- washing soda
- chalk powder and sand.

Procedure: Add a pinch of chalk powder in the first test tube, a pinch of sugar in second test tube, a pinch of common salt in the third test tube, a pinch of sand in the fourth test tube, and a pinch of washing soda in the fifth test tube. Pour water into each test tube such that half of each test tube is filled with water. Shake each test tube vigorously and replace in the rack.

Conclusion: We will notice that sugar, common salt and washing soda disappear in water, and hence are soluble substances. Sand and chalk powder do not dissolve in water, and hence are insoluble substances.

Testing Room 3

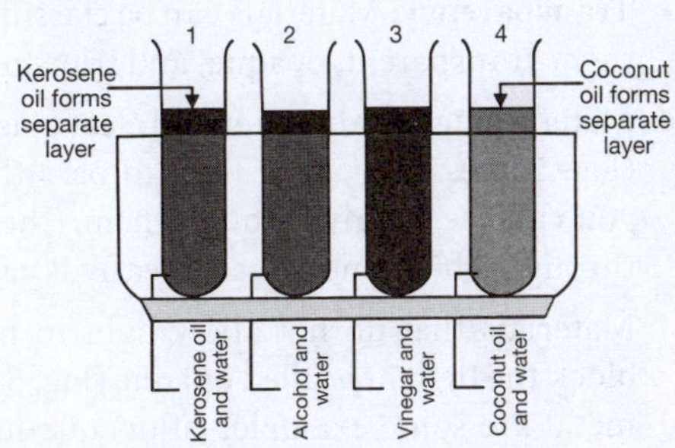

Aim: To prove that some liquids are miscible in water.

Material required:

- A rack of test tubes
- water
- alcohol
- kerosene oil
- vinegar and coconut oil

Procedure: Fill each of the test tubes half with water and place them in the test tube rack. Add a few drops of kerosene oil in the first test tube, a few drops of alcohol in the second test tube, a few drops of vinegar in the third test tube, and few drops of coconut oil in the fourth test tube. Shake each test tube vigorously and replace it in the test tube rack. Wait for 10 minutes

Observation: You will notice that kerosene oil and coconut oil float upon the surface of water and form separate layers. No separate layer is formed in case of vinegar and alcohol.

Conclusion: The activity proves that vinegar and alcohol are soluble in water, and hence are miscible liquids, but kerosene oil and coconut oil are insoluble in water and hence are immiscible liquids.

- **Texture:** The feel of any material is known as its texture. All materials do not feel the same when they are touched. They have different textures. They may be rough or smooth (Fig. 5.4). The surface of paper or a glass tumbler feel smooth since there are no uneven surfaces. The bark of a tree, an unfinished wall, or sandpaper is rough to touch since their surfaces are uneven and bumpy.
- **Floatation**: Substances that are less dense than water or are lighter than water will float in water (Fig. 5.5). For example, paper boats, feathers, and wooden corks float in water. Substances heavier than water such as iron nail or metal coins sink in water.

(a) (b)

Figure 5.4 (a) Rough Substance (b) Smooth Substance

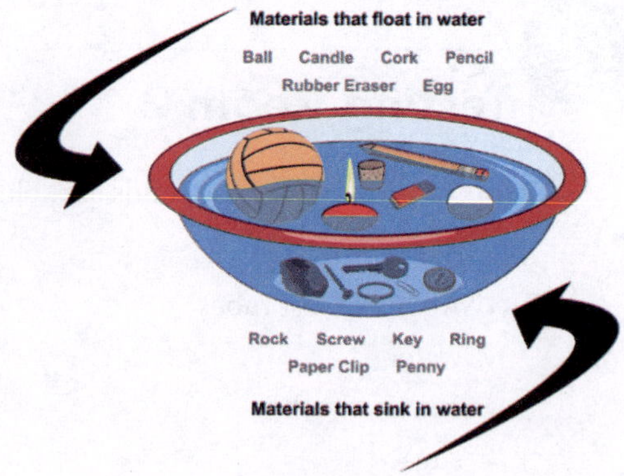

Figure 5.5 Sinking and Floating Substances

Competition Corner

Things that float in air!

Similar to water, an object floats in air when it is less heavy than air, causing enough displacement of air to make room for it's surface, and maintains buoyancy. Paper, kites, gas-filled balloons, hot air balloons, dust, birds, flies, airplanes, satellites, soap bubbles, feathers, dried leaves will all float in air.

- **Transparency:** Materials can be classified into three groups depending on the amount of light that can pass through them-transparent, opaque, and translucent.

  Material such as air, water and clear glass are called transparent (Fig. 5.6(a). They allow light to pass through and as a result, you can see clearly through them. The property of a material through which one can see clearly is called transparency.

  Materials that do not allow light to pass through them and block the light are called opaque (Fig. 5.6(c)). Wood, stone, and metal are some examples of opaque materials. When light is blocked by an object, a shadow is formed. The shadow appears on the side of the object away from the light source.

Keystone

Can animals be transparent?

Yes, some animals are transparent, so predators cannot see them easily. An example of a transparent animal is the jellyfish.

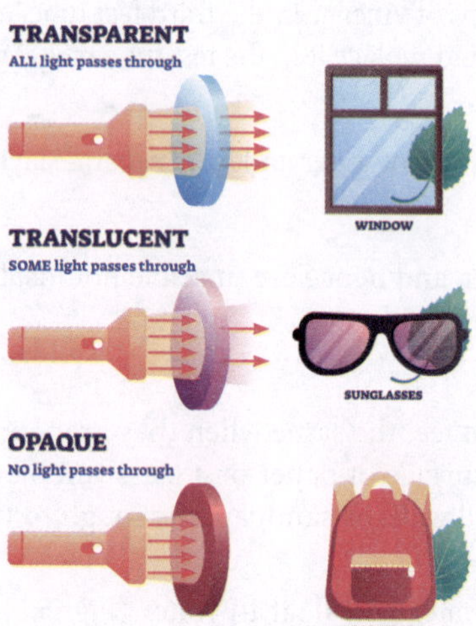

(a) Transparent, (c) Translucent, (b) Opaque

Figure 5.6 Transparency

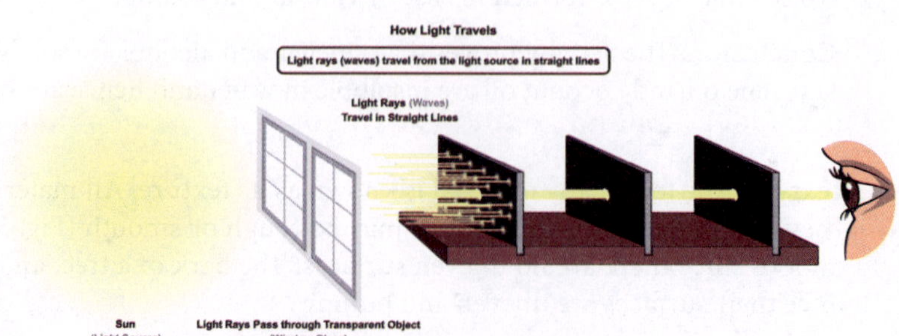

Figure 5.7 Light Can Pass Through

Translucent materials allow only some part of light to pass through (Fig. 5.6(b)). We can see through these materials but not clearly. E.g., oiled paper, ground glass, etc.

❖ INTEXT QUESTION

4. What is common between salt and sand?
   Solution: Both have mass and are in solid state.

Keystone

- Diamond is a naturally occurring substance.
- Diamond is a very good conductor of heat.
- Diamond is a very bad conductor of electricity.

Check Point 2

6. Write any four properties of materials.
7. Is a substance which can be compressed-soft or hard?
8. What are the similarities between iron, copper, and aluminium?
9. Why is water important for our body?
10. Explain the following terms:
    (i) Transparent
    (ii) Opaque
    (iii) Translucent

❖ INTEXT QUESTIONS

5. List three liquids that are transparent.
   Solution: Water, alcohol, and acetone/benzene.
6. List two substances made from leather.
   Solution: Belt and shoes.
7. Name some substances which are made from plastics.
   Solution: Toys, plates, cups, buckets, and baskets.
8. Which is harder, sponge or iron?
   Solution: Iron is harder than sponge.
9. Name two gases which are soluble in water.
   Solution: Oxygen, and carbon dioxide.
10. Name two gases that are insoluble in water.
    Solution: Hydrogen and nitrogen.

STRUCTURAL OUTLINE

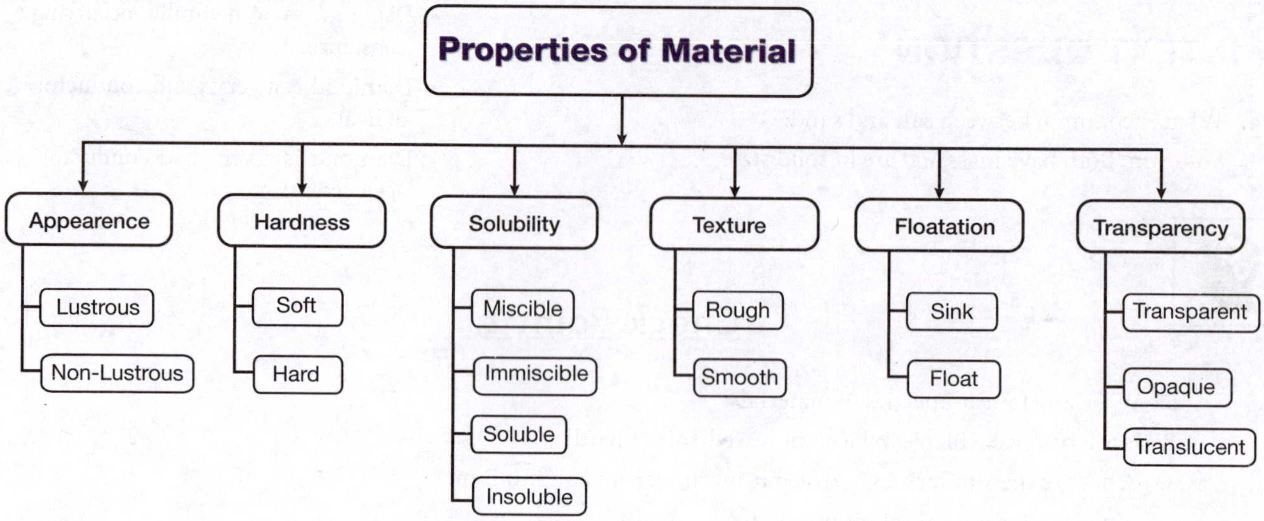

ABRIDGEMENT

- **Attraction towards a magnet:** Materials that are attracted to a magnet are called magnetic materials. This property is called magnetism. Objects made of iron are attracted to a magnet. In addition to iron, nickel and cobalt are also magnetic materials.
- **Conduction of heat:** If you observe the utensils kept in your kitchen, you will notice that though most of them are made of metals, their handles are made of plastic or wood. Why aren't the handles made of metal as well? This is because metals get heated whereas materials such as plastic and wood do not. It would be difficult to handle metal utensil after cooking if the handles were made of metal.

  Materials that allow heat to flow through them are called good conductors of heat whereas those that do not allow heat to flow through them are called bad conductors of heat.

  Generally, metals are good conductors of heat whereas non-metals such as wood, plastic, glass, bamboo, air, and paper are bad conductors of heat.
- **Conduction of electricity:** We get electricity in our homes through cables and wires. An electric cable consists of a number of metals with or without a plastic covering as shown in the figure below. The substances that conduct electricity are called good conductors of electricity or conductors whereas substances that do not conduct electricity are called bad conductors of electricity or insulators.

  For example, metals are good conductors of electricity. Wood, air, and plastic are insulators.

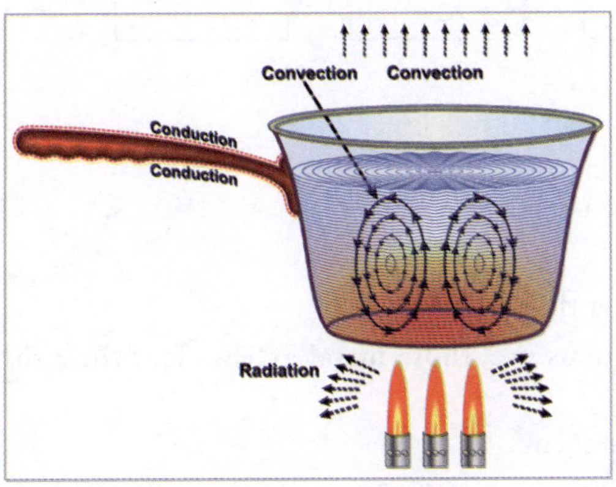

Conduction of Heat

Conduction of Electricity

EXEMPLIFICATION

1. **Why is water called a universal solvent?**

   Solution: Water dissolves a large number of substances in it. Therefore, it is called a universal solvent.
2. **Kerosene, coconut oil, and mustard oil do not dissolve in water even on shaking. They separate after sometime forming two different layers. Explain why.**

   Solution: The molecules of water do not intermingle (mix) with the molecules of oil. The space between the molecules of water is not taken by oil, so they are immiscible in water.
3. **Name a non-metal that has lustre.**

   Solution: Iodine.
4. **Metals generally occur in a solid state and are hard. Name a metal that exists in a liquid state and a metal that is soft and can be cut with a knife.**

   Solution: Mercury is a metal that exists in a liquid state. Sodium and Potassium are soft metals and can be cut with knife.
5. **Name the naturally occurring hardest substance known.**

   Solution: Diamond, it is made up of carbon (non-metal).

6. **Prateek was given a list of some materials—wood, sugar, lemon juice, sand, clay and salt. Name the materials which are water insoluble.**

   Solution: Wood, sand, and clay are water insoluble materials.

7. **What are the properties of material that would be important for their usage?**

   Solution: Appearance, solubility, texture, etc., are the properties of material that would be important for their usage.

8. **Identify objects P to S from the following flow chart.**

   Solution: A is foam, B is rubber ball, C is steel cup, and D is wood.

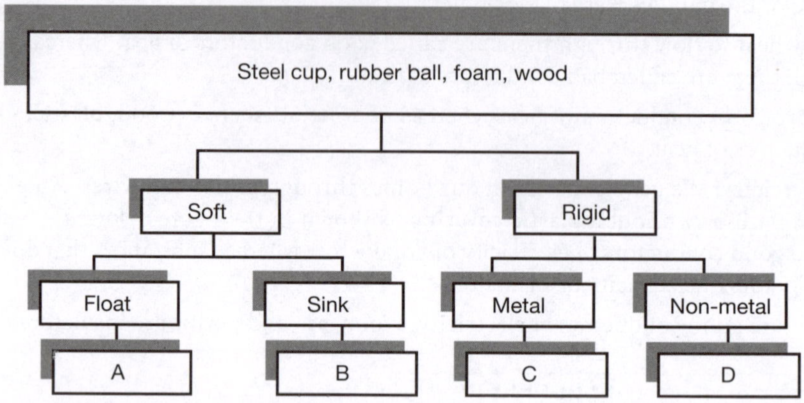

9. **Give any two differences between metals and non-metals?**

   Solution: (i) Metals are lustrous while non-metals are non-lustrous.
   (ii) Metals are rigid while non-metals are non-rigid.

10. **What happens when an iron ball put in water?**

    Solution: The iron ball will sink because iron is heavier than water.

11. **Shweta is having some metal articles. After continuous use, those metal articles lose their shine and appear dull. Why?**

    Solution: Because of the action of air and moisture on them.

12. **Eva spilled some oil in a water bucket. What will be her observation?**

    Solution: She observed that oil floats on water because oil is less dense from water.

13. **What are miscible and immiscible liquids?**

    Solution: When two liquids dissolve in one another such as water and milk, they are known as miscible liquids. Liquids such as mustard oil and kerosene do not dissolve in water but form separate layers. Such liquids are known as immiscible liquids.

NCERT COMPENDIUM

1. Visit your kitchen and observe how your parents have organised various edibles. Can you suggest a better sorting method? Write it in your notebook.
Solution: Pulses such as moong dal, chana dal, urad dal, arhar dal, etc., should be grouped together. Cereals such as rice, dalia, wheat flour, maize flour, etc., should be grouped together.
Spices such as red chilli powder, salt, clove, black pepper, ajwain, cumin (jeera), coriander seeds (dhaniya), turmeric powder, garam masala etc., should be grouped together. Cooking oils and ghee such as mustard oil, soyabean oil, olive oil, cow ghee, etc., should be grouped together.Jams and squashes should be placed together.

2. Unscramble the letters (Column I) and match with their properties (Column II).

Column I	Column II
(i) Tremat	(a) object can be seen clearly through it
(ii) Ulsbelo	(b) occupies the space and has mass
(iii) Tnerpasnart	(c) shiny surface
(iv) Erustl	(d) mixes completely in water

Solution:

Column I	Column II
(i) Matter	(b) occupies the space and has mass
(ii) Soluble	(d) mixes completely in water
(iii) Transparent	(a) object can be seen clearly through it
(iv) Lustre	(c) shiny surface

3. The containers which are used to store materials in shops and at home are usually transparent. Give your reasons for this.
Solution: The containers which are used to store materials in shops and at home are usually transparent so that the materials stored in them can be seen through them and can be found easily.

4. State whether the statements given below are True [T] or False [F], Correct the False statements).
(i) Wood is translucent while glass is opaque.
(ii) Aluminium foil has lustre while an eraser does not.
(iii) Sugar dissolves in water whereas sawdust does not.
(iv) An apple is a matter because it occupies no space and has mass.
Solution: (i) False, Wood is opaque while glass is transparent.
(ii) True
(iii) True
(iv) False, An apple is a matter because it occupies space and has mass.

5. We see chairs made up of various materials, such as wood, iron, plastic, bamboo, cement and stones. Following are some desirable properties of materials which can be used to make chairs. Which materials used to make chairs fulfill these properties the most?
(i) Hardness (does not bend or shake on sitting even after long use).
(ii) Lightweight (easy to lift or to take from one place to another).
(iii) Does not feel very cold when sitting during winters.
(iv) Can be cleaned regularly and made to look new even after long use.
Solution: (i) Iron, cement and stones
(ii) Plastic and bamboo
(iii) Wood and bamboo
(iv) Plastic, iron, cement and stones

6. You need to have containers for collection of (i) food waste, (ii) broken glass and (iii) wastepaper. Which materials will you choose for containers of these types of waste? What properties of materials do you need to think of?
Solution: We can use plastic containers for collection of (i) food waste (ii) broken glass and (iii) waste paper. These containers may have different colours because food waste is biodegradable, broken glass is hazardous and waste paper is recyclable. In case of food waste, the material of the container should not react with food and should be leak proof. For broken glass the material of the container should be hard so that glass should not cut it. For storing waste paper the material of the container should be light and strong.

7. Air is all around us but does not hinder us from seeing each other. Whereas, if a wooden door comes in between, we cannot see each other. It is because air is ________ and ________ the wooden door is ______
Choose the most appropriate option:
(i) transparent, opaque
(ii) translucent, transparent
(iii) opaque, translucent
(iv) transparent, translucent
Solution: (i) transparent, opaque

8. Imagine you have two mysterious materials, X and Y. When you try to press material X, it feels rigid and does not change its shape easily. On the other hand, material Y easily changes its shape when you press it. Now, when you mix both materials in water, only material X dissolves completely, while material Y remains unchanged. What can materials X and Y be? Can you identify whether material X is hard or soft? What about material Y? Justify your answer.

Solution: X can be sugar crystal and Y can be rubber block.

The material X is hard.

The material Y is soft.

9. (i) Who am I? Identify me on the basis of the given properties.

(a) I have luster.
(b) I can be easily compressed.
(c) I am hard and soluble in water.
(d) You cannot see clearly through me.
(e) I have mass and volume, but you cannot see me.

(ii) Make your own Who am I?'

Solution: (i) (a) steel
(b) rubber
(c) sugar
(d) cardboard or plywood
(e) air

(ii) (a) You can see clearly through me
(b) I am soft
(c) I am non-lustrous
(d) I am liquid and insoluble in water
(e) I cannot be compressed easily.

10. You are provided with the following materials—vinegar, honey, mustard oil, water, glucose and wheat flour.

Make any two pairs of materials where one material is soluble in the other. Now, make two pairs of materials where one material remains insoluble in the other material.

Solution: Soluble pairs

(i) Water and glucose
(ii) Water and vinegar

Insoluble pairs

(i) Water and mustard oil
(ii) Water and wheat flour

ASSESSMENT CORNER

LEVEL 1

Fixed Response Type

Multiple Choice Questions

1. Which of the following materials are made up of iron.
(A) Bags, utensils, cars
(B) Chairs, buses, spoons, cars
(C) Umbrella, chair
(D) All of them

2. Which of the following does not belong to the group:
(A) Ink (B) Milk
(C) Honey (D) Oil

3. Sorting of materials is useful as:
(A) it makes studying convenient.
(B) any pattern in their properties can be observed.
(C) properties of a substance can be predicted.
(D) All of these.

4. The property that we use for classifying things depends on the _______ of the classification
(A) grouping (B) purpose
(C) information (D) system

5. Which of the following group of materials have lustrous property?
(A) Iron, gold, Copper
(B) Diamond, gold, silver
(C) Wood, water, honey
(D) Glass, oil, honey

6. Metals can be identified as:
(A) Hard (B) Lustrous
(C) Sonorous (D) All of above

7. A substance is called hard when:
(A) it is easy to scratch and compress.
(B) it is difficult to scratch and compress.
(C) it is shiny and opaque.
(D) it is insoluble in water.

8. Which one of the following liquids is immiscible with water?
(A) Kerosene (B) Vinegar
(C) Glycerine (D) Lemon juice

9. Which of the following is insoluble in water?
(A) Sugar (B) Salt
(C) Kerosene (D) Oxygen

10. Objects which sink in water are:
(A) insoluble and heavier than water
(B) insoluble and lighter than water
(C) soluble and lighter than water
(D) soluble and heavier than water

11. ____ sinks in the water, while _____ floats on the water.
(A) Oil, mercury (B) Oil, petroleum
(C) Mercury, oil (D) Mercury, alcohol

12. When petroleum is mixed with water, it will:
(A) Float (B) Sink
(C) Explode (D) Dissolve

13. Which of the following allow(s) light to pass through it?
(A) Transparent (B) Translucent
(C) Both A and B (D) Opaque

14. Door locks are made of metals because metals:
(A) have lustre.
(B) are hard and strong.
(C) are good conductors of heat.
(D) are opaque.

15. Which of the following objects are not opaque?
(A) Ground glass, water
(B) Brick, iron block
(C) Book, air
(D) Wood,water

16. Which of the following is edible?
(A) Spinach (B) Iron block
(C) Plastic toy (D) Glass

17. Which of the following have different appearance than other ?
(A) Cricket bat (B) Wooden table
(C) Wooden chair (D) Gold

18. Which of the following objects settle down in water?
(A) Ground glass (B) Brick
(C) Book (D) Wood

19. Which of the following object is translucent
(A) Frosted glass (B) Tissue
(C) Butter paper (D) All of them

20. Materials that are attracted to a magnet are called magnetic materials. This property is called magnetism. Objects made of ________ are attracted to a magnet.

(A) Ground glass (B) Sand
(C) Iron (D) Clay

21. Materials that allow heat to flow through them are called:
(A) Bad conductor (B) Good conductor
(C) Semi-conductor (D) Insulator

22. Liquids that do not dissolve or mix with one another are called:
(A) Immiscible liquids (B) Miscible liquids
(C) Both (A)and (B) (D) None of these

23. Which of the following can mix well into water?
(A) Kerosene (B) Vinegar
(C) Coconut oil (D) Mustard oil

24. Which of the following material can be compressed with hands?
(A) Aluminium piece (B) Cotton
(C) Sponge (D) Both (B) and (C)

25. Which of the following object is made up of paper and wood both?
(A) Hammer (B) Rubber
(C) Matchbox (D) Duster

26. What is the similarity between oil and water ?
(A) Both are opaque (B) Both are lustrous
(C) Both float in air (D) Both are liquids

27. Aryan cut a material into two pieces and looked at the freshly cut surface, he noticed that the cut surface appears shiny. The material would be:
(A) Gold (B) Iron
(C) Copper (D) All of these

28. Which of the following is the property of soft material?
(A) Hard to compress
(B) Difficult to mould
(C) Easy to compress
(D) Both (A) and (B)

29. Take two beakers A and B and fill both beakers with 50 ml of water, then add sugar in beaker A and sand into beaker B. Stir well. Which of the following is the correct observation?
(A) Sugar particles settle down at the bottom in beaker A.
(B) Sand particles settle down at the bottom in beaker B.
(C) Sugar disappear in beaker A.
(D) Both (B) and (C).

30. Which of the following materials have smooth texture?
(A) An unfinished wall (B) Bark of a tree
(C) Glass tumbler (D) Sandpaper

Fill in the Blanks

1. The object must be _________or ______ to make a shadow.
2. Materials can be classified as _________ and _____ on the basis of their texture.
3. Liquids which are soluble in one another are called _________ liquids.
4. Substances which are less ________ than water can float on water.
5. ___________ have no definite shape or volume.
6. Material through which objects can be seen, but not clearly, are known as ___________ .
7. Water is a ________ solvent.
8. Some metals often lose their shine and appear dull, because of the action of ___________ and ___________on them.
9. The physical appearance and feel of any material is called ___________.
10. Substances that cannot be dissolved in a liquid are called ___________.
11. When sand and water are mixed with each other, sand particles are ______ dense from water.
12. Plastic and wood are _________ conductor of heat.
13. Gold and silver are _________ conductor of heat.
14. Out of—cotton, sponge, wood, iron and block , ________ is non compressible.
15. Material that are attracted to a magnet are called as magnetic material. This property is called as ________.

True/False

1. Butter paper is transparent while glass is opaque.
2. A notebook has lustre, an eraser does not.
3. When light is blocked by an object, a shadow is formed.
4. A piece of wood floats on water.
5. Oil mixes with water.
6. Sand settles down in the water.
7. Vinegar dissolves in water
8. Silk is obtained from the fleece of sheep or hairy animals.

ASSESSMENT CORNER

9. Materials which can be compressed or scratched easily are called soft materials while some other materials which are difficult to compress are called hard materials.
10. Substances that can be dissolved in a liquid are called soluble substances.
11. Grouping is done in a supermarket by keeping similar items on the same shelf, which makes it easier for us to find the items we need.
12. Classification makes it difficult to study the characteristics of materials and work becomes more systematic.
13. When Sand particles are added to milk, they never settle down at the bottom.
14. Cotton and sponge are non-compressible while wood and iron block are compressible.
15. Orange juice and lemon juice, both are soluble in oil.

Match Type Questions

1.

Column-A		Column-B
1. Soluble	(a)	All metals
2. Lustrous	(b)	Brick
3. Translucent	(c)	Common salt
4. Float	(d)	Frost glass
5. Sink	(e)	Ice cubes

2.

Column-A		Column-B
1. Surgical instruments	(a)	Plastic
2. Newspaper	(b)	Animal product
3. Electrical switches	(c)	Steel
4. Wool	(d)	Plant product

3.

Column A		Column B
1. Stone	(a)	Water soluble
2. Kerosene	(b)	Non compressible
3. Lemon juice	(c)	Compressible
4. Sponge	(d)	Water insoluble

4.

Column-A		Column-B
1. Oiled paper	(a)	Lustrous
2. Aluminium	(b)	Transparent
3. Glass tumbler	(c)	Leather
4. Shoes	(d)	Translucent

5.

Column-A		Column-B
1. Unfinished wall	(a)	Smooth
2. Glass tumbler	(b)	Conductor
3. Plastic	(c)	Rough
4. Metal	(d)	Insulator

6.

Column-A		Column-B
1. Gas	(a)	Sandpaper
2. Rough	(b)	Vinegar
3. Miscible with water	(c)	Nitrogen
4. Lustrous	(d)	Jewellery

7.

Column-A		Column-B
1. Cup	(a)	Iron
2. Table	(b)	Plastic
3. Shirt	(c)	Ceramic
4. Pen	(d)	Cotton

8.

Column-A		Column-B
1. Wooden block	(a)	Good conductor of heat
2. Rocks	(b)	Attracted to magnet
3. Cobalt	(c)	Sink in water
4. Metal utensils	(d)	Float on water

9.

Column-A		Column-B
1. Bucket	(a)	Metal
2. Knife	(b)	Hard
3. Diamond	(c)	Soft
4. Cotton	(d)	Plastic

10.

Column-A		Column-B
1. Substance has a shiny appearance	(a)	Lustrous
2. Substance disappears in water	(b)	Soft
3. Materials which can be compressed	(c)	Soluble substance
4. Liquids that dissolve in one another	(d)	Miscible liquids.

Assertion and Reason Type Questions

Direction: In the following questions, a statement of assertion is followed by statement of reason.

Make the correct choice as:

(A) Both Assertion and Reason are true, and Reason is the correct explanation of Assertion.

(B) Both Assertion and Reason are true, but Reason is not the correct explanation of Assertion.

(C) Assertion is true, but Reason is false.

(D) Both Assertion and Reason are false.

1. **Assertion:** Handles of cooking utensils are made of wood, plastic.
Reason: Metals are bad conductors of heat.

2. **Assertion:** Oil layer floats on water.
Reason: Oil and water are immiscible liquids.

3. **Assertion:** Cotton and sponge are soft materials.
Reason: Cotton and sponge are difficult to compress.

4. **Assertion:** Oil and water can be mixed easily.
Reason: Oil and water are miscible liquids.

5. **Assertion:** Sand settles down in water.
Reason: Sand is heavier than water.

6. **Assertion:** A hot air balloon floats in air.
Reason: Objects floats in air when it is less heavy than air.

7. **Assertion:** All materials can be placed in groups according to similarities in their properties.
Reason: Classification makes it easier to study the characteristics of materials and work becomes systematic.

8. **Assertion:** Materials which can be compressed or scratched easily are called soft materials.
Reason: Cotton is a soft material.

9. **Assertion:** Materials can be separated on the basis of their texture.
Reason: The physical appearance and feel of any material is called texture.

10. **Assertion:** Grouping of objects helps the shopkeeper.
Reason: He can locate the required object easily and quickly.

11. **Assertion:** When a metal rod is heated from one end, after some time you will feel hotness at the other end.
Reason: Metals are good conductors of electricity.

12. **Assertion:** When a metal rod is heated from one end, after some time you will feel hotness at the other end.
Reason: Metals are good conductors of electricity.

13. **Assertion:** Paper, kites, gas-filled balloons, hot air balloons, dust, birds, flies, airplanes, satellites, soap bubbles, feathers, and dried leaves will all float in the air.
Reason: Object floats in the air when they lighter than air.

14. **Assertion:** Chalk powder is insoluble in water.
Reason: Different substances have different solubility.

15. **Assertion:** Sugar and salt are soluble in water.
Reason: Water soluble substances floats into water.

Comprehension Based Questions

Transparency: Materials can be classified into three groups depending on the amount of light that can pass through them—transparent, opaque, and translucent.
Material such as air, water, and clear glass are called transparent. They allow light to pass through and as a result, you can see clearly through them. The property of a material through which one can see clearly is called transparency.
Materials that do not allow light to pass through them and block the light are called opaque. Wood, stone, and metal are some examples of opaque materials. When light is blocked by an object, a shadow is formed. The shadow appears on the side of the object that is away from the light source.
Translucent materials allow only some part of light to pass through. We can see through these materials but not clearly. E.g., oiled paper, ground glass, etc.

1. On what basis can materials be classified into three groups—transparent, opaque, and translucent?
(A) On the basis of texture.
(B) Conduction of heat.
(C) On the basis of light.
(D) On the basis of compressibility.

2. Opaque materials:
(A) block the light.
(B) do not form shadows.
(C) pass the light.
(D) shadow appears on the object itself.

3. Oiled paper and ground glass are examples of:
(A) opaque materials.
(B) transparent materials.
(C) both, transparent and translucent materials.
(D) translucent materials.

Free Response Type

Very Short Answer Type Questions

1. Why do we need to group materials?
2. Group these materials as eatables and non-eatables—water, apple, wood, sugar, balls, and pen.
3. Why is gold used in making ornaments?
4. If a material 'A' scratches material 'B', which is harder?
5. Mention any two materials having smooth or even surface.
6. Name any two liquids that are miscible with each other.
7. Compare the floating properties of oil and water.
8. Give an example each, an opaque and a transparent material.
9. Is a substance which can be compressed soft or hard?
10. Select a lustrous material out of the following substances:

    Wood, paper, aluminium foil, grass, iron nail, plastic jar.
11. Which material is generally used for making pens?

    Wood, aluminium, plastic, cotton
12. Is oil is miscible with water?
13. Can animal be transparent?

Short Answer Type Questions

1. Define classification? Give three examples from everyday life.
2. What are the benefits of classification?
3. When do we say that two liquids are immiscible? Explain taking a suitable example.
4. Differentiate between:
   (a) Miscible and immiscible substances.
   (b) Transparent and translucent substances.
   (c) Hard and soft materials.
5. Write any four properties of materials.
6. Why is a tumbler not made with a piece of cloth?
7. What is the similarities between jellyfish and glass tumbler?
8. Mention some materials which are made of paper.
9. Why is water important for our body?
10. What is the basis for sorting materials?
11. What is the important role of grouping materials in shopping mall?
12. Make a table of objects and the materials they are made of:

Objects	Materials They are Made Of
Plate (*thali*)	
Pen	
Bucket	
Knife	

13. Make a table of different types of objects that are made from the same material.

S. No.	Material	Objects Made of These Materials
1.	Wood	
2.	Paper	
3.	Leather	
4.	Plastics	
5.	Cotton	
6.	Iron	

14. Make a table and find out whether the following materials mix with water: Vinegar, lemon juice, mustard oil, coconut oil, and kerosene.

S. No.	Liquid	Mixes Well/Does Not Mix
1.	Vinegar	
2.	Lemon juice	
3.	Mustard oil	
4.	Coconut oil	
5.	Kerosene	

15. Metals have lustre (shine). Give reasons why some metal articles become dull and lose their lustre.

Long Answer Type Questions

1. Why is a sponge labelled as a soft material?
2. Define floatation. Give five examples of objects that float on water.
3. Mention three properties of the following substances: honey, ice, and iron nail.
4. 'Grouping of objects helps the shopkeeper.' Justify the statement.
5. Describe an experiment to prove that water is transparent.

6. Write an experiment to show that our palm is translucent.
7. How can you show that some solids like sugar and salt are soluble in water whereas solids like chalk powder and sand are not soluble in water?
8. Sugar, salt, mustard oil, sand, sawdust, honey, chalk powder, flower petals, soil, copper sulphate crystals, glucose, wheat flour are some substances given to Paheli. She wants to know whether these substances are soluble in water or not. Help her identify the soluble and insoluble substances in water.
9. Differentiate among opaque, translucent, and transparent materials, giving one example of each.
10. Define the role of oxygen dissolved in water for the survival of aquatic animals and plants?

Numerical Based Question

1. List of Some materials, along with some codes are given to Sudha. She has to calculate the sum of all the codes of materials which are bad conductors of heat.

Material	Code
Bamboo	1
Iron rod	2
Copper wire	3
Air	4
Water	5
Wood	6

Which of the following will be the correct answer given by Sudha?
(A) 16 (B) 11
(C) 7 (D) 10

2. Amrita picked up the wooden scale, glass test tube, oiled paper, and iron block. Out of these materials how many are opaque in nature?
(A) 1 (B) 2
(C) 3 (D) 4

Case Based Questions

If you observe the utensils kept in your kitchen, you will notice that though most of them are made of metals, their handles are made of plastic or wood. Why aren't the handles made of metal as well? This is because metals get heated whereas materials such as plastic and wood do not. It would be difficult to handle metal utensils after cooking if the handles were made of metal.

Materials that allow heat to flow through them are called good conductors of heat whereas those that do not allow heat to flow through them are called bad conductors of heat.

Generally, metals are good conductors of heat whereas non-metals such as wood, plastic, glass, bamboo, air, and paper are bad conductors of heat.

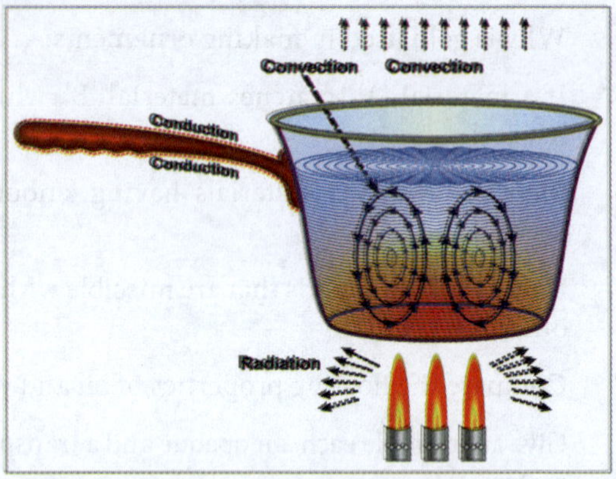

1. What is the characteristic of a good conductor?
(A) Does not allow heat to flow.
(B) Does not allow electricity to flow.
(C) Allows heat to flow.
(D) Both (A) and (B).
2. Which of the following set are bad conductors of heat?
(A) Wood, iron rod, and plastic.
(B) Bamboo, air, and glass.
(C) Aluminium, air, and paper.
(D) Cotton, wood, and metals.
3. Which of the following statements is true?
(A) Metals are good conductors of heat.
(B) Non-metals are bad conductors of heat.
(C) Materials that allow heat to flow through them are called good conductors of heat.
(D) All of these.
4. Air is a/an:
(A) good conductor of heat.
(B) bad conductor of heat.
(C) sometimes good, sometimes bad conductor of electricity.
(D) insulator.
5. Water is a:
(A) good conductor of heat.
(B) bad conductor of heat.
(C) sometimes good, sometimes bad conductor of electricity.
(D) semi-conductor.

ASSESSMENT CORNER

Level 2

Multiple Choice Questions

1. A needle and knife belong to the same group because:
(A) they are transparent.
(B) they are poor conductors of heat.
(C) they float on water.
(D) they are hard and magnetic.

2. Which of the following statements is not correct?
(A) A soft material can be scratched easily.
(B) A soluble material disappears in water.
(C) Oil mixes with water
(D) We should use transparent bottles in kitchens.

3. Milk and water are:
(A) Immiscible liquids
(B) Solvent ans solution
(C) Solute and solution
(D) Miscible liquids

4. Clay is used for making pots and bricks because it is:
(A) Opaque
(B) Non-magnetic
(C) Easily moulded into different shapes
(D) Good conductors of heat

5. What are the characteristics of metals?
(A) Good conductors of electricity and heat; solid at room temperature; transparent, shine brightly when polished.
(B) Good conductors of electricity and heat; solid at room temperature; opaque, except in extremely thin films; do not shine at all when polished.
(C) Bad conductors of electricity and heat; solid at room temperature; opaque, except in extremely thin films.
(D) Good conductors of electricity and heat; solid at room temperature; opaque, except in extremely thin films; shine brightly when polished.

6. Metals lose their shine due to the action of:
(A) Other metals
(B) Water
(C) Air
(D) Both (B) and (C)

7. Wood is different article in-
from a metal
(A) Transparency and lustre
(B) Hardness and solubility
(C) Smoothness and solubility
(D) Hardness and lustre

8. We can see objects through transparent substances because:
(A) transparent substances are hollow.
(B) transparent substances are lustrous.
(C) transparent substances allow light to pass.
(D) transparent substances are colourless.

9. Lokesh took a glass beaker and filled it with clean water. She put a silver coin in it and looked the coin from the top of the beaker. What would be her observation?

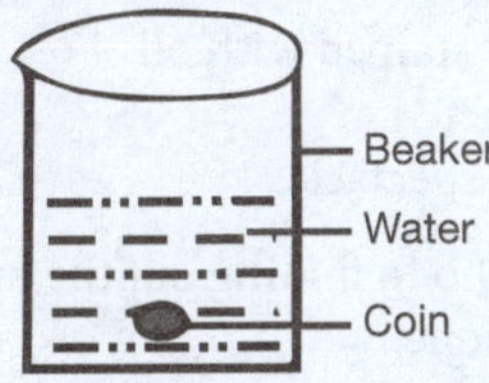

(A) She could not see the coin properly because water is translucent.
(B) She could see the coin clearly because water is opaque.
(C) She could see the coin clearly because water is transparent.
(D) She could not see the coin clearly because the coin is transparent.

10. We should choose a material to make an object depending on its properties and the purpose for which the object is to be used. Based on this knowledge, Ankita made a few choices. Select the incorrect choice made by her.
(A) A window pane made up of glass to look through.
(B) A pan made up of steel to cook food.
(C) A bucket made up of plastic to fill water.
(D) A tumbler made up of cotton cloth to drink water.

11. Which of the following statements is not true:
(A) Materials are grouped for convenience.
(B) Materials are grouped for study their properties.
(C) Materials are grouped for fun.
(D) Materials are grouped for according to their use.

12. Which of the following will sink in water:
(A) A dry leaf (B) A bird feather
(C) A plastic scale (D) A metal key

13. You are provided with following materials:
(i) Magnifying glass
(ii) Mirror
(iii) Stainless steel
(iv) Glass tumbler

Which of the following materials will you identify as transparent:
(A) (i) and (ii) (B) (i) and (iii)
(C) (i) and (iv) (D) (iii) and (iv)

14. An iron nail is kept in each of the following liquids. In which case would it lose it's shine and appear dull?
(A) Mustard oil (B) Soft drink
(C) Coconut oil (D) Kerosene

15. Boojho found a bag containing the following materials.
(i) Mirror
(ii) Paper stained with oil
(iii) Magnet
(iv) Glass spectacles

Help Boojho in finding out the material(s) which is/ are opaque.
(A) (i) only (B) (iv) only
(C) (i) and (iii) (D) (ii) and (iv)

16. While doing an activity in class, the teacher asked Paheli to handover a translucent material. Which among the following materials will Paheli pick and give her teacher?
(A) Glass tumbler (B) Mirror
(C) Muslin cloth (D) Aluminium foil

17. Which pair of substances among the following would float in a tumbler half filled with water?
(A) Cotton thread, thermocol
(B) Feather, plastic ball
(C) Pin, oil drops
(D) Rubber band, coin

18. The bark of tree, an unfinished wall and sandpaper are:
(A) Rough (B) Uneven
(C) Bumpy (D) All of these

19. Kerosene and coconut oil are -
(A) miscible with water
(B) opaque
(C) non lustrous
(D) heavier than water

20. Which of the following is an incorrect reason for grouping materials?
(A) For convenience
(B) To study their properties
(C) For fun
(D) According to their uses

21. Vinegar and alcohol are:
(A) translucent
(B) opaque
(C) heavier than water
(D) miscible with water

22. Which of the following materials is used for making the front glass (wind screen) of a car?
(A) Transparent (B) Translucent
(C) Opaque (D) All the above

23. Which of the following is/are correct statements?
(i) Metals are good conductors of electricity.
(ii) Metals are good conductors of heat.
(iii) Plastics are good conductors of electricity.
(iv) Plastics are insulators.
Which of the following materials will you identify as transparent?
(A) (i) and (ii) (B) (i), (ii), and (iii)
(C) (i), (ii), and (iv) (D) (iii) and (iv)

24. Which of the following is/are correct statements?
(i) Metals are good conductors of electricity.
(ii) Metals are good conductors of heat.
(iii) Plastics are good conductors of electricity.
(iv) Plastics are insulators.
Which of the following materials will you identify as transparent?
(A) (i) and (ii) (B) (i), (ii), and (iii)
(C) (i), (ii), and (iv) (D) (iii) and (iv)

25. Good and glass are different in their
(A) transparency
(B) magnetic nature
(C) conductivity to heat
(D) lustrous nature

26. Some objects given below are grouped based on a certain property.
P: Wooden ruler, copper wire, and plastic cup.
Q: Iron rod and steel spoon
The objects are grouped based on their ability to:
(A) conduct electricity.
(B) conduct heat.
(C) get attracted by a magnet.
(D) reflect light.

27. Two liquids, M and N are poured into a container. Then put three different solids, J, K and L, into the container.

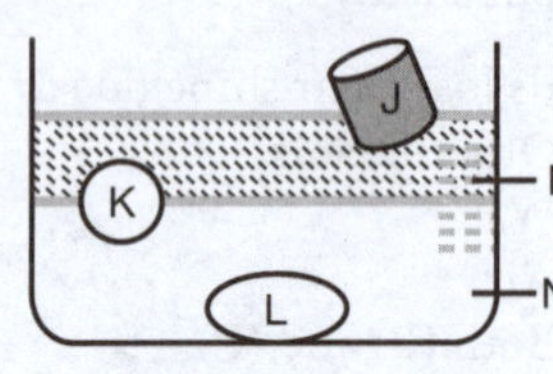

What do you conclude from the above activity?
(A) Solid J will float if it is put into a beaker filled with liquid N only.
(B) Solid K will sink if it is put into a beaker filled with liquid M only.
(C) Solid L has a lower density than solid K.
(D) Both (A) and (B)

28. An insoluble solid from a soluble solid can be separated by mixing the mixture with:
(A) Water, filter and evaporate the water from the resulting filtrate to obtain insoluble solid.
(B) Water, filter and evaporate the sand from the resulting solid.
(C) Oil, filter and evaporate the solid out.
(D) Both (B) and (C).

29. Which set of objects is not grouped correctly?
(A) Saucer, cup, and teapot.
(B) Gold, silver, and jewellery.
(C) Textbook, notebook, and writing pad.
(D) Bedsheet, blanket, and leather handbag.

30. Amrita picked up a wooden scale, glass test tube, and paper basket based on conductivity. Which article will she pick up next?
(A) Steel cup (B) Iron chain
(C) Rubber gloves (D) Copper wire

Higher Order Thinking Skills (HOTS)

1. Why is it difficult to hold a steel glass containing hot tea?

2. Which metal is the best conductor of electricity? Also name a non-metal that conducts electricity.

3. Why plastic or rubber coating is necessary on electrical wires?

4. Mixtures of red chilli powder in water, butter in water, petrol in water, and honey in water were given to Radha, Sudha, Sofia, and Raveena, respectively. Whose mixture is in solution form?

5. It was Paheli's birthday. Her grandmother gave her two gifts made of metal. One old dull silver spoon and a pair of lustrous gold earrings. She was surprised to see the difference in the appearance of the two metals. Can you explain the reason for this difference?

6. On a bright sunny day, Shikha was playing hide and seek with her brother. She hid herself behind a glass door. Do you think her brother will be able to locate her. If yes, why? If no, why not?

7. Take a small cotton ball and place it in a tumbler/bowl filled with water. Observe it for at least 10 minutes. Will it float or sink in water and why?

8. Which among the following materials would you identify as soft materials and why?
Ice, rubber band, leaf, eraser, pencil, pearl, a piece of wooden board, cooked rice, pulses, and fresh chapati.

9. You are provided with the following materials– turmeric, honey, mustard oil, water, glucose, rice flour, and groundnut oil. Make any three pairs of substances where one substance is soluble in the other and any three pairs of substances where one substance remains insoluble in the other substances.

10. Arrange the jumbled words to arrive at the appropriate names of materials and also write two uses of each.
(A) milaunuimn (B) tcaslpi
(C) soekrnee (D) gavnier

11. If you observe the utensils kept in your kitchen, you will notice that though most of them are made of metals, and their handles are made of plastic or wood. Why are not the handles made of metal as well?

12. Anamika take three objects made of iron, nickel and cobalt are kept near a magnet. What will be the observations?

13. What are the factors that affect the solubility of a substance?

14. A student was given a list of materials to classify based on transparency.
Coconut shell, paper plate, thermocol plate, naphthalene balls, computer screen, and glass bottle.
What is the correct list of opaque materials?

15. Compare the floating or sinking nature of cotton and jute fibre?

ARCHIVE CORNER

1. Smriti took four beakers containing equal amounts of water. She wanted to check the solubility of some solids like sugar, salt, chalk powder, and saw dust. She added the solids to each beaker, stirred the contents with stirrer and waited for some time. What did she observe?

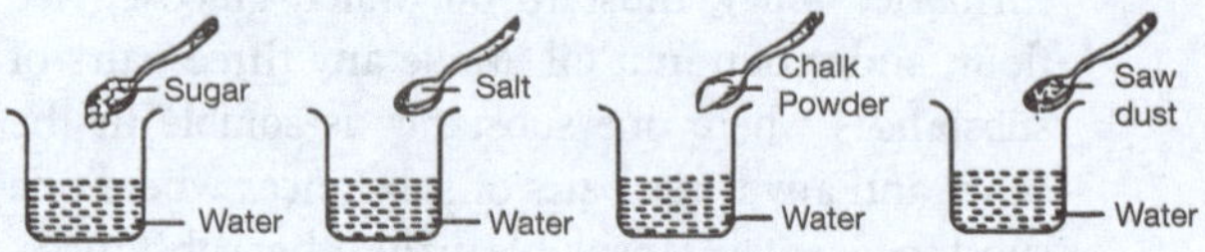

(A) Sugar and chalk powder are soluble in water while salt and saw dust are insoluble.
(B) Sugar, salt, and chalk powder are soluble in water while saw dust is insoluble.
(C) Sugar, salt, chalk powder, and saw dust are soluble in water.
(D) Sugar and salt are soluble in water, while chalk powder and saw dust are insoluble.

2. Identify X and Y in the given Venn diagram.

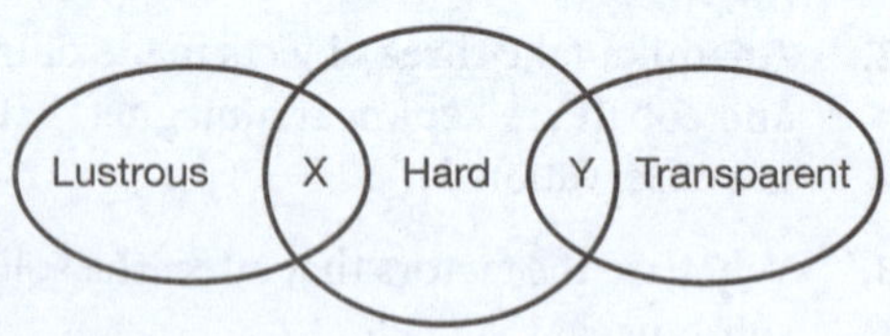

(A) X is wood (B) Y is glass
(C) X is iron (D) Both (B) and (C)

3. Sumant, Raman, and Neha mixed few liquids with water and recorded their observations in the following table:

× – Not mixed well
✓ – Mixed well

	Sumant	Raman	Neha
Vinegar	×	✓	✓
Orange juice	✓	✓	✓
Coconut oil	✓	×	×
Cold drink	✓	✓	✓
Kerosene	✓	×	✓

Which of them recorded all the observations correctly?
(A) Raman (B) Sumant
(C) Neha (D) None of them

4. Sunita classified various materials based on their properties. Which of the following sets are correctly matched?

Set	Hard	Opaque	Floats in Water	Insoluble in Water
I	Sponge	Butter paper	Glass marble	Honey
II	Steel	Wooden board	Ice	Mustard oil
III	Iron nail	Glass	Grass	Sugar candy
IV	Lump of sugar	Thermocol	Hair	Glass powder

(A) II and IV (B) I and II
(C) III and IV (D) All of these

5. Shreya made a cup of hot tea and put a metal spoon in the cup so that the tea would cool down faster.

Which of the following statements best describes the cooling of tea faster?
(A) The metal spoon absorbs the coldness from the surroundings and transfers the coldness to the hot tea.
(B) The metal spoon absorbs heat from the hot tea and transfers the heat to the surrounding.
(C) The metal spoon absorbs heat from the cup and transfers the heat to the surroundings.
(D) None of these.

6. Study the given flowchart carefully and fill in the blanks:

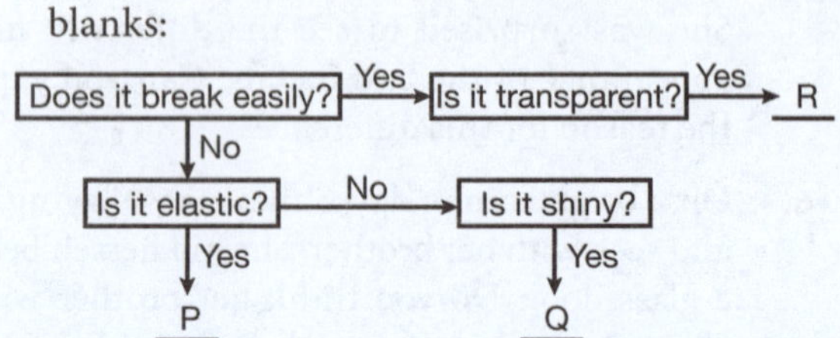

	P	Q	R
(A)	Rubber band	Steel	Electric bulb
(B)	Electric bulb	Rubber band	Steel
(C)	Electric bulb	Steel	Rubber band
(D)	Steel	Electric bulb	Rubber band

7. Complete the following statements by selecting the appropriate option:
(1) A cotton ball initially (i) and then (ii) as is absorbs water
(2) Groundnut oil is (iii) in water while sugar is (iv) in milk.
(3) Hand lens is (v) whereas oiled paper is (vi)

	(i)	(ii)	(iii)	(iv)	(v)	(vi)
(A)	Floats	Sinks	Insoluble	Soluble	Trans-lucent	Trans-parent
(B)	Floats	Sinks	Soluble	Insoluble	Trans-parent	Trans-lucent
(C)	Floats	Sinks	Insoluble	Soluble	Trans-parent	Trans-lucent
(D)	Sinks	Floats	Soluble	Insoluble	Trans-parent	Trans-lucent

8. Study the given flowchart carefully.

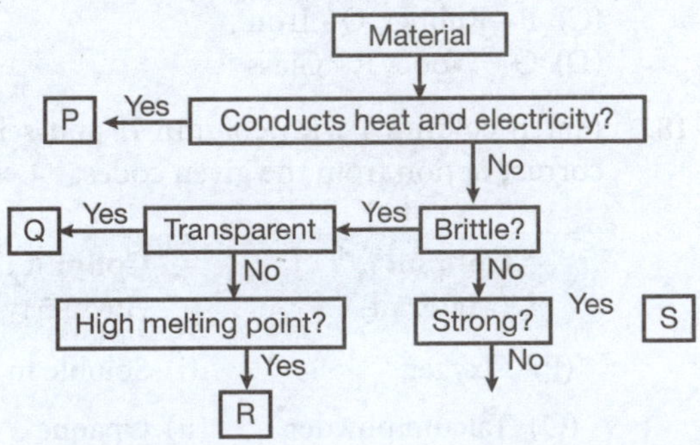

Identify the four groups of materials P, Q, R and S.
(A) P-Metals, Q-Ceramics, R-Plastic, S-Glass
(B) P-Ceramics, Q-Glass, R-Metals, S-Plastic
(C) P-Plastics, Q-Metals, R-Glass, S-Ceramics
(D) P-Metals, Q-Glass, R-Ceramics, S-Plastics

9. Which of the following affects the solubility of a substance?
(I) Type of solvent
(II) Temperature
(III) Size of the particles
(A) I and II (B) I and III
(C) II and III (D) I and III

10. Sumit performed the scratch test with three types of minerals X, Y, and Z. The results are shown here.

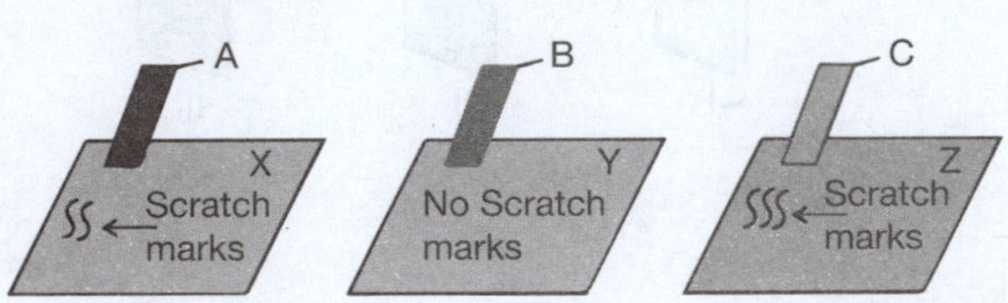

Select the option that correctly arranges these minerals in ascending order of hardness.
(A) X < Y < Z (B) Z < Y < X
(C) Z < X < Y (D) Y < Z < X

11. Rashmi, a class 6 teacher listed the given materials on the board and asked students to classify them based on transparency.
(I) Window glass (II) Oily paper
(III) Metal sheet (IV) Thin muslin cloth
(V) Concrete wall
Which of the following represents the correct classification?
(A) I, IV-transparent; II-translucent; III, V-opaque
(B) I, II-translucent; III-opaque; IV, V-transparent
(C) I-transparent; II, IV-translucent; III, V-opaque
(D) V-opaque; II, III-translucent; I, IV-transparent

12. Which of the following statements are incorrect?
I. Vinegar and lemon juice form a separate layer on water.
II. Freshly cut surfaces of metals are lustrous.
III. Oxygen gas is transparent while milk is opaque.
IV. Wax when mixed with water forms a solution.
(A) I and II only (B) I and IV only
(C) III and IV only (D) None of these

13. The given table shows the rank of three different minerals on the scale of hardness

Material	Rank of hardness
X	5
Y	3
Z	8

Based on the above data, which of the following results of scratch test will be obtained?

(A) 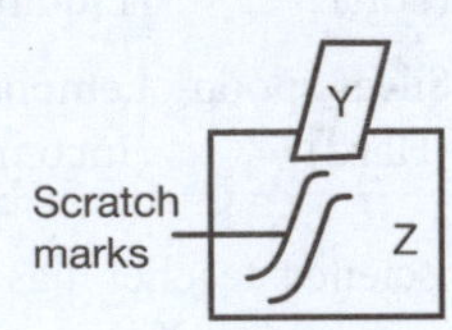

(B) 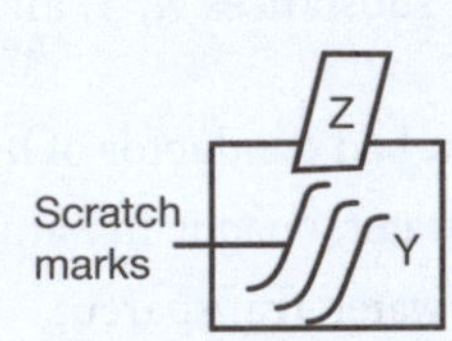

(C) 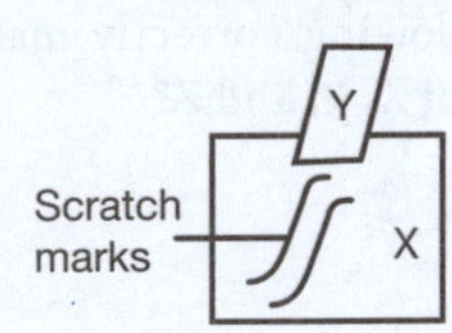

ARCHIVE CORNER

(D) 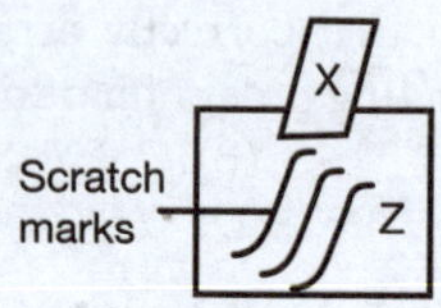

14. Match column I with column II and select the correct option from the given codes.

Column-I	Column-II
P. Air	(i) Insulator
Q. Aluminium	(ii) Transparent
R. Wood	(iii) Opaque
S. Milk	(iv) Magnetic
T. Iron	(v) Conductor

(A) P - (v), Q - (iii), R - (i), S - (ii), T - (iv)
(B) P - (iv), Q - (ii), R - (iii), S - (i), T - (v)
(C) P - (ii), Q - (v), R - (i), S - (iii), T - (iv)
(D) P - (i), Q - (iv), R - (v), S - (ii), T - (iii)

15. Various substances around us are grouped as follows:

Group I: Book, copper, aluminium, gold.

Group II: Cotton ball, silk cloth, sponge, silver spoon.

Group III: Paper, petrol, CNG, lemonade.

Identify the odd-one out in each group and its property which makes it odd.

	Group I	Group II	Group III
(A)	Aluminium (Non-lustrous)	Silver spoon (Hard)	Paper (Solid)
(B)	Book (Non-lustrous)	Silver spoon (Metallic)	CNG (Gas)
(C)	Gold (Noble-metal)	Cotton ball (Soft)	Lemonade (Liquid)
(D)	Book (Non-metallic)	Silver spoon (Hard)	Lemonade (Incombustible)

16. Ms Rashmita, a science teacher has written a few properties of substances X, Y, and Z on the blackboard as:

X: Floats on water, bad conductor of heat.

Y: Soft, floats on water, opaque in nature.

Z: Hard, sinks in water, transparent.

Which of the following correctly matches with the descriptions of X, Y, and Z?

	X	Y	Z
(A)	Cardboard	Rubber ball	Plastic mug
(B)	Steel spoon	Cork	Paper weight
(C)	Pen	Plastic bottle	Eraser
(D)	Plastic mug	Thermocol	Glass bowl

17. Study the given table:

Material	Water-proof	Conducts Electricity	Elastic
P	✓	×	✓
Q	✓	✓	×
R	✓	✓	✓

Select the option that correctly identifies any two of them.

(A) P - Rubber, R - Wood
(B) Q - Copper, R - Plastic
(C) P - Rubber, Q - Iron
(D) Q - Wood, R - Glass

18. Match column I with column II and select the correct option from the given codes.

Column I (Material)	Column II (Property)
(P) Oxygen	(i) Soluble in water
(Q) Talcum powder	(ii) Opaque
(R) Aluminium	(iii) Transparent
(S) Glass	(iv) Conductor
	(v) Malleable

(A) P- (i), (iii); Q - (ii), (v); R - (ii), (iv); S - (i), (iii)
(B) P - (i), (iii); Q - (ii); R - (ii), (iv), (v); S - (iii)
(C) P - (iii); Q - (i), (ii); R - (iii), (v); S - (iii)
(D) P - (iv), (v); Q - (i), (iii); R - (ii); S - (iv)

19. Manu placed three different types of materials I, II, and III in front of letters P, Q, and R as shown in the figure and tried to look from the other side of each.

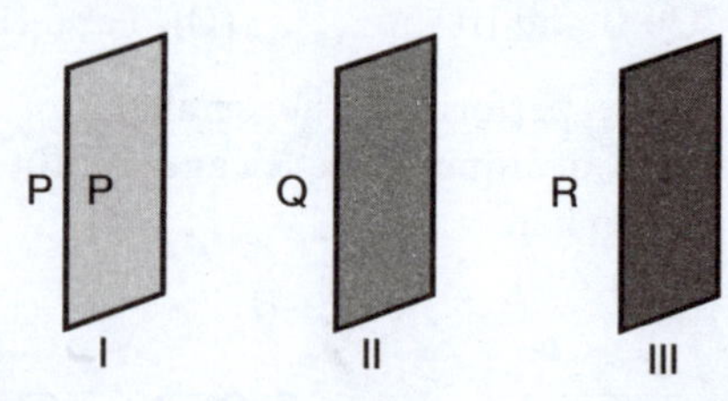

Which of the following is correct?
(A) Material II is frosted glass.
(B) Material I is glass window.
(C) Material III is wooden door.
(D) All of these.

20. The given flow chart was prepared by Sakshi for sorting materials into different groups. Fill in the blanks by selecting an appropriate option.

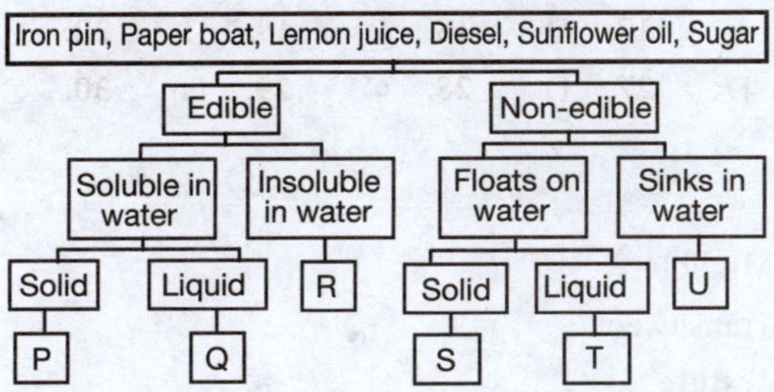

	P	Q	R
(A)	Sunflower oil	Lemon Juice	Sugar
(B)	Sugar	Sunflower oil	Lemon juice
(C)	Paper boat	Lemon juice	Sunflower oil
(D)	Sugar	Lemon juice	Sunflower oil

	S	T	U
(A)	Iron pin	Diesel	Paper boat
(B)	Iron pin	Paper boat	Diesel
(C)	Sugar	Diesel	Iron pin
(D)	Paper boat	Diesel	Iron pin

21. Hitesh has classified some common items based on their properties as shown in the table:

S. No	Item	Compressible	Opaque	Hard	Sinks in Water
1.	Steel spoon	×	✓	✓	✓
2.	Cotton ball	×		×	×
3.	Glass jar	×	×	✓	✓
4.	Thermocol	✓	×	×	
5.	Wooden block	×	✓	✓	✓

Which of the given items are not correctly classified?
(A) II and III only (B) I and IV only
(C) II, IV, and V only (D) None of these

22. Read the given statements and select the correct option.

Assertion: Handles of cooking utensils are made of metals like copper, aluminium, or iron.

Reason: Metals are bad conductors of heat.

(A) Both Assertion and Reason are true, and Reason is the correct explanation of Assertion.
(B) Both Assertion and Reason are true, but Reason is not the correct explanation of Assertion.
(C) Assertion is true, but Reason is false.
(D) Both Assertion and Reason are false.

23. Saransh made the following flow chart on the blackboard and asked his friend to identify objects P to S.

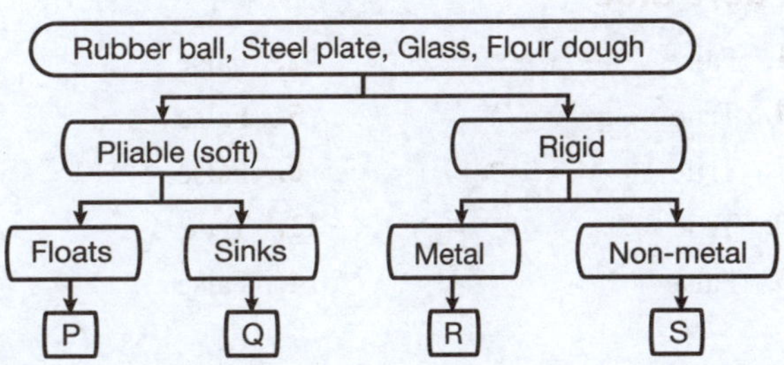

P, Q, R, and S are, respectively:
(A) Rubber ball, flour dough, glass, and steel plate
(B) Flour dough, steel plate, glass, and rubber ball
(C) Glass, rubber ball, flour dough, and steel plate
(D) Rubber ball, flour dough, steel plate, and glass.

ANSWER KEY

Level 1

Fixed Response Type

Multiple Choice Questions

1. B 2. D 3. D 4. A 5. A 6. D 7. B 8. A 9. C 10. A
11. C 12. A 13. C 14. B 15. A 16. A 17. D 18. B 19. D 20. C
21. B 22. A 23. B 24. D 25. C 26. D 27. D 28. C 29. D 30. C

Fill in the Blanks

1. Opaque, translucent 2. Rough, smooth 3. Miscible
4. Dense 5. Gases 6. Translucent
7. Universal 8. Air, moisture 9. Texture
10. Insoluble substance 11. Less 12. Bad
13. Good 14. Wood, iron block 15. Magnetism

True/False

1. False 2. False 3. True
4. True 5. False 6. True
7. True 8. False 9. True
10. True 11. True 12. False
13. False 14. False 15. False

Match Type Questions

1. 1-c, 2-a, 3-d, 4-e, 5-b 2. 1-c, 2-d, 3-a, 4-b 3. 1-b, 2-d, 3-a, 4-c 4. 1-d, 2-a, 3-b, 4-c
5. 1-c, 2-a, 3-d, 4-b 6. 1-c, 2-a, 3-b, 4-d 7. 1-b, 2-a, 3-d, 4-b 8. 1-d, 2-c, 3-b, 4-a
9. 1-d, 2-a, 3-b, 4-c 10. 1-a, 2-c, 3-b, 4-d

Assertion and Reason Type Questions

1. C 2. A 3. C 4. D 5. A 6. A 7. A 8. B 9. A 10. A
11. A 12. A 13. C 14. A 15. C

Comprehension Based Questions

1. C 2. A 3. D

Free Response Type

Numerical Based Question

1. A 2. B

ANSWER KEY

Case Based Questions

1. C **2.** B **3.** D **4.** B **5.** A

Level 2

Multiple Choice Questions

1. D **2.** C **3.** D **4.** C **5.** D **6.** D **7.** D **8.** C **9.** C **10.** D
11. C **12.** D **13.** C **14.** B **15.** C **16.** C **17.** B **18.** D **19.** D **20.** C
21. D **22.** A **23.** C **24.** C **25.** A **26.** C **27.** D **28.** A **29.** D **30.** C

Archive Corner

1. D **2.** D **3.** A **4.** A **5.** B **6.** A **7.** C **8.** B **9.** A **10.** C
11. C **12.** B **13.** B **14.** C **15.** D **16.** D **17.** C **18.** B **19.** B **20.** D
21. C **22.** D **23.** D

CHAPTER 6

Method of Separation in Everyday Life

Learning Outcomes

After reading this chapter, you will be able to:

- explain the chemical classification of matter.
- explain why there is a need for separation of different components of mixtures.
- explain the various separating techniques used for separating components.

Geekspeak

- Pure substance
- Mixture
- Homogeneous mixture
- Heterogeneous mixtures
- Handpicking
- Threshing
- Winnowing
- Sieving
- Magnetic separation
- Sublimation
- Sedimentation and decantation
- Loading
- Filtration
- Evaporation
- Condensation
- Centrifugation
- Separating funnel
- Saturated solution
- Unsaturated solution
- Supersaturated solution
- Crystallization
- Fractional distillation

Introduction

There are numerous things around us which we see and feel. For example, we can see a book in front of us. A book occupies some space. The space occupied by the book is called its volume. If we pick up the book, we can also feel its weight. So, we conclude that the book has some mass. We cannot see the air around us, yet if we fill a balloon with air and then weigh it carefully, we will find that not only does air occupy space (bounded by the balloon), but it also has mass.

Matter

Matter: Anything that has mass and occupies space is called matter.

- All materials or substances are made of matter
- All matter is made up of tiny particles like atoms or molecules.
- Matter mainly have three states: solid, liquid and gas (Fig. 6.1)

  Classification is the grouping together of things that are similar to each other in some of their properties. For instance, if we are given some items—pencil, chalk, skirt, blouse, ink, shirt, pen, and trousers, we would group or classify the similar items as follows.

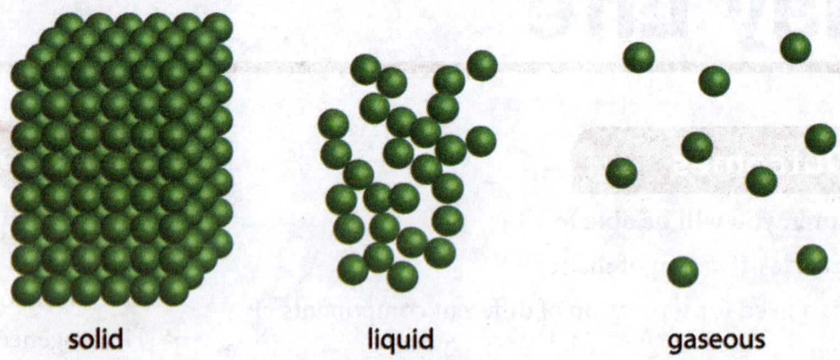

Figure 6.1 State of Matter

Classification of Matter

(a) **Pure Substance:** A homogeneous material which contains particles of only one kind and has a definite set of properties is called a pure substance.

Examples: Iron, silver, oxygen, sulphur, carbon dioxide etc., are pure substances because each of them has only one kind of particles.

(b) **Mixture:** When two or more substances (elements, compounds or both) are mixed together in any proportion, such that they do not undergo any chemical change, but retain their individual characteristics, the resulting product is called a mixture.

An example of mixture of seeds is shown in Fig. 6.2.

Figure 6.2 Mixtures

Types of Mixtures

There are essentially two types of mixtures–Homogeneous and Heterogeneous.

Homogeneous Mixture

If we mix a spoonful of salt in a glass of water, we cannot see the particles of salt with our naked eye as they get uniformly dissolved in water.

"Mixtures that have the same uniform composition throughout are called homogeneous mixtures." Some examples of homogeneous mixture are—salt mixed in water, juice, tea (Fig. 6.3(a)), and air.

Heterogeneous Mixture

If you take a spoonful of sand and mix it in one glass of water, the particles are visible and settle down when left undisturbed for some time. "Mixtures that do not have a uniform composition throughout are called heterogeneous mixtures". Some examples of heterogeneous mixture are mud mixed in water, mixture of oil in water (Fig. 6.3(b)), and soil.

(a)

(b)

Figure 6.3 Types of Mixture (a) Homogeneous Mixture (b) Heterogeneous Mixture

Keystone

Alloys are the homogeneous mixture of two or more metals.

❖ INTEXT QUESTION

1. **What is mixture?**
   Solution: When two or more than two substances are mixed in any ratio, it is called a mixture.

Check Point 1

1. How can we conclude that air is a matter?
2. Explain why the cold cannot be considered as matter.
3. What do you mean by pure substance?
4. Explain how a mixture of salt and water is a homogeneous mixture.
5. Explain heterogeneous mixture with two examples.

Separation of the Components of a Mixture

It is sometimes essential to separate the constituents of a mixture. For example, one must remove impurities from water to make it fit for drinking. Tea leaves are separated from tea using a strainer. Gardeners remove stones from the soil. Stones and husk are removed from rice before cooking.

Need of Separation

- To obtain two different but useful components of a mixture (E.g., butter is a useful component which is separated from milk by churning).
- To remove harmful components or impurities of a mixture (E.g., small pieces of stones and husk are separated from rice or dal before cooking).
- To remove useless components of a mixture (E.g., tea leaves are separated from tea).

Method of Separation

Many substances found in nature are mixed with certain other substances. Therefore, to use them, we separate them by various methods. Separation can be done based on difference in physical properties like—weight, size, magnetic property, solubility, melting point and boiling point.

Separation of Two or More Solid Mixtures

Solid constituents of a mixture can be easily separated if there is a marked difference in their size or colour. Other physical properties such as magnetic nature or solubility in a particular solvent are also helpful. The following techniques can be used to separate the constituents of a mixture of solid.

- **Handpicking:** This method can be used when the components of the mixture differ in size, shape, or colour and are present in small quantities (Fig. 6.4). In this method, components of the mixture are separated by hand. For example, stones can be removed from rice by handpicking.

Figure 6.4 Handpicking

- **Threshing:** The process of separating the grain from the stalk is called threshing (Fig. 6.5). Beat the stems to remove the grain seeds. Sometimes threshing is carried out with the help of cows. Machines are also used to thresh bulk grain.

Figure 6.5 Threshing

Testing Room 1

Aim: To separate components of a mixture of two or more solids

Materials required: Dals of different colours.

Procedure: Bring about one tablespoonful each of different dals (yellow, green, black, pink, etc.) to the class. Mix them in bowl. Now, try to separate the different dals. Were you able to separate them? How did you do that?

Conclusion: We can separate a mixture of different coloured dals by hand.

- **Winnowing:** This method is used to separate heavy and light components of a mixture by wind or air blowing. This method is often used by farmers to separate light hull particles from heavy kernels. Shell particles are carried by the wind. The grains are separated and form a heap near the sieving platform (Fig. 6.6). The separated hides are used for various purposes, such as animal feed.

Figure 6.6 Winnowing

- **Sieving:** In mills, impurities such as husks and stones are removed from wheat before it is ground (Fig. 6.7). Sacks of wheat are usually poured through an inclined sieve. Screening removes stones, stems and husks that may remain in the wheat after threshing and screening. Similar screens are used on construction sites to separate pebbles and rocks from sand.

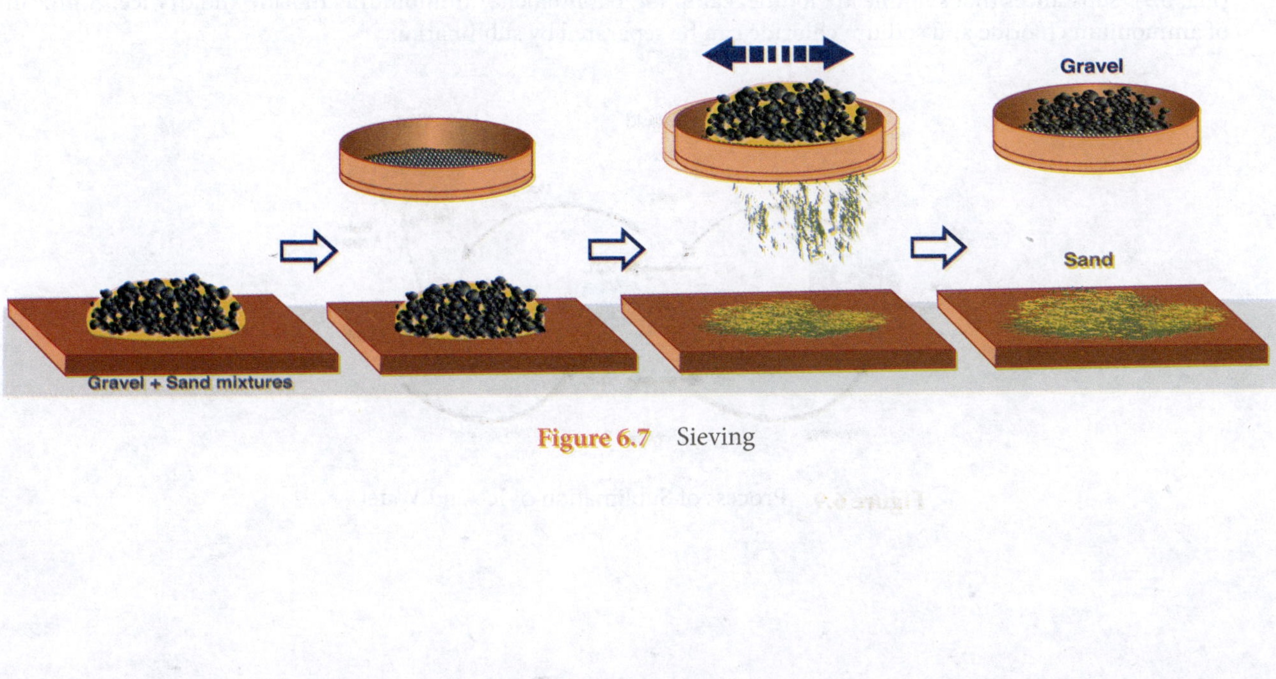

Figure 6.7 Sieving

(v) Magnetic Separation: A mixture of solids can be separated by magnetic separation if one of the constituents of the mixture is a magnetic substance, i.e., it can be attracted by a magnet (Fig. 6.8).

In an iron ore, iron metal is separated from the non-magnetic impurities using the method of magnetic separation. Since iron particles are magnetic in nature, they are attracted by a magnet and collected on one side. The impurities are left behind and form a separate pile. Let us perform the following activity to separate a mixture of iron filings and sand using a magnet.

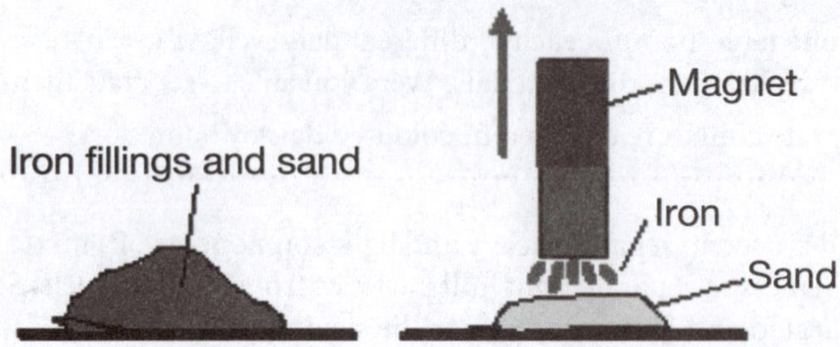

Figure 6.8 Magnetic Separation

Testing Room 2

Aim: To separate components of a mixture of two or more solids

Materials required: Bowl, iron filling, sand, magnet bar.

Procedure: Take a bowl and mix some sand and iron filings in it. Now take a magnet bar and roll it gently over the mixture. The iron filing will be attracted by the magnet. Brush the iron filings off the magnet and collect them separately. Repeat this procedure several times there are no more iron filing left in the original mixture.

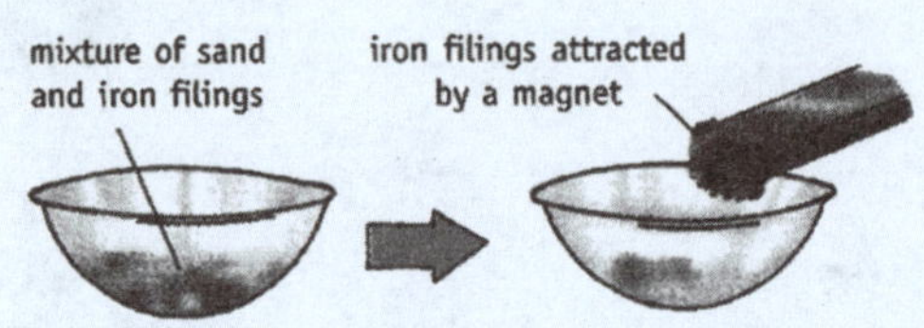

Separation by a magnet

Conclusion: We can separate a mixture of different magnetic element.

(vi) Sublimation: This technique of separation of a mixture of solids can be used if one of the constituents of the mixture sublimes, that is, on heating, it changes directly to gaseous state without passing through the liquid state (Fig. 6.9). Substances that sublime are iodine, camphor, naphthalene, ammonium chloride and dry ice. A mixture of ammonium chloride and sodium chloride can be separated by sublimation.

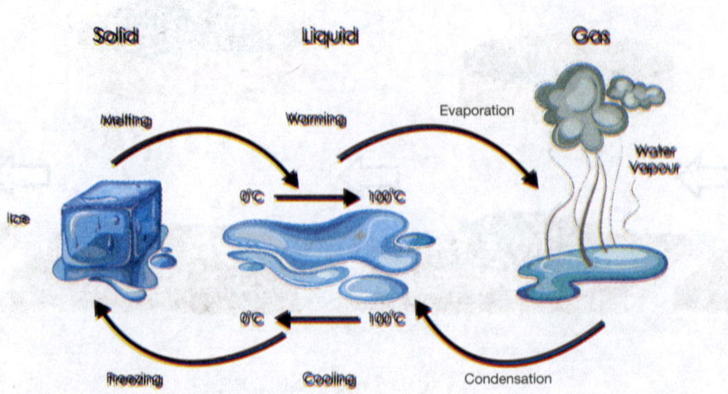

Figure 6.9 Process of Sublimation of Ice and Water

Separation of Insoluble Solid in Liquids

Solids such as chalk powder, sand and dust particles are insoluble in water. Particles of this type can be separated from their solutions using one of the following methods–(i) sedimentation and decantation, (ii) filtration, and (iii) loading.

- **Sedimentation and Decantation:** Sometimes, it may not be possible to separate components of a mixture by winnowing and handpicking. For example, there may be lighter impurities like dust or soil particles in rice or pulses. Rice or pulses are usually washed before cooking. When you add water to these, the impurities like dust and soil particles get separated. These impurities go into water, which becomes a little muddy (Fig. 6.10(a)).

  When the heavier component in a mixture settles after water is added to it, the process is called sedimentation. When the water (along with the dust) is removed, the process is called decantation (Fig. 6.10(b)).

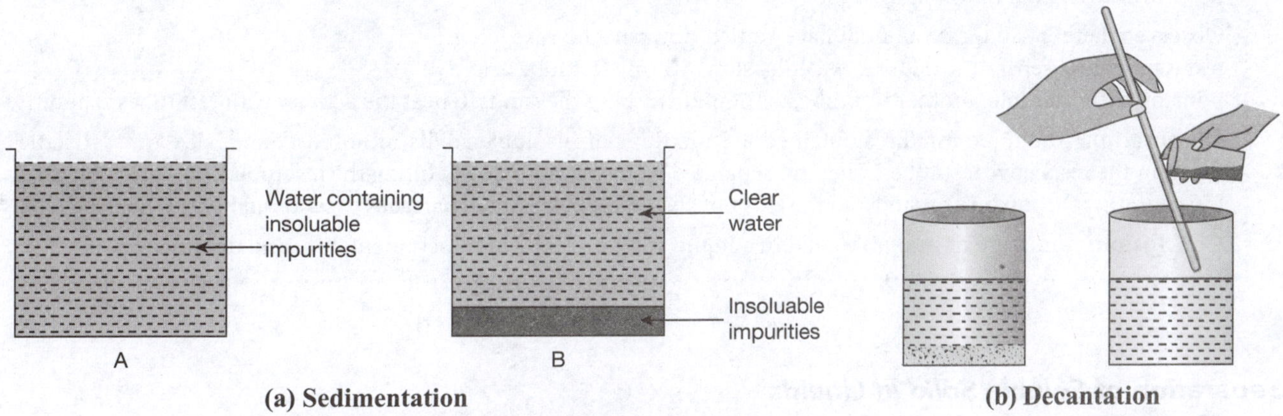

Figure 6.10 Sedimentation and decantation

- **Loading:** This method is used to separate very fine particles of insoluble solids that remain suspended in a liquid (Fig. 6.11). Due to their tiny sizes, their sedimentation takes a very long time. Loading is commonly used to get clear water from such dirty water. Loading is method in which a special substance called alum is used to load the suspended particles to make them heavy and increase their sedimentation speed.
- **Filtration:** The process of separation of insoluble solids from their solutions using a filter is called filtration. The filter allows the liquid to pass through and retains the solid particles. The filter used may be a filter paper, a fine muslin cloth, or a fine mesh. The solid particles retained by the filter form the residue (Fig. 6.12). The clear liquid collected after the filtering process forms the filtrate. The strainer, used to remove tea leaves from tea, is an example of a filter.

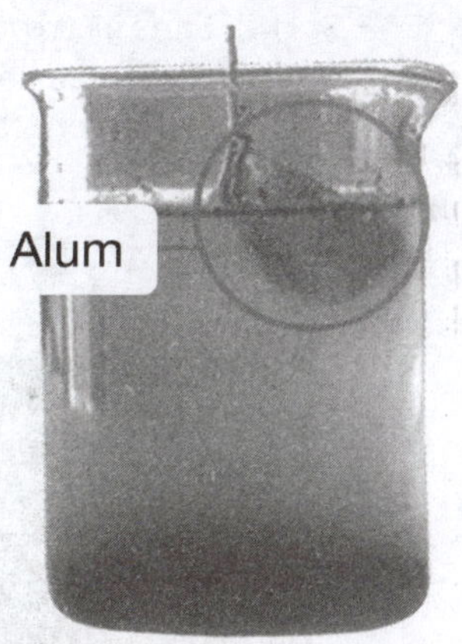

Figure 6.11 Loading

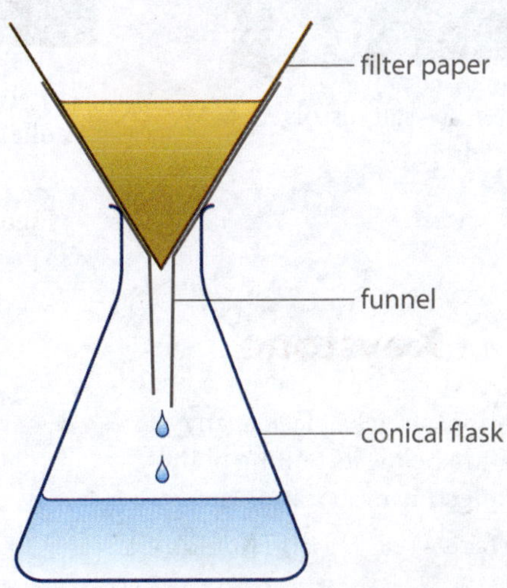

Figure 6.12 Filtration

Testing Room 3

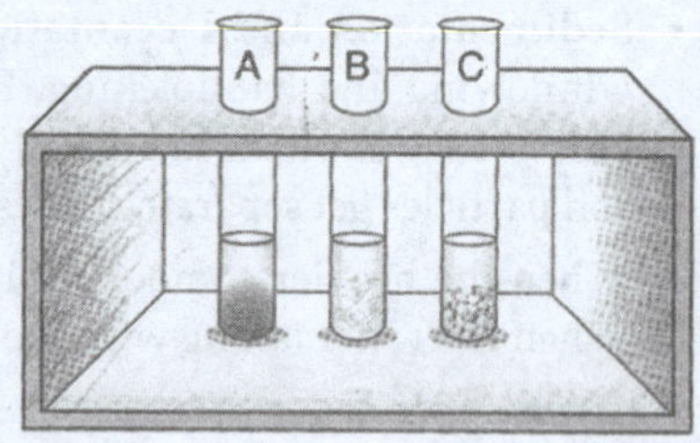

Aim: To separate the mixture of insoluble solids in liquids by sedimentation and decantation.

Materials Required: Six test tubes, sand, rice, dal, water, test tube stand.

Procedure: Take three test tubes and make these mixtures.

- Mixture of sand in water (Test tube A)
- Mixture of rice in water (Test tube B)
- Mixture of dal in water (Test tube C)

Observe whether sand, rice and dal have settled down in the respective test tubes. Now, separate sand from water by slowly tilting test tube A and pouring the water into another test tube, without disturbing the sand. Repeat the activity with test tubes B and C.

Observation: The three mixtures obtained are mixtures of insoluble solids in liquids. Sand, rice and dal settle down in the respective test tubes. They are separated from water by slowly tilting the test tube. The water obtained by separating the mixture of sand and water is not absolutely clear. Small particles of sand can be seen floating in it.

Conclusion: A mixture of insoluble solid in a liquid can be separated by sedimentation and decantation.

Separation of Soluble Solid in Liquids

(i) Evaporation: The process of conversion of water into its vapour below its boiling point is called evaporation. The process of evaporation takes place continuously wherever water is present. Sea water contains many salts mixed in it. One of these salts is the common salt. When sea water is allowed to stand in shallow pits, water gets heated by sunlight and slowly turns into water vapour, through evaporation (Fig. 6.13). In a few days, the water evaporates completely leaving behind the solid salts. Common salt is then obtained from this mixture of salts by further purification.

(a) Seawater has salt dissolved in it.

(b) To obtain salt, seawater is collected in shallow pits and allowed to stand.

(c) Sun's heat evaporates the water. Salt, which is left behind, is collected.

(d) Collection of salt

Figure 6.13 The Story of Salt

Keystone

Evaporation can take place at any temperature below its boiling point. Factors affecting evaporation are:

(i) Surface Area (ii) Humidity

(iii) Temperature (iv) Wind speed

(ii) **Condensation:** Have you ever noticed that water drops condense under the metal lid that has been used to cover a vessel containing just boiled vegetables or milk? It is because the hot milk or vegetables give out water vapour. These vapours on coming in contact with the relatively cold metal lid, liquify to form droplets of water. This process of changing water vapour into the liquid state on cooling is called condensation.

❖ INTEXT QUESTIONS

1. **What is a strainer?**
   Solution: A strainer is a kind of sieve which is used to separate a liquid from solid.
2. **What types of material can we separate by handpicking?**
   Solution: Materials having different size and colour can be separated by handpicking.
3. **Name the other methods used to separate solid materials of different size.**
   Solution: Sieving.
4. **Name the process used to separate heavier and lighter components of a mixture.**
   Solution: Winnowing.
5. **Can the above stated method be used if both the components have same weight?**
   Solution: No, this method cannot be used.
6. **What is evaporation?**
   Solution: The process of conversion of water into vapour is called evaporation.
7. **Name the method by which we get salt from ocean water.**
   Solution: Evaporation.
8. **Define condensation.**
   Solution: The process of conversion of water vapour into liquid form is called condensation.

Check Point 2

6. Define the terms handpicking and threshing by giving examples.
7. How can a mixture of iron filling and sulphur powder be separated?
8. Which property among ammonium chloride and sodium chloride is different?
9. Give two examples of solids which are soluble and insoluble in water.
10. Why are water droplets seen on the surface of a water bottle containing cold water?

Separation of Liquid in Liquid

- **Centrifugation:** Visit a nearby dairy and observe the process of obtaining cream by churning of milk (Fig. 6.14). The technique of centrifugation is used in this process.

  Centrifugation is a technique used to speed up sedimentation of fine particles suspended in a solid-liquid mixture.

  The principle of centrifugation is that an object, when spun at a high speed, experiences an outward force away from the centre of rotation.

  The mixture is placed in a centrifuge tube. When this tube is rotated at high speed in a centrifuge machine, the solid particles move towards the bottom of the centrifuge tube. The liquid on top (supernatant liquid) can be poured off and in this way the solid particles are separated from the mixture.

Figure 6.14 Churn

- **Separating Funnel:** The separation of two immiscible liquids is based on the difference in their densities. The apparatus used for separation is separating funnel. It is a long glass tube provided with a tap at its bottom (6.15).

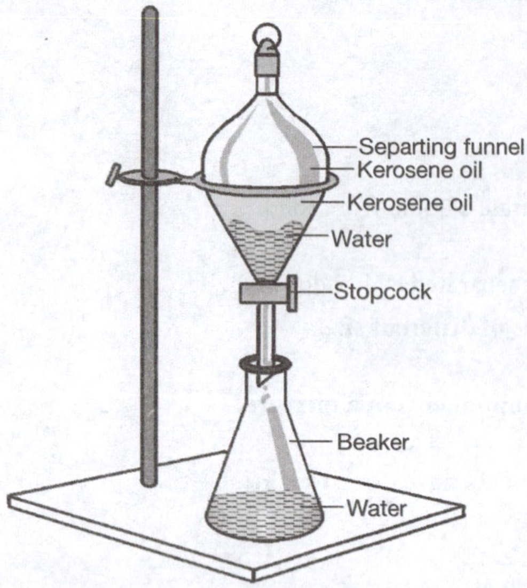

Figure 6.15 Separating Funnel

Keystone

The supernatant liquid may be centrifuged again at greater speeds to extract less dense fractions.

Check Point 3

11. Define the principle of the centrifugation technique.
12. Write two applications of the centrifugation technique.
13. Why is the separating funnel not implemented for separation of two miscible liquids?
14. Among mixtures of benzene and water, identify the bottom layer and top layer in a separating funnel.
15. How can the mixture of benzene, water, and mercury be separated?

Solution

Mixtures in which the components dissolve in each other completely are called solutions.
Each solution has two parts—a solute and a solvent. The substance that dissolves is called the solute, and the substance into which it dissolves is called the solvent. For example, in a salt-water solution, salt dissolves in water, so salt is the solute, and water is the solvent.
An unsaturated solution is one in which more solute can be dissolved in the given amount of solvent.
On the other hand, a solution in which no more solute can be dissolved in the given amount of solvent is called a **saturated solution**.
Many substances dissolve in water and form a solution. Solutions made with water are called **aqueous solutions**.
Solutions which contain more amount of substances dissolved in it than required to form a saturated solution is called **super saturated solution**.

❖ INTEXT QUESTIONS

9. **Name the process opposite to evaporation.**
   Solution: Condensation.
10. **Name the factors Affecting Solubility.**
    Solution: Temperature and Particle size
11. **Name the method used to separate cream from curd.**
    Solution: Centrifugation.
12. **How will you separate mango from a mixture of mango and apple?**
    Solution: By picking.
13. **You are given a mixture of salt and sand. Can you separate them by picking?**
    Solution: No, we cannot separate them by picking.
14. **Name the method used to separate the pieces of stone from grain.**
    Solution: Handpicking.
15. **How can you separate grains from stalk?**
    Solution: We separate grains from stalk by threshing.

Check Point 4

16. Explain the term solute and solvent.
17. Give an example of a non-aqueous solution.
18. What is difference between unsaturated and super saturated solutions?
19. Write down the differences between a saturated and an unsaturated solution.
20. How will you find out if a solution is super saturated?

STRUCTURAL OUTLINE

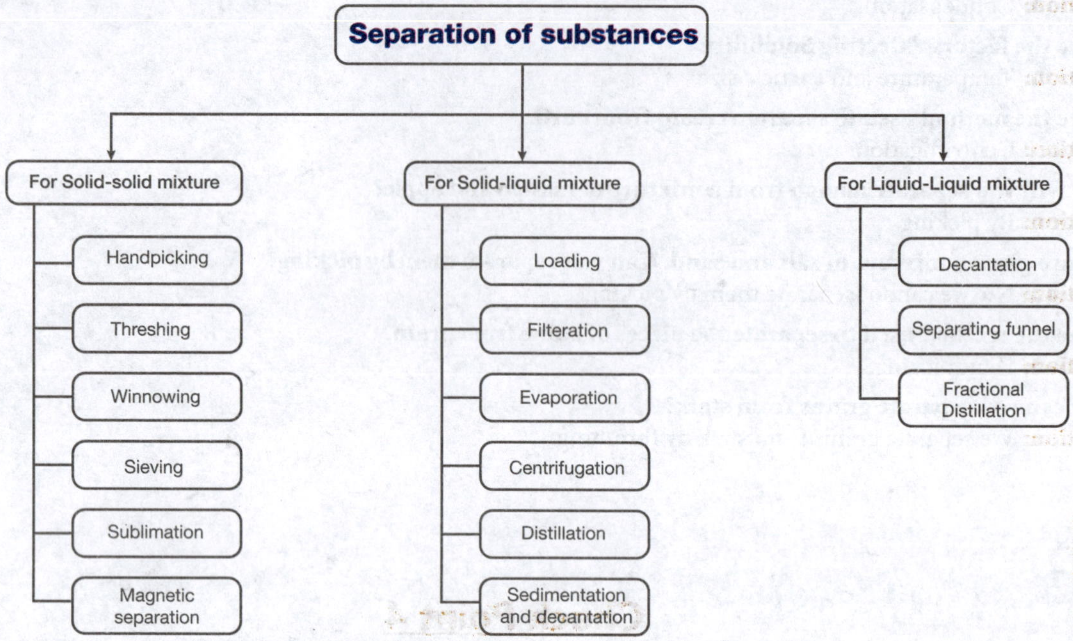

ABRIDGEMENT

Solubility

Solubility is defined as the amount of solute that can be dissolved in a given amount of solvent.

Factors Affecting Solubility

(i) Temperature **(ii)** Particle size

Crystallization

The process by which an impure compound is converted into its crystals is known as crystallization. This is based upon the principle that when a crystal is formed, it tends to exclude the impurities which remain in the solution.

Advantages of crystallization over evaporation: Crystallization is a better technique than evaporation to purify a solid because of the following reasons:

- During evaporation, the solution is heated to dryness. During this heat treatment, some solids may decompose or some solids, like sugar, may get charred.
- Both for evaporation or crystallization the solution of the impure solid is prepared in water or any other suitable solvent. This solution is then filtered to remove insoluble and suspended impurities. However, some soluble impurities may still be present even after filtration. Therefore, when such a solution is evaporated, the impurities get deposited along with the solid, contaminating the solid. In contrast, when the solution is allowed to stand for crystallization, crystals of the pure solid separate out leaving the impurities in the solution.

Fractional Distillation

The process of separating two miscible liquids from one another by heating (on the basis of their boiling point) them at controlled temperature. Petrol, diesel, kerosene etc., are obtained by this process from petroleum which is a mixture of all these constituents.

The difference in boiling points of liquids should be less than 25°C.

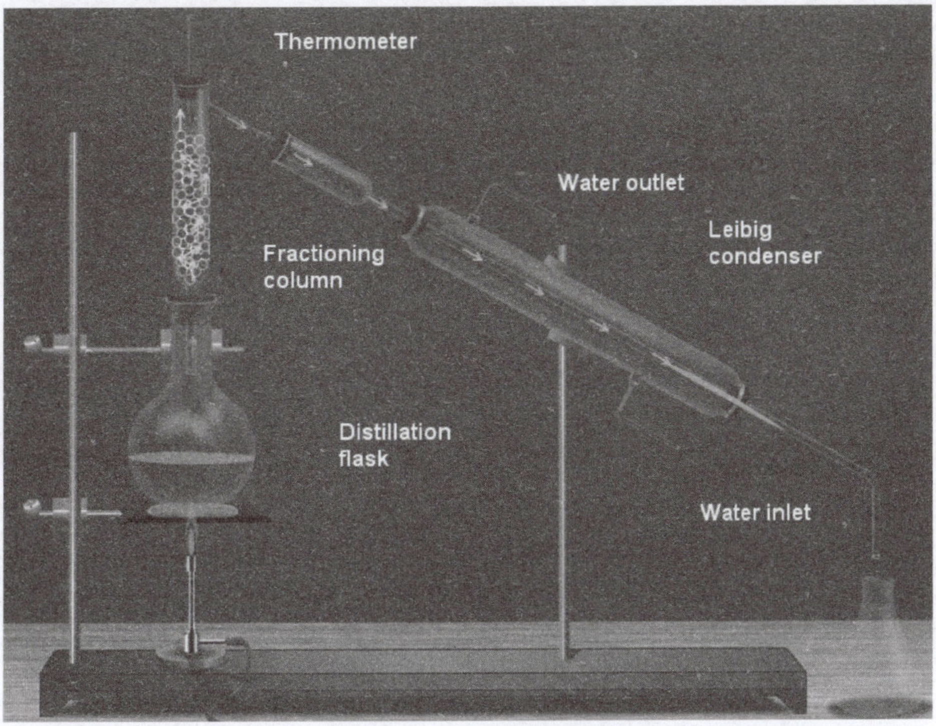

Fractional Distillation

Crude oil is a mixture of many useful things. Petroleum and other substances like diesel and kerosene can be extracted from crude oil with the help of fractional distillation.

- Condensation is the process by which water vapour changes into the liquid state on cooling.
- The technique of centrifugation is used to separate cream from milk.
- Separating funnel is a type of funnel provided with a tap, used for separating two immiscible liquids.
- A solution in which no more amount of solute can be dissolved is called a saturated solution.
- A solution that contains less amount of solute than required to form a saturated solution is called an unsaturated solution.
- A solution that contains more amount of solute than required to form a saturated solution is called a super saturated solution.

EXEMPLIFICATION

1. Filtration is a method to separate the components of a:
   (A) Solution (B) Mixture of a liquid and an insoluble substance
   (C) Both (A) and (B) (D) Pure substance

   Solution: (B) Components of solution cannot be separated by this method.
2. Threshing is done by:
   (A) Beating (B) Bullocks
   (C) Machines (D) All of these

   Solution: (D) All the three methods can be used for threshing.
3. The components of a solution (say sugar in water) can be separated by:
   (A) Filtration (B) Evaporation
   (C) Sedimentation (D) Decantation

   Solution: (B) By evaporation, the volatile component is evaporated which is then condensed.
5. A mixture of ammonium chloride and sand is separated by
   (A) Evaporation (B) Decantation
   (C) Sublimation (D) Filtration

   Solution: (C) Ammonium chloride is separated by a sublimation process.
6. Which of the following processes is used to remove tea from brew?

   Solution: Filtration is used to remove tea from brew.
7. Name the techniques used to separate the following:
   (A) Butter from curd.
   (B) Salt from seawater.

   Solution:
   (A) A process known as centrifugation is used to separate butter from curd. The process is governed on the principle of density.
   (B) We can use the simple evaporation technique to separate salt from seawater. Distillation causes water to evaporate leaving solid salt behind, hence the production of salt.
8. What is the procedure and principle for separation of wheat grains from husk?

   Solution: The differentiating property between husk and wheat is their mass. If treated with a small amount of wind energy, a remarkable variation in the moving distance is noticed. Hence to separate them, the winnowing procedure can be applied.
9. How can we separate small pieces of metal in the engine oil of a car?

   Solution: Tiny chunks of metal pieces in engine oil of car can be manually filtered.

10. Jojo finds a few fine mud particles suspended in drinking water. How can Jojo separate fine mud particles from water?

Solution: Due to the property of water, sand or fine mud particles tends to sink in the bottom as it is denser, provided they are undisturbed. Through the process of sedimentation/ decantation water can be separated from fine mud particles as the technique is established on obtaining clear water by tilting it out.

12. Why is the separating funnel method suitable to separate oil from water?

Solution: To separate oil from water which are two immiscible liquids which vary in their densities, separating funnel can be an effective method.

13. Name the method of separation of Butter from curd.

Solution: The technique of centrifugation can be applied to separate butter from curd. It is based on the concept of difference in density.

NCERT COMPENDIUM

1. What purpose does handpicking serve in the process of separation?
   (i) Filtration
   (ii) Sorting
   (iii) Evaporation
   (iv) Decantation

   Solution: (ii) Sorting

2. Which of the following substances are commonly separated using the churning method?
   (i) Oil from water
   (ii) Sand from water
   (iii) Cream from milk
   (iv) Oxygen from air

   Solution: (iii) Cream from milk

3. Which factor is usually essential for the filtration?
   (i) Apparatus size
   (ii) Presence of air
   (iii) Pore size
   (iv) Temperature of the mixture

   Solution: (iii) Pore size

4. State with reason(s) whether the following statements are True [T] or False [F]. Also, correct the False statements).
   (i) Salt can be separated from ' salt solution by keeping it under the Sun.
   (ii) Handpicking should be used only when the quantity of one component is less.
   (iii) A mixture of puffed rice and rice grains can be separated by threshing.
   (iv) A mixture of mustard oil and lemon water can be separated by decantation.
   (v) Sieving is used to separate a mixture of rice flour and water.

   Solution: (i) True
   Reason: The water will evaporate leaving the salt behind.
   (ii) True
   Reason: It is easier to handpick small quantities.
   (iii) False
   Reason: Process of threshing is used to separate the grains from the stalks.
   Correct statement: This mixture can be separated by handpicking or winnowing.
   (iv) True
   Reason: The oil and water will form separate layers which can be decanted.
   (v) False
   Reason: Sieving is done to separate solid-solid mixture of different particles size.
   Correct Statement: Filtration is used to separate a mixture of rice flour and water.

5. Match the mixtures in Column I with their method of separation in Column II.

Column I	Column II
(i) gram flour mixed with black gram	(a) handpicking
(ii) chalk powder mixed with water	(b) magnetic separation
(iii) corn mixed with potatoes	(c) decantation
(iv) iron powder mixed with soda	(d) sieving
(v) oil mixed with water	(e) filtration

   Solution:

Column I	Column II
(i) gram flour mixed with black gram	(d) sieving
(ii) chalk powder mixed with water	(e) filtration
(iii) corn mixed with potatoes	(a) handpicking
(iv) iron powder mixed with soda	(b) magnetic separation
(v) oil mixed with water	(c) decantation

6. In what situations wouldyou use decantation instead of filtration to separate solids from liquids?

   Solution: Decantation is used when the solid particles are heavy and settle down at the bottom of the container, allowing the clear liquid to be poured off without disturbing the solid sediment. For example separating sand from water.

7. Can you relate the presence of nasal hair to any separation process?

   Solution: Nasal hair acts like a natural filter, trapping dust, pollen, and other particles from the air we breathe, similar to how a filtration process works to remove solid impurities from a liquid.

8. During the COVID-19 pandemic, all of us wore masks. Generally, what material are they made of? What is the role of these masks?

   Solution: Masks are generally made of materials like cotton, synthetic fibers, or polypropylene.

Their role is to filter out airborne particles, including viruses and bacteria, to prevent their inhalation and spread.

9. A mixture containing potatoes, salt and sawdust has been given to you. Outline a stepwise procedure for separating each component from this mixture.

Solution: Step-1 : Handpick the potatoes
Step-2: Add water to the remaining mixture to dissolve the salt
Step-3: Filter the mixture to separate the sawdust from the salt solution.
Step-4: Evaporate the water from the salt solution to obtain the salt.

10. Read the following story titled 'Intelligent Leela' and tick the most appropriate options. Protnde a suitable title of your choice for the paragraph.

Leela was working in the farm with her father when she realised that they left their drinking water at home. Before her father felt thirsty/ hungry, she went to the nearby pond to fetch some water/ grains. After obtaining some water in the container, she noticed that the water was muddy and fit/unfit for drinking. To purify the water, she kept it for some time and then she filtered/churned the muddy water using a piece of paper/ muslin cloth. Leela, then, cooled/ boiled the water for about 10 minutes in a covered pan. After cooling/boiling, she filtered/churned it again and made it fit/unfit for drinking. She served this water to her father while having food, who blessed her and appreciated her efforts.

Solution:

1. Thirsty
2. Water
3. Unfit
4. Filtered
5. Muslin Cloth
6. Boiled
7. Cooling
8. Filtered
9. Fit

NCERT COMPENDIUM

ASSESSMENT CORNER

LEVEL 1

Fixed Response Type

Multiple Choice Questions

1. Which of the following is a property of solids?
(A) Not rigid (B) No fixed volume
(C) No fixed shape (D) Fixed volume

2. Which among the following is homogeneous mixture
(A) Sand and water
(B) Chalk powder and water
(C) Oil and water
(D) None of these

3. Homogeneous mixture
(A) Have uniform composition
(B) Do not have uniform composition
(C) May or may not have uniform composition
(D) None of these

4. Pure substance are those substances
(A) Made of only one kind of particles
(B) Cannot be separated by physical process
(C) Can be separated by physical process
(D) Both (A) and (B)

5. Handpicking method can be used for separating mixture of
(A) Sugar powder and salt
(B) Red and blue coloured balls of different size
(C) Oil and water
(D) Milk and cream

6. Which of the following are pure substances?
(A) cake (B) Ice candy
(C) Ink (D) Gold

7. The method used to separate heavier and lighter components of a mixture is
(A) Handpicking (B) Threshing
(C) Winnowing (D) Sieving

8. Grain and husk can be separated by
(A) Handpicking (B) Threshing
(C) Winnowing (D) Sieving

9. Sieving is used to
(A) Separate impurities from wheat.
(B) Separate pebbles and stones from sand.
(C) Separate impurities from flour.
(D) All of these.

10. Mixture of salt and iron powder is separated by-
(A) Handpicking
(B) Magnetic separation
(C) Sieving
(D) Churning

11. Alloys are:
(A) homogeneous mixture
(B) pure substances
(C) heterogeneous mixture
(D) both (A) and (B)

12. The process used for separating constituents while preparing fruit juice is
(A) Condensation (B) Evaporation
(C) Threshing (D) Filtration

13. The difference between sieving and filtration is
(A) Size of particles (B) Phase of particles
(C) Density (D) None of these

14. We can obtain sugar from sugar solution by
(A) Sedimentation (B) Evaporation
(C) Filtration (D) Decantation

15. On evaporation of sea water _________ obtained?
(A) sugar (B) acid
(C) salt (D) base

16. When steam comes in contact with a cold surface, it converts into water. The process is called -
(A) Evaporation (B) Condensation
(C) Sublimation (D) Melting

17. Cream is separated from milk by _______________ and tea leaves are separated from tea by _________
(A) filtration, decantation
(B) winnowing, filtration
(C) decantation, filtration
(D) decantation, decantation

18. The mixture of sand, salt, and water can be separated by
(A) Sublimation (B) Filtration
(C) Distillation (D) (B) followed by (C)

19. The spinner in washing machine dries clothes works on the principle of:
(A) Evaporation (B) Sedimentation
(C) Filtration (D) Centrifugation

20. Separating funnel used to separate:
(A) two miscible liquids
(B) two gases
(C) two solids
(D) two immiscible liquids

21. After centrifugation when sublimate settles, clear liquid:
(A) can be allowed to rest.
(B) can be allowed to form crystals.
(C) can be decanted off.
(D) can be evaporated.

22. A solution is prepared by dissolving sodium chloride in water. It is called a:
(A) Non-aqueous solution
(B) Aqueous solution.
(C) Alcoholic solution.
(D) Heterogeneous solution.

23. When more quantity of salt is added to saturated solution of salt, then it:
(A) Settles down at the bottom of the container
(B) Remains suspended in the solution
(C) Starts evaporating
(D) Reacts with the solvent (water)

24. Factors affecting solubility of a substance:
(A) temperature (B) nature of solute
(C) both (A) and (B) (D) None of these

Fill in the Blanks

1. A pure substance has_________ of matter.

2. The composition and properties of a___________ mixture is uniform throughout.

3. An ____________ is a homogeneous mixture of two or more metals.

4. Chalk powder added in water is an example of a ____________.

5. When the heavier component in a mixture settles after water is added to it, the process is called ____________.

6. Dry Ice converted directly into vapours __________.

7. _________ can be separate from stalk by threshing.

8. Corn is separated from husk by the process _____________.

9. Simplest way of separating broken rice from whole rice is _____________.

10. A ______________ cannot dissolve more of a given substance at a given temperature.

11. ______________ is commonly used to get clear water from dirty water.

12. Evaporation can take place at any temperature below its ______________.

13. ____________ is a process which is used in flour mill or at construction sites.

14. Within a mixture of kerosene and water, ______ will be the bottom layer in separating funnel.

15. Sugar can be separated from wheat flour by the process of ___________.

True/False

1. A mixture of milk and water can be separated by filtration.

2. A mixture of powdered salt and sugar can be separated by winnowing.

3. Separation of sugar from tea can be done with filtration.

4. Iron filling in salt can be separated by handpicking.

5. On heating, solid changes directly to gaseous state without passing through the liquid state. This process is called sublimation.

6. Solid particles in the mixture pass through it and do not remain on the filter paper.

7. Liquid wax and water are immiscible liquids.

8. Stone and rice can be separated by winnowing.

9. A separating funnel is used to separate lemon juice and water.

10. A mixture of iron and gold pieces can be separated by magnet.

Match Type Questions

1.

Column-A	Column-B
(i) Separation of mixture of sand and water	(a) Sieving
(ii) Rice and suji	(b) Example of mixture
(iii) Two immiscible liquids	(c) Oil and vinegar
(iv) Process of making sedimentation of dust particles faster.	(d) Filtration
(v) Milk, ink, and pickle	(e) Loading

ASSESSMENT CORNER

2.

Column-A	Column-B
(i) Stone and rice	(a) Decantation
(ii) Water and rice	(b) Handpicking
(iii) Water and oil	(c) Winnowing
(iv) Sand and Sawdust	(d) Filtration

3.

Column-A	Column-B
(i) Colourful stones	(a) Centrifugation
(ii) Milk and butter	(b) Separating funnel
(iii) Kerosene and oil	(c) Handpicking
(iv) Husk and seeds	(d) Winnowing

4.

Column-A	Column-B
(i) Threshing	(a) Separating butter from milk
(ii) Evaporation	(b) Conversion of water vapour into liquid
(iii) Condensation	(c) Conversion of water into its vapour
(iv) Churning	(d) Separating grains from its stalks

5.

Column-A	Column-B
(i) Handpicking	(a) Separation by wind or by blowing air
(ii) Winnowing	(b) Separating larger sized impurities
(iii) Sieving	(c) Settling of heavier components at bottom
(iv) Sedimentation	(d) Separating bran from flour

6.

Column-A	Column-B
(i) Mixtures that have uniform composition	(a) Evaporation
(ii) Conversion of water vapour into liquid	(b) Heterogeneous mixtures
(iii) Conversion of water into vapour	(c) Condensation
(iv) Mixtures that have non-uniform composition	(d) Homogeneous mixtures

Assertion and Reason Type Questions

In the following questions, a statement of assertion is followed by statement of reason.

Mark the correct choice as:

(A) Both Assertion and Reason are true, and Reason is the correct explanation of Assertion.

(B) Both Assertion and Reason are true, but Reason is not the correct explanation of Assertion.

(C) Assertion is true, but Reason is false.

(D) Both Assertion and Reason are false.

1. **Assertion:** Evaporation can be used to separate a solid dissolved in a liquid.
Reason: Evaporation is the process in which a liquid gets converted into its vapour.

2. **Assertion:** Husk and stones could be separated from grains by handpicking.
Reason: Husk is separated from heavier seeds of grains by winnowing.

3. **Assertion:** The principle of centrifugation is that an object, when spun at high speed, experiences an outward force away from the centre of rotation.
Reason: Centrifugation is a technique used to speed up sedimentation of fine particles suspended in a solid-liquid mixture.

4. **Assertion:** Water mixture can be separated by using separating funnel.
Reason: Kerosene being heavier than water, will float on it.

5. **Assertion:** When steam comes in contact with a metal plate cooled with ice, it condenses and forms gaseous water.
Reason: The process of conversion of liquid water into its vapour form is called condensation.

6. **Assertion:** While churning milk to obtain butter, we throw away impurities.
Reason: The purpose of separation is to remove non useful components.

7. **Assertion:** Winnowing is used to separate two heavier and lighter components of a mixture.
Reason: Winnowing is used to separate husk and seeds.

8. **Assertion:** When the heavier component in a mixture settles after water is added to it, the process is called sedimentation.
Reason: When water (along with the dust) is removed, it is called decantation.

ASSESSMENT CORNER

9. **Assertion:** Fruit and vegetable juices are usually filtered before drinking to separate the seeds and solid particles of pulp.
Reason: Solid particles in the mixture do not pass through it and remains on the filter paper.

10. **Assertion:** A mixture of ammonium chloride and sodium chloride can be separated by sublimation.
Reason: On heating, a solid changes directly into its gaseous state without passing through the liquid state. This process is called sublimation.

Comprehension Type Questions

Read the given passage.

Centrifugation is a technique used to speed up sedimentation of fine particles suspended in a solid-liquid mixture.

The principle of centrifugation is that an object when spun at high speeds, experiences an outward force away from the centre of rotation.

The mixture is placed in a centrifuge tube. When this tube is rotated at high speed in a centrifuge machine, the solid particles move towards the bottom of the centrifuge tube. The liquid on top (supernatant liquid) can be poured off and in this way the solid particles are separated from the mixture.

Visit a nearby dairy and observe the process of obtaining cream by churning of milk. The technique of centrifugation is used in this process.

1. Separation of butter from milk is based in the principle of
(A) Filtration (B) Centrifugation
(C) Churning (D) Sedimentation

2. Centrifugation method is used for separation of-
(A) Solid-solid mixture
(B) Solid-gas mixture
(C) Liquid-liquid mixture
(D) Solid-liquid mixture

3. During the separation of a mixture, centrifugation tube is rotated at high speeds in a centrifuge machine. The solid particles move towards the bottom of the centrifuge tube. The liquid on top is called-
(A) Superficial liquid (B) Decant
(C) Supernatant liquid (D) Filtrate

4. Centrifugation is a technique used to:
(A) Slow down sedimentation of fine particles suspended in a solid-liquid mixture.
(B) Slow down sedimentation of fine particles suspended in a solid-gas mixture.
(C) Speed up sedimentation of fine particles suspended in a solid-gas mixture.
(D) Speed up sedimentation of fine particles suspended in a solid-liquid mixture.

5. The principle of centrifugation is:
(A) An object, when spun at high speeds, experiences an inward force away from the centre of rotation.
(B) An object, when spun at low speeds, experiences an outward force away from the centre of rotation.
(C) An object, when spun at high speeds, experiences an outward force away from the centre of rotation.
(D) An object, when spun at high speeds, experiences an outward force away from the gravitation.

Free Response Type

Very Short Answer Type Questions

1. What are the main criteria for a substance to be pure or impure?
2. Name the types of mixtures that can be separated by filtration.
3. What is the role of sieving technique in mills?
4. Name the apparatus that can be used to separate a mixture of mustard oil and water.
5. What are aqueous solutions?

Short Answer Type Questions

1. Give any four examples of mixtures used in our daily life.
2. Why do we need to separate different components of a mixture?

ASSESSMENT CORNER

3. Why is loading used to separate suspended impurities?
4. What is evaporation? How is it useful to us?
5. Name any two methods, which are used to separate:
   (a) Solid-solid mixtures
   (b) Liquid-solid mixtures
6. Write various methods of separation of components from their mixture.
7. Define the term handpicking.what is the principle of hand packing?
8. What do you mean by threshing? Where is it used?
9. Write three methods of separation of substances.
10. How will you separate oil and water from their mixture?
11. What is evaporation?
12. What is the role of winnowing in agriculture or farming?
13. What do you mean by sieving? Give an example.
14. Match the column:

Separation Process	Purpose for which we do the Separation	What Do We Do with the Separated Components?
1. Separate stones from rice	(a) To separate two different but useful components.	(i) We throw away the solid component.
2. Churning milk to obtain butter	(b) To remove non-useful components.	(ii) We throw away the impurities.
3. Separate tea leaves	(c) To remove impurities or harmful components.	(iii) We use both the components.

Long Answer Type Questions

1. Why is salt a pure substance whereas, salt solution is considered to be a mixture?
2. Name and briefly describe a method which can be helpful in separating a mixture of husk from grains. What is the principle of this method?
3. Draw a well-labelled diagram for the setup used for filtration. Explain its working.
4. Name the method of separation that can be used in the following situations.
   (A) Accidental mixing of mustard oil and water.
   (B) Adulterated urad dal having papaya seeds in it.
   (C) You visit a village were the water drawn from the well is not transparent.
   (D) If you find that your *bhel puri* has large number of cut green chilies.
5. Differentiate between each of the following pairs:
   (A) Homogeneous and heterogeneous solutions
   (B) Pure and mixed substance
   (C) Solute and solvent
   (D) Sedimentation and decantation
6. Lemonade is prepared by mixing lemon juice and sugar in water. You wish to add ice to cool it. Should you add ice to the lemonade before or after dissolving sugar? In which case would it be possible to dissolve more sugar?
7. What is thresher in agriculture?
8. Describe the method to obtain salt from sea water.
9. What is decantation?
10. What are the main factors affecting evaporation?
11. How will you prepare cheese (paneer)?
12. Explain the method that can be used for separating the following mixture:
   (i) Sand and husk
   (ii) Wheat, sugar and stalk
   (iii) Water and petrol
   (iv) Rice and salt
   (v) Sand and salt
13. Write the steps you would use for making tea. Use the words solution, solvent, solute, dissolve, soluble, insoluble, filtrate, and residue.

Numerical Based Questions

1. A 250 gm of a mixture of sand and water is taken in a beaker and filtered through a very fine porous filter paper. 225 gm of filtrate is obtained after filtration, calculate the amount of sand obtained as a residue.
(A) 125 gm
(B) 25 gm
(C) 50 gm
(D) No residue obtained

2. 47 ml of sugar solution is taken and kept for evaporation. After evaporation 8.5 gm of solid sugar is obtained. Find the amount of water evaporated from the solution.
(A) 37.5 gm (B) 38gm
(C) 38.5gm (D) 39.5 gm

Case Based Questions

Kunal separated components of a mixture with two or more solids. He took a bowl of iron filling, sand, and a magnet bar.
Then, he took a bowl and mix the sand and iron filings in it. Then. he took a magnet bar and rolled it in the mixture. The iron filing were attracted by the magnet. Brush the iron filings off the magnet and collected them separately. He repeat this procedure several times till there were no more iron filing left in the original mixture.

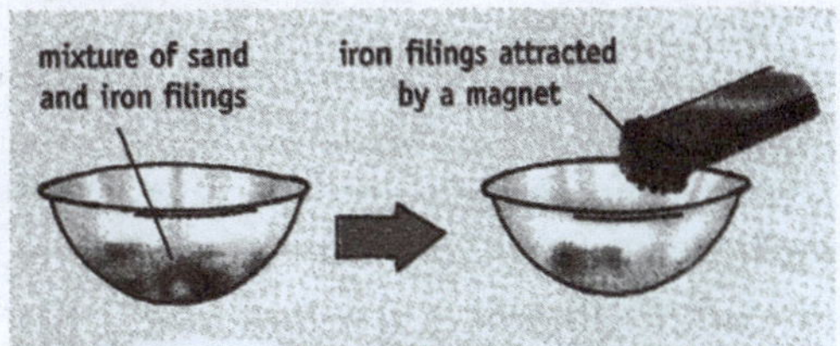

Separation by a magnet

1. Kunal separated sand and iron filling. Which property was used for the separation?
(A) Solubility (B) Density
(C) Magnetic separation (D) Centrifugation

2. Can we separate a mixture of aluminium powder and salt from the above method?
(A) Yes we can, because aluminium has magnetic properties.
(B) Yes we can, because salt has magnetic properties
(C) No we cannot, because aluminium has magnetic properties
(D) No we cannot, because aluminium does not have magnetic properties

3. Which of the following is/are separated by magnetic separation?
(A) Iron nails from saw dust
(B) Iron filling, iodine, and salt
(C) Salt and sugar
(D) Both (A) and (B)

Level 2

Multiple Choice Questions

1. Solutions are:
(A) heterogeneous mixtures
(B) compounds
(C) homogeneous mixtures
(D) elements

2. Winnowing is the method used to separate:
(A) chaff from grain
(B) stones from rice
(C) oil from water
(D) salt from sand

3. During filtration the substance left behind on the filter paper is called:
(A) Distillate (B) Filtrate
(C) Sublimate (D) Residue

4. A mixture of rice and water can be separated by using:
(A) Threshing (B) Sedimentation
(C) Winnowing (D) Sieving

5. Loading is a process in which:
(A) Impurities become heavy and sink to the bottom.
(B) Impurities float on the top.
(C) Impurities vaporize.
(D) None of these.

6. Fractional distillation is used to separate liquids having an appreciable difference in their:
(A) Size and shape (B) Solubility
(C) Boiling points (D) None of these

7. The constituents of a mixture are present in:
(A) A fixed ratio (B) A variable ratio
(C) The ratio of 2: 1 (D) None of these

8. How can a saturated solution be made unsaturated?
(A) By increasing temperature
(B) By adding more amount of solvent
(C) Both (A) and (B)
(D) By decreasing temperature

9. The methods of separating components of a given mixture are based on the:
(A) Physical properties and state of the components.
(B) Colour of the components only
(C) State of the components.
(D) None of these.

10. Which of the following is an example of mixture?
(A) Gold (B) Pickle
(C) Silver (D) Copper

11. Paheli bought some vegetables such as French beans, lady's finger, green chillies, brinjals, and potatoes all mixed in a bag. Which of the following methods of separation would be most appropriate for her to separate them?
(A) Winnowing (B) Sieving
(C) Threshing (D) Handpicking

12. Boojho's grandmother is suffering from diabetes. Her doctor advised her to consume *lassi* with less fat content. Which of the following methods would be most appropriate for Boojho to prepare it?
(A) Filtration (B) Decantation
(C) Churning (D) Winnowing

13. Which of the following can be used in the filtration to separate the mixture of sand and water?
(A) Filter paper (B) Muslin cloth
(C) Fine mash (D) All of these

14. Which amongst the following methods would be most appropriate to separate grains from bundles of stalks?
(A) Handpicking (B) Winnowing
(C) Sieving (D) Threshing

15. Four mixtures are given below.
(i) Kidney beans and chickpeas
(ii) Pulses and rice
(iii) Rice flakes and corn
(iv) Potato wafers and biscuits
Which of these can be separated by the method of winnowing?
(A) (i) and (ii) (B) (ii) and (iii)
(C) (i) and (iii) (D) (iii) and (iv)

16. While preparing chapatis, Paheli found that the flour to be used was mixed with wheat grains. Which out of the following is the most suitable method to separate the grains from the flour?
(A) Threshing (B) Sieving
(C) Winnowing (D) Filtration

17. You might have observed the preparation of ghee from butter and cream at home. Which method(s) can be used to separate ghee from the residue?
(i) Evaporation
(ii) Decantation
(iii) Filtration
(iv) Churning
Which of the following combinations is the correct answer?
(A) (i) and (ii) (B) (ii) and (iii)
(C) (ii) and (iv) (D) (iv) only

18. In the activity, a teacher dissolved a small amount of solid copper sulphate in a tumbler half-filled with water. Which method would you use to get back solid copper sulphate from the solution?
(A) Decantation
(B) Evaporation
(C) Sedimentation
(D) Condensation

19. During summer, Boojho carries water in a transparent plastic bottle to school. One day he left his bottle in the school. The bottle still had some water left in it. The following day, he observed some water droplets on the inner surface of the empty portion of the bottle. These droplets of water were formed due to
(A) Boiling and condensation
(B) Evaporation and saturation
(C) Evaporation and condensation
(D) Condensation and saturation.

20. Paheli asked for a glass of water from Boojho. He gave her a glass of ice-cold water. Paheli observed some water droplets on the outer surface of the glass and asked Boojho how these droplets of water were formed. Which of the following should be Boojho's answer?
(A) Evaporation of water from the glass.
(B) Water that seeped out from the glass.
(C) Evaporation of atmospheric water vapour.
(D) Condensation of atmospheric water vapour.

21. Which of the following is an example of heterogeneous mixture?
(A) salt + water
(B) kerosene + water
(C) sugar + water
(D) lemon juice + water

22. The principle behind fractional distillation technique in separation of two liquids is:
(A) Difference in melting point
(B) Difference in boiling point
(C) Difference in concentration
(D) Difference in solubility

23. Which of the following methods is used for separation of different components of petroleum?

(A) Fractional distillation
(B) Sublimation
(C) Centrifugation
(D) Simple distillation

24. A mixture of alcohol and water can be separated by:
(A) Separating funnel
(B) Fractional distillation
(C) Simple distillation
(D) Sublimation

25. A mixture of ammonium chloride and sodium chloride can be separated by
(A) Chromatography
(B) Handpicking
(C) Sublimation
(D) Centrifugation

26. Which of the following is the correct statement?
(A) Winnowing is used to separate heavier and lighter components of a mixture by wind or by blowing air.
(B) The seeds of grains get separated and form a heap near the platform through winnowing.
(C) Petrol, diesel, kerosene, etc., are separated by fractional distillation from petroleum.
(D) All of these.

27. When ammonium chloride converted from solid into gas, the process called
(A) Decantation (B) Sublimation
(C) Condensation (D) Sedimentation

28. Sieving technique used for the separation of
(A) flour and bran of wheat
(B) tea and tea leaves
(C) mixture of iron filling and sand
(D) salt solution

29. Study the given table of mixtures:
(i) Grains + Husk
(ii) Iron fillings + Sand
(iii) Ammonium chloride + common salt
Which of the following techniques are correct to separate the given mixtures?

	(i)	(ii)	(iii)
(A)	Filtration	Sedimentation	Decantation
(B)	Handpicking	Sedimentation	Filtration
(C)	Winnowing	Magnetic	Sublimation separation
(D)	Evaporation	Distillation	Sublimation

30. Study the given table of methods:
(i) Sublimation
(ii) Filtration
(iii) Magnetic separation
Which of the following techniques are correct to separate the given mixtures?

	(i)	(ii)	(iii)
(A)	Oil + Water	Salt + Water	Iron fillings + Sand
(B)	Stone + Pebbles	Ammonium chloride + Salt	Salt + Water
(C)	Ammonium chloride + Salt	Stone + Pebbles	Kerosene + Water
(D)	Ammonium chloride + Salt	Salt + Water	Iron fillings + Sand

31. An insoluble solid from a soluble solid can be separated by mixing the mixture with?
(A) water, filter, and evaporate the water from the resulting filtrate to obtain soluble solid.
(B) water, filter, and evaporate the sand from the resulting solid.
(C) oil, filter, and evaporate the solid out.
(D) Both (B) and (C).

32. Which of these occurs due to condensation?
(A) The drying of wet clothes.
(B) Water drops appearing on the outer side of a cool water bottle.
(C) Steam rising from wet clothes when they are ironed.
(D) Black board gets dried after it is wiped with wet cloth.

33. Which of the following statements is not true?
(A) No more salt can be dissolved in a saturated solution of salt water without heating.
(B) Water dissolves different amounts of soluble substances in it.
(C) A mixture of milk and water can be separated through filtration.
(D) Salt is separated from sea water through evaporation.

34. A mixture contains tiny particles of three different substances X, Y, and Z. They are of same size, shape, and colour. X particles are heavy, insoluble, and non-magnetic. Y particles are very light, insoluble, and non-magnetic. Z particles are heavy and magnetic. Which of the following methods can be used to separate X, Y, and Z?
(A) Winnowing followed by filtration.
(B) Sieving followed by winnowing.

ASSESSMENT CORNER

(C) Winnowing followed by magnetic separation.
(D) Handpicking followed by magnetic separation.

35. Which of the following method is used to separate water particles from clothes while drying in washing machines?
(A) Magnetic separation
(B) Filtration
(C) Evaporation
(D) Centrifugation

Higher Order Thinking Skills (HOTS)

1. Ananya got an sample of salt containing some water soluble impurities. She need to separate pure salt crystals from the given impure sample, what will be the better technique to get pure crystals?

2. Sheela, Saima, and Ravi have to dissolve maximum amount of sugar in the same amount of milk so as to win in a game. Ravi took hot boiling milk while Saima took ice cold milk. Sheela managed to get milk at room temperature. Whom do you think would win the game and why?

3. During summer, Boojho carries water in a transparent plastic bottle to his school. One day he left his bottle in school. The bottle still had some water left in it. The following day, he observed some water droplets on the inner surface of the empty portion of the bottle. What is the phenomenon responsible for the formation of these water droplets?

4. Both Sarika and Mohan were asked to make a salt solution. Sarika was given a teaspoonful of salt and half a glass of water, whereas Mohan was given twenty teaspoons full of salt and half a glass of water.
(i) How would they make salt solutions?
(ii) Who would be able to prepare a saturated solution?

5. A mixture of iron nails, salt, oil, and water is provided to you. Give stepwise methods to separate each component from this mixture.

6. Paheli was feeling thirsty but there was only one pot of water at home which was muddy and unfit for drinking. How do you think Paheli would have made this water fit for drinking if the following materials were available to her. [Alum, tub, muslin cloth, gas stove, thread, pan, and a lid.]

7. Read the story titled "WISE FARMER" and answer the question.
A farmer was sad/happy to see his healthy wheat crop ready for harvest. He harvested the crops and left it under the sun/rain to dry the stalks. To separate the seeds from the bundles of the stalk he handpicked/threshed them. After gathering the seed grains, he wanted to separate the stones and husk from it. His wife winnowed/threshed them to separate the husk and later sieved/handpicked them to remove stones from it. She ground the wheat grains and sieved/filtered the flour. The wise farmer and his wife got a good price for the flour. Can you tell why?

8. You are provided with a mixture of salt, sand, oil, and water. Write the steps involved in the separation of salt, sand, and oil from the mixture by giving an activity along with the diagram.

9. A mixture of iron nails, salt, oil, and water is provided to you. Give stepwise methods to separate each component from this mixture.

10. Can we separate alcohol dissolved in water by using a separating funnel? If yes, then describe the procedure. If not, explain.

ARCHIVE CORNER

1. Observe the given figures carefully.

X Y

Identify X and Y respectively.
(A) Decantation, Sieving
(B) Sieving, Decantation
(C) Winnowing, Threshing
(D) Threshing, Winnowing

2. Kanya has a material X, whose molecules are separated by large distances or spaces. Nidhi has a material Y, which takes the shape of its container.
Gagan has a material Z, which has no definite volume.
Which of the three materials is/are in gaseous state?
(A) X (B) Y
(C) Both X and Y (D) Both X and Z

3. When a block of ice is dropped gently into a glass of juice, the liquid level in the glass rises.
We can conclude from this observation that the block of ice ___________.
(A) occupies space
(B) has a fixed mass
(C) can be compressed
(D) has a definite shape

4. Ritika mixed lemon juice with water to prepare lemonade. She added ice to cool it. After adding a few spoons of sugar to this solution, she found that _________ sugar can be dissolved. The solution is now said to be ___________. This is because ___________ amount of sugar dissolves in water on _________.
(A) more, pure, high, heating
(B) less, saturated, low, heating
(C) large, impure, more, cooling
(D) no more, saturated, less, cooling

5. Ravi wrote two terms 'X' and 'Y' about a solution.
'X' means 'no more will dissolve'.
'Y' means 'how much will dissolve'
(A) Insoluble, Amount
(B) Saturated, Solubility
(C) Solubility, Volume
(D) Insolubility, Saturated

6. Heat from the sun changes, water from liquid to gas. This process is called –
(A) Evaporation (B) Saturation
(C) Distillation (D) Condensation

7. Fill in the blanks by choosing the correct option.
A mixture contains different substances P, Q and R, P is a liquid which is insoluble in water. Q particles are small and soluble while R particles are small, heavy, and insoluble in water. Substance P is separated from the mixture by _________. Substance R is separated from the mixture by _________. Substance Q is recovered from water by _________.
(A) handpicking, magnetic separation, decantation
(B) Decantation, filtration, evaporation
(C) Winnowing, decantation, filtration
(D) Sieving, handpicking, decantation

8. Which of the following mixture cannot be separated on the basis of difference in weight of components in a mixture?
(A) kidney beans, and chickpeas
(B) potato wafers and biscuits
(C) rice flakes and corns
(D) saw dust and sand

9. Four identical towels were hung out to dry under different conditions.

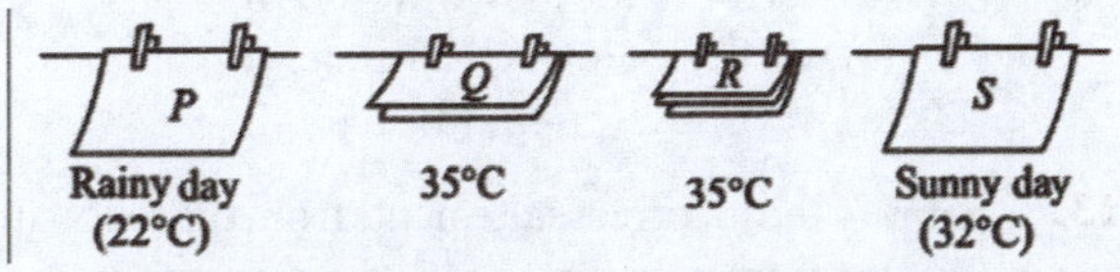

Arrange them in order, beginning with the towel that would take the longest time to dry.
(A) P, Q, R, S (B) P, R, Q, S
(C) R, P, Q, S (D) S, Q, R, P

10. Ritu has 500 cm^3 of oxygen in a small tank and she wants to transfer all of it to another container. Which of the following containers would be able to hold all the oxygen gas?

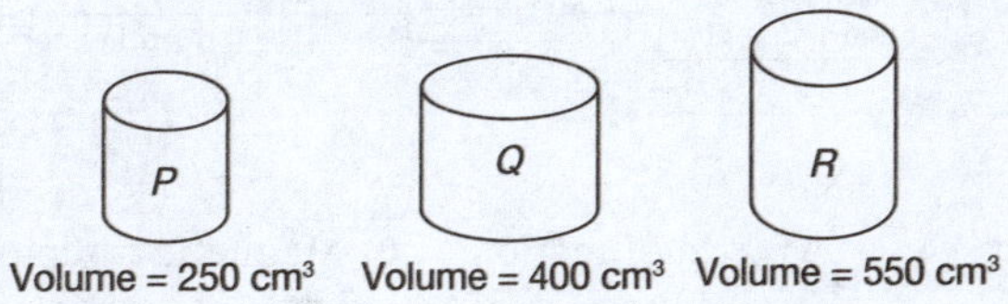

(A) R only (B) Q and R
(C) P, Q, and R (D) None of these

11. A mixture of four different powders is taken in a petri dish. The properties of the powders are listed below in the table.

Powder	Colour	Soluble in Water	Magnetic in Nature	Conductor of electricity
1	Grey	No	Yes	Yes
2	Blue	Yes	No	Yes
3	White	Yes	No	No
4	White	No	No	No

Which pair of substances would be most difficult to separate?

(A) 2 and 4 (B) 2 and 3
(C) 3 and 4 (D) 1 and 2

12. Match the Column-I with Column-II and select the correct option from the codes given below:

Column-I (Mixture)	Column-II (Methods)
(a) Flour and Iron powder	(i) Decantation
(b) Pulses and Rice flour	(ii) Evaporation
(c) Kidney bean and Lady's fingers	(iii) Handpicking
(d) Coconut oil and water	(iv) Sieving
(e) Sugar dissolved in water	(v) Magnet

(A) (a)–iv, (b)–i, (c)–ii, (d)–iii, (e)–v
(B) (a)–i, (b)–ii, (c)–iv, (d)–v, (e)–iii
(C) (a)–v, (b)–iii, (c)–iv, (d)–ii, (e)–i
(D) (a)–v, (b)–iv, (c)–iii, (d)–i, (e)–ii

13. Identify the incorrect statements from the following:

(A) Interparticle distance is more in gas.
(B) Solid has a definite shape and volume.
(C) Ice is heavier than water.
(D) Matter can be changed from one form to another.

14. Study the given flowchart and identify the processes P, Q, R and S involved in the separation of the mixture:

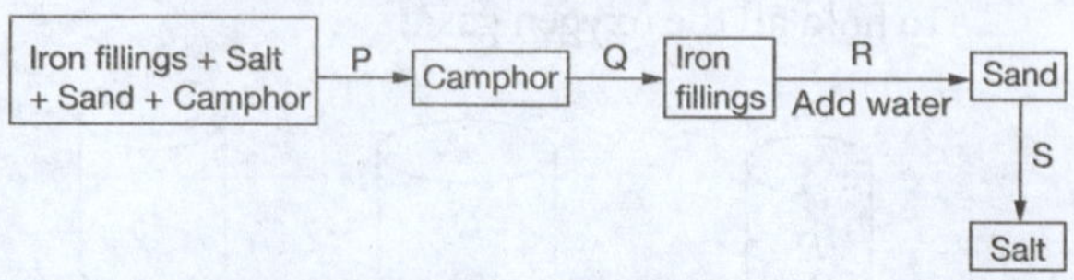

(A) P-Sublimation; Q-Magnetic separation; R-Filtration; S-Evaporation
(B) P-Magnetic separation; Q-Filtration; R-Sublimation; S-Evaporation
(C) P-Evaporation; Q-Magnetic separation; R-Filtration; S-Sublimation
(D) P-Sublimation; Q-Magnetic separation; R-Evaporation; S-Filtration

15. A mixture contains three different substances X, Y, and Z. They are of same size and colour. X particles are heavy and nonmagnetic, Y particles are light and nonmagnetic while Z particles are magnetic. Which of the following methods can be used to separate these particles?

(A) Handpicking followed by filtration.
(B) Winnowing followed by magnetic separation.
(C) Magnetic separation followed by sieving.
(D) Sublimation followed by distillation.

16. Which of the following is correctly matched?

(i) No more salt can be dissolved: Saturated solution.
(ii) Milk and water can be separated by: Filtration.
(iii) To separate heavier and lighter components: Winnowing.
(iv) To obtain butter from milk: Sieving.

(A) i and iii (B) ii and iv
(C) i, iii, and iv (D) All of these

17. A funnel is fitted into a stopper that closes the mouth of a flask as shown in the given diagram. Virag wants to fill the flask with water, but water does not flow in when it is poured into the funnel. This is because _________.

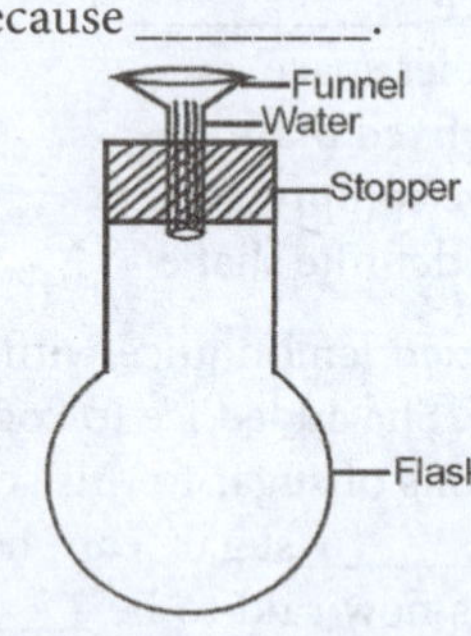

(A) The air pressure inside the flask is lower than the pressure of water in funnel.
(B) The space in the flask is occupied by air.
(C) The funnel is too small for water to flow through.
(D) The mouth of the flask is not sealed tightly enough.

18. The given diagram shows a method by which a solid can be separated from solid-water mixture. Which one of the following could be that solid?

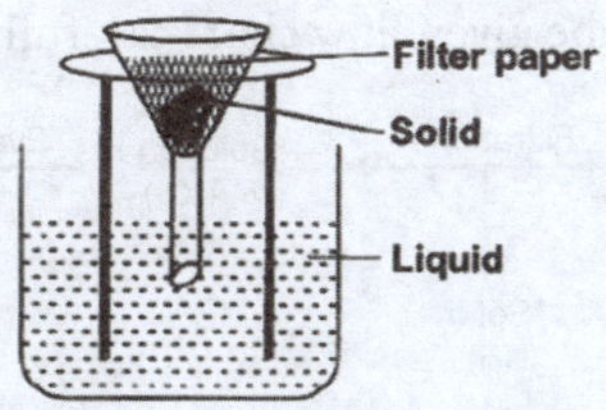

(A) Salt (B) Sugar
(C) Sand (D) Ice crystals

19. The given diagrams represent two elements:

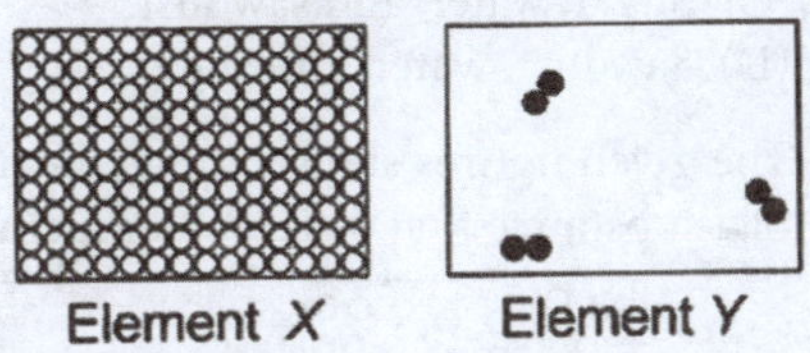

Which of the following statements is true about X and Y?
(A) Particles of element X can move freely in all directions.
(B) Element Y is incompressible in nature.
(C) Element X is a solid, and element Y is a gas.
(D) Element X is less dense than element Y

20. Substances W, X, Y, and Z are obtained from different types of mixtures by using appropriate separating processes as shown in the given flowchart:

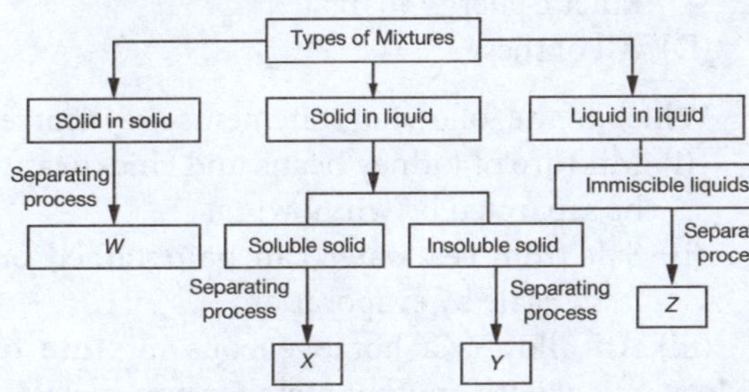

Separating processes used to obtain W, X, Y, and Z respectively are
(A) Winnowing, filtration, sedimentation, and evaporation.
(B) Sedimentation, winnowing, filtration and separating funnel.
(C) Handpicking, sedimentation, winnowing and evaporation.
(D) Sieving, evaporation, filtration, and separating funnel.

21. The given diagram describes the changes that take place between different states of matter:

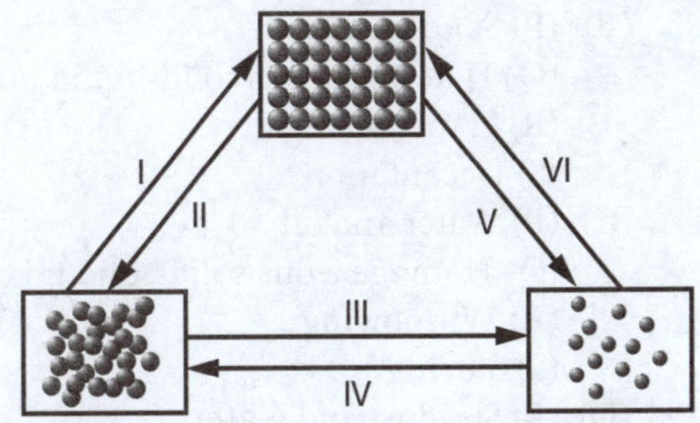

The processes in which energy is given out are
(A) I and III only (B) I, IV, and V only
(C) I, II, and IV only (D) None of these

22. Sonali mixed a packet of salt in a small amount of sand and then tried to recover the salt by the usual processes of sedimentation, decantation or filtration followed by evaporation. To her surprise, she could recover only a small part of the salt that she had taken. The possible reasons could be
(i) Salt also got evaporated along with water.
(ii) The quantity of salt was much more than that required to form a saturated solution.
(iii) The undissolved salt remained mixed with sand.
(iv) The quantity of water taken was insufficient to dissolve all the salt.
(A) II and III only (B) I and IV only
(C) II, III and IV only (D) All of these

23. Fill in the blanks in the given table by choosing an appropriate option.

Type of Mixture	Method of Separation	Example
A heterogeneous solid-liquid mixture in which solid is lighter than liquid.	Filtration	P
Q	Sieving	Bran and Flour
A heterogeneous solid-solid mixture containing one soluble component.	R	Sand and Salt
A heterogeneous liquid-liquid mixture.	S	Water and mustard oil

(A) (P) Husk and water
(Q) Heterogeneous solid-solid mixture
(R) Filtration and evaporation
(S) Separating funnel

ARCHIVE CORNER

(B) (P) Sand and water
(Q) Heterogeneous solid-liquid mixture
(R) Handpicking
(S) Decantation

(C) (P) Water and oil
(Q) Homogeneous solid-solid mixture
(R) Winnowing
(S) Sieving

(D) (P) Sawdust and water
(Q) Heterogeneous solid-solid mixture
(R) Distillation
(S) Separating funnel

24. The table given below shows the amount of water in five identical beakers at the start of an experiment. It also shows the time required for the water in each beaker to go down by 20 mL.

Beaker	Amount of Water at Beginning (mL)	Time Taken for Water to Reduce by 20 mL (min)
P	60	50
Q	60	30
R	80	60
S	90	60
T	100	70

What can we conclude from the table?

(A) Water in beaker Q evaporates faster than in beaker P.
(B) Water in beaker T evaporates faster than in beaker Q.
(C) Water in beaker T evaporates faster than in beaker P.
(D) Beakers R and S will have the same amount of water after 60 min.

25. Which of the following statements are incorrect?

(i) Evaporation of water at ordinary temperature is a physical and slow change.
(ii) Germination of seeds is a chemical and fast change.
(iii) Bursting of a balloon is a chemical and fast change.
(iv) Glowing of a bulb is a physical and fast change.
(v) Digestion of food is a physical and slow change.

(A) II and III only (B) IV and V only
(C) I and IV only (D) II, III, and V only

26. Study the given flow chart carefully.

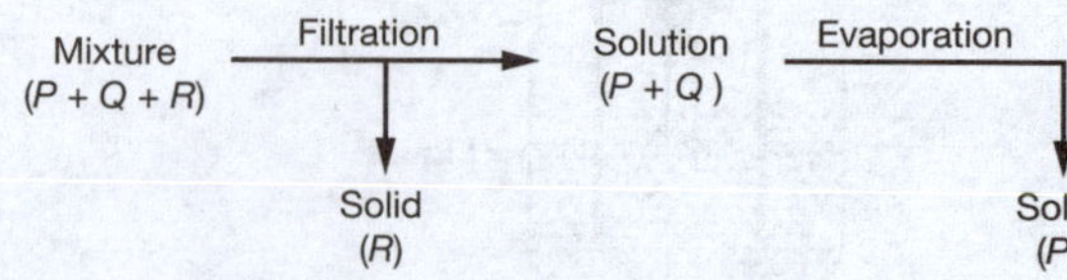

P, Q, and R could be respectively

(A) Chalk powder, water, and sawdust.
(B) Salt, water, and sugar.
(C) Sugar, water, and sawdust.
(D) Sawdust, water, and sugar.

27. The given figures show arrangement of particles of a substance X at different temperatures.

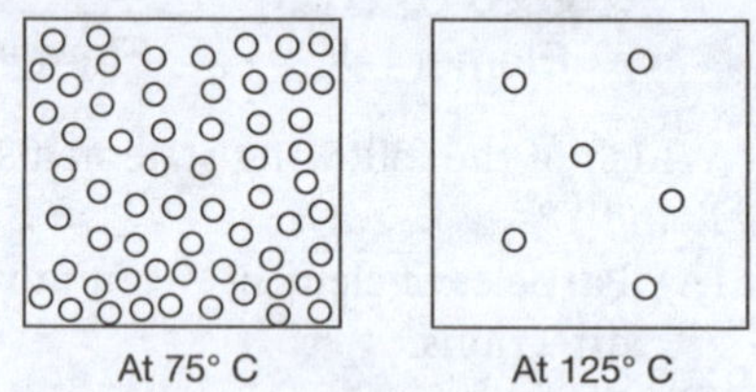

Which of the following statements is correct?

(A) The boiling point of the substance X is between 75°C and 125°C.
(B) The melting point of the substance X is below 75°C.
(C) Particles of substance X at 125°C have more kinetic energy than at 75°C.
(D) All of these.

28. Which of the following statements are incorrect?

(i) Mixture of kidney beans and chickpeas can be separated by winnowing.
(ii) Salt from sea water can be obtained on a large scale by evaporation.
(iii) An alloy is a homogeneous mixture of a metal with another metal or non-metals.
(iv) Seeds of wheat can be separated from a bundle of wheat stalks by sieving.

(A) II and III only (B) I and IV only
(C) I, III, and IV only (D) None of these

29. Read the given statements and select the correct option.

Statement 1: When sea water is allowed to stand in shallow pits, water gets heated by sunlight and slowly turns into water vapour through evaporation.

Statement 2: Boiling takes place at all temperatures.

(A) Both statements 1 and 2 are true, and statement 2 is correct explanation of statement 1.
(B) Both statements 1 and 2 are true, but statement 2 is not the correct explanation of statement 1.
(C) Statement 1 is true, but statement 2 is false.
(D) Both statements 1 and 2 are false.

30. Three identical towels were hung out to dry under different conditions.

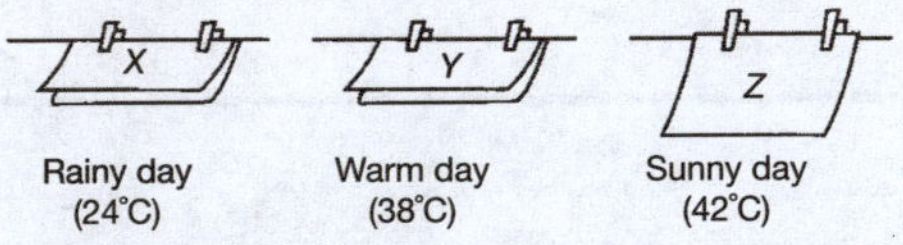

Arrange them in order, beginning with the towel that would take the shortest time to dry.

(A) X, Y, Z (B) Z, X, Y
(C) Z, Y, X (D) Y, X, Z

31. Identify the incorrect statement from the following.

(A) Interparticle distance is more in helium than in gold.
(B) Nitrogen has no definite shape as well as no definite volume.
(C) Mercury is lighter than water.
(D) Potassium is a reactive metal.

32. The given figures show arrangement of particles of a substance 'P' at different temperatures.

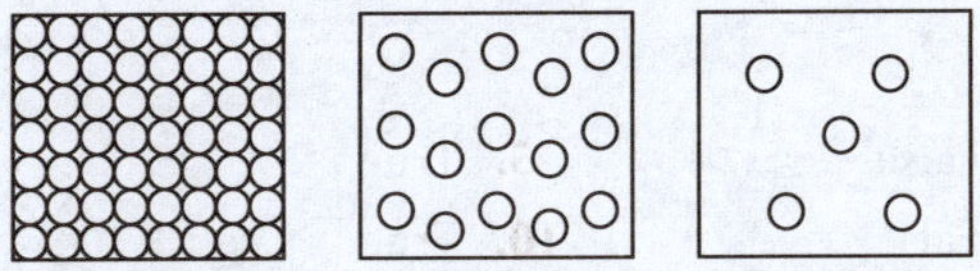

At 42°C At 65°C At 115°C

Which of the following statements is correct?

(A) Melting point of the substance 'P' is below 42°C.
(B) Particles of the substance 'P' at 115°C have less kinetic energy than at 65°C.
(C) Boiling point of the substance 'P' is between 65°C and 115°C.
(D) All of these.

33. Rashu deliberately mixed rice, all pins, biscuits, pebbles, and powdered sugar into a bowl in equal proportions and gave the mixture to her brother Kunal. She asked him to separate each component of the mixture without using water. Select the correct sequence of the methods of separation that you think Kunal should use.

(A) Sieving, threshing, and then handpicking.
(B) Magnetic separation, handpicking, filtration, and then sieving.
(C) Handpicking, centrifugation, and then winnowing.
(D) Handpicking, magnetic separation, and then sieving.

34. Observe the given heating curve of ice carefully and select the correct statement(s) about it.

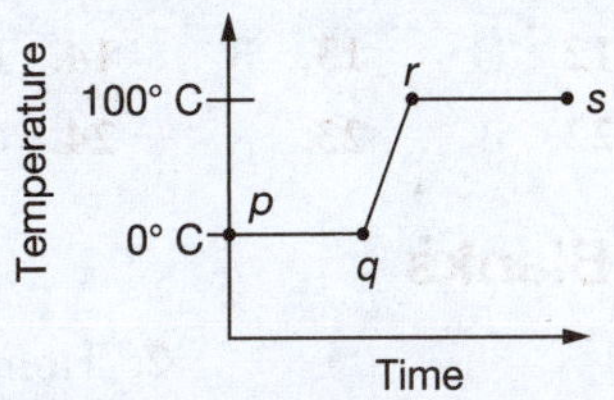

(i) Point p is the freezing point of water.
(ii) Between the points q and r, water exists in liquid state.
(iii) After points, water vapours condense back to liquid water on further increasing the temperature.
(iv) Point r is the boiling point of water.

(A) (ii) and (iii) only
(B) (iii) only
(C) (i) and (iv) only
(D) (i), (ii), and (iv) only

35. Match column I with column II and select the correct option from the given codes.

Column-I	Column-II
(P) Milk	(i) Has definite shape and volume
(Q) Air	(ii) Undergoes sublimation
(R) Ammonium chloride	(iii) Has definite volume
(S) Brick	(iv) Homogeneous mixture

(A) P-(iii); Q- (iv); R- (i), (ii); S- (i)
(B) P-(iii); Q-(ii); R-(i); S-(iv)
(C) P-(i); Q-(ii), (iii); R-(iv); S-(ii)
(D) P-(iv); Q-(i), (iii); R-(iii); S-(ii)

36. Read the given passage and fill in the blanks by selecting an appropriate option. Change in temperature and pressure plays a very important role in changing the state of matter. A gas gets liquefied with __(i)__ and __(ii)__ while camphor undergoes sublimation with __(iii)__ and __(iv)__ .

(i)	(ii)	(iii)	(iv)
(A) Increase in pressure	Decrease in temperature	Decrease in temperature	Decrease in pressure
(B) Increase in pressure	Decrease in temperature	Increase in pressure	Decrease in temperature
(C) Decrease in temperature	Increase in pressure	Increase in temperature	Decrease in pressure
(D) Decrease in pressure	Increase in temperature	Increase in pressure	Decrease in temperature

ANSWER KEY

Level 1

Fixed Response Type

Multiple Choice Questions

1. D 2. D 3. A 4. D 5. B 6. D 7. C 8. C 9. D 10. B
11. A 12. D 13. B 14. B 15. C 16. B 17. C 18. D 19. D 20. D
21. C 22. B 23. A 24. C

Fill in the Blanks

1. One kind 2. Homogeneous 3. Alloy
4. Heterogeneous mixture 5. Sedimentation 6. Sublimation
7. Grains 8. Winnowing 9. Sieving
10. Saturated solution 11. Loading 12. Boiling point
13. Sieving 14. Water 15. Sieving

True/False

1. False 2. False 3. False 4. False 5. True
6. False 7. True 8. False 9. False 10. True

Match Type Questions

1. 1-d, 2-a, 3-c, 4-e, 5-b 2. 1-b, 2-d, 3-a, 4-c 3. 1-c, 2-a, 3-b, 4-d
4. 1-d, 2-c, 3-b, 4-a 5. 1-b, 2-a, 3-d, 4-c 6. 1-d, 2-c, 3-a, 4-b

Assertion and Reason Type Questions

1. A 2. B 3. B 4. C 5. D 6. D 7. B 8. B 9. A 10. A

Comprehension Type Questions

1. B 2. D 3. C 4. D 5. C

Free Response Type

Numerical Based Questions

1. B 2. C

Case Based Questions

1. C 2. D 3. D

ANSWER KEY

Level 2

Multiple Choice Questions

1. C	**2.** A	**3.** D	**4.** B	**5.** A	**6.** C	**7.** B	**8.** C	**9.** A	**10.** B
11. D	**12.** C	**13.** D	**14.** D	**15.** D	**16.** B	**17.** B	**18.** B	**19.** C	**20.** D
21. B	**22.** B	**23.** A	**24.** C	**25.** C	**26.** D	**27.** B	**28.** B	**29.** C	**30.** D
31. A	**32.** B	**33.** C	**34.** C	**35.** D					

Archive Corner

1. D	**2.** D	**3.** A	**4.** D	**5.** B	**6.** A	**7.** B	**8.** A	**9.** B	**10.** C
11. B	**12.** D	**13.** C	**14.** A	**15.** B	**16.** A	**17.** B	**18.** C	**19.** C	**20.** D
21. D	**22.** C	**23.** D	**24.** A	**25.** D	**26.** C	**27.** D	**28.** B	**29.** C	**30.** C
31. C	**32.** C	**33.** D	**34.** D	**35.** A	**36.** C				

CHAPTER 7

A Journey Through States of Water

Learning Outcomes

After reading this chapter, you will be able to:

- explain the importance of water to human beings.
- explain availability of water and sources of water.
- explain physical properties of water and also the role of water as a solvent.
- explain the water cycle, water table, and reasons responsible for water table depletion.
- explain methods to conserve the water.

Geekspeak

- Hydrological cycle
- Ice caps
- Potable water
- Freezing point
- Boiling point
- Organic compounds
- Inorganic compounds
- Universal solvent
- Water table
- Drought, scarcity
- Famine
- Flood
- Rainwater harvesting
- Water pollution
- Hard water
- Soft water
- Distilled water

Introduction

We all depend on the same important substance: water. It is diverse in nature, solid, vapour and liquid. They exist in the air, on the ground, and in soil, and they are constantly changing, creating dramatically diverse natural ecosystems.

For the planet's inhabitants, resource diversity also means a big difference in prosperity and development.

When we degrade water quality and alter the natural ecosystems on which people and life depend, we threaten our own survival.

Water

Water is the most widely occurring substance on this planet. Globally distributed by the hydrological cycle, driven by the energy cycle, circulation of water powers most other natural cycles and conditions the weather and climate. Water has shaped the Earth's evolution and continues to fashion its programmes.

Availability of Water

Water precipitates from the atmosphere onto land, where it is stored in liquid or solid form, and can move laterally, vertically, and between one phase and another through evaporation, condensation, freezing, and thawing at the surface of the earth.This water can move at very different speeds, usually in predictable paths that change slowly over time. Almost all water (about 71%) on Earth is contained in oceans, seas, rivers, lakes, ice caps, groundwater and the atmosphere. However, most of this water is not suitable for human consumption.

Sources of Water

Water covers over 70% of the Earth's surface. However, only 3% is fresh water, out of which 77% is frozen in glaciers and polar caps. The remaining unfrozen freshwater is found primarily as groundwater, with only a small portion existing above ground or in the air.

- **Rainwater:** The main source of water is rain. When the water vapour in the air condenses, it rains. Although rainwater is pure water, it becomes polluted when it falls to the ground, mixing with atmospheric dust and other pollutants.
- **Groundwater:** When it rains, a part of the rainwater evaporates back into the atmosphere, another part forms streams or rivers, and the remaining percolates into the ground to form ground water. As water passes through several layers of sand and rocks, it gets naturally filtered and gets free from suspended impurities. About 30% of the total fresh water found on Earth exists as groundwater. We can obtain groundwater by digging wells and tube wells. Pollution, seawater pollution and overfishing threaten this precious resource.
- **Surface water:** Sources of surface water include all the water collected above the ground such as rivers, lakes, ponds, and oceans. The water bodies usually get their supply of water from rainwater as well as melting snow. Some surface water sources are also supplied by underground aquifers. Surface water accounts for 80% of the water we use.
- **Ocean water:** Rivers flow into oceans and thus river water is a source of water for oceans. Although ocean water makes up nearly 97% of the entire water present on the Earth, it is not a viable source of potable water since it contains salt and other impurities.
- **Ice caps and glaciers:** About 70% of the small amount of freshwater present is locked in glaciers and ice caps. Siachen Glacier, in India, is an example of a glacier.

Keystone

We all know that the human body is made up of about 70% water. But did you know that this is constantly changing at different times in your life.A human embryo has about 95% of it in the first few months, 77% of it at birth, and 60-60% in adulthood. 70% is water. A person weighing 70 kg needs about 42 liters of water.

Composition of Water

Water is a compound. It's constituent elements are hydrogen and oxygen. Water is a stable compound, but it breaks down into hydrogen and oxygen when an electric current is passed through it. Its chemical formula is H_2O. The ratio between hydrogen and oxygen in water is 1:8 by mass.

Physical Properties of Water

The properties of water are different from those of oxygen and hydrogen. For example, water puts out fire, but oxygen supports combustion, and hydrogen pops and burns.

- Pure water is a colourless, odourless, tasteless, and transparent liquid.
- Water exists in all the three states, solid (as ice), liquid (as water) and gas (as water vapour).
- Pure water boils at 100°C at 760 mm of mercury pressure. The boiling point of water depends on the pressure. At low pressure, the boiling point decreases and at high pressures, the boiling point increases.
- Pure water freezes at 0°C at 760 mm of mercury pressure. Impurities decreases the freezing point of water.
- Pure water is a bad conductor of heat and electricity.
- Density of water is 1g/cc at 4°C, which is the maximum density of water.
- Water dissolves inorganic compounds (usually electrovalent compounds), certain organic compounds (carbohydrates, proteins), and a large number of gases and hence, it is called a universal solvent.

Water as a Solvent

One of the best known solvents is water. Solutions made with water are termed aqueous solutions. So, as solution of copper sulphate in water is written as $CuSO_4(aq)$. The symbol 'aq' stands for aqueous.

Gases as well as solids dissolve in water. Natural water contains dissolved gases like oxygen, nitrogen, and carbon dioxide. Oxygen dissolved in water is the main source for survival of aquatic life. Carbon dioxide dissolved in water is utilized to produce food via photochemical reactions. Nitrogen dissolved in water is converted into nitrogenous compounds. This is acted upon by the bacteria in sea water, which acts as a mode of nourishment for water plants.

Gases can be made to dissolve better when pressure is applied. For example, in fizz drinks, once the pressure is released, the dissolved carbon dioxide gas oozes out of the solution. Uses of Water Besides being essential for life, water is used for many other purposes. In India, about 70% of the total water available is used for agriculture, 20–22% by industries, and only 8% is used for personal or domestic needs. Let us learn more about the various uses of water.

- **Agricultural needs:** Our country depends a lot on agricultural crops such as wheat and paddy. Many a times, rainfall is not sufficient to water these crops, and farmers have to use artificial watering systems, referred to as irrigation.
- **Industrial needs:** Factories use a large amount of water every day–as raw material, for cleaning, heating, cooling, generating electricity (e.g. water turbines), etc. The amount of water required depends on the kind and size of the factory.
- **Personal/domestic needs:** We need water to drink. Water that is suitable for human consumption is called potable water. We also need water to bath, wash clothes and dishes, clean our house, and to water plants.

> **Keystone**
>
> Hot water freezes faster than cold water which is known as the Mpemba Effect.

Apart from these uses, water is also used for transportation and recreation. It also regulates the climate of a place and provides homes to many plants and animals.

❖ INTEXT QUESTIONS

1. State the sources of water on Earth.
   Solution: Sources of water on the Earth are: Seas, Oceans, Rivers, Springs, Tube wells, etc.
2. In which form does water exist on the Earth?
   Solution: Water exists on the Earth in all three physical forms: ice, water, and water vapour.

3. What is ground water?

Solution: When it rains, a part of rainwater evaporates back into the atmosphere, another part forms streams or rivers, and the remaining percolates into the ground to form ground water. As water passes through the several layers of sand and rocks, it gets naturally filtered and gets free from suspended impurities.

Check Point 1

1. In which forms does water exist on Earth?
2. Which is largest source of water on the Earth?
3. Name any five sources of water.
4. Write the composition of water.
5. What is the freezing point and boiling point of pure water?

Circulation of Water on Earth

The supply of water in nature does not run out. This is because water is continuously recycled in the water cycle. The journey of water from the oceans to the atmosphere and then back to the ocean is called the water cycle.

- Heat from the sun causes the water on the Earth's surface to evaporate (Fig. 7.1). The vapour rises, cools, and condenses to form tiny water droplets. These droplets form clouds. When the temperature of air increases, it expands (i.e., its particles move away from one another). This makes the air lighter, and it rises in the atmosphere, taking water vapour with it. As the air rises, it begins to cool.

  The water vapour condenses on dust particles present in the atmosphere to form millions of tiny droplets. Tiny ice crystals will be formed instead if it is very cold. This cluster of tiny water droplets floating in air is what we call a cloud.
- The clouds get carried along by air currents. They cool and the droplets join to form larger drops. These fall as mist.
- If the temperature in the region is very low, these water droplets fall as hail, sleet, or snow.
- Some of the rainwater flows along the ground as streams. Soak through the ground and then reappears as springs. Streams and springs join to form rivers. Rivers flow back into the sea. Thus, the water cycle is complete.

Figure 7.1 Water Cycle

Water Table

Upper surface of ground water below which soil is saturated with water that fills all void is called water table as shown in Fig. 7.2.

Depletion

Increase in population, industrial and agricultural activities are some common factors affecting water table. Scanty rainfall is another factor that may deplete the water table.

Increasing Population

Increasing population creates demand for construction of houses, shops, offices, roads and pavements. This decreases the open areas like parks and playgrounds. This, in turn, decreases the seepage of rainwater into the ground. Moreover, a huge amount of water is required for construction work. Groundwater is often used for this purpose. So, on one hand we are consuming more groundwater, and on the other we are allowing lesser water to seep into the ground.

Figure 7.2 Water Table

Increasing Industries

Water is used by all the industries. Almost everything that we use needs water somewhere in its production process. The number of industries is increasing continuously. Water used by most of the industries is drawn from the ground.

Competition Corner

- **Composition of Water:** Water is a compound. Its constituent elements are hydrogen and oxygen. Water is a stable compound but can be broken into hydrogen and oxygen when electric current is passed through it. Its chemical formula is H_2O. The ratio between hydrogen and oxygen in water is 1:8 by mass.
- When iron reacts with water and oxygen present in the atmosphere, it gets rusted.

  This process is known as rusting or corrosion. Rust is hydrated iron (III) oxide. ($Fe_2O_3 . xH_2O$)

  $4Fe + 3O_2 + xH_2O \rightarrow 2Fe_2O_3.xH_2O$

❖ INTEXT QUESTIONS

4. What is transpiration?
   Solution: Loss of water in the form of water vapour through stomata of leaves is called transpiration.
5. How are the clouds formed?
   Solution: Clouds are formed by the condensation of water vapour at high altitude.
6. During winters why do we see more fog in close areas where there are lots of trees?
   Solution: Due to lots of trees, air at that place contains much more water vapour during winters. These vapours condense on dust or smoke particles forming thick fog.

Check Point 2

6. Name two main processes which transfer water present on Earth into water vapour continuously.
7. How are clouds formed?
8. Explain the term 'water table.'
9. What do you mean by depletion of the water table?
10. Give some causes of depletion of water table.

Drought, Flood and Water Conservation

Water is a critical resource, yet its availability is often unpredictable due to natural extremes such as droughts and floods. Both phenomena pose significant challenges to water management systems worldwide.

Drought

Water scarcity can be defined as a lack of sufficient water, or not having access of safe water supplies (Fig. 7.3).

Sometimes, it does not rain for a long time-for an entire month, two months, the whole season, two years, etc. The abnormally long period of insufficient or no rainfall at all is called drought. The lack of food in a region for a long period is called famine.

Effects of Drought

- Drought causes plants and animal to wither away.
- Crops cannot be grown, and already sown crops fail to grow.
- Energy production is reduced.
- Groundwater levels fall, leading to acute water crisis.
- Prices of all commodities go up.
- Erosion of soil by wind takes place (wind erosion).

Figure 7.3 Drought

Flood

Overflowing of water from the rivers and streams into fields and homes is called flood. Some of the consequences of floods are given below.

Effect of Flood

- **Panic, injuries, and deaths:** Heavy rains, as seen in recent floods in Mumbai, cause panic among the people. Many old people, children and physically weak persons suffer from injuries and even die on account of panic.
- **Water level:** Water level in rivers, lakes and ponds rises.
- **Soil erosion:** Heavy floods bring about erosion of soil from the fields, making them barren and infertile.
- **Damage to crops:** Crops get submerged under water, leading to loss of production of useful food items.
- **Diseases:** Floods leads to diseases due to the mixing of floodwater with the waste materials and waste water.
- **Loss of habitats of plants and animals:** Due to floods, the living places of many animals and plants are lost, causing much damage to the flora and fauna of the affected area.

Conservation of Water

Since only a small percentage of water on our planet is usable, it is very important that we use water carefully. The conservation of water can be done by building dams, avoiding wastage of water at homes, both indoors and outdoors, harvesting rainwater, and preventing pollution of water.

Figure 7.4 Dam

Building a Dam

A dam is a structure built to hold back water in order to prevent floods (Fig. 7.4), and to provide water for irrigation and storage. Building a dam is a solution to both drought and flood.

Dams are also used to produce electricity. Built on rivers, a dam has high walls and has many openings or gates to both let in and hold back water. During heavy rainfall, when the rivers fill up, water enters the dam when water is needed later, the gates are opened to let out water.

Rainwater Harvesting

The process of collecting and storing rainwater from roofs or a surface catchment is called rainwater harvesting. Storing rainwater that collects on roofs instead of letting it go down the drain, is a practical solution in case of droughts. This technique is known as rooftop rainwater harvesting. This involves collecting rainwater from rooftops in dugout ponds, vessel, or underground tanks to store water for long periods (Fig. 7.5). Another option is to allow water to go into the ground directly from the roadside drains that collect rainwater. The stored rainwater is treated before use because it may contain bird faeces, chemical and other pollutants, which need to be removed before use.

Figure 7.5 Rainwater Harvesting

Methods of Rainwater Harvesting

- Rooftop rainwater harvesting. In this system, the rainwater from the rooftop is collected in a storage tank, through pipes.
- Another method, a big pit is dug near house for collecting rainwater. This pit is filled with different layers of bricks, coarse gravels and sand or granite pieces.

Preventing Water Pollution

Another method to conserve water is to safeguard our freshwater bodies from pollution. Garbage and harmful chemical pollute the water and make it unfit for use (Fig. 7.6). Polluted water is also very bad for aquatic life. Plants and animals in and around polluted water consume the contaminate fish, etc., they are also pose a risk of disease.

Figure 7.6 Water Pollution

Check Point 3

11. What is water scarcity?
12. What is drought?
13. What is famine?
14. List two effects of drought.
15. State one advantage of rainwater harvesting.

STRUCTURAL OUTLINE

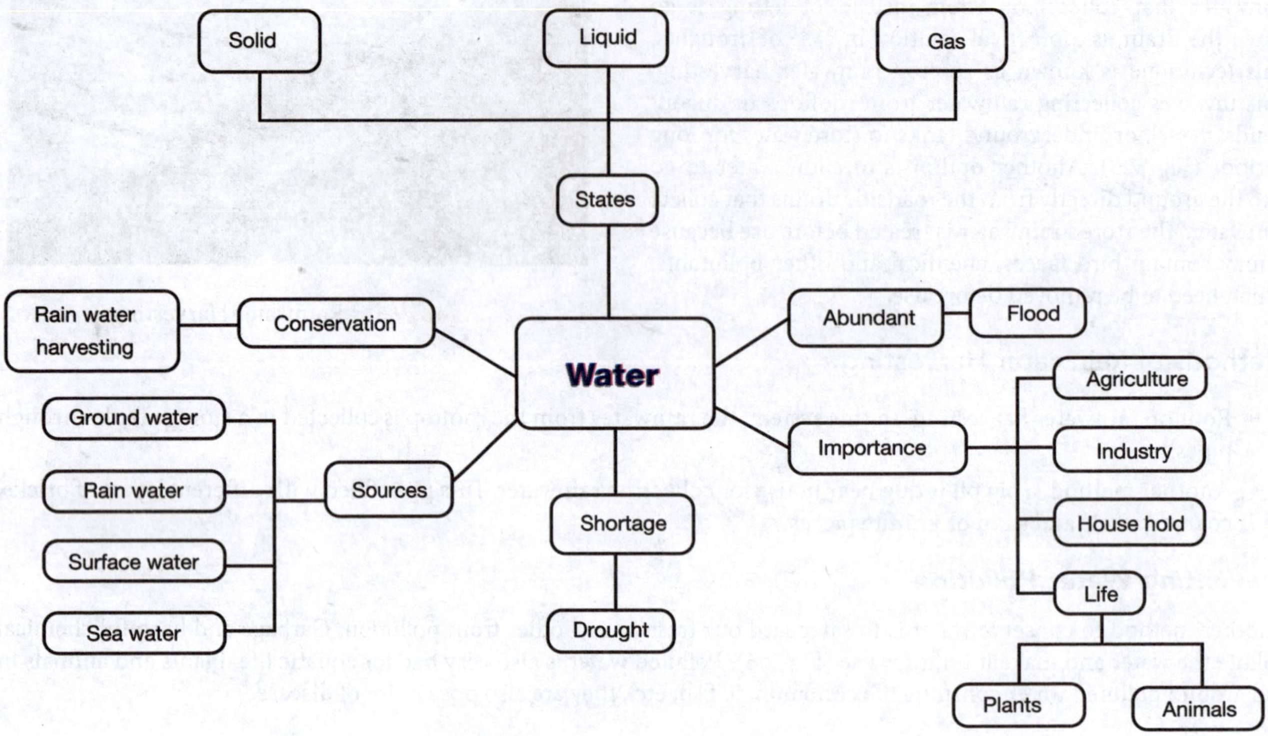

ABRIDGEMENT

- **Hard and soft water**

  Underground water is the main source of water used for various purposes. Since this water remains in the bottom layers of Earth's crust for a long time, it contains dissolved salts. Depending on the type of dissolved salts, water can be classified into two types:

  Soft water: Water which can freely form lather with soap is called soft water.

  Hard water: Water which does not form lather with soap and forms a precipitate or scum is called hard water.

- **Causes of Hardness**

  If the sample of water contains calcium and magnesium bicarbonates, and sulphates, they do not allow the formation of much lather. Therefore, these salts cause hardness of water.

- **Distilled Water**

  Since most of the chemical reactions take place in water, laboratory work requires pure water for carrying out various tests and reactions. For this purpose, the dissolved salts should be removed from water to get pure water. This is done by subjecting water for purification by the process of distillation.

EXEMPLIFICATION

1. **Mention two main functions of water for living organisms.**

   Solution: Two main functions of water for living organisms are:

   (i) Water is essential for the germination of seeds, growth of plants, and in photosynthesis.

   (ii) Water is used for transportation of people and goods.

2. **Why is ocean water not suitable for domestic use?**

   Solution: Sea and ocean water contains large amounts of various salts. It is due to these salts the ocean water is salty and cannot be used for drinking, washing and for irrigation purposes.

3. **Define flood.**

   Solution: Overflowing of water from the rivers and streams into fields and homes is called a flood.

4. **Write any two activities which require less than one bucket of water.**

   Solution: The two activities which require less than one bucket of water are:

   (i) For brushing teeth.

   (ii) For washing hands.

5. **Look at figure given below:**

   Write down activities shown in this figure in which water is being used.

   Solution: The activities shown in the given figure in which water is being used are:

   (i) Water is used for bathing.

(ii) Water is used for washing clothes.

(iii) Water is lifted from the well to store water and for drinking purposes.

6. Write any two activities which require more than a bucket of water.

Solution: The two activities which require more than a bucket of water are:

(i) For irrigation purpose, we require more water.

(ii) For washing a large number of clothes.

7. Why does the water split on the floor disappear after some time?

Solution: Due to evaporation the water split is changed into water vapour. So it disappears after some time.

Water Cycle

8. How does heavy rain affect us?

Solution: Heavy rains may cause:

1. A rise of water level in dams, rivers, lakes, etc.
2. Waterlogging and floods.
3. Floods cause damage to property, crops, and animals.

9. Why do wet clothes placed on a clothes line dry after some time? Explain.

Solution: Wet clothes placed on a clothesline get dry after some time because, on exposing to sunlight, water present in wet clothes gets converted into water vapour due to evaporation, resulting in dry clothes.

10. Water kept in the sunlight gets heat from sun and is evaporated. But how does water kept under the shade of a tree also get evaporated? Explain.

Solution: Water gets evaporated when kept under the shade of a tree during daytime due to the air around the tree also gets heated up from the presence of sunlight, so water gets evaporated from the heated air.

11. What is meant by the conservation of water?

Solution: Careful, economical, and wise use of water and avoiding the wastage of water is called conservation of water.

12. What is rainwater harvesting? Describe the method of rainwater harvesting.

Solution: Rainwater harvesting is the collection of rainwater and storing for future use. In this system rainwater in collected from the rooftops by means of pipes into storage tank for later use.

NCERT COMPENDIUM

1. Which of the following best describes condensation?
(i) The conversion of water into its vapour state.
(ii) The process of water changing from a liquid into gaseous state.
(iii) The formation of clouds from tiny water droplets.
(iv) The conversion of water vapour into its liquid state.

Solution: (iv) The conversion of water vapour into its liquid state describes condensation.

2. Identify in which of the given processes, evaporation is very important
(i) Colouring with
(a) crayons
(b) water colours
(c) acrylic colours
(d) pencil colours
(ii) Writing on paper with
(a) pencil
(b) ink pen
(c) ball point pen

Solution: (i) (b) water colours(ii) (b) ink pen

3. We see green coloured plastic grass at many places these days. Space around natural grass feels cooler than space around the plastic grass. Can you find out why?

Solution: Space around natural grass feels cooler because it absorbs moisture from air.

4. Give examples of liquids other than water, which evaporate.

Solution: Milk, oil, whisky, eye drops, sanitizer.

5. Fans move air around, creating a cooling sensation. It might seem strange to use a fan to dry wet clothes since fans usually make things cooler, not warmer. Normally, when water evaporates, it requires heat, not cold air. What do you think about this?

Solution: Fans move the air faster around clothes and help these to dry faster because water evaporates faster.

6. Usually, when sludge is removed from drains, it is left in heaps next to the drain for 3-4 days. Afterward, it is transported to a garden or a field where it can be used as manure. This approach reduces transportation cost of the sludge and enhances the safety of individuals handling it. Reflect upon it and explain how.

Solution: Water (moisture) from the sludge evaporates with time making it handling and transportation easier.

7. Observe the activities in your house for a day. Identify the activities that involve evaporation. How does understanding the process of evaporation help us in our daily activities? ,

Solution: We perform various activities where process of evaporation help us.
(i) We dry our clothes on a sunny and windy environment.
(ii) We can smell the food being cooked even without entering the kitchen.
(iii) Washed utensils dry up after some time.

8. How is water present in the solid state'in nature?

Solution: Ice, snow and frost are the solid state of water present in nature.

9. Reflect on the statement "Water is our responsibility before it is our right." Share your thoughts.

Solution: Only a small portion of water available on earth is fit for use by plants, animals and humans.Most of the water is available in the oceans which we cannot use directly. We need water for drinking and many other activities. With increasing population the availability of safe water is decreasing. Though it is our right to get water for our existence but at the same time it is our responsibility to keep water bodies free from pollution.

10. The seat of a two-wheeler parked on a sunny day has become very hot. How can you cool it down?

Solution: To cool down the hot seat of a two-wheeler parked on a sunny day, we can:
- Cover it with a wet cloth: Place a damp cloth or towel over the seat. The water will absorb heat as it evaporates, cooling the seat.
- Sprinkle water on it: Lightly sprinkle water directly on the seat. The evaporating water will help to lower the temperature.
- Use a sunshade or cover: If available, use a sunshade or seat cover to protect the seat from direct sunlight, which will help keep it cooler.
- Park in the shade: If possible, move the two-wheeler to a shaded area to reduce the seat's exposure to direct sunlight.

ASSESSMENT CORNER

LEVEL 1

Fixed Response Type

Multiple Choice Questions

1. Pure water, belongs in the category of;
(A) an element (B) a compound
(C) a mixture (D) none of these

2. What percentage of water present in human body?
(A) 30% (B) 70%
(C) 20% (D) none of these

3. How much of the Earth surface is covered with water?
(A) About 1/3rd (B) About 1/4th
(C) About 3/4th (D) None of these

4. The purest form of natural water is:
(A) Rainwater (B) Ground water
(C) Surface water (D) None of these

5. Which of these is the surface water?
(A) Lakes and rivers (B) Wells
(C) Distilled water (D) None of these

6. The ratio of the number of hydrogen atoms and those of oxygen in water is:
(A) 2:1 (B) 1:2
(C) 2:2 (D) None of these

7. At room temperature, water exist in –
(A) solid state (B) liquid state,
(C) gaseous state (D) none of these.

8. Water exists in three physical states:
(A) Solid (B) Liquid
(C) Gas (D) All of these

9. The boiling point of water on plains is 100°C. On hills it will be ______.
(A) 100°C (B) more than 100°C
(C) less than 100°C (D) None of these

10. Water has maximum density at:
(A) 0°C (B) 10°C
(C) 4°C (D) None of these

11. Which of these statements is true?
(A) Density of ice is more than the density of water.
(B) Volume of ice is more than the volume of water.
(C) Temperature of ice is more than the temperature of water.
(D) None of these

12. Water is called universal solvent because:
(A) It can dissolve all the liquids in the universe.
(B) It can dissolve all the gases in the universe.
(C) It can dissolve a large number of solids, liquids, and gases.
(D) None of these.

13. Solubility of sugar in water:
(A) decreases with increase in temperature.
(B) increases with increase in temperature.
(C) is not affected by temperature.
(D) None of these.

14. Solubility of gases in water:
(A) increases with increase in temperature.
(B) decreases with decrease in temperature.
(C) decreases with increase in temperature.
(D) None of these.

15. Two liquids mixed with each other to form a uniform mixture are called;
(A) insoluble liquids (B) miscible liquids
(C) immiscible liquid (D) none of these

16. When water vapour turns back into liquid, it is called:
(A) Evaporation (B) Precipitation
(C) Condensation (D) Sunshine

17. What is evaporation?
(A) Water freezes.
(B) Water vapour meets cold air and change back into liquid.
(C) Water gets warm and change from liquids water to water vapour.
(D) Plants take in water from the soil.

18. What is the correct term for moisture that falls to the ground from cloud?
(A) Condensation (B) Precipitation
(C) Evaporation (D) None of these

19. Which of the following is the reason for depletion of water table?
(A) Planting more trees (B) Heavy rain fall
(C) Industrialisation (D) Rainwater

20. Situation in which there is an occurrence of more rainfall than normal is:
(A) Drought (B) Monsoon winds
(C) Flood (D) Earthquake

21. Which of the following will not help in the conservation of water?

(A) Drip irrigation
(B) Planting more trees
(C) Water treatment plants
(D) Cutting trees to check water loss to transpiration

22. Which of the following will lead the depletion in water table:
(A) plantation
(B) rainwater harvesting
(C) constructing more lakes
(D) increase in population

23. Which one of the following is not responsible for water shortage:
(A) Rapid growth of industries
(B) Increasing population
(C) Heavy rainfall
(D) Mismanagement of water resource

24. Careful management of water means:
(A) More desertification
(B) More deforestation
(C) Less waste of water
(D) More waste of water

Fill in the Blanks

1. Water is colourless, odourless, and ________.
2. Water is a substance made of _________ and ________.
3. The different water sources of the Earth get their water supply from ____________.
4. The use of large amounts of herbicides, pesticides, and fertilisers by the farmers in their farms leads to ____________.
5. Water freezes faster than the cold water, which is known as__________ .
6. In hydroelectric power plants, __________ is used for generating electricity.
7. The water in the oceans and seas has many salts dissolved in it — the water is __________.
8. Water boil that 100° C at __________mm of mercury pressure.
9. Water vapour enters the air through the processes of__________ and __________.
10. A part of the rainwater gets __________ by the ground and seems to disappear in the soil.
11. The circulation of water between ocean and land is a continuous process and called as __________.
12. Most of the rain fall occurs during the __________ season.
13. One way of increasing the availability of water is to collect rainwater. Collecting rainwater in this way is called __________.
14. The basic idea behind rainwater harvesting is "____________________"
15. Excessive rains may cause__________, while lack of it for long periods may cause __________.

True/False

1. Water is a non-renewable natural resource.
2. Water does not play any role in the germination of seeds.
3. Water covers over 90% of the Earth's surface.
4. Oxygen dissolved in water is the main source of survival of aquatic life.
5. Water pollution occurs when a body of water is adversely affected due to the addition of large amounts of materials to the water.
6. Rainwater harvesting is a technique to check water pollution.
7. Solution made with water are termed as aqueous solution.
8. Water vapour gets added to air by evaporation and transpiration.
9. The demand for water is decreasing day-by-day as the number of people using water is decreasing with rising population.
10. Most of the water is in the oceans and it can be used directly.
11. The clouds get carried along by air currents. They cool and the droplets join to form larger drops. These fall as mist.
12. The circulation of water between ocean and land is a non-continuous process.
13. Overflowing of water from rivers and streams into fields and homes is called drought.
14. The total amount of water on Earth remains the same, but the water available for use is very limited and is decreasing with over usage.
15. The water may then spread over large areas causing drought.

Match Type Questions

1.

Column-A		Column-B
1. Oceans	(a)	Rainwater harvesting
2. Wells	(b)	Salty water
3. Plants	(c)	Aquatic
4. Lotus	(d)	Transpiration
5. Conservation of water	(e)	Groundwater

2.

Column-A		Column-B
1. Ground water	(a)	Solid form of water
2. Snow	(b)	Wastage of water
3. Leaking taps	(c)	Rainwater harvesting
4. Water saving method	(d)	Water table

Assertion and Reason Type Questions

In the following questions, a statement of assertion is followed by statement of reason.

Mark the correct choice as:

(A) Both Assertion and Reason are true, and Assertion is the correct explanation of Assertion.

(B) Both Assertion and Reason are true, but Assertion is not the correct explanation of Assertion.

(C) Assertion is true, but Reason is false.

(D) Both Assertion and Reason are false.

1. **Assertion:** In fizz drinks, once the pressure is released, the dissolved carbon dioxide gas oozes out of the solution.
   Reason: Gases can be made to dissolve better when pressure is applied.

2. **Assertion:** Water evaporates into air from oceans, rivers, and lakes but not from the soil.
   Reason: Water vapour is present in air only during monsoon.

3. **Assertion:** About 71% of the Earth's surface is covered with water.
   Reason: Almost all the water on the Earth is contained in the seas, oceans, rivers, lakes, ice caps, as groundwater and in the atmosphere.

4. **Assertion:** Density of water is 1g/cc at 4°C, which is the maximum density of water.
   Reason: Pure water is a bad conductor of heat and electricity.

5. **Assertion:** The supply of water in nature does not run out.
   Reason: This is because water is continuously recycled through the water cycle.

6. **Assertion:** The clouds get carried along by air currents.
   Reason: They cool, and the droplets join to form bigger drops. These fall as mist.

7. **Assertion:** If we dig a hole in the ground near a water body, we may find that the soil is moist.
   Reason: The moisture in the soil indicates the presence of water underground

8. **Assertion:** Increase in population, industrial, and agricultural activities are some common factors affecting the water table.
   Reason: Scanty rainfall is another factor that may deplete the water table.

9. **Assertion:** Solutions made with water are termed aqueous solutions.
   Reason: Plants do not need water to get nutrients from the soil to prepare their food.

10. **Assertion:** Natural water contains dissolved gases like oxygen, nitrogen, and carbon dioxide.
    Reason: Nitrogen dissolved in water is the main source for survival of aquatic life.

Comprehension Type Questions

Comprehension-1 Water as a Solvent

One of the best known solvents is water. Solutions made with water are termed aqueous solutions. So, as solution of copper sulphate in water is written as $CuSO_{4(aq)}$. The symbol 'aq' stands for aqueous.

Gases as well as solids dissolve in water. Natural water contains dissolved gases like oxygen, nitrogen, and carbon dioxide. Oxygen dissolved in water is the main source for survival of aquatic life. Carbon dioxide dissolved in water is utilized to produce food via photochemical reactions. Nitrogen dissolved in water is converted into nitrogenous compounds. This is acted upon by the bacteria in sea water, which acts as a mode of nourishment for the water plants.

Gases can be made to dissolve better when pressure is applied. For example, in fizz drinks, once the pressure is released, the dissolved carbon dioxide gas oozes out of the solution. Uses of Water Besides being essential for life, water is used for many other purposes. In India, about 70% of the total water available is used for agriculture,

20–22% by industries, and only 8% is used for personal or domestic needs.

1. The symbol 'aq' stands for:
   (A) Solid (B) Liquid
   (C) Aqueous (D) Gas
2. Natural water contains dissolved gases like:
   (A) Oxygen, (B) Nitrogen
   (C) Carbon dioxide (D) All of these
3. Gases can be dissolved in water at:
   (A) Low pressure (B) High pressure
   (C) Any pressure (D) All of these

Free Response Type

Very Short Answer Type Questions

1. Name a source of surface water.
2. Is sea water potable?
3. What is the chemical formula of water?
4. Define condensation.

Short Answer Type Questions

1. Why is water called a life giving liquid?
2. What is the chemical composition of water?
3. What is the chemical formula of water?
4. Write any four methods to conserve water at home.
5. Explain how ground water is recharged.
6. You have been asked to maintain a garden. How would you minimise the use of water?

Long Answer Type Questions

1. List the physical properties of water.
2. Explain water cycle with the help of a diagram.
3. Explain how, heavy rains may cause floods. What damage is caused by floods? How are the animals which normally live in water affected by floods?
4. Differentiate between:
   (a) Water pollution and water conservation.
   (b) Surface water and groundwater.
5. Write a short note on water pollution and mention its sources.
6. What is meant by conservation of water? Suggest three methods to conserve water.
8. How does the failure of rainfall affect people on the Earth?
9. Name two processes responsible for the formation of clouds.
10. Why is there a need for conserving water? Give two reasons.

Numerical Based Questions

1. If there are 42 litres of water present in a body of 70 kg person than calculate the amount of water present in the body of a person having a body weight of 50 kg?
   (A) 42 ltr (B) 35 ltr
   (C) 20 ltr (D) 30 ltr
2. The human embryo constitutes around 95% water for the first months. Calculate the amount of water present in the embryo having weight 20 gm only.
   (A) 20 gm water (B) 19 gm water
   (C) 25 gm water (D) 95 gm water
3. Water consumption for a family of four persons in a month of 30 days is 6000 litres. What is the water consumption per head per day?
   (A) 40 *l* (B) 50 *l*
   (C) 60 *l* (D) 70 *l*

Case Based Questions

Water Cycle

The supply of water in nature does not run out. This is because water is continuously recycled in the water cycle. The journey of water from the oceans to the atmosphere and then back to the ocean is called the water cycle.

- Heat from the sun causes the water on the Earth's surface to evaporate. The vapour rises, cools, and condenses to form tiny water droplets. These droplets form clouds. When the temperature of air increases, it expands (i.e., its particles move away from one another). This makes the air lighter, and it rises in the atmosphere, taking water vapour with it. As the air rises, it begins to cool.

  The water vapour condenses on dust particles present in the atmosphere to form millions of tiny droplets. Tiny ice crystals will be formed instead if it is very cold. This cluster of tiny water droplets floating in air is what we call a cloud.
- The clouds get carried along by air currents. They cool and the droplets join to form larger drops. These fall as mist.

- If the temperature in the region is very low, these water droplets fall as hail, sleet, or snow.
- Some of the rainwater flows along the ground as streams. Some soak through the ground and then reappears as springs. Streams and springs join to form rivers. Rivers flow back into the sea. Thus, the water cycle is complete.

1. Which of the following play an important role in water cycle?
(A) Solar system (B) Moon
(C) Sun (D) Mercury

2. Mist is formed by:
(A) evaporation of water droplets.
(B) cool droplets join to form larger drops.
(C) cool droplets join to form smaller drops.
(D) condensation of alcohol.

3. Continuous recycling of water is called:
(A) Cater scarcity
(B) Water cycle
(C) Water condensation
(D) Water evaporation

Level 2

Multiple Choice Questions

1. Water cycle is a:
(A) Continuous process
(B) Drinking process
(C) Non-continuous process
(D) Non-cyclic process

2. The main source of water for perennial rivers is in the form of:
(A) Lakes (B) Rainwater
(C) Snow (D) Dams

3. The melting point of ice is:
(A) 0°C (B) 37°C
(C) 4°C (D) 100°C

4. The density of water is:
(A) 0.1g/cm^3 (B) 1g/cm^3
(C) 100 g/cm^3 (D) 1 kg/m^3

5. Which of the following is potable water?
(A) A glass of water fit for drinking
(B) Water in a pot
(C) Sea water
(D) Water with bacterial and chemicals

6. At what pressure water boils at 100° Celsius?
(A) 76mm of Hg (B) 700 mm of Hg
(C) 760mm of Hg (D) 760° C

7. When hydrogen and oxygen combine to form water, they form:
(A) An unstable compound
(B) A stable mixture
(C) An unstable mixture
(D) An extremely stable compound

8. Water is a kind of a/an __________ oxide.
(A) acidic (B) basic
(C) neutral (D) metal

9. Cloud seeding is a technique used to induce rain that was first used by USA in 1946. It has also been done in Karnataka and other places in India. What is it?
(A) An agricultural practice that depends on clouds.
(B) Introduction of particles in clouds to increase condensation.
(C) Making clouds and placing them in the sky.
(D) Trimming the clouds into seed like structures.

10. Arrange the terms in sequence of water cycle starting from water bodies.
(1) Precipitation
(2) Condensation
(3) Water vapour
(4) Infiltration
(5) Groundwater table
(A) 54231 (B) 32145
(C) 35412 (D) 52314

11. Pure water is –
(A) Colourless (B) odourless
(C) transparent (D) all of these

12. In which of the following activities will you use a minimum amount of water?
(A) Bathing
(B) Brushing teeth
(C) Washing clothes
(D) Mopping a room

13. The quantity of water required to produce one page of your book is:
(A) 1 bucket
(B) 10 buckets
(C) 2 glasses
(D) Few drops

ASSESSMENT CORNER

14. Pure water is –
(A) good conductor of electricity
(B) opaque
(C) occur as a solid at room temperature
(D) bad conductor of electricity

15. In which of the following case evaporation of water will be slowest?
(A) A tray of water kept in sunlight.
(B) A kettle of water kept on a burner.
(C) A glass of water kept in a room.
(D) A bucket of water kept on rooftop.

16. Transpiration is a process in which plants:
(A) receive water from soil.
(B) absorb water vapour from air.
(C) prepare food from water.
(D) release water vapour.

17. Clouds are:
(A) tiny drops of water floating in air.
(B) mixture of dust and water vapour.
(C) particles of water vapour.
(D) rain drops in air.

18. Wells are fed through:
(A) Pond water
(B) Lake water
(C) Rain water
(D) Groundwater

19. Floods causes extensive damage to:
(A) Crops.
(B) Property and human life.
(C) Domestic animals.
(D) All of the above.

20. "Catch water where it falls" is the basic idea behind:
(A) recycling of water.
(B) making dams to store water.
(C) rainwater harvesting.
(D) condensation of water vapour.

21. Which of the following is the correct sequence of the stages in the change of state of water in water cycle?
P – Sea water
Q – Cloud
R – Rain
S – Water vapour
(A) $P \rightarrow Q \rightarrow R \rightarrow S$
(B) $P \rightarrow R \rightarrow Q \rightarrow S$
(C) $P \rightarrow S \rightarrow Q \rightarrow R$
(D) $P \rightarrow R \rightarrow S \rightarrow Q$

22. We have a lot of water in seas, then why is the amount of usable water limited?
(A) Sea water is not fit for all our uses.
(B) Sea water cannot be used directly by us for drinking.
(C) Sea water cannot be used directly for growing crops.
(D) All of the above.

23. In a cloud, the size of droplets increases causing rainfall because:
(A) They become heavier.
(B) They become lighter.
(C) They are converted into steam.
(D) Of reflection of light.

24. Shilpa sprinkles water in a dirty room before sweeping. Why?
(A) Sprinkling water is fashionable.
(B) Sweeping water is easier.
(C) Water coagulates the dust particles.
(D) Water repels dust particles.

25. Through which of the following processes in water vapour added directly to atmospheric air?
(i) Evaporation
(ii) precipitation
(iii) Condensation
(iv) Transpiration
(A) Only (i), (ii), and (iii)
(B) Only (ii), (iii), and (iv)
(C) Only (i), (ii), and (iv)
(D) Only (i) and (iv)

26. Water scarcity is increasing day by day,:
(A) as water cycle has stopped functioning.
(B) as the total amount of water on Earth has decreased.
(C) as the consumption of water has increased.
(D) as there is an increasing frequency of floods.

27. How can we universally overcome the problem of water scarcity?
(A) By overusing water from water bodies.
(B) By keeping taps open, even after filling the containers.
(C) By reducing pressure in public water taps in a locality.
(D) By better water management.

28. Which of the following statements is false about ground water?
(A) It is not generally pure and potable.
(B) It is used in agriculture.
(C) It has many salts dissolved in it.
(D) it is constant at all places.

29. Which of the following correctly defines an aquifer?
(A) Water percolates into the soil and provides as moisture.
(B) Clouds bring fresh water as rain to the land.
(C) The groundwater is stored between layers of hard rock below the water table.
(D) Rainwater is used to recharge ground water.

30. The amount of rainfall at a place depends on:
(A) Terrain
(B) Geographic location
(C) Nature of soil
(D) Proximity to sea

Higher Order Thinking Skills (HOTS)

1. Distinguish between hard water and soft water.

2. Explain the cause for hardness of water.

3. Why is distilled water not suitable for drinking?

4. How do areas covered with concrete affect the availability of groundwater?

5.

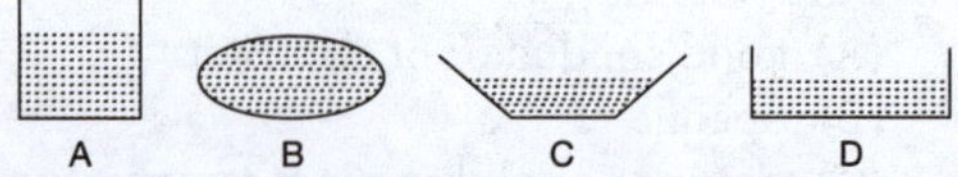

There are 4 containers A, B, C, and D with same amount of water in each. Answer the following based on them.
(a) Name the container in which water will evaporate faster than all others.
(b) Name the container in which water will evaporate very slowly.

Give reason for your answer.

6. Most of the water that falls on the land as rain and snow, sooner or later it goes back to a sea or an ocean. Explain how it happens.

7. Dissolve two spoons of common salt in half a cup of water. Now if you want to get the salt back, what will you do?

ARCHIVE CORNER

1. Match the column-I with column-II and mark the correct from the codes given below

Column-A	Column-B
1. Nitrogen gas + oxygen gas	(a) 99% of air
2. Loss of water by plants	(b) Water cycle
3. Drought	(c) Transpiration
4. Replenishment of water	(d) Scarcity of ground water

(A) (a)-(i), (b)-(ii), (c)-(iii), (d)-(iv)
(B) (a)-(iii), (b)-(ii), (c)-(i), (d)-(iv)
(C) (a)-(iv), (b)-(i), (c)-(ii), (d)-(iii)
(D) (a)-(i), (b)-(iii), (c)-(iv), (d)-(ii)

2. Which natural calamity leads to famine?
(A) Flood (B) Drought
(C) Earthquake (D) All of these

3. Select the incorrect statement:
(A) Water particles on heating become free from their existing arrangement to move faster and escape into the air.
(B) In summer, due to heat, electric cables expand and hang loosely from poles.
(C) Cooling a substance slows down the movement of its particles.
(D) Water expands on heating, thus ice occupies more space.

4. Read the given passage.

Heat of the sun causes (i) of water from the surface of the Earth, oceans, lakes, rivers, and other water bodies. Water vapour is also continuously added to the atmosphere through (ii) from the surface of the leaves. These vapours (iii) to form tiny droplets of water. These droplets floating in the air along with the dust particles form (iv).

Select the option that correctly fills the blanks in the above passage.
(A) (i)-transpiration, (ii)-condense, (iii)-clouds, (iv)-larger droplets
(B) (i)-transpiration, (ii)-evaporation, (iii)-condense, (iv)-clouds
(C) (i)-evaporation, (ii)-transpiration, (iii)-condense, (iv)-clouds
(D) (i)-condense, (ii)-transpiration, (iii)-evaporation, (iv)-larger droplets

5. Three flasks, each containing a different liquid are cooled in a basin of cold water. In the beginning of the experiment, all the three liquids are at the same level in the glass tubes. However, upon cooling, each liquid falls to a different level as shown below:

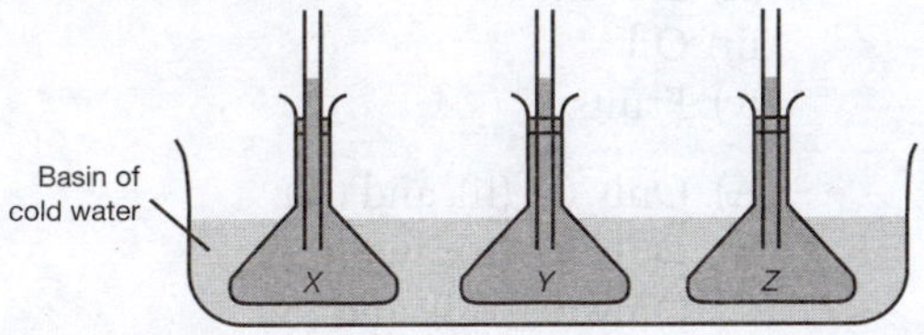

From the results of this experiment, we can conclude that ________.
(i) liquid X contracts more than liquid Y.
(ii) liquid Y does not contract as much liquid Z.
(iii) liquid Z contracts less than liquid X.

(A) (i) only (B) (ii) and (iii)
(C) (i) and (iii) (D) (i), (ii), and (iii)

6. Which of the following will cause a decrease in the water table in the future?
(A) Lack of rainwater harvesting infrastructure
(B) Emigration
(C) Cloud seeding
(D) Growing trees

7. Water is the stable compound, but can be broken into hydrogen and oxygen. when –
(A) Boiling
(B) Freezing
(C) Condensed
(D) Electric current is passed

8. Why is mineral water better than distilled water for drinking?
(A) Mineral water is cheap.
(B) Mineral water is easily available.
(C) Mineral water contains dissolved salts.
(D) Mineral water is colourful.

9. Flood causes:
(A) Soil erosion
(B) Increase in water level
(C) Damage to crops
(D) Both (A) and (D)

10. Which of the following causes water to change from one state to another?
(A) Pressure (B) Concentration
(C) Temperature (D) Volume

ARCHIVE CORNER

11. Rainwater harvesting is an important method for:
(A) Treating sewage water.
(B) Recycling water from factories.
(C) Raising ground water level.
(D) Industrial purposes.

12. Which of the following substances contain water?
(i) Milk
(ii) Blood
(iii) Oil
(iv) Fruits

(A) Only (i), (ii), and (iv)
(B) Only (i), (ii), and (iii)
(C) Only (ii), (iii), and (iv)
(D) Only (i), (iii), and (iv)

13. Which of the following combines with water vapour of rainwater to form acid rain?
(A) Dust (B) Carbon particles
(C) Oxygen (D) Sulphur dioxide

14. Most of the well water and spring water are replenished by:
(A) Dams (B) Floods
(C) Ground water (D) All of these

15. Which of these constituents present in air leads to the formation of fog and mist?
(A) Nitrogen
(B) Oxygen
(C) Water vapour
(D) Carbon dioxide

16. The process of collecting rainwater in huge, cemented pits is called:
(A) Storing of water
(B) Filtration of water
(C) Transpiration of water
(D) Rain water harvesting

ANSWER KEY

Level 1

Fixed Response Type

Multiple Choice Questions

1. B 2. B 3. C 4. A 5. A 6. A 7. B 8. D 9. C 10. C
11. B 12. C 13. B 14. C 15. B 16. C 17. C 18. B 19. C 20. C
21. D 22. D 23. C 24. C

Fill in the Blanks

1. Tasteless, liquid
2. Hydrogen, oxygen
3. Rainwater
4. Water pollution
5. Mpemba effect
6. Water
7. Saline
8. 760
9. Evaporation , transpiration
10. Absorbed
11. Water cycle
12. Monsoon
13. Rainwater harvesting
14. Catch water where it falls
15. Floods, droughts

True/False

1. False
2. False
3. False
4. True
5. True
6. False
7. True
8. True
9. False
10. False
11. True
12. False
13. False
14. True
15. False

Match Type Questions

1. 1-b, 2-e, 3-d, 4-c, 5-a
2. 1-d, 2-a, 3-b, 4-c

Assertion and Reason Type Questions

1. A 2. D 3. A 4. B 5. A 6. B 7. A 8. B 9. C 10. C

Comprehension Type Questions

1. C 2. D 3. B

Free Response Type

Numerical Based Questions

1. D 2. B 3. B

Case Based Questions

1. C 2. B 3. B

Level 2

Multiple Choice Questions

1. A	2. C	3. A	4. B	5. A	6. C	7. D	8. C	9. B	10. B
11. D	12. B	13. C	14. D	15. C	16. D	17. A	18. D	19. D	20. C
21. C	22. D	23. A	24. C	25. D	26. C	27. D	28. D	29. C	30. B

Archive Corner

1. D	2. D	3. D	4. C	5. D	6. A	7. D	8. C	9. D	10. C
11. C	12. A	13. D	14. C	15. C	16. D				

CHAPTER 8

Nature's Treasure: Fossil Fuel

Learning Outcomes

After reading this chapter, you would be able to:

- classify natural resources on the basis of their abundance and availability.
- explain the formation of coal, composition of coal, different varieties of coal and also the carbon content present in different types of coal, different products formed during destructive distillation of coal and different ways in which coal is useful to us.
- understand the formation of petroleum, process involved in refining of petrol, properties and uses of different products formed during fractional distillation of petroleum.
- describe the need of conservation of fossil fuels.

Geekspeak

- Natural resources
- Deposit
- Lignite
- Formation
- Producer gas
- Ethyl Mercaptan
- Conservation
- Fossil fuel
- Carbonization
- Bituminous
- Destructive distillation
- Petroleum
- Fractional distillation
- Coal
- Peat
- Anthracite
- Water gas
- Refining
- Natural gas

Introduction

Natural resources are the big assets of a country. The variety of substances that man gets from earth and nature to meet his basic needs are called natural resources. The word resource means a source of supplying a material generally presented or stored in reserve. Natural resources are both living and non living. Some of these resources are found in abundance, while others are found in limited quantities and present in some restricted parts of our land. For this reason, the natural resources have to be widely used. However, in reality it is not so. They are being used indiscriminately.

Natural Resources

Natural resources are materials or substances that occur in nature and can be used for economic gain or to support life. E.g., solar energy, mountains (Fig. 8.1), forest, wind (Fig. 8.2), etc.

Figure 8.1 Natural Resources

Figure 8.2 Renewable Natural Resources

Types of Natural Resources

Depending upon the abundance and availability, natural resources are categorized into following two types:

- Inexhaustible natural resources
- Exhaustible natural resources

Natural Resources

Inexhaustible

- Resources that are in unlimited quantity.
- Resources that are not likely to be exhausted by human activity or their use.

Examples: Air, water and solar radiations.

Exhaustible

- Resources that are in limited quantity.
- Resources that are not likely to be exhausted by human activities.

Renewable

- Can replenish themselves by quick recyling and replacement within a reasonable time.
- Not likely to be exhausted.
- Examples: Soil, Forests and Wild life.

Non-Renewable

- Cannot replenish themselves by recycling and replacements.
- These may be exhausted.
- Examples: Minerals, Fossil fuels

Fossil Fuels

Exhaustible natural resources like coal, petroleum or natural gas were formed from the dead remains of living organisms (fossils). So, these are called fossil fuels. Coal and petroleum are very important natural resources and play a significant role in our daily life. They are found in the earth's crust. Their availability and specific characteristics make them very important in the growth of industry. At present they are the vital sources of energy worldwide.

Coal

Coal is one of the fuels used to cook food. Earlier it was used in thermal power plants for production of electricity and also in railway engines to produce steam to run steam engines. Coal is a mineral of dark brown or black colour formed from the remains of plants buried in the earth's crust millions of years ago.

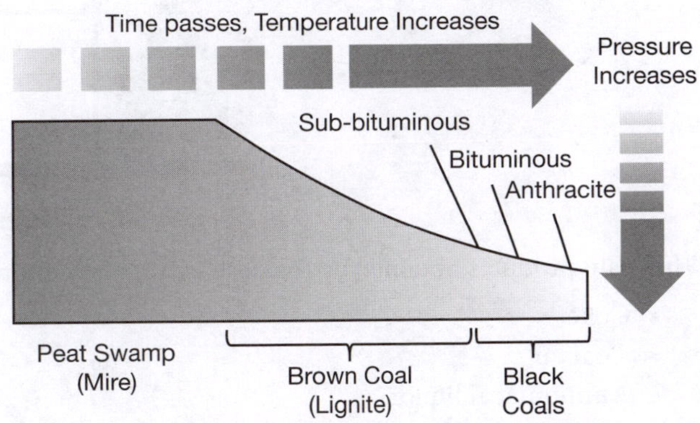

Figure 8.3 Coal Formation

Composition: Coal is a very impure form of carbon. It mainly consists of atoms of carbon, hydrogen and oxygen. A small amount of sulphur is also present in it.

Deposits: The distribution of coal deposits is not uniform in the earth's crust. To the total coal reserves in the world, Asia contributes about one third, whereas North and South America contribute more than half. India has large deposits of coal. It is estimated that India has about 80 billion tonnes of proven coal deposits. The coal deposits are spread over in the states of Jharkhand, Madhya Pradesh and West Bengal.

Keystone

Coal occurs in four main varieties, viz., peat, lignite, anthracite and bituminous. Peat is the most inferior while anthracite is the most superior quality of coal among various varieties of coal.

Formation: It has been found that millions of years ago, the large area of the forests denude by natural forces such as earthquakes and volcanoes. The forests were buried in the chasms or those deep cracks. Thus, the plants had no contact with oxygen and sunlight. Successive layers of sediments sealed the buried plants. Over millions of years these deposits were subjected to high pressure and heat which transformed them into coal. The chemical process involved in the transformation of plant matter into coal is called the carbonization of plant matter (Fig. 8.3). Different type of coal are given in the below flow chart and their calorific value in Table 8.1

Peat [dead plant material]

↓

Lignite[brown coal]

↓

Bituminous coal [household soft coal]

↓

Anthracite[hard coal]

Table 8.1 Coal, its Carbon Content and their Calorific Value

Type of coal	% of carbon content	Calorific value
Peat	50 – 60	10.5 – 12.6 kJ/g
Lignite	60 – 70	14.7 – 18.9 kJ/g
Bituminous	75 – 80	28 – 31 kJ/g
Anthracite	90 – 95	31 – 33 kJ/g

Destructive Distillation of Coal

The process of heating coal in the absence of air is called the destructive distillation of coal (Fig. 8.4). Coal contains a number of elements such as carbon, hydrogen, oxygen, nitrogen and sulphur. When coal is heated in the absence of air, a number of products are obtained.

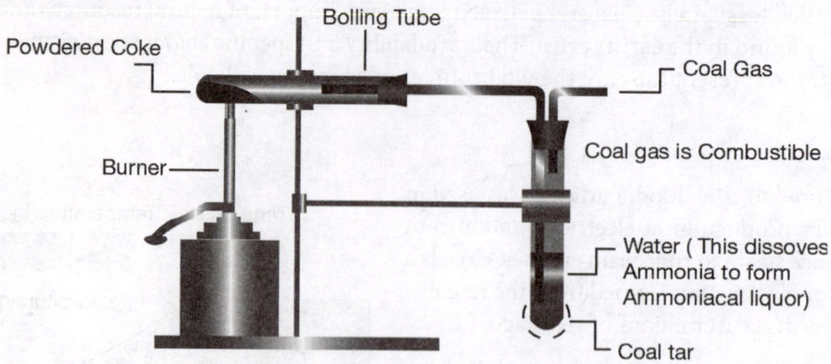

Figure 8.4 Destructive Distillation of Coal

The main products obtained by the destructive distillation of coal are as follows:

- Coke
- Coal tar
- Ammoniacal liquor
- Coal gas

- **Coke:** Coke contains 98% carbon. It is porous, tough, black and the purest form of coal. It is very similar to charcoal which is a good fuel and burns without smoke. But it is seldom employed as a fuel because it can be put to more valuable use. Coke is used in the manufacture of steel and extraction of many metals. It is also used for the preparation of some important fuel gases like water gas and producer gas.

  It is obtained by passing steam over red-hot coke.

  $$\underset{\text{Coke}}{C} + \underset{\text{Water}}{H_2O} \rightarrow \underset{\text{Water gas}}{(CO + H_2)}$$

  It is obtained when air is passed over red-hot coke.

  $$2C + O_2 + 4N_2 \rightarrow \underset{\text{Producer gas}}{(2CO + 4N_2)}$$

- **Coal Tar:** Coal tar is a mixture of different carbon compounds. It is a thick, black liquid with unpleasant smell. Many important chemical substances are obtained from fractional distillation of coal tar which are used as raw materials for the preparation of synthetic dyes, explosives, perfume, paints, drugs, plastics, pesticides and synthetic fibres. Some of these chemicals are benzene, phenol, aniline, toluene and naphthalene. Naphthalene is generally used in our daily life to repel moths and other insects.

> **Keystone**
>
> Bitumen a petroleum product is used in place of coal tar in making of roads.

- **Ammoniacal Liquor:** The ammonia gas produced as a result of destructive distillation of coal is absorbed in water. The aqueous solution of ammonia, i.e., ammonium hydroxide solution, is called Ammoniacal liquor. It is also used as a raw material for fertilizers such as ammonium sulphate and ammonium superphosphate.

- **Coal Gas:** Coal gas is obtained during the processing of coal to get coke. It is mainly a mixture of hydrogen, methane and carbon monoxide. The gases present in coal gas are combustible and hence, it is an excellent fuel. It has high calorific value. Earlier (until 1950), It was used for lighting houses, factories and streets in Mumbai. It was also used for cooking until recently.

Uses:

- Coal is used as a fuel to convert water into steam to run thermal power plants for the generation of electricity. It is also used as a fuel in homes and factories and to run steam engines.

> **Keystone**
>
> Coal gas was used for street lighting for the first time in London in 1810 and in New York around 1820. Now-a-days, it is used as a source of heat rather than light.

- Coal is used in the preparation of fuel gases, such as coal gas.
- Coal is used in the preparation of synthetic petrol.
- Coal is also used in preparation of synthetic natural gas.
- The destructive distillation of coal gives coke, coal tar, coal gas, etc.
- Coal is the source from which a number of organic compounds such as benzene, toluene, phenol, aniline, naphthalene and anthracene are obtained.

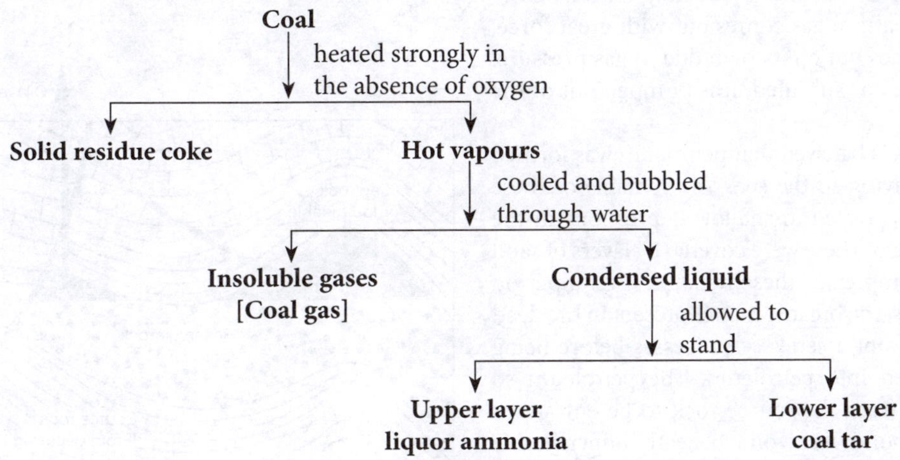

❖ INTEXT QUESTION

1. What is ammoniacal liquor?
   Solution: The aqueous solution of ammonia, i.e., ammonium hydroxide solution is called ammoniacal liquor.
2. What are fossil fuels?
   Solution: Exhaustible natural resources like coal, petroleum or natural gas were formed from the dead remains of living organisms (fossils). So, these are called fossil fuels.
3. What is water gas?
   Solution: Water gas is an equimolar mixture of carbon monoxide and hydrogen.

Check Point 1

1. What are the sources of energy in nature?
2. Which form of energy is used in the production of electricity?
3. Ammonia gas is water soluble or not?
4. What is a chemical formula of ammonium sulphate and ammonium super phosphate?
5. What is the ratio of CO and H_2 in water gas?

Petroleum

Petroleum is a naturally occurring oil that consists chiefly of hydrocarbons with some other elements such as sulphur, oxygen and nitrogen. The unrefined form of petroleum is called crude oil.

Deposits: The major reserves of petroleum are in Saudi Arabia (largest producer of petroleum), Kuwait, Iraq, Russia, China, USA, Libya, etc. The oil is obtained by drilling an oil well (Fig. 8.5). When a well is drilled, natural gas comes out with great force. The crude oil comes out on its own due to gas pressure. After the pressure has subsided, it is pumped out of the well.

Formation: It is believed that petroleum was formed from organisms living in the sea. The remains of these organisms were deposited in shallow depressions in the seabed long long ago. These were covered by layers of sand and clay which compressed these remains. Over a period of millions of years, the organic matter present in the dead organisms underwent a series of processes before being finally transformed into petroleum. The petroleum so formed migrated from the source rock to be entrapped in large underground reservoirs beneath impermeable rocks. It often floats over a layer of water and is held in this position under pressure beneath a layer of natural gas.

Refining: Petroleum is a mixture of several hydrocarbons. It is a foul-smelling brown-black liquid. It also contains water, salt and rocky materials. It cannot be used in this crude form either as a fuel or as a basic material to produce other useful components. Before being put to use, it has to be purified or refined. The process of separating the various components of petroleum from one another is known as the refining of petroleum. This is done by a process called fractional distillation which is based on the fact that the different components of petroleum have distinctly different boiling points.

Keystone

Petroleum is also called rock oil, i.e., petra = rock, oleum = oil.

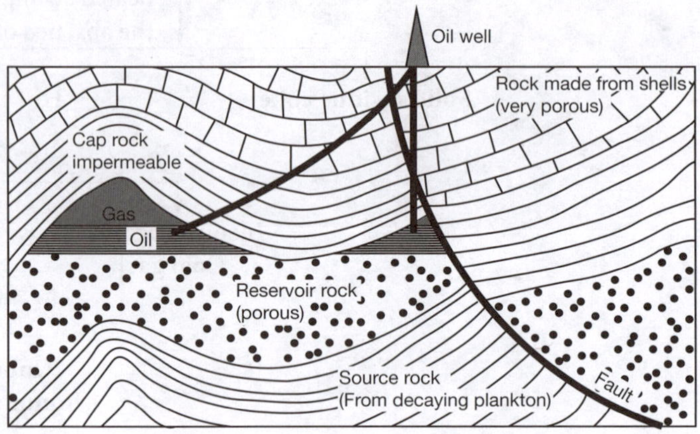

Figure 8.5 Deposits of Petroleum

Keystone

The first oil well was found in Pennsylvania in USA in 1859. India's first oil well was found in 1867 in Digboi, Assam.

Separation

The components of petroleum are separated in a large fractionating column (Fig. 8.6). Crude oil is piped to the refinery from a well. It is washed with acid and alkali (like solution) solutions to remove the basic and acidic impurities, respectively. Crude oil is now heated to about 673K and fed at the base of fractionating column. All the components except asphalt are converted in the vapour state. As the mixture of hot vapours rises up in the column, it begins to cool. The component with the highest boiling point condenses first and is collected. Those with low boiling points condense later. The residual gases escape uncondensed from the upper part of the column. The various components condensed at different heights of the column are collected separately. The components obtained at different heights in order from the bottom are asphalt, lubricating oil, paraffin wax, fuel oil, diesel, kerosene, petrol and petroleum gas.

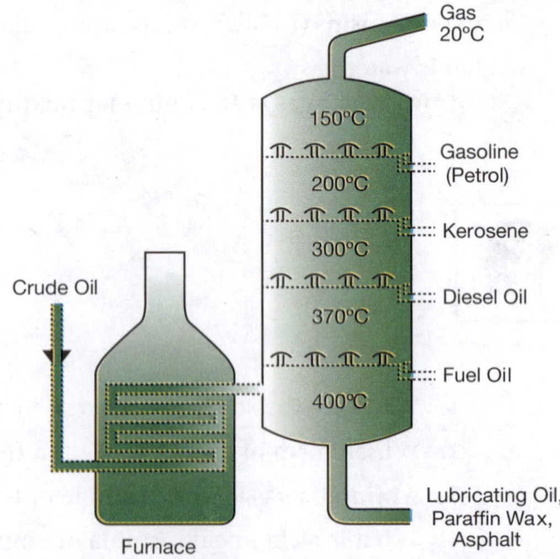

Figure 8.6 Fractional Distillation of Petroleum

- **Products:**
  - **Residual oil:** The residual oil obtained from the primary distillation of petroleum is known as reduced crude. Reduced crude is distilled in vaccum to yield bitumen (asphalt) as residue. Bitumen is largely used in making road surfaces, and also for coating cables to provide electrical insulation.
  - **Paraffin Wax:** It is obtained by the fractionation of residual oil. It is used for making candles, ointments, vaseline, grease, polishes etc. It is also used for water proofing of paper cartons.

- **Lubricating Oil:** It is obtained by the fractionation of residual oil. It is used for lubricating machinery.
- **Fuel Oil:** It is used in industries to heat boilers and furnace. It is a better fuel than coal because it burns completely leaving behind no ash, whereas coal burns producing a large amount of ash which has to be removed regularly.
- **Diesel Oil:** It contains straight chain alkanes with the number of carbon atoms varying from 16 - 20. It is used in cars, trucks, buses and locomotives. It is also used to run pumps in fields and in electric generators.
- **Kerosene:** It contains straight chain alkanes with 11–16 carbon atoms. It is used for domestic purpose, for lighting petromax, lanterns, lamps, stoves, etc. It is also used for making oil gas. A special grade of kerosene is used as aviation fuel in aeroplane jet engines.
- **Petrol:** It is also called gasoline. It contains straight chain alkanes with 7–9 carbon atoms. It is used as a fuel in two-wheelers, three-wheelers and cars. It is also used as a solvent for the dry-cleaning of clothes.
- **Petroleum Gas:** It is a mixture of ethane, propane and butane. Its main constituent is butane which burns by giving off a lot of heat (Fig. 8.7). Butane is easily liquefied under high pressure. In the liquid form it is supplied in cylinders and is commonly known as Liquefied Petroleum Gas (LPG). It is a colourless, odourless and inflammable gas. A domestic gas cylinder contains about 14.2 kg of LPG. A strong-smelling substance called ethyl mercaptan (C_2H_5SH) is added to LPG to detect the leakage of gas from the cylinder. On being lighted, it burns with a blue flame. One gram of LPG produces about 50 kJ of heat.

  LPG should be used with care. Any accidental leakage can cause an explosion. If there is any leakage of gas from the cylinder, the following precautions should be immediately taken:

- Any open flame in the vicinity of the gas should immediately be extinguished.
- All doors and windows of the room in which the cylinder is kept should be opened to allow the gas to escape.
- The tube and joints attached to the cylinder should be systematically checked for defects.

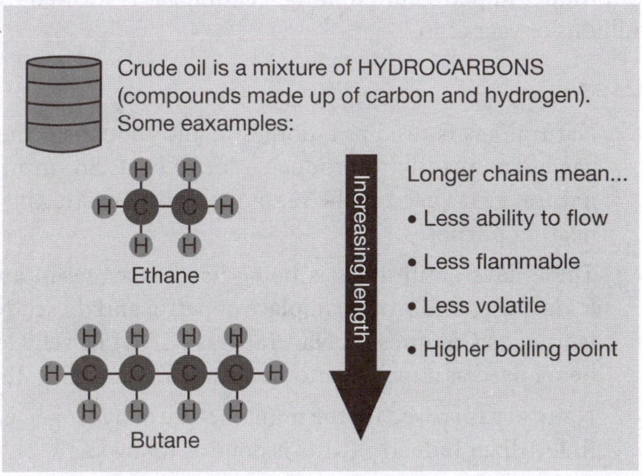

Figure 8.7 Hydrocarbons and Crude Oil

All product obtained from fractional distillation of petroleum and there uses are summarised in Table 8.2.

Table 8.2 Product from fractional distillation of petroleum

Fraction	Approximate Composition	Uses
Gases	$C_1 - C_5$	As fuel, manufacture of carbon black, gasoline and rubber.
Crude Naphtha on refractionation yields	$C_5 - C_{11}$	
(i) Petroleum ether	$C_5 - C_7$	As a solvent for dry cleaning.
(ii) Petrol or gasoline	$C_7 - C_9$	As motor fuel, dry cleaning, for making petrol gas, etc.
(iii) Benzene	$C_9 - C_{11}$	For dry cleaning.
Kerosene Oil	$C_{11} - C_{16}$	As fuel, illuminant, manufacture of oil gas, etc.
Fuel oil or Heavy oil	$C_{16} - C_{20}$	As fuel for diesel engines, cracked to yield more gasoline, furnace fuel, etc.
Residual Oil refractionated to give	C_{20} upwards	
(i) Lubricating oil	$C_{20} - C_{24}$	As lubricant.
(ii) Paraffin wax	C_{24} upwards	For making candles, boot polishes, ointments, water proofing, etc.
(iii) Asphalt or pitch black (terry residue)	$C_{30} - C_{40}$	In paints and varnishes, for water proofing, tarring roads, etc.
(iv) Petroleum coke	$C_1 - C_5$	As fuel.

Natural Gas

Natural gas is a naturally occurring mixture of gaseous hydrocarbons. It is found in porous sedimentary rocks in the earth's crust, usually in association with petroleum deposits. In India, natural gas has been found in Tripura, Rajasthan, Maharashtra and in Krishna-Godavari delta.

Natural gas consists mainly of methane (CH_4) (about 85%), ethane (C_2H_6) (up to about 10%), propane (about 3%) and butane. Carbon dioxide, nitrogen, oxygen, hydrogen sulphide and sometimes helium may also be present.

> **Keystone**
>
> The Indian Petrochemical Corporation Limited (IPCL) in Vadodara (Baroda) is one of the largest petrochemical units in the world.

Natural gas may be obtained from the earth's crust by digging wells in prospective areas. There are some wells which give out only natural gas but most wells produce natural gas as well as petroleum. In fact, natural gas is obtained as a co-product in petroleum mining. Natural gas is formed from the decomposition of organic matter buried under seabeds millions of years ago.

Uses

- Natural gas is used as a domestic and industrial fuel. Natural gas burns readily to produce a lot of heat. So, in many areas, natural gas is used as the main fuel for domestic and industrial heating purposes.
- These days natural gas is being used as a fuel in automobiles (cars, buses and trucks) in place of petrol and diesel. Natural gas is used as Compressed Natural Gas (CNG) in vehicles. CNG is being used as a fuel in automobiles to reduce air pollution.
- Natural gas is used for the manufacture of hydrogen gas (needed in fertilizer industry). This is done as follows:

> **Keystone**
>
> Natural gas is called a clean fuel because it burns without producing smoke and causes no air pollution. Natural gas also does not produce any poisonous gases on burning. Moreover, it does not leave behind any residue on burning.

  - Natural gas is heated with steam at a temperature of 900°C in the presence of nickel catalyst to form a mixture of carbon monoxide and hydrogen gas.

$$\underset{\text{Methane (Natural gas)}}{CH_4} + \underset{\text{Steam}}{H_2O} \rightarrow \underset{\text{Carbon Monoxide}}{CO} + \underset{\text{Hydrogen}}{3H_2}$$

  - This hydrogen gas is heated with nitrogen under pressure and in the presence of finely divided iron and molybdenum as catalyst to make ammonia gas.

$$\underset{\text{Nitrogen}}{N_2} + \underset{\text{Hydrogen}}{3H_2} \xrightarrow[\text{200 atm}]{\text{Fe + Mo; 450°C}} \underset{\text{Ammonia}}{2NH_3}$$

  The combination of nitrogen and hydrogen to form ammonia is called Haber's process. The temperature required in this reaction is 450°C and pressure is 200 atmospheres. The ammonia thus produced is used for manufacturing nitrogenous fertilizers (like ammonium sulphate, ammonium nitrate, etc.) by treatment with suitable acids.

- Natural gas is used as a source of carbon needed in tyre industry. When natural gas is heated strongly, then methane present in it decomposes to form carbon and hydrogen.

$$\underset{\text{Methane (Natural gas)}}{CH_4} \xrightarrow{\text{Strong heating}} \underset{\text{Carbon}}{C} + \underset{\text{Hydrogen}}{2H_2}$$

  The carbon thus formed is called 'carbon black' and it is used as a 'filler' in the manufacture of tyres.

> **Keystone**
>
> Natural gas is an almost ideal fuel. It produces large amount of heat (calorific value 55 kJ/g) when burnt.

❖ INTEXT QUESTION

4. What is the composition of natural gas?
   Solution: Natural gas consists mainly of methane (CH_4) (about 85%), ethane (C_2H_6) (up to about 10%), propane (about 3%) and butane. Carbon dioxide, nitrogen, oxygen, hydrogen sulphide and sometimes helium may also be present.
5. What is gasoline?
   Solution: Petrol is also called gasoline.
6. What is refining of petroleum?
   Solution: The process of separating the various components of petroleum from one another is known as the refining of petroleum.

Check Point 2

6. What is a fuel?
7. What are the different constituents of petroleum?
8. Which is the largest petrochemical unit in the world?
9. Why natural gas is an ideal fuel?
10. Why ethyl mercaptan is added to LPG?

Conservation of Fossil Fuels

Coal and petroleum are fossil fuels, which took millions of years to form, will last only a few hundred years. This is so because they are being used recklessly. Moreover, burning of these fuels is a major cause of air pollution. It is thus necessary to use these fuels only when absolutely necessary.

In India, the Petroleum Conservation Research Association (PCRA) has provided some tips to advise people how to save petrol/diesel. These tips are:

- Drive at a constant and moderate speed as far as possible.
- Switch off the engine at traffic lights or at a place where you have to wait.
- Ensure correct tyre pressure.
- Ensure regular maintenance of the vehicle.

Why should we Conserve Natural Resources

As we know that nature provides all the basic needs which are necessary to us but we are overexploiting or overusing these resources. If we go on overexploiting the nature, there will be no more resources available in the future. So, there is an urgent need to conserve the nature. Some needs are given below:

- To maintain ecological balance for supporting life.
- To preserve different type of biodiversity.
- To preserve the natural resources for the present and future generations.

❖ INTEXT QUESTION

7. Why should we conserve natural resources?
   Ans: To maintain ecological balance for supporting life and to preserve different type of biodiversity.

8. Why do we ensure regular maintenance of the vehicle?
Ans: Because in India, the Petroleum Conservation Research Association (PCRA) has advised people to save petrol/diesel.

Check Point 3

11. How to save fossil fuel in automobiles?
12. 'Fossil fuels are limited in nature.' Explain this.
13. Why is petroleum called as fossil fuel?
14. Write the full form of PCRA.
15. Which association has provided tips to save petrol/diesel?

Competition Corner

- The total fossil fuel used in the year 1997 is the result of 422 years of all plant matter that grew on the entire surface and in all the oceans of the ancient earth.
- Many museums use natural gas-fueled equipment not only to keep the lights on, but also to help maintain the proper humidity for conservation of art, fabrics and historic papers.
- Sugarcane is fermented to make alcohol which can be burnt to generate power. Alternatively, the cane can be crushed and the pulp (called bagasse) can be burnt to make steam to drive turbines.
- When coal is preserved under the right pressure and temperature for ten thousand years, you may get diamonds from these coal pieces. Diamond and coal are both made up of carbon particles. Diamond is one of the purest forms of carbon.
- Coke may burn with little or no smoke under combustible conditions while bituminous coal would produce much smoke.
- The electricity formed by using coal is known as thermal electricity and about 50% of the electricity in the United States is generated from coal.

STRUCTURAL OUTLINE

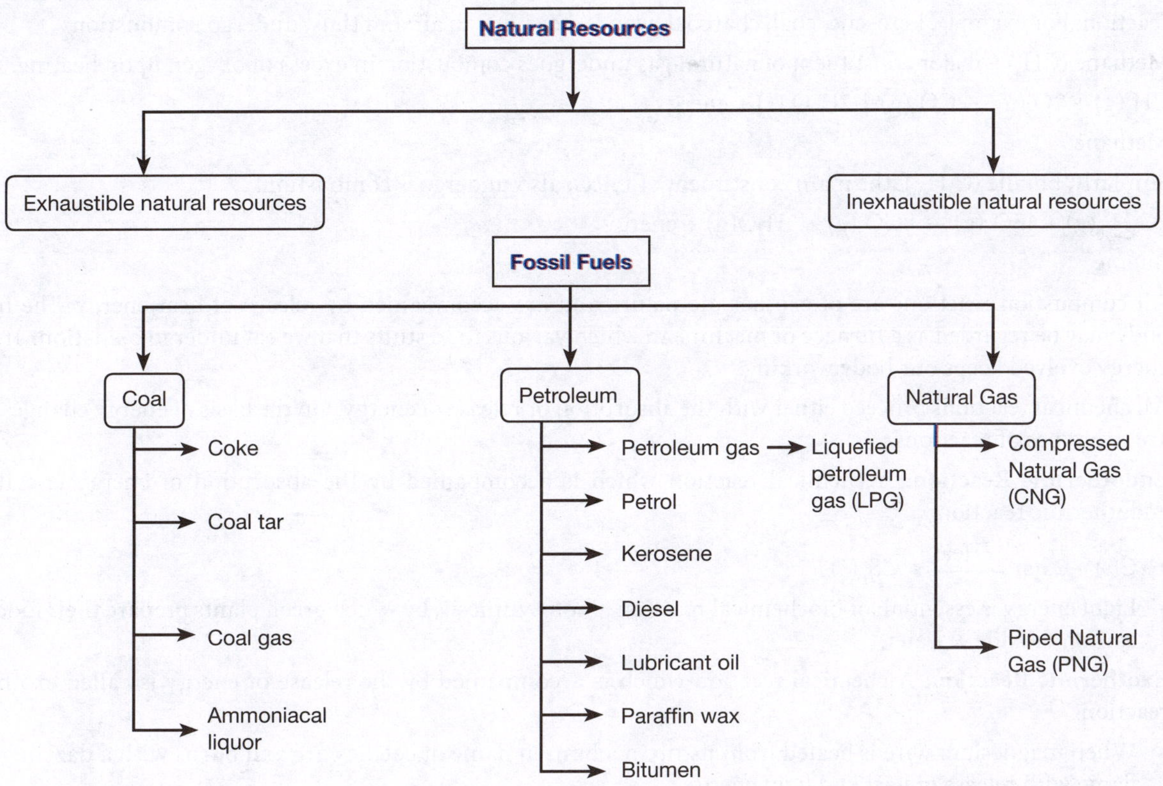

ABRIDGEMENT

Combustion Reactions

- A chemical reaction in which a substance burns or gets oxidized in the presence of air or oxygen is called combustion reaction. For example, kerosene, coal, charcoal, wood, etc., burn in air and thus, undergo combustion.

  Methane (CH_4) a major constituent of natural gas undergoes combustion in excess of oxygen upon heating.

  $\underset{\text{Methane}}{CH_4(g)} + 2O_2(g) \rightarrow CO_2(g) + 2H_2O(\ell) + \text{energy}$

  Similarly, butane (C_4H_{10}), the main constituent of L.P.G. also undergoes combustion.

  $\underset{\text{Butane}}{2C_4H_{10}(g)} + 13O_2(g) \rightarrow 8CO_2(g) + 5H_2O(g) + \text{energy}$

  All combustion reactions are of exothermic nature and are accompanied by release of heat energy. The human body may be regarded as a furnace or machine in which various food stuffs that we eat undergo oxidation. The heat energy evolved keeps our body working.

  All chemical reactions proceed either with the absorption or release of energy. On the basis of energy changes, there are two types of reactions :

- **Endothermic Reaction:** A chemical reaction which is accompanied by the absorption of energy is called an endothermic reaction.
  - $C(s) + 2S(s) \xrightarrow{\text{Heat}} CS_2(\ell)$
  - Light energy is essential for biochemical reaction, photosynthesis, by which green plants prepare their food from carbon dioxide & water.
- **Exothermic Reaction:** A chemical reaction which is accompanied by the release of energy is called exothermic reaction.
  - When magnesium wire is heated from its tip in a bunsen flame, it catches fire and burns with a dazzling white flame with release of heat and light energy.

    $$2Mg(s) + O_2(g) \xrightarrow{\text{Heat}} 2MgO(s) + \text{Energy}$$
  - When quick lime (calcium oxide) is placed in water, the water becomes very hot and sometimes starts boiling. It is because of release of heat energy during the reaction.

    $$\underset{\text{Calcium oxide}}{CaO(s)} + \underset{\text{Water}}{H_2O} \rightarrow \underset{\text{Calcium hydroxide}}{Ca(OH)_2(aq)} + \text{Heat energy}$$

EXEMPLIFICATION

1. Make a list of various materials used by us in daily life and classify them as natural and man-made.
Materials: Air, clothes, fan, forests, cosmetics, cement, water, plastics, minerals, sunlight

Solution: **Natural:** Air, sunlight, water, minerals, forests

Man-made: Plastics, fan, cement, cosmetics, clothes

2. Name the petroleum product used for surfacing of roads.

Solution: Bitumen.

3. What is the slow process of conversion of dead vegetation into coal called?

Solution: Carbonization.

4. Explain why fossil fuels are exhaustible natural resources.

Solution: Fossil fuels are exhaustible natural resources because they will be exhausted by human activities as they are limited in nature.

5. What are natural resources?

Solution: Material obtained from nature are called natural resources.

6. Classify the following as exhaustible and inexhaustible natural resources: air, sunlight, water, forests, wildlife, coal.

Solution: Exhaustible resources – forests, wildlife, coal.

Inexhaustible resources – air, sunlight, water.

7. Define carbonization.

Solution: The slow process of conversion of dead vegetation into coal is called carbonization.

8. What name is given to the process of heating a substance in absence of air?

Solution: Destructive distillation.

9. How is coke obtained?

Solution: Coke is obtained by heating coal in the absence of air.

10. How is coal tar formed?

Solution: When destructive distillation of coal is done, the vapours which condense in the water form coal tar.

11. Why is petroleum called a fossil fuel ?

Solution: Petroleum is called a fossil fuel as it is obtained from the bodies of dead organisms.

NCERT COMPENDIUM

1. What are the advantages of using CNG and LPG as fuels?

Solution: The advantages of using CNG and LPG as fuels are:
- They burn with a smokeless flame and so does not cause any pollution.
- They leave no ash on burning.
- They are easy to handle and convenient to store.

2. Name the petroleum product used for surfacing of roads.

Solution: Bitumen

3. Describe how coal is formed from dead vegetation. What is this process called?

Solution: Millions of years ago, trees, plants, ferns and forests got buried below the rocks, soil and sand due to natural processes like flooding, earthquake, etc. Slowly, as more soil deposited over them, they were compressed. This led to the conditions of high pressure and heat. These conditions along with the anaerobic conditions turned the carbon-enriched organic matter of wood into coal.
This slow process of conversion of wood into coal is called carbonization.

4. Fill in the blanks:
(a) Fossils fuels are ______, ______ and ______.
(b) Process of separation of different constituents from petroleum is called ______.
(c) Least polluting fuel for vehicle is ______.

Solution:
(a) coal, petroleum, natural gas
(b) refining
(c) CNG

5. Write True/False against the following statements.
(a) Fossil fuels can be made in the laboratory.
(b) CNG is more polluting fuel than petrol.
(c) Coke is an almost pure form of carbon.
(d) Coal tar is a mixture of various substances.
(e) Kerosene is not a fossil fuel.

Solution:
(a) False (b) False
(c) True (d) True
(e) False

6. Explain why fossil fuels are exhaustible natural resources.

Solution: Fossil fuels take millions of years to be formed. They are limited in nature and cannot be replenished easily, once consumed. Hence, they are considered as exhaustible natural resources.

7. Describe the characteristics and uses of coke.

Solution: Characteristics of coke:
- Coke is 98% pure carbon.
- It is a tough, porous and black substance.
- It produces a very little smoke.

Uses of coke:
- Coke is very useful as fuel.
- It is a good reducing agent.
- It is widely used in metallurgical processes to reduce metals from their oxides.
- It is used for producing water gas.

8. Explain the process of the formation of petroleum.

Solution: Petroleum is formed by the burial of aquatic plants and animals below the seabed. The marine animals and plants died thousands of years ago and settled down in the bottom of sea. In anaerobic conditions, microorganisms decompose this organic matter. Due to high pressure and heat, the dead remains of tiny plants and animals were slowly converted into petroleum.

9. The following table shows the total power shortage in India from 2004-2010. Show the data in the form of a graph. Piet shortage percentage for the years on the y-axis and the year on the x-axis.

S. No.	Year	Shortage (%)
1.	2004	7.8
2.	2005	8.6
3.	2006	9.0
4.	2007	9.5
5.	2008	9.9
6.	2009	11.2
7.	2010	10.0

Solution:

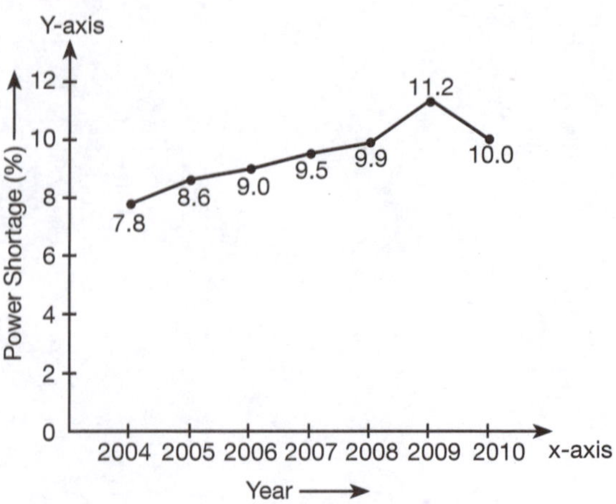

ASSESSMENT CORNER

Level 1

Fixed Response Type

Multiple Choice Questions

1. Main constituents of coal gas are:
(A) H_2O, C_2H_6, O_2
(B) CH_4, CO_2, O_2
(C) CH_4, H_2, CO
(D) C_2H_6, N_2, O_2

2. Ammoniacal liquor is:
(A) ammonia absorbed in water
(B) ammonium hydroxide
(C) aqueous solution of ammonia
(D) All of the above

3. Which of the following products obtained by destructive distillation of coal is not properly matched?
(A) Coal tar – Dyes, explosives, paints
(B) Coal gas – Fuel
(C) Coke – Drinking purposes
(D) Ammoniacal liquor – Fertilizers

4. Which of the following type of coal have highest percentage of carbon?
(A) Anthracite (B) Peat
(C) Lignite (D) Bituminous

5. Least carbon containing coal is:
(A) Peat (B) Lignite
(C) Bituminous (D) Anthracite

6. Which of the following names represents the foul smelling, black, thick, viscous liquid obtained from destructive distillation of coal?
(A) Coke (B) Coal tar
(C) Coal gas (D) None of these

7. Formation of coal from plant matter is called:
(A) destructive distillation
(B) carbonization
(C) both (A) and (B)
(D) none of these

8. Coal and petroleum are:
(A) inexhaustible resources
(B) fossil fuels
(C) renewable resources
(D) all of these

9. Heating of coal in the absence of air is called:
(A) destructive distillation
(B) carbonization
(C) both (A) and (B)
(D) none of these

10. Producer gas is a mixture of:
(A) CO and H_2 (B) CO and N_2
(C) CO and H_2 (D) none of these

11. The distillation of crude petroleum to obtain various commercially useful fraction is called:
(A) compression (B) refining
(C) mining (D) none of these

12. Which of the following is used for refining of petroleum?
(A) Steam distillation
(B) Distillation under reduced pressure
(C) Solvent extraction
(D) Fractional distillation

13. Which one of the following is not a petroleum product?
(A) Kerosene (B) Gasoline
(C) Asphalt (D) Bees wax

14. The amount of LPG in a domestic gas cylinder is about:
(A) 14.2 Kg (B) 13.2 Kg
(C) 12.2 Kg (D) 11.2 Kg

15. CNG stands for:
(A) Conventional Natural Gas
(B) Coal and Natural Gas
(C) Compressed Natural Gas
(D) Commercial Natural Gas

16. Which of the following following hydrocarbon is main constituent of natural gas?
(A) Butane (B) Ethane
(C) Propane (D) Methane

17. Which of the following is household soft coal?
(A) Peat (B) bituminous
(C) Lignite (D) Anthacite

18. The substance added to detect the leakage of LPG is:
(A) methyl mercaptan
(B) ethyl mercaptan
(C) both (A) and (B)
(D) none of these

19. Which of the following is used as a household fuel?
(A) Gasoline (B) Paraffin wax
(C) Kerosene (D) All of these

20. Which of the following is not true for natural gas?
(A) It is generally found with petroleum deposits.
(B) It can be liquefied under pressure.
(C) It is a rich source of hydrogen.
(D) It has a low calorific value.

21. The head of a safety matchstick contains:
(A) antimony trisulphide and potassium chlorate
(B) antimony chloride and potassium sulphide
(C) antimony carbonate
(D) potassium sulphide

Fill in the Blanks

1. The resources that are naturally regenerated after consumption are called ____________ resources.
2. Fractional distillation takes place because the different substances in the mixture have different ____________.
3. The slow process of conversion of dead vegetation into coal is called ____________.
4. On burning, coal produces carbon dioxide, nitrogen dioxide and large amount of ____________.
5. ____________ has highest carbon content, between 86 and 98% and has highest heat value.
6. ____________ is a mixture of various constituents like petroleum gas, petrol, diesel, lubricating oil, paraffin wax, etc.
7. Petroleum is mixture of several________ .
8. Sunlight is ____________ natural resources.
9. Major reserves of petroleum are in __________.
10. Paraffin wax is a constituent of ____________.

True/False

1. Petroleum is a renewable resource that can be recycled.
2. In a fractionating column, the fractions having high boiling points are present at the bottom of column.
3. Coal tar is a white thick liquid with a pleasant smell.
4. Coal is pure form of carbon.
5. Time and technology can change substances into resources.
6. Soil, forest, and wild life are renewable natural resources.
7. Conservation is the improper management of resources.
8. Diesel is used as fuel for light motor vehicles and electric generators.
9. Use of fossil fuels has led to our industrial development.
10. Using pressure cookers save lots of energy in cooking.

Match Type Questions

Direction: There are two columns provided. Choices for column I are given in column II. Match the correct pairs.

1.

Column I (Type of coal)	Column II (% of carbon content)
1. Peat	(a) 90 -95
2. Lignite	(b) 50 -60
3. Anthracite	(c) 75 -80
4. Bituminous	(d) 60 -70

2.

Column - I	Column–II
1. Used for road surfacing	(a) Black gold
2. Natural gas	(b) Vasline and candles
3. Petroleum	(c) Bitumen
4. Paraffine wax	(d) CNG

Assertion and Reasons Type Questions

In the following questions, a statement of assertion is followed by statement of reason.
Mark the correct choice as:
(a) Both assertion and reason are true and reason is the correct explanation of assertion.
(b) Both assertion and reason are true but reason is not the correct explanation of assertion.
(c) Assertion is true but reason is false.
(d) Both assertion and reason are false.

1. **Assertion:** Petrochemicals are useful substances obtained from petroleum.
Reason: They are used in the manufacture of detergents, fibres, polyethylene and other plastics.

2. **Assertion:** In India, natural gas has been formed in Tripura,in the Krishna Godavari Delta.
Reason: propane and butane are the components of natural gas.

3. **Assertion:** Petroleum was formed by the sedimentation of dead remains of microscopic marine plants and animals, which were buried under the surface of the earth, millions of years ago.
Reason: All solid fuels are formed from petroleum.

4. **Assertion:** Fossil fuels are renewable sources of energy because once exhausted they can be recreated in a short period of time.
Reason: Coal is a better fuel than LPG because it does not cause pollution.

5. **Assertion:** The unit of calorific value of combustion of fuels is kilojoule/kilogram.
Reason: LPG is having very high calorific value.

Comprehension Type Questions

Comprehension 1

Natural Gas

Natural gas is a naturally occurring mixture of gaseous hydrocarbons. It is found in porous sedimentary rocks in the earth's crust, usually in association with petroleum deposits. In India, natural gas has been found in Tripura, Rajasthan, Maharashtra and in Krishna-Godavari delta.

Natural gas consists mainly of methane (CH_4) (about 85%), ethane (C_2H_6) (up to about 10%), propane (about 3%) and butane. Carbon dioxide, nitrogen, oxygen, hydrogen sulphide and sometimes helium may also be present.

Natural gas may be obtained from the earth's crust by digging wells in prospective areas. There are some wells which give out only natural gas but most wells produce natural gas as well as petroleum. In fact, natural gas is obtained as a co-product in petroleum mining. Natural gas is formed from the decomposition of organic matter buried under seabeds millions of years ago.

1. The major constituent of natural gas is:
(A) butane
(B) ethane
(C) propane
(D) methane

2. Find the correct statement about natural gas
(A) Natural gas is obtained as a co-product in petroleum mining.
(B) Natural gas may be obtained from the earth's crust by digging wells in prospective areas.
(C) Natural gas is a naturally occurring mixture of gaseous hydrocarbons.
(D) All of these

Free Response Type

Very Short Answer Type Questions

1. Give an example of exhaustible natural resource.
2. Write the name of best quality of coal which contain maximum amount of carbon among all the varieties.
3. What is the main constituent of coal?
4. By which substance, coal tar is being replaced now-a-days?
5. Name the gas found when air is passed over red hot Coke?
6. What is the calorific value of clean fuel?
7. What is crude oil?
8. What is the approximate composition of carbon for kerosene oil?
9. Where was the first oil well drilled?
10. Which country is largest producer of petroleum?
11. You are provided with a mixture of petroleum and water. Can you suggest a method to separate the two?
12. What does CNG stand for and why is it considered to be a better fuel than petrol?
13. Name the petroleum product used as fuel for stoves, lamps and jet aircrafts.
14. Sunlight and air are inexhaustible natural resources. Comment.
15. Some natural resources are given below. Classify them into the exhaustible and inexhaustible natural resources.
Air, coal, natural gas, sunlight, petroleum, minerals, forests, oxygen

Short Answer Type Questions

1. Write the products obtained by processing of coal.
2. Name the products obtained from destructive distillation of coal?
3. What are the fossil fuels? Explain with examples.

4. Why should we use the fossil fuels economically and wisely?
5. Explain the term carbonization?
6. What is destructive distillation of coal?
7. Write the important uses of coal.
8. Write two ways to conserve fossil fuels.
9. Why petrol is exhaustible natural resources whereas sunlight is not? Explain.
10. Write the chemical formula of producer gas.
11. Write two important uses of coke.
12. Write the characteristics and some important uses of coal.
13. Look at the figure where petroleum and natural gas deposits are shown. Why do we find oil layer above water layer?

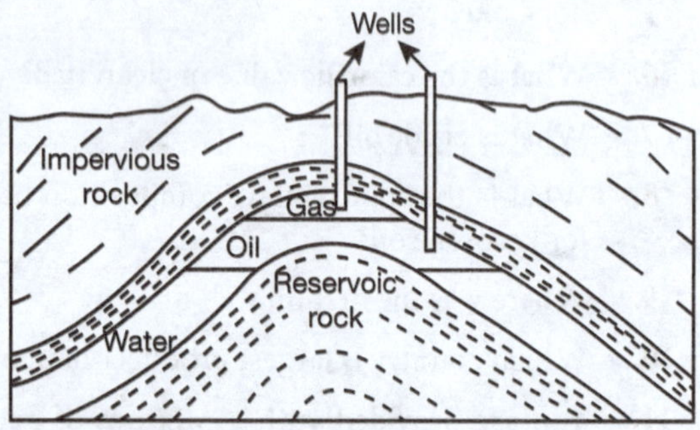

14. Name the products obtained and their uses when coal is processed in industry.
15. Write some important uses of the various constituents of petroleum.

Long Answer Type Questions

1. Differentiate between inexhaustible and exhaustible natural resources.
2. Give the uses of the following:
   (i) coke (ii) coal tar
   (iii) coal gas
3. Name and describe the different varieties of coal.
4. Write a short note on the formation of coal.
5. Explain the term petroleum refining in detail.
6. Give the uses of the following:
   (i) Kerosene (ii) Lubricating oil
   (iii) Paraffin wax (iv) Diesel
7. Fill in the blanks and complete the story.
   About 300 million years ago, the earth had dense ________ in low lying wetland areas. Due to natural processes like ________, these forests got buried under the ________. As more ________ deposited over them, they were compressed. The ________ also rose as they sank deeper and deeper. Under high ________ and high ________, dead plants got slowly converted into coal.
8. We say fossil fuels will last only for a few hundred years. Comment.
9. We read in newspapers that burning of fuels is a major cause of global warming. Explain why?
10. While driving, what are the tips we must follow to save petrol/diesel/natural gas?
11. Why is petrol exhaustible natural resource whereas sunlight is not? Explain.

Numerical Type Questions

1. In an experiment, 2 kg of the fuel was completely burnt. The heat produced was measured to be 180 kJ. Calculate the calorific value of the fuel.
   (A) 90 kJ/kg (B) 180 kJ/kg
   (C) 260 kJ/kg (D) 360 kJ/kg
2. Eva used of cow dung cake for cooking food in a traditional *chullha*. She needs to produce 17500 kJ heat for cooking food. Calculate the amount of cow dung cake required to cook the food. Calorific value of cow dung cake is 7000kJ/kg.
   (A) 2 kg (B) 1 kg
   (C) 2.5 kg (D) 1.5 kg

Case Based Questions

Case-1

Coal: Coal is one of the fuels used to cook food. Earlier, it was used in railway engines to produce steam to run the engine. It is also used in thermal power plants to produce electricity.

Coal is a mineral of dark brown or black colour formed from the remains of plants buried in the earth's crust millions of years ago.

Composition: Coal is a very impure form of carbon. It mainly consists of atoms of carbon, hydrogen and oxygen. A small amount of sulphur is also present in it.

Deposits: The distribution of coal deposits is not uniform in the earth's crust. To the total coal reserves in the world, Asia contributes about one third, whereas North and South America contribute more than half. India has large deposits of coal. It is estimated that India has about 80 billion tonnes of proven coal deposits. The coal deposits are spread over in the states of Jharkhand, Madhya Pradesh and West Bengal.

Formation: It is believed that millions of years ago, the ground below the forests was split open by natural forces such as earthquakes and volcanoes. The forests were buried in the chasms. Thus, the plants had no contact with oxygen. Successive layers of sediments sealed the buried plants. Over millions of years these deposits were subjected to tremendous pressure and heat which finally transformed them into coal.

The chemical process involved in the transformation of plant matter into coal is called the carbonization of plant matter.

1. What are the necessary conditions for the formation of coal?
   (A) High pressure
   (B) Low pressure and low temperature
   (C) High temperature
   (D) Both (A) and (C)

2. The chemical process involved in the transformation of plant matter into coal is:
   (A) Calorific value (B) Chasms
   (C) Deposition of coal (D) Carbonization

Level 2

Multiple Choice Questions

1. Which of the following does not leave behind any residue on burning?
   (A) petrol (B) diesel
   (C) CNG (D) coal

2. An example of exhaustible natural resource is:
   (A) air (B) forests
   (C) rocks (D) sunlight

3. Petrol or gasoline used as automobile fuel is a mixture of:
   (A) hydrocarbons
   (B) alcohols
   (C) carbohydrates
   (D) hydrocarbon and alcohols.

4. Mark the incorrect statement.
   (A) CNG and LPG are clean fuels.
   (B) Petroleum is refined in a petroleum refinery.
   (C) Petroleum products are called petrochemicals.
   (D) Coal does not cause any pollution when burnt.

5. Various materials which are obtained from nature are called natural resources. Which of the following is not a natural resource?
   (A) Minerals (B) Water
   (C) Soil (D) Plastic

6. Air is a natural resource and cannot be exhausted by human activities. It is known as inexhaustible natural resource. Which of the following is another inexhaustible natural resource?
   (A) Coal (B) Petroleum
   (C) Sunlight (D) Minerals

7. Which of the following is a pair of exhaustible natural resources?
   (A) Coal and soil
   (B) Air and sunlight
   (C) Water and petroleum
   (D) Wildlife and minerals

8. Coal is processed in industries to get some useful products. Which of the following is not obtained from coal?
   (A) Coke (B) Coal tar
   (C) Coal gas (D) CNG

9. Exhaustible natural resources are:
   (A) unlimited in quantity
   (B) not dependent on nature
   (C) limited in quantity
   (D) not exhausted by human activities

10. Fossil fuels are obtained from:
    (A) remains of non-living materials
    (B) dead remains of birds only
    (C) dead remains of insects only
    (D) dead remains of living organisms

11. Coal is formed from the remains of:
    (A) vegetation only
    (B) animals only
    (C) both vegetation and animals
    (D) neither vegetation nor animals

12. Which substance is formed by the carbonization of dead vegetation?
    (A) Coal (B) Coke
    (C) Coal gas (D) Coal tar

13. Naphthalene balls are obtained from coal tar and are used as:
    (A) mosquito repellant (B) honeybee repellant
    (C) moth repellant (D) snake repellant

14. Which of the following is not a constituent of petroleum?

(A) Paraffin wax (B) Lubricating oil
(C) Petrol (D) Coke

15. Coal gas is made up of –
(A) Hydrogen (B) Methane
(C) Carbon monoxide (D) All of these

16. Choose the correct statement from the following.
(A) It is difficult to transport natural gas through pipes.
(B) The disadvantage of natural gas is that it cannot be used directly for burning in homes.
(C) Natural gas is stored under high pressure as compressed natural gas.
(D) Natural gas cannot be used for power generation.

Higher Order Thinking Skills (HOTS)

1. Write down the process to form carbon black used for tyre industries?
2. Write the composition of coal gas.
3. When coke and coal are burnt, which produces the smoke and why?
4. How is diamond formed in the nature?
5. Coal reserves are said to be enough to last for another hundred years. Do you think we need to worry in such case? Why or why not?
6. Imagine that all the exhaustible natural resources are exhausted by human activities. Do you think survival of living beings would be possible? If yes, why? If not, why not?
7. How is natural gas formed?
8. What is meant by fractional distillation? What is the principle on which it is based?

ARCHIVE CORNER

1. 'P' is processed in industries to get some useful products such as 'Q', 'R' and 'S'. 'S' is obtained during the processing of 'P' to get 'Q', 'R' is a mixture of about 200 substances. Identify 'P', 'Q' 'R' and 'S'.

	P	Q	R	S
(A)	Coal	Coal tar	Coke	Coal gas
(B)	Coke	Coal	Coal tar	Coal gas
(C)	Coal	Coke	Coal tar	Coal gas
(D)	Coke	Coal	Coal gas	Coal tar

2. Which of the following is not a renewable energy?
(A) Nuclear energy (B) Hydropower energy
(C) Geothermal energy (D) Solar energy

3. Which of the following is an incorrect match?
(A) An oily liquid formed when coal is heated in absence of air – Coal tar
(B) A gas found along with petroleum in reservoirs under the ground – Natural gas
(C) A thick black liquid found trapped in underground rocks – Petroleum
(D) A residue left behind when destructive distillation of coal is carried out – Charcoal

4. Read the following statements carefully and identify P, Q and R.

P: Obtained from petroleum and natural gas and used in the manufacture of man-made plastics.

Q: Due to its great commercial importance, it is also called 'black gold'.

R: Obtained from natural gas and used in the production of fertilizers.

	P	Q	R
(A)	Petrochemicals	Petroleum	Hydrogen gas
(B)	Coke	Coal	Coal tar
(C)	Paraffin wax	Coal tar	Diesel
(D)	Bitumen	Coke	Coal gas

5. Match the Column-I with Column -II and select the correct option given below.

Column-I	Column-II
(a) Coal tar	(i) Metalling the roads
(b) Petrol	(ii) Manufacture of steel
(c) Coal gas	(iii) Source of heat
(d) Bitumen	(iv) Vaseline
(e) Coke	(v) Naphthalene balls
(f) Paraffin wax	(vi) Dry cleaning

(A) a–(v), b– (vi), c– (iii), d– (i), e– (ii), f– (iv)
(B) a– (i), b– (iv), c– (iii), d– (ii), e– (v), f– (vi)
(C) a– (iii), b– (v), c– (i), d– (iv), e– (ii), f– (vi)
(D) a– (iv), b– (i), c– (vi), d– (iii), e– (v), f– (ii)

6. Petroleum is:
(A) lighter than water and soluble in it
(B) heavier than water and insoluble in it
(C) lighter than water and insoluble in it
(D) heavier than water and soluble in it

7. The residue left behind after the dry distillation of coal:
(A) coal tar (B) coal gas
(C) coke (D) ammoniacal liquor

8. Which of the following property is not a characteristic of a good fuel?
(A) High ignition temperature
(B) Low cost
(C) Causes minimum pollution
(D) Readily available

9. Producer gas is not a good fuel because:
(A) it contains CO which is poisonous.
(B) it contains CO_2.
(C) it contains CO_2 which does not burn
(D) it contains N_2 which does not burn.

10. Plants store solar energy in the form of:
(A) electric energy (B) thermal energy
(C) chemical energy (D) bio energy

11. Biogas is a mixture of:
(A) methane + CO_2 (B) methane + CO
(C) ethane + CO_2 (D) ethane + CO

12. Water gas is a mixture of:
(A) H_2 and N_2 (B) H_2 and CO_2
(C) CO_2 and N_2 (D) CO and H_2

13. Aerobic fermentation is a process which helps in formation of:
(A) Coal gas (B) Natural gas
(C) Water gas (D) Petroleum

ARCHIVE CORNER

14. Which of the following is most harmful for human body?
(A) CO (B) CO_2
(C) Oxides of nitrogen (D) Lead compounds

15. What should be the characteristic for a rocket fuel?
(A) Light and compact (B) High calorific value
(C) Should burn rapidly (D) All of the above

16. By which chemical, combustion in a matchstick is started?
(A) Antimony sulphide (B) Potassium chlorate
(C) Phosphorus (D) Starch and wool

17. Fill in the blanks left in the classification of the fossil fuels.

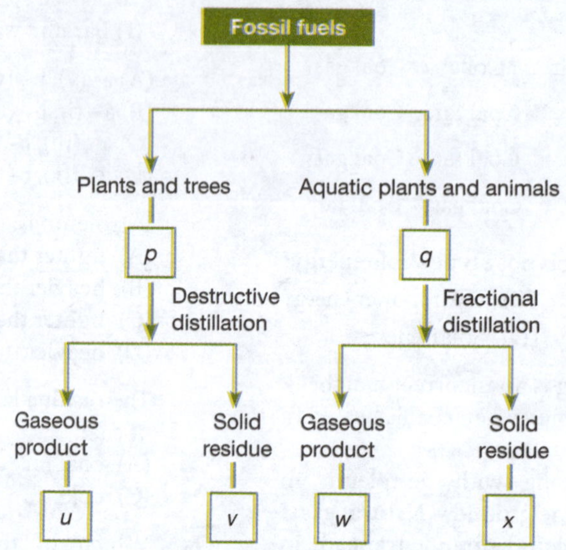

	p	q	u	v	w	x
(A)	Petroleum	Coal	Petroleum	Bitumen	Coal gas	Coke
(B)	Coal, Petroleum	Coal	Coke	Petroleum	Bitumen	Gas
(C)	Coal	Petroleum	Coal gas	Coke	Petroleum gas	Bitumen
(D)	Petroleum	Coal	Gasoline	Bitumen	Natural gas	Coke

18. A brief information about a few substances is given as:

X : It is the residue left behind after destructive distillation of coal.

Y : It is a mixture of hydrogen, methane, carbon monoxide and other gases.

Z : It contains several carbon compounds which are used to make pesticides, explosives, synthetic fibres, perfumes, etc.

X, Y and Z, respectively, are:
(A) Kerosene, CNG and Ammoniacal liquor
(B) Bitumen, Coal gas and Coal tar
(C) Coke, Coal gas and Coal tar
(D) Petrol, CNG and Bitumen

19. The given figure represents a fractionating column used in refineries. Which of the following statements are correct?

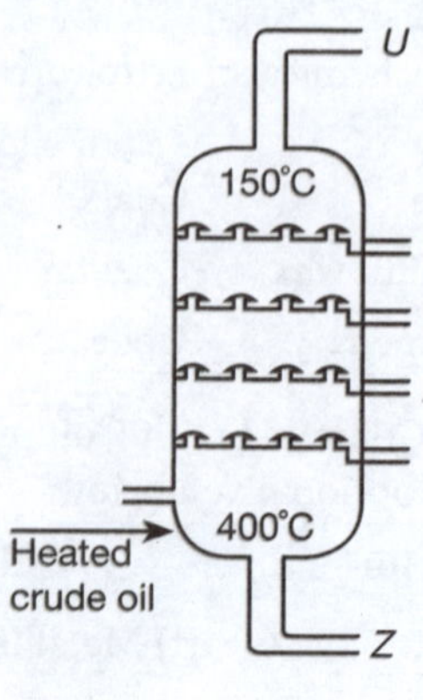

ARCHIVE CORNER

I. Substance U has the highest boiling point among all the fractions while substance Z has the lowest boiling point.
II. Substance U is used as a domestic fuel while substance Z is used for lubrication.
III. U, V, W and X all are used as fuels.
IV. V is used in power stations while X is used as a fuel for lamps and stoves.

(A) I and IV only (B) II and III only
(C) I, III and IV only (D) I, II, III and IV

20. Consider the following statements:
I. Natural gas can be supplied to homes and factories through pipes.
II. Natural gas is obtained by fractional distillation of petroleum.
III. Natural gas is a cleaner fuel, on burning it does not produce any ash or smoke.
IV. Natural gas is an exhaustible source of energy like fossil fuels.

The correct statements are:
(A) I and III only (B) II and III only
(C) I and IV only (D) I, III and IV only

21. Match Column-I with Column-II and select the correct option from the given codes.

Column-I	Column-II
(a) Kerosene	(i) Road surfacing
(b) Paraffin wax	(ii) Fuel for vehicles
(c) Bitumen	(iii) Manufacturing candles
(d) Gasoline	(iv) Jet engine fuel

(A) a-(ii); b-(iv); c-(iii); d-(i)
(B) a-(iii); b-(ii); c-(iv); d-(i)
(C) a-(iv); b-(ii); c-(i); d-(iii)
(D) a-(iv); b-(iii); c-(i); d-(ii)

22. Read the given statements and select the correct option.
Statement 1: Petroleum is a fossil fuel.
Statement 2: Kerosene is not obtained as a fraction of fractional distillation of petroleum.

(A) Both statements 1 and 2 are true and statement 2 is the correct explanation of statement 1.
(B) Both statements 1 and 2 are true but statement 2 is not the correct explanation of statement 1.
(C) Statement 1 is true and statement 2 is false.
(D) Both statements 1 and 2 are false.

23. The given figure represents the fractionating column used in refining of petroleum.

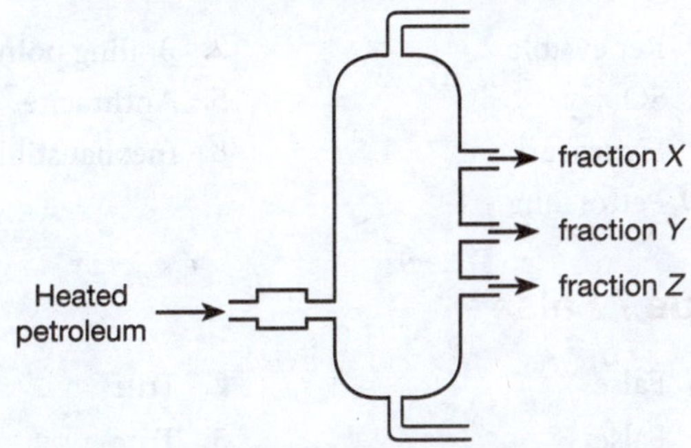

Which of the following statements about the fractions X, Y and Z is/are incorrect?
I. The order of their densities is X > Y > Z.
II. The fraction Z will condense first and the fraction X will condense at the last.
III. The order of their boiling points is X < Y < Z.
IV. X can be heavy oil, Y can be light oil while Z can be gasoline and naphtha.

(A) I and IV only (B) I only
(C) II and III only (D) None of these

ARCHIVE CORNER

ANSWER KEY

Level 1

Fixed Response Type

Multiple Choice Questions

1. C 2. D 3. C 4. A 5. A 6. B 7. B 8. B 9. A 10. B
11. B 12. D 13. D 14. A 15. C 16. D 17. B 18. B 19. C 20. D
21. A

Fill in the Blanks

1. Renewable 2. Boiling point 3. carbonization
4. SO_2 5. Anthracite 6. Petroleum
7. Hydrocarbon 8. Inexhaustible 9. Saudi Arabia
10. Petroleum

True / False

1. False 2. True 3. False
4. False 5. True 6. True
7. False 8. True 9. True
10. True

Match Type Questions

1. 1–b, 2–d, 3–a, 4–c 2. 1–c, 2–d, 3–a, 4–b

Assertion and Reasons Type Questions

1. A 2. C 3. C
4. D 5. B

Comprehension Type Questions

1. D 2. D

Free Response Type

Numerical Type Questions

1. A 2. C

Case Based Questions

1. D 2. D

ANSWER KEY

Level 2

Multiple Choice Questions

1. C	2. B	3. D	4. D	5. D	6. C	7. D	8. D	9. C
10. D	11. A	12. A	13. C	14. D	15. D	16. C		

Archive Corner

1. C	2. A	3. D	4. A	5. A	6. C	7. C	8. A	9. D
10. C	11. A	12. D	13. B	14. D	15. D	16. C	17. C	18. C
19. C	20. D	21. D	22. C	23. A				

CHAPTER 9

Fibre to Fabric

Learning Outcomes

After reading this chapter, you will be able to:

- explain the relation between fibre, yarn, and fabric.
- classify fibres based on their origin (natural fibres and synthetic fibres).
- further classify natural fibres in the categories of plants and animal fibres.
- explain how natural fibres are converted into fabrics.
- tell the characteristic smell obtained during burning test of natural and synthetic fibres.
- explain why the texture of some fabrics is different from others.

Geekspeak

- Fabrics
- Fibre
- Yarn
- Spinning
- Knitting
- Weaving
- Natural fibres
- Synthetic fibres
- Fruit fibres
- Bast fibres
- Leaf fibres
- Picking
- Ginning
- Retting
- Coir
- Silk cotton
- Kapok
- Hemp
- Flax

Introduction

The three most important needs of life are food, clothing, and shelter. Food is essential for survival and protection from diseases. A house is important to live in and for protection against heat, rain, cold, and storm, but why is it necessary to wear clothes? We wear clothes for protection against weather conditions such as rain, snow, extreme heat, or cold. They also offer protection against insect bites. People all over the world wear different kinds of clothing. It usually depends on the weather conditions of that particular place.

Clothing Material and their Variety

Clothing has undergone many changes over the years. Several varieties, textures, and colours of fabrics are seen in markets these days.

Development of Clothing Material

Primitive people did not wear any clothes initially. Later on, as humans migrated to new places, they started covering their bodies with animal skins, leaves, or barks of trees to protect themselves from cold, heat and rain as shown in Fig. 9.1. Some evidence suggest that human beings may have begun wearing clothes as far back as 1,00,000 to 5,00,000 years ago. After people began to settle in agricultural communities, they started weaving twigs and grass into long strands. Slowly they began to weave these strands into fabric. Around 50,000 years ago, the invention of the needle and the spinning wheel revolutionized clothing.

Figure 9.1 Development of Clothing Material

Variety in Fabrics

You must have gone to a cloth shop with your parents to buy dress material for your clothing. You must have noticed that clothing has a wide variety of fabrics. Some dress materials are made from cotton, some from wool, and some from silk. Then there is dress material made from synthetic materials like nylon terylene, polyester, etc. All these materials are called fabrics.

Keystone

New innovative fabrics are being developed for more eco-friendly and sustainable production methods. One of these new fibers is called Qmilch. Made from proteins found in sour milk, it's much more sustainable than cotton and synthetics, and uses less water and chemicals.

Fibre

The material that is used to make a particular type of clothing is called fibre. If you go to a cloth shop to buy cloth or fabric for your dress, you will see a variety of fabrics like—silk, cotton, velvet, satin, and so on. What are these made of?

Take a piece of cloth and pull out a thread from one end. Untwist to loosen this thread. You will see that it is made up of smaller threads or hair like strands. This single hair like strand is called a fibre. A number of fibres twisted together make a yarn.

The fibers are so fine and small that they cannot be processed directly into cloth. So they are first transformed into longer, thicker and stronger threads. We use these threads to make fabrics.

Spinning: The process of twisting the fibres so as to make a stronger thread (Fig. 9.2) is called spinning.

Figure 9.2 Spinning

Knitting: It is method by which a single thread or yarn may be turned into cloth with the help of hand or machine (Fig. 9.3).

Weaving: The process of arranging two sets of yarns together to make a fabric with the help of a handloom or power loom is called weaving (Fig. 9.4).

Figure 9.3 Knitting

Figure 9.4 Weaving

Source of Fibre

Fibres are obtained from various sources such as plants, animal hair, insects, and crude oil. Cotton and jute are obtained from plants (Fig. 9.5). Silk is obtained from the cocoons of silk moths. Wool is obtained from sheep. The fibres obtained from natural sources such as plants and animals are known as natural fibres. Synthetic fibres are obtained from crude oil that is processed into chemical substances and changed to fibre.

Fibre **Yarn** **Fabric**

Figure 9.5 Journey of Fibre to Fabric

Testing Room 1

Visit a nearby tailoring shop. Collect cuttings of fabrics left over after stitching. Feel and touch each piece of fabric. Now try to label some of the fabrics as cotton, silk, wool or synthetic after asking for help from the tailor.

Do you wonder what these different fabrics are made of? When you look at any fabric, it seems a continuous piece. Now, look at it closely. What do you notice?

Testing Room 2

We can separate a mixture of different coloured fibre. Take out a yarn from a piece of cotton fabric. Place this piece of yarn on the table. Now, press one end of the yearn with your thumb.
Scratch the other end of the yarn along its length with your nails as shown in Fig. Do you find that at this end, the yarn splits up into think strands?

Splitting the yarn into thin strands

Yarn split up into thin strands

❖ INTEXT QUESTIONS

1. **Name two types of fabric materials commonly used.**
   Solution: Cotton, silk/wool.
2. **What are fabrics?**
   Solution: Fabrics mean a woven material, textile, or other materials resembling woven cloth.
3. **Name some fabrics in your surroundings.**
   Solution: Bedsheets, blankets, curtains, table clothes, towels, and dusters
4. **Name the thing which is used to make fabric.**
   Solution: Yarns.
5. **What are yarns made of?**
   Solution: Yarns are made up of thin strands called fibres.
6. **What do you observe when you visit your local tailor shop?**
   Solution: At the tailor's shop, you'll find lots of fabric cuts left over after sewing. Some are made of cotton, silk, or wool, while others are made of synthetic fibres.
7. **List the steps involved in the preparation of fabric.**
   Solution: Fabric production includes the following steps: (i) obtain the fiber; (ii) manufacture of yarn from fibers by spinning; (iii) In the case of two pairs of yarns, the yarns are woven on a loom and he makes one cloth. In the case of single yarn, it is knitted to make the fabric.
8. **Describe the process of the formation of yarn from cotton wool.**
   Solution: The cotton wool is obtained from cotton plants. The cotton plants are grown in fields. They are usually grown at the places having black soil and warm climate. The fruits of the cotton plants are called cotton bolls, they are about the size of lemons. After maturing, the bolls burst open, and seeds covered with cotton fibres can be seen. From the cotton bolls cotton is handpicked. Fibres are then separated from the seeds by combing. This process is called ginning of cotton. It is done by hand or by machines. These fibres are then converted into a yarn.

Check Point 1

1. Why is it necessary to wear clothes?
2. Name four type of fabric used by us.
3. What is meant by: (i) Fibre (ii) Fabric
4. What is spinning?
5. Name the process used to prepare fabrics from yarns.

Fibre

Fibres are broadly classified into two types-natural and synthetic. Natural fibres are obtained from either plant or animal sources while synthetic fibres are obtained from chemical substances. Plant fibres include cotton, jute, hemp, coir, etc., whereas animal fibres include wool, silk, etc. Nylon and polyester are examples of synthetic fibres.

Natural Fibres

The natural fibres can be further classified as below

Plant Fibres

Fibres found on some part/parts of plants are called plant fibres.

Examples of plant fibres:

- Cotton has fibres on its seed (Fig. 9.6).
- Coconut has fibres on its fruit.
- Banana tree has fibres on its leaves. Here, it is useful to know that almost all plant leaves have fibres.
- Flax and jute have fibres on their stem.

Figure 9.6 Cotton .

Plant fibres are classified into three categories, depending on the part of the plant they are extracted from.

- **Fruit fibres:** These fibres are obtained from the fruits of the plant. Examples are cotton and coir (coconut fibres). The fruits of these plants are usually light, hairy and allow the wind to carry the seeds.
- **Bast fibres:** These fibres are found in the stem of the plant and provide strength to the plant. They are generally very long. Examples of bast fibres are jute and flax.
- **Leaf fibres:** Fibres obtained from the leaves are rough and sturdy. For example, sisal which is a moisture-resistant fibre is used in making ropes, mats, and carpets.

Cotton: Cotton is the world's most popular natural fibre. It is considered to be the undisputed king of the global textile industry. Cotton fibre is obtained from the cotton plant which is a shrub growing well in black soil and warm climate.

The cotton plant bears fruits called cotton balls. When they are ripe, the balls burst exposing the seeds which are surrounded by cotton fibres. The fibres are then used to create the yarn involving the following steps:

- **Picking:** The process involves handpicking the cotton fibres from the ripe cotton balls (Fig. 9.7(a)).
- **Ginning:** The cotton fibres are separated from the seeds by this process. Earlier, ginning was done by hand, but now, machines are used for this purpose (Fig. 9.7(b)).
- **Spinning:** It is a process by which cotton fibres are spin to form cotton yarn using spinning machines (Fig. 9.7(d)). Most of the cotton we grow is used to manufacture cotton textiles and undergarments. These days, the cotton yarn is blended with polyester to form fine fabric which are crease resistant and last longer.

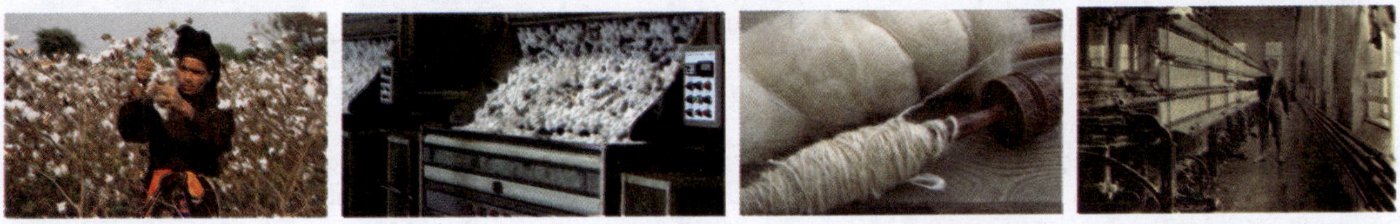

(a) Cotton Picking **(b) Ginning** **(c) Spinning by Hand** **(d) Spinning with Machine**

Figure 9.7 Manufacturing of Cotton

Jute: Jute is a natural fibre with a golden, silky shine and therefore, popularly known as the golden fibre. It is obtained from the bast or skin of the plant stem and is the second most important plant fibre after cotton. It is biodegradable and recyclable and thus, environment friendly.

Jute plant mainly grows in places that have high temperatures and plenty of rainfall. It grows best in soil that has presence of sand, silt, and clay. Jute is cultivated during the rainy season and is generally harvested when it is in the flowering stage. The process of obtaining jute yarn from the plant is as follows:

- **Retting:** The bark of the jute plant is usually glued together by a sticky substance that has to be removed to obtain the fibres. The harvested stalks of the plant are soaked in water for a few days until they start rotting. Then the fibres are separated by hand from the rotting stems. This process is called retting.
- **Spinning:** The fibres are made into yarn by twisting the strands together. This process of making yarn from fibre is called spinning.

The strong threads made from jute fibres are used in making sacks and help to sustain the livelihoods of millions of small farmers. Jute yarn and twines are also woven into curtains coverings, carpets, and rugs.

Keystone

- The name cotton comes from the Arabic word "Qutn," which means fancy. Cotton was once known as vegetable wool.
- Cotton is made up of cellulose.

Animal fibres

These fibres are obtained from animals. Some common examples of animal fibres are wool and silk.

- **Wool:** Wool is obtained from the fleece of sheep or hairy animals (Fig. 9.8) (for example, yaks, camels, cashmere goats, and angora rabbits). The fleece is sheared, washed, dried, and then spun into yarn. This yarn is then woven or knitted to make clothes. Wool is flexible, absorbs moisture, and is dirt and flame resistant. It is used for making fine clothing and in bedding, upholstery, and carpets.
- **Silk:** Silk is produced from cocoons of silkworms which feed on mulberry leaves (Fig. 9.9). It secretes an unbroken fibre around itself, which is the cocoon. The cocoon is boiled and unwound to form the fibre which is then spun. Silk is the strongest natural fibre. It dries quickly, does not shrink, retains its shape, drapes well, has a natural shine, and can be easily dyed. The silk fibre is made into fabrics such as satin, velvet chiffon, crepe, and brocades.

Figure 9.8 Sheep Bearing Wool

Figure 9.9 White Cocoon and Silkworm

Synthetic Fibres

Fibres made by human beings from chemical substances are called synthetic or man-made fibres. These fibres are made from chemical substances processed from crude oil. Examples of synthetic fibres are polyester, nylon, and acrylic. The chemical substances are first heated so that they melt and then forced through spinnerets that have fine pores. The long threads that come out from these pores are allowed to cool and solidify. These threads are then twisted together to form yarn which is ultimately used to make fabric.

This synthetic cloth so formed is strong, does not get wrinkled and dries easily. However, since they have lesser air spaces within them, the fabric does not absorb sweat and is unsuitable to be used in hot and humid climate. Thus, synthetic fibres are usually mixed with other natural fibres such as cotton or wool to make cloth (Fig. 9.10).

Figure 9.10 Synthetic Fibres

Keystone

- Bamboo is a grass that has been used to create a fabric that hangs much like heavy linen.
- Manila Hemp, aka Abaca, was long the best fibre for making ship ropes and rigging. It was also the favoured material for making Manila envelopes, hence the name. These days it is about to enjoy a resurgence as a greener, kinder alternative to the glass fibre used in cars.
- The angora is an old world domestic rabbit breed, whose fur grows twice as fast as other rabbits. The resulting hollow fibre is classified as a wool.

Testing Room 3

Aim: To demonstrate the burning test of fibers.

Material required: Candle, matchstick, pieces of cotton, silk, wool, acrylic, nylon, and polyester.

Procedure: Separate a yarn from each of the sample fabrics. Burn one end of each sample on the flame of the candle and make the following observations:

- How the fiber catches fire
- Type of flame
- Smell after burning
- Ash left behind

Observation:

Table showing the different types of fibre, their flame, smell and Ash

Fiber	Type of Flame	Smell	Ash
Cotton and Rayon	Catch fire easily and contiue to burn with a bright yellow flame.	Smell of burning Paper	Light, feathery ash
Silk and wool	Do not catch fire easily. Burn with a yellow flame but do not continue to burn.	Smell of burning Hair	Black, crushable bead
Nylon, Polyester, Acrylic	Do not catch fire easily. Shrink away from the flame and melt.	No definite smell	Hard, uncrushable bead

Conclusion: Natural fibers burn with a yellow flame and synthetic fibers melt on burning.

❖ INTEXT QUESTIONS

8. **How many types of fibres are there?**
   Solution: There are two types of fibres:
   (i) Natural fibres (ii) Synthetic fibres
9. **Name two natural fibres.**
   Solution: (i) Cotton (ii) Jute

10. Name two synthetic fibres.
Solution: (i) Polyester (ii) Nylon

11. What material you use for making wicks for oil lamps?
Solution: Cotton wool.

12. Where does cotton and wool come from?
Solution: Cotton wool comes from cotton balls.

13. What are fruits of cotton plants called?
Solution: Cotton balls.

14. What type of soil is used to grow cotton plants?
Solution: Black soil.

15. Define ginning of cotton.
Solution: The process of separating fibres from the seeds of cotton is called ginning of cotton.

16. What is jute?
Solution: Jute is a fibre obtained from the stem of a jute plant.

17. Name the states where jute plants are mainly grown in India.
Solution: West Bengal, Bihar, and Assam.

18. What is spinning?
Solution: The process of making yarn from fibre is called spinning.

19. Name two hand-operated devices used for spinning.
Solution: (i) Takli (ii) Charkha

20. How are fabrics prepared?
Solution: Fabrics are prepared from the yarns by weaving or knitting.

21. Name the process used to prepare fabrics from yarns.
Solution: The processes which used to prepare fabrics are: (i) weaving and (ii) knitting.

22. What is weaving?
Solution: The process of arranging two sets of yarns together to make a fabric is called weaving.

23. What is knitting?
Solution: The process in which a single yarn is used to make a piece of fabric is called knitting.

24. Name two methods of knitting.
Solution: (i) By hand (ii) Using machines

25. Where were cotton and flax plants cultivated in ancient Egypt?
Solution: Cotton and flax plants were cultivated near the river Nile in ancient Egypt.

26. Name some modem fabrics formed by unstitched piece of fabric.
Solution: Saree, dhoti, lungi, and turban.

27. How are natural fibres better than synthetic fibres?
Solution: Natural fibres absorbs sweat and gives cooling effect and comfort in any season.

28. Are all fibres produced by plants?
Solution: No.

29. Cotton on burning gives a paper burning smell and cotton is obtained from plants. Is paper also obtained from plants?
Solution: Yes, paper is also obtained from plants.

30. What are natural fibres? Explain with examples.
Solution: The fibres obtained from plants and animals are called natural fibres. For example, cotton from cotton bolls, jute from jute plant, silk from cocoon of silkworm and wool from hair of animals like sheep or goat.

31. What are synthetic fibres?
Solution: The fibres which are made from chemical substances, or which are not obtained from the plant and animal sources are called synthetic fibres. For example, polyester, nylon, and acrylic, etc.

32. Why are cotton clothes rough compared to silk, rayon, or polyester?
Solution: Clothes are woven from threads and the threads are spun from the natural or synthetic fibres. The fibres of cotton and wool have many folds and uneven surface. It is the presence of these folds and uneven surfaces on the fibre,

it makes them rough. In case of silk, the folds are minute and the surface of fibres is not very uneven. Thus, silk is soft to touch. In case of rayon or polyester there are no folds and surface of the fibre is smooth. Thus, they are soft to touch. Jute fibre has a highly uneven surface and hence jute products are very rough. The coconut fibres are very hard and highly uneven. They cannot be spun to a very high degree. Thus, the yarn from coconut fibre is used for making carpet, foot mats and ropes.

Check Point 2

6. What are natural fibres? Explain with an example.
7. What is retting? How is it done?
8. Name any two states in which jute is grown.
9. How silk is obtained from silkworms?
10. What are synthetic fibres? Give examples.

Competition Corner

There are other important plants fibres as well.

Coir: Coir is the fibre obtained from the outer covering of the fruit of the coconut palm. Usually, coconuts are left in water for a few months. The husk is then separated from the nut and beaten with wooden mallets to get the fibre. The fibre thus obtained is then spun and dyed and is ready for weaving. There are various qualities of coir. Coir is used to make several household products like ropes and floor coverings. Some varieties are used as a stuffing in mattresses and pillows.

Coir is Obtained from Coconut Tree

Silk cotton: There is another plant fibre that is commonly used as a stuffing in pillows, sleeping bags, and life jackets. This fibre is known as silk cotton. Silk cotton is obtained from the silk cotton tree, also called kapok.

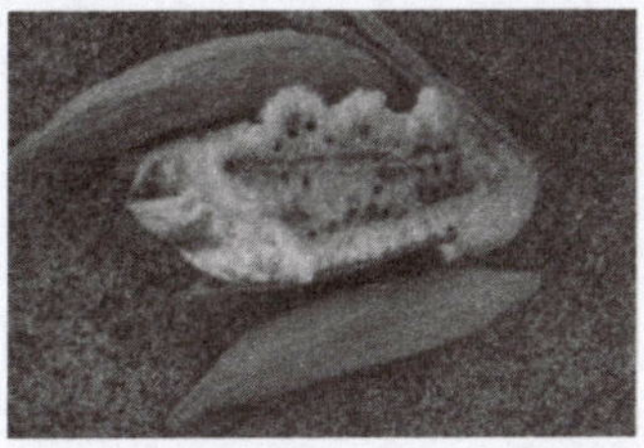

Silk Cotton is Obtained from Kapok Tree

Hemp: Hemp fibres are obtained from the stem of the hemp plant. Hemp plants grow best in loamy soil. Hemp fibres are used in the production of ropes, carpets, nets, clothes, and paper.

Hemp Plant

Flax: Fibres obtained from the stem of the flax plant are woven to make a fabric called linen. Flax fibres are also used in the production of ropes and high-quality paper.

Flax Spindle

STRUCTURAL OUTLINE

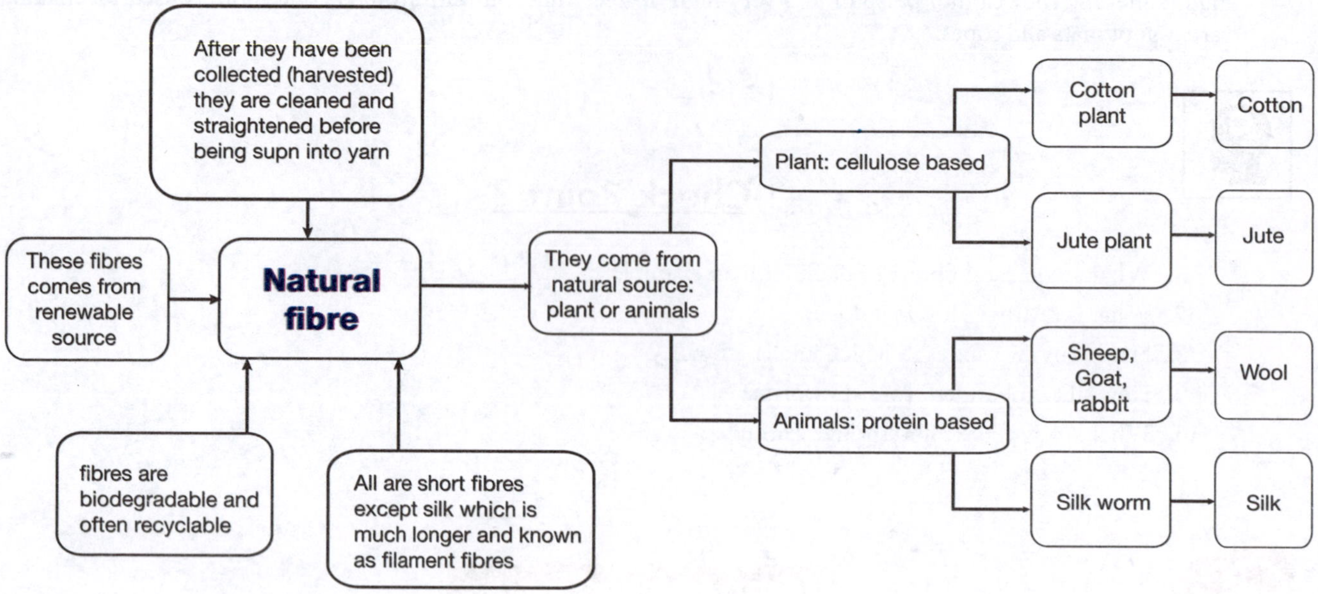

ABRIDGEMENT

Types of fibres:

- Fibres may be of three types -

  (i) Natural fibres

  Natural fibres: Fibres obtained from plants and animals are known as natural fibres. Natural fibres are usually short fibres.

  Examples: Wool, cotton, silk (it can be obtained up to 1 km length)

  (ii) Synthetic fibres

  Synthetic fibres: Fibres synthesized by human beings are known as synthetic fibres. Synthetic fibres are continuous filament fibres.

  Examples: Nylon, Polyester, Acrylic, Spandex etc.

  (iii) Semi-synthetic fibres

  Semi-synthetic fibres: Modified natural fibres are known as semi-synthetic fibres.

  Examples: Rayon or Viscose.

EXEMPLIFICATION

1. **Explain how jute is obtained from jute plants.**

   Solution: The jute plant is normally harvested at flowering stage. The stems of harvested plants are bundled and immersed in water for 10 to 15 days. The stems rot (the process is called retting) and fibres are separated by hand. These fibres are converted into yarns to make fabrics.

2. **What are looms?**

   Solution: The devices on which fabrics are woven are called looms. Looms are either hand operated or power operated.

3. **What happens when a yarn from a torn sock is pulled?**

   Solution: When we pull a yarn from a torn sock then a single yarn gets pulled out continuously as the fabric unravels. Socks are made up of knitted fabrics from a single yarn.

4. **What were the materials used by people in ancient times in place of clothes?**

   Solution: It appears that in those days people used the bark and big leaves of trees or animal skin and furs in place of clothes.

5. **What happened when people began to settle in agricultural communities?**

   Solution: When people began to settle in agricultural communities, they learnt to weave twigs and grass into mats and baskets. Vines, animal fleece or hair were twisted together into long strands. These strands were woven into fabrics.

6. **When we burn wool, why do we get the smell of hair burning?**

   Solution: Wool is obtained from the fleece of sheep, goat, yak etc. This is the why burning wool resembles the smell burning hair.

7. **When we burn nylon, why we do not get the smell of burning paper or burning hair?**

   Solution: Nylon is a synthetic fibre made from chemicals. On burning nylon these chemicals don't produce the smell of burning paper or hair which are natural substances.

8. **Describe the process of spinning and weaving.**

   Solution: The process of making yarn from fibres is called spinning. In this process fibres from a mass of cotton wool are drawn out and twisted. These fibres come together to form a yarn. Spinning can be done by hand, by takli and charkha. On a large scale, spinning is done with the help of machines.

   The process of arranging two sets of yarns together to make a fabric is called weaving. The process of weaving can be done on looms. The looms are either-hand operated or power operated.

KNOWLEDGE COMPENDIUM

1. Classify the following fibres as natural or synthetic: nylon, wool, cotton, silk, polyester, jute.
Solution: Natural fibres: wool, cotton, jute, silk. Synthetic fibres: nylon, and polyester.

2. State whether the following statements are 'true' or 'false':
(a) Yarn is made from fibres.
(b) Spinning is a process of making fibres.
(c) Jute is the outer covering of coconut.
(d) The process of removing seeds from cotton is called ginning.
(d) Weaving of yarn makes a piece of fabric.
(e) Silk fibre is obtained from the stem of a plant.
(f) Polyester is a natural fibre.
Solution: (a) True(b) False (c) False
(d) True (e) True (f) False
(g) False

3. Fill in the blanks:
(a) Plant fibres are obtained from____________ and____________ .
(b) Animal fibres are____________ and____________ .
Solution: (a) cotton plants, jute plants
(b) wool, silk

4. From which part of the plant cotton and jute are obtained?
Solution: (i) Cotton – Cotton bolls (from the surface of cotton seeds) (fruit)
(ii) Jute – Stem

5. Name two items that are made from coconut fibre.
Solution: (i) Ropes (ii) Mats

6. Explain the process of making yarn from fibre.
Solution: Yarns are made up of thin strands called fibres. The process of making yarn from fibres is called spinning. In this process, a mass of cotton wool is drawn out and twisted. This brings the fibres together to form yarns.

ASSESSMENT CORNER

Level 1

Fixed Response Type

Multiple Choice Questions

1. Which materials were used for clothes in ancient times?
(A) Animal Skins (B) Grass
(C) Vines (D) All of these

2. This is made up of a number of fibres twisted together:
(A) Cloth (B) Yarn
(C) Fibre (D) Fabric

3. The process of making yarns from fibres is known as:
(A) Bailing (B) Spinning
(C) Retting (D) Ginning

4. Fabric can be made from yarn by the process:
(A) Knitting (B) Spinning
(C) Weaving (D) Both (A) and (C)

5. Silk is the natural fibre obtained from
(A) Birds (B) Insects
(C) Reptiles (D) Yak

6. What is the process of removing seeds from cotton called:
(A) Knitting (B) Retting
(C) Ginning (D) Seeding

7. Jute is obtained from which part of patsun?
(A) Leaves
(B) Root
(C) Stem
(D) Both leaves and stem

8. Wool is not an:
(A) Protein fibre
(B) Artificial fibre
(C) Animal fibre
(D) Natural fibre

9. Wool burns with the smell of burning hair:
(A) as it is obtained from hair of sheep and goat.
(B) because it is a natural fibre.
(C) because it is synthetic fibre.
(D) None of these.

10. Pashmina shawls are obtained from the skin of which animal?
(A) Kashmiri Goat (B) Camel
(C) Yak (D) None of these

11. Process of removing hair of a sheep is called:
(A) Weaving (B) Shearing
(C) Spinning (D) Ginning

12. Yak wool is obtained in -
(A) Kerela (B) Uttar Pradesh
(C) Madhya Pradesh (D) Ladakh

13. Woollen clothes keep us warm as:
(A) wool is an animal fibre.
(B) wool is made up of proteins.
(C) wool traps air and air is a good conductor of heat.
(D) wool traps air and air is a poor conductor of heat.

14. Which among these bodies or organizations produce high quality wool?
(A) International wool supply
(B) International wool secretariat
(C) Indian wool status
(D) None of these

15. The fabric made from used wool by carding and spinning is called:
(A) Shoddy (B) Kemp
(C) Coarse Wool (D) Fleece

16. Wool is soluble in:
(A) Alcohols
(B) Aldehydes
(C) Acids and bases, both
(D) None of these

17. Main constituent of silk fibre is:
(A) Fats (B) Proteins
(C) Carbohydrates (D) Vitamins

18. The stage in the life cycle of an insect excludes:
(A) Pupa (B) Caterpillar
(C) Sericulture (D) None of these

19. The disease most common among the workers of sericulture industry is:
(A) Respiratory and skin diseases
(B) Cancer

(C) Tuberculosis
(D) Low and high blood pressure

20. While bursting crackers it is safe to wear clothes made of:
(A) Nylon (B) Polyesters
(C) Cotton (D) Silk

21. Which of the following is a natural polymer?
(A) Cellulose (B) Nylon
(C) Polythene (D) PVC

22. Which of the following fibres are soft and smooth to touch?
(A) Wool, cotton (B) Cotton, rayon
(C) Silk, polyester (D) Cotton, jute

23. Man-made fibres are known as:
(A) Blast fibres
(B) Synthetic fibres
(C) Natural fibres
(D) Semi-synthetic fibres

24. __________ is made into fabrics such as satin, velvet chiffon, crepe, and brocades.
(A) Silk fibres (B) Hemp fibres
(C) Coir fibres (D) Cotton fibres

25. New innovative fabrics are being developed for sustainable production methods called:
(A) Silk fibres (B) Bamboo
(C) Coir fibres (D) Qmilch

26. A single yarn is used in:
(A) Twisting (B) Knitting
(C) Spinning (D) Weaving

27. Weaving of fabric is done using:
(A) Handloom (B) Power loom
(C) Both (A) and (B) (D) Takli

28. The hair of which of the following animals is used for making woollen clothes?
(A) Alpaca (B) Fox
(C) Rat (D) Cat

29. Which of the following statements is true for synthetic fibres?
(A) Synthetic cloth so formed is strong.
(B) Synthetic cloth does not get wrinkled.
(C) Synthetic cloth dries easily.
(D) All of these.

30. Which of the following the fabrics do not absorb sweat and is unsuitable to be used in hot and humid climate?
(A) Natural fibre
(B) Synthetic fibre
(C) Semi-synthetic fibre
(D) All of these

31. Which statement out of the following is incorrect?
(A) Use of charkha was popularized by Mahatma Gandhi as a part of the independence movement.
(B) In India, jute is mainly grown in Kerala and Punjab.
(C) To make fabric, fibres are first converted into yarns.
(D) Sufi saint Kabir was a weaver.

32. Which of the following materials did people use in ancient times for making clothes?
(i) Leaves of trees
(ii) Newspaper
(iii) Metal foils
(iv) Animal skins and furs
(A) (i) and (ii) (B) (i) and (iii)
(C) (ii) and (iii) (D) (i) and (iv)

33. Which of the following group does not belongs to the same category?
(A) Cotton, Silk (B) Jute, Wool
(C) Nylon, Rayon (D) Flax,Coir

34. A student went to a cloth shop. There he found a fabric which was smooth to touch, had vibrant colour and shine. The fabric could be:
(A) Cotton (B) Wool
(C) Silk (D) Jute

35. Yarn is woven to get fabric using:
(A) Charkha
(B) Spinning machines
(C) Looms
(D) Knitting needles

36. The correct sequence to get cloth is
(A) Fibre → fabric → yarn
(B) Fibre → yarn → fabric
(C) Fabric → yarn → fibre
(D) Yarn → fibre → fabric.

37. Beera is a farmer. His field has black soil, and the climate is warm. Which fibre yielding plant should he grow in his field?
(A) Jute (B) Cotton
(C) Coconut (D) Wool

38. Boojho wants to make yarn from fibre at home. Which of the following will he use to carry out the task?
(A) Power loom (B) Handloom
(C) Charkha (D) Knitting needles

Fill in the Blanks

1. Weaving is done on ___________ .
2. _________is obtained from the bast or skin of the plant stem.
3. Invention of the __________________________ wheel revolutionised clothing.
4. ___________ is the process by which fibres are spun to form cotton yarn using spinning machines.
5. Jute is __________ and recyclable and thus, environment friendly.
6. Coir is the fibre obtained from the outer covering of the fruit of the ________ .
7. The fabric of cotton saree is made by weaving cotton________, which in turn is made by spinning thin cotton______.
8. Two main processes by which fabrics are made from yarn are ________ and ________.
9. Fibres found on some part/ parts of a plant are called ______ .
10. Natural fibres are modified by the treatment with chemicals are known as ________ fibres.
11. ______ come in a variety of colours, texture, and materials. They are made from fibres.
12. A single hair like strand, resembling a thin thread is called______ .
13. For obtaining silk, the ______ of silkworm are boiled and unwound to separate the fibre which is then spun.
14. Kapok fibre is also called as ________.
15. Hemp fibres are obtained from the ______of the hemp plant.

True/False

1. Semi synthetic fibres are obtained from crude oil.
2. Spinning is a process of making fibre.
3. Jute is the outer covering of coconut.
4. The process of removing seed from cotton is called ginning.
5. Weaving of yarn makes a piece of fabric.
6. Coir fibre is obtained from the stem of a plant.
7. Polyester is a natural fibre.
8. Silk is obtained from the fleece of sheep or hairy animals.
9. Jute is obtained from the leaves of a plant.
10. Weaving is a process of arranging two sets of yarn together.
11. Cotton yarn on burning gives an odour similar to that of burning paper.
12. Hemp plants grow best in loamy soil.
13. The coconut fibres are very soft and highly even.
14. Modified natural fibres are known as semi-synthetic fibres.
15. The process of separation of cotton fibre from the seed is called retting.

Match Type Questions

1.

Column-A	Column-B
1. Jute	(a) Coconut
2. Coir	(b) Black Soil
3. Cotton plant	(c) Ginning
4. Cotton	(d) Linen
5. Flax	(e) Bangladesh

2.

Column-A	Column-B
1. Sweater	(a) Cotton
2. Cotton bolls	(b) Wool
3. Dhoti	(c) Ginning
4. Gunny bags	(d) Jute

3.

Column-A	Column-B
1. Weaving	(a) A single yarn used to make a fabric.
2. Knitting	(b) Combing of cotton fibres to remove seeds.
3. Spinning	(c) Process of arranging two sets of yarns together to make a fabric.
4. Ginning	(d) Process of making yarn from fibres.

ASSESSMENT CORNER

4.

	Column-A		Column-B
1.	Fibre	(a)	Made from thin strands.
2.	Yarn	(b)	Spun from fibres and then used to make fabrics.
3.	Retting	(c)	Handpicking the cotton fibres from the ripe cotton bolls.
4.	Picking	(d)	Stalks of the plant are soaked in water.

5.

	Column A		Column B
1.	Twig and grass	(a)	Wool
2.	Animal fleece	(b)	Mats
3.	Semi synthetic	(c)	Crude oil
4.	Synthetic	(d)	Modified natural fibre

Assertion and Reason Type Questions

1. **Assertion:** Cotton ropes are preferred over nylon ropes due to their high strength.
   Reason: Cotton, wool and rayon are some important natural fibres.
   (A) Both assertion and reason are true and reason is the correct explanation of assertion.
   (B) Both assertion and reason are true and reason is not correct explanation of assertion.
   (C) Assertion is true and reason is false.
   (D) Both assertion and reason are false.

2. **Assertion:** Cotton clothes absorb moisture easily.
   Reason: Cotton traps air in the pockets formed between the individual fibres.
   (A) Both assertion and reason are true, and reason is the correct explanation of assertion.
   (B) Both assertion and reason are true, but reason is not the correct explanation of assertion.
   (C) Assertion is true, and reason is false.
   (D) Reason is true, and assertion is false.

3. **Assertion:** Silk is obtained from the cocoons of silk moths.
   Reason: Silk is a plant fibre.
   (A) Both assertion and reason are true, and reason is the correct explanation of assertion.
   (B) Both assertion and reason are true, but reason is not the correct explanation of assertion.
   (C) Assertion is true, and reason is false.
   (D) Reason is true, and assertion is false.

4. **Assertion:** Coir is a blast fibre.
   Reason: Blast fibres are found from the fruits of plant.
   (A) Both assertion and reason are true and reason is the correct explanation of assertion.
   (B) Both assertion and reason are true and reason is not correct explanation of assertion.
   (C) Assertion is true and reason is false.
   (D) Both assertion and reason are false.

5. **Assertion:** Jute is a natural fibre.
   Reason: Fibres obtained from plants and animals are called as natural fibres.
   (A) Both assertion and reason are true, and reason is the correct explanation of assertion.
   (B) Both assertion and reason are true, but reason is not the correct explanation of assertion.
   (C) Assertion is true, and reason is false.
   (D) Reason is true, and assertion is false.

6. **Assertion:** Synthetic fibres are obtained from crude oil.
   Reason: Natural fibres are obtained from plants or animals.
   (A) Both assertion and reason are true, and reason is the correct explanation of assertion.
   (B) Both assertion and reason are true, but reason is not the correct explanation of assertion.
   (C) Assertion is true, and reason is false.
   (D) Reason is true, and assertion is false.

7. **Assertion:** Jute and flax are blast fibres.
   Reason: These fibres are found in the stem of the plant and provide strength to the plant.
   (A) Both assertion and reason are true, and reason is the correct explanation of assertion.
   (B) Both assertion and reason are true, but reason is not the correct explanation of assertion.
   (C) Assertion is true, and reason is false.
   (D) Reason is true, and assertion is false.

8. **Assertion:** Fibres obtained from the stem of the flax plant are woven to make a fabric called linen
Reason: Flax fibres are also used in the production of ropes and high-quality paper.
(A) Both assertion and reason are true, and reason is the correct explanation of assertion.
(B) Both assertion and reason are true, but reason is not the correct explanation of assertion.
(C) Assertion is true, and reason is false.
(D) Reason is true, and assertion is false.

9. **Assertion:** Cotton is the king of the global textile industry.
Reason: Cotton plant is a shrub growing well in black soil and warm climate.
(A) Both assertion and reason are true, and reason is the correct explanation of assertion.
(B) Both assertion and reason are true, but reason is not the correct explanation of assertion.
(C) Assertion is true, and reason is false.
(D) Reason is true, and assertion is false.

10. **Assertion:** Fibres obtained from the fruit are called fruit fibres.
Reason: Sisal is an example of fruit fibre.
(A) Both assertion and reason are true, and reason is the correct explanation of assertion.
(B) Both assertion and reason are true, but reason is not the correct explanation of assertion.
(C) Assertion is true, and reason is false.
(D) Reason is true, and assertion is false.

Comprehension Type Questions

1. ***Read the given passage:***
Fibres are obtained from various sources such as plants, animal hair, insects, and crude oil. Cotton, and jute are obtained from plants. Silk is obtained from the cocoons of silk moths. We get wool from sheep. The fibres obtained from natural sources such as plants and animals are known as natural fibres. Synthetic fibres are obtained from crude oil that is processed into chemical substances and changed to fibre.
(i) Petrochemical/ crude oil is the raw material for-
(A) Natural fibre.
(B) Synthetic fibre.
(C) Semi-synthetic fibre.
(D) None of these.

2. Refer to the given paragraph.
The yarn produced from fibres can be converted into fabric by processes X and Y. In process X, two sets of yarns are arranged together whereas in process Y, a single yarn is used.
(i) Identify processes X and Y and select the correct statement regarding them.
(A) Process X could be done by handlooms whereas, process Y could be done by power looms.
(B) Takli and charkha could be used for process Y.
(C) X could be spinning whereas process Y could be weaving.
(D) None of these.

3. ***Read the given passage:***
Plant fibres are classified into three categories, depending on the part of the plant they are extracted from.
- **Fruit fibres:** These fibres are obtained from the fruits of the plant. Examples are cotton and coir (coconut fibres). The fruits of these plants are usually light and hairy and allow the wind to carry the seeds.
- **Bast fibres:** These fibres are found in the stem of the plant and provide strength to the plant.

  They are generally very long. Examples of bast fibres are jute and flax.
- **Leaf fibres:** Fibres obtained from leaves are rough and sturdy. An example is sisal which is a moisture-resistant fibre used in making ropes, mats, and carpets.

(i) Cotton and coir are:
(A) Leaf fibre (B) Blast fibre
(C) Fruit fibre (D) Animal fibre
(ii) Jute and flax are:
(A) Leaf fibre (B) Blast fibre
(C) Fruit fibre (D) Animal fibre
(iii) Moisture resistant fibre is:
(A) Sisal (B) Jute
(C) Coir (D) Both (B) and (C)

Fixed Response Type

Very Short Answer Type Questions

1. Name any two fibres which are obtained from nature.

2. Name one example each of plant fibre and animal fibre.

ASSESSMENT CORNER

3. From which part of a plant is cotton obtained?
4. Write two characteristic properties of cotton.
5. Why can't a cotton garment keep us as warm in winter as a woollen sweater can?

Short Answer Type Questions

1. Write down the complete process of manufacturing of fabrics and fibres.
2. Classify the following fibres as natural or synthetic: Nylon, wool, cotton, silk, polyester, and jute.
3. How is Cotton obtained from fruits of a cotton plant and jute is obtained from the stem of a jute plant.
4. What type of soil and climate is good for growing cotton? Name any two states of our country where cotton is mainly grown.
5. Explain the following terms:
   (i) Retting
   (ii) Spinning

Numerical Based Questions

1. Equal sized square pieces of three different fabrics X, Y, and Z were taken and spread out on a floor. Three small similar metal balls were each rolled with equal force from one end diagonally to the other end of the fabric piece. Time taken by the balls to reach the other end of the fabric was noted to be as follows:

X	Y	Z
2.5 sec	2 sec	4 sec

Now, select the correct option regarding this.
(A) Fabric Z can be obtained from seeds of a plant, and fabric Y can be obtained from stem of a plant.
(B) Fabric Z can be obtained from the stem of a plant, and fabric Y can be obtained from larva of an animal.
(C) Fabric Y can be obtained from the fur of an animal, and fabric X can be obtained from larva of an animal.
(D) Fabric Y can be obtained from the fur of an animal, and fabric Z can be obtained from larva of an animal.

2. Alisha took four beakers—A, B, C, and D and poured 30 ml of water in each of them. He soaks same-sized piece of fabric of cotton, wool, silk and polyester in the beakers A, B, C, and D respectively and kept them for five minutes. Now he removed all the fabric pieces from the beakers and measured the amount of water left in each of the four beakers. Which of the following is the correct observation of Alisha?
(A) Maximum amount (approx. 25 ml) of water is left in beaker D, followed by beakers C, A, and B.
(B) Minimum amount (approx. 5 ml) of water is left in beaker D, followed by beakers C, A, and B.
(C) Maximum amount (approx.25 ml) of water is left in beaker B, followed by beakers A, C, and D.
(D) Minimum amount (approx. 5 ml) of water is left in beaker B, followed by beakers D, C, and A.

Case Based Questions

Cotton, one of the world's leading agricultural crops, is plentiful and economically produced, making cotton products relatively inexpensive. Cotton is grown in the field. Cotton plants are usually grown in areas having black soil and warm climate. The fruits of the cotton plant (cotton bolls) are about the size of lemon. After maturing, the bolls burst open the seeds covered with cotton fibres can be seen. A cotton field that is ready for picking, looks like a field covered with snow. From these bolls, cotton is usually picked by hand. Fibres are then separated from the seeds by combing. The process is called ginning of cotton. Ginning was traditionally done by hand. These days, machines are also used for ginning.

Jute fibres are bast fibres. We get jute fibres from the stem of jute plants. It is a long, shiny, and soft fibre. It is stronger than fibres such as cotton. It is one of the most affordable fibres. It is used in the twine, rope, bags, doormats etc. Jute plant mainly grows in places that have high temperatures and plenty of rainfall. Jute is cultivated during the rainy season and is generally harvested when it is in the flowering stage. The harvested stalks of the plants are soaked in water for a few days until they start rotting. The fibres are made into yarn by twisting the strands together. This process of making yarn from fibre is called spinning.

1. Which soil type on which cotton plant is usually grown?
(A) Red (B) Black
(C) Alluvial (D) Both (B) and (C)

2. From which part of a plant are cotton and jute fibres are obtained respectively?
(A) Root, stem (B) Fruit, root
(C) Stem, Fruit (D) Fruit, stem

3. Jute fibres are an example of:
(A) Flax fibres (B) Blast fibres
(C) Natural fibres (D) Both (B) and (C)

LEVEL 2

Multiple Choice Questions

1. Which of the following sequence is correct in making fabric?
(A) Weaving-Ginning-Spinning
(B) Ginning-Spinning-Weaving
(C) Spinning-Weaving-Ginning
(D) Ginning-Weaving-Spinning

2. Which of the following materials is grouped wrongly in the chart given below?

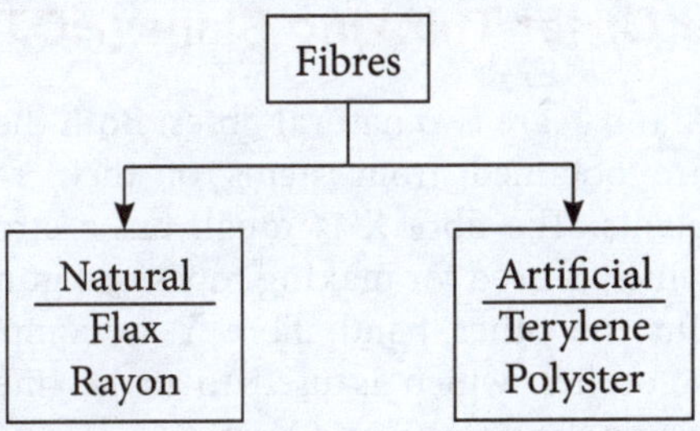

(A) Flax (B) Rayon
(C) Terylene (D) Polyester

3. Complete the given correlation:

Silk: Cocoon, Wool: ?

(A) Hair of rabbit (B) Cotton plant
(C) Fleece of sheep (D) Jute of hemp

4. Which of the following statements is not true?
(A) Fabric is made of yarn.
(B) Jute is the outer covering of coconut.
(C) Polyester is a synthetic fibre.
(D) Silk fibre is obtained from silkworms.

5. Which of the following takes place when fibres are twisted before being made into yarns or thread:
(A) Make them more absorbent.
(B) Make them strong
(C) Make them smoother.
(D) Add air spaces inside the fibre.

6. Cotton and woollen clothes are rough when compared to silk. Which of the following statements supports the above statement?
(A) They have many uneven folds.
(B) They have many even folds.
(C) The folds are small and even.
(D) The fibres are smooth.

7. Silk worm feeds on:
(A) Blueberry leaves (B) Mango Leaves
(C) Mulberry leaves (D) Cotton fruit

8. Which of the following fibre is most suitable for high quality paper ?
(A) Cotton (B) Wool
(C) Flax (D) Nylon

9. The box given below shows characteristics of fibres. Fabric made from above fibre is comfortable to use during which of the following seasons?

- Allow free movement of air
- High water absorption capacity

(A) Winter season (B) Spring season
(C) Summer season (D) Rainy season

10. Which of the following property is applicable on woolen fibre?
(A) poor insulator of heat
(B) good insulator of heat.
(C) does not absorb water.
(D) cheaper than cotton.

11. If P represents fibre and Q represents fabric, find out the correct order in which Q is made from P.
(A) P, Weaving, Spinning, Obtained from source, Yarn, Q.
(B) P, Obtained from source, Spinning, Weaving, Yarn, Q.
(C) P, Obtained from source, Spinning, Yarn, Weaving Q.
(D) None of the above.

12. Refer to the given key carefully and identify fabrics P, Q, R, and S.
1. (i) Fabric made from natural fibres ..... Go to 2.
(ii) Fabric made from man-made fibres ...... Go to 3.

2. (i) Fibre obtained from plants ....[P]
   (ii) Fibre obtained from animals ....[Q]
3. (i) Shrinks away from flame on burning ....[R]
   (ii) Leaves hard beads on burning ....[S]

	P	Q	R	S
(A)	Cotton	Polyester	Silk	Nylon
(B)	Acrylic	Wool	Rayon	Nylon
(C)	Cotton	Wool	Silk	Polyester
(D)	Cotton	Silk	Nylon	Polyester

13. Refer to the given flowchart and select the correct option:

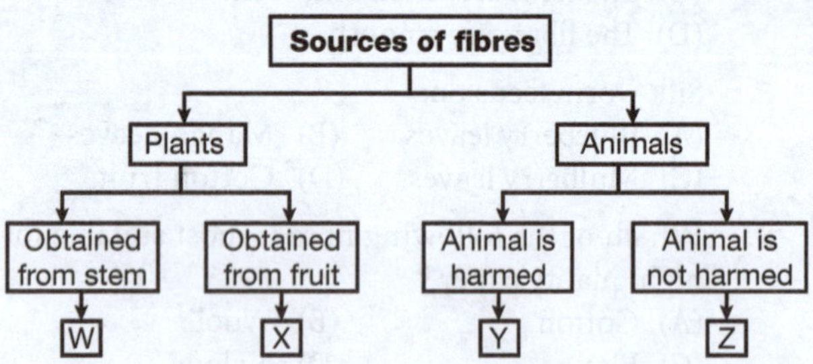

(A) X-Flax, Y-Silk (B) W-Cotton, Y-Silk
(C) W-Flax, Z-Wool (D) X-Jute, Z-Wool

14. Select the incorrect statement out of the following.
(A) Weaving and knitting are the two methods of converting yarn into fabric.
(B) Synthetic fibres absorb less water compared to natural fibres.
(C) Jute plants are harvested at the flowering stage to obtain fibres.
(D) Cotton fibres are sourced from seed hair and thus burn with smell like that of a burning hair.

15. Refer to the given groups (i)- (iv). Each group contains one wrong member. Identify the odd members and select the correct option.
(i) Flax, Coir, Wool, Sisal
(ii) Cotton, Jute, Flax, Hemp
(iii) Polyester, Nylon, Acrylic, Silk
(iv) Shahtoosh, Wool, Silk, Coir

	(i)	(ii)	(iii)	(iv)
(A)	Sisal	Hemp	Acrylic	Shahtoosh
(B)	Flax	Jute	Nylon	Silk
(C)	Wool	Cotton	Silk	Coir
(D)	Coir	Flax	Nylon	Wool

16. Find the incorrect statement.
(i) Ginning is used for cotton.
(ii) Retting is used for jute.
(iii) Cotton and wool are blast fibres.
(iv) Coir is semi synthetic fibre.
(A) (i) and (iii) (B) (ii), (iii), and (iv)
(C) (i), (iii), and (iv) (D) (iii) and (iv)

17. Which of the following property is common for cotton and Rayon ?
(A) Does not catches fire easily
(B) Catches fire and burn with yellow flame.
(C) gives smell of burning hair.
(D) Shrink away from the flame and melt.

18. Sonalika wanted to buy a gift made of animal fibre obtained without killing the animal. Which of the following would be the right gift for her to buy?
(A) Woollen shawl (B) Silk scarf
(C) Animal fur cap (D) Leather jacket

19. Which of the following pair of fibres are manmade?
(A) Wool, nylon (B) Silk, rayon
(C) Nylon, polyester (D) Flax, jute

Higher Order Thinking Skills (HOTS)

1. X and Y are two natural fibres. Both these fibres are obtained from stems of their respective plants. The fibre X is rough but a strong fibre which is used for making ropes and gunny bags. On the other hand, fibre Y is comparatively smoother, which is used to make linen cloth. Name the fibres X and Y.

2. A and B are the two natural fibres. Fibre A is very soft and smooth which is separated from seeds by process C. Fibre A is used for making wicks of oil lamps lit on Diwali. Fibre B is very rough which is present as an outer covering on the ripened fruit D which occurs mainly in coastal areas. Fibre B is also known by another name E. This fibre is used for making ropes and mats.
(A) Name the fibre A.
(B) What is the process C known as?
(C) Name the fibre B.
(D) What is the name of fruit D?
(E) Write the name E.

3. Compare the composition and structure of cotton fibres and silk fibres.

4. Rohan prepared a list of cellulosic fibres obtained from the stem of a plant. By mistake he put some wrong fibres in the list. Select the option that groups only the cellulosic fibres obtained from a plant stem.
(i) Linen (ii) Hemp
(iii) Shahtoosh (iv) Mink

(v) Kapok (vi) Jute
(vii) Coconut (viii) Cotton
(ix) Rayon (x) Acrylic

5. The following is an answer given by Boojho to a question asked by his teacher- "Cotton, wool, silk and jute are classified as natural fibres whereas nylon and polyester are classified as synthetic fibres". Can you tell what question the teacher has asked?

6. Once, Paheli visited a tailor shop and brought home some cuttings of fabric to study their properties. She took two pieces and found that one of the pieces were shrinking when it was burnt with a candle. However, the other did not shrink on burning. Can you help her to find out which of the two was a cotton fabric and which a silk fabric?

7. X,Y and Z are three different natural fibres. X and Y fibres are plant products while Z is an animal product. X is obtained from the outer covering of fruit of a plant and used as a stuffing in mattresses. Y is also used as a stuffing in pillows but obtained from silk cotton tree. Z is soluble in acid and base both and obtained from fleece of hairy animals.
   (i) Name the fibres X,Y and Z.
   (ii) Write the name of fruit from which X can be obtained.
   (iii) Name the process by which Z is obtained?

8. Boojho with perfect eyesight was finding it difficult to pass a thread through the eye of a needle. What can be the possible reason for this?

9. In ancient times stitching was not known. People used to simply drape fabrics around different parts of their body. Even today a number of unstitched fabrics are used by both men and women. Can you give four such examples of clothes?

ASSESSMENT CORNER

ARCHIVE CORNER

ARCHIVE CORNER

1. Which of the following materials upon burning smells like burning paper?
   (i) Cotton (ii) Silk
   (iii) Flax (iv) Wool
   (v) Fur (vi) Jute
   (A) (i), (iii), & (vi) (B) (ii), (iv), & (v)
   (C) (i), (ii), (iv), & (vi) (D) (iv) & (v)

2. Identify X in the given Venn diagram.

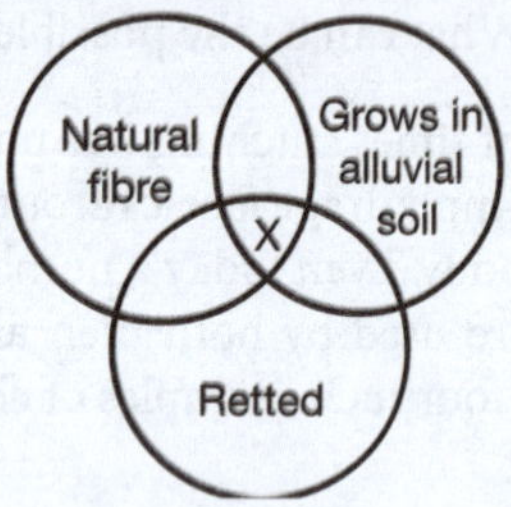

   (A) Silk (B) Wool
   (C) Nylon (D) Jute

3. Ali took four beakers—P, Q, R, and S and poured equal amounts of water in each of them. He soaks same-sized piece of fabric of cotton, wool, silk, and polyester in beakers P, Q, R, and S respectively and kept them for five minutes. He then removed all the fabric pieces from the beakers and measured the amount of water left in each of the four beakers. Which of the following is the correct observation of Ali?
   (A) Maximum amount of water is left in beaker S, followed by beakers R, P, and Q.
   (B) Minimum amount of water is left in beaker S, followed by beakers R, P, and Q.
   (C) Maximum amount of water is left in beaker Q, followed by beakers P, R, and S.
   (D) Minimum amount of water is left in beaker Q, followed by beakers S, R, and P.

4. Read the given statements and select the correct option.
   Assertion: Clothes made from natural fibres are stronger than the clothes made from synthetic fibres.
   Reason: Cotton, wool, and rayon are some important natural fibres.
   (A) Both assertion and reason are true, and reason is the correct explanation of assertion.
   (B) Both assertion and reason are true, and reason is not correct explanation of assertion.
   (C) Assertion is true, and reason is false.
   (D) Both assertion and reason are false

5. If P represents the fibre and Q represents the fabric, find out the correct order in which Q is made from P.
   (A) P, Weaving, Spinning, Obtained from source, Yarn, Q.
   (B) P, Obtained from source, Spinning, Weaving, Yarn, Q.
   (C) P, Obtained from source, Spinning, Yarn, Weaving Q.
   (D) None of the above.

6. Refer to the given key carefully and identify fabrics P, Q, R and S.
   1. (i) Fabric made from natural fibres ..... Go to 2.
      (ii) Fabric made from man-made fibres ...... Go to 3.
   2. (i) Fibre obtained from plants ....[P]
      (ii) Fibre obtained from animals ....[Q]
   3. (i) Shrinks away from flame on burning .... [R]
      (ii) Leaves hard beads on burning ....[S]

	P	Q	R	S
(A)	Cotton	Polyester	Silk	Nylon
(B)	Acrylic	Wool	Rayon	Nylon
(C)	Cotton	Wool	Silk	Polyester
(D)	Cotton	Silk	Nylon	Polyester

7. Refer to the given flowchart and select the correct option:

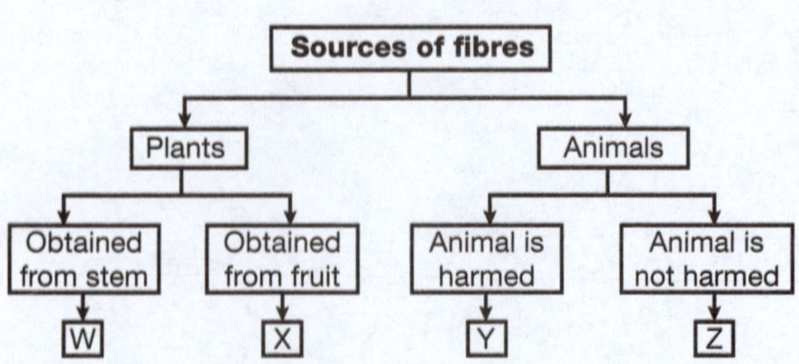

   (A) X-Flax, Y-Silk (B) W-Cotton, Y-Silk
   (C) W-Flax, Z-Wool (D) X-Jute, Z-Wool

8. Read the given statements and select the correct option.
Assertion: Woollen clothes provide warmth in cold weather.
Reason: Woollen fibres trap air in the pockets formed between the individual fibres.
(A) Both assertion and reason are true, and reason is the correct explanation of assertion.
(B) Both assertion and reason are true, but reason is not the correct explanation of assertion.
(C) Assertion is true, and reason is false.
(D) Reason is true, and assertion is false.

9. Refer to the given chart and select the option that correctly identifies the fibres P, Q and R.

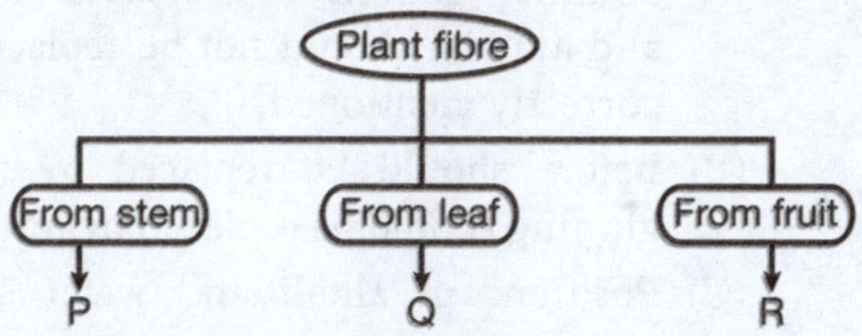

(A) P-Cotton, Q-Jute, R-Flax
(B) P-Flax, Q-Coir, R-Cotton
(C) P-Jute, Q-Banana, R-Coir
(D) P-Cotton, Q-Terylene, R-Jute

10. Select the incorrect statement out of the following.
(A) Weaving and knitting are the two methods of converting yarn into fabric
(B) Synthetic fibres absorb less water compared to natural fibres.
(C) Jute plants are harvested at the flowering stage to obtain fibres.
(D) Cotton fibre is sourced from seed hair and thus, burn with smell similar to burning hair.

11. In the textile industry, the given tool was used earlier to produce____ from____.

(A) Fibre, Yarn (B) Yarn, Fibre
(C) Fabric, Yarn (D) Yarn, Fabric

12. Refer to the given groups (i)-(iv). Each group contains one wrong member. Identify the odd members and select the correct option.
(i) Flax, coir, wool, sisal.
(ii) Cotton, jute, flax, hemp.
(iii) Polyester, nylon, acrylic, silk.
(iv) Shahtoosh, wool, silk, coir.

	(i)	(ii)	(iii)	(iv)
(A)	Sisal	Hemp	Acrylic	Shahtoosh
(B)	Flax	Jute	Nylon	Silk
(C)	Wool	Cotton	Silk	Coir
(D)	Coir	Flax	Nylon	Wool

13. Match column I with column II and select the correct option from the given codes.

Column-A	Column-B
(i) Ginning	(a) Cleaning and disentangling the fibres.
(ii) Combing	(b) Brushing and straightening of fibres.
(iii) Carding	(c) Bolls.
(iv) Seed pods	(d) Cotton fibres after being separated from seeds.
(v) Lint	(e) Separating fibres from seeds.

(A) (i)-(e); (ii)-(b); (iii)-(a); (iv)-(c); (v)-(d)
(B) (i)-(d); (ii)-(e); (iii)-(b); (iv)-(a); (v)-(c)
(C) (i)-(e); (ii)-(a); (iii)-(b); (iv)-(c); (v)-(d)
(D) (i)-(d); (ii)-(a); (iii)-(b); (iv)-(c); (v)-(e)

14. Refer to the given graph plotted for three different fabric pieces of equalize P, Q, and R on the basis of their water absorbing capacity and select the correct statement.

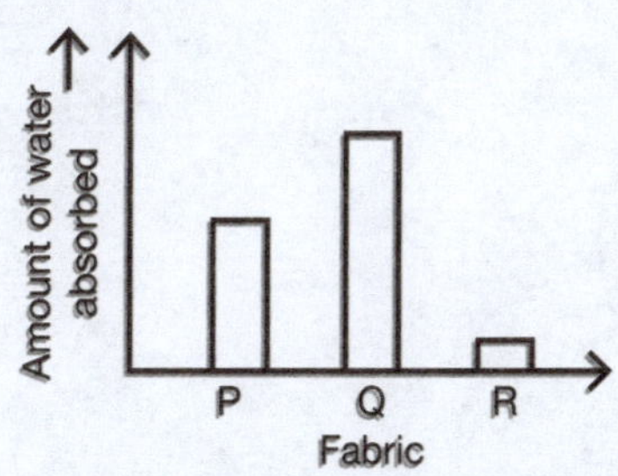

(A) P is made up of fibres obtained from Gossypium plant whereas R is made up of fibres obtained from an insect.
(B) Q is made up of protein fibres obtained from an insect whereas R is made up of cellulose fibres obtained from a flower of a plant.
(C) R is made up of fibres obtained from a plant stem by retting whereas P is made up of fibres obtained from plant seeds by ginning.

(D) P is biodegradable whereas, Q and R are non-biodegradable.

15. Ruchir took four equal sized containers P, Q, R, and S containing equal amounts of water and dipped four different equal sized fabrics in them. After five minutes, he took out all the fabrics from the containers. The given graph shows the amount of water remaining in each container.
Select the correct statement regarding the given graph.

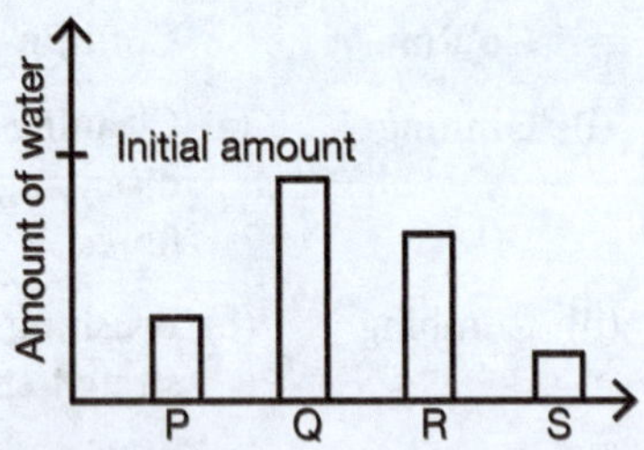

(A) Fabric dipped in Q has base fibre cellulose whereas, fabric dipped in S has base fibre petroleum.

(B) Fabric dipped in P could be made of chemicals whereas, fabric dipped in S could be made of cellulose.

(C) Fabrics dipped in S and R may be obtained from mammal and insect, respectively.

(D) Fabric dipped in P is used for making raincoats whereas, fabric dipped in R is used as winter clothing.

16. Read the given passage.

Jute is a summer season crop and grows best in alluvial soil. Jute plants are harvested before flowering. After harvesting the stalks of the plants, they are tied into bundles and soaked in alkali for few days. This leads to softening of tissues so that fibres get easily separated. The process is called ginning. The fibres are then washed in water and hung up to dry.

Select the correct option regarding this.

(A) Summer should be replaced by winter, and alluvial should not be replaced as it is correctly mentioned.

(B) Before should be replaced by after, and ginning should be replaced by retting.

(C) Positions of alkali and water should be interchanged.

(D) None of these.

ANSWER KEY

Level 1

Fixed Response Type

Multiple Choice Questions

1. D	2. B	3. B	4. D	5. B	6. C	7. C	8. B	9. A	10. A
11. B	12. D	13. D	14. B	15. A	16. C	17. B	18. C	19. A	20. C
21. A	22. C	23. B	24. A	25. D	26. B	27. C	28. A	29. D	30. B
31. B	32. D	33. C	34. C	35. C	36. B	37. B	38. C		

Fill in the Blanks

1. Looms
2. Jute/Flax
3. Needle and spinning wheel
4. Spinning
5. Biodegradable
6. Coconut
7. Yarn, fibres
8. Weaving, knitting
9. Plant fibres
10. Semi-synthetic
11. Fabric
12. Fibre
13. Cocoons
14. Silk cotton
15. Stem

True/False

1. False
2. False
3. False
4. True
5. True
6. False
7. False
8. False
9. False
10. True
11. True
12. True
13. False
14. True
15. False

Match Type Questions

1. 1-e, 2-a, 3-b, 4-c, 5-d
2. 1-b, 2-c, 3-a, 4-d
3. 1-c, 2-a, 3-d, 4-b
4. 1-a, 2-b, 3-d, 4-c
5. 1-b, 2-a, 3-d, 4-c

Assertion and Reason Type Questions

1. D	2. C	3. C	4. D	5. A	6. B	7. A	8. B	9. B	10. D

Comprehension Type Questions

1. (i) B
2. (i) D
3. (i) C (ii) B (iii) A

Free Response Type

Numerical Based Questions

1. B
2. A

Case Based Questions

1. B 2. D 3. D

Level 2

Multiple Choice Questions

1. B 2. B 3. C 4. B 5. B 6. A 7. C 8. C 9. C 10. B
11. C 12. D 13. C 14. D 15. C 16. D 17. A 18. A 19. C

Archive Corner

1. A 2. D 3. A 4. D 5. C 6. D 7. C 8. A 9. C 10. D
11. B 12. C 13. A 14. A 15. C 16. B

CHAPTER 10

Air Around Us

Learning Outcomes

After reading this chapter, you will be able to:

- understand the presence of air.
- explain the importance of air for plants, animals, humans, as well as aquatic life.
- explain the oxygen cycle.
- describe the different reasons responsible for air pollution.
- define some new terms like acid rain, global warming, and greenhouse gases.

Geekspeak

- Atmosphere
- Troposphere
- Stratosphere
- Mesosphere
- Thermosphere
- Exosphere
- Respiration
- Photosynthesis
- Breathe
- Weather phenomena
- Hydrilla
- Acid rain
- Global warming
- Greenhouse effect

Introduction

The Earth is surrounded by a layer of air called atmosphere which extends up to 200 km above the surface of Earth but oxygen is available only up to 30km. Without an atmosphere, the Earth would be very hot. It also helps in movement of air, as the surface temperature varies from one place to another, and cool wind blows due to this temperature difference. The phenomenon of water cycle takes place due to the atmosphere. The water from the surface of the Earth gets evaporated, moves up, forms clouds with water vapour and then causes rain. Thus, the water gets recycled and helps not only in agriculture but also in sustenance of plant and animal life. Air is present everywhere around us. The presence of air can be felt by a simple activity.

What is Air Made of

Air is a mixture of several gases, water vapour and fine dust. Air contains mainly nitrogen, oxygen and smaller amounts of argon, carbon dioxide, water vapour, and traces of helium, neon, krypton and xenon.

- **Water Vapour:** Moisture exists in the atmosphere as water vapour. Water vapour rises high in the atmosphere, cools and forms clouds. This makes it rain both on land and at sea. Snow is produced in cold regions. Water vapour controls our climate conditions. The presence of moisture is prominent in our daily life. When air contacts a cold surface, it condenses and forms water droplets on the cooled surface. This indicates the presence of water in the air.

Keystone

A person breathes almost 16 kg of air every day. As a comparison, we take about 0.7 kg of food and 1.4-2.3 kg of water daily. Therefore, the air quality around us has a great impact on our health.

Testing Room 1

Aim: To know the presence of air

Material required: Empty glass bottle, bucket filled with water

Procedure:

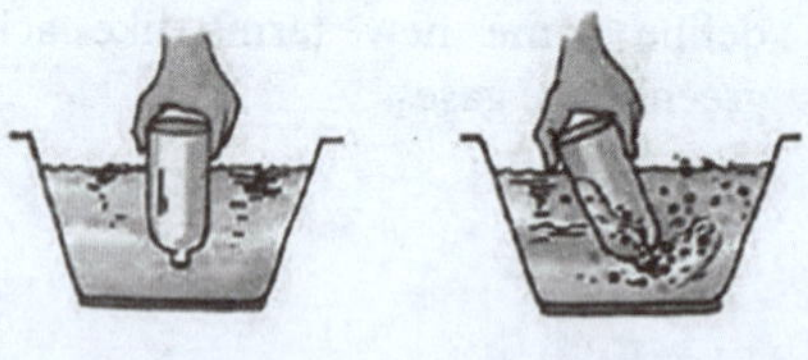

1. Take an empty glass bottle. Turn it upside down. Now dip the open mouth of the bottle into a bucket filled with water as shown in the figure. We observe that water does not enter the bottle.
2. Now till the bottle slightly. We observe that now water enters the bottle and we can see bubbles coming out of the bottle with a bubbly sound.
3. This shows that air was present in the bottle. The bottle was not empty at all. In fact it was filled completely with air even when it is upside down. That is why water does not enter the bottle when it is pushed in an inverted position as there was no space for air to escape.
4. When the bottle was tilted the air was able to come out in the form of bubbles and water filled up the empty space that the air has occupied.

Conclusion: Air is present everywhere around us. It fills all the empty space. It has no colour and one can see through it. It is transparent.

- **Oxygen:** One-fifth of the air is made up of oxygen. Life would not be possible without oxygen, as we need oxygen for respiration. During respiration, we breathe in oxygen and exhale carbon dioxide. Another very important function of oxygen is that it supports burning. If you invert a glass tumbler over a burning candle, you will notice that the candle extinguishes after a short while. This is because the oxygen that supports the burning is cut off when it is covered by the tumbler, and hence, the candle stops burning.
- **Nitrogen:** Nitrogen is one of the major constituents of air as shown in Fig. 10.1. It neither supports burning nor burns itself. But the presence of a huge quantity of nitrogen in the atmosphere is a blessing for us. It slows down any burning. It has many other uses. It is used on a large scale to manufacture fertilizer to be used in cultivation.

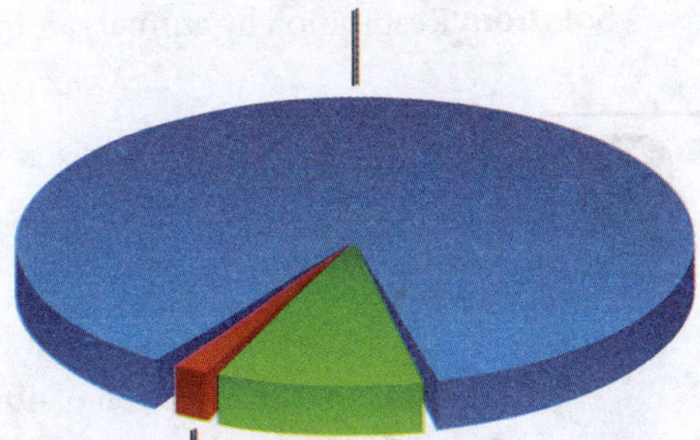

Figure 10.1 Composition of Air

- **Carbon dioxide:** When something is burning in an enclosed space, we feel suffocated. This is due to excess carbon dioxide that can accumulate in the room. Carbon dioxide makes up a small part of the air around us. Plants and animals use oxygen to breathe and produce carbon dioxide. Plants and animals also consume oxygen when they burn, producing primarily carbon dioxide and other gases. Contained in carbohydrates, fats, proteins, nucleic acids, enzymes and hormones. Carbon dioxide molecules reflect thermal radiation and prevent the earth from radiating heat rapidly at night. Carbon dioxide is partially soluble in water and helps form carbonates. These add flavor to spring water. Carbon dioxide is essential for photosynthesis.
- **Dust and Smoke:** Particles in air can be seen when sun rays entering into a room is viewed through a small opening. Similarly, when something is burning, it produces smoke. The smoke contains certain gases and dust particles which are harmful for us. To prevent this, factories have long high chimneys to discard smoke and dust. If you live in a city, you may have noticed that crowded streets are filled with smoke and dust due to pollution caused by automobiles. If you breathe polluted air (air with harmful gases, smoke, and dust) you will feel sick. The composition of air varies from place to place. For example, the air near an industry may be polluted with smoke and dust while the air on the top of a mountain or in the countryside, will be refreshing as it contains more oxygen.

  Air is also present (dissolved) in water and soil. Organisms living in water or underground use the oxygen present in this air for respiration.
- **Inert gases:** Inert or noble gases are present in air in miniscule amounts. These gases do not react with any substance but are useful in many ways.

  From this we can conclude that air contains gases, water vapour and dust particles. The gases in air are mainly—nitrogen, oxygen small amount of carbon dioxide, and many other gases. However, there may be slight differences in air composition from place to place. It turns out that air contains mainly nitrogen and oxygen. In fact, these two gases together make up 99% of air. The remaining 1% is made up of carbon dioxide and other gases, water vapour and dust particles.

❖ INTEXT QUESTIONS

1. **Name the main component of air.**
   Solution: Nitrogen gas
2. **What is the source of oxygen gas in air?**
   Solution: Photosynthesis by green plants is source of oxygen gas in air.
3. **What is the percentage of nitrogen in air?**
   Solution: 78.1%
4. **What is the percentage of oxygen in air?**
   Solution: 20.9%

5. **What is the source of carbon dioxide in air?**
Solution: Respiration by animals and plants and burning of fuel.

Check Point 1

1. What is the composition of air?
2. Name two main gases present in air.
3. Apart from nitrogen and oxygen, name two other gases present in air.
4. Which gas in atmosphere do not support burning? Mention its use.
5. Why does a person feel suffocated when material is burnt in a closed room?

Atmosphere

The transparent, thick, and invisible envelope of air surrounding us is called, the atmosphere. It consists of a uniform mixture of permanent gases called dry air and varying amounts of other materials including organic and inorganic impurities such as smoke, pollen grains, and dust particles.
The atmosphere is divided in various layers to facilitate the study of it.
The different layers of our atmosphere (starting from the surface of Earth) are troposphere, stratosphere, mesosphere, thermosphere, and exosphere (Fig. 10.2).

- **Troposphere:** This is the lowest layer of our atmosphere. It extends to about 11 km above the Earth's surface. All weather phenomena, such as clouds, fog, rainfall, snowfall, storms, and lightning occur here. In this layer the temperature of air decreases with increase in height at the rate of 1°C for every 165m. As the troposphere is the lowest and the densest layer of the atmosphere, it absorbs maximum heat radiated by the Earth's surface and keeps the Earth warm.
- **Stratosphere:** This layer lies above the troposphere, and it extends to a height of about 50km above the Earth's surface. There is virtually no clouds and very little dust and water vapour convection. The stratosphere contains Ozone which absorbs the harmful ultraviolet radiation of the sun.
- **Mesosphere:** The layer lies above the stratosphere, and it extends to about 80km above the Earth's surface. In the mesosphere, temperature decreases as the altitude increases.
- **Thermosphere:** This layer lies above the mesosphere, and it extends up to 480 km above the Earth's surface. This layer contains electrically charged particles called 'Ions', so it is also called the Ionosphere. These particles reflect radio waves back to the Earth's surface and facilitates wireless communication.
- **Exosphere:** The uppermost layer of the atmosphere is called the exosphere. It extends to about 1600 km above the Earth's surface and gradually merges with the interplanetary space.

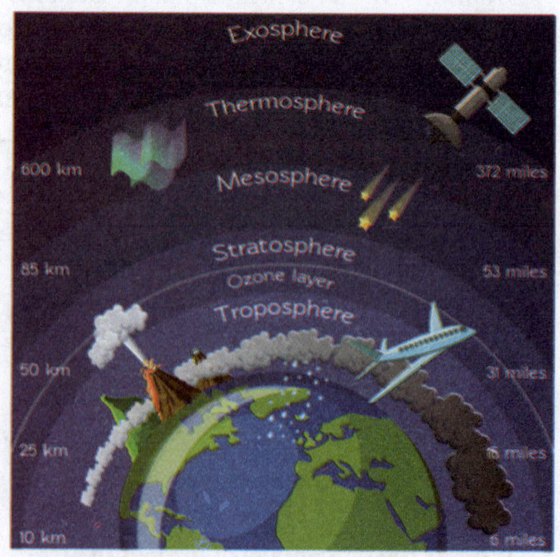

Figure 10.2 Layers of Atmosphere

Importance of Air

We all need air to survive. Air contains oxygen and carbon dioxide, which is useful to plants and animals. Plants use carbon dioxide present in the air to make their own food by a process called photosynthesis. Let us see how air supports life in plants and animals.

- **In Plants:** Plants have tiny pores stomata, found on the underside of a leaf. Air containing carbon dioxide and oxygen enters the plant through these opening where carbon dioxide is used for photosynthesis and oxygen in respiration.
- **In Animals:** All animals need to respire, be it a cockroach, a fish, or an elephant. It is just that they used different organs and mechanism for respiration.

Keystone

The stratosphere, mesosphere, and lowest part of the thermosphere are collectively referred to as the "middle atmosphere"

- **In Aquatic Animals and Plants:** Most aquatic animals such as fish, tadpole, crab, and shrimp have special organs for respiration called gills. Gills help to take in oxygen and give out carbon dioxide. Few aquatic animals such as dolphins and whales come to the surface of the water regularly to take in air since they breathe with the help of lungs.

  Aquatic plants such as 'Hydrilla' also breathe in oxygen dissolved in water through their surface.
- **In Amphibians:** Amphibians such as frog, newt, and salamander need breathing systems for both air and water. Crocodile and alligator swim through water with part of their snout above the water surface to breathe easily through nostrils.
- **In Birds:** Birds have an efficient respiratory system as they need high levels of oxygen during flight. Birds have a pair of lungs with air sacs that remain open all the time, so that air can easily pass through them.
- **In Mammals:** Most mammals breathe with the help of lungs. They take in oxygen and exhale carbon dioxide.

Testing Room 2

Aim: To show the presence of oxygen in water.

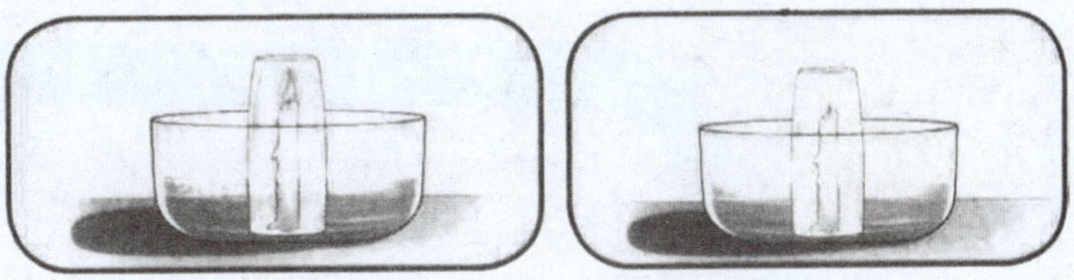

Material needed: Big bowl, water, a candle, a matchbox, and a glass

Procedure:

1. Take a candle and place it in a big bowl.
2. Now fill the bowl with some water.
3. Light the candle and cover it with an inverted glass.

Observation: The candle keeps burning for some time. After some time, the candle blows off.

Conclusion: Oxygen help in burning. When the oxygen inside the glass is used up, the candle blows off.

❖ INTEXT QUESTIONS

6. **Mention one necessary condition for combustion to take place.**
   Solution: Presence of air.
7. **Why is air considered as a mixture?**
   Solution: Air contains oxygen and nitrogen as its major constituents. These gases retain their properties in air. So, the air is called a mixture.
8. **What is the lowest layer of our atmosphere?**
   Solution: Troposphere is the lowest layer of our atmosphere. It extends to about 11 km above the Earth's surface.

Check Point 2

6. Explain the term atmosphere.
7. State the various layers of our atmosphere.
8. What is meant by 'ionosphere'?
9. What is photosynthesis?
10. How does oxygen become available to the animals and plants living in water?

Oxygen Cycle

The percentage of oxygen in the air almost remains constant even though it is continuously used for respiration and burning. This is because during photosynthesis plants take in carbon dioxide from the air and release oxygen (Fig. 10.3). Plants, animals, and human beings use oxygen for respiration during the day as well as during night. The rate of photosynthesis is immense during the daytime. Plants produce and release more oxygen than they consume during respiration and thus the amount of oxygen in the atmosphere is sufficient for the respiration of animals as well as human beings. Plants and animals are thus interdependent on each other and help to maintain the oxygen cycle.
Deforestation and excessive burning of fuel can upset this delicate balance. Therefore, we should plant more trees and use fuel economically.

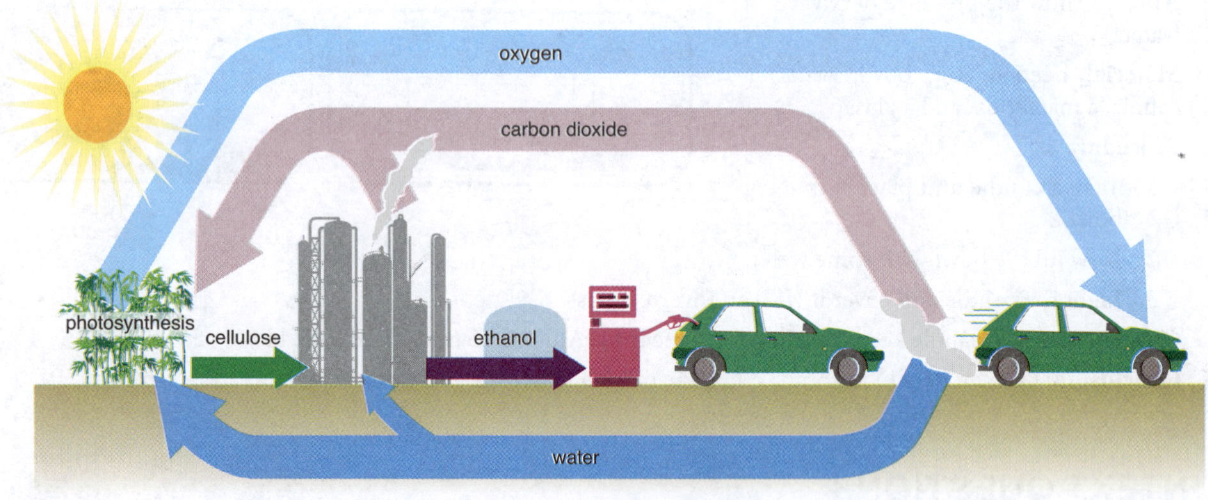

Figure 10.3 Oxygen Cycle

❖ INTEXT QUESTIONS

9. What is the main use of oxygen gas in plants, animals and humans?
   Solution: Plants, animals, and human beings use oxygen for respiration during the day as well as during night.
10. At what time is the rate of photosynthesis very high?
    Solution: The rate of photosynthesis is very high during the daytime.

Check Point 3

11. State the name of the gas which is useful for plants in making food.
12. Why does percentage of oxygen in the air remain constant, even though it is continuously used for respiration and burning?
13. How are plants and animals interdependent on each other?
14. State any two reasons which can cause disruption to the oxygen cycle.
15. What practices can be implemented to maintain balance to the oxygen cycle?

Air Pollution

The addition of substances in the environment in quantities that are harmful to living beings is termed as pollution. Our air is constantly polluted due to various human activities. Burning of fuels such as coal and petroleum, excessive burning of fuels such as wood, smoke and harmful gases released from industries (Fig. 10.4), smoke released by vehicles, and machines releasing gases are the major causes of air pollution. These gases mix in the air and spoil the quality of air, thereby making it impure.

Air pollution has major adverse effects on plants, animals as well as human beings. Harmful gases present in the polluted air make breathing difficult. Air pollution also leads to a rise in lung diseases such as asthma and lung cancer. Air pollution also damages crops. If we do not start looking after the quality of air around us, oxygen and carbon dioxide levels will no longer be balanced and living beings will be the ones getting affected.

There are a number of ways by which we can reduce air pollution. Some of them are, planting more trees, recycling plastics, regular checking of vehicles for the emission of harmful gases, etc.

Figure 10.4 Air Pollution

Keystone

- The popular idea that polluted air can be dangerous to human dates back to the middle ages. Clear evidence of harmful effects from the dirty air started to accumulate after the first use of coal around an early 14th century.
- In our daily lives, everybody contributes to air pollution. Everything we do, and each product we purchase creates pollution. We all bear considerable responsibility for lowering air pollution.

Competition Corner

- **Thunderstorms and cyclones**
Thunderstorms develop in hot, humid tropical areas, like India, very frequently. The rising temperatures produce strong upward rising winds. These winds carry water droplets upwards, where they freeze, and fall down again. The swift movement of the falling water droplets along with the rising air create lightning and sound. It is this event that we call a thunderstorm.
- **How a thunderstorm becomes a cyclone?**
Before cloud formation, water takes up heat from the atmosphere to changes it into vapour. When water vapour changes back to its liquid form as raindrops, this heat is released to the atmosphere. The heat released to the atmosphere warms the air around. The air tends to rise and causes a drop in pressure. More air rushes to the centre of the storm. This cycle is repeated. The chain of events ends with the formation of a very low-pressure system with very high-speed winds revolving around it. It is this weather condition that we call a cyclone. Factors like wind speed, wind direction, temperature, and humidity contribute to the development of cyclones.

❖ INTEXT QUESTIONS

11. What is the harmful effect of air pollution on humans?
Solution: Harmful gases present in the polluted air make breathing difficult.

12. How can we reduce air pollution?
Solution: There are a number of ways by which we can reduce air pollution. Some of them are: planting more trees, recycling plastics, regular checking of vehicles for the emission of harmful gases, etc.

Check Point 4

16. What is pollution?
17. Name two gases which cause air pollution.
18. Write any three reasons that can cause air pollution.
19. Name any two diseases which are caused by air pollution.
20. Write any three consequences of air pollution.

STRUCTURAL OUTLINE

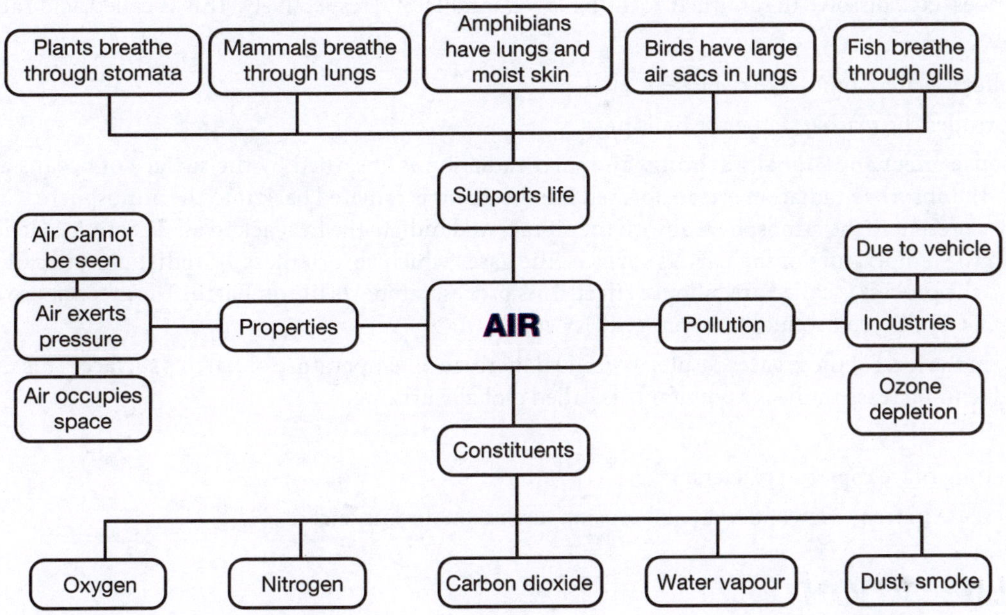

ABRIDGEMENT

- **Acid rain:** The gases such as NO_2 and SO_2 that are released from factory chimneys, burning of fossil fuels, eruption of volcanoes, etc., dissolve in rainwater forming HNO_3 and H_2SO_4 respectively. This is called acid rain.

  Causes:

  (i) Pollutes water bodies like river, seas, etc.

  (ii) Corrodes the marble statues or buildings.

- **Greenhouse effect and global warming:** The solar radiation is absorbed by the surface of oceans and vegetation on land. The absorbed radiation is transformed into heat and is radiated back into the atmosphere. Certain gaseous molecules present in the atmosphere absorb the IR rays and radiate the heat ack in all directions. Hence, these gases maintain the temperature of the Earth's surface. The gases which absorb these IR radiations are called greenhouse gases and the process is called greenhouse effect. This process supports life on Earth. The greenhouse gases are CO_2, H_2O, N_2O, CH_4, O_3, chlorofluorocarbons (CFCs), etc.

  Increase in the level of these gases results in gradual increase of temperature of Earth's surface. This increased effect caused due to increase in the air pollutants is called global warming.

  Causes:

  (i) Melting of ice caps and glaciers.

  (ii) Increase in frequency of floods, soil erosion, unseasonal rains, etc.

EXEMPLIFICATION

1. **Describe the balance of oxygen in air.**

   Solution: The oxygen in air is used by the organisms present in air, water, or soil or on Earth for their respiration. During respiration carbon dioxide gas is released, but green plants during photosynthesis use carbon dioxide of air for preparing food and they release oxygen gas in the air. Thus, the balance of oxygen in air is maintained.

2. **Why is carbon-dioxide gas used to extinguish fire?**

   Solution: It is because carbon-dioxide does not support combustion. When sprayed on a burning object it stops the supply of oxygen and extinguishes fire.

3. **How will you prove that soil contains air in it?**

   Solution: Take a glass tumbler add some soil in it, then pour some water on the soil slowly, the air-bubbles comes out of the soil. This proves that soil holds air in it.

4. **Why do we see the sky and air clear and clean after rainfall?**

   Solution: The dust particles which remain suspended in air get loaded and come down on the ground due to rainfall. This is the reason that the sky and the air look clean and clear after rainfall.

5. **Explain why mountaineers carry oxygen cylinders with them.**

   Solution: As you go up, above the sea-level the atmospheric pressure goes on decreasing and the amount of oxygen also decreases at higher altitude.

6. **Name the major gas present in (a) inhaled air (b) exhaled air.**

   Solution: (a) Oxygen (b) Carbon dioxide.

7. **Write the necessary conditions for rusting of iron to take place.**

   Solution: Rusting of iron takes place in the presence of moisture and oxygen. So, the presence of oxygen and water vapour in air are two necessary conditions for rusting of iron.

8. **Name a device which uses wind energy to generate electricity.**

   Solution: Windmills use wind energy to convert wind energy into electrical energy

9. **What is wind energy? Mention its two advantages.**

   Solution: Blowing air is called wind. Wind possesses kinetic energy. The kinetic energy possessed by wind is called wind energy.

Uses of Wind Energy are:

(i) Wind energy is used to pump ground water.

(ii) Wind energy is used to generate electricity with the help of windmills.

10. Mention two uses of air.

Solution: The two uses of air are as below:

(a) For respiration all organisms need air.

(b) For burning of any substance air is needed.

KNOWLEDGE COMPENDIUM

1. **What is the composition of air?**
   Solution: Air is mixture of nitrogen, oxygen, carbon dioxide, water vapour and a few other gases. Some dust particles may also be present in it.

2. **Which gas in the atmosphere is essential for respiration?**
   Solution: Oxygen.

3. **How will you show that air supports burning?**
   Solution: Take a small burning candle. Cover the burning candle with a glass jar. After few minutes the candle is extinguished as the supply of air is stopped due to glass jar. This experiment proves that air supports burning.

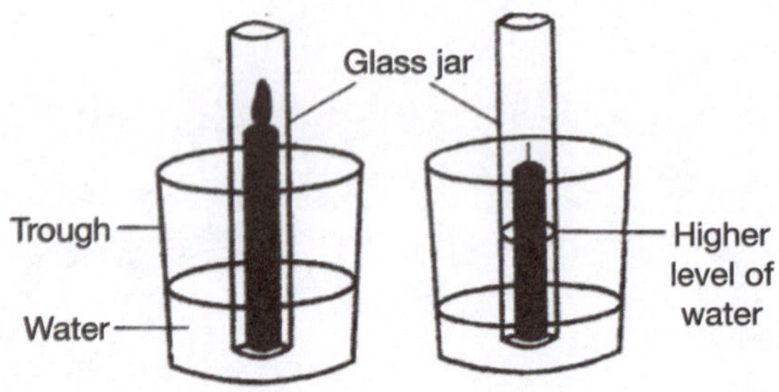

Experiments to Show That Air Supports Burning

4. **How will you show that air is dissolved in water?**
   Solution: Take some water in a glass vessel or beaker. Heat it slowly on a tripod stand. Before the water begins to boil, look carefully at the inner surface of the vessel. You will see tiny bubbles on the inside. On heating, air dissolved in water escapes in the form of these bubbles.

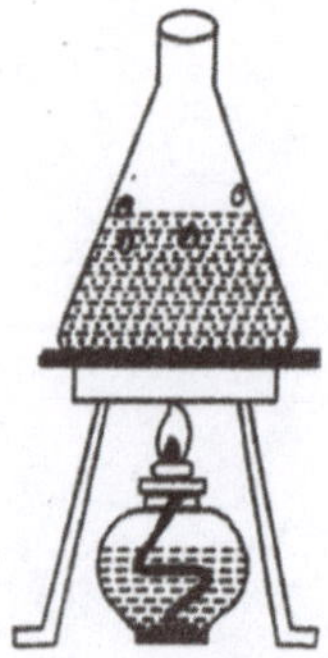

Water Contains Air

5. **Why does a lump of cotton wool shrink in water?**
   Solution: A lump of cotton wool has air among the gaps of cotton fibres. When water replaces the air from these gaps, the cotton lump becomes heavy and also shrinks.

6. **The layer of air around the Earth is known as ______**
   Solution: Atmosphere

7. **The component of air used by green plants to make their food, is ______**
   Solution: Carbon dioxide.

8. **List five activities that are possible due to the presence of air.**
   Solution: The activities that are possible due to the presence of air, are:
   (a) To make a simple firki.
   (b) To make a weathercock.
   (c) To breathe for survival.
   (d) For burning of substance.
   (e) For photosynthesis.

9. **How do plants and animals help each other in the exchange of gases in the atmosphere?**
   Solution: Animals and plants use oxygen from air during respiration and release carbon dioxide gas in air. But green plants also release oxygen gas by using carbon dioxide during photosynthesis. Thus, we can say that animals and plants help each other with the exchange of gases.

ASSESSMENT CORNER

LEVEL 1

Fixed Response Type

Multiple Choice Questions

1. Air is a/an -
(A) Element (B) Compound
(C) Mixture (D) None of these

2. The main constitute of air, which neither supports burning nor burn itself is:
(A) nitrogen (B) oxygen
(C) argon (D) water vapours

3. In a desert, water vapour content is:
(A) High (B) Low
(C) Constant (D) None of these

4. Which of the following is a variable component of air, which controls over climate condition –
(A) nitrogen
(B) oxygen
(C) water vapours
(D) carbon dioxide

5. Which of the following represents correct order of abundance of various gases in air?
(A) Nitrogen > Oxygen > Carbon dioxide > Argon
(B) Nitrogen > Oxygen > Argon > Carbon dioxide
(C) Oxygen > Nitrogen > Carbon dioxide > Argon
(D) Carbon dioxide > Nitrogen > Oxygen > Argon

6. The percentage composition of oxygen in air is:
(A) $\frac{1}{4}^{th}$ of the volume (B) $\frac{1}{6}^{th}$ of the volume
(C) $\frac{1}{5}^{th}$ of the volume (D) $\frac{1}{3}^{rd}$ of the volume

7. The constituent of air that supports combustion is-
(A) Oxygen (B) Nitrogen
(C) Carbon dioxide (D) Both (A) and (B)

8. Which gas is used in packaging of chips?
(A) Nitrogen (B) Argon
(C) Helium (D) Krypton

9. The true statement about greenhouse effect is that it is:
(A) Caused by combination of many gases
(B) Caused by CO_2
(C) Caused by CO_2, CH_4, NO_2 gases
(D) None of these

10. Which of these is an example of natural air pollution?
(A) Acid rain
(B) Vehicle emission of harmful gases
(C) Volcanic eruptions
(D) Burning of fuel

11. In which of the following cities would there be maximum water vapour in the air on a sunny day in December?
(A) Srinagar (B) Delhi
(C) Bhopal (D) Mumbai

12. Carbon dioxide is essential for –
(A) breathing
(B) to generate electricity
(C) photosynthesis
(D) burning of fuel

13. Layer of atmosphere that absorbs UV rays from the sun is called
(A) Thermosphere (B) Stratosphere
(C) Mesosphere (D) Exosphere

14. The atmospheric layer nearest the Earth's surface is the -
(A) Stratosphere (B) Ionosphere
(C) Troposphere (D) Mesosphere

15. Which of the following is layer of atmosphere next to troposphere?
(A) Ionosphere (B) Stratosphere
(C) Mesosphere (D) Thermosphere

16. Oxygen is consumed from the atmosphere in which of the following processes:
(A) Combustion of fuel
(B) Absorbed by green plants during photosynthesis
(C) Biological fixation by symbiotic bacteria
(D) Cultivation of land

17. A gas present in air and useful in making fertilizer is:
(A) O_2 (B) CO_2
(C) N_2 (D) Argon

18. What are the inert gases?
(A) these are major constituent of air
(B) present in 1/5 amount in air
(C) these support burning
(D) these do not react with any substance

19. The rate of photosynthesis is very high during:
(A) Daytime (B) Night
(C) Evening (D) Midnight

20. Photosynthesis increases concentration of oxygen in air which is necessary for all:
(A) Living organisms (B) Fossils
(C) Birds only (D) Animals only

21. Glucose and oxygen combine to form CO_2, water, and
(A) Oxygen (B) Energy
(C) Neon (D) Nitrogen

22. Which of the following components of air cannot be consumed directly by plants?
(A) Oxygen (B) Nitrogen
(C) Carbon dioxide (D) None of these

23. What happens when humans burn oil and other fuels?
(A) All animals will die.
(B) CO_2 is released.
(C) Quality of air will improve.
(D) CO_2 is not released.

24. Long term effects of air pollution include:
(A) Fever
(B) Headache
(C) Nausea
(D) Permanent lung damage

25. Causes of air pollution includes:
(A) Chlorofluorocarbons (CFCs)
(B) Cars and motor vehicles
(C) Power plants and industries
(D) All of these

Fill in the Blanks

1. ____________________ in air supports burning.

2. Air occupies ________ and has _________.

3. Aquatic plants such as __________ also breathe in oxygen dissolved in water through their surface .

4. We all need _____________ for respiration.

5. The thin layer of air around the Earth's surface is called __________.

6. The stratosphere contains_________ which zone the harmful ultraviolet radiation of the sun.

7. When humans burn oil and other fuels, quality of air __________.

8. __________ gas produced while burning of fuel.

9. One-fifth of the air is made up of __________.

10. Inert or noble gases are present in air in very __________ amount.

11. A person feel suffocated when material is burnt in a closed room due to presence of __________ gas.

12. __________ is the lowest layer of our atmosphere.

13. __________ lies above the troposphere and it extends to about 50 km above the Earth's surface.

14. __________ lies above the mesosphere and it extends up to a height of 480 km.

15. The uppermost layer of the atmosphere is called __________.

True/False

1. Nitrogen and oxygen, these two gases together make up 99% of air

2. Carbon dioxide is the major component of air

3. Nitrogen is an important constituent of all fertilizers.

4. Plants use oxygen for respiration during the daytime only.

5. The air we breathe out is rich in oxygen.

6. Thermosphere contains electrically charged particles called 'Ions'.

7. Exosphere extends to a height of about 50km and gradually merges with the interplanetary space.

8. Plants have tiny pores called stomata, found on the underside their leaves.

9. Gills help to take in carbon dioxide and give out oxygen.

10. Crocodiles and alligators swim through water with part of their snout above the water surface to breathe easily.

11. Birds have a pair of lungs with air sacs that remain open all the time so that air can easily pass through them.

12. During photosynthesis plants take in carbon dioxide from the air and release oxygen.

13. The addition of substances in the environment in quantities that are not useful to living beings is called pollution.

14. The gases which absorb the IR radiations are called greenhouse gases.

15. Melting of ice caps and glaciers are due to global warming.

Match Type Questions

1.

Column-A	Column-B
1. Major component of air	(a) Carbon dioxide
2. Component of air used by plants during photosynthesis	(b) Nitrogen
3. Dust particles	(c) Oxygen
4. For respiration we require	(d) Dissolved oxygen
5. Aquatic animals use	(e) Composition varies

2.

Column-A	Column-B
1. Greenhouse gas	(a) O_2
2. Respiration	(b) NO_2
3. Acid rain	(c) CFC
4. Chlorofluorocarbon	(d) CO_2

3.

Column-A	Column-B
1. Stomata	(a) Fish
2. Gills	(b) Salamander
3. Nostrils	(c) Plant leaf
4. Lungs	(d) Mammals

4.

Column-A	Column-B
1. Thermosphere	(a) 11 km
2. Mesosphere	(b) 50 km
3. Troposphere	(c) 80 km
4. Stratosphere	(d) 480 km

5.

Column-A	Column-B
1. Weathercock	(a) Gases and fine dust particles
2. Mountaineers	(b) Prevent dust particles
3. Fine hair inside the nose	(c) Oxygen cylinders
4. Smoke	(d) Direction of air flow

Assertion and Reason Type Questions

Direction: In the following questions, a statements of assertion is followed by statement of reason.
Mark the correct choice as:

(A) Both Assertion and Reason are true, and Reason is the correct explanation of Assertion.
(B) Both Assertion and Reason are true but, Reason is not the correct explanation of Assertion.
(C) Assertion is true but Reason is false.
(D) Both Assertion and Reason are false.

1. **Assertion:** The percentage of oxygen in the air almost remains constant even though it is continuously used for respiration and burning.
Reason: This is because during photosynthesis, plants take in carbon dioxide from the air and release oxygen.

2. **Assertion:** Plants, animals, and human beings use oxygen for respiration during the day as well as during night.
Reason: The rate of photosynthesis is very high during night-time.

3. **Assertion:** Birds have a pair of lungs with air sacs that remain open all the time.
Reason: The air can easily pass through their lungs with air sacs.

4. **Assertion:** Plants make their own food by a process called photosynthesis.
Reason: During photosynthesis oxygen present in the air is used by plants.

5. **Assertion:** This layer lies above the troposphere, and it extends to about 480 km above the Earth's surface.
Reason: The stratosphere contains nitrogen which absorbs the harmful ultraviolet radiation of the sun.

6. **Assertion:** Plants, animals, and human beings use oxygen for respiration during the day as well as during night.
Reason: The rate of photosynthesis is very high during the night-time.

7. **Assertion:** Oxygen slows down any burning.
Reason: Oxygen neither supports burning nor burns itself.

8. **Assertion:** Plants, animals, and human beings use oxygen for respiration during the day as well as during the night.
Reason: The rate of photosynthesis is very high during the night-time.

9. **Assertion:** Water has dissolved gases which are used by aquatic life for respiration and photosynthesis.
Reason: Plants and animals use oxygen for respiration.

10. **Assertion:** Air is a mixture of gases.
Reason: Carbon dioxide and inert gases are present in large amounts in air.

Comprehension Based Question

Case-1 The percentage of oxygen in the air almost remains constant even though it is being continuously used for respiration and burning. This is because during photosynthesis plants take in carbon dioxide from the air and release oxygen. Plants, animals, and human beings use oxygen for respiration during the day as well as during night. The rate of photosynthesis is very high during day-time. Plants release much more oxygen than they consume during respiration and thus, the amount of oxygen in the atmosphere is sufficient for respiration of animals, plants, as well as human beings. Plants and animals are thus interdependent on each other and help to maintain the oxygen cycle.
Deforestation and excessive burning of fuel can upset this delicate balance. Therefore, we should plant more trees and use fuel economically.

1. Which of the following factors can upset ecological balance?
(A) Deforestation (B) Burning of fuel
(C) Respiration (D) Both (A) and (B)

2. The percentage of ___________in the air almost remains constant even though it is continuously used for respiration and burning.
(A) Oxygen (B) Dust
(C) Smoke (D) CO_2

3. The rate of photosynthesis is very high during:
(A) Evening time (B) Daytime
(C) Night-time (D) Winter

Free Response Type

Very Short Answer Type Questions

1. What is the composition of air?
2. Which gas present in air is essential for burning?
3. What fraction of air is comprised of oxygen?
4. Why does a balloon grow in size when we blow air into it?
5. What name is given to the layer of air which surrounds the Earth?

Short Answer Type Questions

1. Name any four inert gases present in the atmosphere.
2. What is smoke? How is it produced?
3. Differentiate between:
(a) Respiration and breathing
(b) Air and wind
4. What is the role of air in the water cycle?
5. Why plantation is necessary?

Long Answer Type Questions

1. Explain why a burning candle stops burning after sometime when covered with an inverted jar.
2. Write the chemical change involved in respiration.
3. Describe an activity to show the presence of water vapour in air.
4. Discuss the importance of photosynthesis in our life.
5. How can we reduce air pollution?
6. Demonstrate through a simple experiment that the air mainly contains nitrogen and oxygen in the volume ratio of 4:1.
7. Air is a mixture. Prove this statement.
8. Explain why during an incident of fire, one is advised to wrap a woollen blanket over a burning object.
9. What is air? Name the major constituents of air and give their volume proportions for the same.
10. Explain the following observations very briefly.
(A) A firki does not rotate in a closed area.
(B) The arrow of a weathercock points towards a particular direction at a particular moment.
(C) An empty glass is in fact, not empty.
(D) Breathing through your mouth may harm you.
11. Write just a few sentences for an imaginary situation if any of the following gases disappear from the atmosphere.
(A) Oxygen
(B) Nitrogen
(C) Carbon dioxide

Numerical Based Questions

1. Total 100 gm of fuel + oxygen are taken during the combustion of a fuel. If 28 gm of oxygen gas is required for combustion, then calculate the total amount of fuel taken.
   (A) 100 gm (B) 96 gm
   (C) 72 gm (D) Can't be calculated

2. Swati inflated a balloon with air, total weight of the balloon is 20 gm. If the mass of an empty balloon is 5 gm, then calculate the mass of air filled in the balloon ?
   (A) 15 gm (B) 25 gm
   (C) 5 gm (D) 30 gm

Case Based Questions

1. Air pollution has major adverse effects on plants, animals as well as human beings. Harmful gases present in the polluted air makes breathing difficult. Air pollution also leads to a lot of lung diseases such as asthma and lung cancer. Air pollution also damages crops. If we do not start looking after the quality of air around us, oxygen and carbon dioxide levels will no longer be balanced and living beings will be the ones affected by it.
   There are a number of ways by which we can reduce air pollution. Some of them are: planting more trees, recycling plastics, regular checking of vehicles for the emission of harmful gases, etc.

   (i) ________ leads to a lot of lung diseases such as asthma and lung cancer.
   (A) Air pollution
   (B) Noise pollution
   (C) Water pollution
   (D) Both (A) and (B)

   (ii) Which of the following is correct way by which we can reduce air pollution.
   (A) Planting trees
   (B) Increasing automobile usage
   (C) Recycling plastics
   (D) Both (A) and (C)

Level 2

Multiple Choice Questions

1. Which of the following statement is/are true?
   (A) In a large container, the air will expand.
   (B) In a small container, the air will get compressed.
   (C) Volume of air in a container, is the same as the volume of the container.
   (D) All of the above.

2. Arrange the following layers of the atmosphere in the decreasing order of their altitudes.
   (1) Stratosphere (2) Troposphere
   (3) Mesosphere (4) Exosphere
   (5) Ionosphere

   (A) 34512 (B) 45312
   (C) 42531 (D) 21354

3. In the process of photosynthesis, plants give out ________ and ________.
   (A) nitrogen; carbon dioxide
   (B) oxygen; water vapour
   (C) food; oxygen
   (D) food; carbon dioxide

4. Global warming takes place due to the increase of ________ in the air.
   (A) nitrogen (B) carbon dioxide
   (C) oxygen (D) carbon monoxide

5. Which of the following plays an important role while drinking soft drinks with a straw?
   (A) Humidity
   (B) Temperature
   (C) Atmospheric pressure
   (D) Composition of air

6. Air is a renewable source of energy. It can be used for -
   (A) Generating electricity
   (B) Moving a windmill
   (C) Pumping water
   (D) All of the above

7. We cannot feel the pressure of the atmosphere because
   (A) pressure increases with increase in altitude.
   (B) pressure decreases with increase in altitude.
   (C) pressure acts in all directions equally.
   (D) pressure is negligible.

8. Which of the following statement is true?
   (A) Energy is stored when air is compressed.
   (B) Compressed air exerts a force.
   (C) Water cannot be compressed.
   (D) All of the above.

9. Read the two sentences carefully and answer the question?
   (i) Compressed air in a tyre exerts a force large enough to lift a heavy car.
   (ii) In a syringe, the plunger compresses the liquid.
   (A) Both statements are true.
   (B) Both statements are false.
   (C) Statement I is true but II is false.
   (D) Statement I is false but II is true.

10. Glass panels usually appear hazy because -
   (A) water vapour settles on the tiny dust particles on the panel.
   (B) of chemical reactions.
   (C) it is the property of all transparent substances.
   (D) the glass is old.

11. Usha took a lump of dry soil in a glass and added water to it till until it was completely immersed. She observed bubbles coming out. The bubbles contain:
   (A) Water vapour (B) Only oxygen gas
   (C) Air (D) None of these.

12. How is air pollution on the roads reduced?
   (A) Widening the roads.
   (B) Having more traffic lights on the roads.
   (C) Having less traffic lights on the roads.
   (D) Reducing the number of vehicles on the road.

13. Seema took two balloons. She has blown one balloon with her mouth. She filled another balloon with the vapours coming out of boiling water. When the balloons are released, she observed that the balloon with the hot vapours raised higher than the other balloon. What can she learn from this experiment?
   (A) Hot air has more weight than the cold air.
   (B) Boiling water gives energy to the balloon.
   (C) Air likes hot balloons.
   (D) Hot air has less weight.

14. Which of the following statements is incorrect?
   (A) All living things require air to breathe.
   (B) We can feel air, but we cannot see it.
   (C) Moving air makes it possible to fly a kite.
   (D) Air is present everywhere but not in soil.

15. Wind does not help in the movement of which of the following?
   (A) Firki (B) Weathercock
   (C) Ceiling fan (D) Sailing yacht

16. What is not true about air?
   (A) It makes the windmill rotate.
   (B) It helps in the movement of aeroplanes.
   (C) Birds can fly due to presence of air.
   (D) It has no role in water cycle.

17. Mountaineers carry oxygen cylinders with them because:
   (A) there is no oxygen on high mountains.
   (B) there is deficiency of oxygen on mountains at high altitude.
   (C) oxygen is used for cooking.
   (D) oxygen keeps them warm at low temperature.

18. Boojho took an empty plastic bottle, turned it upside down, and dipped its open mouth into a bucket filled with water. He then tilted the bottle slightly and made the following observations.
   (i) Bubbles of air came out from the bottle.
   (ii) Some water entered the bottle.
   (iii) Nitrogen gas came out in the form of bubbles and oxygen got dissolved in water.
   (iv) No bubbles formed, only water entered the bottle.
   Which observations is / are correct?
   (A) (i) and (ii) (B) (iv) only
   (C) (iii) and (iv) (D) (i) only

19. Factor/s responsible for the development of cyclone:
   (A) wind speed and direction
   (B) temperature
   (C) humidity
   (D) all of these

20. The components of air which are harmful to living beings are:
   (A) Nitrogen and carbon dioxide
   (B) Dust and water vapour
   (C) Dust and smoke
   (D) Smoke and water vapour.

Higher Order Thinking Skills (HOTS)

1. How air pollutants can affect the atmosphere in the form of acid rain?

2. What is the greenhouse effect? Explain.

3. How air pollution is responsible for global warming and their effects?

4. What happens if the percentage of oxygen in the air reaches to 70%?

5. What happens if the percentage of carbon-dioxide increases in the air?

6. You must have seen during the rainy season, animals like earthworms, snakes, snails, etc., are commonly seen. Explain why?

7. In a number of musical instruments, air plays an important role. Can you name such instruments?

8. In the boxes of column I the letters of some words are jumbled. Arrange them in the proper form in the boxes given in column II.

Column-I	Column-II
(a) DILLMWIN	
(b) YNOGXE	
(c) MESKO	
(d) TUDS	

9. Make sentences using the given set of words.
   (a) 99%, oxygen, nitrogen, air, together
   (b) Respiration, dissolved, animals, air aquatic
   (c) Air, wind, motion, called

10. Garima observed that when she left her tightly capped bottle full of water in open sunlight, tiny bubbles were formed all around inside the bottle. Help Garima to know why it happened?

11. Paheli kept some water in a beaker for heating. She observed that tiny bubbles appeared before the water started to boil. She boiled the water for about 5 minutes and filled it in a bottle up to the brim and kept the bottle airtight till it cooled down to room temperature.
    (a) Why did the tiny bubbles appear?
    (b) Do you think tiny bubbles will appear on heating the water taken out from the bottle? Justify your answer.

12. On a Sunday morning Paheli's friend visited her at home. She wanted to see some flowering plants in the nearby garden, so the both of them went to the garden. While returning from the garden they also observed some flowering plants on the roadside. But to their surprise they found that the leaves and flowers of these roadside plants were comparatively very dull. Can you help them to know why?

ARCHIVE CORNER

1. The given experiment shows:

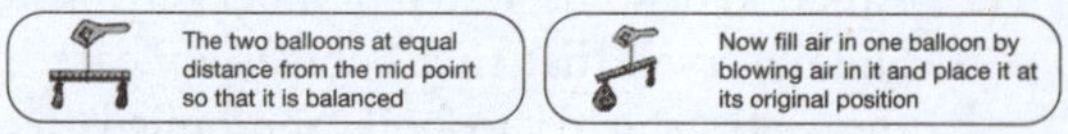

(A) Air contains dust particles
(B) Air occupies space
(C) Air has mass
(D) Air is colourless

2. Garima took a plant found on the land and carefully put it inside a jar of water as shown by tying it to stones. She added the minerals required by the plant in the water and kept it in sunlight. After some days the plant died. What could be the probable reason for its death?

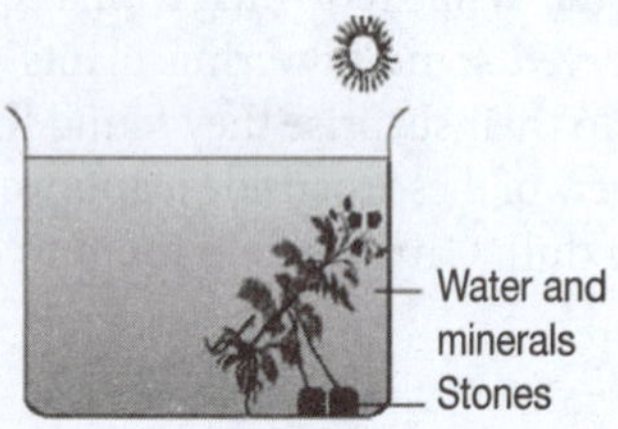

(A) The plant was not able to absorb oxygen for respiration inside the water.
(B) The plant was not able to absorb carbon dioxide for photosynthesis inside water.
(C) The plant did not get sunlight to perform photosynthesis inside water.
(D) Both (A) and (B)

3. Smita set up an apparatus as shown in the figure given below. After keeping the apparatus for some time in the Sun, she found that some gas has collected in the top part of the test tube. Which gas could it be?

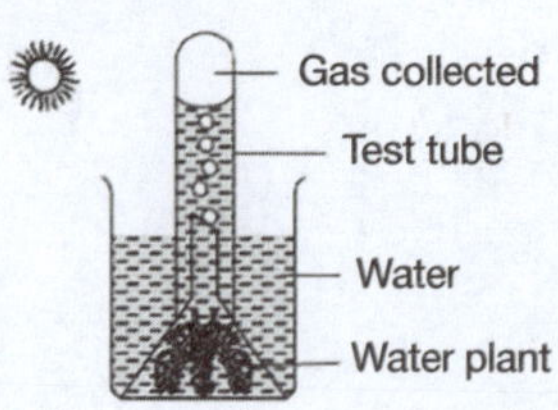

(A) Oxygen (B) Hydrogen
(C) Carbon dioxide (D) Nitrogen

4. Arjun conducted an experiment as shown in figure. What conclusion could you draw from the observation?

(A) Air contains dust particles
(B) Air contains oxygen
(C) Air contains water vapour
(D) Air contains carbon dioxide

5. Read the following statements:
(i) I am present in air
(ii) I enter your lungs when you breathe in
(iii) Your body needs me to produce energy

These statements are regarding _________.
(A) Carbon dioxide (B) Nitrogen
(C) Hydrogen (D) Oxygen

6. Which of the following activities would show that air is dissolved in water?
(A) Press a piece of cotton wool into the bottom of a tumbler. Hold the tumbler upside down and insert it into a bowl of water, without tilting it.
(B) Press steel wool into the bottom of the gas jar. Invert the gas jar into the bowl of water on two small wooden blocks so that there is space between the gas jar and the bowl.
(C) Take some water in a pan. Heat it gently on a gas burner. Observe the water as it begins to heat.
(D) None of these

7. Which of the following statements is correct regarding the atmosphere?
(A) Wind blows, clouds build up, and weather changes take place in stratosphere.
(B) The ozone layer, which acts as huge shield protecting us from the harmful ultraviolet rays of the Sun lies in the thermosphere.
(C) Stratosphere is a clear, cloudless layer where airplanes fly.

(D) Exosphere is very thin and very hot layer that has electrically charged particles which help radios to work.

8. Match Column-I with Column-II and select the correct option from the codes give below:

Column-I	Column-II
(A) Oxygen	(i) Condense into tiny drops
(B) Nitrogen	(ii) Does not support combustion
(C) Carbon dioxide	(iii) Formed by burning of fuel
(D) Smoke	(iv) Constituent of fertilizers
(E) Water vapour	(v) Supports combustion

(A) (a)-(ii), (b)-(iv), c-(v), d-(iii), (e)-(i)
(B) (a)-(v), (b)-(iv), c-(iii), d-(ii), (e)-(i)
(C) (a)-(iv), (b)-(v), c-(ii), d-(iii), (e)-(i)
(D) (a)-(v), (b)-(iv), c-(ii), d-(iii), (e)-(i)

9. Beena sets up two experiments, as shown in the diagram below. She placed both the set-ups in sunlight for 9 hours. On noting down her observations for both set-ups she found that there was more oxygen collected in test tube X as compared to test tube Y. What conclusion could she best draw from this experiment?

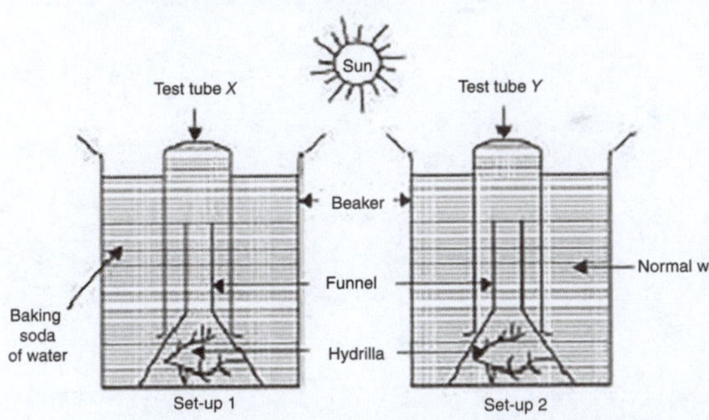

(A) The rate of photosynthesis decreased when there was more carbon dioxide.
(B) Baking soda is required for photosynthesis.
(C) Carbon dioxide is required by the plant for photosynthesis.
(D) The rate of photosynthesis increases when there is more carbon dioxide.

10. Read the following statements:
(i) Air dissolved in water cannot be removed from it.
(ii) Density of air decreases with increasing altitude.
(iii) Air is an element that surrounds the Earth and makes Earth hospitable for living organisms.
(iv) Air helps in pollination of several flowers and in the dispersal of seeds.

Which of the above statements are correct?
(A) (i) and (ii) (B) (ii) and (iv)
(C) (i) and (iii) (D) (iii) and (iv)

11. Refer to the given flow chart and identify the components X, Y and Z of air?

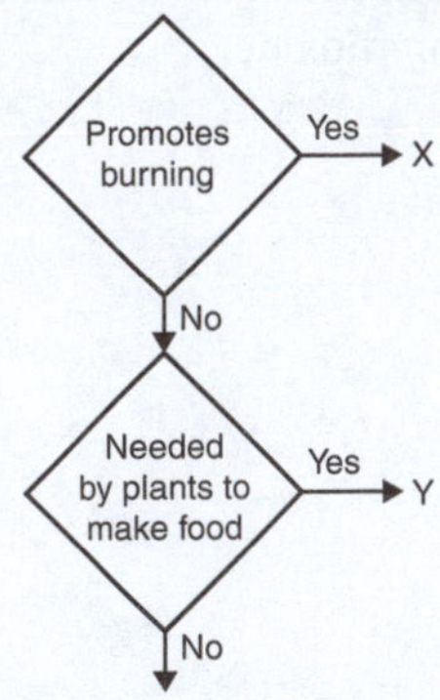

(A) X - Nitrogen, Y - Oxygen
(B) Y- Carbon dioxide, Z - Oxygen
(C) X- Oxygen, Z - Nitrogen
(D) Y- Nitrogen, Z - Carbon dioxide

12. Refer to the given flow chart.

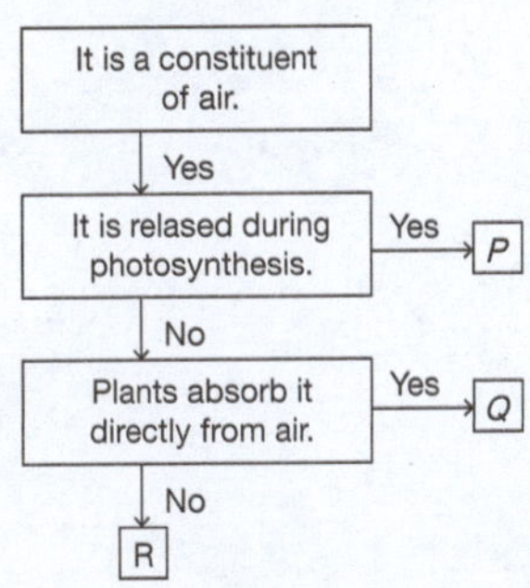

Identify P, Q, and R and select the incorrect statement.
(A) During the process of burning, P is used up and Q is given out.
(B) Autotrophs could be the only source of P in the atmosphere.
(C) Q is used in fire extinguishers as it extinguishes fire.
(D) In atmospheric air, R is present in highest percentage whereas P is present in lowest percentage.

13. On a cold winter day, Sohan put a room heater near his aquarium, which made water in the aquarium warm but not hot.
What could happen due to this?
(A) Fishes would feel more comfortable in warm water due to more availability of oxygen.
(B) Fishes would suffocate due to less availability of oxygen for breathing.
(C) Fishes would die due to decrease in amount of carbon dioxide dissolved in warm water.
(D) Fishes would feel more comfortable in warm water due to decrease in amount of dissolved carbon dioxide.

14. The gas X is only about 20 parts out of 100 parts of air in the atmosphere. It is needed for decomposition of organic matter. The gas X is
(A) Carbon dioxide (B) Water vapour
(C) Oxygen (D) Nitrogen

15. What is/ are the factor/s which can upset the delicate balance of a gas, which makes 1/2 part of air?
(A) Plantation
(B) Photosynthesis
(C) Respiration
(D) Deforestation

ANSWER KEY

Level 1

Fixed Response Type

Multiple Choice Questions

1. C **2.** A **3.** B **4.** C **5.** B **6.** C **7.** A **8.** A **9.** C **10.** C
11. D **12.** C **13.** B **14.** C **15.** B **16.** A **17.** C **18.** D **19.** A **20.** A
21. B **22.** B **23.** B **24.** D **25.** D

Fill in the Blanks

1. Oxygen **2.** Space / mass **3.** Hydrilla
4. Oxygen **5.** Atmosphere **6.** Ozone
7. Decreases **8.** CO_2 **9.** Oxygen
10. Small **11.** CO **12.** Troposphere
13. Stratosphere **14.** Thermosphere **15.** Exosphere

True/False

1. True **2.** False **3.** True
4. False **5.** False **6.** True
7. False **8.** True **9.** False
10. True **11.** True **12.** True
13. True **14.** True **15.** True

Match Type Questions

1. 1-b, 2-a, 3-e, 4-c, 5-d **2.** 1-d, 2-a, 3-b, 4-c **3.** 1-c, 2-a, 3-b, 4-d
4. 1-d, 2-c, 3-a, 4-b **5.** 1-d, 2-c, 3-b, 4-a

Assertion and Reason Type Questions

1. A **2.** C **3.** A **4.** C **5.** D **6.** C **7.** D **8.** C **9.** B **10.** C

Comprehensive Based Questions

1. D **2.** A **3.** B

Free Response Type

Numerical Based Questions

1. C **2.** A

Case Based Questions

1. (i) A (ii) D

Level 2

Multiple Choice Questions

1. D	2. B	3. C	4. B	5. C	6. D	7. C	8. D	9. C	10. A
11. C	12. D	13. D	14. D	15. C	16. D	17. B	18. A	19. D	20. C

Archive Corner

1. C	2. D	3. A	4. C	5. D	6. C	7. C	8. D	9. D	10. B
11. C	12. D	13. B	14. C	15. D					

Part 1: Mindful Eating

CHAPTER 11

Food: Where Does It Come From?

Learning Outcomes

After reading this chapter, you will be able to:

- classify types of organisms.
- discuss food ingredients.
- explain foods from different places.
- discuss the importance of different kind of foods.

Geekspeak

- Nectar
- Herbivore
- Autotroph
- Heterotroph
- Legumes
- Nutrients

Introduction

Food is essential for everyone to give nourishment. Foods have some chemical substances called nutrients. Nutrients are required for the following purposes:

(i) They give us energy for all vital activities.

(ii) They are required for growth and reproduction.

(iii) They provide immunity.

(iv) They are required to heel our worn out cells and tissues.

Variety of Food

Important function of food is providing energy, immunity, raw material for growth and reproduction. Food eaten in the morning is called breakfast. Food eaten in the afternoon is called lunch. Food eaten in the evening or night is called dinner. Food ingredients - Materials which are used to prepare different type of dishes are called food ingredients. E.g., vegetables, salt, oil, etc.

Testing Room 1

Make a list of food items of any 5 states of India and try to find out what ingredients are used to prepare them.

Record your findings in the below table:

S. No.	State	Food Item	Ingredients Used

Types of Animals

On the basis of eating habits animals are divided into following types:

Herbivores (Herbi: Plant; Vore: Eater)

- Herbivorous are those animals which eat only plants or plant products (as shown in Fig. 11.1). For example, Rabbit, Buffalo, Elephant, etc.
- Plants are not easy to digest. Herbivores such as horses have wide teeth to grind the food before it is swallowed.
- Most rodents, such as squirrels, have a pair of broad, sharp-edged front teeth (incisors) in each jaw. They use these teeth to gnaw food such as nuts.

Figure 11.1 Herbivores Animals (a) Horse, (b) Squirrel, (c) Butterfly, and (d) Humming Bird

- Herbivores such as butterflies and humming birds don't need to worry about chewing their food. They have mouthparts shaped like straws to suck nectar from flowers.

Carnivores (Carni: Meat; Vore: Eater)

- Carnivorous are those animals which eat only other animals (as shown in Fig. 11.2). For example, lion, tiger, jackal, etc.
- Some carnivores have sharp claws and powerful jaws (E.g., lion and tiger), which allow them to tear into flesh.
- A flexible lower jaw and numerous joints in the skull allow snakes to swallow animals much larger than themselves.

> **Keystone**
>
> Carnivores have strong and developed canines to tear into food. Herbivores have elongated small intestine that help with digestion.

- Not all carnivores have teeth to chew their food. The owl either swallow an animal whole or tears it down into large chunks before swallowing. The owl then coughs up what it can't digest in the form of a ball called a pellet.
- Vultures belong to a class of carnivores called 'scavengers'. Instead of hunting, they feed on animals that already dead.

Figure 11.2 Carnivores Animals (a) Tiger, (b) Snake, (c) Owl, and (d) Vulture

Omnivores (Omni: All; Vore: Eater)

- Omnivorous are those animals which eat both plants and animals (as shown in Fig. 11.3). For example, bear, crow, human, etc.
- Omnivores aren't too fussy about what they eat. Many, like this raccoon, wouldn't think twice
- Before eating your garbage.

- Crows are very intelligent birds. The New Caledonian crow is known to drop snails and nuts from a height onto large stones to break their hard shells.
- Bears sometimes steal honey from beehives.

Figure 11.3 Omnivores animals (a) Raccoon, (b) Crow, and (c) Bear

Scavengers

Vultures, Jackals, Hyenas, etc. are carnivores, but they do not prey. They eat the flesh animals that are already dead. Such animals are called scavengers.

Keystone

Human beings have both sharp and flat teeth. This allows them to eat both plants and flesh.

Decomposers

Fungi and bacteria secrete digestive juices and there digestive juices decomposes dead organism. They decompose their bodies into simpler substances and then absorb them. Therefore, they are called decomposers.

Competition Corner

- Animals that feed on detritus or dead organic remains, are called detritivores animals. E.g., earthworm.
- Animals which feed on fruits, are called frugivorous animals. E.g., parrot, monkey, birds.
- Organisms that feed on insects are called insectivorous animals. E.g., bats, lizards, spiny ant eater, pitcher plant. Insectivorous plants feed on insects to fulfil their nitrogen requirements.

❖ INTEXT QUESTIONS

1. How have carnivores adapted to consume their food?
   Solution: Carnivores eat flesh of other animals. They have sharp canines for tearing into flesh.
2. Give examples of 3 omnivores animals.
   Solution: Human, crow, and squirrel.

Food Material and Their Sources

Human beings are omnivorous in nature so plant and animals both are good sources of food. Plants provide us fruit, vegetables, grains, pulses etc. as food products. From animals we get milk, cheese, egg, flesh, etc. as food products.

Plant Sources

Plants are autotrophs they synthesize their own food with the help of photosynthesis. Different parts of the plants serve as sources of food for human beings. Fruits, vegetables, cereals, and pulses that we eat, are obtained from different plant parts (as discussed in Table 11.1). Some edible plant parts are as follows:

- **Stem:** In some plants, the stem is an edible plant part. For example, sugar cane, banana stem, etc. Some underground stems like potato, onion, etc. are chief foods that are part of our daily lives.
- **Root:** Carrot, radish, beetroot, etc. are roots which are edible parts of plants. All the parts of Raddish can be eaten.
- **Leaf:** Green leafy vegetables like spinach, lettuce, etc. are edible parts of plants.
- **Flowers:** Flowers of certain plants are also eaten. For example, cauliflower.
- **Fruits and vegetables:** Plants also provide us fruits and vegetables. a fruit is a modified ovary of flower and has seeds. Thus, tomatoes, peas, and beans are fruits and not vegetables. Scientists consider non-seed-containing plants parts such as roots and leaves, as vegetables. Ex. Broccoli, Rose petals etc.

Table 11.1 Parts of a Plant We Eat

Part of Plant	Examples
Root	Carrot, turnip
Leaves	Cariander, spinach, tea
Seeds	Rich, maize, coffee, cumin
Stem	Sugarcane, potato, ginger
Spices	Red chili, mustard
Fruits	Mango, apple, banana
Vegetables	Aubergine, bitter gourd

❖ INTEXT QUESTIONS

3. How do plants prepare their food?
   Solution: In the presence of sunlight and chlorophyll plants use CO_2 and water, to perform photosynthesis, producing glucose or food.
4. In following plants, state the part of the plant that is edible.

Solution: Potato-stem Onion-stem Ginger-root

Check Point 1

1. What is the difference between autotrophs and heterotrophs?
2. What is the role of decomposers in cleaning the environment?
3. What adaptation does the tiger have for eating flesh?

Plant Products as Source of Food

Varieties of food materials are gained by plants like, cereals, pulses, sugar, tea, coffee, oil, vegetable, fruits, spices, etc.

Cereals

They are a main and important food source for animals and humans. They are rich sources of carbohydrates. E.g., wheat, rice, and maize (as shown in Fig. 11.4).

Figure 11.4 Cereals

Pulses or legumes

They are commonly known as "daals". They are rich sources of protein. E.g., pea, bean, moong bean, chickpea, and soyabean (as shown in Fig. 11.5). Roots of leguminous plants have root nodules with Rhizobium which increases fertility of soil.

Figure 11.5 Pulses

Testing Room 2

Take some dry seeds of moong or chana. Put a small quantity of seeds in a container filled with water and leave this aside for a day. The next day, drain the water completely and leave the seeds in the vessel. Wrap them with a piece of wet cloth and it set aside. The following day, do you observe any changes in the seeds?

Take down your observations and write down the results.

____

____

____

____

Vegetables

They are rich sources of minerals, vitamins, and roughage. The various vegetables are shown in the Fig. 11.6. Vegetables are mainly of the following types:

- Leaf vegetables (E.g., Spinach),
- Root vegetables (E.g., Carrot),
- Stem vegetables (E.g., Potato),
- Flower vegetables (E.g., Broccoli)

Figure 11.6 Vegetables

Fruits

They have high water content, and low caloric value. They are rich in minerals and vitamins.
E.g., grapes, banana, guava, pineapple, apple, kiwi, papaya, mango (as shown in the Fig. 11.7).

Figure 11.7 Fruits

Spices

Generally, spices do not have food value. They are only added in food to increase the taste and flavour. E.g., cloves (laung), ginger (*adrak*), turmeric (*haldi*), pepper (*kali mirch*), cumin (*jeera*), asafoetida (*heeng*), coriander (*dhaniya*), chillies (*mirch*), thyme (*ajwain*), cardamom (*ilaichi*), and saffron (*kesar*) (as shown in the Fig. 11.8).

Figure 11.8 Spices

Keystone

Many spices have medicinal value and very useful in our daily life.
E.g., Turmeric increases our immunity.
Ginger is helpful in treating cold and cough.
Tea, coffee, and tobacco are considered as cash crops.

Tea and Coffee

They are used as beverages. Tea is obtained from leaves and coffee is obtained from seeds. They have a stimulant called caffeine.

Competition Corner

- Coffee has more caffeine than tea.
- Brazil produces the most coffee in the world.
- Coffee beans are seeds from which we make coffee.

Animal Products as a Source of Food

Animal products such as meat, eggs, honey, milk, cheese, butter, and curd (as shown in the Fig. 11.9) are eaten by human beings.

Meat

Flesh of some animals such as goat, chicken, and fish is eaten by human beings. Goat were among the first domesticized animals. Apart from milk their hair and milk are also used.

Eggs

Chicken egg is the most commonly eaten bird egg in the world. Chicken eggs are a rich source of proteins and vitamins.

Figure 11.9 Food Products Obtain from Animals (a) Eggs, (b) Fish, and (c) Goat

Egg can be boiled, baked, scrambled, poached, or fried. Most commonly eaten bird eggs are those of—chicken, goose, and duck. Omelette, a popular egg dish, is made by cooking beaten eggs with butter or oil. A single ostrich egg can make omelettes for about ten people. In India, seafood is very popular in West Bengal, Orissa, Kerala, and Andhra Pradesh. Goats were among the first domesticated animals. Apart from meat, their hair and milk is used for various purposes.

Honey

Honey is a sweet liquid made by bees from the nectar of flowers. It is often eaten with bread. Honey can also be used in cooking and baking.

Keystone

- Cow milk has less fat than buffalo milk.
- Cow milk is good source of protein, calcium, and other nutrients. It is easy to digest.

Milk

Milk is obtained from animals such as cow, buffalo, and goat. It is a very nutritious substance and is a rich source of proteins. Milk also contains calcium (as shown in the Fig. 11.10), which is required for healthy bone growth and nerve function.

Figure 11.10 Milk

❖ INTEXT QUESTIONS

5. Suggest any two ways by which you can avoid wastage of food.
   Solution:
   (i) Serve less amount of food at a time.
   (ii) Finish that which you have taken in your plate.
   (iii) Spread awareness among people about the importance of food.
6. Name any 3 products which we obtained from plants and animals.
   Solution: Plant products-Cereals, vegetables, and pulses.
   Animal products-milk, honey, and paneer.
7. How are honeybees useful to us in our daily life?
   Solution: Honeybees play important role in daily life in the following ways-
   (i) They are insects, thus, helpful in pollination.
   (ii) They prepare honey which has a high nutritional and medicinal value.
   (iii) Other products of beehives like bee wax, etc. are commercially important.

Check Point 2

4. What are cash crops?
5. What do you mean by white revolution? Who was the father of white revolution in India?

Competition Corner

- Rearing of honeybees for honey production at the commercial level is called apiculture. The quality of honey depends on the nectar (flower juice) collected by honeybees.
- Honey is very good source of vitamins and minerals. It has great medicinal value.
- India is the world's largest milk producer. Sahiwal is the best Indian cow breed which produces 1500-2500 litre milk per lactation.

Food Miles

The total distance a bag of rice or other food travels from producer to consumer is called food miles. Reducing food miles is important because it helps reduce costs and pollution during transportation, supports local farmers and at the same time produces our fresh and healthy food.

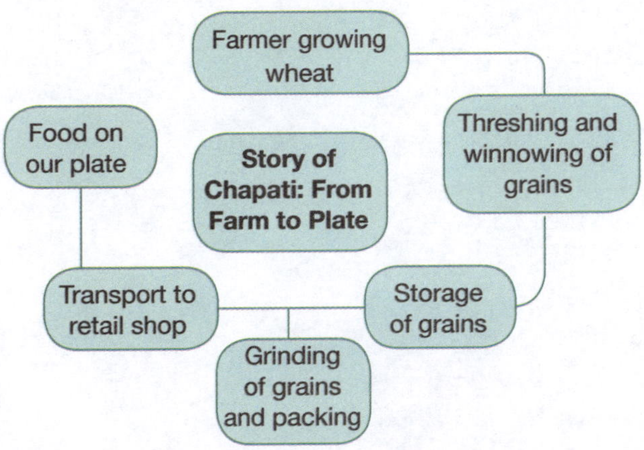

STRUCTURAL OUTLINE

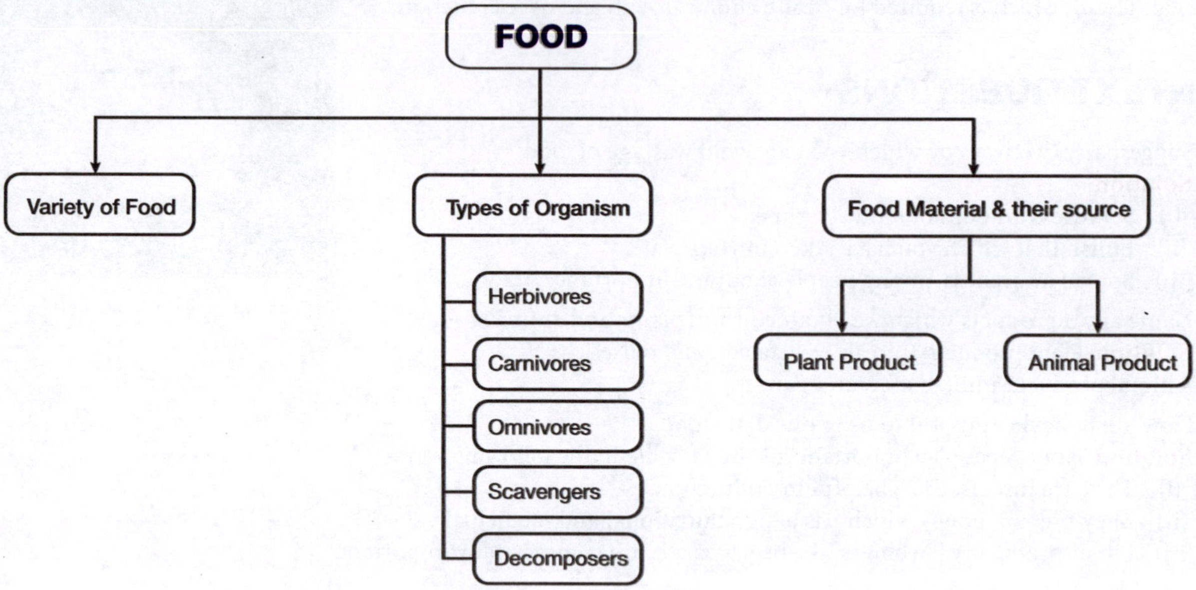

EXEMPLIFICATION

1. **State the names of oils used for cooking in North India and South India respectively.**

   Solution: In southern part of India, people use coconut, groundnut, and sesame oil for cooking. Whereas, in northern part of India, people use mustard oil for cooking.

2. **Define the terms vegetarian and non-vegetarian.**

   Solution: People who do not eat meat, egg, etc. and eat vegetables, cereals, and fruits, etc. are called vegetarians. People who also eat meat, egg, etc. are called non-vegetarians.

3. **Why sprouts have more nutritional value compared to normal food?**

   Solution: After sprouting, seeds are richer in vitamins, and proteins. They are easily digestible therefore, sprouts are more nutritional compared to normal food.

4. **State whether the given statement is true or false. Give reason to support of your answer.**

   'We eat flower part of a cabbage.'

   Solution: The given statement is false because, we eat the leaf part of a cabbage.

5. **Which substances are used to preserve food items?**

   Solution: Preservatives such as baking soda and cream of tartar used for storing food items.

6. **What is the significance of the food chain?**

   Solution: A food chain describes the transfer of energy from one level of organisms to another level of organisms.

7. **Which type of animal receives minimum amount of energy and why?**

   Solution: Carnivores receive minimum amount of energy because they are at higher level of food chain.

NCERT COMPENDIUM

1. Do you find that all living beings need the same kind of food?

Solution: No, all living beings do not need same kind of food.

2. Name five plants and their parts that we eat.

Solution: The names of five plants and their parts that we eat are:

(i) Paddy: seeds
(ii) Wheat: seeds
(iii) Mustard plant: seeds and leaves
(iv) Brinjal plant: fruits
(v) Potato plant: stems

3. Match the items given in column A with those in column B.

Column-A	Column-B
Milk, curd, paneer, ghee	eat other animals
Spinach, cauliflower, carrot	eat plants and plant products
Lions and tigers	are vegetables
Herbivores	are all animal products

Ans.

Column-A	Column-B
Milk, curd, paneer, ghee	are all animal products
Spinach, cauliflower, carrot	are vegetables
Lions and tigers	eat other animals
Herbivores	eat plants and plant products

4. Fill up the blanks with the words given: herbivore, plant, milk, sugarcane, carnivore.

(a) Tiger is a__________ because it eats only meat.
(b) Deer eats only plant products and so is called______________ .
(c) Parrot eats only__________.
(d) The__________ that we drink, which comes from cows, buffaloes and goats is an animal product.
(e) We get sugar from____________ .

Solution:

(a) carnivore (b) herbivore
(c) plant (d) milk
(e) sugarcane

ASSESSMENT CORNER

LEVEL 1

Fixed Response Type

Multiple Choice Question

1. Dogs eat porridge as well as bones. Therefore, they are:
(A) Herbivores (B) Carnivores
(C) Insectivores (D) Omnivores

2. What is 'mindful eating'?
(A) Eating food while watching TV
(B) Eating very fast
(C) Paying full attention to the food while eating
(D) Eating junk food

3. An edible root is:
(A) Ginger (B) Potato
(C) Carrot (D) Onion

4. The part of a chill plant that is used as a spice is the:
(A) Seed (B) Fruit
(C) Leaves (D) Flower

5. The product obtained only from animals-
(A) Flour (B) Fruits
(C) Pulse (D) Milk

6. Food is required because-
(A) It provides us growth.
(B) It provides us energy.
(C) It provides us immunity.
(D) All of these.

7. Rearing of honeybees for honey is called-
(A) Sericulture
(B) Apiculture
(C) Aquaculture
(D) All of these

8. Why should we chew our food properly?
(A) To eat quickly
(B) To make food taste worse
(C) To help with digestion and enjoy the food
(D) To make noise

9. Which of these foods is best for a healthy body?
(A) Fruits and vegetables
(B) Chips and soft drinks
(C) Chocolates
(D) Fried snacks

10. Animals that feed on rotton food are –
(A) Omnivores (B) Carnivores
(C) Detritivores (D) Herbivores

11. Fungi are:
(A) Autotrophs (B) Heterotrophs
(C) Saprophytic (D) Holozoic

12. Cuscuta is:
(A) Endoparasite of sheep.
(B) Endoparasite of human beings.
(C) A parasitic plant.
(D) A parasite on fishes.

13. Which organisms feed on blood?
(A) Omnivores (B) Frugivorous
(C) Sanguivorous (D) Insectivores

14. Heterotrophs are organisms that depend on:-
(A) Living hosts (B) Dead matter
(C) Sunlight (D) Both (A) and (B)

15. The insectivorous plant is:
(A) Mustard (B) Cuscuta
(C) Nepenthes (D) Neem

16. The organism that has sharp canines to tear into food:
(A) Rabbit (B) Lion
(C) Cow (D) Sheep

17. On the first level of the food chain is:
(A) Omnivores (B) Carnivores
(C) Consumers (D) Producers

18. Which of the following are carnivores:
(A) Dog and lion (B) Crow and sheep
(C) Lion and tiger (D) None of these

19. What should you do when you feel full?
(A) Keep eating
(B) Eat faster
(C) Stop eating and listen to your body
(D) Drink soda

20. The plant product added to samosa is:
(A) Milk (B) Potato
(C) Sugar (D) Spinach

21. Mindful eating helps prevent:
(A) Overeating
(B) Enjoying food
(C) Eating fruits and vegetables
(D) Drinking water

22. What should you do when you feel full?
(A) Keep eating
(B) Eat faster
(C) Stop eating and listen to your body
(D) Drink soda

23. Animals which provide egg and meat, both are called-
    (A) Milch animals (B) Carnivores
    (C) Poultry animals (D) Consumers

24. To make *gajar ka halwa*, select the plant part of carrot used.
    (A) Root (B) Stem
    (C) Seed (D) Leaf

25. Organism that obtain their food from plants are called:
    (A) Autotrophs (B) Heterotrophs
    (C) Scavengers (D) Detritivores

26. Sprouted seeds give energy:
    (A) More than dry seeds
    (B) Less than dry seed
    (C) Equal to dry seed
    (D) None of these

27. Which of the following is lowest calorie cereal:
    (A) Wheat (B) Rice
    (C) Maize (D) Jowar

28. Name a non-green plant that we eat:
    (A) Okra (B) Spinach
    (C) Mushroom (D) Algae

29. An example of a balanced diet food is:
    (A) Vegetables (B) Chapati
    (C) Daal and chawal (D) Milk

30. Mushroom is a/an
    (A) Animals product (B) Plant product
    (C) Non green plant (D) None of these

Fill in the Blanks

1. Vulture is a ________ because it eats only meat of dead animals.
2. Deers eat only plant products, therefore, they are called ________.
3. A meal eaten during the night is called ________.
4. ________ of a plant forms fruit.
5. Honeybees synthesize ________ with the help of________.
6. Organism which feed on dead and decaying matter, are called as_____.
7. Substances which are used to prepare food called food ________
8. The component of food that does not provide any nutrient to our body but are essential for flavour and aroma are called ________.
9. Chicken egg is rich source of ________
10. Mung and chana are ________; and wheat and rice are ________
11. ________ is found in roots of leguminous plants.
12. Sprouted gram is rich in vitamin ______.
13. Mung is good source of ________
14. Idli is a ________ food.
15. Peacock is an ______ animal.
16. Honey is produced by ________
17. Parrot is a ________
18. ________ are called natural cleaning agents.
19. Substances which we can eat are called________
20. Honey is an animal product which is rich in________

True/False

1. Sweet potato is used to make sugar.
2. Human beings, lions, birds, insects, etc. eat the same type of food.
3. Frog eats only plant products.
4. Lion is omnivores.
5. Plants give us more varieties of food than animals.
6. In different states of India different kinds of food is consumed.
7. Food taken in day time is called breakfast.
8. We get coffee from leaves and tea from seeds.
9. Groundnut & mustard seeds give us oil.
10. Leaves absorb sunlight and prepare food using chlorophyll.
11. Deers eat only plant products, therefore, they are called herbivores.
12. We get sugar from sugar cane.
13. Brinjal is a fruit.
14. Man belongs to omnivores animals.
15. All organisms need a balanced diet for proper growth.

Match Type Questions

1. Match the following items given in column A with those in column B.

Column-A	Column-B
(i) Rat	(a) Animals
(ii) Man	(b) Plants
(iii) Lion	(c) Grains
(iv) Butterfly	(d) Both plants and animals

(A) (i)-(c), (ii)-(d), (iii)-(a), (iv)-(b)
(B) (iv)-(c), (ii)-(d), (iii)-(a), (i)-(b)
(C) (iii)-(c), (ii)-(d), (i)-(a), (iv)-(b)
(D) (i)-(c), (iii)-(d), (ii)-(a), (iv)-(b)

2. Match the following items given in column Awith those in column B

Column-A	Column-B
(i) Honeybees	(a) Cow
(ii) Meat And Eggs	(b) Hens
(iii) Milk, Rice, Sugar	(c) Nectar
(iv) Flour and Water	(d) Kheer
(v) Ghee And Milk	(e) Roti

(A) (i)-(c), (ii)-(b), (iii)-(d), (iv)-(e), (v)-(a)
(B) (v)-(c), (ii)-(b), (iii)-(d), (i)-(e), (iv)-(a)
(C) (i)-(c), (ii)-(b), (iii)-(d), (iv)-(e), (v)-(a)
(D) (i)-(c), (iii)-(b), (ii)-(d), (iv)-(e), (v)-(a)

3. Match the following items given in column A with those in column B

Column-A	Column-B
(i) Sources Of Food	(a) Human Being
(ii) Mustard, Groundnuts	(b) Plants And Animals
(iii) Herbivore	(c) Cow
(iv) Carnivore	(d) Seeds
(v) Omnivore	(e) Lion

(A) (iv)-(b), (ii)-(d), (iii)-(c), (i)-(e), (v)-(a)
(B) (i)-(b), (ii)-(d), (iii)-(c), (iv)-(e), (v)-(a)
(C) (iii)-(b), (ii)-(d), (i)-(c), (iv)-(e), (v)-(a)
(D) (i)-(b), (ii)-(d), (iii)-(c), (v)-(e), (iv)-(a)

4. Match the following items given in column A with those in column B

Column-A	Column-B
(i) Mung Daal	(a) Animal
(ii) Silk Worm	(b) Honeybee
(iii) Wax	(c) Plant
(iv) Salt	(d) Silk
(v) Egg	(e) Sea

(A) (i)-(c), (ii)-(d), (iii)-(b), (iv)-(e), (v)-(a)
(B) (i)-(a), (ii)-(d), (iii)-(b), (iv)-(e), (v)-(c)
(C) (i)-(c), (ii)-(e), (iii)-(b), (iv)-(d), (v)-(a)
(D) (i)-(b), (ii)-(d), (iii)-(c), (iv)-(e), (v)-(a)

5. Match the column:

Column-A	Column-B
(i) Lion	(a) Herbivores
(ii) Rabbit	(b) Carnivore
(iii) Human	(c) Omnivore
(iv) Parrot	(d) Frugivores

(A) (i)-(d), (ii)-(a), (iii)-(c), (iv)-(b)
(B) (i)-(b), (ii)-(c), (iii)-(a), (iv)-(d)
(C) (i)-(c), (ii)-(a), (iii)-(b), (iv)-(d)
(D) (i)-(b), (ii)-(a), (iii)-(c), (iv)-(d)

Assertion and Reason Type Questions

In the following questions, a statement of Assertion is followed by a statement of Reason.

(A) If both Assertion and Reason are true, and the Reason is the correct explanation of the Assertion.
(B) If both Assertion and Reason are true, but the Reason is not the correct explanation of the Assertion.
(C) If Assertion is true but Reason is false.
(D) If both Assertion and Reason are false.

1. **Assertion**: Lion and tiger are both carnivores.
Reason: Lion and tiger both eat flesh of other animals.

2. **Assertion:** Spices are essential for health because they have high nutritional value.
Reason: Spices are a good source of carbohydrates.

3. **Assertion**: Plants are known as autotrophs.
Reason: Plants perform photosynthesis.

4. **Assertion**: Animals are called consumers.
Reason: Animals are dependent on plants for their food.

5. **Assertion**: Herbivorous animals have sharp canines.
Reason: Herbivores eat only animal products.

6. **Assertion:** We eat different plant parts as a food.
Reason: Spinach, methi, and bathua are leaves of plants.

7. **Assertion**: Decomposers and scavengers are biological cleaning tools of Nature
Reason: Decomposers and scavengers feed on dead and decaying organic matter of organisms.

8. **Assertion:** Prepared food has different type of ingredients.
Reason: All ingredients of food have their different nutritional value.

9. **Assertion:** Food is essential for health.
Reason: Food gives us energy, growth, and immunity.

10. **Assertion**: Cheese, paneer, and milk are animal products.
Reason: Vegetables & fruits are plant products.

Comprehension Type Questions

Honeybees collect flower juice (sweet juices) from flowers, convert it into sweet liquid and store it in their hive. Flowers and their nectar may be available only for a part of the year, so bees store this nectar for their use all through the year. Honeybees also form different types of other products except sweet liquid which have many commercial values.

1. Give the name of sweet liquid which is formed by bees using nectar.
2. Write down the medicinal value of the product of a beehive.
3. Why do bees store nectar for use throughout the year?
4. How many types of bees are found in a hive?

Free Response Type

Very Short Types Questions

1. Define the term 'food'.
2. What are ingredients?
3. Write down any one difference between autotrophs and heterotrophs.
4. What is germination?
5. Why plants are called producers?
6. Define poultry animals.
7. Define photosynthesis.
8. Which is edible part of radish.
9. Name three plants whose stems are edible.
10. Give examples of foods which are good to eat for blood formation.
11. Name five products we derive from milk.
12. Why do boiled seeds not sprout?
13. Give three examples of milch animals.
14. Name two ingredients which we obtained from neither plant nor animal.
15. What is honey comb?

Short Answer Type Questions

1. Explain the importance of food for living organisms.
2. Why do we eat cooked food?
3. Give 2 examples of plants which have 2 or more edible parts.
4. Give two examples of vegetables which have edible fruit.
5. Name the main ingredient of aalu parantha.
6. Write a short note on milch animals.
7. Mention types of organisms based on their feeding habits.
8. Why are scavengers and decomposers known as natures' cleaners?
9. Can you name some insectivorous plants?
10. Can you give examples of edible seeds which can be eaten raw and are rich in proteins and fats.

Long Answer Type Questions

1. Write down edible parts of following plants- Mustard, potato, okra, apple, coriander, mung, brinjal, sugarcane, beetroot, and mango.
2. Write down short note of the variety of food and apiculture.
3. Why do insectivorous plants eat insects?
4. Define the food chain. How is it important to the environment?

5. Define following terms-
   (a) Omnivore (b) Detritivore
   (c) Ingredients of food (d) Decomposer
   (e) Consumer
6. What is honey? What is its importance?
7. What do you know about vegetarian and non-vegetarian habits.
8. What do you mean by source of food, explain.
9. Write down 4 edible parts of plants with their examples.
10. Why are scavengers essential to the environment?

Case Based Questions

We eat different types of foods on a daily basis. For growth and maintenance of good health, our diet should have all components in a balanced form. This is called a balanced diet. The diet should also contain a good amount of roughage and water for proper digestion of food.

Pulses, groundnut, soyabean, sprouted seeds (moong and Bengal gram), fermented foods (idli, dosa), a combination of cereal (missi roti, thepla), banana, spinach, sattu, jaggery, available vegetables, and other such foods provide many nutrients. These foods have different nutritional value and different food components. Food habits of a particular area depend on atmosphere of that place.

1. Give two examples of energy giving foods which form the main constituent of our daily diet.
2. Give an example of fermented foods and where it is consumed.
3. Find out combination of foods mainly eaten in Gujrat.
   (A) Idli, dosa, parantha, and khaman.
   (B) Khaman, thepla, fafada, with jalebi.
   (C) Dhokla, parantha, thepla, and chas.
   (D) Idli, muthiya, parantha, and khaman
4. Define a balanced diet.
5. Give one example of foods that gives us roughage.

Level 2

Multiple Choice Questions

1. Organisms which can synthesise their own food are known as:
   (A) Saprophyte (B) Autotroph
   (C) Heterotroph (D) Parasite
2. What do we call animals that eat both plants and animals?
   (A) Carnivores (B) Herbivores
   (C) Omnivores (D) Frugivores
3. Nectars are found in
   (A) Leaf (B) Fruits
   (C) Flower (D) Seed
4. Honey bees helps in the conversion of nectar to-
   (A) Pollen grains (B) Egg cell
   (C) Honey (D) None of these
5. Which of the following plants store food in their roots?
   (A) Sweet potato (B) Potato
   (C) Guava (D) Tomato
6. Which part of the tomato plant is eaten as food?
   (A) Flower (B) Root
   (C) Stem (D) Leaves
7. How can you eat mindfully?
   (A) By eating slowly and chewing well
   (B) By eating when you are not hungry
   (C) By skipping meals
   (D) By eating in front of a screen
8. Match the column:

	Column-I	Column-II
(i)	Milk	(a) Mustard
(ii)	Herbivores	(b) Hen
(iii)	Edible leaves	(c) Animal product
(iv)	Honey	(d) Root
(v)	Plants	(e) Plant eating animals
(vi)	Eggs	(f) Autotrophs
(vii)	Sweet potato	(g) Bee
(viii)	Nectar	(h) Flower juice

   (A) (i)-(c), (ii)-(e), (iii)-(g), (iv)-(a), (v)-(f), (vi)-(d), (vii)-(b), (viii)-(h)
   (B) (i)-(b), (ii)-(e), (iii)-(h), (iv)-(g), (v)-(f), (vi)-(c), (vii)-(d), (viii)-(a)
   (C) (i)-(c), (ii)-(e), (iii)-(a), (iv)-(g), (v)-(f), (vi)-(b), (vii)-(d), (viii)-(h)
   (D) (i)-(c), (ii)-(a), (iii)-(e), (iv)-(g), (v)-(b), (vi)-(f), (vii)-(d), (viii)-(h)

9. Match the items given in Column A with that in Column B.

Column-A	Column-B
(i) Milk, curd, and paneer	(a) eat other animals.
(ii) Spinach, carrot	(b) eat plants and plant products.
(iii) Lions and tigers	(c) are vegetables.
(iv) Herbivores	(d) are all animal products.

(A) (i)-(a), (ii)-(c), (iii)-(d), (iv)-(b)
(B) (i)-(d), (ii)-(c), (iii)-(a), (iv)-(b)
(C) (i)-(b), (ii)-(c), (iii)-(a), (iv)-(d)
(D) (i)-(c), (ii)-(d), (iii)-(a), (iv)-(b)

10. The edible parts of mustard plant are-
(A) One only (B) Two only
(C) Two or more (D) None of these

11. Blood sucking animals are called-
(A) Herbivores (B) Carnivores
(C) Scavengers (D) Sanguivores

12. Match the column:

Column-A	Column-B
(i) Herbivores	(a) Amarbel
(ii) Carnivores	(b) Yeast
(iii) Omnivores	(c) Cow
(iv) Saprophytes	(d) Lion
(v) Parasite	(e) Cat

(A) i-a, ii-d, iii-e, iv-b, v-c
(B) i-c, ii-b, iii-e, iv-d, v-a
(C) i-e, ii-d, iii-a, iv-b, v-a
(D) i-c, ii-d, iii-e, iv-b, v-a

13. How many statements are false?
(i) Plants are heterotrophs.
(ii) Lion is an herbivore.
(iii) Fungi is an autotroph.
(iv) Pulses are seeds of a plant.
(v) Tomato is a fruit.
(vi) Beetroot is a stem.
(vii) Crow is an omnivore.
(viii) In a *methi* plant, 3 parts are edible.
(ix) Spinach is an iron rich vegetable.
(x) Potato is a root.
(A) 4 (B) 5
(C) 6 (D) 7

14. Milk giving animals are known as –
(A) Producers (B) Heterotrophs
(C) Herbivores (D) Milch animals

15. Ingredient of food which add flavor on food-
(A) Carbohydrate (B) Protein
(C) Cinnamon (D) Vegetables

16. Given below are three statements (a-c) each with one or two blanks. Select the option which correctly fills up the blanks in two statements.
(a) In cacti, the (i) is thick, fleshy, and green. It carries out photosynthesis.
(b) The male reproductive part of a flower is (i).
(c) The coloured (i) of a flower attract insects for pollination
(A) (a) - (i) Root, (b) - (i) Pistil
(B) (b) - (i) Stamen, (c) - (i) Petals
(C) (a) - (i) Root, (c) - (i) Sepals
(D) (a) - (i) Root, (b) - (i) Stamen

17. Which of the following is incorrect regarding herbs, shrubs, and trees?

	Herbs	Shrubs	Trees
(A)	Tomato	Lemon	Mango, guava
(B)	Usually short	Medium sized	Tall in size
(C)	Plants with hard stem, not very thick	Plants with green and tender stems	Plants with thick brown stem
(D)	Branches are few	Stem branches Out near base	Stem branches out in the upper part

18. Tripti made four sets of different plants based on their edible parts as shown here.

Set	Stem	Root	Leaf	Seed
(I)	Potato	Turnip	Lettuce	Rice
(II)	Turmeric	Ginger	Spinach	Sesame
(III)	Colccasia	Onion	Broccoli	Mustard
(IV)	Ginger	Radish	Cabbage	Almond

Which of these sets are correct?
(A) I and III only
(B) II and IV only
(C) I and II only
(D) I and IV only

19. Read the following statements carefully and find out incorrect statements:
(i) Curd is main constituent of kheer.
(ii) Potato is a rich source of carbohydrate.
(iii) All insects feed on plants.
(iv) Herbivores eat plant products only.
(v) Green vegetables give us minerals.

(A) (i), (ii), and (iii)
(B) (i), (iv), and (v)
(C) (ii), (iv), and (v)
(D) (i), (iii), and (v)

20. Which of following are animal products:
Milk, potato, spinach, honey, paneer, curd, pulse, cereal, fish, and egg.
(A) Milk, honey, spinach, curd, fish, and egg.
(B) Potato, honey, spinach, curd, fish, and egg.
(C) Milk, honey, paneer, curd, fish, and egg.
(D) Milk, honey, potato, curd, fish, and egg.

Higher Order Thinking Skills (HOTS)

1. Read the following statements and select correct options for fill ups-
(i) A Meal eaten during the day is called ________.
(ii) Eating too much of fat rich foods may lead to a condition called ________.
(iii) We get oil from ________.

(A) Breakfast, malnutrition, seed.
(B) Lunch, obesity, leaf.
(C) Lunch, dinner, stem.
(D) Lunch, obesity, seed.

2. Harshit took some dry seeds of moong and soaked them for overnight. He then boiled the seeds and kept them for 24hrs in a wet cloth. After 24 hrs he observed that the seeds did not germinate. Why did the seeds not germinate?
(A) Seeds should not be boiled.
(B) Seeds should not be soaked overnight.
(C) Seeds should be wrapped in a dry cloth.
(D) Everything was ok.

3. Which of the following food has more than two ingredients-
(A) Plain Paratha
(B) Potato paratha
(C) Kheer and halwa
(D) Both B and C

4. Select correct edible plant parts-
(A) Potato-leaf
(B) Tomato-stem
(C) Coriander-leaf
(D) Apple-seed

5. Which of the following group has only autotrophs-
(A) Plant, BGA, and grass.
(B) Plant and earthworm.
(C) Plant, bacteria and virus.
(D) None of the above.

6. Match the plants to what they provide us:

Column-A	Column-B
(a) Oil and Fat	(i) Cabbage
(b) Pulses	(ii) Apple
(c) Vegetables	(iii) Barley
(d) Fruits	(iv) Pea
(e) Cereals or Grains	(v) Mustard

(A) (a)-(iii), (b)-(iv), (c)-(ii), (d)-(v), (e)-(i)
(B) (a)-(i), (b)-(iv), (c)-(ii), (d)-(v), (e)-(iii)
(C) (a)-(iii), (b)-(v), (c)-(ii), (d)-(iv), (e)-(i)
(D) (a)-(v), (b)-(iv), (c)-(i), (d)-(ii), (e)-(iii)

ARCHIVE CORNER

1. Which of the following is an incorrect statement regarding the above given animals?

P

Q

R

(A) P and R are omnivores, while Q is an herbivore.
(B) P and Q are herbivores, while R is an omnivore.
(C) P, Q, and R are carnivores.
(D) All of these

2. Which of the following statements is incorrect for the given food item?

(i) The ingredients used to prepare this food are obtained from both plant and animal sources.
(ii) The major nutrients in this food are carbohydrates and proteins
(iii) This food is also a source of vitamin C.
(iv) The ingredient sourced from plants is actually a seed.

(A) (i) and (ii) (B) (iii) only
(C) (ii) and (iv) (D) None of these

3. We use different parts of different plants as food sources. Refer to the labelled figure of a typical plant and select the option that correctly matches an edible plant part with its example.

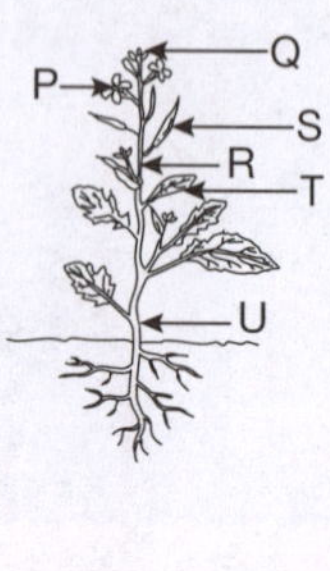

(A) P - Broccoli. Q - Cinnamon
(B) R - Cabbage, S - Chilli
(C) T - Cabbage. U - Spinach
(D) Q - Clove. T – Lettuce

4. Refer to the given figure showing a typical plant with its parts labelled as U, V, W, and X and read the following paragraph.

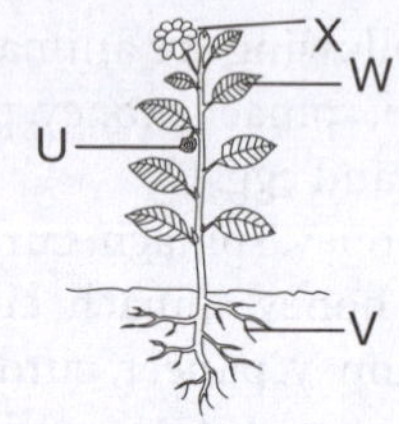

P is a plant where part U is edible, plant Q has edible part W, plant R has edible part X whereas plant S has edible part V.
Select the option that correctly identifies these plants.

	P	Q	R	S
(A)	Clove	Mustard	Cumin	Ginger
(B)	Pomegranate	Rose	Orange	Turmeric
(C)	Spinach	Pomegranate	Clove	Radish
(D)	Cumin	Rose	Spinach	Potato

5. The given relationship is based on eating habits of animals.

Deer → Sparrow → Lion

Which of the following options satisfies the same relationship?
(A) Tiger: Bear: Ant
(B) Cow: Crow: Tiger
(C) Lion: Goat: Leopard
(D) Sheep: Panther: Bear

6. Tripti made four sets of different plants based on their edible parts as shown here.

Set	Stem	Root	Leaf	Seed
(I)	Potato	Turnip	Lettuce	Rice
(II)	Turmeric	Ginger	Spinach	Sesame
(III)	Colccasia	Onion	Broccoli	Mustard
(IV)	Ginger	Radish	Cabbage	Almond

Which of these sets are correct?
(A) I and III only
(B) II and IV only
(C) I and II only
(D) I and IV only

7. Smita set up an apparatus as shown in the given figure. After keeping the apparatus for some time in the Sun, she found that some gas has collected in the top part of the test tube. Which gas could it be?

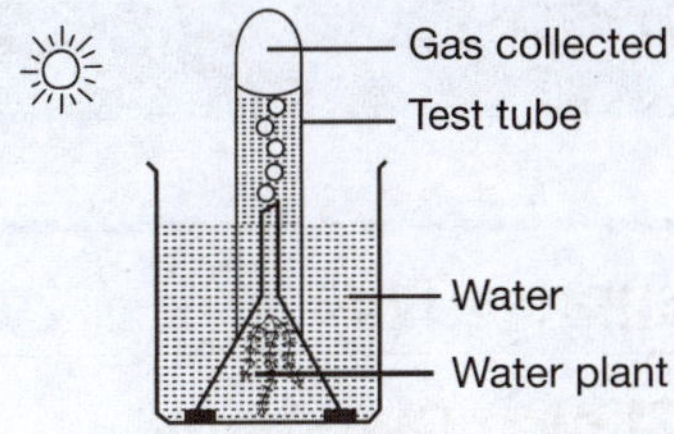

(A) Oxygen (B) Hydrogen
(C) Carbon dioxide (D) Nitrogen

ARCHIVE CORNER

ANSWER KEY

Level 1

Fixed Response Type

Multiple Choice Questions

1. D 2. C 3. C 4. B 5. D 6. D 7. B 8. C 9. A 10. C
11. C 12. C 13. C 14. D 15. C 16. B 17. D 18. C 19. C 20. B
21. A 22. C 23. C 24. A 25. B 26. A 27. D 28. C 29. D 30. C

Fill in the Blanks

1. Scavenger
2. Herbivore
3. Dinner
4. Flower
5. Honey, nectar
6. Decomposers
7. Ingredients
8. Spices
9. Protein
10. Pulses, cereal
11. Rhizobium
12. Vitamin K
13. Protein
14. Fermented food
15. Omnivorous animals as it eats plant products and insects both
16. Honeybees
17. Frugivore animal
18. Scavengers
19. Edible
20. Carbohydrate

True/False

1. False 2. False 3. False 4. False
5. True 6. True 7. False 8. False
9. True 10. True 11. True 12. True
13. True 14. True 15. True

Match Type Questions

1. **A** (i)-(c), (ii)-(d), (iii)-(a), (iv)-(b)
2. **C** (i)-(c), (ii)-(b), (iii)-(d), (iv)-(e), (v)-(a)
3. **B** (i)-(b), (ii)-(d), (iii)-(c), (iv)-(e), (v)-(a)
4. **A** (i)-(c), (ii)-(d), (iii)-(b), (iv)-(e), (v)-(a)
5. **D** (i)-(b), (ii)-(a), (iii)-(c), (iv)-(d)

Assertion and Reason Type Questions

1. A 2. D 3. A 4. A 5. D 6. B 7. A 8. A 9. A 10. B

Level 2

Multiple Choice Questions

1. B 2. C 3. C 4. C 5. A 6. A 7. A 8. C 9. B 10. B
11. D 12. D 13. B 14. D 15. C 16. B 17. C 18. D 19. C 20. C

Higher Order Thinking Skills (HOTS)

1. D 2. A 3. D 4. C 5. A 6. D

Archive Corner

1. D 2. B 3. D 4. A 5. B 6. D 7. A

CHAPTER 12

Components of Food

Learning Outcomes

After reading this chapter, you will be able to:

- discuss the basic components of food.
- recognize the diet needed for an individual for good health.
- identify the process of testing food.
- recognize the diet needed to control deficiency diseases.

Geekspeak

- Meals
- Food habits
- Sources
- Carbohydrates
- Proteins
- Fats
- Vitamins
- Minerals
- Balanced diet
- Deficiency
- Balanced diet

Introduction

In previous chapters we have discussed from where our food comes. We eat different types of food, and they have different nutritional values necessary for our health.

Components of Food

We know that each dish is usually made up of one or more ingredients, which we derive from plants or animals. These ingredients contain some components that are needed for our body. These components are called nutrients. Our food contains mainly five major kinds of nutrients namely—vitamins, minerals, carbohydrates, proteins, and fats (as shown in Fig. 12.1). Additionally, food also contains water and dietary fibres/roughage and water which are also required by our bodies.

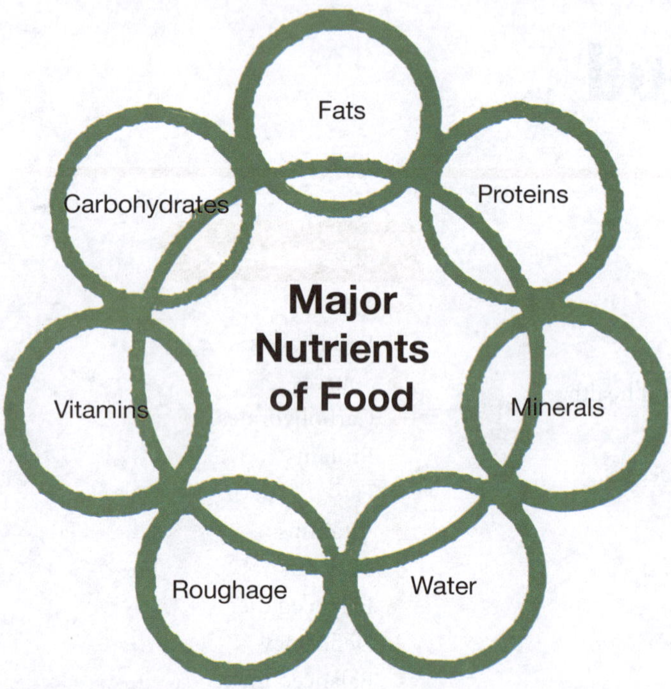

Figure 12.1 Major Nutrients of Food

Keystone

- Coluthur Gopalan (1918-2019) identified the nutritional value of over 500 Indian foods and suggested a diet suitable for India.
- He conducted research on the nutritional status of the Indian population and discovered deficiencies in protein, energy and other nutrients. This led to the implementation of the 'One Day Meal Scheme' in 2002 and now the 'PM POSHAN' initiative to provide equitable food to our government and public school aids.

Carbohydrates

Carbohydrates are the major group of nutrients and form a major part of our diet. Foods containing carbohydrates are known as energy giving foods.

Sources

Cereals and other food items such as bananas, apples, peas, beans, potatoes, vegetables, and dry fruits are food sources of carbohydrates.

Types of Carbohydrates

The types of carbohydrates are discussed as follows:

- **Simple carbohydrates:** These are small units of carbohydrates which are sweet in taste and are soluble in water. They are commonly called Sugars E.g., Glucose, Fructose, Sucrose, Lactose.
- **Complex Carbohydrates:** These are long chain of smaller sugar units. They are tasteless, and insoluble in water. E.g., Starch, cellulose, glycogen, etc.

There are two major types of carbohydrates in food: sugar and starch. Sugars are also called simple carbohydrates. The sources of sugar (are shown in Fig. 12.2).

Figure 12.2 Sources of Sugar

Following are some sources of sugars:

- Table sugar, which is often added to tea, coffee, cold drinks, etc., is made from sugarcane or sugar beet. Table sugar is also called sucrose.
- Sugar found in milk is called lactose.
- Fruits such as apples are natural sources of sugars. Sugar found in most fruit is called fructose.

Note: Though candies and chocolates contain sugars, it is healthier to eat natural sources of sugars such as fruits. This is because fruits also contain vitamins and other important substances that candies do not. Also, eating too many candies and chocolates can be harmful for your teeth!

Keystone

- Due to high sugar content, honey never goes bad.
- Our brain is dependent on only carbohydrates for its proper functioning.

If excess amount of carbohydrates is present in the body, they are converted into fats and stored under the skin, causing obesity.

Functions

They are an important source of energy for our system. One gram of carbohydrate gives nearly 4 kilocalories of energy.

Testing Room 1

Aim: To test the food sample for the presence of carbohydrates/sugars.

Material required: Food sample, water, mortar and pestle, Benedict's solution, burner, and test tube.

Procedure: Take a small piece of food sample in a mortar and make its paste using water. Add 2-3 mL of water to the paste and prepare the extract. Take 1 mL of this extract in a clean test tube and add 2-3 drops of Benedict's solution. Heat the solution. (Do not boil it.)

Observation and conclusion: If red or orange coloured precipitate appears, the given food sample contains sugar.

Testing Room 2

Aim: To test food sample for the presence of starch.

Materials required: Food sample, water, white tile, mortar and pestle, iodine solution, and a dropper.

Procedure: Take a small sample of food item and make its fine paste in a mortar using water. Place a few drops this paste on a clean white tile. Add a few drops of iodine solution with the help of a dropper.

Observation and conclusion: If the paste turns blue-black, the food sample contains starch because starch turns blue-black on coming in contact with iodine.

Proteins

- Proteins are long chain of amino acids which are connected by peptide bonds.The main sources of protein are mung bean, chickpea, red lentils, soya bean, green pea etc. (as shown in Fig. 12.3)
- Pulses and soyabean are plant proteins.
- Meat, fish, egg etc. are animal proteins.
- There are 20 different amino acids which take place in the formation of proteins.
- An adult needs 50-60 gm protein per day.

Cowpea

Green peas

Red lentils

Mung bean

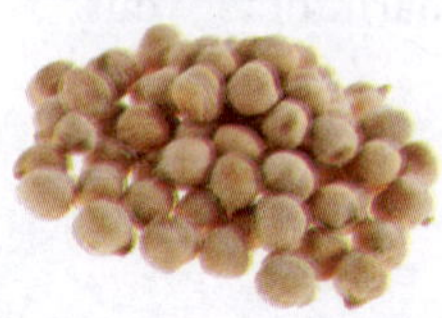

Chickpea

Soya bean

Figure 12.3 Sources of Protein

There are 20 different amino acids which take part in the formation of proteins.

Sources

Pulses, groundnuts, beans, and dry fruits are the sources of plant proteins.
Soyabean is the richest source of protein for vegetarians. Milk, fish, meat, eggs, and cheese are the main sources of animal proteins (as shown in Fig. 12.4).
Our body does not store proteins so protein intake is essential in our daily diet.

Figure 12.4 Sources of Animal Proteins

Functions

- Proteins are called body building units of our body. They form muscles, skin, hair, and nails.
- They are needed for growth and formation of new cells and repairing damaged tissue.
- Our blood contains a protein called haemoglobin which carries oxygen from lungs to the cells.
- When our food does not have sufficient carbohydrates and fats, our bodies burn proteins to provide energy.

Testing Room 3

Aim: To test the food sample for the presence of protein.

Materials required: Food sample, mortar and pestle, water, test tube, dropper, copper sulphate solution, and sodium hydroxide solution.

Procedure: Take a small piece of food item in a mortar. Mash it into a thin paste and add some water to make a suspension. Pour 2 mL of this suspension in a test tube. With a dropper, add two drops of copper sulphate solution and 10 drops of sodium hydroxide solution (caustic soda) to it. Shake the test tube gently and leave for few minutes.

Observation and conclusion: If the solution becomes purple, the given food sample contains protein. If the solution remains blue, the food does not contain protein.

Competition Corner

- BMR: it is defined as the rate at which your body uses energy when you are resting in order to keep vital functions ongoing, such as breathing.
- Basic units of proteins are amino acids. These are of 2 types-
- Essential - They are not made in our bodies and therefore, required with diet.
- Non-essential – They can be made by our bodies.

Fats

Fats is the energy reserved by our body. They store energy for future use.

Sources

They are obtained from both plants and animals.

- Fats of Plant Origin: These are unsaturated fats. They are liquid at room temperature and are called oils. They are considered healthy for human use. Mustard oil, groundnut oil, coconut oil, sunflower oil and other vegetable oils are obtained from plants. Dry fruits like almonds, walnuts, and cashew nuts are also good sources of plant fats.
- Fats of Animal Origin: These are saturated fats. They are solid at room temperature, E.g., butter and ghee. Milk cream, meat, fish, egg-yolk, and cheese are also major sources of animal fats.

Keystone

- Proteins have a short life span.
- It keeps us full for a long time, so in case of weight loss, it is that most favourable food component.

Testing Room 4

Aim: To test the food sample for the presence of fat.

Materials required: Food sample, clean white paper, and a source of light.

Procedure: Rub some crushed pieces of food on a plain white paper. Let it dry, Now, hold the paper against a source of light and look through the spot.

Observation and conclusion: The spot on white paper formed by rubbing the food pieces is oily and light is visible through it. This means fat is present in the food.

Functions of Fats

- Fats are rich sources of energy.
- Fats are stored in our body and are used whenever our body needs extra energy.
- Fat stored under the skin acts as an insulator and prevents loss of heat from the body in cold weather.
- Fats also act as a cushion for the body organs.
- Fats are obtained from both plants and animal sources.

Competition Corner

- The simplest unit of carbohydrates is glucose. All carbohydrates finally break to form glucose. Glucose is carried by our blood to the liver where it is stored in form of glycogen in humans to fulfil our body's energy requirement.
- Fat is deposited in our cell in fat globules and also work as a cushion for protection of organs.
- Sometimes consumption of high fat content in diet becomes harmful for our heart. Extra fat is converted into cholesterol and is deposited in our arteries and causes heart diseases like heart attacks and more.
- An adult requires about 70-80 gm fats/day.

Check Point 1

1. On what basis are macronutrients and micronutrients classified?
2. What are the primary sources of energy in our body?
3. Name the primary sources of fats.
4. What is the basic unit of protein?
5. Why are proteins called the building blocks of our body?

Vitamins

- Vitamins are protective nutrients. They do not provide energy to the body. They are needed in very small quantities.
- Vitamins help in protecting our body against diseases. Vitamins also help in keeping our eyes, bones, teeth, and gums healthy.
- Vitamins are of different kinds known by different names. Some of these are Vitamin A, Vitamin C, Vitamin D, Vitamin E, and Vitamin K. There is also a group of vitamins called Vitamin B-complex. Our body needs all types

of vitamins in small quantities. Vitamin A keeps our skin and eyes healthy. Vitamin C helps body to fight against many diseases. Vitamin D helps our body to use calcium for bones and teeth.

- Vitamins are of two types-
    - **Water-Soluble Vitamins:** Vitamin B and C are soluble in water. They are absorbed in the blood stream and excess amounts are thrown out of the body. These vitamins are not stored in the body. They need to be regularly supplied through food.
    - **Fat-Soluble Vitamins:** Vitamin A, D, E, and K are fat soluble vitamins. These are stored in body fat and are used only when the body needs them.

Sources

The sources of vitamins are discussed in table 12.1.

Table 12.1 Functions of Vitamin and Sources of Food

Vitamin	Functions	Sources of Food
I. Fat-soluble Vitamins		
A	Keeps skin healthy and maintains normal night vision.	Cod-liver oil, egg yolk, milk and dairy products, mangoes, carrots, tomatoes, and green leafy vegetables.
D	Aids in the normal growth of bones in children.	fish, eggs, cod-liver oil, and milk. Sunlight also helps our body to produce vitamin D.
E	Aids in normal reproduction and keeps the skin healthy.	Whole grain cereals, corn, cotton seed oil, milk, meat and egg yolk.
K	Helps in blood clotting.	Green leafy vegetables, tomatoes, sprouts, wheat germ oil, spinach, egg yolk, cabbage, and other green leafy vegetables.
II. Water-soluble Vitamins		
B1	Helps in digestion and maintenance of our nervous system.	Eggs, meat, milk, sprouts, green vegetables, wheat, and whole grains.
B2	Keeps skin and buccal cavity healthy.	Eggs, milk, green leafy vegetables, peas, cherries, and resins.
B6	Essential for normal functioning of our brains.	Yeast, whole grains, fish, meat, and legumes.
B9	Formation and maturation of blood cells.	Green leafy vegetables, fruits, yeast, liver, and kidney.
B12	Helps in the formation of RBCs.	Meat, eggs, fish, and milk.
C	Provides resistance to infections.	Citrus fruits like lemon, orange and lime. Tomatoes, guava, amla, and sprouts.

Functions

- Vitamins help in protecting our body against various diseases.
- They control many metabolic reactions.

Competition Corner

- Vitamin D is also called the sunshine vitamin.
- Most vitamins are not made by our body.
- Vitamin E is also called the beauty vitamin as it has antioxidant properties.

Minerals

- Minerals are also protective nutrients. Our body needs them in small amounts.
- All of them are essential for proper growth and maintenance of good health.
- They are of two types according to their requirement-
    - Macronutrients: Minerals which are needed in large quantities. E.g., Iron, Calcium, Phosphorus, Sulphur, Potassium, Chlorine, Sodium, Magnesium, and Iodine.
    - Micro-minerals: Minerals or trace minerals which are required in very small quantities, E.g., Copper, Zinc, Cobalt, Fluorine, Manganese, etc.

Water

Water is essential for life. About two-thirds of our body weight is made of water.

Sources

Normally, we get most of the water required by our body from the liquids we drink, such as water, milk, tea, etc. All fruits and vegetables also contain large amount of water. Grapes are rich in water content. They contain more than 50 per cent water by weight. Watermelon has the richest water content.

Functions

Water is an essential natural resource that serves numerous purposes for us, such as:

- Water maintains our body temperature.
- It is needed in the excretion of body wastes.
- It acts as a medium for biochemical reactions taking place in the body. It helps in the transportation of nutrients in the body.
- It helps to absorb nutrients from food.

Keystone

- Bananas are potassium rich foods which is healthy for our nervous system.
- Banana peels are very good macro-nutrients for plants. Therefore, they are used as fertilizers.

Roughage

Dietary fibres are also known as roughage. It is mostly provided by plant products like whole grains pulses, fresh fruits, and vegetables. Although it does not provide any nutrients, it is an essential component of our food because it helps in proper digestion. It is advised to eat more roughage in case of constipation.

Roughage helps in easy bowel movement and get rid of the undigested food.

Competition Corner

- Calorific Value of Food. Calorific value is the amount of energy released when 1 gm of a food item is oxidized.
- Requirement of food is different for different persons according to their energy requirements. It depends on following factors-
- Age: Growing children and teenagers need more energy than adults. They are in the developing phase, so they need protein-rich diet for proper growth and development.
- Gender: In general, women need different nutrients compared to men of the same age group.
- Type of work done: A person doing heavy physical work like a labourer, or a rickshaw puller will need more energy than a person sitting on a chair and working. People who do physical work require a carbohydrate rich diet for proper growth and development of their body.

Check Point 2

6. Deficiency of which vitamin causes night blindness?
7. Nausea and dehydration are symptoms of deficiency of which elements?

❖ INTEXT QUESTIONS

1. **Name two types of carbohydrates found in our daily food.**
   Solution: Potato & chapati are good sources of carbohydrates.
2. **Define calorific value.**
   Solution: The amount of energy released when 1 gm of a food item is oxidized in our body is called calorific value.
3. **If we put iodine solution on potato slice then it turns blue-black in colour. Why does this happen?**
   Solution: When iodine reacts with starch it gives blue black colour. When we put iodine solution on a potato slice it reacts with starch and gives a blue-black colour which assures the presence of starch in a potato slice.
4. **Why is iodine essential for body?**
   Solution: Iodine is a mineral which is mainly found in salt. It is essential for proper growth and functioning of the thyroid gland. The thyroid gland secrets the thyroxine hormone which controls our basal metabolic rate (BMR).

Balanced Diet

The food we normally eat in a day is our diet. A balance diet is one which provides proper amount and ratio of carbohydrates, fats, proteins, minerals, vitamins (as shown in Fig. 12.5) which are important for survival of life and help in growth and maintenance of body.

- It varies from person to person depending on age, gender and living style.
- A growing child, a pregnant woman, and a nursing mother need more proteins.
- A labourer and a sportsperson need more carbohydrates and fats.
- An ill person requires more vitamins and minerals to fight against diseases.

Figure 12.5 Components of Balance Diet

Pulses, groundnuts, soyabean, sprouted seeds (moong and Bengal gram), fermented foods (South Indian foods such as idlis), a combination of flours (missi roti, thepla made from cereals and pulses), banana, spinach, sattu, jaggery, available vegetables and other such foods provide many nutrients. Therefore, one can eat a balanced diet without expensive food materials.

Need for a Balanced Diet

- It provides sufficient amount of energy required by our body.
- It provides materials to repair the damaged cells or tissues of the body.
- It provides nutrients required for growth and reproduction.

Cooking of Food

Eating the right kind of food is not enough. It should also be cooked properly so that its nutrients are not lost. Using wrong cooking methods we can cause the loss of their nutritional value, which is not good for our health. If the vegetables and fruits are washed after cutting or peeling them, it may result in the loss of some vitamins. The skins of many vegetables and fruits contain vitamins and minerals. Similarly, repeated washing of rice and pulses may remove some vitamins and minerals present in them. Many useful proteins and considerable amounts of minerals are lost if excess water is used during cooking. Vitamin C gets easily destroyed by heat during cooking. So, vitamin C should not be cooked in any dish. For vitamin C we should use vegetables and fruits in raw form.

Competition Corner

Good nutrition is not just a matter of selecting the right food to eat. It is also important to prepare these food items in the ways that maintain their nutritional benefits. Choose the methods of cooking that retain the flavour, colour, and nutrients of the food items.

- Steam the vegetables instead of boiling them.
- Avoid cooking at high temperatures (quick stir frying) and long cooking time.
- Experiment with a variety of vegetable salads.
- Use whole grain flour for bread and biscuits.

Healthy Eating Practice

- Try more fruit desserts instead of cakes and cookies.
- Choose frozen yoghurt, sherbet and sorbet instead of ice cream.
- Serve cakes with fruits instead of frosting or whipped cream.

Junk Food

- Food items like burgers, chips, fries, pizzas, samosas, pakoras, cold drinks, have very less nutritive value. They also have very high calorie content. Such food items are called junk food.
- Eating junk food on a regular basis leads to obesity.

Deficiency Diseases

A person may be getting enough food to eat, but sometimes the food may not contain a particular nutrient. If this continues over a long period of time, the person may suffer from its deficiency. Intake of this kind of food causes malnutrition. Diseases that occur due to lack of nutrients over a long period of time are called deficiency diseases.

Deficiency of Carbohydrates

Carbohydrate is a main source of energy for our bodies. This energy is used in various functions of our body. Deficiency of carbohydrate in body leads to:

- Weakness.
- Decreased stamina.
- Feeling unhealthy.
- Increased blood sugar levels.
- Feeling dizziness.

Deficiency of Protein

Protein is body builder component of our body. For proper growth it is the most important component of our system.

Kwashiorkor

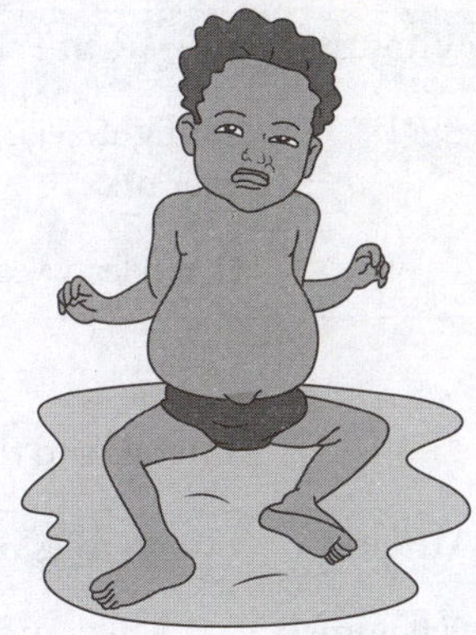
Figure 12.6 Kwashiorkor

Deficiency of proteins leads to a disease called kwashiorkor (as shown in Fig. 12.6). It is common in underdeveloped countries. Its symptoms include:

- Stunted growth.
- Swelling of face and ends of limbs (especially the feet).
- Skin diseases.
- A large pot-like belly.
- Mental retardation, and
- Diarrhoea.

Improving calorie and protein intake may correct kwashiorkor provided that treatment is not started too late. However, full height and growth potential will never be achieved in children who have this condition.

Marasmus

Deficiency of proteins along with carbohydrate deficiency is called Protein Energy Malnutrition (PEM). It leads to marasmus. It is more common among infants and children under five years of age. Its symptoms include:

- Thin physique
- Lack of energy
- Mental retardation
- Poor muscle development
- Slow body growth
- Loss of appetite
- Weak legs
- Poor resistance to diseases

These diseases are more common in rural areas where there is less awareness. To prevent these diseases, the Government of India has started programmes such as the Integrated Child Development Scheme (ICDS) and the mid-day meal scheme in schools.

Deficiency of Different Vitamins and Minerals

Deficiency of different vitamins and minerals may also result in certain diseases or disorders as discussed in Table 12.2 and Table. 12.3.

Table 12.2 Vitamins and their Deficiency Diseases

Vitamin	Sources of Food	Needed For	Deficiency Diseases
A	Carrot, green and yellow vegetables, milk and milk products, and fish liver oil.	Healthy hair, skin, and eyes.	Dryness of hair and skin, and night blindness (difficulty to see in dim light).
B1	Whole grains, liver, cabbage, spinach, yeast, egg and milk	Digestion and functioning of nervous system	Beriberi
B2	Milk, cheese, yeast, cereal, legumes, egg, and liver	Carbohydrates and protein metabolism	Cracking of skin and soreness in the eye
B3	Milk, meat, egg, and lemon.	Functioning of the nervous system.	Pellagra
B12	Liver, kidney, leafy vegetables, meat, egg, milk, and whole grains.	Formation of red blood cells, haemoglobin and functioning of nervous system.	Anaemia
C	Citrus fruits, tomato, gooseberry, and cabbage.	Development of immunity.	Scurvy

(Continued)

Vitamin	Sources of Food	Needed For	Deficiency Diseases
D	Sunlight, egg, fish, and fish liver oil.	Healthy bones and teeth.	Rickets
K	Green leafy vegetables and liver.	Helps in clotting of blood.	Haemorrhage

Table 12.3 Minerals and their Deficiency Diseases

Mineral	Sources of Food	Functions	Deficiency Diseases
Calcium	Milk and milk products, Egg, and green vegetables.	Helps in formation of bones and teeth, clotting of blood, and muscle contraction.	Rickets, weak bones, and excessive bleeding.
Iodine	Iodized salt, bread, and sea food.	Controls physical and mental growth, and the development and synthesis of the hormone, thyroxine.	Goitre
Iron	Meat, liver, egg, and Green leaves.	Formation of blood clotting factor and haemoglobin.	Anaemia
Phosphorus	Egg, meat, sea food, milk products, and potato.	Formation of bones and teeth.	Weak bones and teeth
Potassium	Red meat, egg, and milk products	For proper functioning of the Nervous system.	Improper functioning of nervous system
Sodium	Red meat, egg, and milk products.	Maintaining fluid balance and proper functioning of nerves and muscles.	Nausea, dehydration and fatigue
Sulphur	Onion, garlic, radish, and turnip.	Formation of proteins.	Poor hair and nails

All deficiency diseases can be prevented having a balanced diet.

❖ INTEXT QUESTIONS

5. **Why do you need a balanced diet every day?**
   Solution: The right quantities of essential nutrients are required for a healthy body. Carbohydrates are required in the largest quantity, followed by proteins and then fat. Vitamins and minerals are required in very less quantities. Deficiency of one or more nutrients leads to poor health and makes the body prone to diseases. A diet that contains all essential nutrients required by the body in correct proportions is called a balanced diet. A balanced diet ensures proper functioning of the organ systems, growth and -repair of the body, gives us the ability to do work, and builds immunity.
6. **Write down source function and deficiency diseases of following minerals:**
   (A) Iodine (B) Iron (C) Calcium
   Solution: Deficiency of iodine causes goitre (Malfunctioning of thyroid gland).
   Deficiency of Iron causes anaemia.
   Deficiency of calcium causes rickets.
7. **Name various types of vitamins.**
   Solution: Fat soluble vitamins: Vitamin A, Vitamin D, Vitamin E, Vitamin K. Water soluble vitamins: Vitamin B and Vitamin C.

STRUCTURAL OUTLINE

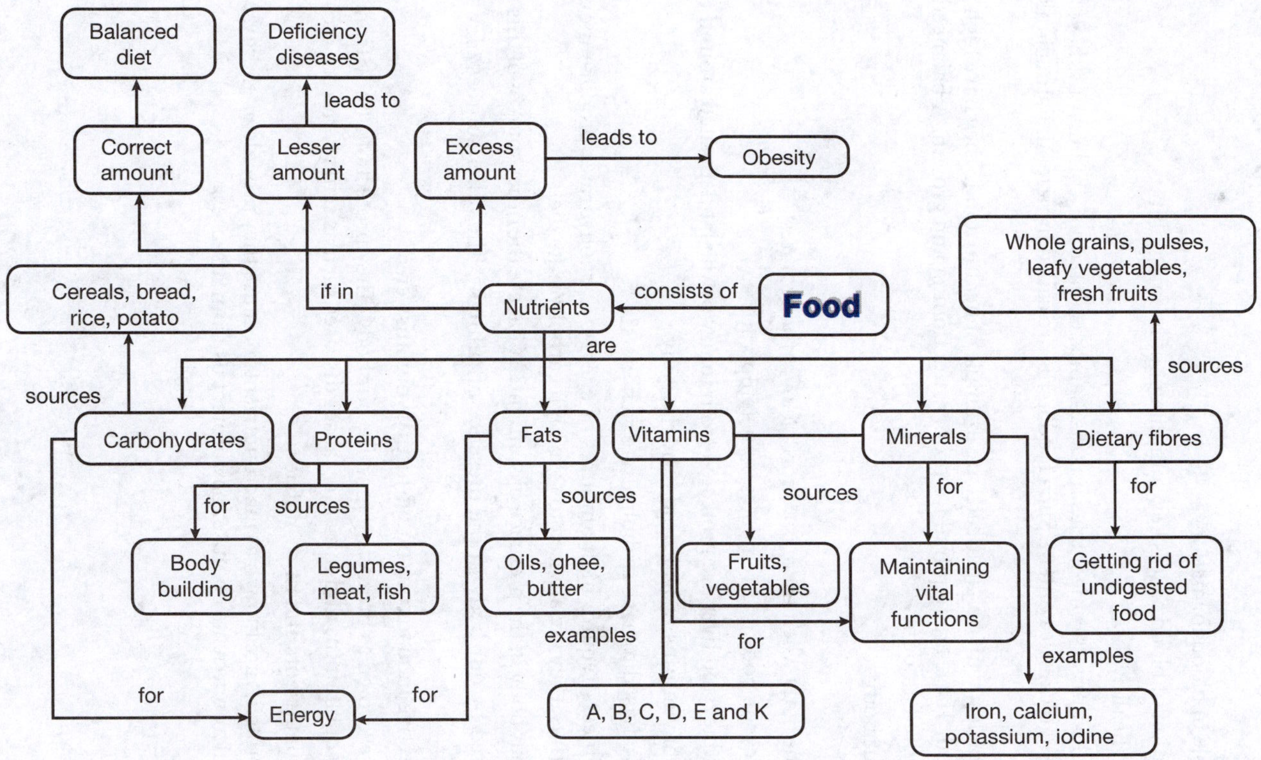

EXEMPLIFICATION

1. What is the role of roughage in our diet?

   Solution: Roughage mainly consists of fibres. All vegetables and fruits are rich sources of fibre. The human digestive system lacks the enzyme required to digest fibre. The importance of roughage in our daily life is:

   - It provides bulk to the food we eat.
   - It helps in the movement of food along the food pipe and intestines and thus, ensures proper bowel movement and prevents constipation.

2. Which mineral plays an essential role in blood formation?

   Solution: Iron is essential for formation of blood as it is key component of haemoglobin.

3. Differentiate between junk food and healthy food.

   Solution: Junk food - Food items like burgers, chips, fries, pizzas, samosas, pakoras, cold drinks, have very less nutritive value. They also have very high calorie content. Such food items are called junk food. Eating junk food on a regular basis leads to obesity.

   Healthy food - Food items like vegetables, fruits, chapati, etc. are example of healthy food. They have high nutritive value and less calories then junk food. These are required for proper functioning and growth. A balanced diet has all good components of food in required amounts.

4. Write down importance of fats in our body.

   Solution: Importance of fats-

   - They act as energy reserves for the body when there is a shortage of carbohydrates.
   - Stored fat under the skin insulates the body and regulates body temperature.
   - Internal organs like stomach, kidney and liver are protected from injury by the fat deposited around them.
   - Fats are required for absorption of vitamins A, D, E, and K by the body.

5. Why are athletes and mountaineers advised to have carbohydrate rich diets?

   Solution: The athletes and mountaineers require high amounts of energy. Carbohydrates produce more energy than proteins and fats in the body. Thus, they are advised to take high carbohydrate diets.

6. Which vitamin can be prepared by our body in the presence of sunlight? What are the other sources of this vitamin?

   Solution: Vitamin D can be prepared by our body in the presence of sunlight. The other sources of Vitamin D are—fish-liver oil, milk, and butter.

7. Which nutrients are known as protective food for our body? Justify your answer.

   Solution: Vitamins and minerals are known as protective food for our body. They protect our body from diseases and make us healthy. The deficiency of vitamins and minerals causes diseases such as scurvy, rickets, etc.

8. Name the various nutrients as macronutrients and micronutrients.

   Solution: Carbohydrates, fats, and proteins are known as macronutrients because they provide us energy. Minerals, vitamins, and water are known as micronutrients because they protect us from diseases.

NCERT COMPENDIUM

1. Name the major nutrients in our food.

Solution: The major nutrients in our food are carbohydrates, proteins, fats, vitamins, minerals, dietary fibres, and water.

2. Name the following:
   (A) The nutrients which mainly give energy to our body.
   (B) The nutrients that are needed for the growth and maintenance of our body.
   (C) A vitamin required for maintaining good eyesight.
   (D) A mineral that is required for keeping our bones healthy.

Solution:

(A) Carbohydrates (B) Proteins
(C) Vitamin A (D) Calcium

3. Name two foods each rich in:
   (A) Fats
   (B) Starch
   (C) Dietary fibre
   (D) Protein

Solution:

(A) Ghee and butter.
(B) Raw potato and rice.
(C) Spinach, cabbage, carrot, or ladies finger (any two).
(D) Milk, egg, fish, meat, or pulses (any two).

4. Tick (✓) the statements that are correct, cross (×) those which are incorrect.
   (A) By eating rice alone we can fulfil the nutritional requirement of our body.
   (B) Deficiency diseases can be prevented by eating a balanced diet.
   (C) Balanced diet for the body should contain a variety of food items.
   (D) Meat alone is sufficient to provide all nutrients to the body.

Solution:

(A) × (B) ✓
(C) ✓ (D) ×

5. Fill in the blanks:
   (A) ________ is caused by deficiency of Vitamin D.
   (B) Deficiency of__________ causes a disease known as beriberi.
   (C) Deficiency of Vitamin C causes a disease known as________________.
   (D) Night blindness is caused due to deficiency of________________ in our food.

Solution:

(A) Rickets (B) Vitamin B_1
(C) Scurvy (D) Vitamin A

NCERT COMPENDIUM

ASSESSMENT CORNER

Level 1

Fixed Response Type

Multiple Choice Questions

1. Soyabean is a:
   (A) Carbohydrate rich food
   (B) Protein rich food
   (C) Fat rich food
   (D) Vitamin rich food

2. Which major nutrient is present in cooked toor *daal*?
   (A) Starch (B) Protein
   (C) Fat (D) None of these

3. Which statement is incorrect?
   (A) Calcium and chlorine is example of protein.
   (B) Carbohydrates are a rich source of energy.
   (C) Protein is a body building food.
   (D) Iron is essential for the formation of haemoglobin.

4. Varun is his school's best Football player, and he is advised to eat food stuffs which give energy. He should eat more of:
   (A) Vitamin & Minerals
   (B) Carbohydrates
   (C) Proteins
   (D) Fibres

5. Fish is a:
   (A) Carbohydrate rich food
   (B) Protein rich food
   (C) Vitamin rich food
   (D) Fat rich food

6. Which component of food is essential for all life processes and helps regulate body temperature?
   (A) Carbohydrates (B) Water
   (C) Fats (D) Vitamins

7. Select correct pairs:
   (A) Crabohydrates-Banana, jowar, wheat and maize
   (B) Protein-Milk,paneer,meat and rice
   (C) Fat-Mil, ghee, oil, mango
   (D) Vitamin-A, B, C, G

8. Foods rich in Carbohydrates are:
   (A) Ghee and butter
   (B) Raw potato and rice
   (C) Cabbage and carrot
   (D) Egg and fish

9. Fruits should be eaten in raw form because:
   (A) They are more effective in their raw form.
   (B) Their taste will change after cooking.
   (C) Vitamins are destroyed after cooking.
   (D) All of the above.

10. Which vegetable is good for blood formation:
    (A) Carrot (B) Spinach
    (C) Tomato (D) Chill

11. By sunbathing we can receive:
    (A) Vitamin A (B) Vitamin B
    (C) Vitamin D (D) Vitamin K

12. Which of the above food items are 'energy giving foods'?
    (I) Wheat (II) Ghee
    (III) Iodised salt (IV) Spinach (Palak)

    (A) (i) and (iv) (B) (ii) and (iv)
    (C) (i) and (ii) (D) (iii) and (iv)

13. Select mismatched pair of following:
    (A) Marasmus-Carbohydrate deficiency disease
    (B) Beriberi-vitamin deficiency disease
    (C) Iodine is essential for the thyroid gland.
    (D) Blood clotting-protein deficiency disease.

14. Which vitamin is produced by our skin in sunlight?
    (A) Vitamin A (B) Vitamin B
    (C) Vitamin C (D) Vitamin D

15. Which mineral is required for the formation of haemoglobin?
    (A) Copper (B) Nitrogen
    (C) Magnesium (D) Iron

16. A person intakes a balanced diet on regular basis which consists of mainly carbohydrates, fats, and proteins. Out of these major components what is the fate of proteins after digestion?
    (A) Stored in form of glycogen.
    (B) Used as building blocks for body.
    (C) Stored beneath the skin.
    (D) Removed from the body by kidneys.

17. Functions of Vitamins are-
    (A) Protecting our body against diseases
    (B) Help in keeping our eyes and bones strong
    (C) Help in keeping our teeth and gums healthy.
    (D) All of these.

18. Which components of diet should be given more to children?
(A) Carbohydrates (B) Minerals
(C) Fats (D) Protein

19. In males infertility occurs due to deficiency of:
(A) Vitamin A (B) Vitamin-E
(C) Vitamin-C (D) Vitamin-D

20. Which of the following is not a nutrient?
(A) Protein (B) Water
(C) Vitamin (D) Oxygen

21. Cellulose is an example of:
(A) Vitamins (B) Fats
(C) Roughage (D) Carbohydrates

22 Tocopherol is also called as:
(A) Vitamin D (B) Vitamin K
(C) Vitamin E (D) Vitamin C

23. Haemoglobin is vital for the transportation of _____ in our blood.
(A) Oxygen (B) Carbon dioxide
(C) Nitrogen (D) Chlorine

24. Which of these nutrients helps keep the body warm and stores energy?
(A) Vitamins (B) Carbohydrates
(C) Fats (D) Water

25. What is the main function of vitamins and minerals?
(A) Provide energy
(B) Build muscles
(C) Help the body fight diseases
(D) Make the body heavy

27. Read following statements and answer
(I) It is example of sugar
(II) It is also called table sugar
(III) It is obtained from sugarcane.
(A) Protein (B) Fat
(C) Sucrose (D) Mineral

28. How many amino acids are essential for protein formation-
(A) 20 (B) 10
(C) 25 (D) 40

29. Which vitamin helps our body to use calcium for strong bones and teeth?
(A) Vitamin E (B) Vitamin D
(C) Vitamin K (D) Vitamin C

30. Lack of which nutrient causes anaemia?
(A) Calcium (B) Iodine
(C) Iron (D) Protein

Fill in the Blanks

1. Deficiency of vitamin k leads to _____________.
2. _____________ is/are rich in animal protein.
3. ________ is stored food in animals
4. ____________ are immunity builders.
5. Vegetables and fruits are rich in ___________ .
6. Cereals are rich sources of ___________.
7. ___________ gives double the amount of energy compared to carbohydrates.
8. Unsaturated fats are___________ at room temperature.
9. Vitamin D is also called as ____________.
10. ___________ is required for synthesis of the hormone, thyroxine.
11. ___________ disease occurs due to vitamin C deficiency.
12. Sugar is obtained from ___________ and ___________
13. Mustard seeds are rich sources of _______.
14. ___________ and ___________ forms a fat molecule.
15. ___________ are rich in proteins.

True/False

1. A balanced diet has all essential components of food.
2. Eating any seasonal fruit makes you healthier.
3. Growing children and teenagers need less proteins than adults.
4. Roughage helps in bowel movement and prevents constipation.
5. Water regulates the body temperature.
6. Junk food has high calorie content.
7. Essential amino acids need to be taken through the diet.
8. Deficiency of vitamin A causes night blindness.
9. Vitamin C is a oil soluble vitamin.
10. High calorie food is good for health.

11. Putting iodine on potato gives it a blue black colour which confirms presence of starch.
12. Anaemia is caused due to calcium deficiency.
13. Goitre is caused due to vitamin B deficiency.
14. Water soluble vitamins are stored in our body.
15. The components of food are called nutrients.
16. Diseases caused due to overeating is a deficiency disease.
17. Vitamin B is responsible for poor vision.
18. Roughage is good source of energy.
19. Onion is a good source of sulphur.
20. Vitamin B_{12} is required for maturation of RBC.

Match Type Questions

1. Match the column and find right answer:

Column-A	Column-B
(i) Carbohydrates	(A) Amino acid
(ii) Proteins	(B) Fatty acid and glycerol
(iii) Fats	(C) Sugar
(iv) Food components	(D) Product of digestion

(A) (i)-(c), (ii)-(d), (iii)-(b), (iv)-(a)
(B) (i)-(b), (ii)-(a), (iii)-(c), (iv)-(d)
(C) (i)-(c), (ii)-(a), (iii)-(b), (iv)-(d)
(D) (i)-(a), (iii)-(c), (ii)-(b), (iv)-(d)

2. Match the column and find the answer:

Column-A	Column-B
(i) Vitamin C	(A) Infertility
(ii) Vitamin E	(B) Scurvy
(iii) Vitamin B_2	(C) Goitre
(iv) Calcium	(D) Cheilosis
(v) Iodine	(E) Bone & tooth decay

(A) (i)-(b), (ii)-(a), (iii)-(d), (iv)-(e), (v)-(c)
(B) (i)-(a), (ii)-(b), (iii)-(d), (iv)-(e), (v)-(c
(C) (i)-(b), (ii)-(c), (iii)-(d), (iv)-(e), (v)-(a)
(D) (i)-(b), (ii)-(a), (iii)-(c), (iv)-(e), (v)-(d)

3. Match the column and find answer:

Column-A	Column-B
(i) Cane sugar	(A) Vitamin D
(ii) Iodine solution	(B) Sucrose
(iii) Calciferol	(C) Vitamin C
(iv) Ascorbic acid	(D) Testing for carbohydrates

(A) (i)-(c), (ii)-(a), (iii)-(b), (iv)-(d)
(B) (i)-(a), (ii)-(b), (iii)-(c), (iv)-(d)
(C) (i)-(b), (ii)-(d), (iii)-(a), (iv)-(c)
(D) (i)-(c), (iii)-(a), (ii)-(d), (iv)-(b)

4.

Column-A	Column-B
(i) Energy giving food	(A) Vitamins and minerals
(ii) Body building food	(B) Iodine
(iii) Protective food	(C) Fats, carbohydrates
(iv) Test for carbohydrate	(D) Copper sulphate and caustic soda

(A) (i)-(a), (ii)-(b), (iii)-(c), (iv)-(d)
(B) (i)-(c), (ii)-(d), (iii)-(a), (iv)-(b)
(C) (i)-(d), (ii)-(b), (iii)-(c), (iv)-(a)
(D) (i)-(a), (ii)-(c), (iii)-(b), (iv)-(d)

Assertion and Reason Type Questions

In the following questions, a statement of Assertion is followed by a statement of Reason.

(A) If both Assertion and Reason are true, and the Reason is the correct explanation of the Assertion.
(B) If both Assertion and Reason are true, but the Reason is not the correct explanation of the Assertion.
(C) If Assertion is true, but Reason is false.
(D) If both Assertion and Reason are false

1. **Assertion:** A balanced diet makes us healthy.
Reason: A balanced diet contains all the components of food in the right proportion.
2. **Assertion:** Protein are body building foods, so they required in high amounts for teenagers.
Reason: Teenagers are growing children. They need a proper diet for proper growth of their bones, muscles, etc.
3. **Assertion:** Junk food is low calorie food.
Reason: These are required for growing children specially.

4. **Assertion:** Vitamin C is a water soluble vitamin and cannot be stored in our body.
Reason: Vitamin C is essential for the development of bones.

5. **Assertion:** Fats are a good source of energy.
Reason: Intake of excess fat is harmful for our heart.

6. **Assertion:** Fruits are rich sources of roughage.
Reason: Roughage is good for proper digestion as they help in elimination of undigested food.

7. **Assertion:** Proteins are made up of amino acids.
Reason: All types of amino acids are synthesized by our body.

8. **Assertion:** Balanced diet has each and every healthy component in the required amount.
Reason: For each person balanced diet is fixed either male or female.

9. **Assertion:** We get all type of proteins from animals only.
Reason: Proteins are a primary source of energy as we get energy from proteins only.

10. **Assertion:** Minerals are obtained from fruits and vegetables.
Reason: Minerals are essential for good health as they perform various functions in our body.

11. **Assertion:** During any wound, clotting of blood is essential to avoid blood loss.
Reason: Vitamin K is essential for blood clotting.

Comprehension Type Questions

Foods containing fats and carbohydrates are also called 'energy giving foods'. Proteins are involved in the formation of body structure, that's why they are called body building foods. Vitamins help in protecting our body against diseases. Vitamins are water soluble and fat soluble. Our body needs all types of vitamins in small quantities. Vitamin A Gives us good vision. Vitamin C helps body to fight against many diseases. Vitamin D helps our body to use calcium for bones and teeth. However, in a given raw material, one particular nutrient may be present in much larger quantity than in others. Therefore, people suggest eating some foods in their raw forms. Besides these nutrients, our body needs dietary fibres and water. Dietary fibres are also known as Roughage. Roughage is mainly provided by fruits, vegetables, whole grains, pulses, etc.

1. Vitamin which keeps our eyes and skin healthy:
(A) Vitamin A (B) Vitamin C
(C) Vitamin E (D) Vitamin D

2. Name the nutrient needed for the growth and repair of the body.
(A) Carbohydrates (B) Roughage
(C) Minerals (D) Proteins

3. Give one word for following statements.
(i) Immunity boosting food
(ii) Instant energy source
(iii) Insulator food
(iv) Simplest sugar

4. What are Roughages?

Free Response Type

Very Short Answer Type Questions

1. Write down protein and carbohydrate deficiency diseases.
2. Why is water important for our body?
3. Name any two sources of Vitamin B.
4. Name the pulse which has maximum protein.
5. Deficiency of which vitamin causes rickets?
6. Which mineral is essential for the proper functioning of our nervous system?
7. Which food is the most energy giving food?
8. Mention 4 names of vitamin C rich food.
9. Name two important minerals and their functions.
10. Which food content is essential for proper digestion of food?
11. Name two immunity increasing food.
12. In which form do animals store their food?
13. Give two examples of vitamin A rich food.
14. Name the vitamin which is essential for the formation of reproductive cells.
15. Fish oil is a rich source of which vitamin?
16. Fruit which has maximum water content.
17. Which disease occurs due to the deficiency of phosphorus?
18. Name the nutrient involved in repairing worn out tissue.
19. Do junk foods contain required nutrients?
20. Name a vitamin that represents a group of vitamins.

21. Give two examples of roughage rich foods.
22. What is anaemia? Which nutrient deficiency causes it?
23. What is another name for vitamin B_1?
24. Name a fat soluble vitamin.
25. Name the two nutrients which protect us from diseases.

Short Answer Type Questions

1. Why water soluble vitamin should take daily according to requirement.
2. What is malnutrition? What are its harmful effects?
3. Can a deficiency disease be an epidemic? If yes, explain.
4. What is the difference between saturated and unsaturated fats?
5. Why are carbohydrates important to us? Name the two types of carbohydrates.
6. Name the main components of food.
7. Differentiate between kwashiorkor and marasmus.
8. Is a balanced diet is same for everyone? Explain.
9. Why is vitamin B_{12} and iron necessary in our diet? What are their roles in our body?
10. Mention the disadvantages of over cooked food.
11. State the scientific name of the following vitamins-
(A) Vitamin A (B) Vitamin C
(C) Vitamin D
12. Why ORS is given to patients those have desentry.
13. What precautions should we take while cooking food?
14. Which kind of food nutrient is available in the following food and what is its role in hair growth?

Long Answer Type Questions

1. What are deficiency diseases? Describe any two diseases caused due to deficiency of proteins.
2. Prepare a diet chart to provide a balanced diet to a twelve year old child. The diet chart should include food items which are not expensive and are commonly available in your area.
3. Write short note on following-
(A) Presence of water in our system.
(B) Functions of fat.
(C) Uses of roughage.
4. Explain the different types of vitamins with their source and diseases caused due to their deficiency.
5. Give brief idea about carbohydrates.
6. Write down role of following mineral and their sources in our daily diet.
(A) Calcium (B) Iodine
(C) Iron (D) Sodium
(E) Potassium
7. Write down the negative impact of excess use of the following foods.
(i) Junk food
(ii) Fatty food
(iii) Carbohydrates

Case Based Questions

The tests for the presence of carbohydrates, proteins, and fats are simpler to do as compared to the tests for other nutrients. Their presence can be determined by special types of tests. Take a small quantity of a food item or a raw ingredient. Put 2-3 drops of dilute Iodine solution on it. Observe if there is any change in the colour of the food item. A blue-black colour shows presence of starch.

To test the presence of proteins in food we need to take a small quantity of a food sample item. If you take a solid sample, then grind it to make paste/powder. Put some of this in a clean test tube, add 10 drops of water to it and shake the test tube. Now add two drops of copper sulphate solution and ten drops of caustic soda solution to the test tube. Shake well and let the test tube stand for a few minutes. You will see that the contents of the test tube will turn violet. A violet colour indicates presence of proteins in the food item.

For fats, take a small quantity of the food item. Wrap it in a piece of paper and crush it. Take care that the paper does not tear. Now straighten the paper and observe it carefully. If you see an oily patch on paper, it proves that the food item contains fat.

1. Which colour indicates the presence of starch in food items?

2. We put drops of copper sulphate solution to test the presence of-
(A) Glucose (B) Starch
(C) Vitamin (D) Protein

3. If the colour of the food item turns blue-black, then it contains fat.
(A) False (B) True

4. Solutions of Copper sulphate and caustic soda are used to test the presence of which nutrient? Write down the process to test this nutrient.

Level 2

Multiple Choice Questions

1. Identify X
(i) X is necessary for immunity
(ii) Found in citrus fruits
(iii) Destroy during cooking
(A) Vitamin D (B) Vitamin A
(C) Vitamin C (D) Vitamin K

2. Eating excess amount of fat deposits in blood vessels and causes:
(A) Liver disease (B) Heart disease
(C) Kidney disease (D) None of these

3. Read following statements and select the correct options for 1&2.
(i) It is an animal product and contributes to a balanced diet.
(ii) It is rich in fibre and has high nutritional value.
(A) Mango and wheat (B) Milk and apple
(C) Maize and fat (D) Cheese and paneer

4. During the digestion of various components of food, carbohydrates are eventually broken down into ___A___ , and proteins into ___B___. A and B are respectively.
(A) Fructose, Amino acids
(B) Sucrose, Fatty acids
(C) Glucose, Amino acids
(D) Amino acids, Glucose

5. Which of the following are good sources of vitamin and minerals
Egg, curd, pulse, fruit juice, onion, yogurt, cheese
(A) Milk, meat, soyabean and grains
(B) Egg, curd, pilse and fruit juice
(C) Broccoli, fruits, carrot, and spinach
(D) Onion, yogurt, cheese and pulses

6. Examine the following statements.
(A) Iron is necessary for the human body and is abundantly found in green vegetables.
(B) Zinc is one of the essential trace elements required for the human body.
(C) Fats and minerals are not the essential nutrients for a balanced diet of humans.
(D) The foods that generate energy in the body after complete oxidation are in the form of carbohydrates, fats, and proteins.

Which one of the following statements is wrong?
(A) A (B) B
(C) C (D) D

7. Which one of the following statements is wrong?
(A) Quinine an anti-malarial drug is obtained from the plant cinchona.
(B) Pulses are rich sources of starch and minerals.
(C) Sunflower is a good source of vegetable oil.
(D) Green vegetables are good sources of vitamins and minerals.

8. Iron helps our body by:
(A) Making bones strong
(B) Improving eyesight
(C) Forming red blood cells
(D) Making us grow tall

9. Select the correct one:

	Mineral	Source	Disease
(A)	Iodine	Spinach	Goitre
(B)	Iron	Green Vegetables	Anaemia
(C)	Calcium	Milk	Night Blindness
(D)	Sodium	Water	Beriberi

10. Read the statements and select the correct option:
(i) Required in very less amounts.
(ii) It is found in whole cereals and fish.
(iii) It is required for proper functioning of the digestive system.
(iv) Its deficiency causes pellagra.
(A) Vitamin K (B) Vitamin B_3
(C) Vitamin D (D) Vitamin C

ASSESSMENT CORNER

11. What do we call a diet that contains all nutrients in the right amounts?
(A) Junk food (B) Balanced diet
(C) Rich diet (D) Energy diet

12. Galactose is an example of
(A) Fat (B) Protein
(C) vitamin (D) carbohydrate

13. In case of low BP which mineral should be provided to patient?
(A) Sodium (B) Sulphur
(C) Potassium (D) Iron

14. Which of these is important but not considered a nutrient?
(A) Fibre (Roughage) (B) Carbohydrate
(C) Protein (D) Fat

15. PME disease is:
(A) Marasmus (B) Kwoshiokore
(C) Anaemia (D) Goitre

16. Fish oil is a rich source of:
(A) Vitamin K (B) Vitamin B3
(C) Vitamin D (D) Vitamin A

17. Haemorrhage occurs due to deficiency of:
(A) Vitamin D (B) Vitamin B_3
(C) Vitamin K (D) Vitamin C

18. If a person is facing hair growth then which mineral should he increase in diet-
(A) Sodium (B) Sulphur
(C) Potassium (D) Zinc

19. Immunity booster vitamin is:
(A) Vitamin D (B) Vitamin B_3
(C) Vitamin K (D) Vitamin C

20. Butter is a good source of:
(A) Vitamin K (B) Vitamin B_3
(C) Vitamin D (D) Vitamin C

Higher Order Thinking Skills (HOTS)

1. Read the given paragraph and select the correct option for P, Q, R, and S. P occurs in children due to deficiency of proteins. Deficiency of Q makes a person lose stamina and get tired easily. R occurs in children due to deficiency of proteins and calories. Deficiency of S causes tooth decay.
(A) P-Kwashiorkor, Q-Calcium, R-Marasmus, S-iodine
(B) P-Marasmus, Q-Iron, R-Kwashiorkor, S-Iodine
(C) P-Kwashiorkor, Q-Iron, R-Marasmus, S-Fluorine
(D) P-Marasmus, Q-Calcium, R-Kwashiorkor, S-Fluorine

2. Given below are four food components (P-S) and their corresponding sources.
P- Meat, fish, and eggs.
Q- Butter, ghee, and margarine.
R- Bread, biscuits, and potatoes.
S- Amla, tomato, and orange.
Select the incorrect statement regarding these.
(A) Deficiency of P causes marasmus in children and kwashiorkor only in adults.
(B) Among P, Q, R, and S, 1 gram of Q produces the maximum energy.
(C) Excess R gets stored in body cells and is used for production of energy whenever required.
(D) Deficiency of S leads to a disease in which gums swell up and bleed.

3. Read the given paragraph.
In the 16th and 17th centuries, sailors who went on long voyages suffered from a disease 'X' as they did not get fresh fruits to eat during the voyage. In the year 1747, a doctor named James Lind discovered that if these sailors were given lemons and oranges, the disease was cured very quickly. This led to the discovery that X is a deficiency disease caused by the deficiency of Y. Identify X and Y in the above paragraph and select the correct option.

X	Y
(i) Pellagra	(A) Vitamin B_1
(ii) Scurvy	(B) Vitamin C
(iii) Goitre	(C) Iodine
(iv) Rickets	(D) Fluorine

4. Refer to the given flow chart

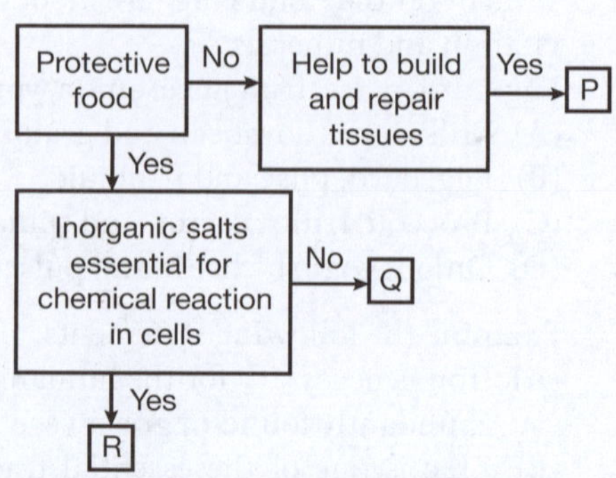

Identify P, Q, and R and select the correct option regarding it.

(A) Deficiency of P can lead to diseases like kwashiorkor and marasmus.
(B) If Q is water soluble then it is not stored in body but if it is fat soluble, it can be stored in body for later use.
(C) Deficiency of R can lead to diseases like anaemia, goitre, rickets, etc.
(D) All of these.

5. Two friends Rohan and Ravi visited a general physician for their respective diseases. Doctor examined them and prepared a chart as shown below to keep a record of their illness.

Name of the Patient	Symptoms of Disease	Treatment
Rohan	Spongy and bleeding gums	Intake of citrus fruits and *amla*
Ravi	Body fatigue, paleness of face and nails	Intake of green leafy vegetables (like spinach) and red meat

Refer to the given chart and select the correct option regarding this.
(A) Rohan is suffering from deficiency of a fat soluble vitamin which helps in formation of bones and teeth.
(B) Ravi is suffering from deficiency of a mineral that is required for formation of haemoglobin that carries oxygen from lungs to body cells.
(C) Rohan is suffering from deficiency of a mineral that also increases immunity against various diseases.
(D) None of these.

6. Refer to the given dichotomous key and select the correct option regarding P, Q, R, and S.
(i) (a) It is a vitamin deficiency disease. – Go to II
(b) It is a mineral deficiency disease. – Go to III
(ii) (a) It is characterized by bleeding gums and aching joints. – P
(b) It is characterised by red rashes, scaly lesions on skin, diarrhoea, etc. – Q
(iii) (a) It affects haemoglobin formation in blood. – R
(b) It affects many metabolic processes of the body and is often characterised by prominent swelling in the neck region. – S

(A) P is caused by vitamin C deficiency whereas Q is caused by vitamin E deficiency.
(B) P is scurvy, Q is pellagra, R is anaemia, and S is goitre.
(C) Person suffering from R should take iodised salt and more of citrus fruits.
(D) Diseases P and Q occur in children only whereas diseases R and S occur only in adults

7. Refer to the given flow chart and select the correct option regarding P, Q, R, and S.

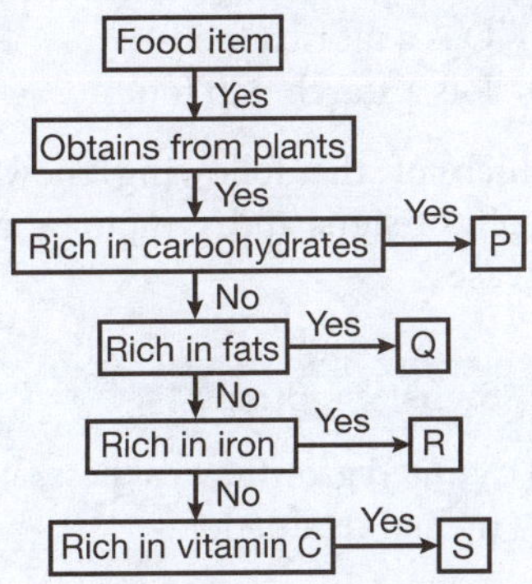

(A) P could be honey or sugarcane whereas Q could be soyabean or maize.
(B) R should be taken in large quantities by patients suffering from goitre.
(C) Deficiency of S leads to bleeding gums and swelling of joints.
(D) Q should be taken in large quantities by patients suffering from kwashiorkor.

8. Maximum amount of vitamin C is found in
(A) Lemon (B) Orange
(C) Amla (D) None

9. Which of the following statements is/are incorrect?
(i) Fats deposited in our body act as shock absorbers and protect us from injury.
(ii) Kwashiorkor is caused by deficiency of proteins, carbohydrates, and fats.
(iii) Roughage neither releases energy nor helps in tissue or body building.
(iv) Starch containing items turns bluish black in colour on undergoing the iodine test.
(A) (i) and (ii) only
(B) (ii) only
(C) (iii) only
(D) (ii) and (iv) only

ARCHIVE CORNER

ARCHIVE CORNER

1. Jahnvi made a paste of two food items—P and Q each. She put them in two test tubes. She added dilute iodine solution to food item P, while copper sulphate solution and caustic soda to food item Q. She observes that P turned blue-black, and Q turned purple.
Which of the following is correct regarding this?
(A) Q is a starch rich food.
(B) P is a protein rich food.
(C) Q is a fat rich food.
(D) P is a starch rich food.

2. Which of the following shows the incorrect match of signs and symptoms of the respective diseases?

Signs/Symptoms	Diseases
(A) Stunted growth, weakness, and mental retardation.	Marasmus
(B) Pale skin, laziness, and weakness.	Anaemia
(C) Bleeding gums and wounds take time to heal.	Scurvy
(D) Brittle bones and bow shaped legs in children.	Rickets

3. The given food items shown in the figure are rich in nutrient X.

Read the given statements regarding X.
(i) 1 gram of X gives 4 calories of energy.
(ii) It helps in protecting our body against diseases.
(iii) Deficiency of X results in diseases such as kwashiorkor and marasmus.
(iv) Test for X is done using Benedict's solution.

Which of the above given statements are correct?
(A) (i) and (iv) (B) (i), (iii), and (iv)
(C) (ii) and (iii) (D) (i) and (ii)

4. Which one of the following is a correct pair of the deficiency disease and its deficient nutrient?

Deficiency Disease	Deficient Nutrient
(A) Scurvy	Vitamin D
(B) Rickets	Vitamin B3
(C) Goitre	Iron
(D) Night blindness	Vitamin A

5. Read the following passage carefully.
P is found abundantly in cod liver oil and is important for visual efficiency. Q is sourced from amla. Tomato and citrus fruits and its deficiency may cause wounds to take longer time for healing. R is formed in our body in presence of sunlight and its deficiency in toddlers may cause deformity of legs.
Now select the incorrect option regarding this.
(A) P can be found in spinach but not R.
(B) In absence of R our body will show calcium deficiency even if it is abundant in our food.
(C) Q is also called B complex as many of its varieties are available.
(D) P cannot be dissolved in water.

6. Rohit's father experienced a heart attack. The doctor told him that his blood vessels have become narrower. What could be the reason for this?
(A) His diet has an excess of roughage and water.
(B) His diet lacks the required amounts of vitamins and minerals.
(C) His diet has an excess of fats and carbohydrates.
(D) His diet lacks required amounts of proteins and carbohydrates

7. Read the given paragraph.
Our food consists of carbohydrates, proteins, fats, vitamins, and P. Carbohydrates may be simple like Q or complex like R. Proteins if deficient in diet can lead to S in children below 1 year of age. P are abundantly present in fruit peels, whole grains, and add bulk to undigested food, easing bowel movements.
Select the correct option regarding this.
(A) P can either be minerals or roughage.
(B) Q can be any of the glucose, fructose, and cellulose.
(C) R can be starch or glycogen
(D) S is pellagra. A deficiency disease of proteins.

8. Which food items from the given choices should be included in our diet to protect us from bleeding gums?
(A) Cheese (B) Yeast
(C) Amla (D) Wheat

9. Match column I with column II and select the correct option from the given codes.

Column-I	Column-II
(A) Iron	(i) Beriberi
(B) Vitamin B1	(ii) Anaemia
(C) Vitamin C	(iii) Scurvy
(D) Vitamin D	(iv) Goitre
(E) Iodine	(v) Rickets

(A) a - (ii), b - (i), c - (iii), d - (v), e - (iv)
(B) a - (i), b - (iii), c - (iv), d - (v), e - (ii)
(C) a - (iii), b - (ii), c - (iv), d - (v), e - (i)
(D) a - (iv), b - (i), c - (v), d - (iii), e - (ii)

10. Following are the properties of four minerals P, Q, R, and S. Identify them and select the correct option regarding them.
P: It is required for proper functioning of the thyroid gland.
Q: It helps in maintaining the body's water balance.
R: It is important for haemoglobin formation.
S: It strengthens bones and teeth and helps in blood clotting.
(A) Deficiency of P causes dryness of eyes and inflammation of the tongue.
(B) Q is also required for the proper functioning of the nervous system.
(C) Deficiency of R causes goitre.
(D) S also helps to fight infections and keeps the skin and mouth healthy.

11. Observe the given experimental figures carefully. What does this experiment prove?

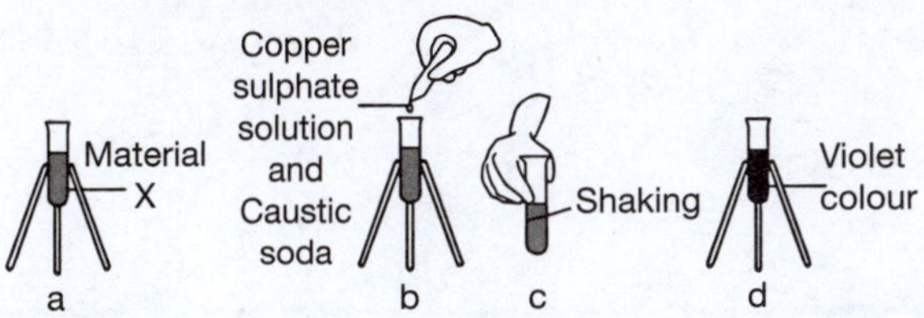

(A) Material X contains proteins.
(B) Material X contains carbohydrates.
(C) Material X contains fats.
(D) Material X contains Vitamin D.

12. Read the given paragraph.
Our food consists of carbohydrates, proteins, fats, vitamins and P. Carbohydrates contain carbon, hydrogen and Q. Proteins if deficient in diet can lead to R in children below 1 year of age. Deficiency of vitamin A can lead to S.
Select the incorrect statement regarding P, Q, R, and S.
(A) P can either be minerals or roughage.
(B) Q is oxygen.
(C) S can be night blindness.
(D) R is pellagra.

13. Saurabh's younger brother Harshit is 3 years old. He is having difficulty in walking due to deformity in his legs as shown. He always complains about body pain. Which of the following can be the reason for it?

(A) His diet is deficient in vitamin C and K due to which his body absorbs excess amount of calcium and phosphorus present in food.
(B) His diet is deficient in vitamin D due to which his body is not able to absorb sufficient amount of calcium and phosphorus present in food.
(C) Major part of his diet is milk and green vegetables.
(D) None of these.

ANSWER KEY

Level 1

Fixed Response Type

Multiple Choice Questions

1. B	2. B	3. A	4. B	5. B	6. B	7. A	8. B	9. C	10. B
11. C	12. C	13. D	14. D	15. D	16. B	17. D	18. D	19. B	20. D
21. C	22. C	23. A	24. C	25. C	26. C	27. C	28. A	29. B	30. C

Fill in the Blanks

1. Delayed blood clotting	2. Meat	3. Glycogen
4. Vitamins	5. Vitamins and minerals	6. Carbohydrates
7. Fats	8. Liquid	9. Sunshine vitamin
10. Iodine	11. Scurvy	12. Sugarcane, beetroot
13. Oil	14. Glycerol, fatty acids	15. Pulses

True/False

1. True	2. True	3. False	4. True
5. True	6. True	7. True	8. True
9. False	10. False	11. True	12. False
13. False	14. False	15. True	16. False
17. False	18. False	19. True	20. True

Match Type Questions

1. C 2. A 3. C 4. B

Assertion and Reason Type Question

1. A 2. A 3. D 4. C 5. B 6. A 7. C 8. C 9. D 10. A
11. A

Comprehension Type Question

1. A 2. D

Level 2

Multiple Choice Questions

1. C	2. B	3. B	4. C	5. C	6. C	7. B	8. C	9. B	10. B
11. B	12. D	13. A	14. A	15. A	16. C	17. C	18. D	19. D	20. C

ANSWER KEY

Higher Order Thinking Skills (HOTS)

1. C **2.** A **3.** B **4.** B **5.** B **6.** B **7.** C **8.** C **9.** B

Archive Corner

1. D **2.** C **3.** B **4.** D **5.** C **6.** C **7.** C **8.** C **9.** A **10.** B
11. A **12.** D **13.** B

Part 2: Diversity in Living Beings and Living Creatures

CHAPTER 13

Getting to Know Plants

Learning Outcomes

After reading this chapter, you will be able to:

- classify the types of plants.
- classify the types of roots.
- explain structure of flower
- discuss the arrangement of veins in leaves.
- explain transpiration.
- explain photosynthesis.

Geekspeak

- Herbs
- Shrubs
- Lamina
- Petiole
- Creeper
- Climber
- Venation
- Midrib
- Transpiration
- Pollination
- Annual rings

Introduction

We are surrounded by plants of different sizes and shapes, which means that plants are all around us. They are living organisms that grow in specific areas. They synthesise food/glucose with the help of water, CO_2, Sunlight, and chlorophyll.

Some plants are so small which cannot be seen by the naked eye, while some trees are very large in size.

Types of Plants

All plants which are found around us can be classified on the basis of the size, shape, etc in following types:

Herbs

- Plants which have soft, green, and destructible stems are called herbs.
- They are generally smaller in size and are almost one meter long in length (as shown in Fig. 13.1).
- They may not have many branches.
- They may live only for 1-2 seasons. Examples: grass, wheat, maize, mint, and mustard. etc.

(a) Mustard

(b) Dahlia

Figure 13.1 Examples of Herbs

Testing Room 1

Look closely at the stem and branches of:

1. Plants much smaller than you.
2. Plants that are about your size, and
3. Plants much taller than you.

Feel their stem and try to bend them gently to see if they are tender or hard.

Shrubs

- These plants have woody stems with branches. Branches develop near the base of the stem.
- They are medium-sized plants which look like bushes.
- The stem is hard but not very thick (as shown in Fig. 13.2).

- They survive for many years, though less than trees.

Example: Hibiscus, Croton, Pomegranate, Jasmine, etc.

(a) Lemon

(b) Rose

Figure 13.2 Examples of Shrubs

Trees

- The trees are very tall and have hard woody stems called trunks.
- They have woody branches, twigs, and leaves.
- Branches arise at some distance above the ground.
- They generally survive for many years. e.g., Banyan, Neem, Mango, Teak, and Oak etc.

Keystone

- Coconut and palm, both are trees but they do not have branches (as shown in Fig. 13.3).
- In India, the oldest tree is a banyan tree which is located in Acharya Jagdish Chandra Bose Botanical Garden in Howrah (Kolkata). It is 700 years old.

Mango

Neem

Coconut

Palm

Figure 13.3 Examples of Trees

Creeper

Plants with weak stems that cannot stand upright and spread on the ground are called creepers. They do not climb up even with the help of support because they have generally heavy fruits (as shown in Fig. 13.4).

Watermelon

Pumpkin

Figure 13.4 Examples of Creeper

Climber

Plants with weak stems which take support on neighbouring structures and climb up are called climbers. E.g., Betel, Grape, Money plants, Beans, etc.

Competition Corner

- Forests are known as the lungs of nature.
- Tropical forests (like the Amazon Forest) have maximum plant diversity on Earth.
- Insectivores plants also perform photosynthesis, but they eat insects to fulfil their nitrogen requirement.
- Some plants complete their life cycle in one season. They are known as annual plants eg Rice,mustard etc

Check Point 1

1. What do you mean by annual plant, biennial plant, and perennial plants?
2. Which are main grains those eat worldwide?
3. Is money plant is creeper or climber and how does it propagate?

Flowering Plants

Developed plants majorly divided into two types:

1. **Non-flowering Plants:** They do not have flowers and fruits. E.g., Pine and Cycas trees.
2. **Flowering Plants:** They have flowers and fruits. Maximum number of plants found around us are flowering plants.

Parts of Flowering Plants

A plant has different parts to perform various functions. These parts are divided into the root system and the shoot system (as shown in Fig. 13.5). The part of a plant that remains under the soil is called the root system. This part of a plant has a number of roots.

The green part of a plant that grows above the ground is called the shoot system. This part of a plant has stem, leaves, buds, flowers, and fruits.

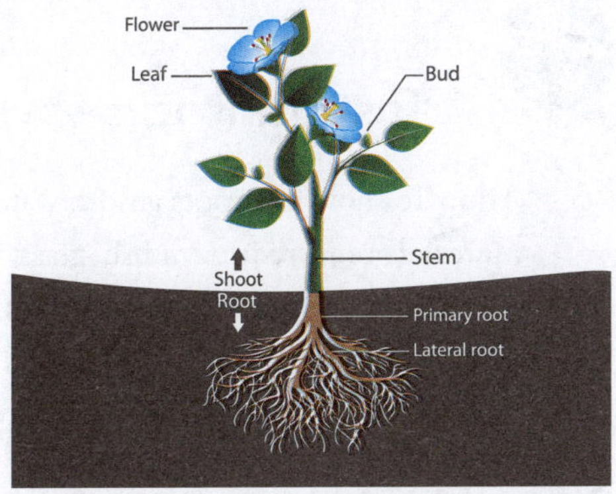

Figure 13.5 Parts of Flowering Plant

Root System

The root system is the underground, nongreen part of a plant. It consists of primary root and its Branches (as shown in Fig. 13.6). The root is a very important component of the plant system. Without the presence of roots the plant cannot survive.

Roots have following features:

- Root develops a part of seed called radicle.
- It has branches called primary, secondary, and tertiary roots.
- It does not have nodes and internodes.
- It grows towards soil and water, and away from sunlight.

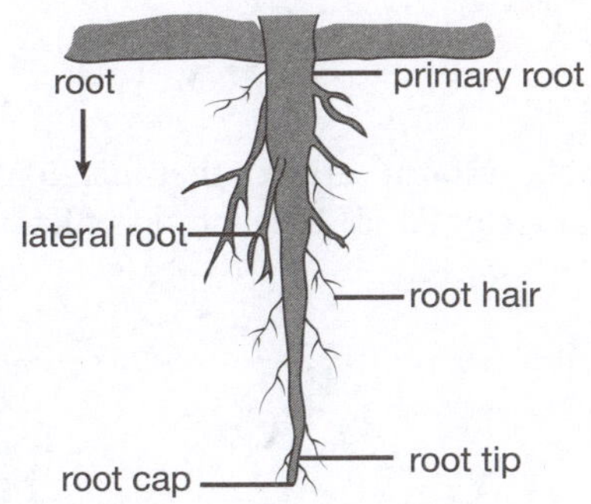

Figure 13.6 Root System

Types of roots: The types of roots are discussed as follows:

- **Tap root:** The main root which is originated from the radicle is called taproot and the smaller roots that grow with this are called lateral roots [as shown in Fig. 13.7 (a)]. Taproot is found in dicot plants. For example—Mustard, Gram, Bean, Pea, Mango, Carrot, Radish, etc.
- **Fibrous root:** In this type of root, the primary root is short lived, so a main root does not exist. All the branches arise from the base of stem and spread out in the soil [as shown in Fig. 13.7 (b)]. Fibrous roots are found in monocot plants. For example— Maize, Wheat, Rice, Barley, Grasses, etc.

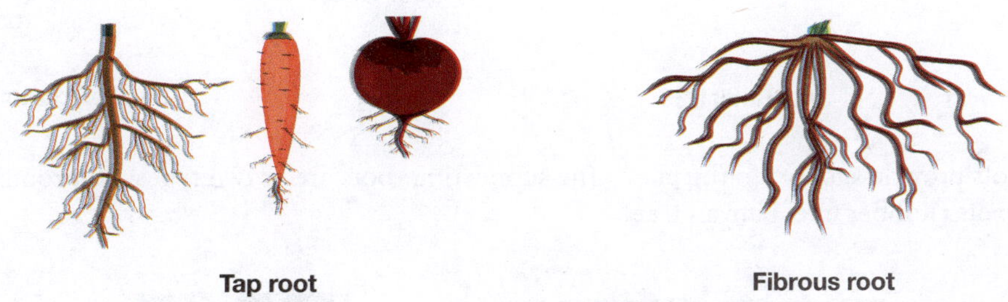

Figure 13.7 Tap Root and Fibrous Root

Functions of root:

- Roots are involved in absorbing minerals and water from the soil and transferring them to the stem.
- Another important function of roots is to firmly anchor the plant in the ground.
- Roots also perform the function of storing important nutrients and food for growth.
- In some plants, roots perform the special function of storing food. Such roots can be seen in a carrot, radish, and sweet potato.
- They bind with soil particles together and prevent them from soil erosion.

Testing Room 2

Aim: To show that roots absorb water

Materials required: A radish, glass, water, red colouring, and a knife.

Procedure: Take a radish. Place it in a glass containing red coloured water.

Leave the set-up for a day. Next day, take the radish out and cut it lengthwise.

Observation: The red colour has spread throughout the radish and red coloured tubes appear extending all along the length of the radish.

Conclusion: The red colour shows the passage of water through the radish. So, it can be concluded that roots absorb water

Competition Corner

Roots perform various other functions except above-

Storage of Food: The taproots of Radish, Turnip, Beetroot, and Carrot store food. So, they are swollen and fleshy.

Carrot

Radish

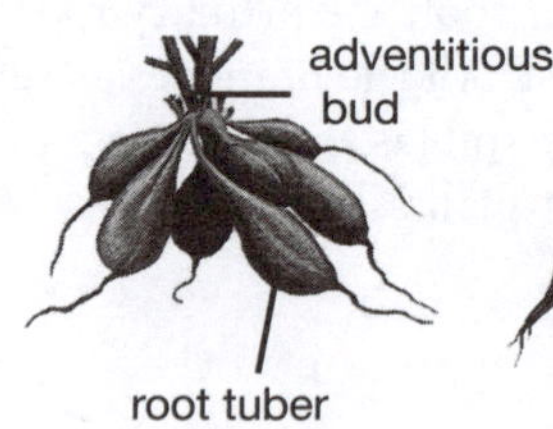

Dahlia

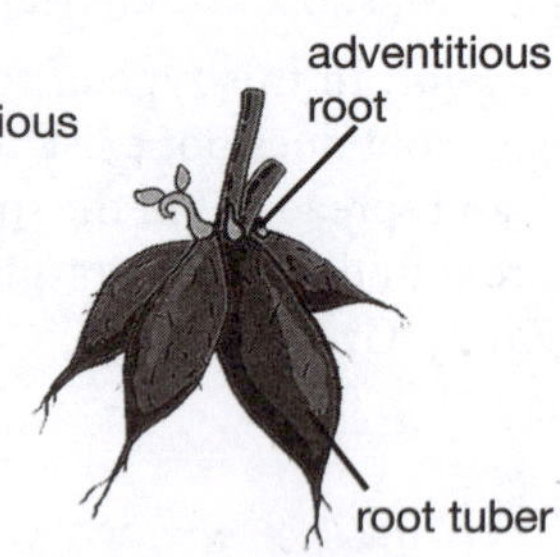

Sweet Potato

Support: Some roots provide support to the plant. The supporting roots are of two types: Stilt roots (E.g., Bamboo, Maize) and Prop roots (Rubber tree, Banyan tree).

Stilt and Prop Root

Keystone

- Pneumatophores are special kind of roots of mangrove plants which participate in gaseous exchange.
- Trapa and Tinospora have aerial roots which have chlorophyll and perform photosynthesis. These kind of roots are called assimilatory roots.
- Some climber like money plant, betal, Ivy etc have climbing/clinging roots for support.

Pneumatophores

Testing Room 3

Aim: To show that roots anchor the plant in soil

Materials required: A pot, garden soil, gram seeds and water.

Procedure: Take a pot filled with garden soil. Place a few gram seeds in it. Water it daily for about a week. After a week, when seeds grow, try to pull out a seedling from the pot. How much force did you need to pull it out? Keep the pot for another week. The seedlings grow into small plants. Now, try to pull a plant from the pot.

How much force did you need to pull the plant out this time?

Observation: More force is needed to pull out the plant second time. This is because the root of the grown up plant is bigger than the root of seedling and has grown deep in the pot.

Conclusion: It is concluded that roots anchor the plant firmly in the soil.

❖ INTEXT QUESTIONS

1. **Define seedling.**
   Solution: A small baby plant grow is called a seedling.
2. **Name the part of a seed that forms the root and shoot in a seedling.**
   Solution: Plumule of seed forms the stem of seedling and radicle forms the root of seedling.
3. **Give 2 examples of herbs, shrubs, and trees.**
   Solution: Herbs- Grass and wheat; Shrubs - Hibiscus and Croton; Trees - Mango and palm.

Check Point 2

4. Why do desert plants have relatively longer roots?
5. What are adventitious roots?
6. What is the white part seen coming out of sprouts?

Shoot System

The part of the plant above the ground is called the shoot system. The Stem is the part of a plant which is responsible for supplying water to all parts of the plant. It is the stem which bears branches, flowers, leaves, fruits, and buds. The root sucks the water and minerals from the soil, and it is the stem's function to push this water upward to other parts of the plant.

Parts of Shoot System

Shoot system consists of stem, leaf and flower. The parts of shoot system are discussed in detail as follows:

Stem

The stem is the main axis of the shoot system. It is green in herbaceous plants but woody and hard in shrubs and trees. The stem of tree is called the trunk.

Stem has following features-

- It has nodes and internodes. New branches and leaves are originate from nodes.
- Stem grows towards light and away from the soil and water.
- Stem bears leaves, branches, buds, flowers, and fruits (as shown in Fig. 13.8).
- Young stems are green but older and woody stems are non-green and hard.
- It provides support to the leaves and exposes them to sunlight.
- It keeps the plant upright.

Figure 13.8 Shoot System

Testing Room 4

Aim: To show that water is conducted through stem.

Materials required: A glass, water, red ink, and a twig with white flower.

Procedure: Take a glass and fill one-third of it with water. Add a few drops of red ink in it and stir well. Now, cut a twig obliquely from a plant having a white flower (like Petunia or Balsam) and put it in the glass. Leave the set-up overnight. Carefully observe the next morning.

Observation: Petals of flower and veins of the leaves have become red.

Conclusion: This shows that red-coloured water has travelled up through the stem into leaves and flowers. The Thin, red-coloured lines are xylem vessels through which water travels from roots to different parts of the shoot.

Balsam stem

Functions of Stem

- It supports all aerial parts of the plant like branches, fruits, flowers, etc.
- It transports water, minerals, and food to all plant parts.
- It bears flowers which gives us fruits.
- In some plants, the stem stores food (as shown in Fig. 13.9).
- In some plants they provide support in form of tendrils (as shown in Fig. 13.10).

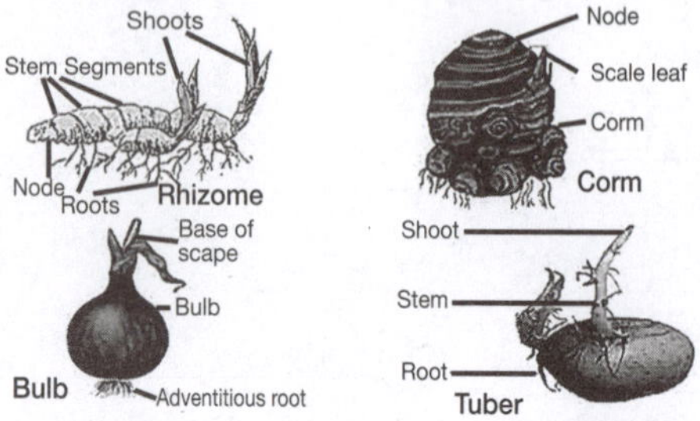

Figure 13.9 Storage of Food by Stem

Figure 13.10 **Support from Tendrils**

Competition Corner

- Transportation of food, water, and minerals in plants is called conduction.
- In stem 2 types of plant tissue are found –
  (i) **Xylem**-it transports water and minerals
  (ii) **Phloem**-It transports food.
- In desert plants, the stem stores water to save the plant in adverse conditions.
- In cacti, it becomes green and performs photosynthesis.

Check Point 3

7. Do stems have pores for gaseous exchange?
8. Give two examples of desert plants.
9. Is sweet potato a stem or a root?

Leaf

- These are also called food factory of plant.
- Different plants have different kinds of leaves which vary in size, shape, colour, texture, and other features.
- Leaves differ from plant to plant (as shown in Fig. 13.11).
- Leaf has following parts-
- **Petiole:** The parts of a leaf by which it is attached to the stem is called petiole.
- **Lamina:** The broad green part of the leaf is called lamina.
- **Midrib:** A thick vein in the middle of the leaf is called the midrib.
- **Veins:** Lines on the leaf are called veins.
- Veins are arranged in different forms in different plants, this arrangement is called leaf venation.
- **Reticulate venation:** If arrangement of veins in a leaf is net like on both sides of midrib the venation called Reticulate.Examples: Leaves of rose mango, etc.
- **Parallel venation:** If veins are arranged parallel to one another in a leaf then venation is called parallel venation. Examples: leaves of wheat, grasses, etc.

Figure 13.11 Parts of Leaf and Leaf Venation

Functions of Leaf

- **Food factory of plants** - Leaves have green pigment called chlorophyll. It absorbs sunlight. Leaves perform photosynthesis in the presence of sunlight, chlorophyll, water, and carbon dioxide.
- **Gaseous exchange** -Small tiny pores means stomata are found in leaves those are involved in gaseous exchange in plants, for photosynthesizes and respiration (as shown in Fig. 13.12).

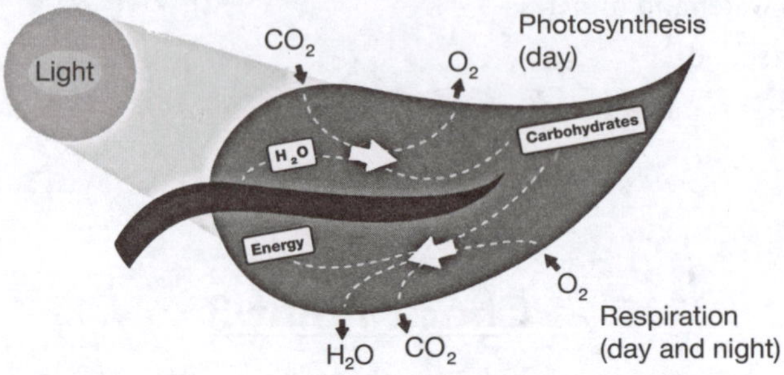

Figure 13.12 Gaseous Exchange by Leaf

- **Transpiration**-Removal of excess amount of water from leaves is called transpiration. It is necessary for absorption of water by roots (as shown in Fig. 13.13).

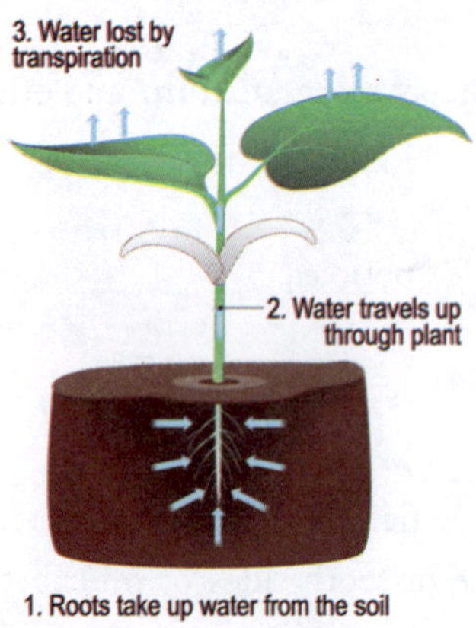

Figure 13.13 Transpiration

Keystone

Giant water lily plants have the largest leaves.
Sometimes plants store their waste products in leaves.
The big banyan tree in Indian botanical garden Kolkata has more than 900 prop roots.It is oldest banyan tree

Testing Room 5

Aim: To check transpiration by leaf

Procedure: Select two or more leaves on the lower branches of a tree or any other plant. Lie a transparent colourless polythene bag on the two leaves and leave it for few days.

Observation: We can see water droplets on inner surface of polythene.

Conclusion: Leaves transpire, and water droplets accumulating on the inner surface of the polythene confirms this.

Competition Corner

- Sometimes leaves are converted into spring like structures and provide support to plants in climbing.
- In cactus leaves are modified into spines to reduce transpiration, as cacti is desert plants.
- In insectivores plants leaves are modified to capture insects.
- In bryophyllum and begonia leaves, they have some bud like structures from which new plant grows.

Venus Fly Trap

Pitcher Plant

Bud at Leaf Notches for Reproduction

❖ INTEXT QUESTIONS

4. **Why leaf is called kitchen of plant?**
Solution: Generally leaves are green in colour, and they have green pigment that is chlorophyll. In the presence of sunlight and chlorophyll leaves perform photosynthesis and synthesise food that is glucose.
5. **What is mid rib why it is important for leaves.**
Solution: Centre thick rib in the leaf is called mid rib. It keeps the leaf in an upright position against strong winds.

Flower

Flower is a modified stem of plant. It is sexual part of the plant meant for reproduction.
The structure of a flower is shown in Fig. 13.14.

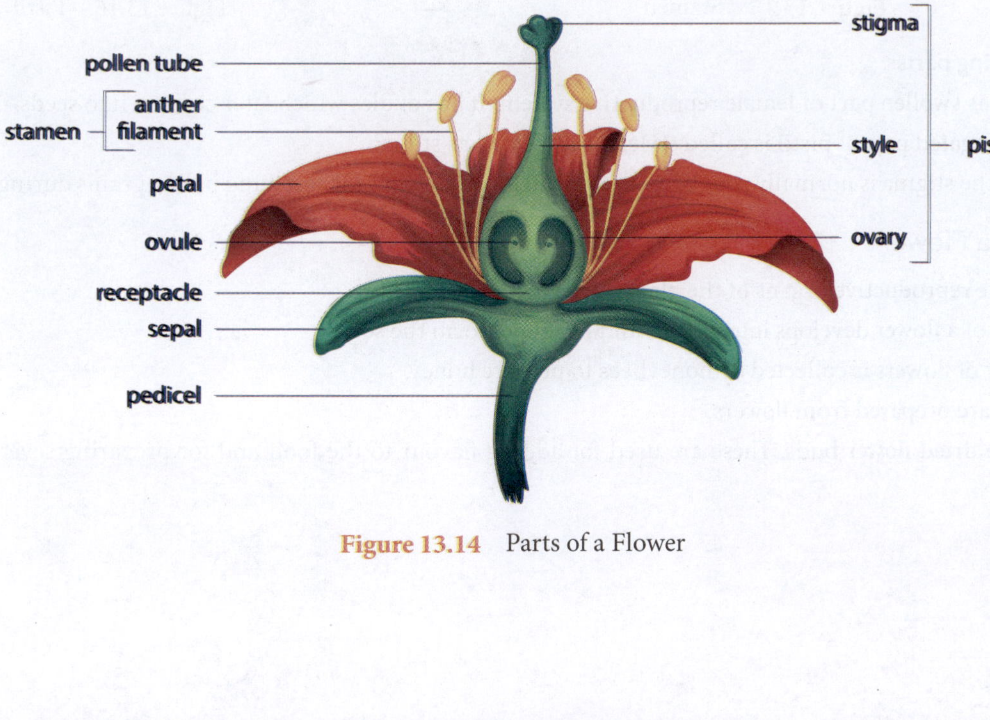

Figure 13.14 Parts of a Flower

- **Pedicel and Thalamus:**
  - Pedicel is a structure by which flower is connected with stem.
  - Thalamus is base swollen part of flower at which flower is situated.
- **Calyx:**
  - It is the First outermost whorl of a Flower.
  - It consists of a leaf like structures called sepals.
  - Sepals are generally green in colour and manufacture food.
  - They also protect the new delicate inner parts of the flower during the bud stage.
- **Corolla:**
  - It is the second whorl of a flower.
  - Each segment of the corolla is known as a petal.
  - Petals are usually brightly coloured due to the presence of pigments.
  - The bright colour, sweet smell, and nectar attract the insect which in turn, help in pollination.
- **Androecium/ stamen/ male reproductive organ:** It is the third floral whorl which is composed of one or more male reproductive organs called stamen (as shown in Fig. 13.15).
- **Gynoecium/ pistil/ female reproductive organ:** It is located in the centre of flower.

The gynoecium is the fourth whorl which is composed of one or more carpels. The freely occurring units of the carpels in a flower are called pistils (as shown in Fig. 13.16).

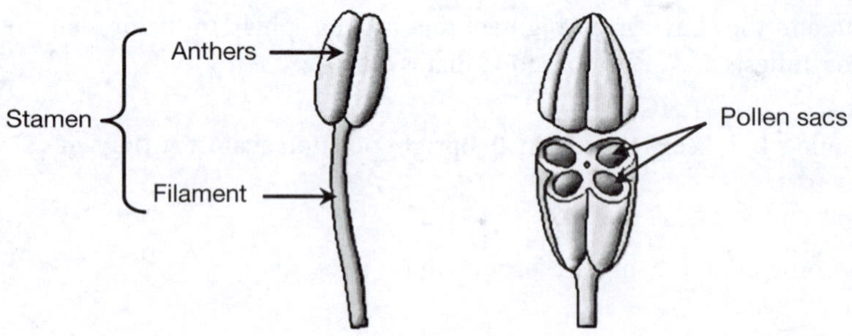

Figure 13.15 Stamen

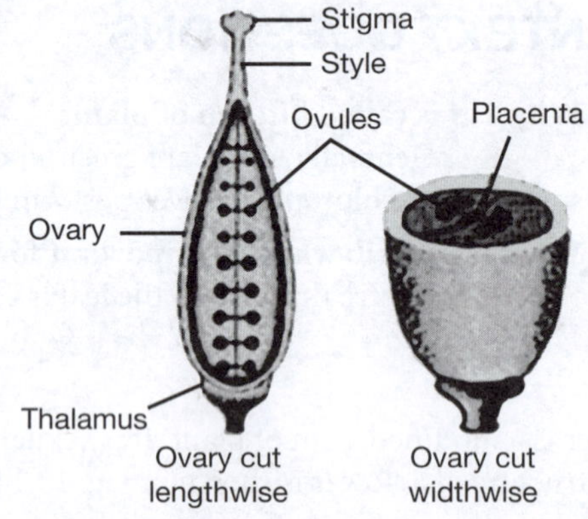

Figure 13.16 Pistil

Pistil has following parts:

- **Ovary** - It is swollen part of female reproductive system. It has ovules which later convert into seeds.
- **Style** - Elongated part of pistil is called style. It's top part has stigma.
- **Stigma** - The stigma is normally rough, hairy, and sticky. It is meant for receiving pollen grains during pollination.

Functions of a Flower

- Flowers are reproductive organs of the plant.
- The ovary of a flower develops into a fruit, and its ovules form the seeds.
- The nectar of flowers is collected by honeybees to prepare honey.
- Perfumes are prepared from flowers.
- Cloves are dried flower buds. These are used for adding flavour to the food and for preparing several ayurvedic medicines.

Competition Corner

- **Pollination:** process of transfer of pollen grains from anther to stigma is called pollination.
- There are two types of pollination.
  - **Self-pollination:** when the pollen grain is transferred from anther to stigma of the same flower.
  - **Cross pollination:** when the pollen grain is transferred from anther to stigma of the different flower.

- **Fertilization:** Fertilization is a process of fusion of male gamete with the female gamete.

The pollen grain contains two male gametes.

After fertilization, ovule changes into a seed and the ovary will change into the fruit.

❖ INTEXT QUESTIONS

6. Define photosynthesis. Write down its equation.

Solution: A process by which plants synthesis their food with the help of water and CO_2 in the presence of sunlight and chlorophyll.

$$6CO_2 + 12H_2O \xrightarrow[Plant]{Light} C_6H_{12}O_6 + 6O_2 + 6H_2O$$

7. What do you mean by bisexual and unisexual flower?

Solution: Unisexual flower - A flower which has only a male or female reproductive system is called unisexual flower. Bisexual flower - A flower which has both, a male and female reproductive system in single flower is called a bisexual flower.

8. What is the role of the stamen in a flower?

Solution: Stamen is the male reproductive part of flower which has an anther at its top region. In the anther, a male reproductive cell, pollen grain is formed.

Check Point 4

10. Do birds also transfer pollens?

11. What are unisexual and bisexual flowers?

12. Can a flower contain more than one carpel?

STRUCTURAL OUTLINE

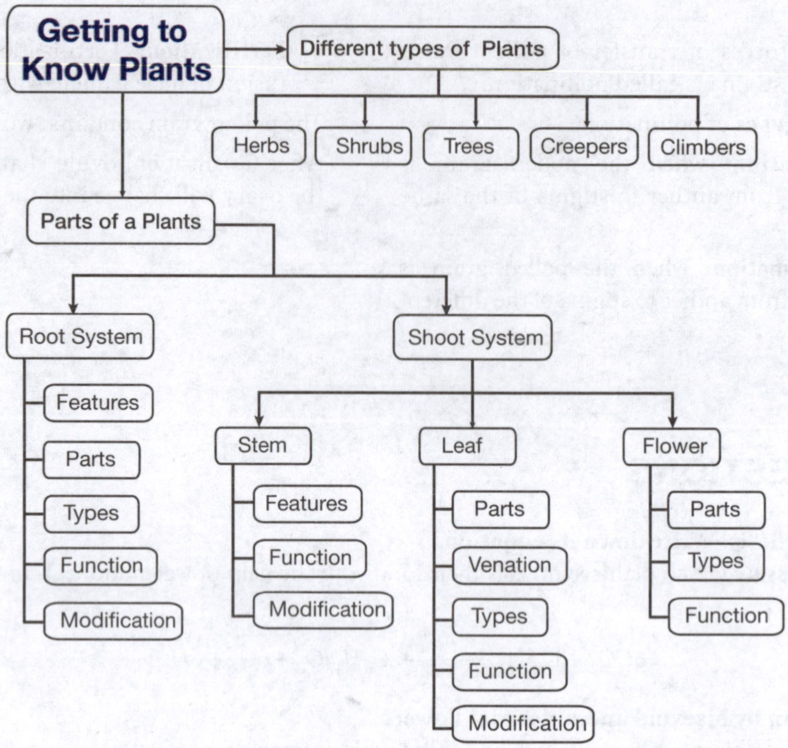

ABRIDGEMENT

- The plants that have flowers are called flowering plants. Most of the flowering plants reproduce by sexual reproduction method involving the fusion of sex cells called gametes. This means that two sexes (male and female) are involved in reproduction in flowering plants.
- Flowers are the reproductive parts of a plant. The reproductive organs (or sex organs) of a plant are in its flowers. In other words, flowers contain the sexual reproductive organs of a plant. In most of the plants, the same flower contains the male organ as well as the female organ.
- The function of a flower is to produce male and female gametes, and to ensure that fertilization takes place to make the seed for growing new plants.
- In other words, flowers perform the function of reproduction in plants by producing seeds of the plant. Thus, flowers are for sexual reproduction in plants.

EXEMPLIFICATION

1. **Define climber and creeper.**

   Solution: Plants with weak stems which take support on neighbouring structures and climb up are called climbers. E.g., betel, grape, money plants, beans, etc.

   Plants with weak stems that cannot stand upright and spread on the ground are called creepers, e.g., sweet potato, pumpkin, watermelon, bottle gourd, and bitter gourd.

2. **Write down difference between tap and fibrous root system.**

   Solution:

   - **Tap root:** The main root which is originated from the radicle is called taproot and the smaller roots that grow with this are called lateral roots.

     Taproot is found in dicot plants, for example Mustard, Gram, Bean, Pea, Mango , Carrot, Radish, etc.
   - **Fibrous root:** In this type of root, the primary root is short lived, so a main root does not exist. All the branches arise from the base of stem and spread out in the soil. Fibrous roots are found in monocot plants. For example—Maize, Wheat, Rice, Barley, Grasses, etc.

3. **What is corolla and how does it help in reproduction of plants.**

   Solution: The corolla is the colourful and fragrance filled part of a flower. It attracts insects for pollination.

4. **What is the role of sunlight in photosynthesis.**

   Solution: Due to the Sun, chlorophyll becomes active and synthesises glucose through photosynthesis.

5. **Explain the activity which shows presence of starch in leaves.**

   Solution:

   - Aim: To test a leaf for the presence of starch
   - Materials Required: Leaf, water, iodine solution and a dropper.
   - Procedure: Take green fresh leaf, boil it in water so the cells of the leaf become softer. Add a few drops of iodine solution with the help of a dropper.
   - Observation and conclusion: If the leaf turns into blue-black, the leaf contains starch because starch turns blue-black on coming in contact with iodine.

6. **How do veins of a leaf help plants?**

   Solution: Veins help in the transportation of water and food. It also provides the support to the leaf.

7. **Discuss the path of transportation of food and water in the plant.**

   Solution: The food is prepared by the green parts of plant (mainly leaves). Thus, the food transports from leaf to the other parts of a plant. The water is absorbed by the roots of plant from the soil. Thus, the water transports from roots to the other parts of a plant.

8. **What are the agents of a pollination in a flowering plant?**

   Solution: Pollination in a flowering plant can be done by wind, water, insects, birds, butterfly, bees, etc.

9. **Which of the following is not an example of stem? Give reason.**

   Ginger, Potato, Carrot, Cactus, Grapevine.

   Solution: Carrot is not an example of a stem because it is a root which stores food and appears swollen and fleshy.

10. **Distinguish between shrubs and trees on the basis of nature of stem.**

    Solution: The stems of shrubs are hard and woody, and the branches arises just above the ground. Whereas, stems of trees are called trunks and their branches arises high up on the stem.

NCERT COMPENDIUM

1. Correct the following statements and rewrite them in your notebook.
(a) Stem absorbs water and minerals from the soil.
(b) Leaves hold the plant upright.
(c) Roots conduct water to the leaves.
(d) The number of sepals and petals in a flower is always equal.
(e) If the sepals of a flower are joined together, its petals are also joined together.
(f) If the petals of a flower are joined together, then the pistil is joined to the petal.
Solution:
(a) Roots absorb water and minerals from the soil.
(b) Roots hold the plant upright.
(c) Stem conducts water to the leaves.
(d) The number of petals and sepals in a flower is usually equal.
(e) If the sepals of a flower are joined together, its petals are not necessarily joined together.
(f) If the petals of a flower are joined together, then the pistil is not necessarily joined to the petal.

2. Draw (a) a leaf, (b) a taproot and fibrous root (c) a flower, you have studied.
Solution:
(a) For Leaf: Refer to Fig. 13.11 on page no. _____
(b) A Taproot and fibrous root: Refer to Fig. 13.7 on page no. ______
(c) A Flower: Refer to Fig. 13.15 on page no. ______

3. Can you find a plant in your house or in your neighbourhood which has a long but a weak stem? State its name. How would you classify it?
Solution: Yes, we found a money plant in our house. It is a climber.

4. What is the function of a stem in a plant?
Solution: A stem performs following functions:
(i) The stem and its branches holds leaves to get maximum sunlight.
(ii) It transports water from roots to different parts of the plant.
(iii) It transports food from leaves to different parts of the plant.
(iv) It bears leaves, flowers, and fruits.

5. Which of the following leaves have reticulate venation? Wheat, Tulsi, Maize, Grass, Coriander (dhania), China rose.
Solution: **Tulsi, China rose.**

6. If a plant has a fibrous root, what type of venation are its leaves likely to have?
Solution: Parallel venation.

7. If a plant has leaves with reticulate venation, what kind of roots will it have?
Solution: Tap root.

8. Is it possible for you to recognise the leaves without seeing them? How?
Solution: We cannot exactly recognise the leaves without seeing them. We may be able to have some idea by touching and smelling them.

9. Write the names of the parts of a flower in sequence, from outside to inside.
Solution: The names of various parts of a flower from outside to inside are:
(i) Sepals
(ii) Petals
(iii) Stamens
(iv) Pistil

10. Which of the following plants have you seen? Of those that you have seen, which one have flowers? Grass, maize, wheat, chilli, tomato, tulsi, pipal, shisham, banyan, mango, jamun, guava, pomegranate, papaya, banana, lemon, sugarcane, potato, and groundnut.
Solution:

S. No.	Name of the Plant	Whether Seen	Whether Have Flowers
1.	Grass	Yes	Yes
2.	Maize	Yes	Yes
3.	Wheat	Yes	Yes
4.	Chilli	Yes	Yes
5.	Tomato	Yes	Yes
6.	Tulsi	Yes	Yes
7.	Pipal	Yes	Yes
8.	Shisham	Yes	Yes
9.	Banyan	Yes	Yes
10.	Mango	Yes	Yes
11.	Jamun	Yes	Yes

(*Continued*)

S. No.	Name of the Plant	Whether Seen	Whether Have Flowers
12.	Guava	Yes	Yes
13.	Pomegrenate	Yes	Yes
14.	Papaya	Yes	Yes
15.	Banana	Yes	Yes
16.	Lemon	Yes	Yes
17.	Sugarcane	Yes	Yes
18.	Potato	Yes	Yes
19.	Groundnut	Yes	Yes

11. Name the part of the plant which produces its food. Name this process.

Solution: Leaves produce food for the plant. This process is called photosynthesis.

12. In which part of a flower you are likely to find the ovary?

Solution: We find ovary in pistil. It is the lowermost part of the pistil.

13. Name two flowers, each with joined and separates sepals.

Solution: Flowers with joined sepals:
(i) Datura
(ii) Loki

Flowers with separate sepals:
(i) Gurhal
(ii) Mustard

ASSESSMENT CORNER

Level 1

Fixed Response Type

Multiple Choice Questions

1. Structure from which new branches originate:
(A) Node (B) Trunk
(C) Scale (D) Internode

2. Which of these trees do not contain branches:
(A) Coconut (B) Apple
(C) Neem (D) Mango

3. Which of these plants store food in their roots?
(A) Balsam (B) Onion
(C) Carrot (D) Zinnia

4. Which part of plant absorbs water and minerals?
(A) Stems (B) Roots
(C) Leaves (D) Flowers

5. Which one of the following has a tap root?
(A) Wheat (B) Rice
(C) Maize (D) Pea

6. The part of the plant that takes part in photosynthesis is:
(A) Stem (B) Leaf
(C) Flower (D) Root

7. The leaves of which of the following plants have reticulate venation?
(A) Wheat (B) Maize
(C) Rose (D) Rice

8. Which part of the plant carries water from roots to leaves?
(A) Phloem
(B) Xylem
(C) Chloroplast
(D) Stomata

9. The male reproductive organ of a flower is the:
(A) Pistil (B) Stamen
(C) Pollen grain (D) Ovule

10. Female reproductive parts of a flower:
(A) Stamens (B) Pistils
(C) Petals (D) Sepals

11. Which part of the flower turns into a fruit-
(A) Sepal (B) Petals
(C) Ovary (D) None of these

12. Prop roots are present in:
(A) Rice (B) Sugarcane
(C) Maize (D) Rubber

13. Breathing roots are present in
(A) Pea (B) Mango
(C) Sugarcane (D) Mangroves

14. A plant having parasitic roots:
(A) Carrot (B) Dodder
(C) Wheat (D) Banyan

15. Which part of the plant helps in climbing and support?
(A) Tendrils
(B) Roots
(C) Leaves
(D) Flowers

16. Tiny pores on the margins of leaves are-
(A) Hydathodes (B) Stomata
(C) Epidermis (D) Buds

17. Which of these plants has aerial roots?
(A) Mango
(B) Banyan
(C) Carrot
(D) Wheat

18. Which part of the plant is responsible for anchoring the plant to the soil?
(A) Root (B) Stem
(C) Leaf (D) Flower

19. When pollen is transferred from anther to stigma of the flower the process is called:
(A) Fertilisation (B) Fusion
(C) Pollination (D) Germination

20. Substances necessary for autotrophic Nutrition are:
(A) CO_2 and H_2O (B) Chlorophyll
(C) Sunlight (D) All of the above

21. Organisms capable of synthesizing their own food are called:
(A) Heterotrophs (B) Autotrophs
(C) Decomposers (D) Parasites

22. Select plant having flowers with large petals-
(A) Hibiscus (B) Tulsi
(C) Wheat (D) Grass

23. Which plant part can be modified into a thorn?
(A) Leaf (B) Root
(C) Stem (D) Flower

24. Chlorophyll contains:
(A) Potassium (B) Iron
(C) Manganese (D) Magnesium

25. Which of the following is represented by X and Y in the given equation?

$$X + Water \xrightarrow[Chlorophyll]{Sunlight} Glucose + Y$$

(A) X - Carbon dioxide, Y- Oxygen
(B) X - Oxygen, Y- Carbon
(C) X - Carbon dioxide, Y- Hydrogen
(D) X - Oxygen, Y - Carbon dioxide

26. How does photosynthesis help to maintain the percentage of oxygen and carbon dioxide in the atmosphere?
(A) By giving off carbon dioxide and absorbing oxygen.
(B) By giving off oxygen and absorbing carbon dioxide.
(C) By releasing oxygen and carbon dioxide.
(D) By absorbing oxygen and carbon dioxide.

27. Which part of the plant helps in vegetative propagation?
(A) Seed (B) Flower
(C) Runner (D) Root hair

28. What role does the insect play in the insectivorous plant?
(A) Fertilization process.
(B) Provides nutrients to the plant.
(C) Dispersal of seeds.
(D) Provides carbon dioxide to the plant.

29. What is the role of the bacteria in leguminous plants?
(A) Convert oxides of nitrogen into soil nitrates.
(B) Convert atmospheric nitrogen gas into soil nitrates.
(C) Convert soil nitrates into gaseous nitrogen.
(D) Convert plant proteins into ammonia.

30. Match column-I with column-II and select the correct option from the codes given below.

Column-I	Column-II
(a) Chlorophyll	(i) Rhizobium
(b) Symbiosis	(ii) Starch
(c) Insectivorous plant	(iii) Lichen
(d) Nitrogen fixing organism	(iv) Mistletoe
(e) Partial parasite	(v) Pitcher plant

(A) (a) - (i), (b) - (iv), (c) - (iii), (d) - (ii), (e) - (v)
(B) (a) - (iii), (b) - (v), (c) - (ii), (d) - (i), (e) - (iv)
(C) (a) - (ii), (b) - (iii), (c) - (v), (d) - (i), (e) - (iv)
(D) (a) - (v), (b) - (iv), (c) - (i), (d) - (ii), (e) - (iii)

Fill in the Blanks

1. __________ is the female reproductive part of the flower.
2. In banyan tree arrangement of veins is ______.
3. Leaves are green as they contain __________ pigment.
4. Plants with tap roots have __________ venation.
5. Ovule grows in the __________.
6. Stamen is __________ reproductive system of flower.
7. Plants are autotrophs because they perform __________
8. The process of release of water from surface of leaves is called ______.
9. Mango is an example of __________
10. The plant which has largest floating leaves is ______.
11. Money plant is an example of __________
12. Bottle guard is an example of ______.
13. Bougainvillea is example of __________
14. Part of flower which protects growing bud is ______.
15. The thick vein in centre of the plant is called __________

True/False

1. Root cap is present on tip of each branch of shoot.
2. Fibrous roots are found in most monocots.
3. Rice plant has a fibrous root system.
4. Sugarcane has prop roots.
5. Sepals in most of the plants are colorful.
6. The broad green part of the leaf is called lamina.
7. The leaf is called the "the food factory" of a plant.
8. Creepers have soft stems.
9. Trees are maximum sized plants which has thick brown color stem.
10. Grape plant is creeper.

Match Type Questions

1. Match the column

	Column-A	Column-B
(a)	Fibrous roots	(i) Dicot
(b)	Plants with soft stem as they climb	(ii) Monocot
(c)	Plants which are very tall and have hard and thick brown stem	(iii) Shrubs
(d)	Have tap roots	(iv) Climber
(e)	Medium height plants	(v) Trees

(A) (a)-(i), (b)-(v), (c)-(iv), (d)-(ii), (e)-(iii)
(B) (a)-(ii), (b)-(iv), (c)-(v), (d)-(iii), (e)-(i)
(C) (a)-(ii), (b)-(iii), (c)-(v), (d)-(i), (e)-(iv)
(D) (a)-(ii), (b)-(iv), (c)-(v), (d)-(i), (e)-(iii)

2.

	Column-A	Column-B
(a)	Sharp prickles	(i) Protect the flower
(b)	Bamboo	(ii) Bougainvillea
(c)	Potato	(iii) Tuber
(d)	Dodder	(iv) Parasitic roots
(e)	Sepals	(v) Prop roots

(A) (a)-(ii), (b)-(v), (c)-(iii), (d)-(iv), (e)-(i)
(B) (a)-(i), (b)-(v), (c)-(iii), (d)-(iv), (e)-(ii)
(C) (a)-(i), (b)-(iv), (c)-(iii), (d)-(v), (e)-(ii)
(D) (a)-(ii), (b)-(v), (c)-(i), (d)-(iv), (e)-(iii)

3.

	Column-A	Column-B
(a)	Roots	(i) Reproductive structure
(b)	Leaf	(ii) Provide support to plant
(c)	Stem	(iii) Food factory
(d)	Flower	(iv) Absorption of water

(A) (a)-(iv), (b)-(iii), (c)-(i), (d)-(ii)
(B) (a)-(i), (b)-(iii), (c)-(iv), (d)-(ii)
(C) (a)-(iv), (b)-(i), (c)-(iii), (d)-(ii)
(D) (a)-(iv), (b)-(iii), (c)-(ii), (d)-(i)

Assertion and Reason Type Questions

In the following questions, a statement of Assertion is followed by a statement of Reason.

(A) If both assertion and reason are true and, the reason is the correct explanation of the assertion.
(B) If both assertion and reason are true, but the reason is not the correct explanation of the assertion.
(C) If assertion is true, but reason is false.
(D) If both assertion and reason are false.

1. **Assertion:** Soft stem plants creep on the surface.
Reason: Trees have hard stems and generally have long lives.
2. **Assertion:** Nodes are those parts of plants from which new branches arise.
Reason: Formation of new branches show a proper growth of a plant.
3. **Assertion:** Roots are very important organs of a plant.
Reason: As roots absorb water & minerals from soil.
4. **Assertion:** Xylem tissue is responsible for transportation of water in a plant.
Reason: Xylem found in the stem.
5. **Assertion:** Leaves are food factories of plants.
Reason: They have a green pigment called chlorophyll.
6. **Assertion:** Flower is the sexual reproductive structure of plant.
Reason: Flower has male & female reproduction structure.
7. **Assertion:** Mid rib is the centre rib of a leaf.
Reason: Climbers have soft stems.
8. **Assertion:** Leaves respire.
Reason: Leaves have tiny pores called stomata that help with respiration.
9. **Assertion:** Arrangements of veins on a leaf is called venation.
Reason: Venation is necessary for transportation.
10. **Assertion:** Tap roots are founds in dicot plants.
Reason: Fibrous roots found in monocot plants.

Comprehension Type Questions

A leaf has various functions like respiration, photosynthesis, etc. To prove photosynthesis takes place, take a leaf in a test tube and pour alcohol on it. Now, place the test tube in a beaker half filled with water. Heat the beaker till all the green colour from the leaf comes out into the alcohol in the test tube. Take out the leaf carefully and wash it with water. Place it on a watch glass and pour some Iodine solution over it. You'll observe that it has turned blue-black, showing the presence of starch in it. Leaves prepare their food in the presence of sunlight and chlorophyll substance present in them. For this, they also use water and carbon dioxide. This process is called photosynthesis. Oxygen is given out in this process.

The food prepared by leaves stored in the form of starch in various plant parts.

1. How do plants synthesise their food?
2. What is starch, and why do plants store it in its leaves.
3. True or false.
   (A) Plants absorb water due to transpiration.
   (B) Chlorine is used to identify presence of starch.
4. Write down equation of photosynthesis.

Free Response Type

Very Short Answer Type Questions

1. Name the two main organ systems in plants.
2. What is photosynthesis? Which plant part performs it?
3. Name any two modifications of a leaf along with their functions and examples.
4. In which part of a flower is the ovary found?
5. Give 2 examples of monocot plants.
6. What is a modified stem? Give an example.
7. Name the part of the pistil that converts into seed.
8. Name the various parts of pistil.
9. Define tap root.
10. What is leaf venation?
11. Give two example of herbs.
12. Where does photosynthesis occur?
13. Why does a white flower bloom at night?
14. What is transpiration and why do plants perform transpiration?
15. What is pollination?

Short Answer Type Questions

1. Classify plants on the basis of their size and give2 examples of each.
2. Differentiate between creeper and climber.
3. What is relation between leaf venation and types of roots?
4. Draw a well labelled diagram of the sexual reproductive structure of a plant.
5. With the help of diagrams, describe the two basic root systems found in plants.
6. Write any two functions of the stem.
7. What are the main parts of the leaves?
8. What is leaf venation? Name its types.
9. Explain an activity by which we can see that stem transports water and minerals.
10. Write down 2 functions of the stem.
11. What do you mean by a complete and incomplete flower?
12. Define following terms-
    (A) Petiole
    (B) Lamina
    (C) Pneumatophore
13. Write down 2 functions of the calyx.
14. Why is transpiration called an essential evil for a plant.
15. Differentiate stem and roots.

Long Answer Type Questions

1. Describe the modification of a stem along with their functions and examples.
2. Describe the functions of a leaf with the help of a labelled diagram.
3. Describe the parts of a typical flower with the help of a diagram.
4. Explain modification of stems with their functions.
5. What are the major functions of flower?
6. Define and explain following terms:
   (A) Pollination (B) Fertilization
7. What are gynoecium and androecium? What role they play in a plant?
8. What do you mean by essential and non essential whrols?

Case Based Questions

(A) Stem of a plant is originated from plumule of seed. It helps in the movement of water. Transportation of water always occurs unidirectionally. The part of leaf by which it is attached to the stem is called petiole. The broad, green part of the leaf is called lamina. The lines on the leaf are called veins. A prominent line in the middle of the leaf is called the midrib. The design made by veins in a leaf is called the leaf venation. If this design is net-like on both sides of midrib, the venation is reticulate. In the leaves of grass, you might have seen that the veins are parallel to one another. This is parallel venation.

1. The network of veins in leaf is called ___________.
   (A) Lamina (B) Petiole
   (C) Vein (D) Venation
2. Green part of leaf is called:
   (A) Venation (B) Midrib
   (C) Petiole (D) Lamina
3. When the veins of leaves of grass are parallel to each other. It is called:
   (A) Parallel venation
   (B) Reticulate venation
   (C) Midrib
   (D) None of the above
4. What is the function a leaf in plants?
5. Explain Reticulate venation in leaves.
6. Draw a well labelled diagram of a leaf with its all parts.

(B) Perform an activity during daytime. Use a healthy, well-watered plant that has been growing in the Sun. Cover a leafy branch of the plant in a polythene and tie up its mouth. Tie up the mouth of another empty polythene cover and keep it also in the sun. After a few hours, observe the inner surface of the covers. You'll observe droplets of water inside the one covering the lead. Water comes out of leaves in the form of vapour by a process called transpiration. Removal of extra amount of water is called transpiration. It is a necessary evil for a plant because it help in absorption of water and minerals from the soil.

1. Water droplets in above activity, what does it show?
2. Leaves have only one function that is of transpiration.
   (A) True
   (B) False
3. Which gas is given out during photosynthesis?
   (A) Carbon dioxide
   (B) Water
   (C) Vapour
   (D) Oxygen
4. Explain the process of transpiration?
5. Why do plants perform transpiration?

Level 2

Multiple Choice Questions

1. Find out the incorrect statements:
   (i) Forest are the kidneys of the Earth.
   (ii) Tap roots are deep and long
   (iii) Monocots are soft and small plants
   (iv) Generally leguminous plants are dicots
   (v) Pea is not involved in nitrogen fixation.
   (A) (ii), (iii), (iv), (v) (B) (i) and (v)
   (C) (ii), (iii), (i) (D) (ii), (i), (iv), (v)
2. Which structure is involved in root formation-
   (A) Bud (B) Plumule
   (C) Radicle (D) Root hairs
3. Which of the following plant parts elongates directly and leads to the formation of roots?
   (A) Bud (B) Radicle
   (C) Plumule (D) Root hair
4. Fibrous root system is found in:
   (A) Monocotyledonous plants.
   (B) Dicotyledonous plants.
   (C) Bryophytes.
   (D) Gymnosperms
5. Pneumatophores are found in:
   (A) The vegetation which is found in marshy and saline lake.
   (B) The vegetation which is found in saline soil.
   (C) Xerophytic condition.
   (D) Hydrophytic condition.
6. Prop roots of a banyan tree are meant for:
   (A) Respiration.
   (B) Absorption of water from soil.
   (C) Providing support to big tree.
   (D) All of the above
7. Stem tendrils are not found in –
   (A) Cucumber (B) Grapevine
   (C) Pumpkin (D) Potato
8. Part of androceum which connect both lobes of anther is-
   (A) Filament (B) Connective
   (C) pollen grain (D) Style
9. Which one of the following structures is not associated with gynoecium?
   (A) Ovary (B) Style
   (C) Stigma (D) Filament

10. Which of the following is the green expanded part of leaf with vein and veinlets?
(A) Petiole (B) Node
(C) Stipule (D) Lamina

11. Which of the following statements are correct about the phloem?
(i) The phloem transports food materials, usually from roots to the other parts of the plant.
(ii) It is composed of a sieve tube element.
(iii) Phloem transports unidirectionally.
(A) Both (i) and (ii) (B) only (iii)
(C) Only (i) (D) only (ii)

12. Identify the following plants are herbs.
Tomato, rice, eucalyptus blue berry, china rose, lavender, mango
(A) Herbs - Tomato, rice, and mango.
(B) Herbs - Tomato, rice, and lavender.
(C) Herbs - Tomato, bluebarry, and lavender.
(D) Herbs - Eucalyptus, rice, and lavender.

13. Which of the following set of plant contain incomplete flower
(A) Hibiscus and petunia
(B) Date palm and Mulberry
(C) Pea and mulberry
(D) Gulmohar and mustard

14. Seed is modification of:
(A) Anther (B) Stigma
(C) Ovule (D) Ovary

15. A stalk by which a plant is connected with stem is called-
(A) Petiole (B) Stigma
(C) lamina (D) Ovary

16. In a food chain producers are kept at-
(A) First trophic level
(B) Second trophic level
(C) Third trophic level
(D) None of the above

17. When we place starch containing leaves in iodine solution it gives _________ colour
(A) Yellow colour (B) Blue black colour
(C) Pink colour (D) green colour

Higher Order Thinking Skill (HOTS)

1. Which of the following are the materials used in photosynthesis?
(i) Water (ii) Sunlight
(iii) Starch (iv) Carbon dioxide
(A) (i) and (ii) only
(B) (i) and (iv) only
(C) (iii) and (iv) only
(D) (i), (ii), and (iv) only

2. Look at the two plants below.

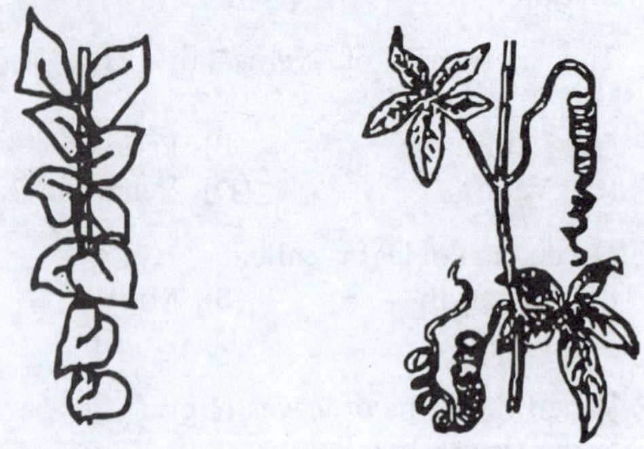

Plant A Plant B

Plant A has clasping roots and Plant B has tendrils. The clasping roots and tendrils are very important because they:
(A) absorb water and minerals.
(B) can grow into young plants.
(C) capture sunlight for making food.
(D) enable the plants to climb and get more sunlight.

3. What is the possible heading for X and Y from the given figure?

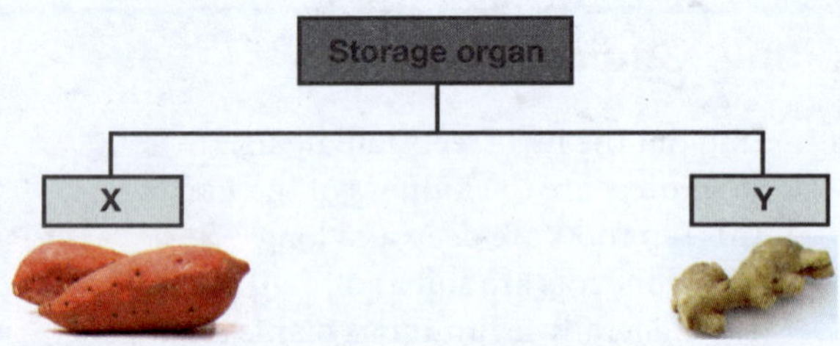

Sweet potato Ginger

	X	Y
(A)	Leaf	Root
(B)	Underground root	Leaf
(C)	Underground stem	Root
(D)	Root	Underground stem

4. Find the matching pair.
Jute: stem ; Cotton: ??????
(A) Flower (B) Fruit
(C) Leaf (D) Seed

5. Which characteristic feature is common to rose, hibiscus, and bougainvillea?
(A) They are shrubs
(B) They are trees
(C) They are climbers
(D) They are herbs

6. I anchor the plant to the ground. I absorb water and mineral salts from the soil. Who am I?
(A) Root (B) Stem
(C) Leaf (D) Flower

7. The diagram shows stomata, which are usually found on the underside of leaves.
Stomata

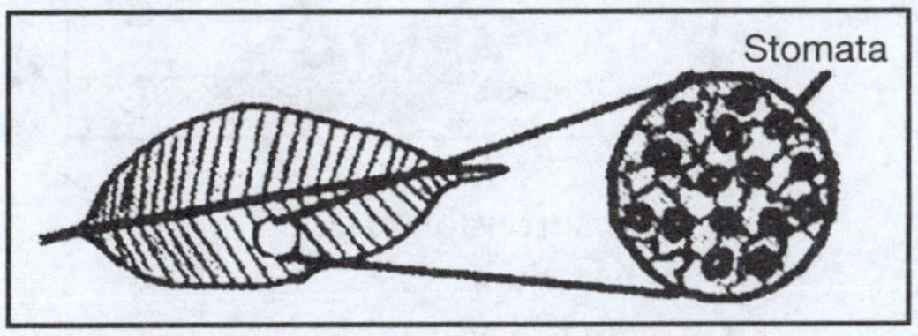

Which of the following is NOT a function performed by them?
(A) Trap sunlight to make food for the plant.
(B) Take in carbon dioxide and give out oxygen.
(C) Take in oxygen and give out carbon dioxide.
(D) Allow excess water to evaporate from the leaves.

8. Which part of broccoli do we eat?
(A) Stem (B) Root
(C) Flower (D) Leaf

9. In which part of the flower are pollen produced?
(A) Pistil (B) Stamen
(C) Anther (D) Ovary

10. Which of the following illustrations correctly demonstrates the process of transpiration in plants?

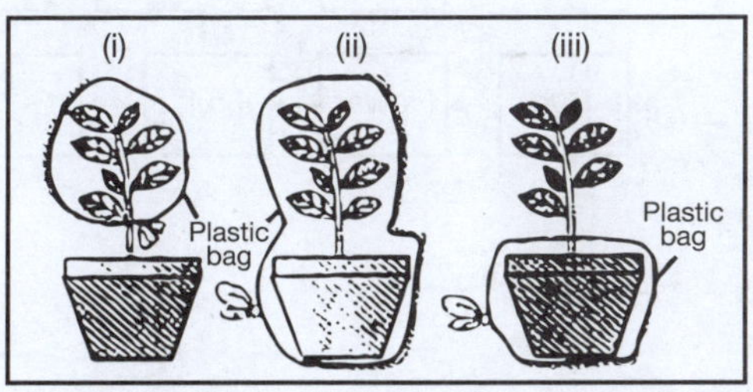

(A) Only (i) (B) Only (ii)
(C) Only (iii) (D) Only (ii) and (iii)

11. The given diagram of a plant shows the movement of substances in the form of arrows.

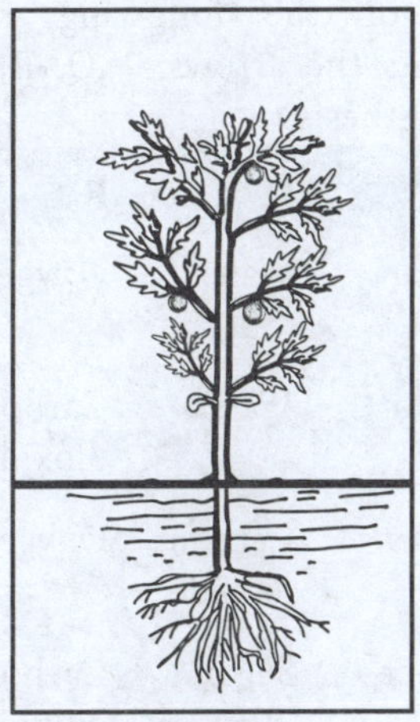

Which of the following substances is/are transported in the given plant as shown by the arrows?
(i) Water
(ii) Mineral salts
(iii) Oxygen
(iv) Sugar

(A) Only (i) and (ii)
(B) Only (ii) and (iii)
(C) Only (i), (ii), and (iii)
(D) (i), (ii), (iiii), and (iv)

12. Which one of the following groups of vegetables includes only roots that are eaten as food is stored in them?
(A) Beetroot, Sugarcane, Ginger, Radish
(B) Potato, Carrot, Radish, Beetroot
(C) Carrot, Turnip, Radish, Beetroot
(D) Colocasia, Potato, Onion, Cabbage

13. Which of the following plants has breathing roots?
(A) Mangrove (B) Maize
(C) Vallisneria (D) Sugarcane

14. The diagram shows a green leaf of a potted plant that is exposed to sunlight.

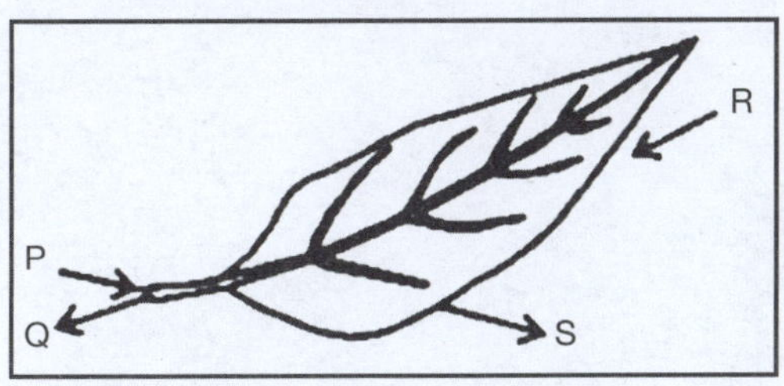

ASSESSMENT CORNER

Which of the following rows correctly represents the arrows P, Q, R, and S during photosynthesis?

	P	Q	R	S
(A)	Sugar	Water	Oxygen	Carbon dioxide
(B)	Sugar	Water	Carbon dioxide	Oxygen
(C)	Water	Carbon dioxide	Oxygen	Water
(D)	Water	Sugar	Carbon dioxide	Sugar

15. Which of the following is an adaptation that helps cuscuta plant to obtain its nutrition (to get its food)?

(A) Stem is modified to take up the function of the leaves.
(B) Roots are modified to suck food from the host.
(C) Stem is modified to suck food from the host.
(D) Leaves trap insects to suck food from them

16. Identify the plant which is harvested in the flowering stage.

(A) Wheat (B) Jute
(C) Maize (D) Paddy

17. The figure given below shows a plant. What is the function of the part labelled 'G' in the given plant?

(A) To absorb moisture.
(B) To breathe.
(C) To absorb sunlight.
(D) To provide support.

18. Which of the following edible root is/are rich in sugar protein and carotene?

(i) Carrot
(ii) Beetroot
(iii) Radish

(A) Only I (B) II only
(C) III only (D) I, II, and III

19. Which of the following is correct sequence for fruit formation:

(A) Fruit → Flower → Dropping of petals → Bud
(B) Fruit → Dropping of petals → Flower → Bud
(C) Bud → Flower → Dropping of petals → Fruit
(D) Bud → Flower → Fruit → Dropping of petals

ARCHIVE CORNER

1. Shruti took a white carnation flower and split its stalk halfway along the length and arranged a setup as shown in the given figure. After some time, she observed that half of the petals turned blue, and the other half turned red. The section through the stem also showed blue and red coloured areas.

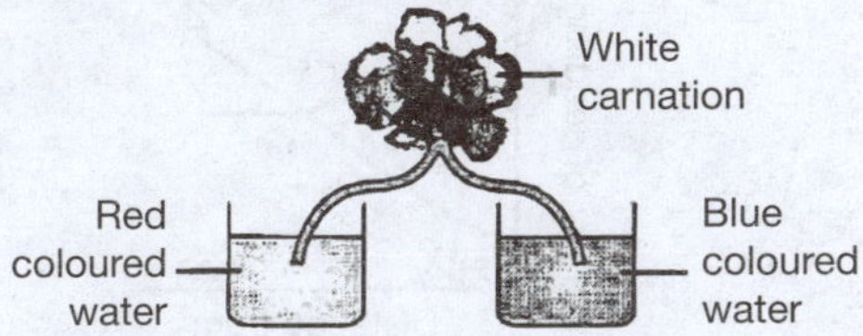

What can she observe from this experiment?
(A) Stem conducts water to all parts of the plant.
(B) Stem has localized structures for conduction of water.
(C) Stem conducts solutes along with water.
(D) All of these

2. Refer the given figure of different parts of a typical flower and select the correct statements regarding it.

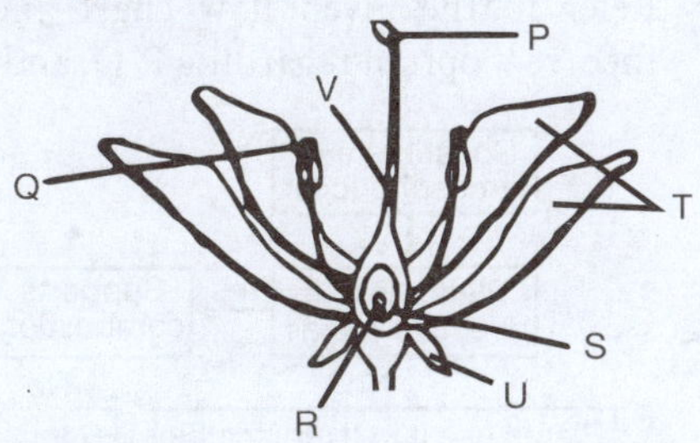

(i) After pollination, 'S' swells up and changes into a fruit and 'R' changes into a seed.
(ii) 'P' contains pollen grains.
(iii) The pollen grains are transferred from 'Q' to 'P' in self -pollination.
(iv) 'U' is brightly coloured and scented to attract insects that help in reproduction.
(v) Different flowers have 'T' of different colours.
(vi) 'P'. 'V' and 'S' form the innermost part of a flower called pistil.

(A) (i), (ii), (iv), and (vi)
(B) (i), (iii), (v), and (vi)
(C) (ii) and (v)
(D) (iii), (iv), and (vi)

3. Refer the given three plants P, Q, and R.

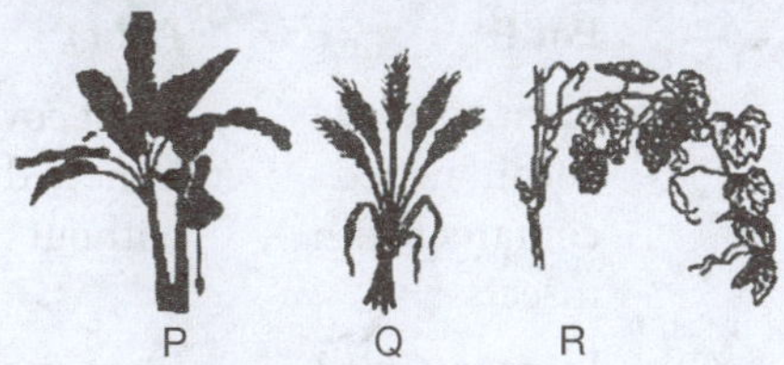

Which of the following is a suitable statement for the given plants?
(A) P and R produce food, while Q does not.
(B) P and Q produce oxygen, while R does not.
(C) P is a shrub, Q is a herb, while R is a tree.
(D) Leaves of P and Q show parallel venation, while that of R shows reticulate venation.

4. He is known as 'Father of Green Revolution.' He produced a high yielding, disease resistant wheat variety and was awarded Nobel Peace Prize in 1970 because of his contributions to world peace by helping to reduce scarcity of food. Who is he?
(A) Dr. Verghese Kurien
(B) Hilaire de Chardonnet
(C) Norman de Kazimodke
(D) Norman Ernest Borlaug

Direction (Q.5 and 6): Refer the given passage and answer the following questions.

In some plants. leaves get modified to perform different functions. For example, in insectivorous plants such as the pitcher plant, the leaf is modified to form a pitcher for capturing insects. These plants have green leaves as well. They grow in regions where the soil is deficient in nitrogen.

5. Which of the following statements is incorrect regarding this?
(A) Photosynthesis that occurs in the green leaves of these plants, produces carbohydrates as their food source.
(B) Photosynthesis does not occur in these plants as they depend only upon insects for their food.
(C) To harvest nitrogen necessary for their growth and development, these plants trap insects and digest them.
(D) Insectivorous plants prepare their food by the following reaction:

$$\underset{\text{(From air)}}{CO_2} + \text{Water} \rightarrow \text{Glucose} + \underset{\text{(From soil)}}{O_2}$$

6. Which of these sets of two different pots (P and Q) should one select to carry out a starch test in order to prove that insectivorous plants are photosynthetic?

	Pot P	Pot Q
(A)	Plant covered within netted container with insects	Plant covered with in netted container without insects
(B)	Plant in sealed wooden container	Plant in sealed glass container
(C)	Plant watered everyday	Plant watered every 3rd day
(D)	Plant with fertilizer	Plant without fertilizer

7. Identify the parts labelled in the given figure. Match them with their respective functions and select the correct option.

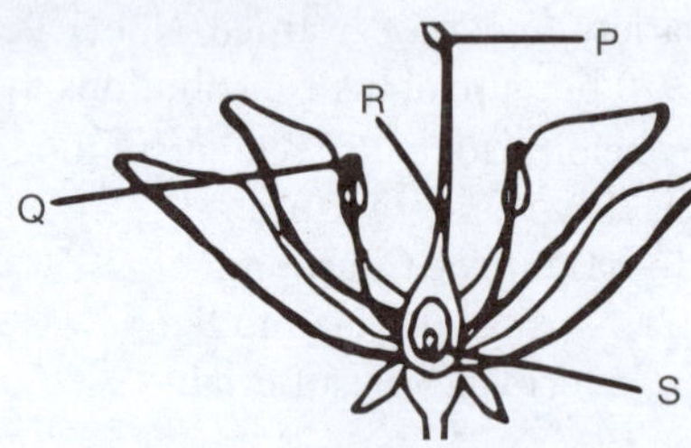

(A) P - Anther - Transfer of pollen grains.
(B) Q - Stigma - Receives pollen grains.
(C) R - Style - Transfer of ovule.
(D) S - Ovary - Involved in fertilization.

8. Which of the following features are useful for desert plants?
(A) Leaf hairs (B) Large flat leaves
(C) Needle like leaves (D) All of these

9. X is a stem modified to store food, while Y is a stem modified to make food. X and Y are respectively
(A) Cactus and sweet potato
(B) Onion and potato
(C) Ginger and cactus
(D) Dahlia and ginger.

10. Phyllotaxy is the arrangement of leaves on the stem. Identify the three types of phyllotaxy shown in the given figures, X, Y and Z.

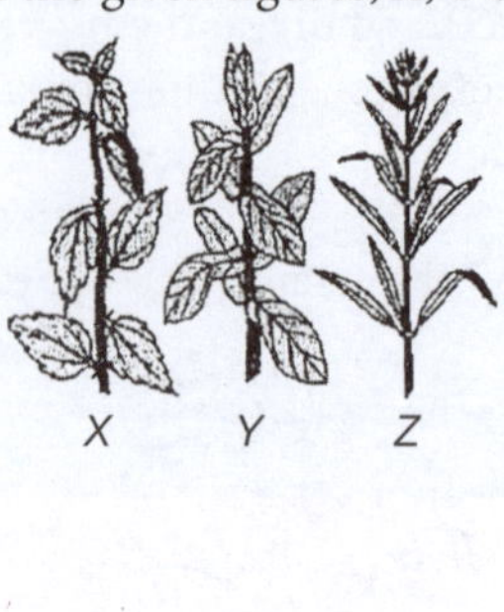

	X	Y	Z
(A)	Alternate	Opposite	Whorled
(B)	Opposite	Whorled	Alternate
(C)	Whorled	Alternate	Opposite
(D)	Opposite	Alternate	Whorled

11. Refer to tile given graph depicting seed dispersal in three different types of plants X, Y, and Z. Select the incorrect option regarding this.

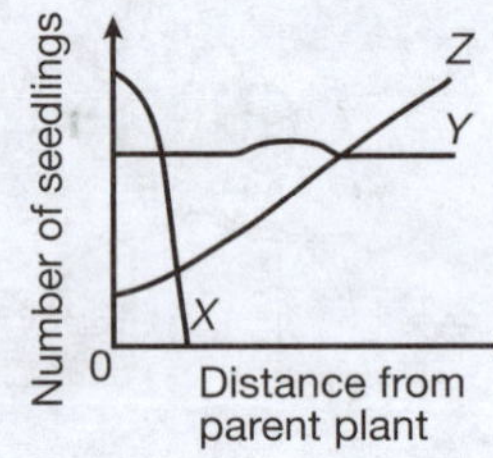

(A) X could be geranium, Y could be Xanthium, and Z could be dandelion.
(B) Y may produce edible fruits or seeds with hooks and spines.
(C) Seeds of X may have hair or wing like structures that enable them to float in air currents.
(D) Seeds of Z are small and light weighted.

12. Refer to the given flow chart and select the incorrect option regarding P, Q, and R

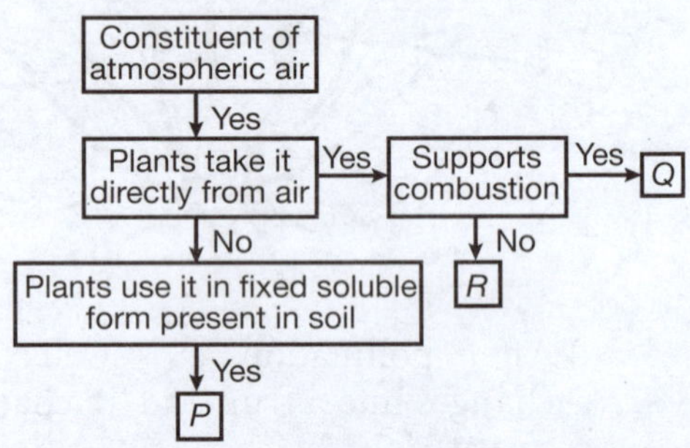

(A) There are some bacteria present in the soil that convert P into simple soluble form which can be taken by plants for manufacturing their proteins.
(B) Q is the gas that is added to atmosphere only by photosynthetic activity of green plants.
(C) Increased R in atmosphere could lead to increased greenhouse effect thereby leading to global warming.
(D) Animals get P directly from atmospheric air to manufacture their proteins.

13. Study the given relationship and select the option that satisfies the same relationship.

Pumpkin :: Rose :: Pea

(A) Money plant:: Hibiscus::Bottle gourd
(B) Mint::Bottlebrush::Grapevine
(C) Watermelon::Hibiscus::Betel
(D) Calliandra::Spinach::Bitter gourd

14. Refer to the given Venn diagram and select the correct option regarding P, Q, R, and S.

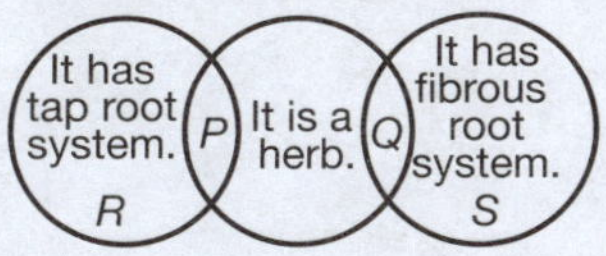

	P	Q	R	S
(A)	Mustard	Wheat	Neem	Palm
(B)	Gram	Pea	Sunflower	Grass
(C)	Maize	Spinach	China rose	Barley
(D)	Mint	Carrot	Mango	Rice

15. Refer to the given flow chart and identify P, Q, R, S, and T.

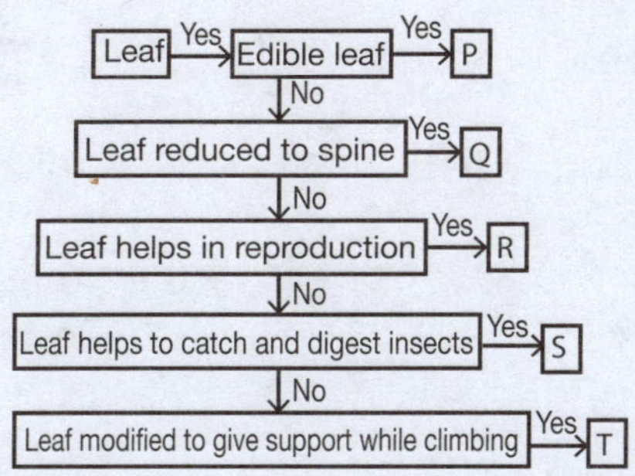

	P	Q	R	S	T
(A)	Lettuce	Aloe vera	Petunia	Mistletoe	Grape-vine
(B)	Fenu-greek	Acacia	Bry-ophyllum	Cuscuta	Grape-vine
(C)	Spinach	Cactus	Begonia	Nepenthes	Pea
(D)	Mint	Dionaea	Hibiscus	Sundew	Pea

16. Refer to the given dichotomous key.

(i) (A) It conducts food, water, and minerals to different parts of the plant. -Go to Il
(B) It absorbs water. -Go to III

(ii) (A) It is modified to climb. ------P
(B) It is modified to store water.------Q

(iii) (A) It is modified to climb.-------R
(B) It is modified to absorb moisture from air.------S

Select the incorrect option regarding P — S.

(A) P could be tendrils of grapevines whereas, S could be prop roots of banyan trees.
(B) Q could be stem of Opuntia whereas, R could be climbing root of betel.
(C) P could be tendril of Cucurhila whereas, R could be climbing root of ivy.
(D) P could be tendril of passion flower whereas, S could be an aerial root of an orchid.

17. Read the following statements and select the option that correctly identify true (T) and false (F) ones.

(i) The number of petals and sepals in a flower is always equal.
(ii) Roots absorb water and minerals from the soil.
(iii) Stamens form the female reproductive part of a flower.
(iv) Petiole is the short stalk that attaches leaf to the stem.
(v) Calyx and corolla form the essential whorls of the flower.

	(i)	(ii)	(iii)	(iv)	(v)
(A)	T	T	F	T	F
(B)	F	T	F	T	F
(C)	F	T	T	T	F
(D)	T	T	F	F	T

18. Identify the figures (P-S) and select the incorrect statement regarding these

P Q R S

(A) P is a modified tap root which stores food.
(B) Edible part of Q is the same as edible part of an onion.
(C) R is a fruit which is eaten as a vegetable.
(D) Edible part of S is the same as the edible part of a turnip.

19. Refer to the given figure and select the incorrect option regarding its parts labelled as P,Q, R, S, and T

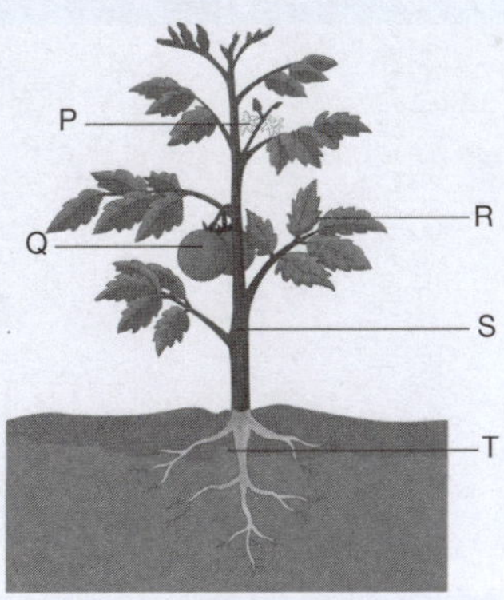

(A) P is the main reproductive organ in plants but in some plants like broccoli and cauliflower it gets modified to store food.

(B) After reproduction, P changes to Q which is always edible in all plants.
(C) T stores food and becomes swollen in plants like asparagus, sweet potato, and Dahlia.
(D) Fenugreek and lettuce have edible R. It is reduced to spines in Opuntia whereas ginger has edible S. It stores water and becomes photosynthetic in some cacti.

ANSWER KEY

Level 1

Fixed Response Type

Multiple Choice Questions

1. A	**2.** A	**3.** C	**4.** B	**5.** D	**6.** B	**7.** C	**8.** B	**9.** B	**10.** B
11. C	**12.** B	**13.** D	**14.** B	**15.** A	**16.** A	**17.** B	**18.** A	**19.** C	**20.** D
21. B	**22.** A	**23.** A	**24.** D	**25.** A	**26.** B	**27.** C	**28.** B	**29.** B	**30.** C

Fill in the Blanks

1. Pistil/carpel

2. Reticulate venetion-Banyan tree is dicotyledon so it has reticulate venation

3. Chlorophyll	**4.** Reticulate	**5.** Ovary	**6.** Male
7. Photosynthesis	**8.** Transpiration	**9.** Dicot	
10. Giant water lily (Victoria regis)	**11.** Climber	**12.** Climber	
13. Large colourful bracts	**14.** Sepals	**15.** Midrib	

True/False

1. False	**2.** True	**3.** True	**4.** True	**5.** False
6. True	**7.** True	**8.** True	**9.** True	**10.** False

Match Type Questions

1. **(D)** (a)-(ii), (b)-(iv), (c)-(v), (d)-(i), (e)-(iii)

2. **(A)** (a)-(ii), (b)-(v), (c)-(iii), (d)-(iv), (e)-(i)

3. **(D)** (a)-(iv), (b)-(iii), (c)-(ii), (d)-(i)

Assertion and Reason Type Question

1. B	**2.** B	**3.** A	**4.** A	**5.** A	**6.** A	**7.** B	**8.** A	**9.** C	**10.** B

Level 2

Multiple Choice Questions

1. B	**2.** C	**3.** B	**4.** A	**5.** A	**6.** D	**7.** D	**8.** B	**9.** D	**10.** D
11. D	**12.** B	**13.** B	**14.** C	**15.** A	**16.** A	**17.** B			

Higher Order Thinking Skill (HOTS)

1. D	**2.** D	**3.** D	**4.** D	**5.** A	**6.** A	**7.** A	**8.** C	**9.** C	**10.** A
11. C	**12.** C	**13.** A	**14.** B	**15.** B	**16.** B	**17.** B	**18.** C	**19.** C	

Archive Corner

1. D	**2.** B	**3.** D	**4.** D	**5.** B	**6.** C	**7.** D	**8.** D	**9.** C	**10.** C
11. A	**12.** D	**13.** D	**14.** C	**15.** A	**16.** C	**17.** B	**18.** D	**19.** B	

CHAPTER 14

The Living Organisms: Characteristics and Surrounding

Learning Outcomes

After reading this chapter, you will be able to:

- define adaptation.
- discuss adaptation in various habitats.
- explain the components of the environment.
- discuss the characteristics of living beings.

Geekspeak

- Growth
- Reproduction
- Habitat
- Adaptation
- Respiration
- Stimuli
- Biotic components

Introduction

All living organisms are dependent on natural resources like water, air, sunlight, etc. Interaction between living and non-living factors is called ecosystem. Living factors of the ecosystem are called **biotic factors** and non-living factors of ecosystem are called **abiotic factors.**

Organisms and their Surrounding

The organisms can survive only in particular surroundings according to their needs. For example, a polar bear can only survive in cold areas and camels can only survive in desert areas.

Habitat

- Many organisms live in our surroundings. Organisms get their food, shelter, air, water, etc. from the environment. These components are required for their survival.
- Living components of this environment are called biotic components and non-living components are called abiotic components. The place where organisms live is called a habitat. A habitat means the dwelling place or the home of an organism.
- Several plants and animals share a habitat. They live together in a delicately maintained balance among themselves.
- Habitat may be of two types:

Terrestrial Habitat

It refers to the land where all plants and animals survive. It includes mountains, deserts, forests, and grasslands.

Aquatic Habitat

It refers to the water where plants and animals survive. Aquatic habitat includes rivers, ponds, lakes, oceans, and swamps.

Check Point 1

1. What is a microorganism?
2. How do some organisms live in extreme heat and cold conditions?
3. Define ecosystem.

Adaptation

Characteristics of organisms which help them to survive in the surroundings in which they are normally found. These special features or habits, which the organisms develop to survive in their habitat, are called **adaptations.**

Testing Room 1

Aim: Pluck a leaf of aak plant and feel what you get?

Result: You will get sticky milky substance, which is the excretory product of plant. It is antioxidant in nature and used in skin problems.

Competition Corner

- Life is raised in the ocean.
- Change that occurs in the body of a single organism in a short period of time to adjust to the changes in the surroundings is called acclimatization.

❖ INTEXT QUESTIONS

1. **What do you understand by ecology?**
   Solution: Ecology is the study of relationships between living organisms and their surroundings.
2. **How can you divide a biotics component of the environment on the basis of the food they obtain?**
   Solution: The biotic components of the environment can be divided into three groups on the basis of food they obtain:
   - Producers
   - Consumers
   - Decomposers
3. **Discuss the role of decomposers in the habitat.**
   Solution: The organisms who feed on the dead remains of plants and animals are known as decomposers. The examples of decomposers are bacteria and fungi. These organisms help in maintaining the balance of nutrients in the soil. They also help in cleaning the environment by disposal of dead animals.

Some Terrestrial Habitat

Terrestrial habitats with the adaptations in plants and animals living there are discussed as follows:

Deserts

Deserts are areas that receive very little rainfall. Deserts are water deplete areas causing plants and animals are adapted for a little less water. E.g., Thar desert. Cactus, camel, kangaroo, rat, etc. are found in the desert. They are adapted to conserve water.

Adaptation in Desert Habitat

- Desert animals like snakes, rats, etc. tend to stay away from intense heat during the day, they stay in burrows deep in the sand. These animals come out only during the night, when it is cooler.
- Camels' nostrils have long hairs to prevent the entry of sand and dust. They have no sweat glands on their skin. They have long legs (as shown in Fig. 14.1 (b)).
- Desert plants lose very little water through transpiration. The leaves in desert plants are either absent, very small, or they are in the form of spines (as shown in Fig. 14.1 (a)).

(a)

(b)

Figure 14.1 **(a) Cactus, and (b) Camel**

- This helps in reducing loss of water from leaves through transpiration. The leaf-like structure you see in a cactus is, in fact, its stem.
- Photosynthesis in these plants is usually carried out by the stems.
- The stem is also covered with a thick waxy layer, which helps to retain water in the cacti. Most desert plants have roots that go very deep into the soil for absorbing water.

Keystone

- A kangaroo rat is a desert animal which dies if it drinks water.
- Camel can survive more many days without water.

Testing Room 2

- Take a potted cactus and a leafy plant to the classroom. Tie polythene bags to some parts of the two plants. Leave the potted plants in the sun and observe after a few hours.
- Take some observations. You will find that the cactus plant shows very less water on polythene as it is a desert plant and it saves water, therefore, rate of transpiration is very low in cacti than other plants.

Check Point 2

4. Give 2 examples of desert plants.

5. Why do cacti store water in it's leaves?

Mountain Regions

These habitats are normally very cold and windy. In some areas, snowfall may take place in winters. There is a large variety of plants and animals living in the mountain regions.

Adaptation in Mountain Regions

- Trees are normally cone shaped and have sloping branches. The leaves of some of these trees are needle-like (as shown in Fig. 14.2). This helps rainwater and snow to slide off easily.

Figure 14.2 **Trees of Mountain Region**

Keystone

- Salim Ali (1896-1987) travelled throughout India to observe different birds. He compiled a list of birds, recorded his journeys and habitats. He listed areas where a large number of bird species were found and took steps for their conservation. Keoladeo National Park in Bharatpur, Rajasthan and Ranganathittu Bird Sanctuary in Mandya, Karnataka are examples of areas he protected. He wrote proof of 10 books on birds of the Indian subcontinent.
- Known as the "*Birdman of India*".
- Received the Padma Shri in 1976.

- There could be trees with shapes very different from these that are also present on mountains. They may have different kinds of adaptations to survive on the mountains.
- Animals living in the mountain regions are also adapted to the conditions there. They have thick skin or fur to protect them from the cold. For example, yaks have long hair to keep them warm (Fig. 14.3).

Figure 14.3 **Animals Living in Mountain Region, (a) Mountain Goat, (b) Polar Bear, (c) Yak**

- Snow leopard has thick fur on its body including feet and toes. This protects it's feet from the cold when it walks on the snow.
- The mountain goat has strong hooves for running up the rocky slopes of the mountains.

Competition Corner

- **Boreal Forests** (Taiga): Boreal forests or taiga found In Canada, Russia, Scandinavia, China, Mongolia, and northern Japan. Boreal forests have moderately warm summers and long, cold winters. The annual snowfall in these regions ranges from 40 to 100 cm.

Grasslands

These habitats are normally windy and dry with low availability of water. Temperature in these regions varies according to the season. In this region, mainly grasses and other herbs are found as shown in (Fig. 14.4). There is a small number of shrubs and trees.

Figure 14.4 **Plants in Grassland Region**

Adaptation in Grassland Regions

- The plants in this region have small leaves to reduce water loss. These plants have strong roots to protect them from the wind.
- Some plants in this region have long roots which go deeper in the soil and helps in absorbing underground water.
- In grassland regions, mainly grazing animals such as zebra, deer, etc. are found. Lion and deer are animals found in grasslands or forests.

Figure 14.5 **Animals in Grassland Region (a) Lion, and (b) Deer**

- A lion lives in a forest or a grassland and is a strong animal that can hunt and kill animals like deer. It is light brown in colour (as shown in Fig. 14.5(a)). It's light brown colour helps it to camouflage in dry grasslands when it hunts for prey (animals to eat).
- Lions have long claws in their front legs that can be withdrawn inside the toes. The eyes in front of the face allow it to have a correct idea about the location of its prey.
- A deer is another animal that lives in forests and grasslands (as shown in Fig. 14.5 (b)). It has strong teeth for chewing hard plant stems of the forest.

Keystone

- Deers have great hearing sense which helps them to save themselves from predators.
- A lion can eat 40-50 kg of flesh at a time.

- A deer needs to know about the presence of predators (animals like lion that make it their prey) in order to run away from them and not become their prey. It has long ears to hear movements of predators.
- The eyes on the side of its head allow it to look in all directions for danger. The speed of the deer helps them to run away from the predators.

Some Aquatic Habitat

The aquatic habitats with the adaptations in plants and animals living there are discussed as follows:

Ocean

- Like fish many other sea animals have streamlined bodies to help them move easily in water (as shown in Fig. 14.6).

- There are some sea animals like squids and octopus, which do not have this streamlined shape. They stay deeper in the ocean, near the seabed and catch any prey that moves towards them.
- However, when they move in water, they mould their bodies in a streamlined shape. These animals have gills to help them use oxygen dissolved in water.
- There are some sea animals like dolphins and whales that do not have gills. They breathe in air through nostrils or blowholes that are located on the upper parts of their heads. This allows them to breathe in air when they swim near the surface of water. They can stay inside the water for a long time without breathing. They come out to the surface from time to time, to breathe in air.

Figure 14.6 Aquatic Animals: Fish

Ponds and Lake

- Some aquatic plants have their roots fixed in the soil below the water. In terrestrial plants, roots normally play a very important role in the absorption of nutrients and water from the soil. However, in aquatic plants, roots are much reduced in size and their main function is to hold the plant in place.
- The stems of these plants are long, hollow, and light. The stems grow up to the surface of water while the leaves and flowers float on the surface of water such as lotus (as shown in Fig. 14.7).
- Some aquatic plants are submerged in water. All parts of such plants are under water. Some of these plants have narrow and thin ribbon-like leaves.
- These can bend in flowing water. In some submerged plants, leaves are often highly divided, through which water can easily flow without damaging them.
- Frogs usually live in ponds. Frogs can stay both inside the water as well as move on land.
- They have strong back legs that help them in leaping and catching their prey (as shown in **Fig. 14.8**).
- They have webbed feet which help them swim in water.

- Frogs usually live in ponds. Frogs can stay both inside the water as well as move on land.
- They have strong back legs that help them in leaping and catching their prey (as shown in Fig. 14.8).
- They have webbed feet which help them swim in water.

Figure 14.7 Pond Plant: Lotus

Figure 14.8 Pond Animal: Frog

Competition Corner

- Coral reefs and Estuaries: Coral reefs are rock-like structures made from the skeletons of small ocean animals called corals. Coral reefs are widely distributed in warm shallow waters. They are also called 'rainforests of the sea' as they provide shelter to a large number of marine organisms.
- Estuaries are regions where saltwater (from the ocean) mixes with freshwater (from rivers or streams). These unique habitats provide shelter to several marine animals and birds.

❖ INTEXT QUESTIONS

4. **What are tropical regions?**
Solution: The regions situated between the equator and the two tropics are known as tropical regions. In this region, the weather is hot and wet all year long resulting in rich vegetation.
5. **What kind of weather do we observe in temperate forests?**
Solution: Temperate forests are also known as evergreen forests. These forests are situated regions with warm summers and cool winters. Most trees in these forests are deciduous.
6. **Which type of region has mostly grasses and herbs? Give reason.**
Solution: The region of large land areas is also known as grasslands, which mostly have grasses and herbs. These regions are windy and dry with less availability of water. Thus, shrubs and trees are found in very less numbers in this region.

Check Point 3

6. Define adaptation.
7. Why are biotic and abiotic factors required in nature?
8. Which kind of habitat a do deer share and why?

Characteristics of Organisms

The characteristics of living organisms are discussed as follows:

Need for Food

- Animals depend on plants and other animals for their food. Food gives organisms the energy needed for them to grow.
- Organisms also need energy for other life processes that go on inside them. Food is the source of energy.
- Therefore, we need to understand the characteristics of living and non-living things in more detail. If we observe them closely, a few characteristics are common to all living beings.
- Birds require energy for flying. While resting, there is no apparent need for energy. But living beings require energy all the time for various life processes going on inside them all the time.

Growth

All living organisms show growth. A chick hatched from an egg grows into a hen or a cock. Young ones of animals also grow into adults (as shown in Fig. 14.9). Little puppies grow up to become dogs.

Figure 14.9 **Growth in Living Organisms (a) Chicken Grows into Adult, and (b) Baby Grows into an Adult**

Competition Corner

- All organisms are formed by a single cell called zygote.
- Cell is the basic unit of life. Many organisms on earth are unicellular and other are multicellular.

Respiration

- When we inhale, the air moves from the outside to the inside of our body. When we breathe out, air moves from inside our body to outside.
- Breathing is part of a process called respiration. In respiration, some of the oxygen of the air we breathe in, is used by the body.
- The mechanism of exchange of gases /respiration may differ in different animals.
- Respiration is necessary for all living organisms. It is through respiration that the body finally obtains energy from the food it takes.
- Some animals may have different mechanisms for the exchange of gases, which is a part of the respiration process. For example, earthworms breathe through their skin. Fish, we have learnt, have gills for using oxygen dissolved in water. The gills absorb oxygen from the air dissolved in water.

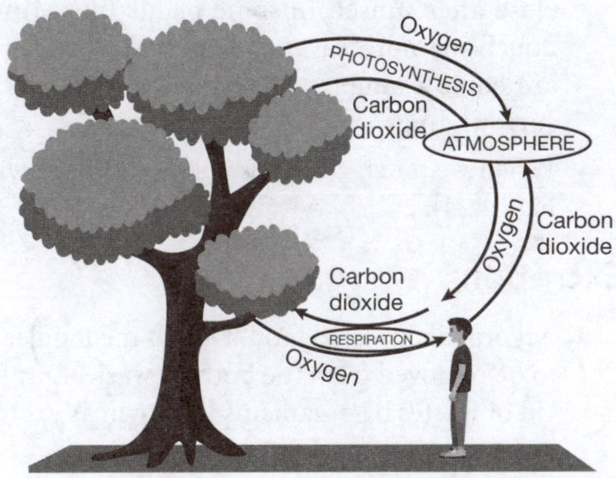

Figure 14.10 **Exchange of Gases**

- Exchange of gases in plants mainly takes place through leaves. The leaves take in air through tiny pores in them and use the oxygen. They give out carbon dioxide to the air.
- The amount of oxygen released in the process of photosynthesis by plants is much more than the oxygen they use in respiration (as shown in Fig. 14.10).

  Respiration in plants takes place during the day.

Testing Room 3

- Collect some dry moong seeds. Keep 20-30 seeds aside and soak the rest in water for a day. Divide the soaked seeds into four parts. Keep one part completely submerged in water for 3-4 days. Do not disturb the dry seeds and those submerged in water. Keep one part of soaked seeds in a sunny room and another in a completely dark region like a cupboard that does not allow any light to come in. Keep the last part in very cold surroundings, say, in a refrigerator or with ice around them.
- Rinse them and replace the water every day.
- Now observe the results and mention them in your notebook with proper explanations.

Competition Corner

- Respiration is a key feature of living being as it gives us energy.
- Energy is produced by oxidation of glucose molecules.
- In living beings, the energy currency is called the ATP.

Response to Stimulus

Figure 14.11 **Response to Stimuli**

- Stimulus is defined as any change in the surroundings or environment of an organism. The reaction of the organism to a change in the environment is called response to stimulus.
- Wild animals run away when bright light is flashed towards them. Similarly, cockroaches begin to move to their hiding places if the light in the kitchen is switched on at night.
- Flowers of some plants bloom only at night. In some plants flowers close after sunset. In some plants like Mimosa, commonly known as 'touch-me-not', leaves close or fold when someone touches them. These are some examples of responses of plants towards changes in their surroundings.
- When we touch a Mimosa plant (also known as *chuimui*), it closes the leaves as a response to stimuli (as shown in Fig. 14.11).

Excretion

- All organisms need food. Not all the food eaten is completely used, only a part of it is utilised by the body. This has to be removed from the body as waste. Our body produces waste in other life processes also. The process of getting rid of wastes by organisms is known as excretion.
- The mechanisms of excretion in plants are a little different. Some plants find it possible to store waste products within their parts in a way that they do not harm the plant as a whole. Some plants remove waste products as secretions.

Check Point 4

9. Name the excretory organ in humans.
10. Which kind of food should we consume to perform all vital activity in a proper manner.
11. Why is food necessary for living beings.

Reproduction

- The phenomenon of generation of organisms of their own kind is called reproduction.
- The mode of reproduction may be different in different animals. Some animals produce their young ones through eggs and some give birth to their young ones.
- Plants also reproduce. Many plants reproduce through seeds. Plants produce seeds, which can germinate and grow into new plants (as shown in Fig. 14.12).
- Some plants also reproduce through parts other than seeds. For example, a part of a potato with a bud, grows into a new plant.

Figure 14.12 **Seed Germination**

Life Cycle of plants

Seeds develop into seedlings that, when mature, produce plants and fruits. The fruit (the pod) contains the seeds that give rise to the next generation of legumes. The entire process from seed to plant to the next generation of seeds is called the life cycle of plants. A plant is considered dead when it stops growing and all life activities gradually cease, even after all the necessary conditions have been met.

Life cycle of a mosquito

Female mosquitoes ared bloodsucking insects that transmit diseases such as malaria, dengue fever and chikungunya. The mosquito life cycle goes through four stages: egg, larva, pupa and adult. Adult mosquitoes can live for 10 to 15 days. Lifeof mosquito begins with an egg (first stage), the egg develops into a larva (second), the larva develops into a pupa (third) and the pupa develops into adult mosquitoes (stage 4)(Fig. 14.13). Adult female mosquitoes lay their eggs directly on or near water and the cycle continues. The shape of the egg is quite different from the larva; the larva appears very different from the pupa. The pupa appears very distinct from the adult mosquito.

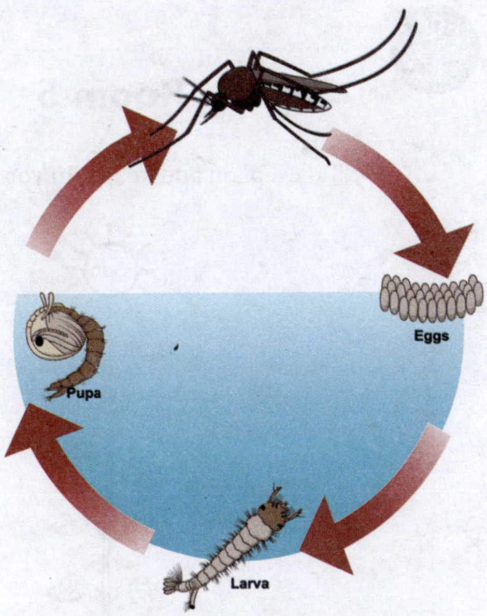

Figure 14.13 Life Cycle of Mosquito

Life cycle of a frog

Life cycle of a frog has following stages— the egg stage, which progresses to the embryo stage; the tadpole stage, consisting of an early stage with a tail and no legs, and a late stage with hind legs; the frog let stage, and the adult frog stage (Fig. 14.14). These four stages of frog are different from each other. The tadpole develops legs but still has a tail. The tail helps them swim in the water. The tadpoles grow and start to resemble small frogs called toads. They still live in the water but start to spend time on land. They still grow and lose their tails completely. Their legs are strong enough to help them jump and land. They develop into adult frogs and live in water and on land.

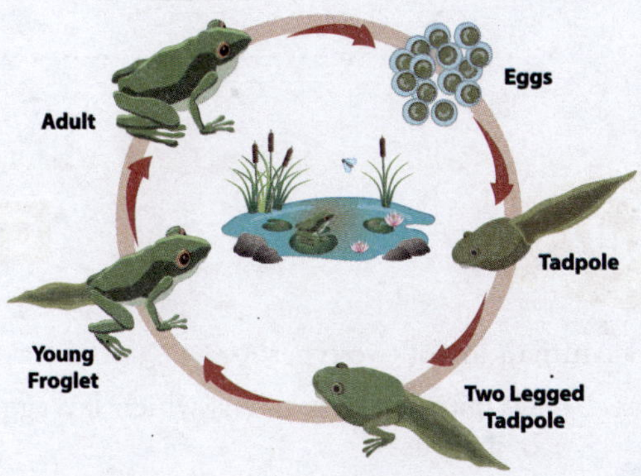

Figure 14.14 Life Cycle of Frog

Testing Room 4

- Take a cutting from a rose or a mint plant. Fix it in the soil and water it regularly and find out the results.
- Perform same activity with potato eye/potato tubers.

Movement

- All living organisms show movement. Animals move from one place to another.
- Their body parts are also capable of independent movements (e.g.: movement of the neck).
- Animals also show movement of substances within their body. Blood in the body transports various nutrients to all parts of the human body.
- Plants are generally anchored to the ground with the help of their roots.
- Plants respond to sunlight and bend over or show growth in the direction of the light.
- The drooping of the touch me-not plant and opening and closing of flowers in response to light are some other examples of plants showing movement.

Testing Room 5

- Take a plant and keep it in your window from where it can get direct sunlight and observe the results.

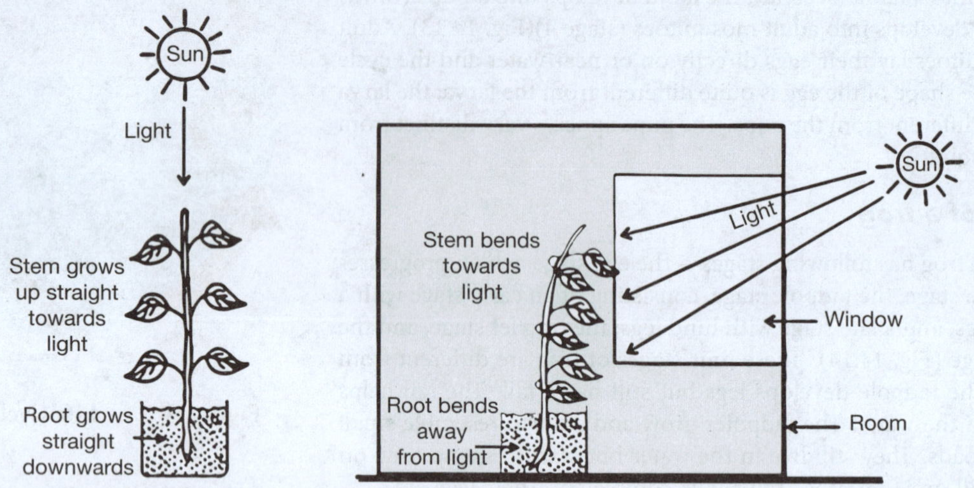

Competition Corner

Animals are of two types:

- **Oviparous:** Organisms which lay eggs are called oviparous.
- **Viviparous:** Organisms which give birth to young once are called viviparous.

A sacred forest is an undisturbed forest. They can range in size from small to very large. There are sacred forests all over India. They are inhabited by many species of plants and animals, including many medicinal plants. These are protected by the local community and no one is allowed to harm any animal, cut down trees in these forests, or disturb the area.

❖ INTEXT QUESTIONS

7. Define following terms:

(i) Excretion

(ii) Respiration

(iii) Reproduction

Solution: (i) The process of getting rid of wastes by organisms is known as excretion.

(ii) Oxidation of glucose/food releases energy. This is called respiration.

(iii) The phenomenon of generation of organisms of their own kind is called reproduction.

8. What do you understand by xerophytic conditions?

Solution: Deserts have xerophytic conditions that receive very little rainfall. Deserts are water deplete areas and therefore plants and animals adapt to these conditions.

What Then is Life?

- Push your hand deep inside a sack of wheat. Do you find it is warm inside? There is some heat being produced inside the sack of wheat. The seeds respire and, in that process, give out some heat.
- We see that respiration is a process that takes place in seeds even when some of the other life processes may not be very active.
- It may not be very easy to answer our question—"what then is life"?
- However, looking at all the diversity of living beings around us, we can conclude that life is beautiful!

Check Point 5

12. Define reproduction. why is it necessary?

13. Why is the mimosa pudica also called the touch me not plant.

Competition Corner

Plants are of following types according to their habitat:

- **Mesophytes:** live in normal conditions.
- **Halophytes:** live in salty water.
- **Xerophytes:** live in deserts.
- **Hydrophytes:** live in water.

STRUCTURAL OUTLINE

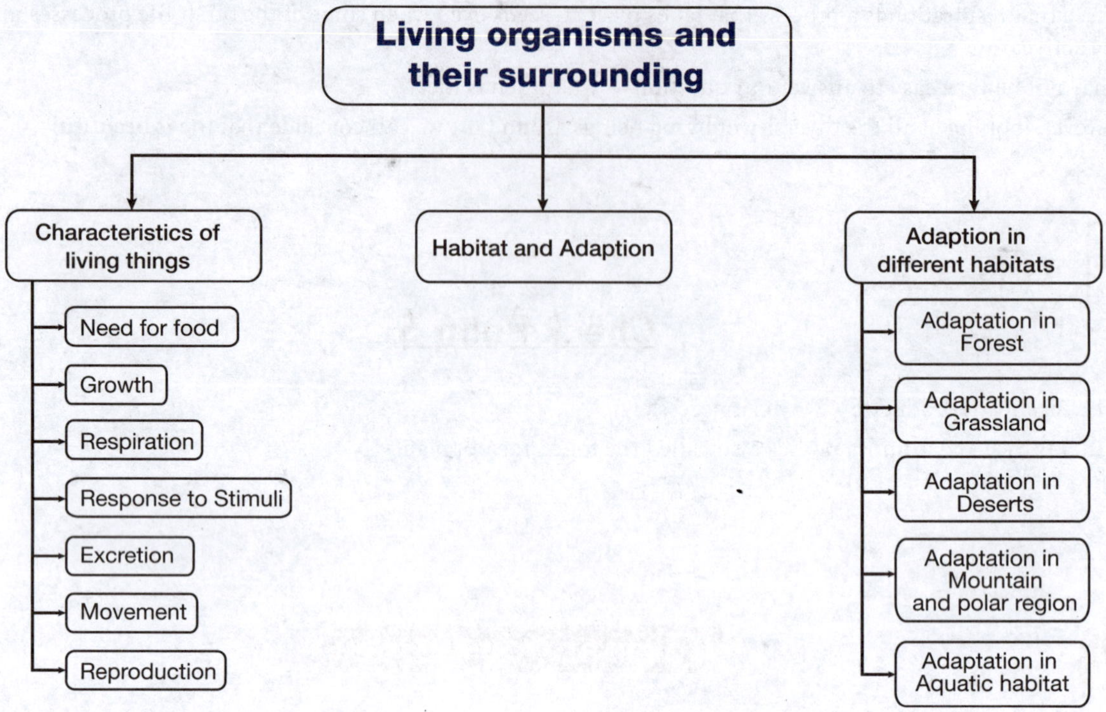

ABRIDGEMENT

- **Food chain:** Transfer of energy between the different organisms of an ecosystem is called the food chain.
- **Food web:** Network of various food chains is called a food web. Organisms show adaptation according to the weather and climate. Adaptation helps an organism to survive in adverse conditions.

EXEMPLIFICATION

1. **Where are conifers generally found?**

   Solution: Generally conifers are found in cold and boreal regions.

2. **Camel excreta or dung is hard and dry. What is the reason?**

   Solution: Camel is a desert animal adapted to survive in that environment. There is water scarcity in the desert water scarcity, therefore, it stores a large amount of water at a time. It excretes highly concentrated urine and excreta to save water.

3. **If an organism fails to adapt to its environment, what could be the possible consequences?**

   Solution: If an organism fails to adapt to its environment, it will struggle for survival and finally die due to adverse conditions.

4. **Differentiate between aestivation and hibernation. How do they help in the survival of an organism.**

   Solution: Aestivation is summer sleep which helps animals to survive in high temperatures and hot environments.

   Hibernation is winter sleep which helps animal to survive in cold environments by reducing their metabolic activities.

5. **Why do polar animals look white? Is it just a coincidence?**

   Solution: The white colour of the polar bear's fur is not a coincidence. It's colour helps camouflage in the snow. They have white colour hair covering their skin.

6. **What are the adaptations developed in birds for flying?**

   Solution: Birds have following adaptations to fly:

   (i) They have hollow bones which makes them lighter.

   (ii) Their forelimbs are modified into wings.

   (iii) They have a streamlined body.

7. **Write down the climatic conditions of polar regions.**

   Solution: The Polar Regions are very cold for most parts of the year and the temperatures fall as low as –37°C. For six months, the sun does not rise and for six months the sun does not set. Some animals found in the polar regions are polar bear, penguins, musk oxen, reindeers, foxes, seals, whales, Siberian crane, etc.

8. **Which features do polar bears adapt to live in extremely cold climate?**

   Solution: Polar bears have following adaptations for survival:

   - They have white fur so that they camouflage into the snow, which helps in catching their prey.
   - They have two layers of fur to protect them from extreme cold.
   - They have a layer of fat under the skin which also protects them from the cold.
   - Their paws are wide and large which help them walk on snow and swim in water.
   - They have a strong sense of smell which helps them catch their prey.

NCERT COMPENDIUM

1. What is a habitat?

Solution: The surroundings where animals live is called their habitat. Organisms depend on their habitat for food, water, air, shelter, and other needs. Habitat means a dwelling place.

2. How are cacti adapted to survive in a desert?

Solution: Cacti have adapted to survive in a desert through:

(i) It's leaves are modified into spines.
(ii) The stem performs photosynthesis, conserving water.
(iii) Their roots go very deep into the soil for water absorption.

3. (a) The presence of specific features which enables a plant or an animal to live in a particular habitat is called

(b) The habitats of the plants and animals that live on land are called __________ habitats.

(c) The habitats of plants and animals that live in water are called ____________ habitats.

(d) Soil, water, and air are the ____________ factors of a habitats.

(e) Changes in our surroundings that make us respond to them are called ____________.

Solution:

(a) adaptation
(b) terrestrial
(c) aquatic
(d) abiotic
(e) stimuli

4. Which of the things in the following list are non-living things?

Plough, mushroom, sewing machine, radio, boat, water hyacinth, and earthworms.

Solution: Plough, sewing machine, radio, boat, and water are non-living things.

5. Give an example of a non-living thing which shows two characteristics of a living thing.

Solution: Clouds are a great example of a non-living thing, and it shows following characters of living:

(i) It grows in size.
(ii) It shows movement.

6. Which of the following non-living things were once part of a living thing?

Butter, leather, soil, wool, electric bulb, cooking oil, salt, apple, rubber.

Solution: Butter, leather, wool, cooking oil, apple and rubber are non-living things which were once part of a living thing.

7. List the common characteristics of living things.

Solution: Some common characteristics of living things are:

1. Growth
2. Reproduction
3. Respiration
4. Responsiveness
5. Excretion
6. Movement

8. Explain why speed is important for survival in the grasslands for animals that live there. (Hint: There are few trees or places for animals to hide in grassland habitats).

Solution: In grassland habitats, there are few trees or places for animals to hide. When predators attack on prey, they have to run fast for survival. If they fail, they lose their life. Therefore, speed is very important for survival of grassland animals.

ASSESSMENT CORNER

Level 1

Fixed Response Type

Multiple Choice Questions

1. All living organisms have the ability to produce young ones of their own kind. The process is called:
(A) Excretion (B) Reproduction
(C) Movement (D) Respiration

2. What is the process by which a seed grows into a new plant?
(A) Photosynthesis (B) Germination
(C) Fertilisation (D) Pollination

3. Interaction between living and nonliving components of environment is called-
(A) Niche (B) Ecosystem
(C) Population (D) None of these

4. When an organism develops certain features/ characters to be adjusted better in the environment the process is called:
(A) Adaptation (B) Stimulus
(C) Response (D) Reproduction

5. What is the first structure to emerge from a germinating seed?
(A) Shoot (B) Root
(C) Leaf (D) Flower

6. Which of these adaptations are for food:
(A) Gills in a fish
(B) Spines in cacti
(C) Long neck in giraffes
(D) Long legs in camels

7. Desert plants have-
(i) Long roots
(ii) Thick cuticle layer
(iii) Board leaves
(iv) Soft stem
(A) (i) and (ii) (B) (i), (ii) and (iii)
(C) (i) & (iii) (D) (i) & (iv)

8. Which condition is not required for seed germination?
(A) Air (B) Sunlight
(C) Water (D) Warmth

9. Whales and dolphins breathe in air through
(A) Blowholes (B) Spiracles
(C) Gills (D) Skin

10. In tadepole respiratory organ is-
(A) Lungs (B) Blowholes
(C) Gills (D) Skin

Fill in the Blanks

1. The white milk-like fluid coming out from rubber plants is called ________.
2. Changes in our surrounding that makes us respond to them are called ________.
3. The process of obtaining energy from food using oxygen is called __________.
4. Lakes, oceans, and ponds are included under __________habitats.
5. Biotic components include all _________ things of the environment
6. The habitats of plants and animals that live in water are called ________ habitats.
7. Desert plants are also known as _________.
8. Microorganisms that feed on dead remains of plants and animals are called________.
9. Water lily plant shows ______________adaptation.
10. Cactus plant is an example of _________.
11. _________ are present in whales for breathing.
12. Plants found in normal environments are __________.
13. Organisms maintain their species count by __________
14. All organisms show response against __________
15. Needle like leaves are found in __________plants.
16. _________ helps aquatic animals respire.
17. Thick skin of polar bears act as _________ to maintain body temperature.
18. The stem is long, hollow, and light. These are key features of __________
19. In desert plants, leaves are modified into _________ to reduce transpiration.

True/False

1. All plants are producers.
2. Temperature is an biotic factor.
3. Organisms living in water are called aquatic animals.
4. A place where an organism lives is called a habitat.
5. Fish is an example of an amphibian.
6. Summer sleep is called aestivation.
7. Earthworm breathe through their gills.
8. Aquatic plants have less developed roots and animals have a streamlined body and breathe through gills.
9. Frogs can stay both inside the pond water as well as on land. Such organisms are called amphibians.
10. Aquatic plants have small roots to absorb water.
11. The phenomenon of generation of organisms of their own kind is called reproduction.
12. The surroundings where plants and animals live is called their habitat.
13. Polar plants and animals have the ability to survive in high temperatures.
14. Excess fat is required for proper growth.
15. Plants exchange gases with the help of stomata and hairs.

Match Type Questions

1. Match the following.

Column-A	Column-B
(a) Xerophytes	(i) Streamlined body
(b) Submerged Hydrophytes	(ii) White fur having fat layer below
(c) Aerial	(iii) Photosynthetic stem
(d) Mountains	(iv) Different shapes of leaves
(e) Aquatic	(v) Hollow bones

(A) (a)-(iii), (b)-(ii), (c)-(v), (d)-(iv), (e)-(i)
(B) (a)-(i), (b)-(iv), (c)-(v), (d)-(ii), (e)-(iii)
(C) (a)-(iii), (b)-(iv), (c)-(v), (d)-(ii), (e)-(i)
(D) (a)-(v), (b)-(iv), (c)-(v), (d)-(ii), (e)-(iii)

2. Match the following.

Column-A	Column-B
(a) Air	(i) Arboreal
(b) Bird	(ii) Stimuli
(c) Monkey	(iii) Abiotic factor
(d) Response	(iv) Streamlined body

(A) (a)-(iii), (b)-(iv), (c)-(i), (d)-(ii)
(B) (a)-(iii), (b)-(i), (c)-(iv), (d)-(ii)
(C) (a)-(iii), (b)-(iv), (c)-(ii), (d)-(i)
(D) (a)-(iv), (b)-(iii), (c)-(i), (d)-(ii)

3. Match the following.

Column-A	Column-B
(a) Mesophytes	(i) Aquatic plants
(b) Hydrophytes	(ii) Desert plants
(c) Xerophytes	(iii) Saline habitat
(d) Halophytes	(iv) Normal surrounding plants

(A) (a)-(iv), (b)-(iii), (c)-(ii), (d)-(i)
(B) (a)-(i), (b)-(ii), (c)-(iii), (d)-(iv)
(C) (a)-(ii), (b)-(i), (c)-(iii), (d)-(iv)
(D) (a)-(iv), (b)-(i), (c)-(ii), (d)-(iii)

4. Match the following.

Column-A	Column-B
(a) Frog	(i) Keep moving big ears to keep body cool
(b) Camel	(ii) Cold blooded animals
(c) Siberian	(iii) Ship of the desert
(d) Polar bear	(iv) migration
(e) Elephant	(v) thick coat of white fur

(A) (a)-(ii), (b)-(iii), (c)-(iv), (d)-(v), (e)-(v)
(B) (a)-(ii), (b)-(iv), (c)-(iii), (d)-(v), (e)-(i)
(C) (a)-(ii), (b)-(iii), (c)-(iv), (d)-(v), (e)-(i)
(D) (a)-(iv), (b)-(iii), (c)-(ii), (d)-(i), (e)-(v)

5. Match the following.

Column-A	Column-B
(a) Desert	(i) Slowest mover
(b) Seal	(ii) Winter sleep
(c) Hibernation	(iii) Camel
(d) Adipose tissue	(iv) Polar region
(e) Snail	(v) Layer of fat deposit

(A) (a)-(i), (b)-(iv), (c)-(ii), (d)-(v), (e)-(iii)
(B) (a)-(iii), (b)-(iv), (c)-(ii), (d)-(v), (e)-(i)
(C) (a)-(iii), (b)-(v), (c)-(ii), (d)-(iv), (e)-(i)
(D) (a)-(iii), (b)-(ii), (c)-(iv), (d)-(v), (e)-(i)

6. Match the following.

Column-A	Column-B
(a) Generation of new organisms	(i) Viviparous
(b) Polar beer	(ii) Fat layer
(c) Human	(iii) Reproduction
(d) Insulator	(iv) Polar region

(A) (a)-(iii), (b)-(iv), (c)-(ii), (d)-(i)
(B) (a)-(iii), (b)-(ii), (c)-(i), (d)-(iv)
(C) (a)-(i), (b)-(iv), (c)-(iii), (d)-(ii)
(D) (a)-(iii), (b)-(iv), (c)-(i), (d)-(ii)

w 7. Match the following.

Column-A	Column-B
(a) Long roots	(i) Xerophytes
(b) Soft stem	(ii) Hydrophytes
(c) Leaves modified in spines	(iii) Cool region
(d) Conifers	(iv) Cactus

(A) (a)-(i), (b)-(ii), (c)-(iv), (d)-(iii)
(B) (a)-(ii), (b)-(iii), (c)-(i), (d)-(iv)
(C) (a)-(i), (b)-(ii), (c)-(iii), (d)-(iv)
(D) (a)-(iv), (b)-(iii), (c)-(ii), (d)-(i)

8. Match the following.

Column-A	Column-B
(a) Summer sleep	(i) Tuber
(b) Kangaroo rat	(ii) Aestivation
(c) Oxidation of glucose	(iii) Desert animal
(d) Potato	(iv) Energy

(A) (a)-(i), (b)-(ii), (c)-(iv), (d)-(iii)
(B) (a)-(ii), (b)-(iii), (c)-(iv), (d)-(i)
(C) (a)-(i), (b)-(ii), (c)-(iii), (d)-(iv)
(D) (a)-(iv), (b)-(iii), (c)-(ii), (d)-(i)

Assertion and Reason Type Questions

In the following questions, a statement of Assertion is followed by a statement of Reason.

(A) If both Assertion and Reason are true, and the Reason is the correct explanation of the Assertion.
(B) If both Assertion and Reason are true, but the Reason is not the correct explanation of the Assertion.
(C) If Assertion is true, but Reason is false.
(D) If both Assertion and Reason are false.

1. **Assertion:** Hydrophytes are aquatic plants.
Reason: They have long primary roots to absorb water.

2. **Assertion:** Reproduction is a process by which all organism maintain their continuity of life.
Reason: Reproduction is one of the key feature of living being.

3. **Assertion:** A polar bear has thick fatty skin.
Reason: Their skin acts as insulator.

4. **Assertion:** Cactus is a desert plant.
Reason: Leaves of cacti modify into spines to reduce transpiration.

5. **Assertion:** Removal of waste from the body is called excretion.
Reason: Respiration is necessary for survival.

6. **Assertion:** Plants are autotrophs.
Reason: Plants perform photosynthesis.

7. **Assertion:** Change in the surrounding is called stimuli.
Reason: Each living organism shows response to stimuli.

8. **Assertion:** Balanced diet is required for growth.
Reason: Growth is feature of a living being.

9. **Assertion:** By respiration, organisms increase their population.
Reason: Human respires through the kidney.

10. **Assertion:** Movement & locomotion are the same.
Reason: Displacement of any living being is called movement.

11. **Assertion:** Frogs are amphibians.
Reason: They can live in water and on land.

12. **Assertion:** Any change in an organism according to their surrounding is called adaption.
    Reason: Adaption is necessary for survival.

13. **Assertion:** Camel is a desert animal.
    Reason: It excretes concentrated urine for survival.

14. **Assertion:** Fish has a streamlined body to survive.
    Reason: Fishes have lungs for breathing.

15. **Assertion:** Lion is a carnivore.
    Reason: It has sharp canines to tear its food.

Comprehension Type Questions

A place where an organism lives is called a habitat. Habitat denotes the home of an organism. In a habitat, both biotic and abiotic components are found. Living components are called biotic components and non-living components are called abiotic components. The habitat provides food, water, air, shelter, and other needful things to organisms. Several kinds of plants and animals live in the same habitat. Organisms that live on land are called terrestrial animals and their habitat is called a terrestrial habitat. Some examples of terrestrial habitats are forests, grasslands, deserts, coastal and mountain regions. Organisms which live in water are called aquatic organisms and their habitat is called aquatic habitat. Lakes, rivers, and oceans are some examples of aquatic habitats. Organisms which live on both water and land are called amphibians. They have adaptation for both type of habitats.

1. Define habitat.
2. An example of a terrestrial habitat is:
   (A) Grassland
   (B) Dwelling place
   (C) Pond
   (D) Sea
3. Which of the following is an aquatic habitat?
   (A) Lakes
   (B) Forest
   (C) Pond
   (D) Both (A) and (C)
4. Living things are the biotic components of a habitat.
   (A) True (B) False
5. Amphibians can live in water.
   (A) True (B) False
6. Give one example of an amphibian and write down it's adaptation.
7. Write a short note on biotic and abiotic components of a habitat.
8. Write down differences between terrestrial and aquatic habitats.
9. How does an organism survive in a habitat?
10. Give names of 2 animals which can live in the desert.

Free Response Type

Very Short Answer Type Questions

1. Define predators and prey.
2. Visit a pond and notice which the kinds of plants you see there.
3. Name the stages in the life cycle of a frog.
4. What do you understand by life cycle and life span of a living organism?
5. What is a tadpole?
6. Write down 2 differences between terrestrial and aquatic habitats.
7. Why does a camel have a hump on it's back?
8. Which kind of animals have blowholes?
9. Define germination. Write down it's importance in a plant's life.
10. If we cover the leaf of a mesophyte with a polythene and place it under sunlight, what can we observe after 3-4 hours?
11. What is an ecosystem?
12. Why is water important in the life cycle of a frog?
13. Do plants show locomotion? If yes, give 2 examples.
14. Give three examples of grassland animals.
15. Select the plants which can propagate by stem cutting:
    Basil, wheat, rice, money plant, potato, bryophyllum, rose, and mint.

Short Answer Type Questions

1. Ans the following questions.
   (i) Name the animal called as the ship of the desert.
   (ii) How do gills help a fish?
   (iii) In which habitats do rats show aestivation?
   (iv) Name animals living in aerial habitats.
2. Why can't all animals live in the same habitat?
3. If we touch mimosa pudica, what kind of movement will it show?
4. State the mountain region adaptation in animals.
5. State the adaptations of lions.
6. What do you mean by acclimatization and estuaries?
7. Name the adaptation undergone by camels which help it to survive in the desert.
8. Differentiate between oceans and ponds with examples of animals which live in these two.
9. What is respiration why it is necessary for a living being?
10. Frogs are amphibians. Which kind of adaptation has it undergone to survive in both environments?

Long Answer Type Questions

1. What features have polar bears adapted to live in extremely cold climates?
2. Explain with an example, polar region adaptations in animals and plants.
3. Write down few adaptations of aquatic plants and animals both.
4. Write down adaptations undergone by camels and kangaroo rats to survive in deserts.
5. Explain characteristics of living beings.
6. What are the differences between biotic and abiotic components?
7. Mention any two types of terrestrial habitats, and their key features.
8. In which type of habitat can a whale live in and what kind of adaptation does it have to survive in that habitat.
9. Explain adaptation of mountain region trees.
10. Differentaite between living and non-living things.

Case Based Questions

Year 2020-21 were very crucial years for the whole world due to COVID. During this time, people were packed in their homes to protect themselves from corona. During this period, their social lives were stuck and travelling completely stopped.

In December 2021, when conditions were normal, we planned to visit a few places in India. First, we visited the Thar desert in Rajasthan. It is very large in size with big sand dunes. Here, I saw some plants which do not have leaves. They have spines on their stems. These stems are green in colour. Only short sized plants were there. Animals of that place were also different in their appearance. I saw ship of the desert there for the first time. Our guide informed us of some specifications about that animal. We also enjoyed camping there in sand. After long time, that was a great trip.

1. Which animal our guide was talking about?
2. Give 1 example of a desert plant and write their features.
3. Why are spines are found instead of leaves in desert plants?
4. Define transpiration. Why do plants perform this?
5. Which kind of habitat is the Thar desert?
6. Long feet of desert animals is also adaptation.
7. Which type of adaptation does a desert plant have?
   (A) True (B) False
8. Hydrilla is an aquatic plant.
   (A) True (B) False
9. Changes at a physical level to survive in a particular habitat is called ____________
   (A) Survival (B) Biotic factor
   (C) Adaptation (D) Abiotic factor
10. ____________ is also called desert of the ship.

ASSESSMENT CORNER

Level 2

Multiple Choice Questions

1. An ecosystem is a:
   (A) Group of components that interact with one another.
   (B) Group of interacting species in one place at one time.
   (C) Biological community and component of the physical environment with which the community interacts.
   (D) A group of interacting chemicals and their cycles.
2. In an ecosystem, abiotic components include which of the following?
   (A) Flow of energy.
   (B) Cycling of materials.
   (C) Consumers.
   (D) Flow of energy and cycling of materials.
3. Food chains differ from food webs in that:
   (A) a food chain is a single sequence of who eats whom in a community.
   (B) food chains better represent the entire community.
   (C) food webs represent the complex interaction among food chains.
   (D) a food chain is the flow of energy in a population.
4. Following are some features of plants:
   (i) They lose a lot of water through transpiration.
   (ii) Their leaves are always broad and flat.
   (iii) They lose very little water through transpiration.
   (iv) Their roots grow very deep in the soil.
   Which of the combination of above features are typical for desert plants?
   (A) (i) and (ii) (B) (ii) and (iv)
   (C) (ii) and (iii) (D) (iii) and (iv)
5. Which of the following are characteristics of living beings?
   (i) Respiration
   (ii) Reproduction
   (iii) Adaptation
   (iv) Excretion
   Choose the correct answer from the options below.
   (A) (i), (ii), (iii), and (iv) only
   (B) (i) and (ii) only
   (C) (ii) and (iv) only
   (D) (i), (ii), and (iii)
6. Which of the following is not an example of response to stimulus?
   (A) Mouth watering when we see delicious food items.
   (B) Closing of leaves of a Mimosa plant when touched.
   (C) Shutting our eyes when an object is suddenly thrown in our direction.
   (D) A chick hatching out of an egg.
7. Which of the following is correct for respiration in plants?
   (A) Respiration takes place only during daytime.
   (B) Respiration takes place only during night.
   (C) Respiration takes place both during day and night.
   (D) Respiration takes place only when plants are not making food.
8. In ecosystem non-living components include which of the following-
   (A) Flow of energy
   (B) Cycling of material
   (C) Consumers
   (D) Flow of energy and Cycling of material
9. Which of the following is the correct sequence of the mosquito life cycle?
   (A) Egg → Pupa → Larva → Adult
   (B) Egg → Larva → Pupa → Adult
   (C) Larva → Egg → Pupa → Adult
   (D) Egg → Larva → Adult → Pupa
10. If you happen to go to a desert, what changes do you expect to observe in the urine you excrete? You would:
    (i) excrete a small amount of urine.
    (ii) excrete a large amount of urine.
    (iii) excrete concentrated urine.
    (iv) excrete very dilute urine.
    Which of the above would hold true?
    (A) (i) and (iii) (B) (ii) and (iv)
    (C) (i) and (iv) (D) (i) and (ii)
11. Refer to the given paragraph where few words/phrases have been italicised and select the correct option.
    Different organisms show different adaptations to adjust to their habitats. Plants inhabiting in deserts have leaves with drip tips which help in draining excess sand sticking to their surfaces. In some plants like aloe vera, leaves are reduced to spines to reduce transpirational loss of water. Plants inhabiting in rain forests are normally cone shaped with sloping branches and needle like leaves, e.g., pine trees.

ASSESSMENT CORNER

Animals found in cold mountainous regions generally become active at night and remain deep in their burrows during daytime. They excrete dilute urine. Animals inhabiting in polar regions possess subcutaneous fat and thick fur to protect them from the cold.

(A) Deserts should be replaced with polar regions whereas sand should be replaced with water.
(B) Aloe vera should not be replaced as it is correctly mentioned whereas pine should be replaced with neem.
(C) The positions of cold mountainous regions and rainforests should be interchanged.
(D) Dilute should be replaced with concentrated whereas subcutaneous fat should not be replaced as it is correctly mentioned.

12. Read the given statements and select the correct option.
Statement 1: Trees growing on high altitudes like mountains have needle-like leaves.
Statement 2: High altitudes are cool regions as temperature decreases with increasing altitudes.
(A) Both statements 1 and 2 are true, and statement 2 is the correct explanation of statement 1.
(B) Both statements 1 and 2 are true, but statement 2 is not the correct explanation of statement 1.
(C) Statement 1 is true, but statement 2 is false.
(D) Statement 1 is false, but statement 2 is true.

13. Which of the following is not characterstics of biotic component of ecosystems-
(A) Living organism are made up of cell
(B) Living organisms grow and mature
(C) Living organisms have an indefinite life span
(D) Living organisms respond to stimulus

14. Megha's brother brought a plant with the following features-
(i) Narrow and thin ribbon like leaves
(ii) Reduced size of roots
(iii) long, hollow,and light stem
Her brother most likely brought this plant is-
(A) Xerophyte (B) Mesophyte
(C) Halophyte (D) Hydrophyte

15. Which stage of the mosquito is active and swims in water?
(A) Egg (B) Larva
(C) Pupa (D) Adult

16. Read the following adaptations of animals for grassland habitat.
(i) They have strong claws that can be withdrawn inside their toes.
(ii) They have eyes on the side of their heads.
(iii) They are light brown in colour.
(iv) They have strong flat hind teeth for chewing.
(v) They move in herds.
(vi) They have eyes in front of their faces.
Select the option that correctly categories the given adaptations for predator and prey animals
Preys Predators
(A) (i), (ii), (vi) (iii), (iv), (v)
(B) (ii), (v) (i), (iii), (iv), (vi)
(C) (ii), (iv), (v) (i), (iii), (vi)
(D) (iii), (v), (vi) (i), (ii), (iv)

17. When people living on plains visit high mountain regions, they experience breathlessness and nausea. This happens because mountains at a high altitude have low levels of oxygen in the atmosphere. Therefore, they have to breathe faster. After some days, they temporarily change to adjust to the newly changed conditions.
Read the given passage and answer the following.
(a) State the term given to such a feature of organisms where they temporarily change to overcome changed environmental conditions.
(b) Select another example of such feature.

A		B
(a)	Adaptation	Thick layer of fur in polar bears.
(b)	Acclimatization	Change in skin colour due to the climate.
(c)	Acclimatization	Bending of plants towards sunlight.
(d)	Adaptation	Streamlined body of birds.

18. Select the incorrect statement:
(i) The Sundarbans delta is the largest mangrove forest in the world.
(ii) Andaman and Nicobar Islands in India have coral reefs.
(iii) The Great Barrier Reef of Australia is the biggest coral reef.
(iv) Mangroves cannot grow in sea water.
(A) (i), (ii), and (iii) (B) (ii) only
(C) (iv) only (D) Both (ii) and (iv)

19. Which of the following are not found in estuaries:
(A) Corals (B) Sea animals
(C) Mangroves (D) Both (A) and (B)

ASSESSMENT CORNER

20. Which of the following is an incorrect match?

	Aquatic plant	Adaptation
(a)	Water hyacinth	Inflated leaf stalks
(b)	Floating moss fern	Spongy leaves
(c)	Water lettuce	Tiny hairs to trap air bubbles
(d)	Duckweed	Large waterproof leaves

Higher Order Thinking Skill (HOTS)

1. Choose the set that represents only the biotic components of a habitat:
(A) Tiger, deer, grass, and soil.
(B) Rocks, soil, plants, and air.
(C) Aquatic plant, fish, frog, and insect.
(D) Sand, turtle, crab, and rocks.

2. Which of the following cannot be called a habitat?
(A) A desert with a camel.
(B) Cultivated land with grazing cattle.
(C) A jungle with wild animals.
(D) A Pond with fishes.

3. Earthworms breathe through their:
(A) Gills (B) Lungs
(C) Skin (D) Stomata

4. Deepak is doing his homework which is given by his teacher. Would you help him to choose the incorrect sentences?
(A) The lion is a strong fast and agile animal which can hunt and kill it's prey.
(B) The lion has eyes in the front of its head which enables it to have a correct idea of the location of it's prey.
(C) The light brown colour helps the lion hide in dry grasslands when it hurts for prey.
(D) None of the above.

5. Study the diagram below.

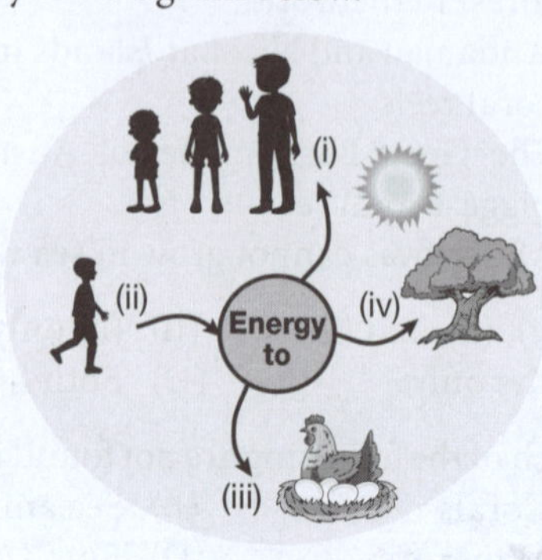

The diagram shows some of the importance of energy to living things. What could (i), (ii), (iii) and (iv) represent?

	(i)	(ii)	(iii)	(iv)
(A)	Growth	Movement	Reproduction	Feeding
(B)	Growth	Movement	Reproduction	Photosynthesis
(C)	Movement	Growth	Digestion	Photosynthesis
(D)	Re-production	Movement	Digestion	Feeding

6. Which of the following organisms has an exoskeleton?

(A)  (B) 

(C)  (D) 

7. Which of the following options represents population?

(A)  (B) 

(C)  (D) 

8. The diagram below shows three animals

Animal P Animal Q Animal R

Animal ________ is most likely found in the desert because it has ________.
(A) P, the ability to climb
(B) Q, large ears to lose heat
(C) Q, large ears to conserve heat
(D) R, a long neck to reach for leaves in tall trees.

9. Which of the following habitats have the given characteristics?

Plants are usually weak stemmed with numerous air spaces

Very thin long and waxy coated leaves
(A) Mesophytes
(B) Bryophytes
(C) Xerophytes
(D) Hydrophytes

10. Look at the diagram given below.

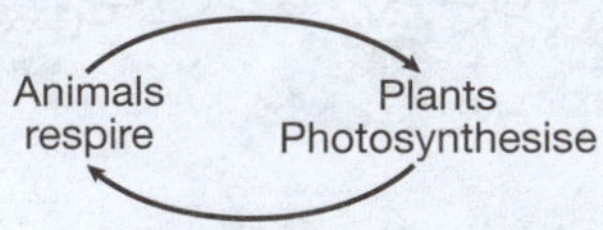

The plants and animals are exchanging ______ for their life processes to take place.
(A) Space (B) Nutrients
(C) Gases (D) Shelter

11. How do desert animals adjust to very high temperatures and lack of water in the area?
(A) They shed their skin.
(B) They become active during daytime.
(C) They lose much water from their bodies.
(D) They use the water stored in their bodies.

12. Which of these plants have a waxy coating so that they do not decay despite being constantly in contact with water?
(A) Water hyacinth (B) Water chestnut
(C) Hydrilla (D) All of the above

13. Which of the following animals shows slithering movements?

(A)  (B) 

(C)  (D) 

14. Which of the following sequences is arranged correctly in an increasing order of complexity in a multicellular organism?
(A) Tissue → Cell → Organ → System
(B) Organ → System → Tissue → Cell
(C) Cell → Tissue → Organ → System
(D) System → Cell → Tissue → Organ

15. An X organism has chitin cover on his body & walk climb on a wall or even can fly-
(A) Cockroach
(B) Snail
(C) Bat
(D) Snake

16. What do the arrows in the given figure represent?

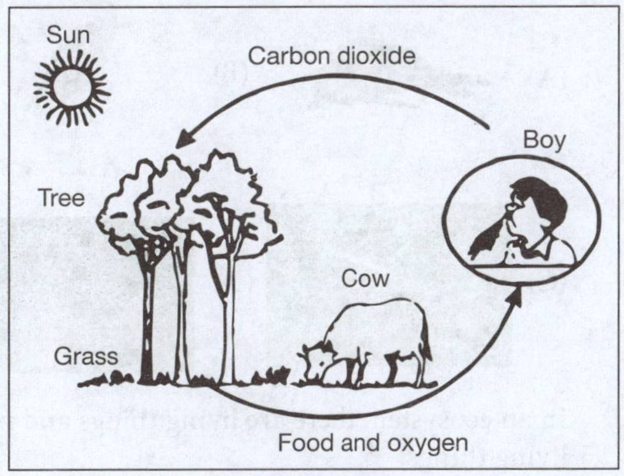

(A) Interdependence between plants only.
(B) Interdependence between animals only.
(C) Interdependence between plants and animals.
(D) Interdependence between abiotic factors.

17. The given figure shows a mimosa plant.

When you step on the mimosa plant, its leaves will close up. This shows that the plant is exhibiting which of the following characteristics of living things?
(A) Growth
(B) Response to stimuli
(C) Reproduction
(D) Locomotion

18. Identify 'X' in the given chart

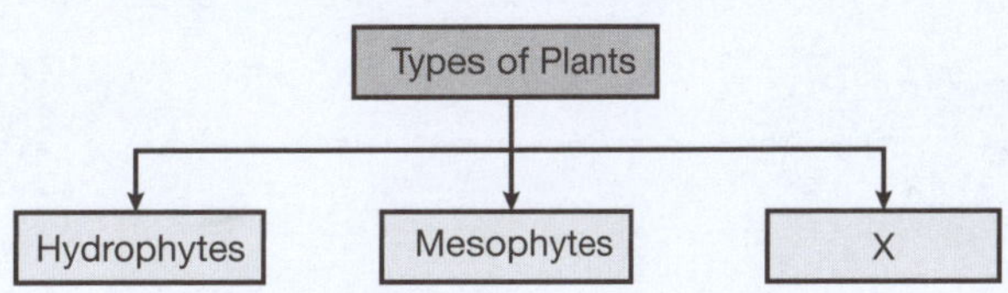

(A) Saprophytes (B) Thallophyte
(C) Xerophytes (D) Bryophytes

19. Study the food chain below.
Grass → X → frog → snake
Which of the following can X be?

(A)  (B) 

(C)  (D) 

20. In an ecosystem there are living things and non-living things.

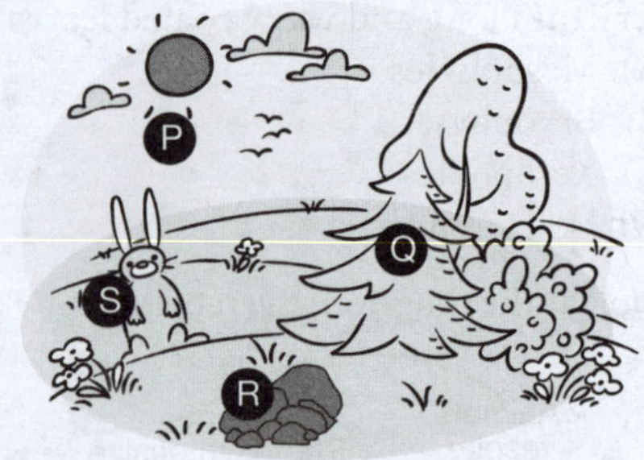

Which labelled part in this ecosystem is an autotroph?

(A) P (B) Q

(C) R (D) S

ASSESSMENT CORNER

ARCHIVE CORNER

1. Which of the following statements does not hold true for the given plants?

(A) Roots are either absent or very poorly developed.
(B) Stomata are present only on the upper surface of leaves to facilitate gaseous exchange.
(C) Body tissue has numerous air spaces.
(D) Leaves are either ribbon-like or highly divided to prevent them from getting torn.

2. Refer to the given flowchart and select the correct option regarding it.

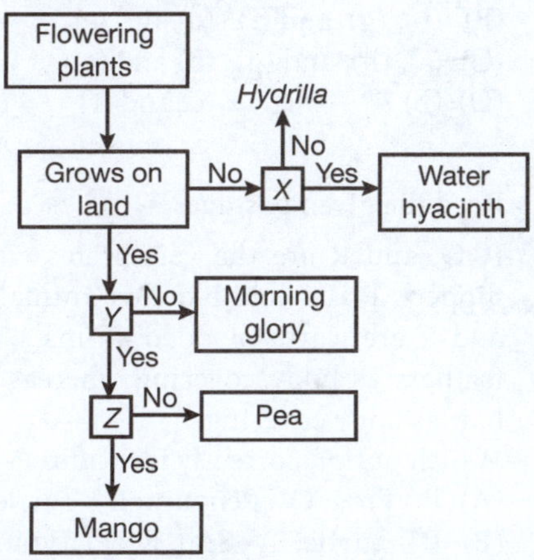

Which of the following can you conclude regarding the habitats of these animals?

	X	Y	Z
(A)	Has spores	Has weak stem	Has poisonous fruits
(B)	Has swollen	Has weak stem	Has fleshy leaf and stalk fruits
(C)	Has fleshy	Has woody stem	Has poisonous fruits
(D)	Floats on water	Has woody stem	Has fleshy fruits

3. Read the given passage.
Animals X, Y, and Z are found in completely different habitats. Animal X is nocturnal and has developed many characteristics to conserve water as much as it can in the body. Animal Y has a furry body with thick skin. It is large in size and has padded feet. Animal Z is adapted to live on trees. Sticky pads on it's feet help it to climb trees.
(A) Animal X lives in a place with annual rainfall of about 80-100 cm.
(B) Animal Y lives in a place where days may be extremely hot, and nights can be very cold.
(C) Animal Z lives in an area with annual rainfall of about 20-25 cm.
(D) Animal Y lives in an area where temperatures sometimes reaches 0°C or falls below it.

4. A science teacher took her students out for a practical activity to teach them more about aquatic plants. She showed the students an underwater leaf and told them that underwater leaves do not have waxy waterproof coating. She asked them the reason for the same.
given below are the replies of the students:
Student P: Unwaxed leaf surface can float easily.
Student Q: Unwaxed leaf surface facilitates gaseous exchange between the plant and water.
Student R: Unwaxed leaf surface can reduce transpiration.
Student S: Unwaxed leaf surface can transport water.
Which of these students replied correctly?
(A) Student P (B) Student Q
(C) Student R (D) Student S

5. Two different animals have the following characteristics in common:
(i) They are aquatic animals.
(ii) They give birth to their young ones and suckle them.
(iii) They have blowholes and breathe through lungs.
The animals are likely to be:
(A) A turtle and a frog
(B) A swordfish and a shark
(C) A dolphin and a whale
(D) A turtle and a penguin

6. Which of the following is paired correctly?
(A) Desert-Dolphin (B) Aquatic-Giraffe
(C) Terrestrial-whale (D) Terrestrial-deer

7. On the basis of body covering, Rohit made four groups of three organisms each. In an attempt of doing so, he classified organisms incorrectly in one of the groups. Identify this group and select the correct option.
(A) Tortoise, snail, and oyster.
(B) Fish, snake, and lizard.
(C) Penguin, ostrich, and bat.
(D) Hippopotamus, whale, and cow.

8. A large number of fur seals and aquatic birds were found dead near a water body. The reason behind their death came out to be the failure of their temperature regulating system.
This indicates the occurrence of a/an _________ recently.
(A) Avalanche (B) Oil spill
(C) Acid rain (D) Flood

9. Refer to the given classification chart and select the correct option regarding it.

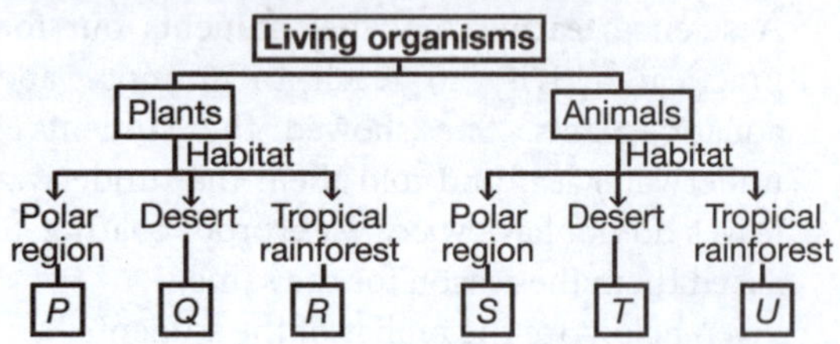

	P S	Q T	R U
(A)	Pine Armadillo	Cactus Caribou	Acacia Spider
(B)	Willow Penguin	Opuntia Kangaroo-rat	Rubber tree Toucan
(C)	Maple Bison	Fern Walrus	Lenina Raccoon
(D)	Tape grass Indian	Sundew Lynx	Teak Arowana

10. The given graphs show number and average biomass of different organisms present in an aquatic ecosystem.

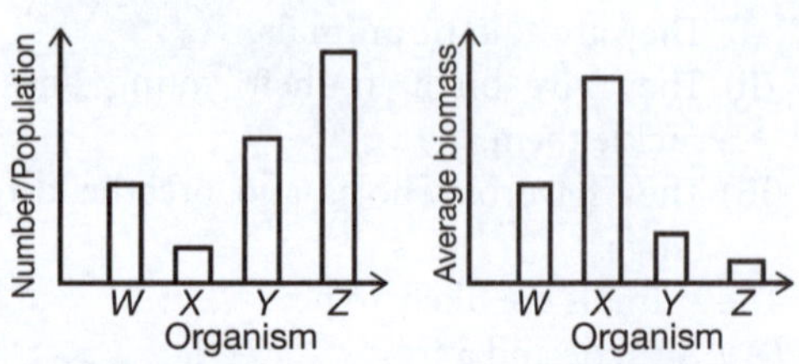

Select the correct option regarding the food chain formed by interlinking organisms W, X, Y, and Z.
(A) X could be a producer and forms the first link in the food chain formed by interlinking these organisms.
(B) Y and W could be primary and secondary consumers respectively in the food chain formed by interlinking these organisms.
(C) The correct relation of these organisms in the food chain is X—W—Z—Y.
(D) If a population of an exotic species is introduced in this community which exclusively feeds on X, then populations of Z and W will be negatively affected.

11. Study the given list of adaptations in plants.
(a) Leaves reduced into spines
(b) Drip tips
(c) Sloping branch
(d) Fleshy stem
(e) Thick waxy layer on stem
(f) Cone shaped trees
(g) Photosynthetic stem
Which of the given adaptations are of plants inhabiting rainforests (X), mountains (Y) and deserts (Z)?

	X	Y	Z
(A)	(g) and (f)	(a), (d), and (e)	(b) and (e)
(B)	(b), (g), and (f)	(d) and (e)	(a) and (c)
(C)	(a), (h), and (g)	(d) and (e)	(c) and (f)
(D)	(b)	(c) and (f)	(a), (d), (e), and (g)

12. Read the given passage.
P, Q, and R are the vertebrates which possess flippers. P is a cold blooded animal whereas, Q and R are warm blooded animals. Q possesses feathers as body covering whereas R possesses hair as body covering.
Which option correctly identifies P-R?
(A) P - Frog; Q - Penguin; R - Turtle
(B) P – Turtle; Q - Seal; R - Platypus
(C) P - Seal; Q - Frog; R - Penguin
(D) P - Turtle; Q - Penguin; R - Seal

13. Refer to the given table and select the correct option.

Animal	Characteristics				
	Hair	Shell	Feathers	Hibernation	Aestivation
P	✓	×	×	✓	×
Q	×	×	✓	×	×
R	×	✓	×	×	✓
S	×	×	×	✓	×

(A) P could be a mammal that possesses thick subcutaneous fat layer whereas, Q could be sparrow that has air filled bones.

(B) R could be a snail that has endoskeleton of bones whereas, S could be reptile that bears poisonous fangs.

(C) P could be an invertebrate whose mouth has thick leathery lining for eating spiny shrubs whereas, Q could be a migratory bird such as an ostrich.

(D) R could be a vertebrate whose body is divisible into head, visceral hump, and foot whereas, S could be an amphibious vertebrate.

ANSWER KEY

Level 1

Fixed Response Type

Multiple Choice Questions

1. B 2. B 3. B 4. A 5. B 6. C 7. A 8. B 9. A 10. C

Fill in the Blanks

1. Latex
2. Stimuli
3. Cellular respiration
4. Aquatic
5. Living
6. Aquatic
7. Xerophytes
8. Dedritivores
9. Aquatic
10. Xerophyte/desert plant
11. Blowholes
12. Mesophytes
13. Reproduction
14. Stimuli
15. Conifers
16. Gill
17. Insulator
18. Aquatic
19. Spines

True/False

1. True 2. False 3. True 4. True 5. False
6. True 7. False 8. True 9. True 10. True
11. True 12. True 13. False 14. False 15. True

Match Type Questions

1. C 2. A 3. D 4. C 5. B 6. D 7. A 8. B

Assertion Reason Type Question

1. C 2. A 3. A 4. A 5. B 6. A 7. A 8. B 9. D 10. D
11. A 12. A 13. A 14. C 15. B

Comprehension Type Questions

1. A 2. A 3. D 4. A 5. A

Level 2

Multiple Choice Questions

1. C 2. D 3. C 4. D 5. A 6. D 7. C 8. D 9. B 10. A
11. D 12. B 13. C 14. D 15. B 16. C 17. B 18. C 19. D 20. D

ANSWER KEY

Higher Order Thinking Skill (HOTS)

1. C	**2.** B	**3.** C	**4.** D	**5.** B	**6.** D	**7.** B	**8.** D	**9.** D	**10.** C
11. D	**12.** D	**13.** C	**14.** C	**15.** A	**16.** C	**17.** B	**18.** C	**19.** C	**20.** B

Archive Corner

1. B	**2.** D	**3.** D	**4.** B	**5.** C	**6.** D	**7.** C	**8.** B	**9.** B	**10.** B
11. D	**12.** D	**13.** A							

Hints and Explanations

CHAPTER 1: MEASUREMENT OF LENGTH AND MOTION

CHECK POINT 1

1. Bus, train
2. Helicopter, aeroplane
3. Boat, ship
4. Primitive mode of transportation was mostly based on simple machines, like wooden cart, wooden rafts made of woods, etc. Also, they use animals to some extent. While modern mode of transportation is mostly using fuels and engines to increase their speed. They are made up of metals.
5. Primitive mode of transportation was made up of wood because at that time, the most easily accessible and available thing was wood which is obtained from trees.
6. (a) $5\ \mu m = 5 \times 10^{-6}$ m
   (b) 3 km $= 3 \times 10^{3}$ m
   (c) 20 mm $= 20 \times 10^{-3}$ m $= 2 \times 10^{-2}$ m
   (d) 73 picometer $= 73 \times 10^{-12}$ m $= 7.3 \times 10^{-11}$ m
   (e) 7.5 nm $= 7.5 \times 10^{-9}$ m
7. 5 metric tonne = 5×10^{3} kg $= 5 \times 10^{3} \times 10^{3}$ gram $= 5 \times 10^{6}$ gram
8. 1 gram = 1×10^{-3} kg
   1560 gram = 1560×10^{-3} kg = 1.560 kg
9. $13.6\ gcm^{-3} = 13.6 \times 10^{-3}\ kg \times (100)^{-3}\ m^{3} = 13.6 \times 10^{-9}\ m^{3}$
10. 1 light year = $3 \times 10^{8} \times 365 \times 24 \times 60 \times 60 = 9.46 \times 10^{15}$ m
11. Volume of cube = $(Side)^{3} = (1\ cm)^{3} = (10^{-2}\ m)^{3} = 10^{-6} m^{3}$
12. $18\ km\ h^{-1} = 18 \times 10^{3} / (60 \times 60) = 5$ m in 1 second

CHECK POINT 2

13. Scale C is suitable for measuring up to 10 cm length.
14. 500 m = 500×10^{-3} km = 0.5 km
15. 1 millimeter < 1 centimeter < 1 meter < 1 kilometer
16. 1.65 m = 1.65×10^{2} cm = 165 cm
    1.65 m = 1.65×10^{3} mm = 1650 mm
17. Perimeter of square park = 4 × side = 4 × 300 m = 1200 m
    Cost of fencing = Cost of 1 meter × Perimeter = Rs. 25 × 1200 = Rs. 30,000

CHECK POINT 3

18. Motion of earth around sun, motion of simple pendulum
19. **(i)** The motion of a swing is an example of oscillatory motion.
    (ii) The instrument used to measure speed is called as speedometer.
20. **(a)** oscillatory motion
    (b) random motion
    (c) combined motion
21. Speed = Distance / Time = 248 km / 4 hours = 62 km/hr
22. Distance travelled = PQ + QR = 2 m + 2 m = 4 m

LEVEL 1

Fixed Response Type

Multiple Choice Questions

1. **(C)** Hand spans depend on the size of the hands of a person which varies from person to person.
2. **(B)** People began the use of animals to haul their loads around 5000 BC.
3. **(B)** People developed boats on the pattern of streamlined shape of fish which help them to move forward easily in water.
4. **(A)** Bullock cart is the slowest mode of transportation.
5. **(B)** The movement of things and people from one place to another is known as transportation.

6. (C) International System of Units is abbreviated as S.I.

7. (A) The S.I. unit of mass is kilogram.

8. (D) 1 kg = 1000 g 1.5 kg = 1.5 1000 g = 1500 g

9. (B) $1\ m^2 = 1\ m \times 1\ m = 100\ cm \times 100\ cm$ = 10,000-centimetre square

10. (C) $1\ cm^2 = 1\ cm\ 1\ cm = 10^{-2}\ m\ 10^{-2}\ m = 10^{-4}\ m^2$ = $1/10000\ m^2$

11. (D) Second is the SI unit of time.

12. (A) Area of rectangle = Length × Breadth

13. (A) 1 cm = 10 mm 1 mm = 1/10 cm

14. (A) $1\ m^3 = 10^6\ cm^3$ which implies $1\ cm^3 = 10^{-6}\ m^3$

15. (B) Meter is the standard unit of length.

16. (C) Vernier calipers are used to measure very small lengths.

17. (A) Here, the bus is moving so it is in motion.

18. (C) kilometer is largest among the options.

19. (B) The position is measured from reference point which can indicate whether a person is in motion or at rest.

20. (B) The S.I. unit of speed is metre/second.

21. (C) Oscillatory and curved motion.

22. (B) State of rest or motion depends on the reference point.

23. (C) Vernier caliper is best suited to measure the diameter of a small ball.

24. (B) The point on the blade will exhibit circular motion.

25. (A) The motion which repeats itself after a regular interval of time is periodic.

Assertion and Reason Type Questions

1. (A) Both A and R are true, and R is the correct explanation of A.

2. (D) In international system of units, the unit of length is meter.

3. (C) Aeroplanes were developed in 1903.

4. (D) Speed cannot be negative. It can be positive and zero only.

Comprehension Type Questions

1. (B) The S.I. system of units is based on metric system.

2. (D) The metric system of units was created by French people.

3. (B) The S.I. unit of length is metre.

4. (A) Chronological order: cycle, train, bus, aeroplane.

5. (C) Steam engines were used in trains.

6. (D) All of these vehicles required wheels.

Free Response Type

Very Short Answer Type Questions

1. The process of travelling/moving people or goods from one place to another is called transportation.

2. A boy is running on a circular track in the park.

3. We can measure the length of curved line using a ruler and a thread.

4. An object is said to be at rest if it does not change its position with respect to its surroundings with the passage of time while A body is said to be in motion if its position changes continuously with respect to the surroundings (or with respect to an observer) with the passage of time.

5. Kelvin is the SI unit of measurement for temperature

6. Distance is the actual path travelled by a body. Its SI unit is m.

7. Odometer is the device used to measure the distance traveled by a vehicle.

Short Answer Type Questions

1. The advantages of modern means of transport are:
   (i) It saves our time.
   (ii) We can cover large distances in very short amount of time.
   (iii) It is convenient and easily available.
   (iv) It is cost friendly.

2. The disadvantages of modern means of transport are:
   (i) We are becoming lazier as we do not walk.
   (ii) We are much prone to get diseases due to lack of exercise.

(iii) It causes pollution which is harming our environment in the long run.

(iv) More deaths are occurring because of accidents.

3. The hands of a clock exhibit circular motion as well as periodic motion as their tips are moving on a circular path repeatedly after a fixed interval of time.

4. When we have to bring fruits, vegetables, etc., from the market then the seller measures their quantity using beam balance and we have to pay him accordingly. The tailor needs exact measurement of our body to stitch our dresses. Also, when go on a picnic we always have an approximation that how much time will be spent on a journey for our convenience. Thus, we can conclude that measurement is important part of everyday life.

5. Divider is used to measure the length of a small object or line drawn.

6. When we stretch the elastic measuring tape, its length increases. This is why, elastic measuring tape is not a reliable tool to measure distance.

7. Speed = Distance/time = 120 km/ 2hr = 60 km/hr

8. A periodic motion in which a body revolves around a fix point on the circular path is called circular motion. Example: Motion of the tip of the clock's arm.

   The to and fro periodic motion of a body is called oscillatory motion. Example: Motion of a simple pendulum.

Long Answer Type Questions

1. Wheel can be treated as a tool which rolls on the surface and help the vehicle move forward. The time taken by a body to travel a long distance can be decreased at great extent. Wheels makes it easy to move a vehicle.

2. We will ask for the driver for the distance covered by us and note the total time taken using stop watch. Then using formula, average speed = (Total distance covered / Total time taken)

3. Let initial reading = 5 cm

   Let final reading = 23.2 cm

   Length of the knitting needle = Final reading – Initial reading = 23.2 – 5 = 18.2 cm

4. The motion that repeats itself after a fixed interval of time is known as periodic motion. For example: the motion of hands of a clock and the motion of moon around the earth are the periodic motion.

5. First, we can measure the length of our foot using a scale. Then we will use our feet to measure the steps from heel to toe by following the entire length of the room. Finally we will multiply the number of steps to the length of one foot to get the length of the room.

6. (i) They both are rotating about the axis imagined passing through them.

   (ii) The type of motion of both is random motion.

7. We can note the occurrence of seasons. The time taken in reaching from one summer season to the next will give the rough idea about the time period of one year.

8. Speed = Distance/time = 20 km/0.5 hr = 40 km/hr

9. (i) 54 km/hr = (54 × 1000 m)/ (60 × 60 sec) = 15 m/s

   (ii) 30 m/s = (30 × 10^{-3} km)/ (1/(60 × 60) hr) = 108 km/hr

Numerical Based Questions

1. Time taken = Distance / Speed = 1000 m / (10m/s) = 100 s

2. AE as starting point is A and ending point is E.

3. Distance moved = AB + BC + CD + DE = 2 cm + 2 cm + 3 cm + 1 cm = 8 cm

Case Based Questions

1. (C) Both tailor and sewing machine remains at rest.

2. (A) Wheel of machine moves with circular motion.

3. (C) The up and down motion of the needle of sewing machine can be classified as periodic motion.

Level 2

Multiple Choice Questions

1. (B) Same scales of measurement will provide same conclusions to ensure consistency in measurements.
2. (D) Measurement means the comparison of an unknown quantity with some known quantity of same kind.
3. (C) The smallest time measured by a wristwatch accurately is 1 second.
4. (C) The observer's eye is not positioned correctly.
5. (B) The standard unit of measuring large distances, such as the distance between cities, is kilometer.
6. (A) It will be curvilinear motion (a type of translatory motion). Striker of carrom board will be in random motion.
7. (C) Both rotational and translational motion.
8. (C) The distance covered by a moving object in unit time is called speed.
9. (D) micrometer is used to measure the length of very small objects like bacteria.
10. (C) Circular/elliptical motion.
11. (B) It can follow the curved surface accurately.
12. (B) Volume of object = $82\ cm^3 - 70\ cm^3 = 12\ cm^3$
13. (B) To measure the thickness of a thin sheet of paper, the most suitable unit would be millimeter.
14. (B) The time taken for one complete oscillation.
15. (B) Symbols used for unit of a physical quantity shouldn't be written in plural forms.
16. (B) Their measurements are different because they are using different unit systems. They should convert all measurements to a common unit to standardize their results.
17. (C) Millimeter is the unit used for measuring very small length.
18. (C) Blades rotate about a fixed axis.
19. (B) Period = 120 seconds ÷ 4 rotations = 30 seconds
20. (A) Motion of a swing is oscillatory motion.
21. (A) Time period = Total time taken/Number of oscillations = 10 / 20 = 0.5 s
22. (C) A measurement consists of number and unit both.
23. (A) Perimeter = 2(25.5 + 18.75) = 88.5 m = 8850 cm
24. (B) The object is moving with uniform speed
25. (B) 23.7 – 5.2 = 18.5 cm
26. (D) 3.75 km = 3.75 × 1,000,000 mm = 3,750,000 mm
27. (B) A child on a swing; because it repeats its motion at regular intervals
28. (B) $\text{Time Period} = \dfrac{\text{Total time}}{\text{Number of oscillations}}$

    $= \dfrac{30}{15} = 2\ \text{seconds}$
29. (A) Ruler; measure once
30. (C) Use vernier calipers and position your eye at the level of measurement.
31. (B) It requires conversion to a common unit to accurately compare
32. (C) Circumference = $2\pi r = 2 \times \dfrac{22}{7} \times 70 =$ 440 meters
33. (B) Speed = Distance/time 60 = d/2.5 d = 150 km
34. (B) Moves backward relative to the bus.
35. (A) 200 cm ÷ 15 cm = 13.33 ≈ 13
36. (C) A falling stone and moving bus on straight road shows rectilinear motion.
37. (B) The object is changing direction
38. (C) Circumference = 60π cm ≈ 188.4 cm; $\text{Rotations} = \dfrac{5000}{188.4} \approx 26.5 \approx 27$
39. (C) At the same level as the measurement mark.
40. (B) 2.5 cm = 25 mm; 25 mm ÷ 200 = 0.125 mm
41. (A) Using a measuring tape
42. (A) The motion of a coin moving over a carrom board can be classified as rectilinear motion.

43. (C) The ball is rolling with uniform speed means constant speed.

44. (B) Division by 1000

45. (C) After 1 hour, Distance travelled by A = 60 km and the distance travelled by B = 40 km

    Total distance between A and B = 60 km + 40 km = 100 km

46. (C) The precautions that has to be taken while taking a measurement of length are the scale be placed in contact with the object and the eye should be placed exactly in front are on the top of the point where the measurement is to be taken.

47. (B) March past of soldiers is an example of periodic motion.

48. (C) 2.5 hours = 150 minutes; Distance $= 12 \times 150 = 1800$ mm

49. (B) Let the tape follow the curved path.

Higher Order Thinking Skills (HOTS)

1. (B) When two bodies moving with some speed hit each other, most likely their speeds and directions changes.

2. (C) Time period (T) is one complete oscillation between P and Q, i.e., pendulum moves from P to Q and then return to P. Here, R is the mid-point of the path P to Q. So, time taken to move from each section will be equal.

   $T = \text{time taken in 1 complete oscillation}$

   $T = \text{Time taken in } (PR + RQ + QR + RP)$

   $T = t + t + t + t$

   $T = 4t$

   $t = T/4$

3. (A) Stick is rotating at fixed point.

4. (C) The balling is rotating as well as moving forward linearly.

5. (A) An object appears to move when its position appears to change with respect to observer.

6. (C) From the ground, the passenger will seems to be in circular motion.

7. (A) As the length of pendulum increases, its time period also increases.

8. (C) No motion relative to the wheel.

9. (B) 20 m = 0.2 km and 30 mm = 3 cm

10. (C) Motion of earth around sun is circular motion as well as periodic motion. Motion of hand of clock is circular motion as well as periodic motion. Motion of simple pendulum is periodic motion as well as oscillatory motion.

11. (C) The pendulum will only raise to the same height in the opposite side from which it was released if there is no loss of energy to surroundings.

12. (B) 0 km/h as the trains are moving with same speed.

13. (B) Car on a bank road – Curvilinear motion; Apple falling from a tree – Rectilinear motion; Moving top – Rotatory motion; Kid on a swing – Oscillatory motion

14. (D) Movement of snake – Curvilinear motion; Kids on see-saw – Oscillatory motion; Players playing football – Random motion; Motion of ceiling fan – Rotatory motion

15. (A) 100 centuries = 10 millennium

16. (C) Different parts of the coin exhibit different combinations of motion.

17. (B) Measurement should be taken directly in front of the mark of the thermometer.

Archive Corner

1. (C) Displacement = Minimum distance between initial and final point = PQ= $2 \times$ radius = 2a

2. (B) Unit of measurement and required precision.

3. (B) In circular motion, the direction of motion changes continuously.

4. (B) Length of thread is almost 15 cm $\times$ 6 = 90 cm = 0.9 m. This should be between 0.50 m-1.0 m

5. (C) Their time periods depend on different factors like length and amplitude.

6. (D) 1 cm = 10 mm. Least count will be 1 cm/20 = 10 mm/20 = 0.5 mm

7. (A) Railway engine – Metric ton; Packet of chilli powder – g; Sack of wheat – Quintal; Huge bag of sand – kg; Aspirin tablet – mg.

8. (B) Periodic as well as oscillatory motion are of simple pendulum.

9. **(B)** Motion of soldiers on march past is linear motion. Every periodic motion is not oscillatory motion. Hockey player running after ball is random motion.

10. **(C)** Length of P = nearly 2 cm, length of Q = nearly 3 cm, length of R = nearly 3 cm, length of S = 2.5 cm

    Average length = (2 cm + 3 cm + 3 cm + 2.5 cm)/4 = 2.6 cm

11. **(A)** Displacement = Minimum distance between initial and final point

12. **(B)** Since the time taken is same, so Rahul covers a longer distance with higher speed to compensate.

13. **(B)** The measurement scale is too large compared to the object being measured.

14. **(B)** Different levels of precision and errors in each method.

15. **(B)** Reproducibility, universality, and appropriate scale.

16. **(C)** To and fro motion of swing is periodic as well as oscillatory. Hands of clock shows periodic as well as rotatory motion. Motion of a top is rotatory.

17. **(D)** Number of oscillations during T seconds is = 10. So, time period is T/10.

CHAPTER 2: EXPLORING MAGNETS

Check Point 1

1. The blade and screw inside a sharpener are made up of iron. So, they are attracted to both poles of magnet.
2. We will use another magnet whose both poles are known. We will bring close the north pole to both the poles of unknown magnet. The pole which repels will be north pole. The opposite will be south pole.

Check Point 2

3. Using magnetic keeper.
4. It will slowly lose its capacity to attract magnetic substances.
5. Stainless steel is non-magnetic in nature. So, it will not be attracted by magnets.

Check Point 3

6. Refer to the heading 'The Magnetic Compass'
7. Lodestone
8. Letters are directions marked on the compass and numbers are degrees. Numbers are marked every 30° and marks are observed every 5°.
9. Yes
10. North pole is marked as red colour on small magnetic needle on magnetic compass.

Level 1

Fixed Response Type

Multiple Choice Questions

1. (C) Copper is non-magnetic.
2. (C) Wool will not be attracted to magnet.
3. (B) The chemical formula of magnetite (natural magnet) is Fe_3O_4.
4. (B) North-South
5. (B) Like poles repel each other.
6. (B) Compass can detect a magnet.
7. (A) Both poles have same capacity to attract.
8. (C) Natural magnets are weaker than the artificial magnets.
9. (C) Poles
10. (A) North pole of a magnet can be identified by another magnet having its poles marked as north pole and south pole.
11. (C) Lodestone
12. (A) Each piece becomes a new magnet
13. (B) Plastic cannot be turned into magnet.
14. (C) Directive property is used in compass.
15. (B) At the ends/poles
16. (A) Space around a magnet is called magnetic field.
17. (D) Triangle
18. (D) On breaking a bar magnet, we will get more magnets equal to number of pieces.
19. (A) ALNICO is permanent magnet.
20. (B) Heating
21. (B) Like poles repel each other.
22. (C) Magnetic compass is a device used by pilots and navigators used to find the direction.
23. (C) Breaking a magnet will give you magnetic pieces.
24. (C) North
25. (B) The direction EAST from direction SOUTH-EAST in magnetic compass is 45 degrees apart.
26. (D) Soft iron can make temporary magnet.
27. (B) The magnetic domains scatter.
28. (C) To prevent loss of magnetism
29. (B) Copper is not a magnetic material.

30. (A) Magnetic field

31. (C) (i) – Magnets, (ii) – Shepherd, (iii) – Magnes, (iv) – Wooden, (v) – Magnetite

32. (C) By testing for repulsion with the marked poles

33. (B) To amplify sound.

34. (B) Like poles repel each other.

35. (C) Magnetic keeper is a piece of soft iron placed across the poles of a magnet.

36. (C) Color doesn't affect magnetic strength.

37. (A) Magnet will attract iron fillings.

38. (B) Because of magnetic force.

39. (C) Earth aligns the compass needle in north-south direction.

40. (C) Magnet

41. (C) North Pole of a magnetic needle is usually painted red.

42. (D) North pole of a magnet can be identified by another magnet having marked north and south pole.

43. (A) Iron nail becomes a temporary magnet

44. (D) South pole of a freely suspended magnet is attracted towards south direction of earth.

45. (D) All of these

46. (D) Like poles repel each other and unlike poles attract each other.

47. (B) The figure in option B shows the correct arrangement.

48. (A) The stronger magnet will attract more iron filings.

49. (B) Heat or hammer

50. (A) Copper wire and iron rod

Assertion and Reason Type Questions

1. (A) Both A and R are true and R is the correct explanation of A.

2. (A) Both A and R are true and R is the correct explanation of A.

3. (B) Bar magnet is made by artificial means.

Comprehension Type Questions

1. (A) Compass has a small magnet.

2. (C) North is shown by coloured end of magnetic needle.

3. (B) Compass has a small magnet which is called magnetic needle.

Free Response Type

Very Short Answer Type Questions

1. Soft iron or steel

2. Very low strength is at the centre of bar magnet.

3. 5 North poles and 5 south poles will be there.

4. Iron, nickel, cobalt

5. Refer to the heading 'Methods of demagnetizing a permanent magnet'

6. Natural and Artificial magnets

7. We can test the 'tea dust' by magnet.

8. Yes

Short Answer Type Questions

1. Refer to the heading 'Electromagnet'

2. Refer to the heading 'Magnetic Substances'

3. Refer to the heading 'Magnetic Substances'

4. Refer to the heading 'Magnetic Substances'

5. Strength of electromagnet depends on (i) number of turns, (ii) value of current (iii) nature of material inside coil

6. Refer to the heading 'Properties of Bar Magnet'

7. (a) a is the strongest magnet as the iron filings attracted to it are highest.

   (b) b is not a magnet as it doesn't attract iron filings.

8. We will use another magnet whose both poles are known. We will bring close both the poles of known magnet to the pole attached to front of car. By repulsion, we can get the poles.

9. We can use iron filings to find out the magnet. Also, we can use magnet of known poles to find out the magnet.

Long Answer Type Questions

1. Refer to the heading 'The Magnetic Compass'
2. Repulsion is the surest test of magnetism. Since a magnet can attract magnet and magnetic substances, but it will always repel the magnet only.
3. Electromagnets are stronger than natural magnets as we can increase the strength of electromagnet to our needs just by changing the current, number of turns and choosing the material of the magnet. This is not the case with natural magnet.
4. Refer to the heading 'Properties of Bar Magnet'
5. Refer to the heading "Electromagnet"
6. We will use another magnet whose both poles are known. We will bring close the north pole to both the poles of unknown magnet. The pole which repels will be north pole. The opposite will be south pole.
7. Refer to the heading 'Methods of magnetizing and demagnetizing'
8. If we bring the north pole of bar magnet near the north pole of magnetic needle, there will be repulsion. Similarly, if we bring the south pole of bar magnet near the north pole of magnetic needle, there will be attraction.

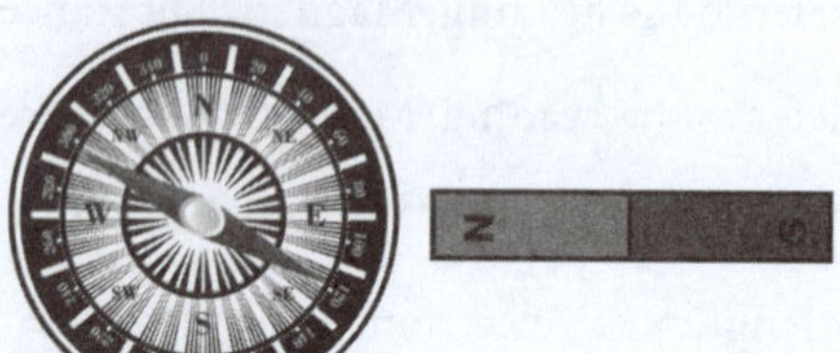

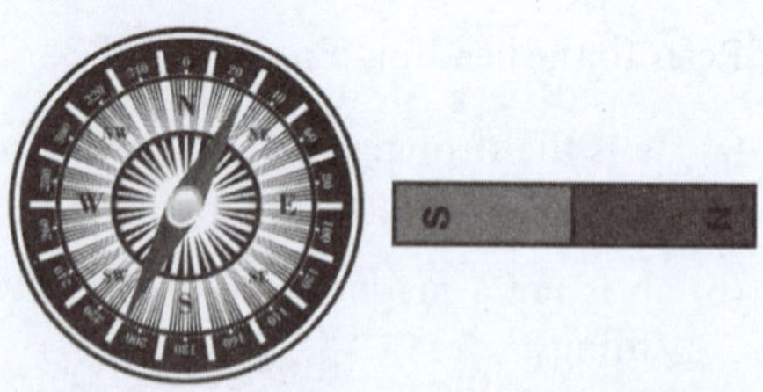

9. We can use single touch method. Refer to the heading 'Methods of magnetizing and demagnetizing'
10. This shows that magnetic substances can be magnetized using magnet.
11. Yes, the two pieces will act as individual magnets. On A, other end will be south pole. On B, the other end will be north pole. We can try to bring the north poles of both the magnets together. If there is repulsion, we can say that both are magnets.
12. U shaped magnet can be stored by putting the magnetic keepers across its poles. To store bar magnet, we will need two magnetic keepers kept on both poles of magnet. But U-shaped magnet will need only one magnetic keeper connecting both the poles.

Numerical Type Questions

1. 2 north poles and 2 south poles will be obtained.
2. 7 north poles and 7 south poles will be obtained.

Case Based Questions

1. **(B)** Magnetic substances can be attracted by magnets but cannot attract other objects.
2. **(B)** Iron, cobalt and nickel are magnetic substances.
3. **(D)** Non-magnetic substances can't be magnetized.

Level 2

Multiple Choice Questions

1. (C) Magnetism
2. (C) Magnetic domains are fully aligned in one direction.
3. (C) Heating or dropping makes the magnet weak.
4. (C) Like poles repel each other.
5. (A) All of the observations are showing that nail was magnetised.
6. (B) Iron filings still get attracted.
7. (A) Thumbtacks are magnetised here. So, the end of the fourth thumbtacks is North. So, it will move towards the south pole of the strong magnet.
8. (B) Magnet Y is weakest here, as the number of paper clips attracted shows its strength. More paper clips, stronger the magnet.
9. (B) Magnetized metal
10. (C) Like poles repel each other.
11. (A) Copper is non-magnetic while iron and steel are magnetic substances.
12. (B) Poles has more attracting capacity.
13. (B) It is hard to magnetize and demagnetize steel.
14. (B) They repel
15. (B) Another strong magnet
16. (B) Large metal structures like bridges, ships, and buildings can create local magnetic fields that can disrupt the compass.
17. (B) Magnetic lines emerge from North pole and enters in south pole.
18. (C) Needle of the compass is made of a magnet because it gets deflected when a magnet is brought near to it and comes to rest in a North-South direction.
19. (C) By rubbing iron piece with another magnet.
20. (A) Alnico is alloy of iron, cobalt, nickel and aluminium.
21. (A) Poles have stronger field
22. (B) Poles exist in pairs
23. (B) Four basic points on compass are classified as cardinal points.
24. (A) Both magnets and magnetic substances can be attracted by a magnet.
25. (A) Magnets can be repelled by magnets only.
26. (C) Copper is non-magnetic.
27. (B) Decreases with distance.
28. (B) Earth has a magnetic field
29. (D) Lodestone is natural magnet. Artificial magnets can be made from magnetic materials only. The north pole of a magnet will repel the north pole of another magnet.
30. (A) It is magnetized by induction
31. (B) A magnet always point when suspended freely in north-south direction.
32. (A) Nearby Magnet which must be deflecting the compass needle.
33. (A) Motor creates heat/vibrations
34. (B) You get two magnets each with both poles
35. (A) Another magnet and a compass can be used to identify magnet and magnetic substances.
36. (B) It becomes weaker.
37. (C) Compass is used to find directions.
38. (A) Their like poles repel
39. (B) Another magnet and a compass can be used to identify magnet and magnetic substances.
40. (A) Bar magnet
41. (B) Gives wrong direction as it will interfere with the compass needle.
42. (A) Repulsion is the sure test of magnetism.
43. (D) Like poles repel each other and unlike poles attract each other.
44. (B) Heat weakens magnets
45. (C) We pivot the compass needle on a sharp pin to minimize the friction so that compass needle rotate freely.
46. (B) Electromagnet is used in electric motor.

47. (B) Like poles repel each other.
48. (C) By making the turns of coil closer.
49. (A) A torch doesn't contain a magnet.
50. (B) To ensure the safety of the contents, magnets in the lids/covers are present.
51. (A) Attractive property.
52. (D) Dry cell doesn't contain a magnet.
53. (C) Magnet aligns itself in north south direction, when suspended freely.
54. (C) Weak magnet will move, and north pole will stick to south pole.
55. (C) Disc magnet has poles at its two sides.
56. (A) Like poles repel each other.
57. (B) Magnetic keepers are used to store magnet.
58. (D) All shapes are possible for magnet.

Higher Order Thinking Skills (HOTS)

1. (A) Nickel is magnetic substance.
2. (B) Repulsion is the sure test of magnetism.
3. (B) The magnetic domains become random.
4. (D) Poles have the strongest magnetic force.
5. (B) Magnetic field lines emerge from north pole and enter in south pole.
6. (D) Magnetic field lines emerge from north pole and enter in south pole.
7. (B) Repulsion is the sure test of magnetism.
8. (D) The number of turns is more, so the iron core will have more strength.
9. (A) More the iron fillings, more the strength of magnet.
10. (A) Keeping the magnet in north south direction might be magnetise it again.
11. (C) Magnetism is induced on iron nail means both the poles will be there.
12. (B) Bar X has deflected the compass needle. Thus, it is a magnet.
13. (C) Magnetic field lines emerge from north pole and enter in south pole.
14. (C) Like poles repel each other.
15. (B) Hammering weakens the magnet.
16. (A) Magnet can be used on the container having one magnetic substance and other non-magnetic substance.
17. (C) It may erase the data on floppy disk.
18. (C) Like poles repel each other and unlike poles attract each other.
19. (A) (i)- Maximum; (ii) – Minimum; (iii) – Opposite; (iv) – Similar.
20. (C) Like poles repel each other and unlike poles attract each other.
21. (C) Magnetic field lines emerge from north pole and enter in south pole.
22. (C) Like poles repel each other and unlike poles attract each other.
23. (B) Both steel pieces will get attracted by the magnet.
24. (A) More the iron fillings, more the strength of magnet.
25. (D) Like poles repel each other and unlike poles attract each other.
26. (D) North pole will induce at the end where the north pole of magnet touches first.
27. (D) Both iron nails will get attracted by the magnet and magnetic properties will be induced.

Archive Corner

1. (D) Magnetic field lines emerge from north pole and enter in south pole.
2. (D) Like poles repel each other and unlike poles attract each other.
3. (D) The magnetic field of the magnets cannot pass through the metal.
4. (B) Poles have maximum strength.
5. (C) Like poles repel each other and unlike poles attract each other.
6. (A) North pole will induce at the end where the north pole of magnet touches first.

7. (D) Like poles repel each other and unlike poles attract each other.

8. (C) Dropping from a height can make magnet to lose its properties.

9. (D) Steel is magnetic substance.

10. (B) Red portion of compass points in north direction.

11. (B) 6 north poles and 6 south poles will be there.

12. (B) Like poles repel each other.

13. (D) Horseshoe magnet has two poles at the ends of the U shaped.

14. (C) Magnetic force may be pulling or pushing.

15. (D) Soft iron must be used to store magnet.

16. (C) Like poles repel each other and unlike poles attract each other.

17. (A) Stainless steel is non-magnetic.

CHAPTER 3: TEMPERATURE AND ITS MEASUREMENT

Check Point 1

1. The difference in temperature of two bodies in the Celsius scale = 1°C.
We know C/100 = (F – 32)/180
C = 5/9(F – 32)
9/5C + 32 = F
F = 9/5C + 32
So, the difference of 1° in the Celsius scale is equal to the difference of 9/5°, i.e., 1.8° in the Fahrenheit scale.

2. T(K) = T(°C) + 273 = 45 + 273 = 318 K

3. Heat will not flow in this case as temperature is same as heat only flow from high temperature to low temperature.

4. He can use a box inside which a layer of insulator of heat like thermocol is present.

5. We have to shake the thermometer before taking the temperature in a clinical thermometer so that the mercury flows back into the bulb.

Level 1

Fixed Response Type

Multiple Choice Questions

1. (C) T(°C) = T(K) – 273 = 293 – 273 = 20°C
2. (B) First convert all the temperatures into Celsius scale. 100 K = –173°C ; For –13°F: C = 5/9 (F – 32) = 5/9(–13 – 32) = –25°C; so, –13°F = –25°C. Thus, highest temperature is –20°C.
3. (A) The normal temperature of human body is 37°C.
4. (A) Fahrenheit scale have 180 parts between two fixed points.
5. (A) C = 5/9 (F – 32) = 5/9(302 – 32) = 150°C
6. (B) Given: C = 0.5 F; Put this value in C = 5/9 (F – 32); 0.5 F = 5/9 (F – 32); F = 320°F
7. (A) Put F = 32 in C = 5/9 (F – 32);
C = 5/9 (32 – 32) = 0°C
8. (C) Heat is closely related with temperature.
9. (A) T(K) = T(°C) + 273 = 55 + 273 = 328 K
10. (D) The measure of degree of hotness or coldness of body is called temperature.
11. (A) When in thermal contact, the quantity of heat lost by the hotter body is equal to the amount of heat gained by the colder body.
12. (A) 1 calorie = 4.2 J
13. (B) As, matter expand on heating.
14. (A) Solids have more strong intermolecular attraction.
15. (A) The difference in the temperatures of the two bodies enables heat to flow from one body to another identical body.
16. (A) Heat is a form of energy. It can convert in one form to another.
17. (D) The wall of glass bulb should be thin to enable mercury in a glass thermometer to respond quickly to changes in temperature.
18. (D) Thermometer measures the degree of hotness and coldness of a body.
19. (B) Mercury is opaque and has a constant coefficient of expansion.
20. (D) Richter scale is used to measure destruction caused by earthquake.
21. (A) Celsius scale has 100 equal parts.
22. (D) The range of a clinical thermometer is 35–42°C.
23. (D) The normal human body temperature is 98.4°F.
24. (A) Since heat energy is provided to molecules, their kinetic energy increases.
25. (D) The measure of degree of hotness or coldness of body is called temperature.
26. (B) The degree of hotness or coldness of a body
27. (C) Mercury contracts as temperature decreases
28. (B) It starts from absolute zero temperature
29. (B) The liquid level will change immediately upon removal

30. (C) Different thermometers may have slight variations in precision
31. (B) The thermal radiation emitted by the object
32. (B) Clinical thermometers are designed specifically for human body measurements
33. (C) Energy is being used to convert liquid to vapour rather than to increase the temperature.
34. (B) Expands uniformly with temperature changes
35. (B) Prevent mercury from flowing back immediately after measurement
36. (C) Laboratory thermometer, because it can measure higher temperatures
37. (C) 298.15 K

Assertion and Reason Type Questions

1. (C) Heat always flow from hot body to cold body.
2. (B) Two body at same temperature can have the different amount of mass and specific heat capacity.
3. (C) Heat always flow from hot body to cold body.
4. (B) We need to associate a number to degree of hotness, so we do it by temperature.

Comprehension Type Questions

1. (D) 39°C is above normal body temperature.
2. (B) We need sometime to read the temperature. After reading, we give it a jerk and it goes back.
3. (D) Thermometer should be washed before and after use, preferably with some antiseptic.

Free Response Type

Very Short Answer Type Questions

1. Refer to the heading 'Introduction'.
2. Refer to section 'temperature'

Short Answer Type Questions

1. Refer to the heading 'Types of Thermometer'
2. Heat will not flow because both the bodies are at same temperature.

Long Answer Type Questions

1. Refer to the section 'Scales of temperature'

Numerical Based Questions

1. $^{\circ}C = \frac{5}{9}(F - 32)$

Put C = 37°C

$\frac{9 \times 37}{5} = F - 32$

$\frac{333}{5} + 32 = F$

$66.6 + 32 = F$

$98.6°F = F$

2. $T(K) = T(°C) + 273.15$

Put T(°C) = 42°C

$T(K) = 42 + 273.15$

$T(K) = 315.15K$

3. $C = \frac{5}{9}(F - 32)$

Put F = 100°F

$C = \frac{5}{9}(100 - 32)$

$C = \frac{5}{9} \times 68$

$C = 37.7°C$

4. $T(K) = T(°C) + 273.15$

Put T(K) = 0K

$0 = T(°C) + 273.15$

$T(°C) = -273.15°C$

5. $T(K) = T(°C) + 273.15$

Also, $T(°C) = \frac{5}{9}(T(°F) - 32)$

$T(K) = \frac{5}{9}(T(°F) - 32) + 273.15$

Put T(°F) = 76°F

$T(K) = \frac{5}{9}(76 - 32) + 273.15$

$T(K) = \frac{5}{9} \times 44 + 273.15$

$T(K) = 297.55K$

Level 2

Multiple Choice Questions

1. (A) $\frac{T_c - 0}{100} = \frac{T_F - 32}{180}$

Let initial atmospheric temperature be $T_F = x°F$

Hence, $\frac{T_C - 0}{100} = \frac{x - 32}{180}$

$\Rightarrow T_C = \frac{5}{9}(x - 32)$

If temperature rises by 18°F

Then, final temperature, $T_F' = (x + 18)°F$

Hence, $\frac{T'_C - 0}{100} = \frac{x + 18 - 32}{180}$

$\Rightarrow T'_C = \frac{5}{9}(x - 14)$

Thus, rise in temperature

$T'_C - T_C = \frac{5}{9}(x - 14 - x + 32) = 10°C$

2. (A) Heat will flow from high temperature to low temperature. After mixing, temperature of mixture will be between both these temperatures.
3. (A) First, temperature will increase but after sometime when conversion of state starts then extra heat will be used in conversion. So, temperature will become constant.
4. (A) When a liquid becomes a gas at its boiling point, the average kinetic energy increases of the molecules.
5. (B) In gas, the molecules are not arranged in any order. They are free to move randomly.
6. (A) Solids expand when gain heat.
7. (B) Cooling the key will contract it and heating the lock will expand it.
8. (C) Both P and Q are at same distance and near from heat source. They will fall first.
9. (D) Heat travels from a hot place to cold place.
10. (B) Infrared thermometer for safety and speed
11. (C) Energy is used for changing state, not increasing temperature
12. (B) 176°F
13. (D) All of the above
14. (B) 39°C
15. (B) Digital cooking thermometer
16. (A) Add 273.15 to get 263.15 K
17. (C) 22°C, 71.6°F, 295.15 K
18. (B) Digital thermometers are faster, safer, and more accurate.
19. (C) Different precision levels and calibration of instruments
20. (B) Clinical thermometers are designed specifically for human body temperature measurement

Higher Order Thinking Skills (HOTS)

1. (A) Heat from warm water will be used in melting of ice. So, the temperature of warm water decreases.
2. (D) Mercury will expand on getting heat, so its volume increases.
3. (B) The temperature will decrease till 4 minutes after that heat will be utilised in changing state. So, it will be mixture of liquid and solid.
4. (D) The water in the kettle started boiling at C. The water took 3 minutes to reach its boiling point, after it was heated. As the kettle is closed so, the vapour must be condensed and amount of water is same. Kettle was heated for 3 minutes as temperature starts rising from B point.
5. (C) Heat may be used to change the state of system.
6. (B) Water vapours convert into liquid by releasing heat.
7. (A) 105°C is less than the melting point of substance. So, it will be in solid state.
8. (B) From the given shapes, all of them have the same mass. The circular plate will be having the largest surface area out of the three. This will help the plate to cool down faster. Out of the three, the sphere will be the shape having the minimum surface area for a given volume. Hence the sphere will be cooling down the slowest.

9. (B) Given heat energy is increasing the kinetic energy of the molecules. So, they will be moving faster.

10. (B) For difference of 100 degree Celsius = (26–2) = 24 mm length of mercury column
For difference of 75 degree Celsius = 24 × 75/100 = 18 mm length of mercury column
Total length of mercury column at 75 degree Celsius = 18 + 2 = 20 mm

11. (A) Metal X is a better conductor of heat than metal Y. Metal X expands while metal Y remains as it is.

12. (B) Wax is a poor conductor of heat, it will melt. Also, the near the wax from source of heat, faster it will fall.

13. (B) Kelvin and Celsius have the same degree size but different zero points

14. (C) Specialised cryogenic thermometer would be needed

15. (B) Contact thermometers measure internal temperature, while infrared thermometers measure surface temperature.

16. (B) It has uniform thermal expansion over a wide temperature range

17. (C) Underground pipes are insulated by soil temperature

18. (B) They break easily and mercury is toxic

19. (B) The Kelvin scale was specifically designed to start from absolute zero

20. (B) The measurements show acceptable precision within instrument error

Archive Corner

1. (A) Wax is a poor conductor of heat, it will melt. Also, the near the wax from source of heat, faster it will fall.

2. (D) Heat gets transferred from hot part of body to cold part.

3. (A) Iron is good conductor of heat.

4. (A) The outer edge of aluminium strip is longer than inner edge of copper. Thus, aluminium expands more than copper.

5. (C) Steel is conductor and ebonite is insulator.

6. (A) If we hold the thermometer by bulb while reading, it can change the reading and will not give accurate result.

7. (C) Both will have same temperature when Celsius and Fahrenheit scale are same.

8. (A) Average kinetic energy increases when a liquid becomes a gas at its boiling point as the molecules receives heat energy.

9. (B) The presence of a kink in clinical thermometers

10. (B) They measure different things—surface vs internal temperature

11. (B) They eliminate the risk of mercury exposure from broken thermometers

12. (B) The ability to measure a wide range of temperatures with good accuracy

13. (B) Molecules move faster and take up more space when heated

14. (B) A Fahrenheit degree is smaller than a Celsius degree

15. (B) Normal measurement uncertainty and instrument precision limits

16. (C) Digital thermometer designed for high temperatures

17. (B) The relationship involves multiplying by $\frac{9}{5}$ and adding 32.

CHAPTER 4: BEYOND EARTH

Check Point 1

1. False, Pole star is a star and stars are not the member of solar system.
2. False, constellation orion can be seen during winters around late evenings. It is one of the most magnificent constellation in the sky, visible to the naked eyes.
3. Constellation
4. Meteors
5. A spinning pinwheel/spiral.

Check Point 2

6. Asteroids and Meteors
7. West to East
8. Mars and Jupiter
9. Uranus
10. Jupiter

Check Point 3

11. True
12. Bhaskara and Rohini
13. Aryabhatta
14. Purnima night
15. Amavasya

Level 1

Fixed Response Type

Multiple Choice Questions

1. (C) Stars are mainly made up of Hydrogen and Helium.
2. (A) Sun is a Star.
3. (C) Stars appear motionless because they are very far away from the earth.
4. (B) Galaxies move away from each other.
5. (B) Any heavenly body having light of its own is called a star.
6. (C) Galaxies are usually classified on the basis of their Shape.
7. (A) Indian name of Milky way galaxy is Akash Ganga.
8. (B) The vast collection of billion of stars is called a Galaxy.
9. (B) The Milky Way galaxy has a Spiral shape.
10. (D) Orion is the name of constellation.
11. (A) The star that lies close to the axis of rotation of the earth is the polar star.
12. (A) The stars forming a group that has a recognizable shape is called constellation.
13. (C) Our earth as well as the sun belongs to the galaxy which has a spiral shape called the Milky way.
14. (B) Stars produce heat energy and light due to the fusion of hydrogen.
15. (C) Distance of star are expressed in light year.
16. (D) The distance of the star proxima centauri from the earth is 4.3 light years.
17. (D) The planet which takes the minimum time to revolve around itself is Neptune.
18. (D) A Star which appear blue will be much hotter than the sun.
19. (A) The average distance of earth from the sun is 150 million kilometers.
20. (C) Time taken by Neptune to complete one revolution around the sun is 165 years.
21. (B) Stars emit their own light while planets reflect light
22. (C) Sirius
23. (B) New Moon

24. (C) The Sun's bright light makes stars invisible

25. (B) It is located close to Earth's axis of rotation

26. (B) During the day, the surface temperature on moon is 100°C.

27. (D) India's 1st satellite put in the space was Aryabhatta.

28. (B) It is only the sunlight, reflected by some parts of the moon that reaches the earth.

29. (A) Geostationary satellite launching vehicle.

30. (B) INSAT means Indian National Satellite.

Assertion and Reasons Type Questions

1. (A) Both A and R are true and R is the correct explanation of A.
2. (B) Venus has trapped CO_2.
3. (B) The amount of light which enters our eyes fluctuates from bright to faint, this is why stars seem to twinkle.
4. (B) Due to smaller size, the moon has less gravity than earth and so it can't hold the gases like earth and thus no atmosphere in it unlike earth.
5. (A) Both A and R are true and R is the correct explanation of A.
6. (A) Both A and R are true and R is the correct explanation of A.
7. (A) Both A and R are true and R is the correct explanation of A.

Comprehension Type Questions

1. (C) Example of natural satellite is moon.
2. (B) Moon is non luminous.
3. (D) It is only the sunlight, reflected by some parts of the moon that reaches the earth.

Free Response Type

Very Short Answer Type Questions

1. Pole star is the star which appears stationary from the earth.
2. Milky way galaxy is the galaxy in which our solar system situated.
3. The twinkling of star is due to atmospheric refraction of star-light.
4. Light year is the distance traveled by light in one year in vacuum.
5. Mars
6. Proxima Centauri
7. Mars and Jupiter are two planet which have asteroid between them.
8. Jupiter, There are approximately 156 known natural satellites.
9. Comet appear as a bright ball with a long glowing tail in the sky.
10. Venus is known as Earth's sister planet because both planets are a lot similar to each other.
11. Halley's comet
12. Indian name of ursa minor is Laghu saptarishi.
13. Venus has longest day.

Short Answer Type Questions

1. A Satellite is an object which revolves around a heavenly body.
2. Refer to the heading 'Asteroids'
3. Many astronomical objects like stars or galaxies are very far away from the earth.
   & giving their distances in the kilometers unit becomes very inconvenient. Light year is a large unit and equals the distance travelled by light in one year. Hence, the large distance is expressed in light years. 1 light year = 9.46×10^{12} km. If the star is located 8 light years away from the earth, it means that the distance between star and the earth is the distance light would travel in eight years.
4. Refer to the heading 'Planets'
5. The atmosphere on Venus and Mars constitutes about 95–97% carbon dioxide.
   Life cannot exist in such a CO_2 rich atmosphere.
6. Venus appears either in the eastern sky before sunrise or in the western sky after sunset.
   When it appear after sunset in the western sky, it is called an evening star.
7. 8
8. Refer to heading 'Comets'

9. The earth's spin axis is tilted with respect to its orbital plane. This is what causes the seasons. When the earth's axis points towards the sun, it is summer for that hemisphere.
When the earth's axis points away,winter can be expected.

10. Refer to the heading 'The Solar System'.

Long Answer Type Questions

1. Refer to the heading 'Our Solar System'
2. Refer to the heading 'The Night Sky'.
3. Refer to the heading 'Satellite'.
4. Refer to the heading 'Motion of Earth'
5. Refer to the heading 'Satellite'.

Numerical Type Questions

1. Earth has only one natural satellite.
2. 2
3. 4.3 light year distance in kilometre = Distance traveled in one light year × Number of light years
$= 9.46 \times 10^{12}$ km × 4.3
$= 40.678 \times 10^{12}$ km
4. Venus don't have any natural satellites.
5. There are eight phases of moon.

Case Based Questions

1. (B) Saturn
2. (A) Mercury
3. (A) Rocks

Level 2

Multiple Choice Questions

1. (C) Both the statements are correct.
2. (A) Ursa major have 7 main stars.
3. (A) Milky way has spiral shape.
4. (D) Sources of energy in the sun is combination of light nuclei.
5. (C) Ceres is an asteroid
6. (C) The tail of a comet usually extends to 800 million kilometer.
7. (D) The number of satellites of venus is zero.
8. (A) Mars is the Red planet.
9. (A) Comet
10. (A) Venus takes the maximum time to rotate on its axis.
11. (B) Galileo
12. (A) Shani is Saturn
13. (A) Mercury has no atmosphere and Venus has a thick atmosphere which can retain the heat.
14. (D) Biggest satellite of Saturn is titan.
15. (A) The biggest star in the sky is Sirius.
16. (A) Moon
17. (B) Orbital plane
18. (C) The earth is slightly bulging in the middle.
19. (B) Equator
20. (C) Indian space research organisation.
21. (A) Geostationary orbit
22. (D) 36000 km.
23. (B) On the day of amavasya, the phase of the moon is New moon.
24. (C) Lunar eclipse occurs when the earth comes between the sun and the moon.
25. (C) Ursa Major
26. (B) Mercury, Venus, Earth, Mars
27. (C) Mercury, Venus, Earth, Mars, Jupiter, Saturn, Uranus, Neptune
28. (B) Full Moon
29. (B) The Big Dipper (part of Ursa Major)
30. (B) Earth's rotation on its axis
31. (D) One side of Earth would always face the Sun, creating permanent day and night sides
32. (B) The Moon's orbit is tilted about five degrees relative to Earth's orbit
33. (B) Presence or absence of a solid surface
34. (C) Constellations would become harder to see

35. (B) Jovian planets

36. (B) A Jovian planet

Higher Order Thinking Skills (HOTS)

11. (B) Different seasons show different constellations due to Earth's orbit

12. (B) Earth casting a shadow on the Moon

13. (B) It would be reclassified as a terrestrial planet

14. (A) Constellations would appear in the same positions all year

15. (B) We would have both solar and lunar eclipses every month

16. (D) Both (B) and (C)

17. (A) Solar eclipse: Moon between Earth and Sun; Lunar eclipse: Earth between Moon and Sun

18. (B) Their strong gravitational fields can capture more objects

19. (B) Jovian planet

20. (B) Closer planets are rocky, farther planets are gaseous

21. (B) The Moon's rotation period equals its orbital period around Earth

22. (B) Constellations remain in relatively fixed positions and can indicate direction.

Archive Corner

1. (D) All the stars of a constellation are at the different distance from us.

2. (B) Meera's father has gone 39 complete turns.

3. (D) Neptune takes 164.8 years to revolve around sun once and takes 16 hours to rotate once on its axis.

4. (C) ROHINI, APPLE, EDUSAT, INSAT 48

5. (D) Decreasing order of time required to complete one revolution around the sun are Uranus, Jupiter, Mars and Earth.

6. (D) Gravitational force is responsible for revolution of earth around sun.

7. (B) Terrestrial planets are denser because they're composed mainly of rock and metal

8. (A) It's made of the same materials as stars but lacks sufficient mass for nuclear fusion.

9. (C) There would be no eclipses because Mars' moons are too small

10. (B) No, Uranus and Neptune are ice giants, not gas giants

11. (B) Jovian planets because they have prominent ring systems

12. (B) Earth's rotation causes the apparent movement

CHAPTER 5: MATERIAL AROUND US

Check Point 1

1. All objects are made of substances called materials.
2. Pencil, chair and table are made of materials like wood.
3. Book, disposable cups, notebook and newspaper are made of paper.
4. Placing similar things together is called grouping.
5. Grouping is done by shopkeeper by keeping similar items on the same shelf, which makes it easier for us to find the items we need.

Check Point 2

6. Appearance, hardness, solubility, texture.
7. Materials which can be compressed or scratched easily are called soft.
8. They are hard and opaque.
9. Water is very important constituent for human body, it regulates all the metabolic activities in human body.
10. (a) **Transparent:** They allow light to pass through

    (b) **Opaque:** They do not allow light to pass through them.

    (c) **Translucent:** They materials allow only some part of light to pass through.

Level 1

Fixed Response Type

Multiple Choice Questions

1. (B) Chairs, buses, spoons, cars are made up of iron.
2. (D) Ink, milk and honey are water soluble.
3. (D) Refer grouping of materials.
4. (A) Materials are grouped for our convenience to study their properties and also observe any patterns in these properties.
5. (A) Iron, gold, Copper metals are lustrous in nature.
6. (D) Metals are hard, lustrous and sonorous.
7. (B) Hard material is difficult to scratch and compress.
8. (A) Kerosene is water soluble.
9. (C) Kerosene is water soluble.
10. (A) Objects which sink in water which are insoluble and heavier than water.
11. (C) Mercury is heavier than water and oil is lighter than water.
12. (A) Petroleum floats on water.
13. (C) Opaque materials do not allow light to pass through it.
14. (B) Metals are hard and strong.
15. (A) Brick, iron block do not allow light to pass through it.
16. (A) Spinach is eatable.
17. (D) Gold is a metal having different appearance than other.
18. (B) Wood floats on water.
19. (D) Frosted glass, tissue, butter paper are translucent .
20. (C) Iron is magnetic in nature.
21. (B) Materials that allow heat to flow through them are called good conductors.
22. (A) Liquids that do not dissolve or mix with one another are called immiscible liquids.
23. (B) Vinegar is water soluble.
24. (C) Cotton and sponges are soft and compressible.
25. (C) Matchbox is made up of paper and wood both.
26. (D) Oil and water both are liquids.
27. (D) All metals are shiny.
28. (C) Soft materials are easy to compress.

29. (D) Sugar is water soluble and sand is water insoluble.

30. (C) Glass tumbler is smooth in texture.

Assertion and Reason Type Questions

1. (C) Metals are good conductor of heat.

2. (A) Oil and water are in miscible liquids. Oil is lighter and floats on water.

3. (C) Cotton and sponge are soft material and easy to compress.

4. (D) Oil and water are immiscible liquids.

5. (A) Sand is heavier than water and it settles down in the water.

6. (A) Hot air is lighter than air, so hot air balloon floats in air.

7. (A) Refer grouping.

8. (B) Refer hardness.

9. (A) Refer texture.

10. (A) Grouping make things easier.

11. (A) Metals are good conductor of heat.

12. (A) Wood is bad conductor of heat.

13. (C) Object floats in the air when they less heavy than air.

14. (A) Different substances have different solubility.

15. (C) Water soluble substances dissolved into water.

Free Response Type

Very Short Answer Type Questions

1. Grouping makes it easier for us to find things when we need them.

2. Eatables: water, apple, sugar,
Non-eatables: wood, balls, pen.

3. Gold is a lustrous metal; and do not get affected by water and air.

4. A is harder than B.

5. Cotton and sponge.

6. Milk and water.

7. Oil is lighter than water.

8. Iron almirah is opaque and glass tumbler is transparent .

9. Soft.

10. Aluminium foil, iron nail.

11. Plastic or metal.

12. Oil does not dissolve in water, so it is insoluble in water but floats on the surface of water.

13. Yes, some animals are transparent,so predators cannot see then easily. Example : Jelly fish

Short Answer Type Questions

1. The process of grouping things on the basis of some similarities and dis similarities is called classification.
(I) living and nonliving things
(II) hard and soft things
(III) heavy and light things

2. Classification makes it easier for us to find things when we need them.

3. When two liquids dissolve in one another such as water and milk, they are known as miscible liquids. Example: Mustard oil and kerosene do not dissolve in water.

4. (a) Miscible and immiscible substances: Refer solubility
(b) Transparent and translucent substances: Refer transparency
(c) Hard and soft materials: Refer hardness

5. (a) Appearance, (b) Hardness, (c) Solubility, (d) Float or sink in water, and (e) Transparency

6. A tumbler made of cloth cannot hold a liquid because cloth piece is not hard enough to hold liquids and cloth piece has very minute pores through which liquid oozes out.

7. Both are transparent.

8. Books, notebooks, newspapers, toys, calendars, etc.

9. Water can dissolve a large number of substances, so it is needed by the body. It is also major part of our body cells.

10. Materials are grouped on the basis of similarities or dissimilarities in their properties.

11. We can locate the required object easily and quickly.

12.

Objects	Materials they are made of
Plate	Steel, glass, or plastic
Pen	Plastic, metal
Bucket	Plastic, metal
knife	Steel/wood, wood/plastic

13.

Objects	Materials they are made of
Wood	Chair, table, bullock cart
Paper	Books, notebooks, newspaper, toys
Leather	Shoes, belts, purses, jackets
Plastics	Buckets, chair, table, bags

14.

Liquid	Mixes well/ Does not mix
Vinegar	Mixes well
Lemon juice	Mixes well
Mustard oil	Does not mix
Coconut oil	Does not mix
Kerosene	Does not mix

15. Metals when exposed to air react with moisture and gases present in it, thereby forming a dull layer of some other compound on it.

Long Answer Type Questions

1. Sponge is porous material.
2. Refer floatation.
3. Honey: Liquid, water soluble, translucent
   Ice: Solid, floats on water, transparent
   Iron nail: Solid, hard, sink into water
4. **(i)** He can locate the required object easily and quickly.
   (ii) He can easily come to know what stocks are going to finish and he should purchase them for his customers.
5. Put a coin in beaker of water. You can clearly see the coin immersed in water. This proves that water is a transparent liquid.
6. In a dark place, cover the torch jar with your palm. Observe from the other side of the palm with a flashlight. The light of the torch passes through your palm, but you can't see it clearly.
7. Observations are :
   Sugar: Disappears completely in water
   Salt: Disappears completely in water
   Chalk powder: Does not disappear in water
   Sand: Does not disappear in water
8. Honey, Salt, Sugar, Copper sulphate crystals, Glucose – Soluble in water
   Mustard oil, Sand, Sawdust, Chalk powder, Petals of flower, Soil, Wheat flour – Insoluble in water
9. An opaque substance is a substance through which objects cannot be seen. For example wood, stone. A translucent substance is a substance through which an object can be seen, but not clearly seen. Eg. Oiled paper, frosted glass. A transparent substance is a substance in which objects can be clearly seen. B. Glass, clear water.
10. Oxygen dissolve in water is used by animals for respiration and by plants for respiration and photosynthesis.

Numerical Based Questions

1. Bamboo + Air + water + wood = 1 + 4 + 5 + 6 = 16
2. Wooden scale and iron block are opaque.

Level 2

Multiple Choice Questions

1. **(D)** A needle and knife are hard and magnetic.
2. **(C)** Oil is insoluble in water.
3. **(D)** Milk and water are miscible liquids.
4. **(C)** Clay can be easily molded into different shapes.
5. **(D)** Metals are good conductors of electricity and heat; and are solid at room temperature.
6. **(D)** Metals lose their shine due to action of air and water.
7. **(D)** Metals are hard and lustrous.
8. **(C)** Transparent substances allow light to pass through them.
9. **(C)** Because water is transparent.
10. **(C)** A bucket made up of plastic to fill water.
11. **(C)** Materials are grouped for easy study.
12. **(D)** Metal is heavier than water.
13. **(C)** Magnifying glass and glass tumbler are transparent.

14. (B) Soft drink are acidic in nature so it can react with iron.

15. (C) Mirror and Magnetare are opaque.

16. (C) Muslin cloth is translucent material.

17. (B) Feather and plastic ball are lighter than water.

18. (D) The bark of tree, an unfinished wall and sandpaper are rough, uneven and bumpy.

19. (D) kerosene coconut oil are immiscible and heavier than water.

20. (C) Metals are good conductors.

21. (D) Vinegar and alcohol are water soluble.

22. (A) Front glass is transparent.

23. (C) Metals are good conductor of heat and electricity while plastics are insulators.

24. (C) Plastics are insulators.

25. (A) Wood is opaque and glass is transparent.

26. (C) Metals get attracted by a magnet.

27. (D) Solid J is lighter than liquid N only and Solid K is heavier than liquid M only.

28. (A) Water can be used to separate the mixture on the basis of solubility.

29. (D) Bedsheet, blanket and leather handbag – all are made up of different materials.

30. (C) Rubber is insulator.

Higher Order Thinking Skills (HOTS)

1. Steel is good conductor of heat.

2. Silver is the best conductor of electricity. Graphite (carbon) is a non-metal which conduct electricity.

3. For the protection from electricity.

4. Honey and water are miscible with each other. Hence, a solution will be formed when honey is mixed with water. Raveena will get the mixture in solution form.

5. Gold is a precious metal. It does not react with gases present in the atmosphere. Silver reacts with some gases, such as hydrogen sulfide, and loses its luster in moist air.

6. Yes, because glass door is translucent. Hence, Shikha can be located.

7. Initially, the cotton ball floats on water. Slowly, it absorbs water and becomes heavy; and sinks in water.

8. Rubber bands, leaves, erasers, rice and fresh chapattis are soft materials that can be easily scratched or squeezed.

9. (i) Soluble pairs: (i) Honey – water
   (ii) Glucose – water
   (iii) Mustard oil – groundnut oil

   (ii) Insoluble pairs: (i) Turmeric – water
   (ii) Mustard oil – water
   (iii) Rice flour – water

10. (a) Aluminium – Foil in food wraps, in making aircraft, etc.
    (b) Plastic – Buckets, pencil box, etc.
    (c) Kerosene – Fuel, solvent, etc.
    (d) Vinegar – Preservative, food ingredients, etc.

11. This is because metals get heated whereas materials such as plastic and wood do not. It would be difficult to handle metal utensil after cooking if the handles were made of metal.

12. Materials that are attracted to a magnet are called magnetic materials. This property is called magnetism.

13. I. Type of solvent
    II. Temperature
    III. Size of the particles

14. Coconut shell, paper plate, thermocol plate, naphthalene balls, computer screen are opaque material.

15. Cotton and jute fibres both are less dense than water, so they can float on water.

Archive Corner

1. (D) Sugar and salt are soluble in water while chalk powder and saw dust are insoluble
2. (D) Glass is transparent; iron is hard and lustrous.
3. (A) Vinegar, orange juice and cold drink are water soluble; and kerosene and coconut oil are water insoluble.
4. (A) Refer properties of materials.
5. (B) The metal is good conductor of heat.
6. (A) Rubber band is elastic; steel is shiny and electric bulb is transparent.
7. (C) Refer solubility and floatation.
8. (D) Metals are good conductors and ceramic have high melting point.
9. (A) Type of solvent and temperature affect the solubility of substance.
10. (C) More scratches, less hard metal.
11. (C) Refer transparency.
12. (B) Vinegar and lemon juice are miscible. Wax and water are immiscible.
13. (C) More scratches, less hard metal.
14. (C) Refer properties of materials.
15. (D) Refer properties of materials.
16. (D) Plastic mug: Floats on water, bad conductor of heat

    Thermocol: Soft, floats on water, opaque in nature

    Glass bowl: Hard, sinks in water, transparent
17. (C) Rubber: Waterproof and elastic

    Iron: Waterproof, electricity conductor and elastic
18. (B) Oxygen: Soluble in water

    Talcum powder: Opaque

    Aluminium: Opaque, conductor, malleable

    Glass: Transparent
19. (B) Glass is transparent.
20. (D) Refer properties of materials.
21. (C) Refer properties of materials.
22. (D) Metals are good conductors of heat.
23. (D) Refer properties of materials.

CHAPTER 6: METHOD OF SEPARATION IN EVERYDAY LIFE

CHECK POINT 1

1. Air has mass and occupies space.
2. Cold is the measurement of temperature, have no mass and occupy space.
3. Pure substance is made up of same kind of atoms.
4. They mixed uniformly.
5. Mixtures are called heterogeneous mixtures as they do not have a uniform composition throughout. Examples: Mud mixed in water, mixture of oil and water, and soil.

CHECK POINT 2

6. Stones can be removed from rice by handpicking on the basis of difference in size.
   Stalks and seeds are separated by threshing.
7. Iron fillings and sulphur powder can be separated by magnetic separation.
8. Ammonium chloride and sodium chloride is different in the property of sublimation.
9. Sugar and salt are soluble in water.
   Chalk powder and sand are insoluble in water.
10. Water droplets are seen on the surface of water bottle containing cold water due to condensation of water vapours present in atmosphere.

CHECK POINT 3

11. The principle of centrifugation is that an object, when spun at high speed, experiences an outward force away from the centre of rotation.
12. (i) Separation of cream by churning of milk.
    (ii) Separation of blood sample.
13. Because separating funnel is used for separation of two immiscible liquids due to difference in their density.
14. Benzene will be in top layer and water will be in bottom layer.
15. Mixture of benzene, water and mercury can be separated by separating funnel.

CHECK POINT 4

16. The substance that dissolves, is called solute, and the substance into which it dissolves, is called solvent.
17. Benzene and chloroform mixture.
18. An unsaturated solution is one in which more solute can be dissolved in the given amount of solvent.
    Solution which contains more amount of substances dissolved in it than required to form a saturated solution is called super saturated solution.
19. A solution in which no more solute can be dissolved in the given amount of solvent is called a saturated solution.
    An unsaturated solution is one in which more solute can be dissolved in the given amount of solvent.
20. On cooling a super saturated solution, excess amount of solute settle down at the bottom.

LEVEL 1

Fixed Response Type

Multiple Choice Questions

1. (D) Solid have Fixed volume
2. (D) All are heterogeneous mixture.
3. (A) Homogeneous have uniform composition.
4. (D) Pure substance are those substances which are made of only one kind of particles and cannot be separated by physical process.
5. (B) Red and blue colour balls of different size can be separated by handpicking method.
6. (D) Gold is pure substance while cake, ink and ice candy are mixtures.

7. (C) The method used to separate heavier and lighter components of a mixture is winnowing.
8. (C) Grain and husk can be separated by winnowing.
9. (D) Sieving is used to separate pebbles and stones from sand.
10. (B) Iron powder is magnetic in nature.
11. (A) Alloys are homogeneous mixture of metals.
12. (D) Filtration is used for separating constituents while preparing fruit juice.
13. (B) The difference between sieving and filtration is of phase of particles.
14. (B) Evaporation method is used to separate sugar from sugar solution.
15. (C) Evaporation method is used to separate salt from seawater.
16. (B) The process of converting vapours into liquid is called condensation.
17. (C) Cream is separated from milk by decantation and tea leaves are separated from tea by filtration.
18. (D) Filtration can be used to separate sand; and then salt and water can be separated by distillation.
19. (D) The spinner in washing machine dries clothes works on the principle of centrifugation.
20. (D) Separating final, is used to separate immiscible liquids on the basis of density.
21. (C) After centrifugation when sublimate settles, clear liquid can be decanted off.
22. (B) Aqueous solution contains water as a solvent.
23. (A) When more quantity of salt is added to saturated solution, salt settles down at the bottom of the container.
24. (C) Solubility, depends on temperature and nature of solute.

Assertion and Reason Type Questions

1. (A) Refer evaporation.
2. (B) Handpicking is used to separate on the basis of difference in size and winnowing is used to separate on the basis of difference in weight.
3. (B) Refer centrifugation.
4. (C) Separating funnel is used to separate immiscible liquids.
5. (D) Conversion of water liquid into its vapour is called boiling.
6. (D) Cream is separated from milk by churning.
7. (B) Refer winnowing.
8. (B) Refer sedimentation and decantation.
9. (A) Refer filtration.
10. (A) Refer sublimation.

Free Response Type

Very Short Answer Type Questions

1. When a substance is made up of single component, it belongs to the category of pure substance.
2. Separation of insoluble solids from their solutions can be done by filtration.
3. In mills, impurities such as husk and stones are removed from wheat before it is ground.
4. Separating funnel can be used to separate a mixture of mustard oil and water.
5. Solutions which contain water as a solvent are called aqueous solutions.

Short Answer Type Questions

1. Vinegar, milk, soap, detergent
2. It is sometimes essential to separate the constituents of a mixture.
3. This method is used to separate very fine particle of an insoluble solid that remains suspended in a liquid. Due to their tiny sizes, their sedimentation takes a very long time.
4. The process of conversion of water into its vapour below its boiling point is called evaporation. The process of evaporation takes place continuously wherever water is present.
5. (a) Solid-solid mixtures: Winnowing, handpicking

   (b) Liquid-solid mixtures: Filtration, evaporation.
6. Handpicking, threshing, winnowing, sedimentation, decantation, filtration, evaporation, condensation

7. The process of separating slightly larger particles from the mixture by hand is called handpicking. The principle is difference in the size of components.

8. Threshing is the process of separating the grain from the stalk. This method is used by farmers to separate gram, wheat, rice and mustard grains in their fields.

9. Handpicking, threshing and winnowing.

10. Oil, which is lighter than water, floats. Two distinct layers are formed and the oil is slowly poured into another container to separate it from the water. Using a separating funnel he can also separate the two.

11. The process by which water turns into steam is called evaporation. This process takes place continuously wherever water is present. This method extracts table salt from seawater.

12. It is the best method used to separate heavier components from the lighter components. Example: grains from husk.

13. Sieving allows the finer powder particles to pass through the sieve holes, while the larger particles and impurities remain in the sieve. For example, mills remove impurities such as husks and stones from wheat before it is ground.

14. (1)-(c)-(ii) (2)-(a)-(iii) (3)-(b)-(i)

Long Answer Type Questions

1. Salt is a pure sodium chloride compound while salt solution is mixture of salt and water.

2. Mixture of husk from grains can be separated by winnowing. Winnowing is used to separate heavier and lighter components of a mixture by wind or by blowing air.

3. Refer filtration.

4. (a) Separating funnel
   (b) Handpicking
   (c) Loading
   (d) Handpicking

5. (a) Mixtures that have uniform composition throughout are called homogeneous mixtures.

   Mixtures are called heterogeneous mixtures as they do not have a uniform composition throughout.

   (b) Pure substances are made up of single components.

   Mixed substances are made up of more than one component.

   (c) Solute: Substance which is present in small amount in a solution.

   Solvent: Substance which is present in larger amount in a solution.

   (d) Sedimentation: When the heavier component in a mixture settles after water is added to it, the process is called sedimentation.

   Decantation: When the water (along with the dust) is removed, the process is called decantation.

6. No, at low temperature, it would be difficult to dissolve sugar and also it would be more difficult to dissolve more sugar.

7. Threshold is a machine used to separate the edible part of crop from the stalks.

8. Seawater is stored in a shallow hole, and the sunlight evaporates the water, slowly turning it into water vapour. In a few days the water will completely evaporate, leaving behind solid salts.

9. Decanting is the process of separating insoluble solids from liquids. Let the suspension of solid particles in the liquid sit for a while. Solid particles settle to the bottom of the container and clean water rises to the top. Transfer the clean water to another container without disturbing the settled particles.

10. There are four main factories affecting evaporation
    (i) surface area (ii) humidity (iii) temperature (iv) wind speed

11. To make paneer, add a few drops of lemon juice to boiling milk. This gives a mixture of solid paneer and liquid particles. The paneer is then separated by filtering the mixture through a fine cloth or sieve.

12. (i) Sand and husk can be separated by the method of winnowing.
    (ii) Winnowing followed by sieving.
    (iii) Both are immiscible. So, it can be separated by the use of separating funnel.
    (iv) Rice and salt can be separated by sieving.
    (v) By sedimentation and decantation followed by filtration. After that, using evaporation, common salt is separated.

13. (a) Put 1 cup of milk as a solvent in a container and heat it.
(b) Add tea powder or tea leaves to boiling milk acting as a solute. Continue to heat.
(c) Solute, i. H. The tea powder remains undissolved in the milk and can be observed while it is still boiling.
(d) At this stage add sugar to the boiling solution while stirring.
(e) Sugar is a solute, but it dissolves in solvents.
(f) Keep stirring until the sugar is completely dissolved and saturated in the tea solution.
(g) When the tea leaves are no longer fishy and the tea liquor is sufficiently boiled, it is removed from the heat and filtered or strained to separate the tea powder from the tea liquor. The insoluble tea powder remains as residue, while the solute (sugar) and solvent (milk vinegar) pass through the filter media and are collected as filtrate.

Numerical Based Questions

1. (B) Mixture – filtrate = sand
250 – 225 gm = 25 gm
2. (C) Sugar solution = sugar + water
Water = sugar solution – sugar = 47 – 8.5 = 38.5 gm

Level 2

Multiple Choice Questions

1. (C) Solutions are homogeneous mixtures.
2. (A) Lighter particles are separated by heavier particles.
3. (D) Residue is left behind on the filter paper.
4. (B) A mixture of rice and water can be separated by sedimentation.
5. (A) Loading is a process in which impurities become heavy and sink to the bottom.
6. (C) Fractional distillation work on the difference in boiling points.
7. (B) Constituents are present in a variable ratio in a mixture.
8. (A) A saturated solution be made unsaturated either by increasing temperature or by adding more amount of solvent.
9. (A) Mixtures can be separated on the basis of physical properties.
10. (B) Pickle is the example of mixture.
11. (D) Since the vegetables are big in size, handpicking is the best method for separating the vegetables.
12. (C) Butter (fat) is separated by churning the curd and the remaining lassi contains less fat content.
13. (D) Filter, paper, Muslim cloth and fine mash can be used in the filtration to separate the mixture of sand and water.
14. (D) To separate grains from bundles of stalks threshing is the best method.
15. (D) Winnowing is used to separate lighter and heavier components.
16. (B) Sieving is used to separate the components of different size.
17. (B) To separate ghee (which is in liquid form) from the residue (which is in solid form), we can use the method decantation and filtration.
18. (B) To get back solid copper sulphate from the solution, we can use evaporation method. When the solution of copper sulphate is heated, water evaporates leaving behind the solid copper sulphate.
19. (C) The water droplets appear due to condensation.
20. (D) The water droplets appear due to condensation.
21. (B) Kerosene + water is immiscible.
22. (B) The principle behind fractional distillation technique is difference in boiling point.
23. (A) Fractional distillation is used for separation of different components of petroleum.
24. (C) A mixture of alcohol and water can be separated by simple distillation.
25. (C) A mixture of ammonium chloride and sodium chloride can be separated by sublimation

26. (D) Refer winnowing and fractional distillation.

27. (B) Solid converted into gas by the process of sublimation.

28. (B) Tea and tea leaves are separated by sieving.
(C) mixture of iron filling and sand
(D) salt solution

29. (C) Refer winnowing, magnetic separation and sublimation.

30. (D) Refer filtration, magnetic separation and sublimation.

31. (A) Filtration followed by evaporation.

32. (B) Water drops appearing on the outer side of a cool water bottle occurs due to condensation.

33. (C) A mixture of milk and water cannot be separated by filtration.

34. (C) Winnowing followed by magnetic separation.

35. (D) Washing machine dryer work on the principle of centrifugation.

Higher Order Thinking Skills (HOTS)

1. Crystallisation is best technique to get pure crystals from an impure sample.

2. More solute can be dissolved by increasing temperature.

3. Water drops appearing on the outer side of a cool water bottle occurs due to condensation

4. (i) By stirring of salt and water mixture.
(ii) Mohan

5. Magnetic separation, separating funnel and evaporation.

6. Refer filtration, sedimentation and decantation.

7. (i) Happy (ii) Sun
(iii) Threshed (iv) Winnowed
(v) Handpicked (vi) Sieved

A wise farmer and his wife obtained good flour by proper means, so they could get it cheaply.

8. 1. Decantation
2. Filter the mixture.
3. Evaporate the salt solution.

9. Magnetic separation, separating funnel and evaporation.

10. No, a mixture of water and alcohol is miscible and cannot be separated because it forms a solution.

Archive Corner

1. (D) Threshing, winnowing.

2. (D) Gases have large space between molecules and have no definite volume.

3. (A) Block of ice occupies space.

4. (D) Refer types of solutions.

5. (B) In saturated solution, no more solute will dissolve.

Solubility means 'how much solute will dissolve'

6. (A) On heating when a liquid converted into gas, the process is called as evaporation.

7. (B) Decantation, filtration, evaporation.

8. (A) Kidney beans and chickpeas cannot be separated on the basis of difference in weight. They can be separated on the basis of their size by hand picking.

9. (B) High temperature and larger surface area increases evaporation.

10. (C) Gases have large space between molecules and have no definite volume.

11. (B) Copper sulphate is blue in color, soluble in water, non-magnetic and its solution can conduct electricity.

12. (D) Refer separation techniques.

13. (C) Ice is lighter than water.

14. (A) P-Sublimation; Q-Magnetic separation; R-Filtration; S-Evaporation

15. (D) Sublimation followed by distillation.

16. (B) Milk and water cannot be separated by filtration.

To obtain butter from milk, centrifugation method is used.

17. (B) The space in the flask is occupied by air.

18. (C) Sand is water insoluble.

19. (C) Solid have less interparticle space and gases have more interparticle space.

20. (D) Sieving, evaporation, filtration and separating funnel.

21. (B) I, IV and V are exothermic.

22. (C) II, III and IV only

23. (A) (P) Husk and water
(Q) Heterogeneous solid-solid mixture
(R) Filtration and evaporation
(S) Separating funnel

24. (C) Water in beaker T evaporates faster than in beaker P.

25. II. Germination of seeds is a chemical and slow change.
III. Bursting of balloon is a physical and fast change.
V. Digestion of food is a chemical and slow change.

26. (C) Sugar, water and sawdust

27. (D) All statements are correct.

28. (B) I. Mixture of kidney beans and chickpeas can be separated by handpicking.
IV. Seeds of wheat can be separated from a bundle of wheat stalks by threshing.

29. (C) Boiling takes place at boiling point only.

30. (C) At high temperature, evaporation will be faster.

31. (C) Mercury is heavier than water.

32. (C) 'P' will be a gas is between 65°C and 115°C.

33. (D) Handpicking, magnetic separation and then sieving

34. (D) **(i)** Freezing point of water is 0 °C.
(ii) Between 0 °C and 100 °C, water exists in liquid state.
(iv) 100 °C is the boiling point of water.

35. (A) Solids have definite shape and volume.

36. (C) Refer sublimation.

CHAPTER 7: A JOURNEY THROUGH STATES OF WATER

Check Point 1

1. Water exists on the earth in three forms solid, liquid and gas.
2. Sea is the largest source of water on the earth.
3. Seas and oceans, rivers, lakes, ice caps, as groundwater.
4. Water is a compound. Its constituent elements are hydrogen and oxygen.
5. Pure water freezes at 0°C at 760 mm of mercury pressure.

   Pure water boils at 100°C at 760 mm of mercury pressure.

Check Point 2

6. Vapouration and condensation.
7. Water vapour condenses on dust particles in the atmosphere, forming millions of tiny water droplets. Tiny ice crystals will be formed instead if it is very cold. This cluster of tiny water droplets floating in air is what we call a cloud.
8. Upper surface of ground water below which soil is saturated with water that fills all void is called water table.
9. Decreases the amount of water present in water table is called depletion in water table.
10. Increase in population, scanty rainfall, industrial and agricultural activities are causes of depletion of water table.

Check Point 3

11. Water scarcity can be defined as a lack of sufficient water, or not having access of safe water supplies.
12. The abnormally long period of insufficient or no rainfall at all is called drought.
13. The lack of food in a region for a long period is called famine.
14. Drought causes plants and animal to wither away.

    Crops cannot be grown, and already sown crops fail to grow.
15. Rainwater harvesting increases the level of ground water.

Level 1

Fixed Response Type

Multiple Choice Questions

1. (B) Pure water is a compound.
2. (B) 70% of water present in our body.
3. (C) About 3/4th of the earth surface is covered with water.
4. (A) Rainwater is the purest form of natural water.
5. (A) Lakes and rivers is the surface water.
6. (A) The ratio of the number of hydrogen atoms and those of oxygen in water is 2 : 1.
7. (B) At room temperature, water is liquid.
8. (D) Water exists in three physical states solid, liquid and gas
9. (C) At high altitude, boiling point decreases.
10. (C) Water has maximum density at 4°C.
11. (B) Volume of ice is more than the volume of water.
12. (C) Water is called universal solvent because it dissolves large number of solids, liquids and gases
13. (B) Solubility increase with increase in temperature.
14. (C) Solubility of gas decreases with increase in temperature.
15. (B) Liquids that dissolve in water are called miscible liquids.
16. (C) Vapour turn back into liquid is called condensation.
17. (C) During evaporation, liquids water changes to water vapour.
18. (B) Moisture that falls to the ground from cloud is called precipitation.
19. (C) Industrialization is the reason for depletion of water table.

20. (C) Flood is the situation in which occurrence of more rainfall than normal level water.

21. (D) Cutting trees to check water loss to transpiration.

22. (D) Increase in population will lead the depletion in water table.

23. (C) Heavy rainfall is not responsible for water shortage.

24. (C) Careful management of water means less waste of water.

Assertion and Reason Type Questions

1. (A) Gases can be made to dissolve better when pressure is applied.
2. (D) Water vapour is present in air in all seasons.
3. (A) Refer occurrence of water
4. (B) Refer physical properties of water.
5. (A) Water is continuously recycled in the water cycle.
6. (B) This cluster of tiny water droplets floating in air is called cloud.
7. (A) The moisture in the soil indicates the presence of water underground.
8. (B) Increase in population, scanty rainfall, industrial and agricultural activities are factors that may deplete the water table.
9. (C) Plants need water to get nutrients from the soil to prepare their food.
10. (C) Oxygen dissolved in water is the main source for survival for aquatic life.

Free Response Type

Very Short Answer Type Questions

1. Rivers are source of surface water.
2. No, it is salty in nature.
3. H_2O
4. Conversion of water vapours into liquid is called condensation.

Short Answer Type Questions

1. Human body constitutes about 70% of water, so water is called a life-giving liquid.
2. Water is made up of hydrogen and oxygen in 1:8 ratio by mass.
3. Refer rainwater harvesting.
4. Collecting and storing rainwater from roofs or a surface, collecting in tanks or in small pits.
5. Ground water is recharged by collecting rainwater.
6. Use bucket for watering the plants instead of water pipes.

Long Answer Type Questions

1. Refer physical properties of water.
2. Refer water cycle.
3. Water level in rivers, lakes and ponds rises.
   Heavy floods bring about erosion of soil from the fields, making them barren and infertile.
   Crops get submerged under water, leading to loss of production of useful food items.
   Floods leads to diseases due to the mixing of floodwater with the waste materials and wastewater.
4. (A) Refer water pollution and water conservation.
   (B) Refer surface water and groundwater.
5. Refer water pollution.
6. Careful and economical use of water and avoiding its wastage is called conservation of water. Suggestions for conserving water:
   Use only the required quantity of water.
   Trees and forests help in causing rainfall. So, to conserve water, we should plant more and more trees.
   By collecting rainwater in tanks, ponds or by constructing check dams.
8. The failure of rainfall can cause the following:
   (i) The soil becomes dry.
   (ii) Water level in rivers, lakes, dams, etc., may fall. Ponds and canals may even dry up.
   (iii) The ground water level falls.
9. Evaporation and transpiration.

10. (i) With the rise in population, the availability of water is decreasing. The demand for water is increasing day by day. Hence, we need to conserve water for the future.

(ii) The level of groundwater is decreasing drastically due to the change in climate which results in limited usage of water. This would lead to extreme water scarcity and hence we should conserve water for the next generations.

Numerical Based Questions

1. $42 \times 50 / 70 = 30$ ltr

2. $20 \times 95 / 100 = 19$ gm water

3. Consumption for a family of four persons per day = 6000/30 = 200 litres
Consumption per head = 200/4 = 50 litres

Level 2

Multiple Choice Questions

1. (A) Water cycle is a continuous process.

2. (C) The main source of water for perennial rivers is due to melting of snow.

3. (A) The melting point of ice is 0°C.

4. (B) The density of water is $1 g/cm^3$

5. (A) A glass of water fit for drinking

6. (C) Pure water boils at 100° Celsius.

7. (D) Water is an extremely stable compound.

8. (C) Water is a neutral oxide.

9. (B) Introduction of particles in clouds to increase condensation.

10. (B) Water vapour → condensation→ precipitation→ infiltration→ground water table

11. (D) Pure water is colourless, odourless, transparent liquid.

12. (B) Bathing, washing clothes, and mopping a room require a lot of water. A minimum amount of water is required for brushing teeth.

13. (C) To make one sheet of paper, two glasses of water is required.

14. (D) Pure water is bad conductor of electricity.

15. (C) Evaporation is directly proportional to temperature, and as temperature increases so does evaporation. Indoor temperatures are lower than those of sunlight, burners, and roofs. Therefore, a glass of water standing in the room evaporates the slowest.

16. (D) Transpiration is the process by which water is lost in the form of steam, and when part of the plant (mainly the leaves) is exposed, it is called transpiration. Water loss through transpiration is very high.

17. (A) Water vapour present in the air condenses into tiny water droplets that float in the air and look like clouds to us. These small droplets then become larger droplets and become rain.

18. (D) Lakes, ponds, rivers and other bodies of water are replenished by rainwater. Some of the rainwater evaporates back into the air. The remaining soil absorbs water into the soil and is available as groundwater. Wells are therefore fed from this groundwater.

19. (D) Heavy rains raise the water levels of rivers, lakes and ponds. This water spreads over a wide area and causes floods. Instead, fields, forests, villages and towns will be submerged. Floods therefore cause enormous damage to crops, livestock, property, and human life.

20. (C) Rainwater harvesting is a method of collecting rainwater. Storing water can increase the availability of water to collect and store for later use.

21. (C) Sea water → Water vapour → Cloud → Rain

22. (D) Sea water is not fit for all our uses.

23. (A) In a cloud, the size of droplets increases causing rainfall because they become heavier.

24. (C) Water coagulates the dust particles.

25. (D) Evaporation and transpiration.

26. (C) Water consumption causes water scarcity.

27. (D) Water scarcity can overcome by better water management.

28. (D) Ground water is not constant at all places.

29. (C) The groundwater is stored between layers of hard rock below the water table is called aquifer.

30. (B) The amount of rainfall at a place depends on geographic location.

Higher Order Thinking Skills (HOTS)

1. Soft water: Water which can freely form lather with soap is called soft water.

   Hard water: Water which does not form lather with soap and forms a precipitate or scum is called hard water.

2. If the sample of water contains calcium and magnesium bicarbonates, and sulphates, they do not allow the formation of much lather. Therefore, these salts cause hardness of water.

3. Distilled water not suitable for drinking because the dissolved salts should be removed from water to get pure water.

4. Areas covered with concrete affect the availability of groundwater because it reduces the entry of rainwater into the ground, which in turn, reduces the availability of groundwater.

5. (A) C – More is the exposed surface area, more will be evaporation of water. (b) B – As it is closed, no evaporation takes place.

6. Most of the water that falls on land as rain or snow sooner or later returns to the seas and oceans. Because the water that falls on land as snow melts in the summer and flows into rivers and streams, and then into the seas and oceans. Some of the water seeps into the soil and is available as groundwater. Groundwater is pumped for domestic, irrigation, and industrial use, and eventually becomes rivers and finally seas and oceans.

7. There are two ways of getting the salt out of the water again. Either we can heat the brine on a stove or let it evaporate in the sun for a few hours in a plate to remove the water from the brine. Evaporation is the slow change of water to a vapour state. After the water evaporates, add the salt back.

Archive Corner

1. (D) Refer water cycle and water scarcity

2. (D) Flood, drought and earthquake can leads to famine.

3. (D) Water expands on heating, thus ice occupies less space.

4. (C) Refer water cycle

5. (i) Liquid X contracts more than liquid Y.

   (ii) Liquid Y does not contract as much liquid Z.

   (iii) Liquid Z contracts less than liquid X.

6. (A) Lack of rainwater harvesting infrastructure cause a decrease in the water table.

7. (D) Water can be broken into hydrogen and oxygen by passing electric current.

8. (C) Mineral water contains dissolved salts.

9. (D) Flood causes soil erosion and cause damage to crops.

10. (C) Temperature converts water to change from one state to another.

11. (C) Rainwater harvesting is an important method for raising ground water level.

12. (A) Milk, blood and fruits contain water.

13. (D) Sulphur dioxide combine with water vapour of rainwater to form acid rain.

14. (C) Most of the well water and spring water are replenished by ground water.

15. (C) Water vapour present in air leads to the formation of fog and mist.

16. (D) The process of collecting rainwater in huge cemented pits is called rainwater harvesting.

CHAPTER 8: NATURE'S TREASURE: FOSSIL FUEL

CHECK POINT 1

1. Fossil fuels are the sources of energy in nature.
2. Thermal power plants are used in the production of electricity.
3. Yes, ammonia gas is water soluble. The aqueous solution of ammonia, i.e., ammonium hydroxide solution.
4. Ammonium sulphate: $(NH_4)_2SO_4$ and Ammonium super phosphate: $NH_4H_2PO_4$.
5. Water gas is an equimolar mixture of carbon monoxide and hydrogen.

CHECK POINT 2

6. Fuels are the materials which produce heat or energy on burning.
7. Petroleum consists chiefly of hydrocarbons with some other elements such as sulphur, oxygen and nitrogen.
8. Saudi Arabia has the largest petrochemical unit in the world.
9. Natural gas is flammable and produces a lot of heat. It burns smokelessly and does not cause air pollution.
10. A strong-smelling substance called ethyl mercaptan (C_2H_5SH) is added to LPG to detect the leakage of gas from the cylinder.

CHECK POINT 3

11. (a) If possible, drive at a constant, moderate speed.
    (b) Switch off the engine at traffic lights or at a place where you have to wait.
    (c) Ensure correct tyre pressure.
    (d) Ensure regular maintenance of the vehicle.
12. Refer conservation of fossil fuel.
13. Petroleum is a fossil fuel that will last only a few hundred years because it took millions of years to form.
14. Petroleum Conservation Research Association (PCRA)
15. The Petroleum Conservation Research Association (PCRA) has provided some tips to advise people how to save petrol/diesel.

LEVEL 1

Fixed Response Type

Multiple Choice Questions

1. (C) CH_4, H_2, CO are main constituents of coal gas.
2. (D) Ammoniacal liquor is ammonium hydroxide.
3. (C) Coke is not used for drinking purposes.
4. (A)
5. (A) Peat is least carbon containing coal.
6. (B) Coal tar is the foul smelling, black, thick, viscous liquid obtained from destructive distillation of coal.
7. (B) Carbonization is the formation of coal from plant matter.
8. (B) Coal and petroleum are fossil fuels.
9. (A) Heating of coal in the absence of air is called destructive distillation.
10. (B) Producer gas is a mixture of CO and N_2.
11. (B) The distillation of crude petroleum is called refining.
12. (D) Fractional distillation is used for refining of petroleum.
13. (D) Bees wax is not a petroleum product.

14. (A) The amount of LPG in a domestic gas cylinder is about 14.2 kg.

15. (C) Compressed Natural Gas

16. (D)

17. (B)

18. (B) Ethyl mercaptan added to detect the leakage of LPG.

19. (C) Kerosene is used as a household fuel.

20. (D) Natural gas has high calorific value.

21. (A) The head of a safety matchstick contains antimony trisulphide and potassium chlorate.

Assertion and Reasons Type Questions

1. (A) Petrochemicals are used in the manufacture of detergents, fibres, polyethylene and other plastics.

2. (B)

3. (C) Solid, liquid and gaseous fuels are formed from petroleum.

4. (D) Fossil fuels are non-renewable sources of energy. Coal causes pollution.

5. (B) LPG is having very high calorific value.

Free Response Type

Very Short Answer Type Questions

1. Fossil fuels are exhaustible natural resource.

2. Anthracite contain approx 95% carbon.

3. Carbon

4. Now a days, coal tar is replaced by bitumen.

5. Producer gas is a mixture of carbon monoxide and nitrogen.

6. Calorific value of natural gas is 55 kJ/g.

7. The unrefined form of petroleum is called crude oil.

8. Composition of carbon for kerosene oil is C_{11}-C_{16}

9. The first oil well was found in Pennsylvania in USA in 1859.

10. Saudi Arabia is largest producer of petroleum.

11. Decanting can be used to separate oil and water mixtures. Let the mixture stand. Petroleum is lighter than water, so it floats on water. The lighter layers of oil can be carefully injected and separated without disturbing the heavier layers of water.

12. CNG stands for Compressed Natural Gas. It is considered to be a better fuel because it bums with a smokeless flame and causes no air pollution.

13. Kerosene is a petroleum product which is used as fuel for stoves, lamps and jet aircrafts.

14. These resources are present in an unlimited quantity in nature and are not likely to be exhausted by human activities.

15. Exhaustible natural resources are coal, natural gas, petroleum, minerals, forests. Inexhaustible natural resources are air, sunlight, oxygen.

Short Answer Type Questions

1. Coal gas, coal tar, coke and ammoniacal liquor.

2. Coke, coal gas, Ammonical liquor, Coal tar

3. Exhaustible natural resources like coal, petroleum or natural gas were formed from the dead remains of living organisms (fossils). So, these are called fossil fuels.

4. Fossil fuels are exhaustible, so we should use economically and wisely.

5. The chemical process involved in the transformation of plant matter into coal is called the carbonization of plant matter.

6. Heating of coal in the absence of air or oxygen is called as destructive distillation of coal. It is a purification method.

7. Refer uses of coal.

8. Refer conservation of fossil fuels.

9. It's a limited resource. The more limited it is, the more carelessly it's being used by humans. This is the reason why petrol is an exhaustible resource. Whereas, sunlight is a source of energy that is produced by the sun.

10. $CO + N_2$

11. (i) Coke is mainly used as a reducing agent in the extraction of metals like iron, zinc, etc.

 (ii) It is used in the manufacture of steel.

12. Coal has the following properties:
 (i) A hard, black, combustible fuel.
 (ii) It mainly contains carbon
 (iii) An energy source; some important uses of coal are:
  (i) Used as a domestic and industrial fuel and to generate electricity in thermal power plants
  (ii) Used in the production of coal gas and coke
13. Oil is lighter than water, hence floats over it.
14. Refer the destructive distillation of coal.
15. Refer refining of petroleum.

Long Answer Type Questions

1. Refer types of natural resources.
2. Refer the destructive distillation of coal.
3. Peat (50-60% carbon), lignite (60-70% carbon), Bituminous (75-80% carbon), Anthracite (90-95% carbon)
4. Refer the formation of coal.
5. Refer petroleum refining.
6. Refer petroleum refining.
7. Forests, floods, soil, soil, temperature, pressure, temperature.
8. Because they are exhaustible natural resources. If they are consumed faster than they can be formed in nature, they are quickly depleted.
9. Burning of fuels is a major cause of global warming because they produce a lot of greenhouse gas (carbon dioxide) on burning.
10. To save petrol/diesel/natural gas, you should follow these tips:
 (i) Pay attention to correct tire pressure.
 (ii) ensuring regular maintenance of vehicles.
 (iii) Drive at a constant and moderate speed as much as possible.
 (iv) Stop the engine at traffic lights or waiting areas.
11. The natural resources which are present in a limited quantity in nature and can be exhausted by human activities are called exhaustible natural resources, e.g., coal, petroleum, natural gas, minerals, forests, wildlife, etc.

Numerical Type Questions

1. (A) 180/2 = 90 kJ/kg
2. (C) 17500 kJ / 7000 kJ/kg = 2.5 kg

Level 2

Multiple Choice Questions

1. (C)
2. (B) Forests is exhaustible natural resource.
3. (D) Petrol or gasoline used as automobile fuel is a mixture of hydrocarbon and alcohols.
4. (D) Coal does causes pollution when burnt.
5. (D) Plastic is not a natural resource.
6. (C) Sunlight, air and water are inexhaustible natural resources that cannot be depleted by human activity.
7. (D) Wildlife and minerals are natural resources subject to depletion, as they exist in limited amounts in nature and can be depleted by human activity.
8. (D) CNG (Compressed Natural Gas) is not derived from coal.
9. (C) Exhaustible natural resources are present in a limited quantity in nature and can be exhausted by human activities.
10. (D) Fossil fuels come from the remains of organisms (animals and plants) buried underground millions of years ago.
11. (A) Coal is formed by the decomposition of large land plants and trees buried under the earth about 300 million years ago.
12. (A) Coal is formed by the carbonization of dead vegetation.
13. (C) Naphthalene balls are used to repel moths and other insects in stored clothes, etc.
14. (D) Coke is not a component of petroleum. Coke is made by heating coal in the absence of air.
15. (D) Gas is a mixture of hydrogen, methane and carbon dioxide.

16. (C) Natural gas is stored as compressed natural gas under high pressure.

Higher Order Thinking Skills (HOTS)

1. Natural gas is heated strongly, then methane present in it decomposes to form carbon and hydrogen.

2. When natural gas is heated strongly, than methane present in it decomposes into carbon and hydrogen.

3. Coke is good fuel and burns without smoke because it do not contain any impurity.

4. Diamond is formed at high temperature and high pressure when organic matter buries into soil.

5. Yes, known coal deposits only last about 100 years. It takes millions of years to turn dead organisms in nature into fossil fuels.

6. If all exhaustible resources are depleted by human activity, the survival of living things becomes impossible. In fact, fossil fuels are the most important source of energy for us today.

7. Natural gas is produced below the surface. It forms on oil.

8. Petroleum is a mixture of different hydrocarbons with different boiling points. As the number of carbon atoms increases, so does the boiling point. This property is used to separate the various components of petroleum and is called fractional distillation.

Archive Corner

1. (C) Refer destructive distillation of coal.
2. (A) Nuclear energy is not a renewable energy.
3. (D) A residue left behind when destructive distillation of coal is carried out is charcoal.
4. (A) Refer refining of petroleum.
5. (A) Refer refining of petroleum.
6. (C) Lighter than water and insoluble in it.
7. (C) Coke
8. (A) Low ignition temperature is a characteristic property of a good fuel.
9. (D) Producer gas is not a good fuel because it contains N_2 which does not burn.
10. (C) Plants store solar energy in the form of chemical energy.
11. (A) Biogas is a mixture of methane + CO_2.
12. (D) Water gas is a mixture of CO and H_2.
13. (B) Aerobic fermentation is a process which helps in formation of natural gas.
14. (D) Lead compounds are most harmful for human body.
15. (D) Characteristics for a rocket fuel are light and compact, high calorific value and should burn rapidly.
16. (C) Phosphorus is used to start the combustion in a matchstick.
17. (C) Refer destructive distillation of coal.
18. (C) Refer destructive distillation of coal.
19. (C) Refer refining of petroleum.
20. (D) Refer uses of natural gas
21. (D) Refer refining of petroleum.
22. (C) Kerosene is obtained as a fraction of fractional distillation of petroleum.
23. (A) Refer refining of petroleum.

CHAPTER 9: FIBRE TO FABRIC

Check Point 1

1. We wear clothes for protection against weather conditions such as rain, snow, extreme heat, or cold. They also offer protection against insect bites.
2. Cotton, nylon terylene, polyester.
3. (i) The material that is used to make a particular type of clothing is called fibre.
   (ii) Weaving strands or fibres into fabric.
4. The process of twisting the fibres so as to make a stronger thread is called spinning.
5. Weaving is the process of arranging two sets of yarns together to make a fabric with the help of a handloom or power loom.

Check Point 2

6. Fibres which are obtained either from plant or animal sources are known as natural fibres.
7. The separation of jute fibres from jute stem is called retting. In this process, the harvested stalks of the plants are soaked in water for a few days until they start rotting. Then the fibres are separated by hand from the rotting stems.
8. Jute is mainly grown in West Bengal, Bihar and Assam.
9. Silk is produced from cocoons of the silkworm which feeds on mulberry leaves. It secretes an unbroken fibre cocoon around itself. The cocoon is boiled and unwound to form the fibre which is then spun.
10. Fibres made by human beings from chemical substances are called synthetic or man-made fibres. Examples of synthetic fibres are polyester, nylon, and acrylic.

Level 1

Fixed Response Type

Multiple Choice Questions

1. (D) In ancient times, people wear cloths made up of animal skins, grass and vines.
2. (B) Yarn is made up of a number of fibres twisted together.
3. (B) The process of twisting the fibres so as to make a stronger thread is called spinning.
4. (D) Fabric can be made from yarn by knitting and weaving.
5. (B) Silkworm is an insect.
6. (C) The process of removing seeds from cotton called ginning.
7. (C) Jute is obtained from stem of patsun.
8. (B) Wool is an animal fibre obtained from sheep.
9. (A) Wool burns with smell of burning hair as it is obtained from hair of sheep and goat.
10. (A) Pashmina shawls are obtained from the skin of Kashmiri goat.
11. (B) The process of removing hairs of a sheep is called shearing.
12. (D) Yak wool is obtained in Ladakh.
13. (D) Woolen clothes keep us warm as wool traps air and air is a poor conductor of heat.
14. (B) International wool secretariat produce high quality wool.
15. (A) The fabric made from used wool, by carding and spinning, is called shoddy.
16. (C) Wool is soluble in acids and bases.
17. (B) Protein is main constituent of silk fibre.
18. (C) Sericulture is cultivation of silkworm to produce silk.
19. (A) Respiratory and skin diseases are most common among the workers of sericulture industry.
20. (C) While bursting crackers, it is safe to wear clothes made of cotton because they do not catch fire easily.
21. (A) Cellulose is a natural polymer obtained from plants.
22. (C) Silk and polyester are soft and smooth in touch.

23. (B) Man-made fibres are known as synthetic fibres.

24. (A) The silk fibres are made into fabrics such as satin, velvet chiffon, crepe, and brocades.

25. (D) New innovative fabrics is being developed for more environmental and sustainable production methods, is called Qmilch.

26. (B) Single yarn is used in knitting for making sweaters.

27. (C) Power looms and handlooms are used for weaving of fabrics.

28. (A) Alpaca hair is used for making woolen clothes.

29. (D) Synthetic fibres are strong, does not get wrinkled and dries easily.

30. (B) Synthetic fibre does not absorb sweat and is not suitable to be used in hot and humid climate.

31. (B) In India, jute is mainly grown in West Bengal, Bihar, Assam and Andhra Pradesh.

32. (D) In ancient times, people used bark and leaves of trees, skin and fur of animals to cover their bodies. Newspapers and metal foils were not available in those times.

33. (C) Nylon is synthetic fibre while rayon belongs to semisynthetic fibre.

34. (C) Silk fibres are natural animal fibres obtained from the cocoon of silkworm. Silk fabric is very smooth to touch and has vibrant colour and shine.

35. (C) The process of arranging two sets of yarns together to make a fabric is called weaving. Weaving of fabric is done on looms.

36. (B) The process of converting fibre into fabric involves spinning and weaving or knitting. Spinning is the process of making yarn from fibres. Weaving is the process of arranging two sets of yarn together to make a fabric whereas in knitting, a single yarn is used to make a fabric.

37. (B) Cotton plants are usually grown at places having black soil and warm climate.

38. (C) The process of making yarn from fibres is called spinning. In this process, fibres are twisted. This brings the fibres together to form a yarn.

Assertion and Reason Type Questions

1. (D)
2. (C) Cotton is porous, so cotton do not trap air in the pockets formed between the individual fibres.
3. (C) Silk is obtained from silkworm.
4. (D) Coir is obtained from coconut fruit.
5. (A) The fibres obtained from plants and animals are called as natural fibres. Examples: Cotton, jute, wool, silk, etc.
6. (B) Synthetic fibres are obtained from crude oil while natural fibres are obtained by plants or animals.
7. (A) These fibres are found in the stem of the plant and provide strength to the plant. Examples: Jute and flax.
8. (B) Flax fibres are also used in the production of cloths.
9. (B) Both statements 1 and 2 are true.
10. (D) Sisal is an example of leaf fibre.

Free Response Type

Very Short Answer Type Questions

1. Cotton and silk fibre.
2. Cotton is plant fibre and wool is animal fibre.
3. Cotton is obtained from fruit.
4. (i) Cotton fibres are rough.
   (ii) They can absorb moisture.
5. Wool does not allow air to pass through it.

Short Answer Type Questions

1. Fibre obtained from source followed by spinning, yarning and weaving then fabric is obtained.
2. Nylon and polyester are synthetic fibre. Wool, cotton, silk, and jute are natural fibres.
3. Handpicking the ripe cotton bolls → Ginning → Spinning → Manufacture of cotton textiles.
4. Cotton plant is a shrub growing well in black soil and warm climate mainly grow in Punjab, Madhya Pradesh, Rajasthan.

5. **Retting:** The jute fibres are separated by hand from the rotting stems. This process is called retting.

   Spinning: The fibres are made into yarn by twisting the strands together.

Numerical Based Questions

1. Fabric Z are rough and fabric Y are smooth.
2. Polyster (synthetic fibre) absorb less water and natural fibres absorb more water.

Level 2

Multiple Choice Questions

1. (B) Correct sequence in making fabric: Ginning-Spinning-Weaving.
2. (B) Rayon is a semi-synthetic fibre.
3. (C) Wool is obtained from fleece of sheep.
4. (B) Jute is the obtained from stem of patsan.
5. (B) Fibres are twisted before being made into yarns or thread to make them stronger.
6. (A) Cotton and woolen clothes are rough while silk is smooth.
7. (C) Silk worm feeds on mulberry leaves.
8. (C) Flax is most suitable for making high-quality paper.
9. (C) In summer season, fibres must have good absorption capacity of sweat and must allow free movement of air.
10. (B)
11. (C) Fibre obtained from Source → Spinning → Yarn → Weaving → Fabric
12. (D) Cotton obtained from plants.
    Silk from animals.
    Nylon shrinks away from flame on burning.
    Polyester leaves hard beads on burning.
13. (C) Flax is obtained from stem and wool is obtained from sheep without any harm.
14. (D) Cotton fibre burn with smell like that of a burning paper.
15. (C)
    (i) Wool is animal fiber, others are plant fibre.
    (ii) Cotton is fruit fibre.
    (iii) Silk is natural fibre.
    (iv) Coir is plant fibre.
16. (D) Wool are animal fibre and coir is plant fibre.
17. (A) Cotton and rayon do not catches fire easily.
18. (A) Wool is obtained from sheep without harming.
19. (C) Nylon and polyester are man made fibres.

Higher Order Thinking Skills (HOTS)

1. X is jute which is rough but strong fibre while Y is flax. It is comparatively much smooth fibre which is used to make linen cloth.
2. (a) Fibre A is cotton.
   (b) The process C is ginning.
   (c) Fibre B is coconut fibre.
   (d) Fruit D is coconut.
   (e) Coir.
3. Cotton fibres Made up of cellulose and are rough, non-shining, while silk fibres are made up of proteins and soft, smooth and lustrous .
4. Jute, hemp and linen (flax) are cellulosic fibres obtained from the stem of a plant.
5. The teacher must have asked the students to classify the following fibers into natural and synthetic. Jute, Silk, Nylon, Cotton, Wool, Polyester.
6. When burned, silk fabrics shrink due to the presence of proteins, whereas cotton fabrics do not.
7. (i) Coir, Kapok, wool
   (ii) Coconut
   (iii) Shearing
8. May be due to the fault in the thread, the end of the thread was separated into a few thin strands, or the thread was quite thick. Hence, Boojho found it difficult to pass a thread through the eye of a needle.
9. Saree, dupatta, dhoti, lungi, turban, etc., are unstitched fabrics used by both men and women.

Archive Corner

1. (A) Cotton, flax and jute are natural fibre gives smell like burning paper.
2. (D) Jute is a natural fibre and fibres are obtained by retting.
3. (A) Polyester (synthetic fibre) absorb less water and natural fibres absorb more water.
4. (D) Synthetic fibres are stronger than natural fibres. Rayon is semi-synthetic fibre.
5. (C) P, Fibre obtained from source → Spinning → Yarn → Weaving → fabric Q.
6. (D) Cotton, wool and silk are natural fibres. Synthetic fibres shrink away from flame on burning.
7. (C) Flax is obtained from stem and wool is obtained from sheep without any harm.
8. (A) Wool is insulator.
9. (C) Stem fibre-Jute, Leaf fibre-Banana, Fruit fibre-Coir
10. (D) Cotton fibre is fruit fibre and burn with smell like burning paper.
11. (B) Fibre → Spinning → Yarn → Weaving → Fabric
12. (C) Refer types of fibres.
13. (A) Refer plant fibres.
14. (A) P is cotton fibre and absorb lot of water whereas R is silk.
15. (C) R and S are animal fibres.
16. (B) Before should be replaced by after, and ginning should be replaced by retting.

CHAPTER 10: AIR AROUND US

Check Point 1

1. Air contains mainly nitrogen, oxygen; and smaller amounts of argon, carbon dioxide, water vapour; and traces of helium, neon, krypton and xenon.
2. Air contains mainly nitrogen and oxygen.
3. Smaller amounts of argon, carbon dioxide, water vapour; and traces of helium, neon, krypton and xenon in air.
4. Nitrogen do not support burning. It is used on a large scale to manufacture fertilizer to be used in cultivation.
5. A person feels suffocated when some material is burnt in a closed room due to excess of carbon dioxide gas.

Check Point 2

6. The transparent, thick and invisible envelope of air surrounding us is called atmosphere.
7. The different layers of atmosphere (starting from the surface of earth) are troposphere, stratosphere, mesosphere, thermosphere and exosphere.
8. This layer contains electrically charged particles called 'Ions', so it is also called ionosphere. It extends up to a height of 480 km.
9. Plants synthesis their own food in presence of sunlight, chlorophyll and CO_2. This process is called photosynthesis.
10. Oxygen is water soluble which become available to the animals and plants living in water.

Check Point 3

11. Oxygen
12. This is because during photosynthesis plants take in carbon dioxide from the air and release oxygen.
13. Refer oxygen cycle.
14. Deforestation and excessive burning of fuel can unbalance oxygen cycle.
15. Plantation can be used to maintain oxygen cycle balance.

Check Point 4

16. The addition of substances in the environment in quantities that are harmful to living beings is called pollution.
17. Carbon dioxide, sulphur dioxide
18. Burning of fuels, harmful gases released from industries and smoke released by vehicle.
19. Asthma and lung cancer can be caused by air pollution.
20. Make breathing difficult; Asthma and lung cancer.

Level 1

Fixed Response Type

Multiple Choice Questions

1. (C) Air is a mixture.
2. (A) Nitrogen neither support burning nor itself.
3. (B) In desert area, water vapour content is low.
4. (C) Water vapour controls the climate condition or temperature of the atmosphere.
5. (B) Nitrogen > Oxygen > Argon > Carbon dioxide
6. (C) The percentage composition of oxygen in air is $\frac{1}{5}$ th of the volume.
7. (A) Oxygen supports combustion.
8. (A) Nitrogen gas is used in packaging of chips.
9. (C) Greenhouse effect is caused by CO_2, CH_4, NO_2 gases.
10. (C) Volcanic eruptions causes air pollution.
11. (D) Mumbai

12. (C) Carbon dioxide is essential component for photosynthesis.
13. (B) Layer of atmosphere that absorb UV rays from the sun is called stratosphere.
14. (C) The atmospheric layer nearest to the earth's surface is the troposphere.
15. (B) Stratosphere is second layer of atmosphere.
16. (A) Oxygen is consumed from atmosphere during combustion of fuel.
17. (C) N_2 useful in making fertilizer.
18. (D) Gases which do not react with any substance are known as inert gases.
19. (A) The rate of photosynthesis is very high during day time.
20. (A) Oxygen is necessary for living organism.
21. (B) Glucose and oxygen combine to form CO_2, water and energy.
22. (B) Nitrogen cannot be taken directly by plants.
23. (B) CO_2 is released during burning of oil and other fuel.
24. (D) Long term effects of air pollution include permanent long damage.
25. (D) Refer air pollution.

Assertion and Reason Type Questions

1. (A) During photosynthesis, plants take in carbon dioxide from the air and release oxygen.
2. (C) The rate of photosynthesis is very high during the day time.
3. (A) In birds, air can easily pass through the pair of lungs with air sacs.
4. (C) Plants make their own food by a process called photosynthesis by using CO_2 gas.
5. (D) Refer layers of atmosphere.
6. (C) The rate of photosynthesis is very high during the day time.
7. (D) Oxygen supports burning and increases the rate of burning.
8. (C) The rate of photosynthesis is very high during the day time.
9. (B) Refer oxygen cycle.
10. (C) Carbon dioxide and inert gases are present in very small amounts in air.

Free Response Type

Very Short Answer Type Questions

1. Air contains 78% nitrogen, 21 % oxygen, 0.03% CO_2 and other gases in very small amount.
2. Oxygen
3. 21% oxygen
4. By the filling up air.
5. Atmosphere

Short Answer Type Questions

1. Helium, argon, neon and xenon.
2. When something is burnt, it produces smoke. The smoke contains certain gases and dust particles which are harmful for us.
3. (a) Respiration is breakdown of food in presence of oxygen; and breathing is intake and exhalation of respiratory gases.

   (b) Air is the gaseous mixture in our atmosphere; and wind is the horizontal motion of air due to the pressure difference between two places.
4. Air plays a major role in water cycle. Air helps water vapour rise and cloud formation. Evaporation of water, cloud formation and falling of rain, all take place in the atmosphere.
5. Plantation is necessary to reduce air pollution.

Long Answer Type Questions

1. Due to lack of oxygen and presence of CO_2.
2. During respiration, breakdown of food takes place in presence of oxygen and give out carbon dioxide.
3. Take a glass containing ice cold water, after some time small water droplets appear outside of the glass water due to phenomena of condensation.
4. Plants use carbon dioxide present in the air to make their own food by a process called photosynthesis.

   During photosynthesis, plants release oxygen which is important in our life.
5. There are a number of ways by which we can reduce air pollution. Some of them are planting more and more trees, recycling plastics, regular

checking of vehicles for the emission of harmful gases, etc.

6. Refer activity.

7. The components of air are oxygen, nitrogen, water vapour and carbon-dioxide. All these gases can be easily separated and they retain their properties.

8. Blanket cuts the supply of oxygen to the object that is burning, thereby prevents it from further burning.

9. Air is a mixture of gases. The major constituents of air are nitrogen, oxygen, carbon dioxide and argon.

10. (a) Place the Firki or PM wheel in an open area and it will spin due to the ubiquitous moving air. Enclosed areas lack air movement and do not support filki rotation.

(b) A weather vane is an instrument used to indicate wind direction. It consists of an arrow attached to the center of gravity for free movement around a vertical axis. Therefore, at a certain point in time, the arrow points in a certain direction, indicating the final direction of wind movement.

(c) An empty glass is filled with the air

(d) If we breathe through mouth, the harmful dust particles may enter our body and make us ill. Thus, breathing through mouth may harm us.

11. Refer composition of air.

Numerical Based Questions

1. Total amount of fuel minus amount of oxygen is equal to amount of fuel taken
100 – 28 = 72 g of fuel taken.

2. Total weight of ballon – Mass of empty balloon
= 20 – 5 = 15 g

Level 2

Multiple Choice Questions

1. (D) Air have indefinite volume.

2. (B) Exosphere→ ionosphere → mesosphere → stratosphere →troposphere

3. (C) In the process of photosynthesis, plants give out oxygen and water vapour.

4. (B) Global warming takes place due to the increase of carbon dioxide in air.

5. (C) Drinking soft drinks with a straw working on atmospheric pressure.

6. (D) Air can be used for generating electricity, moving a windmill and pumping water.

7. (C) We cannot feel the pressure of atmosphere because pressure acts in all directions equally.

8. (D) Energy is stored when air is compressed, and compressed air exerts a force.

9. (C) In a syringe, the plunger compresses the air.

10. (A) Glass panels usually appear hazy because water vapour settles on the tiny dust particles on the panel.

11. (C) Air bubbles formed.

12. (D) Air pollution on the roads reduced reducing the number of vehicles on the road.

13. (D) Hot air has less weight and rises more height.

14. (D) Air also present in soil.

15. (C) Ceiling fan moves by electricity.

16. (D) Air plays a major role in water cycle.

17. (B) There is deficiency of oxygen on mountains at high altitude.

18. (A) As the bubbles of air came out from the bottle and some water entered the bottle.

19. (D) Wind speed, wind direction, temperature and humidity are factors responsible for the development of cyclone.

20. (C) Dust and smoke are harmful to living beings.

Higher Order Thinking Skills (HOTS)

1. Acidic oxides like NO_2, SO_2 dissolves in water to form acid rain.

2. The increased percentage of carbon dioxide will cause greenhouse effect, As soon as the sun's heat rays enter the Earth's atmosphere, they are reflected back out of the atmosphere. The temperature of the earth rises, the ice on the mountains melts and the water level rises.

3. Refer global warming.

4. If any substance catches fire, it will become difficult to extinguish the fire, as oxygen supports combustion.

5. The increased percentage of carbon-dioxide will cause greenhouse effect.

6. All of these animals live in burrows or remain buried in the ground. They get their oxygen from the air that enters their burrows through the burrow entrance or through pores in the ground. But when it rains, water fills their dwellings and the pores of the ground. So they come out for air.

7. Air plays an important role in many musical instruments such as flute, trumpet, harmonica, chenai, harmonium.

8. (A) Windmill (b) Oxygen (c) Smoke (d) Dust

9. (a) Oxygen and Nitrogen together make up 99% of air.
   (b) Aquatic animals use dissolved air for respiration.
   (c) Moving air is called wind.

10. Due to the heat of the sun, dissolved air in the water begins to escape in the form of small bubbles. This formed small bubbles all over the bottle.

11. (A) Small bubbles appeared before the water boiled because air was dissolved in the water. When the water is heated, the air dissolved in the water becomes bubbles and escapes.

    (B) When water taken from a bottle is heated, small bubbles appear. When you open the cap, a certain amount of air is trapped inside. A certain amount of air is also trapped when transferring water from the bottle to the cookware for heating.

12. The dull colors of foliage and flowers on street trees may be caused by dust and soot from cars, chimneys, factories, etc. These particles may have settled in the plant parts and made them look dull.

Archive Corner

1. (C) Air has mass.

2. (D) The plant was not able to absorb oxygen for respiration inside water.

   Plant was not able to absorb carbon dioxide for photosynthesis inside water.

3. (A) Oxygen gas has collected in the top part of the test tube.

4. (C) Air contains water vapour.

5. (D) Oxygen

6. (C) Take some water in a pan. Heat it gently on a gas burner. Observe the water as it begins to heat.

7. (C) Stratosphere is a clear, cloudless layer where the star shine and airplanes fly.

8. (D) Refer composition of air.

9. (D) The rate of photosynthesis increases when there is more carbon dioxide.

10. (D) (iii) and (iv)

11. (C) X – Oxygen, promotes burning,

    Z – Nitrogen, needed by plants to make food.

12. (D) In atmospheric air, R is present in highest percentage whereas P is present in lowest percentage.

13. (B) Solubility of oxygen decreases on heating, so fishes would suffocate.

14. (C) The gas X is oxygen.

15. (D) Deforestation can upset the delicate balance of air.

CHAPTER 11: FOOD: WHERE DOES IT COMES FROM?

Check Point 1

1. (a) Autotrophic (Auto = self, trophic = food): It is a mode of nutrition in which organisms prepare their own food. Examples: plants, cyanobacteria.

   (b) Heterotrophic (Hetero = different, trophic = food): It is a mode of nutrition in which organisms derive their food from some other animals or plants. Example: Human being.

2. Decomposers are those organisms which decompose biodegradable waste. They clean the environment by decomposing the waste.

3. Tiger has sharp claws, powerful jaw and a set of developed canines for eating flesh.

Check Point 2

4. Crops which are grown for commercial uses and not self consumption are referred as cash crops. Tobacco, tea and coffee are considered cash crops.

5. The increase in milk production has been possible due to the launching of country wide programme called 'operation flood' which resulted in the white revolution in India. Dr. V. Kurien is known as father of white revolution.

Level 1

Fixed Response Type

Multiple Choice Questions

1. (D) Omnivores are animal which eat both plant products and animal flesh.
2. (C) Paying full attention to the food while eating
3. (C) Various parts of plants are edible like stem, root, flower, etc. In carrot, root is edible part.
4. (B) Chilli is modified ovary which is the fruit.
5. (D) Milk is produced by milch animals.
6. (D) Food is required for growth, energy and immunity.
7. (B) Honeybees are insects and play a very important role in nature. They produce honey and various other products which are commercially very useful for us. So, these are cultured artificially too. Their culture is called apiculture.
8. (C) To help with digestion and enjoy the food
9. (A) Fruits and vegetables
10. (C) Bacteria and fungi are those organisms which feed on dead and decay matter and clean the environment.
11. (C) Fungi feed on dead and decay matter.
12. (C) Some plants or animals take their nutrition from other organisms and these are called parasites. Cuscuta is also a parasitic plant.
13. (C) Some organisms derive nutrition from blood, and they are known as sanguivores. Ex.-Mosquito like mosquito.
14. (D) Heterotrophs derive there nutrition from other organisms, like plants, dead matter etc.
15. (C) Insectivores derive there nutrition from insects in order to fulfill their nitrogen requirement. Ex. Nepenthes.
16. (B) Lion is a carnivore, it has sharp canines for tearing flesh.
17. (D) Plants form first trophic level of food chain as they can synthesize food. They are also known as producers.
18. (C) Lion and tiger are carnivorous animals.
19. (C) Stop eating and listen to your body
20. (B) Filling of samosa is spicy mashed potato.
21. (A) Overeating
22. (C) Stop eating and listen to your body
23. (C) Animals which provides egg and meat are known as poultry animals.
24. (A) Root is the edible part of carrot.
25. (B) Organisms those obtain their food from plants are called heterotrophs.
26. (A) Sprouted seeds have more energy than dry seeds.
27. (D) Jowar has low calorie and high fiber content, so it is good for our health.

28. (C) Fungus has cell wall so earlier considered as non-green plant. Mushroom is a fungus.

29. (D) Milk provide all the required nutrients, so it is an example of balanced diet.

30. (C) Mushroom is non green plant and edible fungi. It is very rich in nutrients.

Assertion and Reason Type Questions

1. (A) Carnivores consume other organisms, Example: Lion, tiger, jackal, etc.

2. (D) Generally, spices do not have food value. They are only added in food to increase the taste and flavour. Example: cloves (laung), ginger (adrak), etc.

3. (A) Plants are known as autotrophs because plants perform photosynthesis.

4. (A) Animals are called consumers because animals are dependent on plants for their food.

5. (D) Carnivores has strong and more developed canines to tear food. Herbivores have more elongated small intestine.

6. (A) Various parts of plants are edible like leaf, root, shoot and flower. Spinach, bathua and methi – are green leafy vegetables which are rich in minerals.

7. (A) Decomposers and scavengers are biological cleaning agents of nature because they feed on dead and decaying organic matter of organisms.

8. (B) Prepared food has different type of ingredients and different ingredients of food have their different nutritional value.

9. (A) Food is essential for our heath because it gives us energy, growth and immunity.

10. (A) Cheese, paneer and milk are animal products; and vegetables and fruits are plant products.

Comprehension Type Questions

1. Honey is sweet liquid nectar which is formed by honeybees. Honey has many nutrients like vitamins minerals, sugar, etc. It is used for medicinal purpose and in cosmetics.

2. Honey is used in cough syrups and many ayurvedic medicines.

3. Some plant and flowers are seasonal. They grow in only particular season. So, bees store nectar in flowering time and store it as a food for whole year.

4. In a beehive, three types of bees are found, i.e., queen, worker and drone. They all have different structure and function in beehive. Queen is diploid fertile female and only involve in reproduction, drone is sterile haploid male which is involved in mating with queen during reproduction. Workers are sterile male involved in cleaning of hive, collecting nectar, etc.

Free Response Type

Very Short Answer Type Questions

1. Substances those are eaten by any living being and get energy is called food.

2. Material which are used to prepare different type of dishes are called food ingredients. Examples: Vegetables, salt, oil, etc.

3. Autotrophs can prepare their own food by photosynthesis. Heterotrophs lack chlorophyll, so they cannot synthesize their own food. They are dependent on autotrophs for their food.

4. Sprouting of seed after dormancy is called seed germination.

5. Plants can prepare their own food and they are first trophic level of food chain. So, they are called producers.

6. Poultry is the collective term for domestic birds such as chicken, ducks, pheasants, geese, etc., raised for their egg and meat. Those animals which are used for eggs are called poultry animals.

7. The synthesis of organic compounds like glucose from simple inorganic molecules like CO_2 and H_2O by the cells of green plants having chlorophyll in the presence of sunlight is called as photosynthesis.

8. Radish is modified root and its leaf and root both are edible.

9. Potato, sugarcane and bamboo are edible stem.

10. Green leafy vegetables and beetroot are good for blood formation.

11. Ghee, curd, cheese, khoya and butter are obtained from milk.
12. During the boiling process, embryo of seed is destroyed. So, it is not sprouted.
13. Cow, buffalo and goat are called milch animal.
14. Mushroom and yeast are fungi. These are neither plant and nor animal product.
15. Honey comb is a hexagonal structure made by honey bees with the help of bee wax. These are the places where queen, worker and drone live. In these structures honey bees stores nectar and form different product/byproduct of honey bees.

Short Answer Type Questions

1. All organisms need food, because:
   - They need food for obtaining energy
   - They derive required nutrients for growth, development and repair of damaged cells and tissues.
   - Food provides us immunity to fight against diseases.
2. Some raw food has various kind of bacteria and microorganism which are pathogenic for our health, so it is necessary that we eat certain food in cooked form. Fruits loss their nutritional value during cooking, so it is suggested that fruit should be eaten in raw form.
3. In case of mustard and onion, 2 parts of edible.
4. Cucumber and eggplant.
5. Main ingredients of aalu parantha are allu, wheat flour, salt, green and red chilli, coriander onion ect.
6. Milk producing animals are milch animals. Milk providing animals are cows, buffaloes, goats, camels.
7. Refer types of animals – On the basis of feeding habits
8. Scavengers feed on dead and decaying matter. and fungi and bacteria feed on dead plants and animals. They decompose their bodies into simpler substances and then absorb them. Both scavengers and decomposers are cleaning dead and decay matter of earth, so these are called nature's cleaners.
9. Some example of insectivores plants are venus flytrap,sundews,pitcher plants ect.
10. Chia seeds, sesame seeds and almond are edible seeds. They are rich in fat and protein.

Long Answer Type Questions

1. Mustard – Leaf and seeds; Potato – Stem; Ladyfinger – Fruit; Apple – Receptacle; Coriander – Leaf and seed; Mung – Seed; Brinjal – Fruit; Sugarcane – Stem; Beetroot – Leaf and root; Mango – Fruit.
2. Refer last competition corner.
3. Plants which feed on insects is called insectivorous, e.g., pitcher plant. Insectivorous plants are feed on insect to full fill deficiency of nitrogen.

   Generally, plants absorb nitrogen from soil as normal soil has sufficient amount of nitrogen which is fixed by nitrogen fixing bacteria. But insectivores plant grown in nitrogen deficit areas. To full fill their nitrogen deficiency, they have special type of leafy modifications to trap insects.
4. Refer topic food chain.
5. (a) Organisms which feed on plants and animals both, e.g., dog, human.

   (b) Organisms which feed on detritus or dead organic remains, e.g., earthworm, millipedes, sea cucumber.

   (c) Material which are used to prepare different type of dishes are called food ingredients, e.g., vegetables, salt, oil, etc.

   (d) Organisms which feed on dead and decay matter are known as decomposers, e.g., bacteria
6. Honey is produced by the honey bees(workers) collected nectar and cane sugar. It is formed of levulose, dextrose (23%), maltose (40%), enzymes and pigment (25%), minerals, vitamins and water.

   Honey has following importance:

   (i) It has antibacterial and antioxidant activity.
   (ii) It is good alternative of sugar.
   (iii) It provides us immunity.
   (iv) It is major component of cough syrups.
   (v) It is used in various cosmetic products.

7. Vegetarian habits means eating of plenty full vegetables or plant products like fruits, potato, tomato, leafy vegetables, etc.

   Non-vegetarian habits means eating of meat, flesh of other animals, etc.

8. Refer food material and their resources.

9. Many parts of plants are edible and has different nutritional values.

   Stem: Potato, sugarcane, bamboo

   Leave: Spinach, methi, bathua

   Flower: Cauliflower, rose, broccoli

   Root: Ginger, turmeric, sweet potato

10. Refer to scavengers

Case Based Study

1. Carbohydrates and fats are main constituents of food which give us energy.
2. Idli and dosa are fermented food and these are consumed mainly in south India.
3. (B) Khaman, thepla, fafada with jalebi.
4. A diet which have all components in balanced form is called balanced diet.
5. Cabbage is a good source of roughage.

Level 2

Multiple Choice Questions

1. (B) Autotrophs can synthesise their own food using either chemical energy or light energy; for example, blue-green algae (BGA) and plants.
2. (C) Omnivores are those animals which eat both plants and animals as food.
3. (C) Nectars or fruit juice are found in flower which provides nutrition to insects.
4. (C) Honey
5. (A) Sweet potato store food in their roots.
6. (A) Tomato is modified ovary of flower.
7. (A) By eating slowly and chewing well.
8. (C) 1-c, 2-e, 3-a, 4-g, 5-f, 6-b, 7-d, 8-h
9. (B) 1-d, 2-c, 3-a, 4-b
10. (B) Leaves and seeds are edible part of mustard plant.
11. (D) Blood sucking animals are called sanguivores.
12. (D) i-c, ii-d, iii-e, iv-b, v-a
13. (B) 5
14. (D) Milk giving animals are known as milch animals.
15. (C) Cinnamon is a spice which adds flavor in the food and also good for health.
16. (B) Stamen is male reproductive system of flower, and it has anther, connective and filament. Petals are colorful and fragranceful part of flower which attract insects for pollination.
17. (C) Option C has incorrect traits for herbs, shrubs and trees.
18. (D) I and IV only
19. (C) (ii), (iv), and (v)
20. (C) Milk, honey, paneer, curd, fish, egg are animal products; and potato, spinach, pulses, and cereals are plant products.

Higher Order Thinking Skills (HOTS)

1. (D) Lunch, obesity and seed
2. (A) Due to boiling of seeds, seeds become dormant or inactive. They will not germinate.
3. (D) Potato parantha, kheer and halwa – all have more than two food ingredients.
4. (C) Coriander – leaf.
5. (A) Plants, BGA and grass – all have chlorophyll for photosynthesis, so they are autotrophs.
6. (D) (a)-(v), (b)-(iv), (c)-(i), (d)-(ii), (e)-(iii)

Archive Corner

1. (A) Herbivores are animals which feed on only plant products.

   Carnivores depend on flesh of other animals.

   Omnivores eat both plant and flesh of other animals.

2. (B) For kheer, milk, rice and sugar are main ingredients in which milk is animal product, and rice and sugar are plant products. Rice and sugar are good source of carbohydrate, and milk is a good example of balance diet.

3. (D) Q – Clove, T – Lettuce.

4. (A) Clove Mustard Cumin Ginger

5. (B) Food chain is relation between different organisms to obtain their food. Deer is herbivore and cow is also herbivore. Sparrow is omnivore and crow is also omnivore and lion is carnivore and tiger is also a carnivore.

6. (C) 1 and 2 only

7. (A) Oxygen

CHAPTER 12: COMPONENTS OF FOOD

CHECK POINT 1

1. Nutrients in food can be divided into macronutrients and micronutrients based on their quantity requirement by the body.
2. Carbohydrates are primary energy source in our body.
3. Oil and ghee are primary source of fats.
4. Amino acids are basic unit of protein.
5. Proteins are required by the body for growth and repair of damaged cells, so proteins are known as building blocks of our body.

CHECK POINT 2

6. Deficiency of vitamin A causes night blindness.
7. Nausea and dehydration are symptoms of water deficiency.

LEVEL 1

Fixed Response Type

Multiple Choice Questions

1. (B) Protein rich food
2. (B) Pulses are rich source of proteins and proteins are building blocks our body.
3. (A) Minerals are vitamins are micronutrients which are required in less quantity but they provide us immunity and require for proper functioning of body. Calcium and chlorine are minerals.
4. (B) Varun is a kid and a best player of football. So, he needs energy. Carbohydrates are rich and instant energy sources.
5. (B) Fish is a protein rich food.
6. (B) Water is essential for all life processes and helps regulate body temperature
7. (A) Banana, jowar, wheat and maize-are example of carbohydrates.
8. (B) Potato and rice are source of starch and starch is a carbohydrate.
9. (C) Fruits have high quantity of vitamins and minerals. Vitamins and minerals are denatured at high temperature, so they should be eaten in raw form.
10. (B) Green leafy vegetables are rich source of minerals like iron and iron is essential to form hemoglobin.
11. (C) Vitamin D is also known as sunshine vitamin because it is synthesized by our body in the presence of sunlight.
12. (C) Carbohydrates and fats are energy giving food. Wheat and ghee are carbohydrate and fat, respectively.
13. (D) Kwashiorkor is a protein deficiency disease, and not blood clotting.
14. (D) Vitamin D is also known as the sunshine vitamin.
15 (D) Green leafy vegetables are rich source of minerals like iron and iron is essential to form haemoglobin.
16. (B) Pulses are rich source of proteins and proteins are building blocks of our body.
17. (D) Vitamins are micronutrients and require in less amount. They provide us immunity, keep our eyes bones, teeth and gums healthy.
18. (D) Children are in growing age and they need sufficient amount of healthy and protein rich diet for proper growth.
19. (B) Deficiency of vitamin E causes infertility or low production of gametes in male and female both.
20. (D) Oxygen is a gas which is essential for respiration; it is not a component of nutrients.
21. (C) Cellulose is carbohydrate but it is rich in roughage. So, it is good for proper digestion of our food.
22. (A) Tocopherol is also called as Vitamin D.

23. (A) Haemoglobin acts as a carrier of oxygen because oxygen is needed to oxidize glucose in cell. One haemoglobin molecule carries 4 oxygen molecules at a time.

24. (C) Fats work as an insulator and keep the body warm and store energy.

25. (C) Vitamins and minerals help the body fight diseases.

26. (C) Food additives or preservatives increase shelf life of food stuff.

27. (C) Sucrose is also known as table sugar, and it is derived from sugar cane.

28. (A) Basic unit of protein is amino acid. 20 amino acids are required for protein formation.

29. (B) Vitamin D helps our body to use calcium effectively.

30. (C) Iron is essential to form Haemoglobin and a deficiency of iron causes anaemia.

Assertion and Reason Type Questions

1. (A) A balanced diet contains all the components of food in right proportion which makes us healthy.

2. (A) Teenagers are growing children. They need a proper diet for proper growth of their bones, muscles, etc. Protein are body building food, so they require in high amount in teenage.

3. (D) Both are false

4. (C) Vitamin C increases our immunity and it can get denatured if cooked. It is mainly found in citrus fruits.

5. (B) Fats are a good source of energy but excess fat deposits in our blood vessel and causes heart disease.

6. (A) Roughage are good for proper digestion as they help in elimination of undigested food.

7. (C) Basic unit of proteins are amino acid. Amino acids are of two types essential and non-essential. Non essential amino acids are prepared by the body and Essential amino acids are to be taken from diet.

8. (B) Different amount of food components are required by different people according to their gender, age group and work.

9. (D) We can derive protein from plant sources as well like pulses.

10. (A) Fruits and vegetables are good source of minerals and vitamins.

11. (A) Vitamin K is required for blood clotting.

Comprehension Type Questions

1. (A) Vitamin A keeps eyes and skin healthy.

2. (D) Protein is essential for growth and repair of the body.

3. (i) Vitamin C rich food like amla, lemon orange, etc.
   (ii) Carbohydrates (Glucose)
   (iii) Fats
   (iv) Glucose

4. Dietary fibres are also known as roughage. Roughage is mainly provided by fruits, vegetables, whole grains and pulses, etc.

Very Short Answer Type Questions

1. Marasmus is a protein and carbohydrate deficiency disease. Kwashiorkor a protein deficiency disease.

2. Water helps in digestion, absorption of food, and removal of waste from the body.

3. Meat, eggs, legumes, leafy vegetables, etc., are sources of vitamin B.

4. Urad daal (black lentil) has maximum protein.

5. Deficiency of vitamin D causes rickets.

6. Sodium and potassium are important for normal functioning of nervous system.

7. Fats and carbohydrates are energy giving food, but carbohydrates provide instant energy, so our metabolic system uses carbohydrates first.

8. Amla, oranges, lemon and guava are vitamin C rich foods.

9. • Calcium – for strong bones and teeth
   • Iron – helps in the formation of red blood cells

10. Roughage (fibers) are essential for digestion of food.

11. Vitamin C rich food like amla, oranges are immunity increasing food.

12. Animals store their food in form of glycogen that is carbohydrate.

13. Carrot and papaya are vitamin A rich foods.

14. Vitamin E is essential for gametes formation.

15. Fish oil rich source of vitamin A and vitamin D.

16. Water melon has maximum content of water.

17. Phosphorus in play an important in formation of bones. Due to deficiency of phosphorus bones become weaker.

18. Proteins are necessary in repairing of our worn-out tissues.

19. No, junk food does not contain any nutrient. They are harmful for our body.

20. Vitamin B complex has multiple type of vitamin B.

21. Green vegetables, cabbage give us roughage.

22. Anaemia is caused by a lack of iron and leads to weakness and fatigue.

23. Vitamin B1 also known as thiamin.

24. Vitamin A, vitamin D, vitamin E and vitamina K are fat soluble vitamins.

25. Vitamin C rich food like amla, lemon and other citrus fruits protect us from disease.

Short Answer Type Questions

1. Water soluble vitamins are not stored in the body so it is required to take these vitamin on daily basis.

2. Lack of sufficient amount of nutrients in food causes malnutrition. These nutrients may be carbohydrates, proteins, vitamins and minerals. Malnutrition has various harmful effects like:
   - Deficiency of these causes various disease.
   - Malnutrition stunts the growth growing children.
   - It causes lack of immunity.
   - Affect the growth of brain.

3. Yes, deficiency diseases can be epidemic. Epidemic diseases are those diseases which spread in large number of human or animals at same time. Sometime deficiency of any specific nutrient/mineral in a particular area causes epidemic disease.

4. Fats are of two types:

   (i) Saturated fats: They are solid at room temperature, e.g., butter, ghee, milk, cream, meat, fish, egg-yolk, etc. These are animal origin.

   (ii) Unsaturated fats: They are liquid at room temperature and are called oils like mustard oil, ground nut oil, etc. These are plant origin.

5. Carbohydrates are important main source of energy for our system. One gram of carbohydrate gives 4 kilocalories as energy. Cereals and other food items such as banana, apples, peas, potatoes, vegetable and dry fruits are food sources of carbohydrates.

6. Our food contains mainly five major kinds of nutrients namely vitamins, minerals, carbohydrates, proteins and fats. Additionally, food also contains water and dietary fibres/roughage and water which are also required by our bodies.

7. Kwashiorkor: Deficiency of proteins leads to a disease called kwashiorkor. It is common in underdeveloped countries. Its symptoms include stunted growth, swelling of face and ends of limbs (especially the feet), skin diseases, a large pot-like belly, mental retardation, and diarrhea.

   Improving calorie and protein intake may correct kwashiorkor, provided that treatment is not started too late. However, full height and growth potential will never be achieved in children who have had this condition.

   Marasmus: Deficiency of proteins along with carbohydrate deficiency is called Protein Energy Malnutrition (PEM). It leads to marasmus. It is more common among infants and children under five years of age. Its symptoms include thin physique, slow body growth, lack of energy, mental retardation, poor muscle development, poor resistance to diseases.

8. No, balance diet is not same for all because each age group or person needs different amount of nutrients for proper functioning and growth.

9. Vitamin B12 and iron cannot be synthesized by our body, so they are required in our diet. Iron is essential for formation of hemoglobin and Vitamin B12 is essential for maturation of RBC (Red blood cell).

10. Some disadvantages of overcooked food are as follows:
   - Due to over cooking, various nutrients vitamins are destroyed.
   - It is harder to digest.
   - Sometimes, it becomes the cause of cancer.

11. • Vitamin A-Retinol
• Vitamin C-Ascorbic acid
• Vitamin D-Calciferol

12. Same answer given in ans key

13. We should keep following precautions during cooking of food:
- Steam the vegetables instead of boiling them.
- Avoid cooking at high temperatures (expect for quick stir frying) and long cooking time.
- Experiment with a variety of vegetable salads.
- Do not wash vegetables and fruits after cutting.

14.

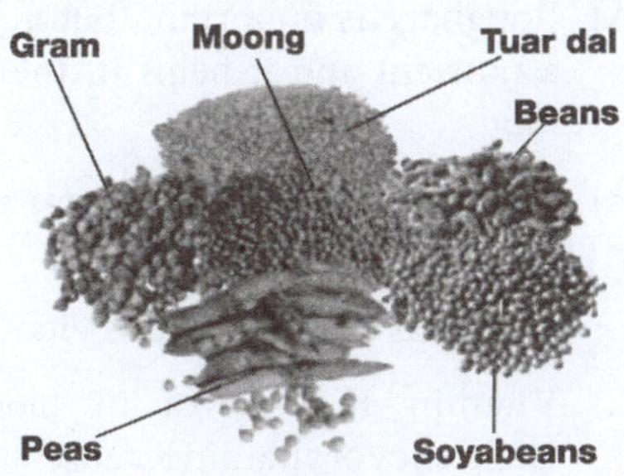

In the given figure, all are pulses and these are rich source of protein. Our hair are made up of keratin protein, so these are good for growth and healthy hairs.

Long Answer Type Questions

1. Refer to deficiency of protein.

2. A twelve-year-old child is teenager and in his growing stage. So, he/she needs balance diet for proper development. It should have all types of nutrients in appropriate amount.

Carbohydrate – Grains, cereals (like wheat, rice, etc.), potato, sweet potato and banana are also rich sources of sugar or carbohydrate.

Proteins – All types of pulses are good source of protein.

Fats – Ghee, butter and vegetable oils are source of fats.

Vitamins and minerals – For vitamins and minerals seasonal fruits and vegetables are good source.

3. (A) Water is essential for life. About two-thirds of our body weight is due to water. Normally, we get most of the water required by our body from the liquids we drink, such as water, milk, tea, etc. All fruits and vegetables also contain large amount of water. Grapes are rich in water content. They contain more than 50 per cent water by weight. Watermelon has the richest water content.

(B) Functions of fat:
- Fats are a rich source of energy.
- Fats are stored in our body and are used whenever our body needs extra energy.
- Fat stored under the skin acts as an insulator and prevents loss of heat from the body in cold weather.
- Fats also act as a cushion for the body organs.

(C) Dietary fibres are also known as roughage. It is mostly provided by plant products like whole grains pulses, fresh fruits and vegetables. Although it does not provide any nutrients, but it is essential component of our food because it helps in proper digestion. It is advised to eat more roughage in case of constipation.

4. Refer to table 12.2

5. Carbohydrate is a biological molecule consisting of carbon (C), hydrogen (H) and oxygen (O) simply known as sugars. Structurally these are polyhydroxy aldehyde or ketone. The term sugar is also known as saccharides.

Source: Sucrose ($C_{12}H_{22}O_{11}$), maltose, etc., are dimers whereas cellulose, starch and lignin are polymers. Monomers and dimers are water soluble but polymers are water insoluble. Monomers group together to form dimers, example - glucose + fructose = sucrose. Many monomers together form a polymer, example n × (glucose) = starch, cellulose, etc.

Functions of carbohydrate: Carbohydrates are the immediate source of energy. Glucose undergoes breakdown to produce energy. Its calorific value is 4.5 Kcal/gm. The storage of carbohydrate in animals is in the form of glycogen and in plants, it is in the form of starch. Other than providing food and energy, they also help in the formation of many useful molecules and are part of enzymes and hormones.

6. (A) Calcium - We get calcium from dairy products like milk, cheese, curd, etc.

(B) Iodine - We get iodine from iodized salt.

(C) Iron - Green and leafy vegetables like spinach methi, etc., are rich source of iron.

(D) Sodium - We get sodium from salt.

(E) Potassium - Banana, apricot, some dry fruits are good source of potassium.

7. (i) Food items like burgers, chips, fries, pizzas, samosas, pakoras, cold drinks, have very less nutritive value. They also have very high calorie content. Such food items are called junk food. Eating junk food on a regular basis could lead to obesity.

(ii) Sometimes consumption of high fat content in diet becomes harmful for our heart, as fat is converted into cholesterol and is deposited in our arteries and causes heart diseases like heart attack.

(iii) If excess amount of carbohydrates is present in the body, they are converted into fats and stored under the skin and cause obesity.

Level 2

1. (C) Vitamin C increases our immunity and gets denatured if we cook it. It is mainly found in citrus fruits.
2. (B) When we take excess fat or carbohydrate, it deposits in our blood vessel and their lumen become narrow. It causes less supply of blood to heart muscles and causes heart attack.
3. (B) Milk is considered as balanced diet as it has all macro and micronutrients. Apple is rich in fibre content or roughage.
4. (C) Simplest unit of carbohydrate and proteins are glucose and amino acid.
5. (C) Broccoli, fruits, carrot, and spinach.
6. (C) Fats and minerals are essential nutrients for a balanced diet of humans.
7. (B) Pulses are rich sources of protein.
8. (C) Iron helps our body by forming red blood cells.
9. (B) Green vegetables have iron which is responsible for formation of blood.
10. (B) Vitamin B3 is required in small amounts and its deficiency cause pellagra.
11. (B) Balanced diet contains all nutrients in the right amounts.
12. (D) Galactose is an example of carbohydrate/sugar.
13. (A) Sodium is a mineral which is responsible for balancing of blood pressure. In case of low BP, sodium is provided to patient and in case of high BP, doctor suggests avoiding more sodium in diet.
14. (A) Roughage is important, but not considered a nutrient and it helps in the digestion of food.
15. (A) Marasmus is a protein energy malnutrition disease.
16. (C) Fish oil is a rich source of vitamin D.
17. (C) Vitamin K involves in blood clotting. Deficiency of vitamin K causes haemorrhage.
18. (D) Zinc.
19. (D) Vitamin C increases our immunity and denatured if we cook it. It is mainly found in citrus fruits.
20. (C) Vitamin D

Higher Order Thinking Skills (HOTS)

1. (C) Kwashiorkor is protein deficiency disease. Iron is involved in formation of hemoglobin and its deficiency causes anemia. Marasmus is PEM. Fluorine prevents tooth decay by making the enamel more resistant to action of acids.
2. (A) P are sources of protein and only deficiency of protein causes kwashiorkor not marasmus.
3. (B) Deficiency of vitamin C causes scurvy. It is also known as gums disease.
4. (D) P is protein.
5. (B) Ravi is suffering from deficiency of iron. It is required for formation of haemoglobin that carries oxygen from lungs to body cells.
6. (B) P is scurvy, Q is pellagra, R is anaemia, and S is goitre.

7. (C) Deficiency of vitamin C causes scurvy. It is also known as gums disease.

8. (C) Amla is great source of vitamin C.

9. (B) Kwashiorkor is caused by deficiency of proteins.

ARCHIVE CORNER

1. (D) In P test tube, carbohydrate or starch rich food is present. When it reacts with iodine, it gives blue black color.

2. (C) Deficiency of vitamin C causes scurvy that is bleeding gums disease but deficiency of vitamin B affects wound healing.

3. (B) 1g of protein gives 4 calorie energy. It helps us in growth and repair, and it protects us from diseases. Deficiency of protein can cause kwashiorkor and marasmus

4. (D) Deficiency of vitamin A causes night blindness.

5. (D) P is vitamin A which is fat soluble vitamin.

6. (C) Excess fats and carbohydrates store in our blood vessel and it is main reason of heart diseases.

7. (C) R is complex carbohydrate. It may be starch or glycogen.

8. (C) Refer question no 2

9. (A) a - (ii), b - (i), c - (iii), d - (v), e - (iv)

10. (B) Q is also required for the proper functioning of the nervous system

11. (A) Copper sulphate and caustic soda when react with protein then it gives purple color.

12. (D) Deficiency of R causes kwashiorkor.

13. (B) Harshit has rickets which occurs due to deficiency of vitamin D.

CHAPTER 13: GETTING TO KNOW PLANTS

CHECK POINT 1

1. (i) Annuals: These are plants with a life span of one year. They are herbs.
   (ii) Biennials: The plants with a life span of two years are called biennials.
   (iii) Perennials: The plants that survive for several years are called perennials. These include shrubs and trees.
2. Wheat and rice main grain which eat worldwide.
3. Money plant is a climber. It is propagated by stem cutting.

CHECK POINT 2

4. Desert is water deficit area, so desert plants have longer roots to absorb water.
5. Roots which are raised except radicle are called adventitious roots.
6. White part coming out from sprouted seed is root.

CHECK POINT 3

7. Yes, green stem has stomata and woody stems have lenticels for respiration.
8. Aloe vera, cactus and pineapple are desert plants.
9. Sweet potato is modified root.

CHECK POINT 4

10. Yes, birds are also pollinating agents. Pollination by birds is called ornithology.
11. Flower which has only either male or female reproductive system is called as unisexual flower; and flower which has both male and female reproductive system is called bisexual flower.
12. Yes, a flower contains more than carpel or pistil.

LEVEL 1

Fixed Response Type

Multiple Choice Questions

1. (A) Branches are originated from nodes.
2. (A) Coconut trees don't have branches.
3. (C) Carrot is modified root which stores food.
4. (B) Roots absorb water and minerals with the help of root hairs from soil.
5. (D) Pea plant is a dicot plant and dicot plants has tap roots.
6. (B) Green leaf and green stem have chlorophyll, so they are involved in photosynthesis.
7. (C) Rose is dicot plant and dicot plants have reticulate venation in their leaves.
8. (B) Xylem
9. (B) Stamen is male reproductive part of flower.
10. (B) Pistil is female reproductive part of flower.
11. (C) After maturation of flower ,all other parts of flower shad off and ovary converts into fruit and ovule forms seed.
12. (B) Prop roots are present in sugarcane.
13. (D) In mangroves, breathing roots are present which are called pneumatophores.
14. (B) Dodder/cuscuta is a parasite plant which get its nutrition from other plant.
15. (A) Tendrils
16. (A) Hydothodes are pores which are found at the side of leaves.
17. (B) Banyan
18. (A) Root
19. (C) When pollen is transferred from anther to stigma of a flower, the process is known as pollination.
20. (D) Substances necessary for autotrophic nutrition are CO_2, H_2O, chlorophyll and sunlight.
21. (B) Organisms capable of synthesizing their own food are called autotrophs.

22. (A) Hibiscus has large petals and both reproductive system of flower is easily visible in this so it is majorly used for study in laboratories.
23. (A) Leaf
24. (D) Magnesium ion stabilizes the chlorophyll molecule.
25. (A) X - Carbon dioxide and Y- Oxygen (equation is of photosynthesis)
26. (B) Plants help maintain atmospheric oxygen and carbon dioxide by giving off oxygen and absorbing carbon dioxide.
27. (C) Runner
28. (B) Insectivorous plants feed on insects for their nutrition.
29. (B) Roots of leguminous plants have root nodules which have nitrogen fixing bacteria.
30. (C) (a) - (ii), (b) - (iii), (c) - (v), (d) - (i), (e) - (iv)

True/False

5. False: Sepals are green coloured false leaves which protect bud and generally green in colour.
9. True: maximum tree has thick brown coloured stem.

Assertion and Reason Type Questions

1. (B) Creepers creep due to soft stem and trees have long life span.
2. (B) Nodes have meristematic tissue from which new branches arise and it shows growth of a plant.
3. (A) Root is important organ of plant because it absorbs water and minerals from soil.
4. (A) Stem transports water with the help of xylem.
5. (A) Leaves has chlorophyll, so it can performs photosynthesis.
6. (A) Flower has one reproductive organ for sexual reproduction.
7. (B) Mid rib found in the centre of leaf and soft stem can easily climb.
8. (A) Plant can respire through stomata.
9. (C) Different kind of venation is found in monocots and dicots.
10. (B) Tap roots are found in dicot and fibrous roots are found in monocot.

Comprehension Type Questions

1. Plants are autotrophs so they can synthesize their own food with help of photosynthesis.
2. Starch is stored food in plant. It is complex carbohydrate which is stored by plant to get energy when photosynthesis is not occurred.
3. (a) True – Transpiration helps in absorption of water.
   (b) False – Iodine is used to identify presence of starch.
4. $6CO_2 + 12H_2O \xrightarrow[\text{Plant}]{\text{Light}} C_6H_{12}O_6 + 6O_2 + 6H_2O$

Free Response Type

Very Short Answer Type Questions

1. Androecium and gynoecium are two important main parts of flower.
2. Photosynthesis is the process by which plants make their food using sunlight. It is performed by the leaves.
3. Sometimes leaves are converted into spring-like structure and provide support to plant in climbing. In cactus, leaves are modified into spines to reduce transpiration as cactus is desert plant.
4. In carpel or pistil, ovary is found.
5. Wheat and rice are example of monocots.
6. A modified stem is a stem that changes its form to perform special functions. Example: Potato.
7. After maturation of flower, ovule is converted into seeds.
8. Stigma, style and ovary are parts of pistil.
9. The main root which is originated from radicle is called taproot.
10. Arrangement of veins on leaf is called leaf venation.
11. Wheat, rice, tomato mustard, etc., are example of herbs.

12. Photosynthesis occurs in chloroplast of a plant cell.

13. Strong smell of flowers attract pollinators for pollination.

14. Removal of excess amount of water from leaves is called transpiration. It is necessary for absorption of water by roots.

15. Pollination is the transfer of pollen from the stamen to the pistil.

Short Answer Type Questions

1. On the basis of size plants are of three types:
   (i) Herbs: Plants which have soft, green and destructible stems are called herbs. They are generally smaller in size; they are almost one meter long in length. Examples: Mustard, wheat, rice, etc.
   (ii) Shrubs: These plants have woody stems with branches. Branches develop near the base of stem. They are medium-sized plants which look like bushes. Examples: Jasmine, croton, hibiscus, etc.
   (iii) Trees: The trees are very tall and have hard woody stem called trunk. They have woody branches, twigs and leaves. Examples: Neem, mango, etc.

2. Creepers: Plants with weak stems that cannot stand upright and spread on the ground are called creepers. Examples: Sweet potato, pumpkin, watermelon, bottle gourd, bitter gourd.

   Climbers: Plants with weak stems which take support on neighboring structure and climb up are called climbers. Examples: Betel, grape, money plants, beans, etc.

3. Arrangement of veins in leaf is called leaf venation. Plants with fibrous root have parallel venation, e.g., monocots. Plants with tap roots have reticulate venation, e.g., dicots.

4. Refer to diagram of flower

5. Refer to root system

6. Refer to functions of stem

7. Leaf has following parts:
   - Petiole: The parts of a leaf by which it is attached to the stem is called petiole.
   - Lamina: The broad green part of the leaf is called lamina
   - Midrib: A thick vein in the middle of the leaf is called the midrib.
   - Veins: Lines on the leaf are called veins.

8. Veins are arranged in different forms in different plants, this arrangement is called leaf venation.
   - Reticulate venation: If arrangement of veins in a leaf is net-like on both sides of midrib the venation called reticulate venation, e.g., leaves of rose mango, etc.
   - Parallel venation: If veins are arranged parallel to one another in a leaf, then venation is called parallel venation, e.g., leaves of wheat, grasses, etc.

9. Refer testing room 4

10. Seed has two germinating parts plumule and radicle. Plumule forms stem and radical forms root.

11. A complete flower has all four whorls of flower that are corolla, calyx, androecium and gynoecium. An incomplete flower has either two or three whorls of flower not all.

12. Petiole: The parts of a leaf by which it is attached to the stem is called petiole. Lamina: The broad green part of the leaf is called lamina. Pneumatophore: Pneumatophores are special kind of roots of mangrove plants, which involve in gaseous exchange.

13. Calyx is the first outermost whorl of a flower.
    - Sepals are generally green in colour and manufacture food.
    - They also protect the new delicate inner parts of the flower during the bud stage.

14. Transpiration me removal of excess amount of water from leaves. When plants perform transpiration, then a root pressure builds on roots which helps in absorption of water and mineral from soil. Transpiration also promotes transportation of water from roots to leaves. So, transpiration is called essential evil for plant.

15. Stem is the main axis of the shoot system. It is green in herbaceous plants but woody and hard in shrubs and trees.
    - It has nodes and internodes. From nodes, new branches and leaves are originated.
    - Stem grows towards light and away from the soil and water.
    - Stem bears leaves, branches, buds, flowers and fruits.

Root develops a part of seed called radiacle.

- It has branches called primary, secondary and tertiary roots.
- It does not have nodes and internodes.
- It grows towards soil and water and away from sunlight.

Long Answer Type Questions

1. Modifications of Stem: In certain plants, stem is modified to carry out special functions besides, support and conduction. These functions are:

   (i) Manufacture of food: The green stem of annual plants synthesizes food by photosynthesis. In cacti and succulents, the stem becomes green and leaf-like to make food, e.g., opuntia.

   (ii) Storage of food: Stem store food.

   Rhizome: In ginger, the underground stem swells up in an irregular form and is called rhizome. It has nodes, internodes, buds and scaly leaves.

   Tuber: Some stems have swollen underground structures used as storage organ for nutrients reserved, which help the plant to survive winter or adverse conditions. It might also have buds, e.g., potato.

   Corms are special tubers with rounded and condensed structure covered with scaly leaves, e.g., gladioli and zimikand.

   (iii) Stem tendril: In some plants like grapevine and passion flower, the stem is weak and some of its branches are modified into thread-like structure coil around the support called stem tendrils.

2. Refer to diagram 14.12 and functions of leaf.
3. Refer to diagram of flower.
4. (i) Simple leaf: A leaf that consist of a single lamina, which is not divided into segments. Plants like mango, guava and money plant have simple leaves.

   (ii) Compound leaf: The leaf in which the lamina is divided into several small segments or leaflet each attached to the same petiole. The leaflet may be arranged on opposite sides of the petiole like in rose and neem or may arise from a common point at the petiole like in palm leaves.

5. Flowers are reproductive organs of the plant.
   - The ovary of a flower develops into fruit and its ovules form the seeds.
   - The nectar of flowers is collected by honeybees to prepare honey.
   - Perfumes are prepared from flowers.
   - Clove is dried flower bud. It adds flavour to the food.

6. Pollination: Process of transfer of pollen grains from anther to stigma is called pollination. There are two types of pollination:
   - Self pollination: When pollen grain is transferred from anther to stigma of the same flower.
   - Cross pollination: When pollen grain is transferred from anther to stigma of the different flower.

   Fertilization: It is a process of fusion of male gamete with the female gamete. Pollen grain contain two male gametes. After fertilization, ovule changes into seed and ovary wall change into fruit wall.

7. Gynoecium / pistil / female reproductive organ: The gynoecium is the fourth whorl which is composed of one or more carpels. The freely occurring units of the carpels in a flower are called pistils. It is female reproductive system of flower. In this, female gamete or egg cell is formed in ovule.

   Androecium / stamen / male reproductive organ: It is the third floral whorl which is composed of one or more male reproductive organs called stamen. A stamen has anther and filament. In anther, male gamete that is pollen grains are produced.

8. Essential and non-essential whorls: Stamens and pistil form the essential whorls of the flower. These are the male and female reproductive organs of the flower and are directly involved in reproduction. On the other hand, calyx and corolla are accessory or non-essential whorls of the flower because these are not associated directly with the reproduction.

Level 2

Multiple Choice Questions

1. (B) Wetlands are the kidneys of the earth and peas are leguminous plant which are involved in nitrogen fixation.
2. (C) Redicle is involved in the formation of root.
3. (B) Radical of stem forms root.
4. (A) Monocots have fibrous root system.
5. (A) Pneumatophores are roots found in mangroves.
6. (D) Additional adventitious roots of banyan tree are prop roots which involves in all functions.
7. (D) Potato is not a climber.
8. (B) Connective tissue is a type of tissue which connects both lobes of anther.
9. (D) Filament is part of stamen.
10. (D) Broad green part of leaf is called lamina which involves in photosynthesis.
11. (D) Phloem does contain sieve tubes.
12. (B) Tomato, rice, lavender are herbs.
13. (B) Date palm and Mulberry.
14. (C) Seed is modified seeds.
15. (A) A stalk by which a leaf is connected with stem is called petiole.
16. (A) First trophic level.
17. (B) When starch reacts with iodine, it gives blue black color.

Higher Order Thinking Skills (HOTS)

1. (D) Water and carbon dioxide are raw material for photosynthesis and sunlight and chlorophyll are essential elements for photosynthesis for sugar formation.
2. (D) Tendrils are supportive structures of plants which helps in climbing and support.
3. (C) Sweet potato is stem and ginger is a root which stores food.
4. (D) Cotton is obtained from cotton seeds.
5. (A) Rose, hibiscus and bougainvillea are small size plants and they are herbs.
6. (A) Roots anchor the plant to the ground and absorb water and mineral salts from the soil.
7. (A) Stomata are tiny pores on leaf which involves in gaseous exchange and chlorophyll absorbs sunlight.
8. (C) Broccoli is a flower which we can consume.
9. (C) Anther is a part of male reproductive system in which male gamete pollens are produced.
10. (A) In first plant, polythene is adjusted in right way and show transpiration.
11. (A) Water and mineral salts
12. (C) Carrot, turnip, radish, beetroot are modified roots which stores food.
13. (A) Mangroves has pneumatophores for respiration.
14. (D) Water and carbon dioxide are raw material for photosynthesis and sunlight and chlorophyll are essential elements for photosynthesis for sugar formation
15. (B) Cuscuta is parasite plant which absorb nutrition from host plant with the help of roots.
16. (B) Jute is harvested in flowering stage because in this stage good, quality of fibre can be obtained.
17. (B) Function of the part is to breathe.
18. (B) Beetroot is rich in sugar, protein and carotene.
19. (C) Fruit is modified ovary which form after maturation of flower.

HINTS AND EXPLANATIONS

Archive Corner

1. (D) Stem has xylem for conduction of water and minerals.
2. (B) S is ovary which modifies into fruit and R are ovules which are modified into seeds. T are petal which are generally different in colors in different flowers. P, V and S form pistil which is female reproductive system of flower.
3. (D) P and Q are monocots, so they have parallel venation while R is dicot, so it has reticulate venation.
4. (D) Father of green revolution of world is Norman Ernest Borlaug. He produced a high yielding, disease resistant wheat variety and was awarded Nobel Peace Prize in 1970.
5. (B) Photosynthesis occurs in insectivorous plants also.
6. (C) Pot P-Plant watered everyday and Pot Q-Plant watered every 3rd day.
7. (D) S is ovary which is involved in fertilization and it modifies into fruit.
8. (D) Desert plants are adapted to survive in desert areas.
9. (C) Ginger is a modified root to store food and in cactus, stem is modified to synthesize food.
10. (C) X- Whorled, Y- Alternate, Z-Opposite
11. (A) It shows seed dispersal by different factors in different plants.
12. (D) P is nitrogen which animals get directly from plants but plants get after nitrogen fixation.
13. (D) Calliandra::Spinach::Bitter gourd
14. (C) P-Maize, Q-Spinach, R-China rose, S-Barley
15. (A) P is leafy vegetable that is lettuce. Aloe vera is desert plant so its leaf are modified into spines to prevent transpiration. R is bryophyllum in which leaf reproduces. S is insectivores plant and T is climber.
16. (C) P could be tendril of Cucurbita whereas and R could be climbing root of ivy.
17. (B)
    - Petals and sepals are different in different plants.
    - Roots absorb water and minerals.
    - Stamen is male reproductive part of flower.
    - By petiole, leaf is attached with stem.
    - Calyx and corolla are non-essential part of flower.
18. (D) In corn, seeds are edible and in turnip, root is edible.
19. (B) In all plants, Q is not edible.

CHAPTER 14: THE LIVING ORGANISMS CHARACTERISTICS AND SURROUNDING

Check Point 1

1. Organisms which are not visible to naked eyes are called microorganism.
2. Some organisms live in extreme cold and heat conditions because they adapted themselves according to their surroundings.
3. Interaction between living and non-living factors is called ecosystem.

Check Point 2

4. Cactus and aloe vera are desert plants.
5. Cactus is xerophyte and in desert, there is scarcity of water. To fulfill its need, it stores water in its leaf. It is an adaptation of xerophytes.

Check Point 3

6. Special features or habits, which the organisms develop in order to survive in their habitat, are called adaptations.
7. All living organisms are dependent on natural resources like water, air, sunlight, etc. Interaction between living and non-living factors is required for survival of living being.
8. Deer shares grass land or forest type of habitat because are herbivore and eat only plants.

Check Point 4

9. Kidneys are primary excretory organ in human.
10. We should eat balanced diet to perform all vital activities in proper manner.
11. Food gives energy which is necessary to perform all vital functions of the body.

Check Point 5

12. A process by which an organism forms its own kind is called reproduction. It is necessary to maintain continuity of life.
13. When we touch mimosa pudica, its leaves are droop down due to water loss, so it is called touch me not plant.

Level 1

Fixed Response Type

Multiple Choice Questions

1. (B) All living organisms have the ability to produce young one of their own kind. The process is called reproduction.
2. (B) Germination
3. (B) Interaction between living and nonliving components of environment is called Ecosystem.
4. (A) When an organism develops certain features/characters to be adjusted better in the environment the process is called adaptation.
5. (B) Root
6. (C) Giraffe's long neck is an adaptation based on food.
7. (A) Desert plant shave long roots for absorption of water and thick cuticle layer to reduce transpiration.
8. (B) Sunlight
9. (A) Whales and dolphins breathe through blowholes.
10. (C) Tadpole leaves in water so it has Gills as a respiratory organ.

Assertion and Reason Type Questions

1. (C) Hydrophytes have smaller roots.
2. (A) Both assertion and reason are correct.
3. (A) Thick skin of polar bear protect it from low temperature.
4. (A) To reduce transpiration, leaves of cactus are modified into spines.
5. (B) Excretion and respiration both are features of living being.

HINTS AND EXPLANATIONS

6. (A) Plants are producers because they perform photosynthesis.
7. (A) Each living being respond to stimuli.
8. (B) Balance diet provide nutrition for growth.
9. (D) By reproduction, organisms increase their count and in human lungs are respiratory organ.
10. (D) Movement and locomotion are different. Displacement of any living being is locomotion.
11. (A) Frogs are amphibian, so they can live in water and land.
12. (A) Adaptation prepares organism for survival in any habitat.
13. (A) Camel excretes concentrated urine to conserve water.
14. (C) Fish has gills for respiration.
15. (A) Carnivores have sharp canines to tear other animals.

Comprehension Type Questions

1. Place where an organism live is called habitat.
2 (A) Grassland is an example of terrestrial habitat.
3 (D) Lakes and pond both are examples of aquatic habitat.
4 (A) Living things are the biotic components of a habitat.
5. (A) Amphibian can live in both water and on land.
6. Frog is an example of amphibian. When it is tadpole, then it has gills for respiration and when it is adult, it has lungs for respiration.
7. Living components of ecosystem are called biotic factors, e.g., plants, animals, etc. Non-living factors of ecosystem are called abiotic factors, e.g., light, temperature, etc.
8. Refer to terrestrial and aquatic habitat from chapter.
9. An organism can survive in a habitat with the help of some adaptation.
10. Camel and lama can survive in desert region.

Very Short Answer Type Questions

1. Prey is an organism which is killed by predator for its food.

   Predator is an organism which hunt another organism for its food.
2. In pond, we can see aquatic plant with hollow soft stem, small leaves and generally, small ribbon shape leaves.
3. The stages are as follows:
   - Egg
   - Tadpole
   - Tadpole with legs
   - Froglet
   - Adult frog
4. Life span is duration between birth to death. Life cycle means biological changes that occurs in an organism from birth to death.
5. A tadpole is the larval stage of a frog that hatches from the egg. It lives in water and breathes through gills.
6. In terrestrial habitat, organism live on land and in aquatic habitat means organism who live in water.
7. Camel stores fat in their hump to use it as food in case of scarcity.
8. Whale has blowholes for respiration.
9. A process by which different plants grow by its seed is called germination. It is necessary for a plant for reproduction.
10. If we cover leaf of a mesophyte by a polythene and place it into sunlight, then we get some droplets at surface of leaf which show process of transpiration in leaf.
11. Interaction between biotic and abiotic factors is called ecosystem.
12. Water is important because eggs and tadpoles need water to survive and develop.
13. No, plants do not show locomotion. They show only movement.
14. Deer, lion and tiger are animals of grassland ecosystem.
15. Money plant, potato, rose and mint can propagate by stem cutting.

Short Answer Type Questions

1. (i) Camel is known as the called ship of desert.
   (ii) Gills are respiratory organ in fish.
   (iii) In terrestrial habitat, rat shows aestivation.
   (iv) Crow and pigeon are examples of aerial habitat organism.
2. All animals have different morphology, anatomy and physiology. So, they cannot live in same kind of habitat.
3. Base of mimosa pudica leaflet has a swollen structure that is called pulvinus. When we touch leaf of *Mimosa pudica*, then its mid rib losses its water and water reach to pulvinus. So, leaves of mimosa pudica droop down for some time.
4. Refer to mountain adaptation from chapter
5. Refer to adaption in lion from terrestrial adaptation
6. Estuaries are regions where saltwater (from the ocean) mixes with freshwater (from rivers or streams). These unique habitats provide shelter to several marine animals and birds.

   Acclimatization: Adaptation of an organism to a new temperature, altitude and other environmental factors is called acclimatization.
7. Refer to desert adaptation of camel from chapter
8. Pond is freshwater resource in which frogs, freshwater fishes, toads, etc., live.

   Ocean is salty water resource in which whale, dolphin, seals, etc., live.
9. Respiration means gaseous exchange between environment and an individual. In respiration, organism inhale oxygen which is necessary for cellular respiration in cell to release energy for survival.
10. Frog is an amphibian so it can live in water and in land both. When it lives in water, it has gills for respiration; and when it lives in land, then it has lungs for respiration.

Long Answer Type Questions

1. Refer to polar bear adaptation from chapter.
2. Refer to polar region adaptation.
3. Refer to aquatic adaptation in plants and animals.
4. Refer to adaptation in camel and kangaroo rat from desert adaptation.
5. Refer to characters of organisms from chapter.
6. Living components of this environment are called biotic components.
   (i) Producers: All the autotrophs of ecosystem are called as producers.
   (ii) Consumers: All the heterotrophs of the ecosystem are known as consumers.
   (iii) Decomposers or micro-consumers: Those living organisms which decompose the dead bodies of producers and consumers and release mineral substances again into the soil are called decomposers.

   Non-living components are called abiotic components, for example, temperature, light, humidity, etc.
7. Refer to terrestrial habitat.
8. Whale live in aquatic marine habitat. It is a mammal and has following adaptations for marine habitat:
   - It has streamlined body which helps in swimming.
   - Its forelimbs are modified into flippers.
   - It has blowholes for respiration.
   - It has blubber for warmth to avoid excess heat loss.
9. Refer to mountain adaptation from content of chapter.

Case Based Questions

1. Camel
2. Cactus is a desert plant. Its leaves are modified into spines and stem modifies for photosynthesis.
3. Spines are found in desert plant for protection.
4. Removal of excess amount of water is called transpiration. Plants perform transpiration for transportation of water.
5. Thar desert is a part of terrestrial habitat.
6. Long feet of desert animals help them to easy walking in sand.
7. They have spiny leaves, modified stem for storage of water.
8. (A) True
9. (C) Changes at a physical level to survive in a particular habitat is called adaptation.
10. Camel

Level 2

1. (C) An ecosystem is a biological community and component of the physical environment with which the community interacts.
2. (D) Abiotic components include flow of energy and cycling of materials.
3. (C) Food web is a network of various food chains. It is more stable than food chain.
4. (D) Plants lose very little water through transpiration and their roots grow very deep in the soil.
5. (A) Respiration, reproduction, adaptation and excretion are necessary for living being.
6. (D) Hatching is a process in birds by which chick or baby develops in birds from egg.
7. (C) Plants respire in day time as well as night time.
8. (D) Flow of energy and Cycling of material.
9. (B) Egg → Larva → Pupa → Adult
10. (A) In desert, urine is passed in small amount and it is concentrated.
11. (D) Adaptation of desert region and cold region are given.
12. (B) High altitude area trees have needle-like leaves to shed off snow. In high altitude, temperature is less.
13. (C) All Living organisms have an definite life span.
14. (D) Hydrophyte.
15. (B) Larva
16. (C) Correct order is (ii), (iv), (v) (i), (iii), (vi)
17. (B) Acclimatization: Change in skin colour due to the climate.
18. (C) Mangroves grow in sea water.
19. (D) Corals and sea anemone both are not found in estuaries.
20. (D) Duckweed are aquatic plants that float on freshwater and wetlands.

Higher Order Thinking Skills (HOTS)

1. (C) All living components are called biotic component.
2. (B) Cultivated land with grazing cattle is not an example of habitat.
3. (C) Earthworms has moist and thin skin for breathing.
4. (D) All the statements are correct.
5. (B) Growth, Movement, Reproduction and Photosynthesis
6. (C) Birds has exoskeleton in form of feathers.
7. (B) Group of penguins depicts population.
8. (D) Animal R (Camel) is most likely found in the desert because it has a long neck to reach for leaves in tall trees.
9. (D) Aquatic plants have soft long stem and waxy leaves.
10. (C) The plants and animals are exchanging gases for their life processes to take place.
11. (D) Desert animals drink a lot of water and store it to adjust high temperature.
12. (D) Water hyacinth, water chestnut and hydrilla – all of them have a waxy coating on their surface.
13. (C) Snake shows slithering or creeping movement.
14. (C) Cell → Tissue → Organ → System
15. (A) Cockroach.
16. (C) Diagram shows gaseous cycle in animals and plants.
17. (B) Mimosa plant show response to stimuli.
18. (C) Hydrophytes are aquatic plants, mesophytes are normal plants, and xerophytes are desert plant.
19. (C) Grasshopper is herbivore and form second trophic level of food chain.
20. (B) Q-plants

Archive Corner

1. (B) These pictures are of monocot plants which have equal stomata at upper and lower both surface.
2. (D) X – Floats on water; Y – Has woody stem; Z – Has fleshy fruit
3. (D) Animal Y is an animal which live in cold region, so it has adaptation according to this.
4. (B) Student Q
5. (C) These all features are of dolphin and whale.
6. (D) Deer is terrestrial animal with terrestrial adaptation.
7. (C) Penguin, ostrich, and bat.
8. (B) Water pollution due to spilling of oil from ships is main cause of death of aquatic organisms.
9. (B) P – Willow; Q – Opuntia; R – Rubber tree; S – Penguin; T – Kangaroo-rat; U – Toucan
10. (B) Y and W could be primary and secondary consumers, respectively, in the food chain formed by interlinking these organisms.
11. (D) All are adaptations of different ecosystems.
12. (D) These all are features of turtle, penguin and seal.
13. (A) P could be a mammal that possesses thick subcutaneous fat layer whereas, Q could be sparrow that has air-filled bones.

Photo Credits

Chapter 1

Page 1.2—**Fig. 1.1**—AL1209646_smereka. Shutterstock; AL1402359_Dimitris Leonidas. Shutterstock; AL1359087_andrey_l. Shutterstock; AL1348313_th_trvlr. Shutterstock; AL1190399_Arne Bramsen. Shutterstock; AL1358983_Vadim Sadovski. Shutterstock; **Page 1.3**—**Fig. 1.2**—AL1193338_Philip Pilosian. Shutterstock; AL1281787_miroslav110. Shutterstock; AL1325232_Photomarine. Shutterstock; AL1376222_surflover. Shutterstock; AL1214711_Nico Smit. 123rf.com; AL1355561_f11photo. Shutterstock; **Page 1.9**—**Fig. 1.5**—AL1530094_Matt Benoit. Shutterstock; **Page 1.11**—123rf.com; AL2003645_Andrey Suslov / Shutterstock; **Fig. 1.9**—AL1431319_alexlmx / 123RF; **Page 1.13**—**Fig. 1.10**—AL1417511_Romrodphoto / Shutterstock; **Fig. 1.11**—AL1408507_Aphelleon / Shutterstock; **Fig. 1.12**—AL1334409_Joe Ravi / Shutterstock; **Page 1.14**—**Fig. 1.13**—AL1137141_Jag_cz. Shutterstock; AL1131816_Racheal Grazias. Shutterstock; **Fig. 1.14**—AL500554_Pablo77 / Shutterstock; **Page 1.15**—**Fig. 1.15**—AL1383385_PhotographyByMK / Shutterstock; **Fig. 1.15**—AL1355836_Aleoks / Shutterstock **Page 1.25**—**Comprehension based- Q3(iii)**_AL2049879_Spreadthesign / Shutterstock; **Page 1.25**—**Comprehension based Q4(i)**_AL2000476_Paul Beebee, Beehive Illustrations / Pearson Education Ltd; **Comprehension based Q4(ii)**_AL2001585_PDQ Digital Media Solutions Ltd / Pearson Education Ltd; **Comprehension based Q4(iv)**_AL1461590_PDQ Digital Media Solutions Ltd / Pearson Education Ltd

Chapter 2

Page 2.3—**Fig. 2.1**—AL1307941_Wlad74. Shutterstock; **Page 2.3**—**Fig. 2.2**—AL1511043_nizozoz. Shutterstock; **Page 2.4**—**Fig. 2.3**—AL1291265_blueringmedia / 123RF; AL1309459_Mohd Suhail. Pearson India Education Services Pvt. Ltd; AL1483176_ShutterStockStudio. Shutterstock; AL1449598_ShutterStockStudio. Shutterstock; **Page 2.6**—**Fig. 2.4**—AL1490862_OSweetNature. Shutterstock; AL1490863_OSweetNature. Shutterstock; AL1192456_Mohammed Ali. Pearson India Education Services Pvt. Ltd; AL8188_HL Studios. Pearson Education Ltd; AL1309459_Mohd Suhail. Pearson India Education Services Pvt. Ltd; AL1195797_Mohammed Ali. Pearson India Education Services Pvt. Ltd; AL1449274_Cico. Shutterstock; AL1101557_Anatoly Maslennikov. Shutterstock; AL1312627_Arvind Singh Negi/Red Reef Design Studio. Pearson India Education Services Pvt. Ltd; AL1210704_Mohd Suhail. Pearson India Education Services Pvt. Ltd; AL1312675_Arvind Singh Negi/Red Reef Design Studio. Pearson India Education Services Pvt. Ltd; AL1449571_Zern Liew. Shutterstock; AL1511043_nizozoz. Shutterstock; **Page 2.12**—**NCERT Compendium Q4**_AL1544151_redknapper / Shutterstock; AL1119549_Roxana Bashyrova / Shutterstock; **Page 2.23**—**Level 2 MCQ Q52**_AL2017217_phototiara / Shutterstock, AL1280650_indigolotos / 123RF, AL1468761_Jakkapan Jabjaiṇai / 123RF

Chapter 3

Page 3.2—**Fig. 3.1(a)**—IM_VISUALS. Shutterstock; **Page 3.2**—**Fig. 3.1(b)**—AlexGreenArt. Shutterstock; **Page 3.4**—**Fig. 3.2(c)**—AlexGreenArt. Shutterstock; **Page 3.5**—**Fig. 3.3**—Fouad A. Saad. Shutterstock; **Page 3.7**—**Fig. 3.4**—Mohd Suhail. Pearson India Education Services Pvt. Ltd; **Page 3.7**—**Fig. 3.5**—Mohd Suhail. Pearson India Education Services Pvt. Ltd; **Page 3.8**—**Fig. 3.7**—photoiconix. Shutterstock; **Page 3.12**—**NCERT Compendium Q6**—BlueRingMedia. Shutterstock; **Page 3.13**—**NCERT Compendium Q6 Solution**—BlueRingMedia. Shutterstock; **Page 3.24**—**Archive CornerQ3 P**—Libor Píška. Shutterstock; **Page 3.24**—**Archive Corner Q3 Q**—Tudor Photography. Pearson Education Ltd; **Page 3.24**—**Archive Corner Q3 R**—MSSA. Shutterstock; **Page 3.24**—**Archive Corner Q4 A**—Patcharapa / Shutterstock; **Page 3.24**—**Archive Corner Q4 B**—Igor Zakharevich. 123rf.com; **Page 3.24**—**Archive Corner Q4 C**—Kostsov. Shutterstock; **Page 3.24**—**Archive Corner Q4 D**—wk1003mike. Shutterstock; **Page 3.25**—**Archive Corner Q10**—photoiconix. Shutterstock; **Page 3.25**—**Archive Corner Q11**—mates. Shutterstock

Chapter 4

Page 4.4—Fig. 4.1—AL1280074_Alex Mit. Shutterstock; AL1449401_Igor Chekalin. Shutterstock; AL1423437_nasaimages. 123rf.com; **Page 4.5—Fig. 4.2**—AL2038033 [Converted] new_ingaclemens / 123RF; **Fig. 4.3**—AL1428541_ Vector FX. Shutterstock; **Page 4.6—Fig. 4.4**—AL1271947_tan4ikk / 123RF; **Page 4.7—Fig. 4.5**—AL1095049_fluidworkshop. Shutterstock; **Fig. 4.6**—AL1129730_xfox01. Shutterstock; **Fig. 4.7**—AL1367195_NASA images. Shutterstock; **Page 4.8—Fig. 4.8**—AL1481976_NASA images. Shutterstock; **Fig. 4.9**—AL1367265_Aphelleon. Shutterstock; AL1496056_ Alones. Shutterstock; AL1333525_Byron W.Moore. Shutterstock; **Page 4.9—Fig. 4.12**—AL498686_Jaan- Martin KuusmannShutterstock; **Fig. 4.13**—AL1495486_grejak. Shutterstock; **Fig. 4.14**—AL1356067_NASA images. Shutterstock; **Fig. 4.15**—AL1481667_Dotted Yeti. Shutterstock; **Fig. 4.16**—AL1438761_muratart. Shutterstock; **Page 4.10—Fig. 4.17**—AL1164416_Paul Fleet. Shutterstock; **Page 4.11—Fig. 4.18**—AL1517192_BlueRingMedia. Shutterstock; **Page 4.12—Fig. 4.19**—AL1481963_tsuneomp. Shutterstock; **Page 4.15**—AL1271718_alhovik. 123rf.com; **Page 4.16**—AL1349394 new 1_BlueRingMedia/Shutterstock; AL1349394 new 2_ BlueRingMedia/Shutterstock; **Page 4.17**—AL1439697 new_ Redsapphire / Shutterstock; **Page 4.19**—AL1439697_Redsapphire/Shutterstock; **Page 4.29**—AL2038033_ingaclemens / 123RF

Chapter 5

Page 5.2—Fig. 5.1—AL1414056_elenabsl / 123RF; **Page 5.3—Fig. 5.2**—AL1218821_Julia Reschke. Shutterstock; Josef Bosak. Shutterstock; **Page 5.4—Fig. 5.3**—AL1346315_Idea tank. Shutterstock; AL27113_Coleman Yuen. Pearson Education Asia Ltd; **Page 5.6—Fig. 5.4**—AL1340399_kritchanut. 123rf.com; AL1213153_Liliia Rudchenko. 123rf.com; **Page 5.6—Fig. 5.5**—AL1532944_udaix. Shutterstock; **Fig. 5.6**—AL2004270_VectorMine / Shutterstock; **Fig. 5.7**—AL1477999_udaix. 123rf.com; **Fig. 5.2**—AL497428_Josef Bosak / Shutterstock; **Page 5.9—Abridgement**_AL1319930_ Fouad A. Saad / Shutterstock; **Abridgement**_AL1448659_bioraven / Shutterstock

Chapter 6

Page 6.2—Fig. 6.1—AL1220667_magnetix / Shutterstock; **Page 6.2—Fig. 6.2**—AL1384358_Emilio100 / Shutterstock; **Page 6.3—Fig. 6.3**—AL1467341_origami cat. Shutterstock; AL1094106_Martyn F. Chillmaid. Pearson Education Ltd; **Page 6.5—Fig. 6.7**—AL2031271_grayjay / Shutterstock; **Page 6.6—Fig. 6.9**—AL1449412_Vecton. Shutterstock; **Page 6.7—Fig. 6.12**—AL5852_Oxford Designers & Illustrators Ltd / Pearson Education Ltd; **Page 6.8—Fig. 6.13**—AL1526304_Nick Greaves. Shutterstock; **Fig. 6.13**—AL1322744_windcoast / Shutterstock; **Fig. 6.13**—AL1485230_Fahroni / Shutterstock; **Fig. 6.13**—AL2003341_1D2B Daniel Budnik / Shutterstock **Page 6.9—Fig 6.14**—AL1342856_czarnybez / 123RF; **Page 6.10—Fig. 6.15**—AL1192527_Mohammed Ali. Pearson India Education Services Pvt. Ltd; AL1215359_Amit John. Pearson India Education Services Pvt. Ltd; AL1415975_Arvind Singh Negi/Red Reef Design Studio. Pearson India Education Services Pvt. Ltd; AL1415977_Arvind Singh Negi/Red Reef Design Studio. Pearson India Education Services Pvt. Ltd; AL1415980_Arvind Singh Negi/Red Reef Design Studio. Pearson India Education Services Pvt. Ltd; AL1192489_ Mohammed Ali. Pearson India Education Services Pvt. Ltd; AL1192527_Mohammed Ali. Pearson India Education Services Pvt. Ltd; AL1415953_Arvind Singh Negi/Red Reef Design Studio. Pearson India Education Services Pvt. Ltd; AL1415980_Arvind Singh Negi/Red Reef Design Studio. Pearson India Education Services Pvt. Ltd; AL1276724_Mohd Suhail. Pearson India Education Services Pvt. Ltd; AL1222784_Mohd Suhail. Pearson India Education Services Pvt. Ltd; AL1415953_Arvind Singh Negi/Red Reef Design Studio. Pearson India Education Services Pvt. Ltd; AL1215359_Amit John. Pearson India Education Services Pvt. Ltd; AL5643_Pearson Education Ltd

Chapter 7

Page 7.4—Fig. 7.1—AL1394623_Artisticco / Shutterstock; **Page 7.5—Fig. 7.2**—AL2070325_designua / 123RF; **Page 7.6—Fig. 7.3**—AL1456699_Galyna Andrushko. Shutterstock; **Page 7.6—Fig. 7.4**—AL1374104_姚 一龙. 123rf.com; **Page 7.7—Fig. 7.5**—AL1536534_Anna Nikonorova / Shutterstock; **Page 7.7—Fig. 7.6**—AL1281144_Toa55 / Shutterstock; **Page 7.10—Exemplification Q7**_AL1394623_Artisticco / Shutterstock

Chapter 8

Page 8.2—Fig. 8.1—makasana photo. Shutterstock; **Page 8.3**—Fig. 8.2—Tony Moran. Shutterstock; **Page 8.6**—Fig. 8.6—Pearson Education Ltd

Chapter 9

Page 9.2—Fig. 9.2—AL1424090_Rob kemp. Shutterstock; **Page 9.3**—Fig. 9.3—AL1123885_littleny. Shutterstock; Fig. 9.4—AL1209244_Fribus Mara. Shutterstock; Fig. 9.5—AL1185845_ermess. Shutterstock; AL1343765_Teresa Levite. Shutterstock; AL1454364_Robert Przybysz. Shutterstock; **Page 9.5**—Fig. 9.6—AL1415986_Arvind Singh Negi/Red Reef Design Studio. Pearson India Education Services Pvt. Ltd; AL1222321_THPStock. Shutterstock; AL1482743_CRS PHOTO. Shutterstock; AL1282629_artbyallyson. 123rf.com; AL1280229_aidart. Shutterstock; AL1299009_Everett Historical. Shutterstock; AL1448710_Lubov Vis. Shutterstock; AL1216417_Sofiaworld. Shutterstock; AL1424083_Martina Simonazzi. Shutterstock; AL1385949_kaband. Shutterstock; AL1290578_vitor costa. Shutterstock; AL1195788_Mohammed Ali. Pearson India Education Services Pvt. Ltd; **Page 9.9**—Competition Corner_AL1493143_Yevhenii Orlov / Shutterstock

Chapter 10

Page 10.3—Fig. 10.1—AL1173009_imagedb.com. Shutterstock; **Page 10.4**—Fig. 10.2—AL1489985_Inna Bigun. Shutterstock; **Page 10.6**—Fig. 10.3—AL6946_Pearson Education Ltd; **Page 10.7**—Fig. 10.4—AL1535786_James Steidl / Shutterstock

Chapter 11

Page 11.5—Fig. 11.1—AL51141_Gareth Boden. Pearson Education Ltd; AL1224061_gradts. 123rf.com; AL1136960_StevenRussellSmithPhotos. Shutterstock; AL1115212_Chesapeake Images. Shutterstock; **Page 11.5**—Fig. 11.2—AL1367189_Vladimir Wrangel. Shutterstock; AL1095818_Skynavin. Shutterstock; AL1342436_Edwin Godinho. Shutterstock; AL1404627_Carmine Arienzo. Shutterstock; **Page 11.6**—Fig. 11.3—AL1210573_Catcher of Light, Inc.. Shutterstock; AL1526927_danyas286. 123rf.com; AL1218237_Stuart Partridge. 123rf.com; AL1319655_Tiger Images. Shutterstock; AL1106847_eye-blink. Shutterstock; AL23443_Coleman Yuen. Pearson Education Asia Ltd; **Page 11.8**—Fig. 11.4—AL1366867_HelloRF Zcool. Shutterstock; AL465872_Repina Valeriya. Shutterstock; **Page 11.8**—Fig. 11.5—AL1357608_Piyaset. Shutterstock; **Page 11.9**—Fig. 11.6—AL1476962_Olga Nayashkova. Shutterstock; Fig. 11.7—AL485543_Serg64. Shutterstock; Fig. 11.8—AL1214816_Jag_cz. Shutterstock; **Page 11.10**—Fig. 11.9—AL1417525_Anthony Shaw Photography. Shutterstock; AL1533762_trexec. 123rf.com; AL1324140_Reinhold Leitner. Shutterstock; **Page 11.11**—Fig. 11.10—AL1448987_5PH. Shutterstock; AL1526927_danyas286. 123rf.com; AL468832_Randy Rimland. Shutterstock; AL2002590_Milan Zygmunt / Shutterstock; AL1221500_Marcin Lukaszewicz. 123rf.com

Chapter 12

Page 12.3—Fig. 12.2—AL31187_Tudor Photography. Pearson Education Ltd; AL1418421_YKTR. Shutterstock; AL455184_Olga Lyubkina. Shutterstock; AL454442_Robert Milek. Shutterstock; AL1483318_Roman Samokhin. Shutterstock; **Page 12.4**—Fig. 12.3—AL1477972_Sirichai Asawalapsakul. 123rf.com; AL1098737_stavklem. Shutterstock; AL1410481_maykal. 123rf.com; AL30563_Coleman Yuen. Pearson Education Asia Ltd; AL463384_Madlen. Shutterstock; AL1221188_kenishirotie. 123rf.com; **Page 12.4**—Fig. 12.4—AL1469407_Oleksandra Naumenko. 123rf.com; **Page 12.9**—Fig. 12.5—AL1115726_ifong. Shutterstock; **Page 12.20**—Short Answer Type Q14_AL1301341_Elena Schweitzer / Shutterstock; **Page 12.24**—Archive Corner Q3_AL1424030_Oleksandra Naumenko / Shutterstock;

Chapter 13

Page 13.4—Fig. 13.1—AL1459536_Ruth Swan. Shutterstock; AL1398537_Olha Solodenko. 123rf.com; **Page 13.5—Fig. 13.2**—AL1413973_Sanyalux Srisurin. 123rf.com; AL1201604_m.wolf. Shutterstock; **Fig. 13.3**—AL1416676_margo1778. Shutterstock; AL1221386_Vinod Kumar Pillai. 123rf.com; AL1115414_Sealstep. Shutterstock; AL1514078_Ayham Shoaib. Shutterstock; **Page 13.6—Fig. 13.4**—AL1211924_tonobalaguer. 123rf.com; AL1302845_ve_ro_sa. Shutterstock; **Page 13.7—Fig. 13.5**—AL1371447_Nikitina Olga. Shutterstock; **Fig. 13.7**—AL2031800_Kazakova Maryia / Shutterstock; **Page 13.8—Competition Corner**_AL484870_Natalie-art / Shutterstock; **Competition Corner**_AL1495880_JIANG HONGYAN / Shutterstock; **Competition Corner**_ AL1414248_Peter Etchells / 123RF; **Competition Corner**_AL1215805_Sean Lema / Shutterstock; **Page 13.9—Keystone**_AL498492_Jon E Oringer / Shutterstock; **Page 13.10—Fig. 13.8**—AL1318875_Dualororua / Shutterstock; **Fig. 13.10**—AL1187004_Le Do / Shutterstock; **Page 13.11—Fig. 13.11**—AL5932_HL Studios / Pearson Education Ltd; AL1507678_Lamyai / Shutterstock; **Page 13.12—Fig. 13.13**—AL1517087_Designua. Shutterstock; AL1294731_Mary Lane. 123rf.com; AL1299881_Pongsak Dithongngam. 123rf.com; AL1412046_Arvind Singh Negi/Red Reef Design Studio. Pearson India Education Services Pvt. Ltd; AL1345476_BlueRingMedia. Shutterstock; AL1289070_jiangdi. Shutterstock; AL23443_Coleman Yuen. Pearson Education Asia Ltd; AL1310405_Swapan Photography. Shutterstock; AL478544_Valentyn Volkov. Shutterstock; AL498117_Valentyn Volkov. Shutterstock; AL1327961_Oleg Roman Ko. 123rf.com; AL1059656_Henu Mehtani. Pearson India Education Services Pvt. Ltd; **Page 13.13—Competition Corner (iii)**_AL1217380_Warayoo / Shutterstock; **Page 13.31—Archive Corner-Q 1**_AL1394927_Teguh Mujiono / Shutterstock

Chapter 14

Page 14.4—Fig. 14.1—AL1544030_Konstantnin. Shutterstock; AL2002952_Alexandra Lande / Shutterstock; **Page 14.5—Fig. 14.2**—AL2003363_Darkangel8688 / Shutterstock; **Page 14.5—Fig. 14.3**—AL1314086_Steve Boice. Shutterstock; AL1115096_VikOl. Shutterstock; AL1325294_Daniel Prudek. Shutterstock; **Page 14.6—Fig. 14.4**—AL1112399_Zack Frank. Shutterstock; **Page 14.6—Fig. 14.5**—AL1311970_mhgallery. 123rf.com; AL1272653_Daniel Schweinert. Shutterstock; Page **14.7—Fig. 14.6**—AL1438645_Rich Carey. Shutterstock; **Page 14.7—Fig. 14.7**—AL1371586_Vasin Lee. Shutterstock; **Page 14.7—Fig. 14.8**—AL1479162_WildlifeWorld. Shutterstock; **Page 14.8—Fig. 14.9**—AL2009501_graphic-line / Shutterstock; **Page 14.10—Fig. 14.11**—AL1398039_sutham / Shutterstock; **Page 14.10—Fig. 14.12**—AL2002723_alexdov / Shutterstock; AL1544263_bamgraphy. Shutterstock; AL1331173_kazoka. Shutterstock; AL1355737_Ondrej Prosicky. Shutterstock; AL1357053_Mirek Kijewski. Shutterstock; AL1324140_Reinhold Leitner. Shutterstock; AL1529378_ondrejprosicky. 123rf.com; AL1452530_Eric Isselee. 123rf.com; AL1357053_Mirek Kijewski. Shutterstock; AL1355737_Ondrej Prosicky. Shutterstock; AL1095818_Skynavin. Shutterstock; AL1331173_kazoka. Shutterstock; AL1328329_huzhiqiang. 123rf.com; AL1324367_Eric Isselee. Shutterstock; AL2002970_Eric Isselee / Shutterstock; AL1385416_Eileen Kumpf. Shutterstock; AL1314606_Kevin M. McCarthy. Shutterstock; **Page 14.11—Fig. 14.13**—AL1544265_AL1544265; **Page 14.11—Fig. 14.14**—AL2059811_OSweetNature / Shutterstock